KT-548-439

LIFE IN
THE
JUNGLE

Also by Michael Heseltine

Where There's a Will
The Challenge of Europe

Michael Heseltine

LIFE IN THE JUNGLE

My Autobiography

Hodder & Stoughton

Copyright © 2000 by Michael Heseltine

First published in Great Britain in 2000 by Hodder and Stoughton
A division of Hodder Headline

The right of Michael Heseltine to be identified as the Author
of the Work has been asserted by him in accordance with the
Copyright, Designs and Patents Act 1988.

10 9 8 7 6 5 4 3 2 1

All rights reserved.
No part of this publication may be reproduced,
stored in a retrieval system, or transmitted, in any form
or by any means without the prior written permission of the publisher,
nor be otherwise circulated in any form of binding or cover other than
that in which it is published and without a similar condition being
imposed on the subsequent purchaser.

British Library Cataloguing in Publication Data
A CIP catalogue record for this title
is available from the British Library

ISBN 0 340 73915 0

Designed by Behram Kapadia
Typeset by Palimpsest Book Production Limited,
Polmont, Stirlingshire
Printed and bound in Great Britain by
Clays Ltd, St Ives plc

Hodder and Stoughton
A division of Hodder Headline
338 Euston Road
London NW1 3BH

To Anne, Annabel, Alexandra and Rupert

Contents

List of Illustrations   ix

Preface   xi

Part One: 1933–1966

1. A Swansea Childhood   3
2. An Undistinguished Schoolboy   13
3. Oxford and the Union   25
4. The Real World   39
5. Candidate for Gower   47
6. Business at the Deep End   59
7. Finding a Seat   95

Part Two: 1966–1979

8. On to the Front Bench   109
9. First Taste of Office   121
10. The National Stage   155

Part Three: 1979–1990

11. Secretary of State   185
12. 'It Took a Riot'   209
13. Cold War Hot Seat   237
14. Managing the MOD   261

15. 'A VERY GOOD RESIGNATION'   293

16. 'SAY NOT THE STRUGGLE NAUGHT AVAILETH'   335

Part Four: 1990–1997

17. BACK TO ENVIRONMENT   377

18. THE COMPETITIVENESS AGENDA   415

19. THE HAND OF FATE   453

20. DEPUTY PRIME MINISTER   485

21. END OF THE ROAD   523

Appendix: Resignation Statement, 9 January 1986   535

Index   545

List of Illustrations

Section One

Our post-war family home: Broughton in Sketty, Swansea
My father, Rupert, taken after the war
My mother in early married life
My sister, 'Bubbles' and myself with our Scottie in 1940
My mother and father on a Mediterranean cruise
Preparing to be Minister for Aerospace at the age of eleven
Moser's Hall house photograph taken at Shrewsbury in 1950
The young undergraduate in 1951
The Oxford Union Debating Chamber in 1954
With Sir Bernard and Lady Docker in 1954
Guardsman Heseltine at Caterham in 1959
At Mons Officer Cadet School alongside my much-prized Jaguar in 1959
In 1960 with my sister 'Bubbles' in Stafford Terrace, London
Clive Labovitch

Section Two

As Tory candidate for Gower in 1959
Campaigning in Coventry North in 1964
I married Anne Williams at Holy Trinity, Brompton, in August 1962
Early days of *About Town* magazine
Pond Lodge on the Earl of Suffolk's estate in Wiltshire
Our young family in the garden of our London home at Chepstow Villas in 1967
Ted Heath visits the Haymarket stand at a magazine exhibition in 1967
Meeting Zhou Enlai on my first visit to China in 1973
Showing HM the Queen over Concorde
The *Sunday Times* reconstruction of the Mace incident of May 1976
Arriving at the House of Commons the day after the Mace incident
Thenford House

Section Three

The London Docklands in 1979

On the streets of Liverpool in 1981

My plans for cutting back on local authority expenditure caused widespread indignation

The BBC showed the 20-year old drama-documentary, *The War Game*, during my time as Secretary of State for Defence

At the Tory Party Conference in 1977

The perils of being Defence Secretary

At Goose Green, the Falklands, in 1983

With US Defense Secretary, Cap Weinberger

Coming out of Cabinet to announce my resignation as Defence Secretary in January 1986

A clutch of Defence Secretaries

Section Four

Panorama comes to Thenford

Announcing for leadership in November 1990

Two cruel cartoons: Mac in the *Daily Mail* and Peter Brookes in *The Times*

Geoffrey Howe, his wife Elspeth, and Norma and John Major join Anne and me at the constituency diner in 1999 marking my 25 years as Henley's MP

Lunching with old friend, Lord Levene

At work in the arboretum

As President of the Board of Trade on a North Sea oil rig

Remembrance Sunday 1995

Surprisingly cheerful after my heart attack in 1993

Engraving the labels to identify the trees in my arboretum

The long, reflective view

Preface

Politicians famously find the task of writing an autobiography not only difficult but daunting. In the first place, there is the understandable human reluctance to draw a line under a career: to serve notice, as it were, that the party is over. But – sensitive as I am to Harold Macmillan's dictum that one should not hang about in the green room once the final curtain has come down – I do not intend the publication of this book to intimate my withdrawal from public life. I continue to hold strong views on a number of issues, particularly concerning Britain's future in Europe – an issue that divides all parties. Although I have announced that I intend to stand down from the House of Commons at the next election, I hope to play an active and energetic part in the national debate on this and other questions for many years to come.

So, disappointing as it may be for my critics, this is not goodbye. I have always had difficulty in imagining myself in the role of an elder statesman. Faced with Walter Bagehot's celebrated distinction between the 'dignified' and the 'efficient' parts of the constitution, I have never had the slightest doubt on which side of the divide I prefer to be.

The public, or so it seems to me, is entitled to know about the influences, pressures and experiences that combine to form the character and outlook of any leading political figure. Anyway, these are the things that have mattered to me. So I have not shrunk from telling the story of my life from its beginnings, not skimping my childhood in South Wales, my less than successful schooldays at Shrewsbury, my compensating time at Oxford or anything else that played a part in shaping the personality of the rather nervous but no doubt brash young man who arrived at the House of Commons at the age of thirty-three.

The most formative part of this background was my political baptism at Oxford University and particularly the Oxford Union, followed by my early adventures in property and publishing – adventures that brought me to the brink of financial disaster in 1961–2 and from which I was able only slowly and painfully to recover before building up the magazine publishing company that is today the Haymarket

Publishing Group. The tale of this struggle for commercial survival is told in Chapters 4 and 6. I am most grateful to my colleagues at Haymarket – especially Lindsay Masters and Simon Tindall, who were there with me throughout the darkest days, and David Fraser, who joined us at the end of the 1960s just in time to experience something of this trauma, from which he helped to extract us – for allowing me the benefit of their memories to check against my own.

Once I became seriously involved in frontbench politics, I had, of course, to abandon all the executive responsibilities for my business, picking up the reins again at Haymarket only after the retirement of Lindsay a year or so after the Conservative defeat at the 1997 general election. But if there was one lesson I learnt even from those early rugged years, it was the advantage to any politician of not being simply a hothouse Westminster plant. When I arrived in the Commons in 1966, I may have been a political *ingénu* but I had already had experience of the world outside politics and I knew how tough it could be. In later years I sometimes found myself wishing that more of my colleagues in the Conservative Party – particularly those who were the most dogmatic and doctrinaire – had faced the same sort of challenges as I had. If they had known more about the world as it is and not how theory says it ought to be, they might have been able to make more temperate and rational contributions to the great economic debate of the 1980s.

Politics, as my family would bear witness, is certainly a jealous taskmistress and I cannot pretend that in my thirty-five years of apprenticeship to the trade in the House of Commons I developed the kind of 'hinterland' of which Denis Healey often boasts. In my role as a minister, I believed in concentrating almost exclusively on the job in hand and, if some readers are surprised by the general absence of 'overview' reflections in this book, then my explanation is that my attention was almost always totally absorbed by the problems to be solved and the choices to be made in the various government departments of which I was in charge. In any event, I suspect that the age of the gentleman amateur in politics – most attractively personified by Sir Alec Douglas-Home – has now gone for good.

Nevertheless, from 1977 our family home at Thenford on the Oxfordshire–Northamptonshire border offered a constant welcome contrast to my weekly Whitehall preoccupations. I hope later on to write further about the arboretum at Thenford which my wife Anne and I devised and planted (and which I sometimes feel will serve as my real memorial), but I trust there is enough in the pages that follow to convince the more open-minded reader that even I sometimes took time off from politics.

I owe an enormous debt to a variety of individuals – civil servants (especially my successive permanent and private secretaries), parliamentary and government colleagues, leaders and officials in local government, officers and members of my constituency associations and old friends – who have assisted me in summoning back the memories of the often turbulent years covered by this book. Many of them expressly did not wish to be named, so it seems only fair to afford them all the blanket cover of anonymity. There must, however, be a few exceptions to that rule.

The staff of the House of Commons library have, as always in my experience, been endlessly helpful and courteous in responding to requests to check facts or verify the record. I am grateful to them all for their fund of information – and their patience.

I was particularly fortunate to discover that, unbeknown to me at the time, diarists were faithfully recording their impressions as events unfolded. Michael Mates' energetic young political researcher Nick Kent let me see his notes made in the late 1980s and the eventful year of 1990. My immensely supportive Parliamentary Private Secretary, Richard Ottaway, kept a detailed account of his conversations with colleagues as speculation increased that I might succeed John Major in the mid-1990s.

I cannot overstress the debt I owe to two other parliamentary colleagues, Michael Mates and Keith Hampson, who from 1986 to 1990 devoted much time and energy to the drudgery – and I hope also shared some of the excitement – of those wilderness years.

Another group of people who gave of their time for inadequate reward were my special advisers. I do not know to this day of their political allegiance, but it was not for party political reasons that I invited them to join me. Each in his way brought a professionalism and an expertise that was not available to me in any other way. Tom Baron, Ed Berman, Peter Levene, Tom Burke, Peter Hall and Alan Kemp all made an invaluable contribution to our achievements.

Eileen Strathnaver first came to work for me in 1966 and, after a gap while she brought up her two daughters, returned to take charge of the political office I set up after my resignation as a result of the Westland affair in 1986. In 1990 she moved with me when I went back into government, becoming my political adviser in Whitehall between 1990 and 1997. The later pages of this book thus tell what is almost a joint story; for this period she certainly brought all the threads together, and this book would have been a much more patchy garment without her very considerable contribution.

The other person who has been at my elbow throughout the task of writing has been Tony Howard. We have known each other for forty-eight years and I am glad to say that our friendship has survived what could have been a high-risk endeavour. Whether the credit for this is due to his fortitude in making forthright criticisms of my tendency towards prolixity or to my forbearance in receiving (although not always acting upon) them, I am unclear. He initially demurred at my suggestion that he might like to assist me in producing the book but, once I had overcome his reservations – which I suspect were based on no more than the fact that we happen to hold opposing political views – he heroically threw himself into the enterprise.

My thanks also go to my family, who were unfailingly supportive throughout. Anne, in particular, made a number of suggestions and emendations, all of which have improved the text, and my son Rupert suggested the title. Any lapses in prose style that remain are entirely my responsibility – as are mistakes whether of fact or judgement, misunderstandings of other people whether of their actions or of their motives and all other examples of personal failure whether of comprehension or compassion.

MICHAEL HESELTINE
Westminster, June 2000

Part One:
1933–1966

Chapter 1

A SWANSEA CHILDHOOD

M y arrival in this world attracted scant notice and what little it did took the form of a paid advertisement in the *South Wales Evening Post* announcing the birth on 21 March 1933 of a son to Rupert and Eileen Heseltine of Shirley, 22 Eaton Crescent, Swansea. They had married a year before, in February 1932, and I was to be their only son. I was christened Michael Ray Dibdin Heseltine and was joined by my sister, Yvonne, some eighteen months later. She was born with a mass of curly blonde hair, and the nickname 'Bubbles' (after the popular Millais painting of that name) remains with her to this day.

So I was born in Wales and throughout my life have been proud of my Welsh roots. But, as with so many of our countrymen, the background is more complex. My paternal grandfather, born in 1872, was brought up in fairly affluent circumstances in Hampstead but, following the suicide of his father (beset by financial troubles) in 1890, he became at the age of eighteen responsible not just for his mother but for five younger brothers and sisters. Holding the family together was quite a task, and for a time they were separated. But they were eventually reunited in Huntingdon, before moving to South Wales just before the turn of the century. This was essentially an English family that had settled in Swansea.

My grandfather, John William Dibdin Heseltine, was not an easy man. But as the years went by – he died in 1953 – I came to appreciate something of the strength of character he displayed in facing the trauma of a lost family fortune. His mother, of whom he was always very protective, was born Eve Mary Dibdin, a direct descendant of a minor Victorian watercolourist, Thomas Colman Dibdin, and, further back still, of Charles Dibdin, the songwriter ('Tom Bowling' is probably the best known of his works today), an actor at the Drury Lane Theatre and later at Sadler's Wells, where he staged 'aquatic spectacles' including the Siege of Gibraltar in 1804 – I have no doubt they were stirring stuff. My grandfather married in 1898 Marie Berthe Lefauve, one of three daughters of a French shipowner who had left Grimouville in Normandy to live in Swansea. I have no recollection at all of her as she died when I was only two. At the time of his marriage my grandfather, out of deference to his wife's family, converted to the Roman Catholic faith. All his children, including my father, were brought up in it.

In Swansea my grandfather had found a job as a representative of Robbins Tea, a tea-import company. He probably owed this position to his father's former connections in the grocery business – the man who lost the family fortune had been an original partner in the firm of Heseltine, Kearley and Tonge (a company long since absorbed into today's Gateway Supermarkets). Life cannot have been easy for my grandfather, and I suspect that if it had not been for his father's tragedy – precipitating him into family responsibilities at a very early age – he would have chosen a different career for himself.

My father, Rupert Dibdin Heseltine, was one of his seven children and the eldest of the four who survived to adult life. He was born and spent his entire youth in Swansea. Educated at Swansea Grammar School, he left in his mid-teens to train as a structural engineer in the drawing office of Rees and Kirby, a Swansea firm.

I was much closer to my maternal grandparents. They lived at 4 Nyanza Terrace – 200 yards away from the new home at 1 Uplands Crescent to which my parents had moved just after I was born. We saw a great deal of them. My mother's father, James Pridmore, was a self-made entrepreneur, born in Swansea in 1879. By his own initiative and enterprise he had risen from humble origins. His father had been an illiterate general labourer – or so I assume from the 'X' for a signature on my grandfather's birth certificate. James married Mary Marie Bevans, my mother's mother, in 1903. They had three children: my mother, Eileen Ray, was their only daughter and was born in 1906. In early life my grandfather worked a small colliery and owned some coasters, enabling him to build up a substantial business as a coal merchant. (He was the local coal controller for Swansea in the 1914–18 war and again during the 1926 general strike.) He barely survived the slump that followed the Great Crash of 1929 and the prosperity that he achieved in the first two decades of the twentieth century was never quite to be repeated. But he lived comfortably and was generous with one-pound notes when a pound bought much more than it does today, thus making a valuable contribution to our family's living standard up to the time of his death in the early 1950s.

No. 1 Uplands Crescent was a prosperous town house, built around the turn of the century, of no architectural merit but of great comfort. There was a staff of two, the Davies sisters – Gwen served as cook, Betty as nanny. It was from here that I set forth at the age of four and a half, for mornings only, to Oakleigh House, then under the formidable leadership of Mrs Bartlett-Williams and her sister. It was an admirable kindergarten, well run and disciplined, full of children of my parents' friends, and just round the corner from where we lived. What we learnt I do not remember, but I recall the school with fondness.

I suffered from all the usual childhood illnesses – one form of rash or spots succeeded by another. Yet one childhood illness nearly ensured that this book would never be written. At the age of five I contracted meningitis. My birthday was on a Monday; the Oakleigh House form came to tea. The next Monday I had meningitis. In those days it was even more of a killer than it is today. My mother recalls that I had none of the obvious symptoms. My nanny detected that there was something wrong at 7 a.m. and I was unconscious most of that day. In the evening my father telephoned the doctor. My life was saved by Dr Elwyn James and the consultant he called in, a Mr Sladden, the pathologist at Swansea Hospital. They debated whether I should be given what was then a new experimental drug. (Was it Prontosil? Anyway, it was later withdrawn.) My mother remembers very clearly the resulting conversation. Mr Sladden recommended giving me double the children's normal dosage. 'Give him the adult dose,' he said, murmuring as an afterthought the words 'kill or cure'. The two doctors looked at each other and discussed which of them would authorise the decision – 'Are you giving it or am I?' Eventually Elwyn James took the responsibility. There was only enough of the drug available in Swansea to give me one injection. Dr James rang up Great Ormond Street Children's Hospital and arranged for a further supply. He met the train. I regained consciousness at three o'clock the following morning. My nanny to this day remembers me uttering the words: 'Please pass me some goggy.' Oranges were duly squeezed. The worst was over. At the time I was unaware of the stress this medical crisis had inflicted on my parents. But dimly, at the back of my mind, I can recollect the process of recovery: three weeks in bed and then we took a house at Porthcawl for a month while I recuperated.

I can also just remember listening to Chamberlain broadcast his bleak declaration of war against Germany on Sunday, 3 September 1939. I did so at my nanny's home in Grovesend as my father was in the Territorial Army and had already been summoned to the colours. He had always had military connections, joining the TA at the age of twenty in 1922. He had started his training as a structural engineer in Swansea and completed it in India between 1925 and 1930. While out there he served in the India Reserve of Officers with the King George's Own Bengal Sappers and Miners. When he returned to Swansea in 1930 he joined the 244 Field Company Royal Engineers, took command of the unit in 1935 and mobilised with them at the outbreak of war. From then on, wherever he went we went with him – when we could.

He was first posted to Narberth in Pembrokeshire, where we stayed with a Miss Lewis-Lloyd at Bloomfield. The house is now a recreation centre and the land has been given to the community of Narberth for rugby and cricket pitches, but then it was very much the home of the lady of the manor. From there we moved to Dundrum in Northern Ireland, then to Clitheroe in Lancashire and finally to Shotover in Oxfordshire, where we stayed at Forest Lodge Guest House in Headington (it is now incorporated into the offices of the Nielsen group of companies). My mother, my sister and I (together with nanny) were simply camp-followers. Only in the last year of the war did my father send us back to Swansea, where we joined my maternal grandparents at 1 Uplands Crescent.

My grandfather James Pridmore's office in Albion Chambers had received a direct hit in a bombing raid early in the war. It happened at night and no one was injured, but he had had to move much of his business activity into his own home in Nyanza Terrace. There wasn't enough room there for both business and family, so my grandparents had come to live at Uplands Crescent. As we were in Northern Ireland at the time, my grandparents' taking over of our Swansea home had presented no inconvenience to anyone.

I was devoted to them and they played a formative role in bringing me up, particularly in the absence of my father. My grandfather would take me for long walks along the Mumbles and Langland beaches. We explored the little stream that runs up the Clyne Valley; we collected cowrie shells at Langland; we watched the elvers fight their way up the stream; we stood to one side to watch the Mumbles train rumble its way along the oldest railway line in the world. It was during these magical outings that I first felt that overwhelming fascination with nature which has stayed with me ever since.

Swansea is the gateway to the Gower Peninsula. The war with its petrol rationing and limited public transport kept us close to the town, but as the years passed, and particularly as a teenager, I came to know and love the wonders of that dramatically beautiful and unspoilt coastline which stretches west past Caswell, Three Cliffs, Horton and on to the best of them all, Rhossili. To the north and east lie the very different Brecon Beacons, the Usk Valley and on up into the higher reaches of the Wye, where with a childhood friend, Geoffrey Hayes, I would clamber to the supposed site of the cave of Twm Shun Catti's – a folklore highwayman – and perhaps drop the odd fly over someone else's river.

Swansea itself was blessed with splendid public parks. My earliest outings took me – pushed uphill by nanny – to Cwmdonkin Park, where, rather like pre-war Kensington Gardens, all the local nannies converged to show off their charges and gossip the hours away. And then there was Brynmill Park. This was about half a mile from Uplands Crescent. There were swings for the children, flowerbeds with accompanying seats for the elderly, ice cream for those so inclined and a bowling green. It was a happy place, made especially so for me by Charlie Moore, the park keeper, a friendly, rather stooped man with only one eye. He looked after the monkeys, the rabbits, the guineapigs and the pheasants. He also had his own private collection of budgerigars, which he was only too pleased to share with those of us on the threshold of what was then known as the 'fancy'.

But at that age it was the lake and the fishing that provided the big attraction. Day after day in the holidays I would walk the half-mile to the park, armed with my fishing rod, to pit my wits against the wary roach, perch and carp. The culmination of the year was the annual angling competition – one class for the seniors and one for the juniors. I entered the two-and-a-half-hour contest for the juniors. After half an hour I had caught nothing. The bread paste invariably fell off the hook; the fish were too wily for my overtures. There was suddenly a voice alongside me: 'Try one of these.' And a hand held out a tin of wriggling maggots. I tried again. Two hours later I had caught thirty-nine fish. At the age of ten or eleven I became the junior angling champion of Brynmill. I was allowed to keep a huge silver cup for the following year and I received 7s 6d in cash as prize money. For the completeness of the record I should add that the total weight of the fish was 11¾ ounces.

Swansea was one of the most heavily bombed towns in the country and, though I was away with my mother and sister for much of the early days of the war, after our return I can remember many nights when the atmosphere was tense, first waiting for the bombing to start and then living through the explosions when it did. We had a little Scottie dog called Angus who played a particular part in the folklore of our wartime experience. Originally owned by a sergeant-major who served under my father in Northern Ireland, Angus was the proud possessor of his own little coat with sergeant's stripes which barred him from entry into the anteroom of the officers' mess of which my father was a member. So he came back to Swansea with us. The German bombers arrived with predictable regularity, and each night at 7.30 Angus was to be found waiting at the top of the stairs leading to our basement, which had been reinforced by pit props to provide us with an air-raid shelter. My sister and I had bunk beds, everyone else easy chairs.

I remember vividly my father on leave, in his dressing gown, surrounded by the family as we all sat there in our shelter, no one ever quite knowing what to expect. But I do not remember fear. The danger was so present and yet so remote. Apart from the damage to my grandfather's office, the closest a bomb ever came to our house was when the local bakery received a direct hit, sending a brick through our roof which landed on my mother's bed. We were in Ireland at the time and heard the news from one of the sappers who had come back from leave.

On another occasion I can remember standing in the garden of 1 Uplands Crescent with my grandfather watching the searchlights stab the night sky, seeking the German planes amid the ghostly silhouettes of the barrage balloons. There were fires everywhere. I was told some were deliberately lit on the mountains, which overshadowed the town, by the local fire brigade in order to distract the bombers' aim. But for Swansea there was no escape. Night after night the town was bombed, and very soon its centre was flattened.

The war drew to an end as I approached my teens. My parents had kept our family together as best they could. As a result, we had lived a somewhat nomadic life, but a happy one, without much of the strain of being apart that affected so many families at this time. There was a war on, as everyone kept reminding each other; but we suffered little of the protracted separations or enforced absences that were so much a part of the wartime experience of others. Some months before the Normandy landings, however, my father was posted to Kent as part of the huge Allied build-up. This move coincided with the indiscriminate targeting of that part of England by Hitler's V2 rockets. At that point my father sent us home to Swansea. Following the successful liberation of Belgium he was posted there for the remainder of the war and was awarded the Order of Leopold for his work in rebuilding that country's roads and bridges. I still have the letter I wrote to him in January 1945 stating that 'I would very much like to come to BELGIUM' and arguing persuasively (I thought) that my French would be so much better as a result, because 'I could learn by listening to the citizens.' Neither ambition was to be fulfilled.

Back in Swansea the family was involved in the war effort like everyone else. My uncle was an air-raid warden, my mother delivered meals on wheels, the iron railings at the front of our house went to be melted down and everyone queued for everything. Even our weekly rationing of sweets was an orderly ritual. But I do not look back with any sense of deprivation. It was not until a few days after D-Day that I actually knew anyone who lost a close relative. I can still remember Colin Cocks, a friend of mine at my prep school, Broughton Hall, being called to the headmaster to be told that his father, a lieutenant-colonel with Southern Command, had been killed during the Normandy landings as he looked out of the turret of the tank he was commanding.

I was still at school at Broughton Hall on that spring day in 1945 when the war in Europe came to an end. I remember it was in the middle of a sports session, in the afternoon, when we heard the news. The sun was shining. But much more dramatic, for me, was VJ Day, the end of the war against Japan in August, the middle of the school holidays. By coincidence, and by remarkable good fortune, my parents had taken me to London for the first time. They had booked rooms in the Regent Palace Hotel, a wedge-shaped building that jutted out towards Piccadilly Circus. My room was at the front, and to this day I can see the crowds, swirling, dancing, overjoyed, around the statue of Eros, as an indescribable release of emotion freed the nation from the horrors of those six destructive years. It was a sight that I will never forget, a moment of history, hopefully never to be repeated, engraved for ever on my memory.

*   *   *

At the end of the European war my father, with so many of his contemporaries, was demobbed and returned to his old firm, Dawnays, a steel fabricating and construction works, as assistant general manager at a weekly salary of £8. He brought with him the coupons entitling him to an overcoat and civilian suit in order to re-embark on his former life. My parents now had to seek a new home and they were very lucky to find a substantial town house built around 1900, but on much older foundations. With a well-planted garden of two acres, full of birds, with greenhouses, a grass tennis court, garages, potting sheds and workshops, Pantysifi (the Welsh for strawberry dell) was another world. It was set in what was then one of the smarter suburbs of Swansea, opposite the police station a hundred yards above Sketty Cross, and became for me a dream home.

My parents bought it for £5,000 and we moved in in 1945 – but not before the name had been changed to Broughton, as a tribute to the happiness of my time at the prep school of that name. In the purchase my parents also acquired four tenanted cottages adjoining our land, in one of which lived Tom and Elvira Bevan. Tom had left the mining industry with chest problems and needed a job. 'Mrs Bev' (as she was affectionately known to us for the rest of her life) became our cook/housekeeper, while Tom went to work at Dawnays as my father's chauffeur. In his spare time he did the garden, along with my parents and, to a lesser extent, myself. I organised two of my friends, Peter Bevan who lived next door (no relation to Tom and Mrs Bev), and David Davies, a local doctor's son, into a fledgling company called Hesdavan and we hired ourselves out to my father for five shillings an hour to clear overgrown scrub.

My parents patiently watched the conversion of a garden hut into an aviary for my collection of budgerigars, started with encouragement from Charlie Moore of Brynmill Park. They tolerated the shanty town for rabbits and guineapigs that developed alongside and, with Tom, faithfully carried out the instructions for their care and maintenance which I left behind when each new term took me away for two or three months at a time.

It is impossible to overstate the happiness that Broughton meant for us as a family. My father was back, and had good prospects for advancement at Dawnays. My mother was devoted to her life as wife and parent; it centred entirely round her husband and children. Their health and happiness were the sum of her ambition for them. We were settled, with a clear future ahead. It gave Bubbles and me a security for which our gratitude is beyond measure.

So I look back with undiminished affection on my early life in a middle-class family in Swansea, conscious that the influences and experiences of those times have lived with me ever since. My love of gardening has its roots in that Welsh soil. My concern for the environment must in part have been inspired by memories of the Gower coast's breathtaking beauty. My commitment to One Nation Conservatism has its origins in the industrial, social and human contrasts of that city and its hinterland. I could not have hoped for a better start in life and remain, to this day, proud of my early days in Wales and of the city which to me was home.

Chapter 2

AN UNDISTINGUISHED
SCHOOLBOY

I was just five when, while still living in Northern Ireland, I started
school at the local primary school, Dundrum Public Elementary.
Then in the Easter term of 1941, just before I was eight, I went
off to a boarding preparatory school, Mourne Grange, at the base
of the Mountains of Mourne, where an elderly Mr Carey presided
over a small establishment for young boys. I was happy enough, but
progress in reading and writing was slow and spelling particularly
caused me difficulty, as my youthful reports made all too clear.

The word 'dyslexic' featured in no one's vocabulary at the time.
Today the problem is recognised and, as far as possible, tackled
at an early age. I still find spelling and punctuation difficult, and
my handwriting has been a constant source of strain for devoted
secretaries who have struggled to interpret my illegible scrawl over
many years. I strongly suspect that the illegibility of my writing started
as a deliberate cover-up through which I learnt to hide my inability to
spell. Many a squiggle has replaced letters about which I felt some
uncertainty, leaving it to the reader's imagination or a secretary's
superior knowledge to fill the gap. I still don't enjoy reading and
have never found it the easiest way to absorb information. In any
case, I did not come from a family background where books were an
accustomed part of everyday life.

Slowly, but increasingly down the years, the suspicion grew in my
mind that I was slightly dyslexic. I do not think that I fully understood
the reality of it, though, until my son Rupert was diagnosed as
suffering from much the same difficulties shortly after he went to
school. Dr Macdonald Critchley, the leading neurologist to whom we
went for advice, spotted that my wife had completed both the forms

that we had been given to fill out, and asked why. 'I hate filling up forms,' I said. He passed them to me to check whether the information was correct. 'Yes,' I said, after a considered pause. 'You do realise that you are a classic dyslexic?' was his response.

Somehow or other at about the same time the *Sunday Express* got hold of a garbled story that I had severe reading difficulties and printed it in its gossip column. Inevitably then came the invitations to address those, or the parents of those, similarly afflicted. I found such approaches embarrassing; I felt a fraud. There is nothing but the most tenuous relationship between the problem I have had and the sort of difficulties and handicaps with which many children have to wrestle. The exam results I achieved (when I tried or was interested) at school and university, my thirty years' survival at the forefront of national politics together with a commercial career of some success hardly entitle me to be treated as a victim. And, as I shall relate later, whatever little disadvantage I may have suffered from in early days prompted me to take steps which in themselves – at least in Whitehall terms – were to prove positively beneficial.

My father's posting to Northern Ireland lasted less than two years and the family next followed him to Clitheroe in Lancashire. I was sent to the junior school of Bromsgrove, then located in Llanwrtyd Wells, under the headmastership of a Mr Hughes. I didn't like it, and I wasn't alone in feeling miserable. The upshot of it all was that, together with one of my Swansea friends, Kellan Scott, I plotted a mass escape. On Saturday afternoons we were allowed out in groups of about thirty for walks in what was then unspoilt countryside. Our plan was to take part in the walk but, once clear of the school, to hitchhike to Swansea, some forty miles away on the other side of the Sugarloaf Mountain. In the end only Kellan and I kept our nerve, but the rest of the boys were very supportive. They conducted a whip-round to help us on our way and, armed with a sixpence or two and a packet of cornflakes, both of us set off on the road home. To our delight, the first car that came along rumbled obligingly to a halt. But our joy was short-lived. The figure in the driving seat was soon revealed to be the headmaster himself. He was looking for us, and we were taken smartly back to school. Fortunately, my parents were less than impressed with the school's explanation of how we had managed to escape undetected in the first place. At the end of the term I was taken away.

I was then sent to Broughton Hall, housed in a magnificent Tudor building in Staffordshire, under the headmastership of George

Kenneth Thompson, aided by his wife Heather and by an admirable assistant, Molly Salter. Mr Thompson, a short, moustachioed man with a military bearing and beady eyes, was a strict disciplinarian, but a very fair one. I was there from 1942 to 1946, and these years were among the happiest of my schooldays. I have to acknowledge, however, that my reports did not make encouraging reading. The one bright and – for the long term – encouraging exception came during the term in which my parents promised me a bicycle if I managed to deliver a significant improvement in performance. I learnt my first lesson about how to run a business. The incentive was there; the improvement followed. But this carrot-led recovery lasted for that one term only.

As a young boy of eight or nine, I was already pretty tall for my age. Inevitably at the order, 'Tallest on the right, shortest on the left,' I was the one on the furthest right. This had both advantages and disadvantages. I had outgrown my strength and frequently found myself (probably once a term) confined to bed in what was a minor form of exhaustion. My arms especially never developed a strength commensurate with my size. In the boxing ring this was a particular handicap. We were taught by an ex-RAF boxing instructor. To us he seemed a giant thug of a man. He would get us into the ring, flex his solar plexus and say: 'Go on, 'it me.' I had no desire to hit him. He had never done anything to me. Anyway, it was a totally pointless exercise. The harder I tried to hit him, the more he laughed, while I became increasingly apprehensive that at any moment he might turn the tables and hit me back, with painful consequences. It soon became apparent to me that boxing was never going to be my strong suit. I was too tall, my arms too weak; I was too heavy for my relative strength. The report on my prowess in the ring got it about right: 'He who fights and runs away lives to fight another day, but that another day has not yet dawned.' My concern was simply to survive to see that other day.

But my size did have its advantages. I could out-stride any of my peers. In each of my last two years at Broughton I was the *Victor Ludorum*. I could run faster and jump higher and further than any other boy in the school. By accumulating a growing number of points in trial after trial, including the unlikely triumph of coming third in throwing the discus, I was twice the winner by a clear margin.

Another memory from my time at Broughton Hall reflects a future interest. I was for the first time in control of my own garden. Each boy was presented with a square yard of mud and a packet of Virginia stock seeds. A few weeks later I had a square yard of multicoloured flowers. I caught the bug, although I could not have known at the time that later in life I would plant on fifty acres in Northamptonshire one of the larger British arboretums created in the second half of the twentieth century.

Broughton's grounds were on a scale appropriate to its noble buildings, and they provided an exciting playground for small boys. It was here that I enjoyed some of my earliest bird-watching and bird-catching experiences. To the uninitiated, sitting in a damp shed clutching the end of a long piece of string attached to a stick that props open a large wire cage may seem pretty dreary stuff. Not so. To spring the trap at exactly the right time in the fleeting moments when the bird is actually inside requires skill and judgement. It has all the thrill of the chase. How much use were the forms we completed recording birds caught, birds ringed, birds released? I never knew or really cared. Throughout my life I have zealously guarded the secret that, in order to organise the bird-watching, I created a group of fellow bird-watchers called the Tit Club. I remember little about this organisation except that we each took the name of one of the tits. There was Long-Tailed Tit, Blue Tit, Marsh Tit, Coal Tit; I blush to say that I was Great Tit.

Our bird-watching had one bizarre consequence. This was wartime. Posters everywhere warned us that walls had ears, the enemy was all around. We were determined to do our bit. The victim of this atmosphere was a young French music teacher. She was to us a foreigner. She had an accent. The word went round that she was a German spy, communicating her messages by a series of Morse code signals disguised as owl calls. Night after night we solemnly recorded the hooting of the numerous owls in order to interpret the messages we believed she was sending to neighbouring spies. Ever more fanciful rumours gained currency. She left the school; who could blame her? Little boys can be merciless, and I fear we were.

Broughton was a happy place, a successful school, with a firm but respected headmaster. Curiously, there was another side to it of which I was virtually unaware until I received an invitation in late 1946 to appear in court in defence of my headmaster. Another school, Brockhurst, from Newbury in Berkshire, owned by one John Fergus Park, had been boarded on us for a couple of years. We apparently had the space and it was commonplace in wartime for schools (particularly evacuated ones) to share premises. But in this case the two headmasters did not get on. Although I have no memory of the Brockhurst boys ever being set against the Broughton boys, Julian Critchley claims that they were. Julian was two years older than me and was the elder son of Dr Macdonald Critchley, the leading neurologist whom I have already mentioned. By coincidence, our lives were to cross and recross many times – at prep school, public school, Oxford, in publishing and finally as Members of Parliament.

That story will unfold in the coming pages, but I have only one, though vivid, memory of him at this stage of our lives. He sold me a model landing barge for 7s 6d, coloured grey and made of rough wood, and in those invasion-focused times a treasured possession. Julian was a Brockhurst boy, but there must have been a measure of fraternisation or this transaction could never have taken place – though we did not at this time know each other well. He has since told me that his headmaster, John Park, actively encouraged animosity between the two schools.

Certainly, the whole saga ended dramatically enough. It culminated in a civil action, which was heard at the Stafford Assize Court in March 1947 just before my fourteenth birthday. By then I had left Broughton to go to Shrewsbury. Three of my former schoolmates and I were invited to appear in the witness box first to be examined by counsel for our old headmaster, Mr Thompson (who was claiming damages for trespass and assault), and then to be cross-examined by Mr Park, who was conducting his own case.

In an earnest croak – my voice was just about to break – I related how Brockhurst boys had shouted 'things' at Broughton boys, and that I had written to my parents to tell them that there was a rumour that Mr Park had bought Broughton and saying, 'If you don't mind, I want to leave immediately.' The questioning seemed to me extraordinarily banal. At one stage, Mr Park asked whether I had ever climbed trees at school, to which I readily replied, 'Yes, often – on the sly.' At this point Mr Justice Wrottesley intervened to ask: 'Did you ever get whacked for it?' 'I never got caught, my Lord,' was my answer to that. It was not exactly F. E. Smith-style repartee, but it still seemed to amuse the court. A report of the proceedings appeared in the *Daily Mail* under the less than original headline 'Battle of the Old School Tie'. It was my first exposure to the national press. My former headmaster won the case and was awarded damages of just over £2,000, the judge commending us schoolboy witnesses for being 'an impressive lot of youngsters'.

Despite the somewhat sceptical observations in my termly reports, the teaching at Broughton ensured that I obtained decent Common Entrance results. This was especially true of mathematics, in which I gained 100 per cent and 98 per cent in two of the three papers. I owed this particularly to I. G. S. Scotchman, who had taught me not just arithmetic but algebra and geometry as well. Years later, when I got into Parliament, he wrote to tell me that he had always known that this was where I was headed – a secret, as a hard taskmaster, he had not shared with me at the time.

My parents were determined to do their best for me. They chose to send me to Shrewsbury, by any standards one of Britain's leading public schools. Situated high on a hill overlooking the town and separated from it by the River Severn – crossed by a toll bridge – the main school buildings are on a majestic site around which are scattered the individual houses where the boarders live. In my day the whole school would assemble regularly either in the Alington Hall, named after a distinguished former headmaster C. A. Alington (who, like Eric Anderson, went on to be headmaster of Eton) or in the school chapel. Specialist facilities ranged from laboratories to a swimming pool, fives courts to a gymnasium and, along the river bank, the boat houses. The river and the playing fields have always been renowned and it is here that the school's reputation for rowing, soccer and cricket – though not rugby – has been forged through successive generations.

The school is structured around the individual houses, of which there are some dozen. Mine, Moser's Hall, had been founded by one of the 'greats' of Shrewsbury's past, Edward Branthwaite Moser, in 1884. Every house was divided into studies containing four boys, each presided over by a study monitor. The most senior of these became house monitors. One or two of the house monitors from each house would in turn become school praepostors. This rather military structure was the administrative backbone to all our lives. We each started life as a 'scum', as new boys were called. In addition to the normal round of lessons and games, we were expected to carry out menial tasks for the senior boys. The scumming system was simple. One of the house monitors would put his head outside the door of the house monitors' room and shout 'Doul!' at the top of his voice, whereupon all the scum would race to the point of call, the last being chosen for whatever was in the great man's mind. 'Find this,' 'Clear that,' 'Go here,' 'Be there.' It was all pretty harmless stuff.

No one suffered from it. There was corporal punishment, most of it administered at house level, but I do not recall any abuse of it. I received my fair share, limited but reasonable in the circumstances, though I was once beaten by the head of school for walking into town wearing a trilby. Some may feel in today's world that that punishment was somewhat over the top. Bullying, such as it was, was no worse than you would find in any school, whether in the state or private sector. No one will ever eliminate the instinct of little boys to behave as a predatory pack, picking on the weaker or more idiosyncratic members. But, with very rare exceptions, the system at Shrewsbury worked. The results were good enough and the school deserved its distinguished reputation.

But personally I was a failure. I cannot look back on my five years at Shrewsbury with the same degree of affection that I felt for Broughton Hall. It is very difficult to know what went wrong, but undoubtedly something did. It would have been hard for anyone to have left Shrewsbury with a less impressive record than mine. The only activity in which I prospered was the CCF, the Combined Cadet Force, where I was promoted to the rank of sergeant. At games I was hopeless – not through lack of energy or interest: I simply wasn't any good at them. I became moderately proficient at tennis, but no more. I did have hopes in one sport, where I thought I had a natural advantage. As I was among the tallest boys in the school, high jumping seemed an activity in which I might shine. So I worked hard at it, practised every evening clearing that wretched bar and thought I was on my way to winning the school high-jumping championship in my last year. The competition was proceeding and, as anticipated, I was well ahead when I caught sight of one of the school's great athletes, Brian Smallwood. He was a joy to watch in any sport in which he played: a natural athlete, with grace and style, a wonderful eye for the ball, a hero to his generation. There he was strolling across from the playing fields in his football boots to enter the high-jumping competition. I came second. To the best of my knowledge, it was the first and only time he took part in a high-jumping event. I did manage, however, to reach the school athletics team, participating not only in high jumping but in relay racing. I trained for this miraculous achievement by combining business with pleasure. Every mid-morning a half-hour break in lessons would be announced by a bell ringing throughout the school buildings. The fastest and most agile of us would be out of the doors to race for the head of the queue to the tuck shop a hundred yards away. Both at getting out of the classroom and at reaching the tuck shop early in the queue I excelled. I suspect this reflected my serious interest in tuck as well as my relative lack of interest in the classroom.

Academically my achievements were adequate, although in one significant way I was fortunate. In my school certificate in the summer of 1948 I achieved five credits and two passes and the following year I gained one higher certificate pass in physics. They were all in the right places to qualify me for matriculation. Round about the age of sixteen I had begun to wonder in what direction I should seek a career, and the post-school certificate year seemed a good time to start planning ahead. My first ambition was to be a doctor or, more specifically, a surgeon. What attracted me to the medical profession I don't know. Possibly my already evident fascination with nature and a certain facility with my hands (I was skilful at building model aeroplanes from kits) persuaded me that this was where my professional future lay. I set out to acquire the necessary academic qualifications. It was a short-lived experiment. I was able to endure cutting away at some hapless frog spreadeagled on the dissecting slab and could even tackle the dogfish, but the rabbit was something else again. It was not so much that I once had pet rabbits and liked them, while having no such feeling for frogs or dogfish. No – it was the smell and the nauseating exposure to multicoloured intestines, which I was expected to prod and poke. It just wasn't for me, and what enthusiasm I had imagined I had for my chosen career took a sharp downward turn. I abandoned my medical ambitions.

Just at that time the powers-that-be at Shrewsbury decided to offer a new option for post-school certificate boys. Under the rather unpromising title of the 'general side', it was in practice a combination of history and economics. I was the only boy of my year to switch from the traditional syllabus to this new venture, although a dozen or so boys one year behind me also made the change and I was combined with them to make up a form. At last I found subjects in which I was interested. Much of the credit for this must go to the teaching of a stocky young New Zealander, Russell Wood, who created in me a zest for work of which hitherto there had been no sign. I took my last exams at Shrewsbury in the summer of 1951 and eventually received a General Certificate of Education recording that in July of that year I got A-levels both in history and in economics and political science, with an O-level in English language.

Yet, on the normal yardsticks by which success is judged in a British public school, I hardly stood out. There was never the prospect that I would achieve the ultimate accolade and become a school praepostor. I did not even become one of the five or six house monitors and had to accept the lowly status of a study monitor, as the final judgement on my leadership abilities. I regarded my failure to move higher up the ladder as a gross misjudgement by the housemaster of the day, A. H. Phillips, known to the boys as 'Bounce', a sobriquet which reflected the fact that his movement from place to place seemed to resemble a series of vertical bounces. One clue to my lack of progress up the school hierarchy may have lain in the fact that we never really hit it off.

The headmaster of Shrewsbury in my day was John Wolfenden. Tall, elegant and immaculately clothed, he cut an arresting figure, and he knew it. His slow, measured delivery was designed to attract and retain attention. Whether he was addressing 600 boys in the school chapel on the undesirability of 'smutty' behaviour – no one quite called a spade a spade in those days – or standing, poised and sophisticated, in the Alington Hall as his less than impressive successor shuffled in from the back, he was a showman and a class act. I remember one interview when he sat in his study, his legs crossed and his feet firmly resting on an open drawer of his spacious desk. Later he became vice-chancellor of Reading University, author of the 1957 report on prostitution and homosexuality which bore his name and eventually a crossbench recruit to the House of Lords. He was married with two sons and two daughters, though this did not stop him appearing remote and aloof to the boys within the school. Yet, as I discovered, he could be warm and approachable as well. He showed a genuine interest when he once spotted me wheeling a cage full of birds across the school grounds. He wanted to know all about this curious hobby of mine and seemed intrigued that I had carried it on determinedly throughout my schooldays.

My interest in birds had followed me from Broughton and developed throughout my career at Shrewsbury. I had built up a finger-tame collection not only of jackdaws and magpies but also of finches of every kind. As a member of the Royal Society for the Protection of Birds, I had become an enthusiastic 'ringer' of wild birds. Hours were spent silently watching carefully prepared traps, into which it was hoped a stray blackbird would foolishly hop. I would also cycle for miles to the home on the fringe of the town of a Mr Lewis, who had a large collection of British finches which he was only too pleased to show me.

I very nearly made a fortune at Shrewsbury. I had discovered the football pools. One Saturday I had completed a coupon for the fourteen results. The challenge is to predict accurately the results of every one of fourteen matches listed on the pools promoter's form. Fourteen correct answers could win very large sums of money. In those days on Saturday at five o'clock the match results were always announced on BBC radio. To my vast excitement, twelve out of my fourteen predicted results were correct. The other two results were not yet available because fog had delayed the start of a couple of games. So in eager anticipation of wealth beyond my dreams I sat for an hour awaiting the last two results. Sadly, I had them both wrong.

One other event from my time at Shrewsbury has always stayed in my memory. There is no real context for it but it left an abiding impression upon me and came floating back to the forefront of my mind during my time in Liverpool in the early 1980s. One evening I had gone from the school site over the toll bridge into the town of Shrewsbury. Out of curiosity I had wandered off the main shopping streets into what could only be described as a low-quality, working-class housing area – probably privately owned, tenanted and rent-controlled. Its image was classically that of the mean and narrow streets of the late-Victorian period. As I turned the corner, I came face to face with a little girl, the spitting image of my sister Bubbles. She was pretty, with the same curly fair hair from which my sister had taken her nickname. But the child was also poorly dressed and dirty, and these mean streets were doubtless where she lived. The contrast between the two images struck a chord with me – just how wide is the gap between those who are born into the relative comfort of the middle classes and those who start life a great deal further down the ladder. I remember that little girl's face today as if I had it in a photograph: simply an early memory that helped to forge a political philosophy which would later see me involved in working with (and, as I like to think, for) those much less fortunate than I have been lucky enough to be.

I left school at the end of the summer term of 1951. Four of us, Robert Wild, with whom I had shared many of my bird-watching experiences, Guy Shepherd and Charlie Fuge, spent two weeks hitchhiking around

Europe. We travelled in pairs, agreeing to meet at prearranged destinations by leaving chalk marks to the right of the main door of the principal post office. It worked in Paris but failed in Marseilles. Robert and I completed two and a half thousand miles in two weeks for under £20. The roadside ditches and the Mediterranean cliffs seemed safe enough for the odd night under the stars, although the local lorry in which we crossed the Swiss border ensured that two soot-covered tramps were ejected from the only restaurant that appeared to be open late in one German town.

I did make one further visit to Shrewsbury shortly afterwards. In the autumn of 1952, at the opening of my second year at Oxford, I went back with Julian Critchley for a debate there. We had been asked – or perhaps it was Julian's typically mischievous suggestion – to propose a motion criticising the way in which public schools were run. Against us, standing guard over our alma mater, and replacing two Old Salopians from Cambridge who had declined to come, were two members of the school staff: Anthony Chenevix-Trench, the housemaster of School House (and later headmaster of Eton and Fettes) and Michael Hoban (subsequently the headmaster of Bradfield and Harrow, where he accepted my son Rupert as a pupil).

It was a dank November night but there was a general air of expectation, and it turned into an exciting evening. Julian and I advanced all the standard anti-public school arguments but with a veneer of sophistication and a fair smattering of Oxford Union jokes which between us we had managed to accumulate. By contrast, Chenevix-Trench, in particular, chose to treat us as a couple of erring schoolboys, thereby probably not doing his side of the argument much good. The vote was so close that there had to be a recount, but in the end, to great cheers and counter-cheers, Julian and I were declared to have won by ten votes. (I have never had the slightest doubt that a significant part of our support was based on the very understandable instinct of young boys to deliver a smack in the eye to their schoolmasters.) The whole thing had been relatively good-humoured and I even went afterwards – as the result of a rather surprising invitation from him – to stay the night with 'Bounce', my former housemaster. The next day, over breakfast, the barometer had dropped dramatically. On his way back into the town, where he had decided to stay, Julian had stopped off at a public call-box and rung the Press Association with news of our triumph. Not surprisingly, the story of public schoolboys rebelling against the system under which they were being educated proved irresistible, not least to non-Tory newspapers like the *News Chronicle* and the *Daily Herald*. I had not long been back at Oxford before I became conscious, in the face of such headlines as 'Public School Votes – Stop the Cane', of a burgeoning chorus of disapproval from the school. There was even talk, though it came to nothing, of our expulsion from the Old Salopian Association.

That was not, however, the end of my embarrassment. Nearly thirty years later, when I was already a Cabinet minister, someone who had been in the audience that evening chose to recall my speech when he appeared on *Any Questions*. He was immensely generous about it, calling it 'brilliant' and explaining how at the age of fourteen his whole attitude to private education had been defined for him by what I had had to say. He claimed not to know what had become of the young 'red revolutionary' he had listened to that night, explaining that he had recently heard 'a foul rumour' that he had joined Margaret Thatcher's Cabinet – 'but I don't believe that kind of smear'. He was fulsome to a fault but, since his name was Paul Foot (nephew of Michael Foot, then leader of the Labour Party), I somehow doubt if it was his purpose to be either helpful or kind.

Chapter 3

OXFORD AND THE UNION

O nce I had abandoned my notional medical vocation, I faced the task – while doing general studies at Shrewsbury – of identifying a fresh 'career path'. The pressure was on as much at home as at school, and relief came only with my announcement that I wanted to become an accountant. My father promptly and efficiently arranged for me to take up articles with the Swansea branch of Deloitte, Plender and Griffiths. I was to be paid £3 a week and the hope was that, after five years' articles, I would become a chartered accountant.

I do not remember precisely what it was that made me think of the university route instead. It meant taking an extra year – three years as an undergraduate and three years in articles thereafter, providing that you had first achieved your degree. I do remember saying to my father that I wondered if we could explore the possibility of a BComm., which was on offer at both Reading and Bristol Universities at the time. My academic record, such as it was, was dispatched to each place. Both universities returned the appropriate forms pointing out the hurdles which I would have to jump before I could be considered for enrolment. First, university entrance examinations were essential. And, second, they were prepared to take me only after I had done my National Service (all able-bodied young men were compulsorily conscripted into the armed forces for two years until the beginning of the 1960s). I decided to look elsewhere.

'Why don't we try Oxford and Cambridge?' I boldly asked my father. I had the advantage of matriculation via the old school certificate, which meant that I was eligible for entrance to both universities. Further letters were duly sent to St John's College, Cambridge, and Pembroke College, Oxford. In those days such distinguished seats of learning had not yet got round to organising the obstacle of a specific entrance exam or even interview by tutors. Pembroke College, Oxford was at that time presided over by the Rev. Frederick Homes Dudden, its seventy-seven-year-old Master, who relied upon his judgement in interviews to select undergraduates. I arrived early after lunch and apparently met with his approval. I was invited to join the college as an undergraduate directly upon leaving school. Indeed, St John's too offered me a place. I now had the luxury of a choice between two of the world's greatest universities. However, Cambridge was insistent upon my doing National Service first and for that project I had no enthusiasm. I was anxious to get on with what, for me, were far more important priorities. So I chose Pembroke, and in October 1951 I set off for Oxford.

I owe a tremendous debt to that university. Born and brought up in the commercial and industrial middle classes of South Wales and educated within the narrow and stereotyped environment of an English public school, I had had little exposure to the range and pace of a generation of contemporaries drawn from every background and every persuasion. I threw myself into my new life as soon as I got off the train from Swansea. On the same day I enrolled in the two organisations which were to dominate the next three years.

My first port of call was the local office of the Oxford City Conservative Association. I had spent the first ten days of October 1951 working in the Swansea West Conservative Association seeking to secure the election to Parliament of one Captain Henry Kerby (later a slightly unorthodox Tory MP for Arundel and Shoreham, with heavy intelligence connections). This is my first remembered link with the Conservative Party. I had been walking towards the town centre of Swansea at the beginning of October – university terms started much later than school ones – when I suddenly saw a large sign on the other side of the road: '1951 General Election Campaign: Henry Kerby Your Conservative Candidate'. I had actually been making my way into town to meet friends over coffee. But on an impulse, and without any particular forethought, I crossed the road and offered to help. They gave me a membership book for the Young Conservatives and told me to start recruiting. I brought in so many members that they there and then made me an honorary member of the local branch. The rest of that ten days passed in the usual range of grassroots political activities: canvassing, stuffing envelopes, attending meetings – one of which, at the rougher end of the constituency, was chaired by my father (who, while not especially active, had always been a loyal Conservative; he was, he told me, the only officer in his mess to vote Conservative in 1945).

Ten days later I went up to Oxford. The general election campaign (it culminated with the return to office of Winston Churchill) still had about two weeks to go and my priority was to rejoin the fray. I signed up with the local Conservatives – for more of the same, this time on behalf of a sitting Member, a paint manufacturer (who later came to a sticky commercial end) called Lawrence Turner. So trusted was I that I even got to look after the candidate's car.

My second visit that first day in Oxford was to the Victorian Gothic offices of the Oxford Union. My previous experience of debating – this, of course, was before Julian Critchley and I undertook our Old Boys' excursion to Shrewsbury – was limited. Occasionally I had spoken in the school debating society but only in a minor way. My final report from Shrewsbury includes references to 'debating skills' and 'thoroughly enjoys a debate', but also comments, 'He has decided opinions about everything' and adds that 'his discussion is apt to develop into controversy'. My side of the story would have been that I actually had views I believed in and which I was prepared to defend with vigour. Although my father chaired the odd meeting in the 1951 election, there was no political background in my family, but I must, however unformed the judgement, have been thinking of such a career myself. It is idle to recreate memories long since faded, but my friends were clear from my earliest Oxford days that in the end I was likely to go into politics.

Of course, it was also necessary to get a degree and, like so many aspiring politicians, I was attracted to the idea of law. My general studies background – such as it was – from Shrewsbury was not, however, the ideal launching pad for this subject, and a short interview with my tutor, Neville Ward Perkins, put a rapid end to such ambitions. 'PPE?' he suggested. I had never heard of this degree course but (combining, as it did, philosophy, politics and economics) it sounded interesting and I accepted his advice. The first hurdle was 'prelims', the preliminary examinations at the end of the second term. I spectacularly managed to fail all three papers. But a kindly system allowed retakes. I passed two of the papers the next term and, finally, the French paper in the spring of the following year, after some serious coaching. Languages have never come easily to me.

So, although I was a freshman at Pembroke College, my interests lay elsewhere. My ten-day immersion in the Swansea West constituency battles of the 1951 election had shown me a new world. On arrival at Oxford, it was to the city and university Conservative associations that I first turned, and to the centre of undergraduate politics, the Oxford Union Society.

If I sought company, it was the company not of the Junior Common Room, with its mix of every undergraduate interest from hearty oarsmen to academics manqués, but of those who shared my fascinations and commitments. Besides, I wasn't living in college, having rented a room at the far end of the Banbury Road. There was very little to draw me to Pembroke when the Union could offer me not just more appealing company but the facilities of a club as well. That is where I was to be found, and it was a pattern that was to persist even when I moved into college at the beginning of my second year.

I had a few introductions to take me into the Oxford political world. One was to Norman St John-Stevas, given to me by the Conservative agent in Swansea West. I turned up at Christ Church to meet this distinguished figure of student politics, a postgraduate who was to serve as secretary of the Oxford Union (having already been president of the Cambridge Union) during my first year. He possessed a sophistication rare even then in undergraduate life, matured by his years at Cambridge and coupled with a confidence built on florid good looks and a fine intellect. He was understandably surprised to find me knocking on his door but received me with courtesy. 'Be circumspect,' he advised me, as I took my leave. Over the years, he may have sometimes felt that his advice fell on stony ground, but he was still good enough to support my candidature for the leadership of the Conservative Party thirty-nine years later.

I was lucky, too, in meeting in my very early days two freshmen who were to play a significant part in my future life. By an extraordinary coincidence, Julian Critchley, whom I had first met at Broughton Hall, turned up at the same college on the same day that I did; a friendship, instead of the mere acquaintanceship at the two schools we had shared together, rapidly grew up between us. Julian brought something of the Sorbonne to Oxford. Handsome, tall, self-assured and possessed of a sharp wit and a ready smile, he stood out from the crowd and provoked conflicting reactions of admiration and envy from others less conspicuously endowed. He held strong convictions which were never to bend in his later years in politics. Ian Josephs I had not known at all before Oxford, but in my second year we decided to share a set of rooms in Pembroke, and it was this association that led to a joint business venture on our coming down from Oxford two years later. Ian was something of an irrepressible imp – mischievous and clever without being energetic, and almost maniacally fascinated by the local bookies.

My second introduction was to George Silver, proprietor of Long John's, a well-known undergraduate haunt at the upper end of the local covered market. George had been my father's catering officer in the Royal Engineers during the war. 'We were well provided for,' was my father's laconic comment. So was I, first at Long John's and later at a rather grander establishment in St Giles called the Regency. George opened an account for me. The bill was rendered by the term. To the best of my recollection, it never bore any relationship to either the quality or the quantity of my consumption. My debt to 'Colonel' Silver remains unpaid.

It was at Long John's – according to Julian Critchley – that I am supposed to have mapped out my future career on the back of an envelope, culminating with the date '1990s' and the words '10 Downing Street' alongside it. Although as an anecdote it has been recycled more times than I care to remember, I have absolutely no memory of any such episode taking place.

It was a new world and I entered into it with enthusiasm. Undergraduates are faced with a bewildering range of clubs. One could listen to people expound on the virtues of witchcraft, the threat of nuclear destruction and more or less any other of the wilder obsessions of the young at the time. Policy lines were not as firmly drawn as they were to be later. Indeed, for about a week in the summer of 1954 I was involved with an all-party group that opposed the H-bomb tests and called on the British government to take the lead in renouncing thermonuclear weapons. A petition circulated in Oxford to that effect and I gave it my support (once a phrase about 'morally wrong' had been withdrawn). Since the aim of the petition was universal, worldwide disarmament, I was only marginally embarrassed when this dark secret from my past was disinterred by the *Guardian* while I was Secretary of State for Defence in 1984. That paper could have discovered far worse – such as my ardent championing in my first bid for the Union presidency in the Trinity term of 1953 of the foreign policy stands then being taken by my fellow Welshman Aneurin Bevan.

Next to the Union, the Oxford University Conservative Association was my principal stamping-ground. OUCA at that time was run by a group of largely Christ Church undergraduates. Drawn for the most part from an upper-class background, they were able, through their membership of the rather snobbish Oxford Carlton Club and the peculiarity of the electoral system, to ensure that they stayed in permanent control. In the way of things this seemed to some of us a less than desirable state of affairs and there developed one of those foretastes of the wider world of Westminster which undergraduate politics just occasionally supplies. At the beginning of my second year, in the autumn term of 1952, Julian Critchley and I formed a pro-democracy movement under the banner of an organisation called the Blue Ribbon Club, in effect a ginger group. Our stated aim was to disseminate Conservative policy more widely. Our activities even attracted the interest of the national press, which linked my name to the word 'split' for the first – but by no means the last – time in my life. In a way, it supplied a curious preview of my later career. I held junior office in the Conservative Association, but, in the absence of a direct election system, it was never possible for me to move beyond that. Ironically, the battle to reform and democratise OUCA ultimately triumphed in the term in which I ended my university career.

But OUCA still taught me a lot. For one thing, it offered – if only in the most rudimentary sense – a degree of professional training. Under its auspices, a determined parson's wife called Stella Gatehouse (her husband was the vicar of the local village of Piddington) would turn up once a week to give speaking lessons to aspirant undergraduate politicians. Encouraged by her advice, we would then descend upon the branches of neighbouring Conservative associations to address groups of elderly ladies whose principal interest was the tea, the rattling of the cups for which would jerk them into action from what had been, as we spoke, almost permanently somnolent positions. But there were also speaking tours further afield. I remember four of us attacking the Labour stronghold of Barrow-in-Furness in the early 1950s, where one of our number, a bluff New College undergraduate called Martin Morton (who went on to flourish in local government), proclaimed in a voice always a good few decibels above the norm that at the forthcoming election Barrow 'will come out true blue'. He was to have to wait some thirty years before the anti-nuclear posture of the Labour Party proved too much for the dockyard workers building Britain's nuclear submarines and ensured that his prophecy, surprisingly, did come true. (But then it was only for the duration of two Parliaments; by 1992, Labour having abandoned its anti-nuclear stance, Barrow returned to its traditional Labour loyalty.)

But, ahead of OUCA or the Blue Ribbon Club, it was always the Union which took first place in my affections. It was not, of course, just a debating society. It had the facilities of a club and it was to this club, with its bars and its dining room, that the politically committed undergraduates of all parties gravitated. In a sense it provided an alternative to the Junior Common Rooms of college life. The first president during my time at Oxford was Ivan Yates (a future journalist on the *Observer*, killed in a road accident in 1974 before he was fifty), followed in the succeeding terms by Peter Blaker, Howard Shuman and then the quietly dignified Paddy Mayhew. These three were all to play a part in my future life. Peter Blaker became Minister of State at the Ministry of Defence, where together we fought off the nuclear disarmers; the American Howard Shuman went on to be the legislative assistant to Senator Paul Douglas of Illinois and, as a champion of NATO and the West in the Cold War, was always assured of a warm welcome in Whitehall; while Paddy Mayhew and I served as Cabinet colleagues together and he was, of course, the Solicitor General during the Westland affair.

I shall never forget the experience of sitting as a freshman in the packed Union debating hall in October 1951. The officers of the Union, with their immaculate white tie and tails and their general air of self-confidence, made a strong impression on me. I was an extremely nervous novice and my early speeches undoubtedly showed it. Ian Josephs insists that when we shared rooms together I spent hours preparing and rehearsing speeches in front of the mirror. I was certainly determined to improve. And, whether by luck or perseverance, I was eventually given my first chance to speak from the dispatch box, 'on the paper' as it is called, at the end of my fourth term, on 27 November 1952. The motion that evening was that 'In the opinion of this House the United Nations Organisation has failed.' I led the opponents – and we won. Perhaps more important to me, though, was that the president of that term, Paddy Mayhew, actually wrote the next week in the *Oxford Magazine* that my performance was 'a great improvement on past form', adding the prediction, 'With a bit more warmth he will be very good.' Suddenly all that posturing in front of the mirror seemed to have been worth while.

There were two committees of the Society, the junior being the

Library Committee and the senior the Standing Committee. Membership of both committees was by election – the ladder leading, hopefully, from Library to Standing Committee and then to becoming a Union office-holder as secretary, treasurer, librarian and ultimately perhaps president. But very few made the jump straight to office without serving their time on one or both these committees.

On 28 November, the day after my first paper speech, I was elected to serve on the Library Committee for Hilary term 1953 and a term later was elected to the grander Standing Committee. It was from there that I took my first risk, resolving to challenge the incumbent librarian, a hereditary baronet named Sir Andrew Cuninghame – he was to die prematurely a few years later as a British diplomat in Djakarta – for the top office of the presidency. I had not expected to win and I did not do so, my speech in the presidential debate being adjudged no more than 'worthy'; but I did go on to come top in the election to Standing Committee for Michaelmas term 1953.

From this jumping-off point, I was elected secretary for Hilary term 1954. The other two candidates were John King-Farlow and Robin Maxwell-Hyslop – both from Christ Church. Robin was to become among the first of my contemporaries to be elected to the House of Commons, winning a by-election at Tiverton in November 1960 (only Robin Cooke – elected at a Bristol by-election in 1957 – and Julian Critchley and Peter Tapsell – both first elected at the October 1959 general election – were to get there before him). John King-Farlow served, two terms later, as secretary of the Union, went on to be librarian and eventually became a professor of philosophy in Canada, writing learned articles with such forbidding titles as 'The Logic of Cognitive States'.

In face of rather more formidable competition from Tony Howard, a left-wing undergraduate at Christ Church, I managed to take the next step up the ladder by being elected treasurer for the Trinity term of 1954. The Union was at that stage in a financial crisis. It was failing to attract the necessary numbers of freshmen – who had the option of paying a life subscription of £11 or instalments of £2 10s in the first term and £1 10s a term thereafter. Its facilities were perceived to be shabby and down-at-heel. There was no spark about the place. The choice was one that is familiar to any business: cut your costs to meet your revenue or invest in and improve your product to build the revenue you need to provide more attractive wares. I was strongly in favour of the latter course. I threw myself into the challenge of attracting a bigger membership. That was my strategy. I succeeded in persuading my fellow committee members, but not the senior treasurer of the Union, George Richardson, a don at St John's, who insisted on resigning his office in protest at what he saw as my profligacy. This was a serious blow as, under the Proctors' regulations, every university club or organisation had to have a a 'senior member' – and the senior treasurer had always counted for that in the case of the Union. Without such a figure we could not function: the situation was as grave as that. Fortunately Richardson's predecessor, Asa Briggs of Worcester College, had just that weekend returned from America and he generously agreed to step into the breach while we looked for a permanent successor. We were lucky enough to find him in Maurice Shock, a young research don at St Antony's then at the outset of his distinguished academic career.

What was immediately dubbed my 'Brighter Union' policy embraced the introduction of a wide-screen, back-projection television set (a huge technological leap forward for its time), the upgrading of the restaurant to provide four-course lunches for 2s 6d and five-course dinners for 3s 6d and a plan for the future conversion of the old wine cellars under the Union building into a nightclub. The results were immediate and spectacular. Undergraduates flocked to the restaurant and received extraordinary value, though I daresay a few corners were cut. I remember, for instance, a conversation I had with the chef one day. Every mealtime, twice a day, fish was on the menu: sole, turbot, halibut, you name it and it was there. 'How is it, chef,' I said, 'that we offer this different range of fish, all the best fish, every day and yet the only bills I ever see are for cod?' 'Ah,' he replied with a smile, 'it's how you carve it!' We also had an equally resourceful head waiter in the person of Mr Duck – the highly camp former janitor at the Examination Schools who, as he fluttered about the dining room, somehow contrived to lend an air of 1920s decadence even to the serving of a *table d'hôte* menu at half a crown.

With that success under my belt, it suddenly seemed likely that I might be able to achieve my ambition and secure the presidency itself in the elections at the end of that academic year. But there was a snag: thanks to my slightly slow start, I had already exhausted my allotted three-year span at Oxford. Would my college allow me an extra term if I stood and was elected? I went well in advance to see the avuncular Vice-Master of Pembroke, R. B. McCallum (Homes Dudden, the Master, being by then virtually incapacitated), explained my dilemma to him and asked whether he would be prepared to let me come up for an extra term. I proposed that, if he did, I would submit an entry for the Gladstone Memorial History Prize. McCallum was soon to take over the mastership of my college and was a man of perception. He said: 'Well, certainly, I'd very happily have you back for one more term, but I wouldn't expect you to worry too much about the Gladstone Memorial Prize.'

The task of presiding over the Union's finances in that summer term of 1954 had undoubtedly aided my candidature for the presidency. Campaigning for any office was forbidden in any formal sense under the rules of the Society and, though a certain amount of illicit activity took place, there was no organised machine to deliver a vote. It is possible that a significant number of politically active members of the University Conservative Association voted the ticket, as people in the University Labour Club or the University Liberal Club also would have done. But there were no official canvassing teams. You hoped, of course, that your friends would turn out on the day and bring their friends with them. It was all pretty amateurish, and I think the rules of the Society at that time were broadly respected. The campaign, such as it ever was, largely consisted of the speeches that one had made, the service one had rendered and the contacts that one had established in other activities as well as in the debating chamber. When the election finally came, two of my closest supporters, Tony Howard and Jeremy Isaacs, a voluble and engaging character with a pronounced Glaswegian accent, were respectively chairman-elect and chairman of the University Labour Club and joined an all-party coalition to support my candidature. Against me were two ex-presidents of the University Liberals, Roger Booth and Bruce Burton, and an ex-chairman of the Labour Club, Jonathan Boswell. I won on the second round – once the bottom candidate, Bruce Burton, had been eliminated after the first ballot. But since I had got double the number of votes of my leading opponent it had been fairly easy. At the same time Jeremy Isaacs was elected librarian and Tony Howard treasurer. We thereby laid the foundations of a lifelong, three-way friendship.

Of course, there was another side to that summer term. It was also the term when I had to take my final exams, 'Schools' as they were called after the Examination Schools building into which we all traipsed for our final date with destiny. I performed competently in most of the subjects. But without the help of John Stewart, a former Union treasurer, I would never have managed the philosophy paper.

I can remember sitting in the window bay of the Union's dining room as he patiently explained to me the nature of logical positivism with a clarity that none of my tutors had ever managed. 'A great but undeserved triumph,' was the comment of my tutor, Neville Ward Perkins, when the examination results were announced. I heard the news in a telegram from Julian Critchley: 'Many congratulations on a second. Just off to catch banana boat.' He had actually achieved an almost unique distinction at Oxford of failing to get a degree at all. He fought back to attain another almost unique achievement: a fourth-class degree at the second attempt a year later. To anyone who knows him these were inexplicable results and quite fail to reflect his true abilities.

So, having been elected president of the Oxford Union for the Michaelmas term of 1954, I found myself free of any responsibilities other than that of the presidency. I had secured excellent digs at 5 Beaumont Street and devoted myself to the Union, as indeed I had largely done for the previous two terms. The task of converting the wine cellars into a nightclub proceeded apace. The old wine cellars were at that time being partially used to store coal. You descended a rickety staircase and there was the coal, in a damp vaulted chamber. The steward, Leslie Crawte, and I helped to move it. The scheme worked. The freshmen came up in October as always and a thousand new members joined that term – a record. The financial gamble had paid off and, looking back, it was my first commercial venture of any significance.

The nightclub was scene to one of my more bizarre undergraduate experiences. I had invited Sir Bernard and Lady Docker to come and open the cellars on Saturday, 30 October 1954. The Dockers were renowned at that time. They were flamboyant, colourful and wealthy figures, seen by some as an extravagant joke and by others as an industrialist with a glamorous wife who had presided over the decline of one of Britain's better-known companies, BSA. But they were a warm-hearted couple who lived life to the full. They arrived in their famous gold-plated Rolls-Royce and, after the most sumptuous dinner the Union could provide (no creative carving of cod on this occasion), we all repaired to the cellars, where I danced with Lady Docker. She looked up at me and said, 'Michael, Bernard and I would like to pay for this. How much did it cost?' I happened, to my good fortune, to know exactly how much it had cost. 'Six hundred pounds,' I said. A few days later a cheque duly arrived. We had got the nightclub for free. The cellars remained a feature of the Union for many years but then gradually went into a decline. However, forty years on from the original opening – to the month – I was invited back to reopen them, expanded, professionally managed and even more popular. The president on that occasion told me that she had spent the morning in the local music shop finding out what had been top of the hit parade at the time of the inaugural opening. The unforgettable voice of Nat King Cole ensured that for me, at least, it was an evening of memories.

One of the first tasks of any newly elected president of the Union is to prepare the 'card' for his or her term in office. The card is, in effect, the programme of debates. Motions have to be chosen and guests invited to participate. By tradition, the first debate of the new academic year, when with the opening of Michaelmas term the freshmen arrive, is that 'This House Has No Confidence in Her Majesty's Government.' This debate is always packed, but the freshmen have to be persuaded to sign up for membership – hopefully for life. The programme is the bait. Like every other student debating society, you invite the stars currently in the firmament of public life or not too long in their eclipse from it. To Oxford they all come: in my term alone we had speakers as varied as the Suez Group leader Julian Amery, the communist R. Palme Dutt, Lady Violet Bonham Carter, the future Taoiseach Liam Cosgrave, my old headmaster John Wolfenden and the television pundit Jacob Bronowski.

Undoubtedly the darlings of the university debating halls of that time were the Bevanites: Barbara Castle, Dick Crossman, Ian Mikado, Michael Foot and, of course, Nye Bevan – although he would never come to the Oxford Union itself. But I did hear him speak once at Oxford, as the guest of Tony Howard, the chairman of the Oxford University Labour Club, who (with a little help from Harold Wilson) persuaded him to come to a meeting, packed to the rafters, which the Labour Club held in the Union debating chamber in November 1954. He was marvellously impressive and I can hear his beguiling Welsh lilt and his oddly compelling stutter to this day.

The quality of the visiting speakers in the Union was generally very high, although they could occasionally go disastrously wrong. For the traditional 'no confidence' debate on 16 October 1954, I was disappointed not to have attracted a top-flight Cabinet minister to defend the government's record. We had been able to secure the services only of David Gammans MP, a former colonial servant who, having been in the House of Commons since 1941, had risen to the giddy heights of Assistant Postmaster-General in Winston Churchill's post-war government. He was to top the bill by speaking last on behalf of the government. I have seldom heard a more dreary, protracted speech then or since. The audience fidgeted and coughed, creating an atmosphere of total unease as the unfortunate man meandered on about home affairs. After forty-seven minutes he said, 'Now I turn to foreign affairs.' A fit of collective giggles broke out. Worse was to come. 'I want to talk about the Cold War,' the speaker proclaimed. 'Some of you may think this has been going on for a long time.' The place shook with laughter. 'I can see no end to it – it will, I fear, last for the rest of my natural lifetime.' There was not a dry eye left in the House. My two officers, Tony Howard and Jeremy Isaacs, sitting in their white ties and tails on either side of me, were in serious danger of falling off their chairs. Alone of the 800 undergraduates, my face was cast in granite, although the tears streamed down my cheeks. It was left, I think, to an ex-president, Bryan Magee, to try to explain to the bewildered Assistant Postmaster-General why they had all laughed so long and loud at his speech. Even the dons' own weekly paper, the *Oxford Magazine*, was to refer to 'an unfortunate series of *double entendres*'. The *Manchester Guardian* did worse by printing in its London Correspondence column a vivid account of the mauling the unfortunate Minister had received, down to and including the brutal comment in *Isis* that he had had to endure the experience of 'hearing the whole House roaring with laughter *at* him'. It says much for the standing of the Churchill administration – or at least for the resilience of the normal Tory majority among Union members – that the government case still carried the day.

This last term was a curious period in a sense. Most of my contemporaries had gone down, having completed their three years. I was to some extent set apart from the life of the body of undergraduates – rather, I suspect, like living to a great age as your contemporaries pass on. I remember at the time feeling an almost Olympian detachment from the battles that raged among the undergraduates. It was the period of the EOKA troubles in Cyprus and of Cheddi Jagan's challenge to the Colonial Secretary in British Guiana. Both issues deeply divided the university. Meetings were held, protests launched, petitions signed. It all seemed to me an irrelevance. It probably wasn't – but part of the excitement and challenge in the past had been the shared companionship with like-minded friends and colleagues, and most of mine had gone. Despite new friendships made in the Union, they had left a vacuum which was never quite filled.

I remember also the battle to admit women into the Union Society, which was, of course, genuine and hard-fought. I recall vividly being deeply involved, although I have no recollection today on which side of the argument I campaigned. It was to make little difference. Women were not finally admitted to full membership of the Union until eight years later in February 1963. Tony Howard thinks I was in favour. Why all these years later should I doubt him, particularly as it appears I may have been, for once, on the side of the angels?

It is said that George IV once remarked to the captain of school at Eton: 'You are greater now than ever I could make you.' There is something of that about being president of the Oxford Union. You have climbed a ladder, in competition with some of the most talented of your generation. You have entertained, on a scale far beyond the normal experience of your age group, a number of distinguished public figures and presided over one of the most illustrious undergraduate societies in the world. The busts of earlier generations of presidents are there to remind you of who has sat where you now sit: Gladstone, Salisbury, Asquith, F. E. Smith. Your most immediate predecessors are already climbing their chosen ladder, often in national politics. The future beckons. You have received the acclaim of a whole-page feature in the university magazine, *Isis*, under the grand, deluding title of 'Idol'. Mine was written by Tony Howard. He dared to forecast the story of my life. Writing in October 1954, he toyed with the notion of a biography eventually being produced about me: 'Perhaps one day it will be written. It will be all about a twentieth-century Dick Whittington who dreamt that there were streets paved with gold and that he was going to walk along them. At the end of the book – which will, of course, be a true life story – he will.' And so I left Oxford in December 1954, feeling then, as I feel to this day, an immense and irredeemable debt of gratitude to the university and all the experience it gave me.

Chapter 4

THE REAL WORLD

M y first day in search of those golden pavements was to be very different from the promise of only a few weeks earlier. I had secured articles to Henry Peat, a partner of Peat, Marwick, Mitchell and Co. of Ironmonger Lane, EC2, one of the world's leading accountancy firms. I arrived in the City of London on 3 January 1955 – long hair, suede shoes, red velvet waistcoat – to meet Derek Palmar, the manager of the department to which I was assigned (later to become chairman and chief executive and subsequently president of Bass the brewers and to receive a knighthood). I suspect he was horrified at so obvious an example of exotic youth fresh from Oxford. I was dispatched to the Angel, Islington, to join the team auditing the accounts of the slaughterhouse owned by the Fatstock Marketing Corporation at the top of the hill. I was given a ledger. It must have been six inches thick. It consisted simply of column after column of figures: the invoice totals of the amounts due to various farmers for their livestock. 'I suggest you start by casting that,' were the instructions. To cast, to an accountant, is to add. Today it is done by computer and yesterday by comptometer operators – girls with adding-up machines. But when I started out it was done mentally. I toiled away at it until about five o'clock and I remember walking out of the office into the night, into the cold, into the snow, clutching my head. The transformation from president of the Oxford Union to articled clerk was complete. It had not taken long – just seven hours.

I still find it difficult to know just when my commercial aspirations really started. Self-evidently both on my mother's and on my father's side of the family there were strong commercial instincts and at an early stage it seemed that I would try to follow in the same direction. Perhaps the first example I can remember was at Shrewsbury, where my lack of prowess at games left me with much spare time. Characteristically, though, that time was not wasted. I would go to the local post office where you could buy a variety of fizzy drinks at a shilling a bottle, four bottles to a crate. As others laboured on the playing fields, I struggled with the bottles – two crates at a time – up the hill to await their return. Together with three colleagues I then sold to our more energetic schoolmates the various coloured liquids by the glass. It didn't make a fortune but it did make me a profit, and it certainly whetted the appetite.

My commercial experience at Oxford, however, was a good deal more formative – involving, as it did, the renovation of the Oxford Union, its finances and its infrastructure. But more important even than that was a decision I took during my last term. I had to decide where to live in London when I began life as an articled clerk. The firm had declared as a matter of policy that they were going out to recruit in the graduate market and so, instead of paying the £3 a week which was then the going rate for articled clerks, they offered – me anyway – £7 a week. However, that £7 was still only about half the £600 a year that my graduate contemporaries at that time could expect to earn.

Over many years my grandparents had built up for me a Post Office Savings Account. They had done so by putting in £1 or £2 at a time and there now stood to my credit at the beginning of 1955 the princely sum of £1,000. I calculated that, spread over the three years, it would add something like £6 a week to the £7 of my earnings. I would be able to live broadly at the same living standard as my contemporaries. But on reflection – this was the calculation which prompted the critical decision – the rather obvious and chilling thought occurred to me that at the end of three years I wouldn't any longer have my £1,000.

It so happened that my old room-mate at Pembroke, Ian Josephs, was in a similar position. He, too, had £1,000. His father owned a number of boarding houses in London and, to the suggestion that he might look out for a similar such venture for his son and myself, he generously acceded. He offered us the prospect of purchasing a thirteen-year lease on the Thurston Court Hotel at 39 Clanricarde Gardens, Notting Hill Gate. The price was £3,750 but £1,750 of it was available on mortgage. Ian and I formed a company, called it Michian Ltd – an amalgam of our two first names – and with Thurston Court as our headquarters we were in business.

The property was in a substantial state of disrepair. The smell as you went through the front door was appalling. A complete overhaul was essential. We gave notice to the dozen or so occupants and, once we had achieved possession, Ian's father renovated the property from top to bottom as part of the purchase arrangements. Ian and I took a room each, leaving us with nine spare rooms. A suitably enticing sales card was produced to advertise the newly renovated facilities. Perhaps particularly attracted by the last sentence on the card, 'opposite Millionaires Row' – meaning Kensington Palace Gardens, home of all the grandest ambassadors' residences – we had no difficulty in finding tenants whose weekly rent of £2 or £3 each gave us some £30 a week. Occasionally, but not often, they were friends of ours. Julian Critchley and Tony Howard were both tenants of No. 39 – and among the most difficult tenants we ever had. (They paid much the lowest rent for a secluded attic room and yet complained incessantly that the roof leaked.) A year later we were amazed to discover that our asset was now worth £5,750 and that we had, effectively, doubled our money. It seemed too good to be true. We seized the opportunity. The house was duly sold, leaving us – after paying off the mortgage – with £4,000 capital.

Ian then found what was a cross between a boarding house and an hotel at 45 Inverness Terrace, Bayswater. Consisting of four converted houses, the New Court Hotel possessed something like thirty-five rooms; later we added a fifth house, giving us a forty-five-bedroom hotel. Again, its condition left much to be desired. But it was a big step up. We paid some £27,000 for it and the owner was prepared to leave £23,000 of it on mortgage. We should have been warned. But we had become the proud owners of a rather rundown hotel in a good, wide Bayswater street.

They were heady days. We had done it once. We could do it again. We had just managed to pay for the property; the problem of working capital had been left to providence. Everything we wanted to do had to be paid for from the revenue, and our revenue barely covered our costs. We couldn't afford builders. We did the work ourselves. I spent the days in the City ticking other people's account books. In the evenings and at weekends it was overalls and a paintbrush, as we slowly, painfully traded up the quality of the rooms. Sometimes we were helped by friends. One such from Swansea, Geoffrey Hayes, organised a group of his fellow medical students from Guy's Hospital to help decorate at £5 per head for the weekend. It was a messy, effective, immensely amusing process. They certainly became better doctors than they were decorators.

The hotel had one significant characteristic. It was built over a tube line. Every few minutes the structure began to tremble. The noise came next and the building shook from top to bottom as the Central Line trains rumbled between Lancaster Gate and Queensway stations. It required a considerable degree of aplomb, when unsuspecting guests arrived, to get them signed in and their luggage whisked to their rooms in the minute or two of silence which separated peak-hour trains roaring under the building. To fail in this was to be confronted by the evident dismay of people suddenly aware that they were going to have to sleep through this process and fearful, anyway, that the building would not survive the night.

The New Court Hotel was not Claridge's. We were on the frontiers of Bayswater, warts and all. All human life was there. There was a small number of long-term residents and a smattering of commercial travellers; business was brisk during the Motor Show, the Smithfield Show for farmers, the Ideal Home Exhibition and regularly on Friday and Saturday nights when the American servicemen arrived. By and large these last were charming, courteous and well behaved and, considering the frustrations they must have had to endure in the impersonal camps in which they were stationed, an amusing and companionable lot. But coping with forty rooms full of American GIs, let out of base for a night on the town, was a long way from the presidency of the Oxford Union and even pretty far removed from the world of an articled clerk in the City of London.

There were some dramatic moments – the night, for instance, when, on my way upstairs to bed, a door flew open and a naked prostitute was flung across the hallway. On another occasion a former member of the British Indian Army, who was visiting London to receive some high military decoration earned on the field of battle, pursued some unfortunate woman with the most blood-curdling yell. It would have terrified any enemy and doubtless was commonly heard on India's North West Frontier. But it seemed excessive on an otherwise quiet evening in springtime London. Mercifully, she escaped. Others have told of the time the Irish chef (to coin a phrase) walked out in the middle of the night, leaving me with the unenviable task of getting up even earlier than usual to cook breakfasts, before setting off for the City. I had always been able to make a passable shot at frying an egg. But faced with the need to fry forty eggs in a very short period of time, I still maintain it was a wonder that the guests and the hotel survived. (I reject, however, the story – much put about by a hostile witness – that every morning I was to be found in the kitchen mixing the butter with the margarine in order to save on catering bills.)

Ian was not the most energetic partner and we would never have managed even to the limited extent that we did had it not been for two invaluable girls, the Swansea-born Jean Taverner and the Canadian Rusty Rouane, who bore between them the day-to-day strain of coping. They kept the show not so much on the road as off the rocks. Then, towards the end of my association with the New Court Hotel, a new figure came to stay: one Major Denny, retired from the British Army and back in this country after service overseas. He was a large, affable enough chap. He was always there. He was willing to fill in, to help out, to man the bar, to sit behind the desk, to answer the telephone. He became one of the family. Week by week he grew ever more absorbed into the running of the hotel. He was to all appearances an officer and a gentleman. Nobody thought to check his references. It was a mistake I later came to regret.

In 1957 Ian and I decided to sell the hotel and go our separate ways. The financial strain had been considerable. It had provided us with accommodation and a living, but we were never going to make a serious success of it. The property was put on the market. One experience lives in my mind: the day I met Peter Rachman, the man who perhaps did more to create the sinister reputation of the property business in the late 1950s and early 1960s than any other single person. One of his managers had come to view the hotel. It so happened that, having shown him the premises, I was standing outside talking to him when a Rolls-Royce parked alongside us. The manager turned to the man behind the wheel, saying, 'A little child was killed this morning, Mr Rachman. She fell off the balcony of one of our properties.' Rachman's reply was brief: 'Are we insured?' 'Yes.' And off he drove.

It was at moments of that sort that I inevitably felt a measure of relief that I had a quite different day-job. But the truth is that at this, too, I was growing restive. After eighteen months with Peat's, helping to audit the books of some of the biggest companies in the land, I had decided to move to a smaller firm of accountants where I felt I would be more likely to get a feel for the whole picture rather than just some tiny part of a giant organisation. With this in mind, I had negotiated to move my articles from Henry Peat to Ken Ive, a partner in Shipley Blackburn, Sutton and Co., a medium-sized West End firm just off the Haymarket. Struggling hard with my intermediate chartered accountant's examinations – I had to take them three times in order to pass them, despite having special coaching lessons – my articles ran out in January 1958 before I was even within sight of taking the finals.

That confronted me with a tough decision. Did I really want to be an accountant? By then I think I had concluded that I was happier working in a commercial environment of my own choosing than pursuing the rigid disciplines of a career in accountancy. Moreover, I was pretty sure that I was already earning more from my other activities – which, now that I had joined up with another old Oxford friend, Clive Labovitch, included publishing – than was the partner to whom I was articled. National Service was approaching. I was committed to my entrepreneurial lifestyle. And, although I had finally passed the intermediate accountancy exams at the third attempt, the prospect of my sitting, let alone passing, the final examinations had simply ceased to be realistic.

It is difficult to be sure to what extent my experience as an articled clerk, particularly my early days in the City, influenced my views. Certainly, it made me question my convictions about the nature of capitalism. There was a scale and a remoteness about the activities of the City that seemed to lose human contact. A great tide of human beings, like ants, flowed into London's railway stations and across London's bridges every morning and flowed out again in the evening. It was a human conveyor belt. Could, I wondered, such a process keep close enough to the legitimate aspirations of the individual in the sort of responsible society in which I believed?

My father's sudden death at the age of fifty-five from a heart attack in April 1957 was the first real tragedy to hit our family. In the early evening of 1 April I had telephoned my parents, only to learn from my mother that my father had suffered a heart attack. Obviously she was worried, but at that time there was no talk of my returning home. Fortunately, I decided to ring our family doctor, Elwyn Jones, the same man who had brought me through meningitis. He explained that my father would need complete rest for the next ten days, during which time there was bound to be a degree of anxiety. We decided that I would not leave London. There was a sound medical reason – to avoid the heightened tensions that my arrival would have caused. We would speak again. A little later I rang Geoffrey Hayes, who, without in any way understating the risks involved, did his best to reassure me. I put the receiver down, having agreed that we, too, would speak again.

But the telephone rang again almost immediately. It was Geoff: 'I think I gave you the wrong advice. I think you should go and, if you like, I'll drive you tomorrow morning.' I owe him an immeasurable debt. We collected Bubbles and arrived at Broughton, our home on the Gower Road, in the early afternoon. I went straight to see my father. I did my rather inarticulate best to reinforce the medical advice I knew he had been given. He looked drawn and tired; the strength had gone from his voice as he thanked me for coming. Our conversation was brief and was interrupted by the arrival of a locum doctor who, together with my father's nurse, conducted an examination. My mother and sister and I stood waiting on the terrace outside the house. The doctor gave us his report on the way out: there was no change. Then, just as he was leaving, the nurse came rushing out to call him back. My father was dead.

It was the most dreadful moment of my life. My parents had been devoted to each other. Bubbles and I had shared and treasured the parental love that had been a constant feature of our lives. And now the rock upon which it all rested was gone. My father had given me a figure to respect, firm but wholly admirable. He had taught me to catch prawns and collect shells, had looked after my budgerigars, built my canoe – all the little things that had made up a happy childhood. He had taken me with him when on Saturdays he walked around the fabricating yards of Dawnays, of which he became the local director and from whose ranks so many had joined him on the outbreak of war. He had scrimped to pay the Shrewsbury fees. He had come to my twenty-first party in the Oxford Union and later stayed in the New Court Hotel, when his expense account would have allowed the best of the West End. He had encouraged me in every way. He had been proud of me, and to me he had been everything a father could and should be. If there was a day when I grew up, it was 2 April 1957. More than forty years on I write this with tears in my eyes.

In a curious way a consequence of my father's death was to reinforce the uncertainties that exposure to City life had first aroused. Virtually every weekend from April 1957 until I joined the Army in January 1959 I drove down to Swansea to see my mother and to try to preserve some remnant of family life. In those days the journey by car from London to Swansea – long before the Heads of the Valley road or the M4 made it possible to avoid the scars of a bygone industrial revolution as epitomised by Ebbw Vale, Merthyr Tydfil and Neath – took one through some of the most derelict areas of Britain. I looked and I questioned. I suppose my grief at the loss of my father compounded my mood. I have long since come to realise that most young people go through some such period when the economic order of society seems to them to cry out for radical reform. My own passed fairly quickly, and not since then have I ever had the remotest doubt that the capitalist system, within a civilised and regulated society, gives a greater diversity of choice and provides a wider opportunity for wealth creation than does any alternative economic structure. My faith in the beliefs of the Conservative Party was strengthened, not weakened, by this early period of misgivings – misgivings that anyway were relatively rapidly resolved. The market itself may know no morality. But to help make sure a moral order prevails is one of the responsibilities of the politician. At its best, that is what makes politics the high-minded and satisfying calling which I have found it to be.

Chapter 5

CANDIDATE FOR GOWER

O n moving to London in January of 1955, I had had four main preoccupations. The first was to complete my articles as an articled clerk. The second was to lay the foundations for financial independence, with a view to pursuing a political career. The third was to sustain a relationship with the Conservative Party, albeit more limited than that in my time at Oxford. And finally there was the issue of National Service.

The day-to-day grind of the City, the need to study for my accountancy exams and the hours devoted to my property interests left little time for the voluntary side of the Conservative Party. I did, however, at the age of twenty-three apply to put my name on the list of Conservative candidates, having secured the support of Ted Heath, the government Chief Whip at the time. (I had first met him during a visit he made to Oxford. I took my chance and wrote to him in October 1956 and by return of post he agreed that I could use his name as a referee.) Paul Bryan, the Tory MP for Howden and the Vice-Chairman of the party in charge of candidates, interviewed me at Conservative Central Office. He told me politely that he thought I was too young and inexperienced to be considered at that time as a candidate for the party at the next general election – which was still some years off. 'If, however, you find that you get selected for a seat, then, of course, we would revise our judgement.'

It wasn't until a couple of years later that I heard that the Gower constituency in South Wales was looking for a Conservative candidate. Of course I knew the area well from my boyhood and my mother was still living in Swansea, the town – now the city – which the Gower Peninsula and the Swansea Valley would look to as their main shopping and communications centre. The constituency itself was one of the safest Labour seats in South Wales. The selection process took place in the Constitutional Club, Swansea, late in the evening, one weekday night. A number of hopeful aspirants to political power had been invited to display their wares to what was virtually the entire Association of National Liberal/Conservatives in Gower – a tiny handful of beleaguered folk. I arrived at my appointed hour, to the huge relief of the selection committee. Nobody else had bothered to turn up. Thus, towards the end of 1958 I was selected unanimously as the National Liberal and Conservative (the label the Gower Conservative Association then used)* prospective parliamentary candidate for Gower.

It was not until the campaign itself that my role in this rock-ribbed Labour seat required any great commitment. There was very little evidence of Conservative activity on the ground, but it was pleasing to know that I was treading in the steps of Alan Lennox-Boyd (later Lord Boyd of Merton and before that a long-serving Conservative Colonial Secretary from 1954 to 1959) who had fought the seat in 1929, a point often referred to by the remnant of the faithful who remembered him vividly even thirty years later.

In London I joined the Coningsby Club, a monthly dining club for Oxbridge graduates which met at the House of Commons to listen to prominent figures of the day. I also joined the Bow Group and a few years later, in 1961, I took my girlfriend and future wife, Anne Williams, on our third date, to listen to the man of the future as he then was to so many of my generation: Ted Heath. Thus I kept in touch with the Conservative Party of the time.

Until 1956 I hadn't been able to afford a car and had had little need of one. Besides, I had long since agreed with myself that I wouldn't buy just any old car. I wanted a Jaguar. They were British. They looked good. It would be worth the wait. The day the British troops entered Suez, the price of petrol had gone through the roof and the price of cars through the floor. It was time to strike. On 21 December 1956, I bought my first second-hand Jaguar for £1,750. Ten miles from the garage on my way to display my proud possession to my parents in Swansea over the Christmas holidays, it broke down. No matter; I

---

* Until 1966, the National Liberal Party – a by-product of Sir John Simon's split away from the Liberal Party over his support of a Commonwealth Tariff Agreement in the national government of 1931 – survived as technically a separate organisation from the Tories. This enabled candidates to be put up as 'National Liberal and Conservative', 'Conservative and National Liberal' or even simply 'National Liberal'.

owned a Jaguar. A year later I traded it in, receiving the price I had paid for it, for a brand-new model.

National Service presented me with a dilemma. I had been brought up to admire and respect the military. My father, throughout his life, devoted much energy and enthusiasm to the Territorial Army and I had seen his commitment as a commanding officer in the Royal Engineers during the war. I was torn in two directions. The first strong conviction was that there were priorities in my life which demanded my attention. There was so much that I wanted to do that the prospect of losing two years to square-bashing was unappealing. On the other hand, I was determined that, if I had to do it, I wanted to serve in one of the foremost regiments of the British Army. My father had secured for me an introduction to the Colonel of the Welsh Guards, Colonel D. G. Davies-Scourfield MC, through a distinguished former member of the regiment, Sir Godfrey Llewellyn. The Colonel saw me in the autumn of 1955 and it was agreed that I would join the brigade squad of potential officers at the Guards Depot, Caterham, when I came to do my National Service. My deferment, granted while I served my articles, expired at the end of 1958, and the papers calling me up for National Service duly arrived, informing me that I was expected to appear, along with some thirty other aspirant officers, on 9 January 1959 before five in the afternoon.

Preparing for National Service required some decisions. I didn't wish to lose touch with the business. By this time Major Denny had become the manager of our property interests, but I was the central player and there were daily decisions to be taken. My solution was simple. I would take a dictating machine with me to send messages in response to tapes which would daily arrive through the post. It seemed a sensible and practical approach – devoid, however, of any sense of reality, as I was soon to discover. I was also concerned that my relatively long hair was not going to provide a bumper harvest for some demon Army barber. After lunch on that bleak January Friday, I set off for the Washington Hotel for my last rendezvous with the man who had been cutting my hair ever since I came to London. 'Take it off,' I said. 'Take it off like an Army barber would take it off. They're not going to make a fool of me.' Almost with tears in his eyes, he faithfully carried out my instructions. I returned to the office to the vast merriment of the assembled staff. Later that same afternoon, driven by Major Denny in my Jaguar, with a great suitcase carrying all manner of paraphernalia (including the overweight dictating machine), and wearing my father's demob overcoat (equally large – an unnecessarily cumbersome attribute), I arrived at the Guards Depot at Caterham, in the dark and in the cold. I went through the gate and was about to inquire where they would like me to go when a voice rasped in my ear, 'Stand still, you 'orrible long-haired monster, you!' That voice, unnecessarily loud and totally devoid of any natural human courtesy, directed me towards a Tarmac road leading off into an ever thickening fog. 'Follow me,' it said and set off at a pace which would have done credit to an Olympic sprinter, expecting me to keep up with suitcase, overcoat and all the consequences of three years' worth of relatively inactive comfort. How I completed that hundred-yard journey remains to this day a mystery to me. But I did, arriving gasping and dishevelled for my first medical examination. I was asked whether I could see the colours of a chart on the wall. I was in no fit state to see the wall, let alone the chart or the colours. But it soon turned out that I had difficulty in distinguishing reds on green, a deficiency which has lived with me ever since and remains something of a handicap in my love of birds and flowers.

There were some thirty of us new recruits; but I was easily the oldest at twenty-five – all the others were eighteen-year-olds. We were corralled into two huts out on the middle of a windswept plain, fifteen to a hut. My hut was under the eye of Trained Soldier Thorpe, a Guardsman whose job it was to teach us the rudiments of that alien world: how to make boots look like polished steel; how to press unyielding cloth into razor-sharp creases; how to stack our pathetic possessions neatly on the bed for daily inspection. For nine weeks Barry Thorpe was to be the indispensable key to our survival.

As we arrived one by one, there was not much conversation among the fifteen people gathered in the first hut. Instead, there was the silence of apprehension. It was fully justified. Suddenly, the door of the hut swung open, allowing an icy blast of winter wind and a terrifying phenomenon, a colour sergeant of the Coldstream Guards, to enter. Every bit of him was polished and creased. His peak cap was slashed so that only the barest sight of two glaring eyes shone out as he surveyed those who were to be his responsibility for the next nine weeks. 'Right then, stand by your beds,' he said in a voice far louder than was necessary to communicate in a closed environment with fifteen people who were desperate to take in every word he uttered. But the impact was the message. 'There are only two ways through the Guards Depot,' he said. 'The 'ard way. That's my way.

And the fucking 'ard way. That's any other way.' And with that, he was gone. This was our introduction to Sergeant Peter Horsfall, the twenty-nine-year-old who was to dominate our lives for the next nine weeks.

Many have described the Guards Depot and I will not seek to add to their vivid descriptions of the toughness and hardness of the course. Rugged it certainly was. It has to be realised, and I certainly came to accept it, that the essential responsibility resting on that colour sergeant was that he had thirty very young and inexperienced men who, once they completed their training at officer cadet school, might become responsible for the lives of a platoon of thirty men on active service. He had to make sure that nobody got through without being able to command sufficient respect to lead men into battle. And, as he had only the initial nine weeks in which to do it, you could hardly fault him for making sure that there were not many mistakes. The recruit in the bed next to me was Johnny Ricketts, later to command the Welsh Guards in the Falklands War. No mistake there.

We drilled, marched, ran, climbed, learnt to assemble rifles, to break down rifles, strip machine guns, fire machine guns – every minute of our day we were kept hard at it. And quite rightly so. The physical strain of it was designed to test you: to see whether you were strong enough; but also to see whether you had the will to go on beyond the limit, almost, of tolerance. I saw one man crack. He couldn't take the pace and he lay on the ground in considerable physical distress. There was no apparent mercy as Sergeant Horsfall stood over him, shouting abuse and telling him to get to his feet. It was cruel, harsh, but the next day the man was gone. As far as Peter Horsfall was concerned, he had ensured that that particular potential officer would never be responsible for men in battle. Who could blame him?

After three weeks we were allowed out on a weekend pass. I decided to have a real break from Caterham. I had been using the Connaught Hotel restaurant for several years; it is one of the world's most sympathetic hotels. I knew the head waiter, Charles, a legendary figure of his time in that profession. I was saluted by the manager and respected, superficially at least, by the hall porter. I was a customer. What else mattered? Or so I thought – until I appeared in a guardsman's uniform (we were not allowed to leave Caterham in mufti on our first leave pass). I had made a reservation by telephone. Naturally, it had been accepted. Nobody had told them that the Michael Heseltine they had served so punctiliously over recent years was now Guardsman Heseltine, the lowest form of military life to the Army officers from whose ranks the Connaught would customarily draw its customers. When I arrived to sign in, there was an acute moment of embarrassment, whispers behind partitions, as they imagined the delicacy of the situation should I come face to face with any of my commissioned superiors. But finally commercial interests and a long-term perspective prevailed. They gave me a room. No officers whatever appeared, and it all passed without mishap. After three days I was back in the Guards Depot. But at least I had been reminded that there was a life after Caterham.

For me, though, my current existence remained a pretty tortured one. Some years before, I had leapt down the last five steps of the stairs of our original boarding house, at 39 Clanricarde Gardens. My ankle had given way and had turned over, leaving me in acute pain. The sprain of course had healed, as sprains do. But it had left me with a permanently weak ankle. Although the doctors had considered this before I went into National Service, they had decided that the ankle was perfectly capable of taking the strain of basic training. It proved to be a misjudgement and I found that I was forced out of some of the physical activity that was an essential feature of basic training. After about four or five weeks at the Guards Depot, the doctor said to me, 'Do you really think you ought to go on? This isn't working.' By that time I was within four weeks of completing the course and I had made up my mind that I would sweat it out and so refused the offer of a medical discharge that was available to me.

After six weeks, we were lined up as usual when Sergeant Horsfall made a joke. It wasn't a particularly funny joke. That was not the point. The psychological shock was immense. This was not a man given to jokes. This was not a man given to anything except a barked command and an instant reprimand. So our first reaction was a rather nervous titter. We were uncertain what the trap was, where the dangers were, fearful of the immediate penalty that was likely to flow if we got the judgement wrong. But it was intended as a joke. It was the beginning of the build-up after the six weeks of breakdown. When, three weeks later, we left the Guards Depot in a truck, there were absolutely no hard feelings as we waved goodbye to Sergeant Horsfall. He was, by then, our friend. Living through that experience, and coming to understand something of the purpose behind it, taught me more about the loyalties of the Brigade of Guards than any book or lecture could ever have done. He had literally taken us, pushed us, to the furthest point of physical endurance, made us hate him, and then – as if we were puppets he was manipulating on a string – pulled us back into a sense of pride and comradeship that formed the basis of our relationship from then on.

I later learnt that four months after we left the Guards Depot one of my contemporaries, the Hon. Tim Tollemache (now Lord Tollemache), newly commissioned, joined the 2nd Battalion of the Coldstream Guards in Kenya towards the end of the Mau Mau troubles. There he found himself commanding a platoon, the sergeant of which was Peter Horsfall, recently released from his responsibilities as scourge of potential officers at Caterham. Sergeant Peter Horsfall went on to take a quartermaster's commission and become Major Peter Horsfall. After retiring from the Army, he was for many years the Staff Superintendent in the House of Lords and received an MBE for his services. We still meet at occasional Brigade squad reunion dinners.

We left the Guards Depot for Mons, the officer cadet school where we were to spend three months before, hopefully, gaining commissions and the posting to our individual units. This time the Jaguar came too. At Mons we came into contact with National Service soldiers from every regiment and corps. It was noticeable just how much better trained and how much more closely bonded we were than any of the others. In that competitive environment there were some from the Royal Marines who stood out, but the bunch always way ahead were from the Brigade. We were proud of it. Our instructors, Company Sergeant-Major Bert Croucher and Sergeant Eric Howard (who later wrote of his experiences in *My Trinity*, published in 1999), were both from the Scots Guards. By the time of the passing-out parade to celebrate our commissioning, one from each of the four companies had been chosen as a junior under-officer, one of whom was to be promoted to senior under-officer and awarded the Sword of Honour. Of the four under-officers selected, three came from the Brigade. I was one of them and received an A-grade. I was told I had not got the Sword of Honour because it was felt that, at my age, I had an unfair advantage over the rest of the intake.

After receiving a commission on 11 June, I reported with other new colleagues from the Welsh Guards, Johnny Ricketts and George Rees (who was subsequently to become a partner in a firm of stockbrokers), to Pirbright where the battalion, under the command of Lieutenant-Colonel John Miller DSO MC, was stationed. I was posted to the Prince of Wales Company, 1st Battalion Welsh Guards. Lieutenant-Colonel

Miller had, as a major, led the Prince of Wales Company as part of the advance party of the Welsh Guards which liberated Brussels in early September 1944. By coincidence, I had an earlier connection with the Miller family. Their home was Shotover House, just outside Oxford. It had been commandeered during the war and became the headquarters of a training battalion of the Royal Engineers. It was to this splendid Georgian house that my father had been posted as commanding officer in 1943. My mother, sister and I had lived in a boarding house, Forest Lodge, in Headington, Oxford. It was just a short walk across the fields from Forest Lodge to Shotover. I made the journey frequently and retain warm memories of many happy hours wandering the grounds with my father or being taken on conducted tours of the demonstration huts housing a wondrous (to a small boy) display of explosive military equipment.

As an Oxford undergraduate, I once told Julian Critchley that my father had been stationed in a splendid house just outside the city. We decided to go and introduce ourselves to the owner, a Major Alastair Miller, an elder brother of John's. We duly arrived, having transported ourselves on Julian's Vespa. The door was opened by the Major. I introduced myself, expecting a warm, friendly reception. It was not to be. It became obvious that we were not to be invited in. We retreated. I mentioned this later to my father before he died, expressing surprise at the reception we got. 'Well,' he replied, 'we had to build those demonstration Nissen huts and the only solid base on which to do it was the tennis courts.' That explained a great deal. But I was to get to know Alastair's younger brother, John Miller, not just as my commanding officer in 1959, but personally later as a friend. I became his Member of Parliament in 1974 and later still, when I went to be sworn in as a Privy Counsellor in 1979, it was Lieutenant-Colonel Sir John Miller who, as Crown Equerry to the Queen, briefed us on the form of things. Then, in the summer of 1994 while I was President of the Board of Trade, he was to give a small, private dinner party at Dukes Hotel for Her Majesty the Queen to which he invited as the only guests three of his subaltern officers from the Pirbright battalion: General Sir Charles Guthrie, future Chief of the Defence Staff; Colonel Johnny Ricketts, who commanded the 1st Battalion in the Falklands, and myself. It was a memorable evening.

I found life at Pirbright as a subaltern officer in the battalion extremely boring. There seemed to be absolutely nothing to do. I had an in-tray in an office. But there was never anything of any interest in it. I remember complaining, or rather asking once if there was anything that I could do, and being told that I could have a foot inspection of my men. It all might have been very different if we had been involved in soldiering in serious circumstances. But the routine daily round of inspection and parade, with long hours off-duty, was frustrating to an extraordinary degree. This was not how I had seen my life panning out.

Fortunately, the 1959 general election was announced on 8 September: the Conservatives under Harold Macmillan were seeking a third successive Tory victory. Under Queen's Regulations I was given the four weeks up to polling day in order to conduct an active campaign. Polling day was to be on 8 October, so I set off almost immediately to fight my seat. In South Wales there was a small group of us political virgins, Hugh Rees, Idris Pearce, Humphry Crum Ewing and myself, who were fighting our first-ever campaigns at that election (Geoffrey Howe was fighting his second at Aberavon). But of that company only Hugh Rees in Swansea West had a remote chance of winning, which he did by just 403 votes.

The Gower constituency in those days comprised two very different communities. In the southern part it consisted of some of the most wonderful coastline of the Gower Peninsula, where I had spent innumerable happy childhood days on the beaches. To this had to be added the coal-mining communities of the Swansea Valley. The Steel Company of Wales had also located its major investment at Velindre, a triumph for the investment policies of the Tory government of the 1950s that seemed to have passed quite unnoticed by the local electorate. I armed myself with a Land Rover, my Alsatian dog Kim, and my then girlfriend, Margaret Vaux, and set out to take the Tory message to parts of Wales which it had not reached for many a long year. With all the enthusiasm and energy I possessed, I penetrated the mining villages and small towns, spreading the 'never had it so good' message of Macmillan's election campaign. The only thing missing was a Conservative audience. There were very few branches, tiny numbers of volunteers and a Labour voting public wholly indifferent to any message other than the one they knew to be their own.

I decided to take the attack to the enemy. There was a new Labour candidate, an industrial consultant called Ifor Davies, in place of the ex-miner Dai Grenfell who had held the seat for thirty-seven years and had briefly served as Secretary for Mines in Churchill's wartime coalition. I adopted the age-old technique of challenging Davies to a public debate. I certainly couldn't get any audiences on my own, so why not share his? He had the good sense not to take me up on my suggestion. But this gave me an admirable headline in the *South Wales Evening Post*: 'Roaring lion or a mouse?' Again, no response. I decided the only thing to do was to turn up at one of his meetings. All was very courteous and well ordered, until I got bored with his message, rapturously applauded by the gathered ranks of the Labour Welsh. I decided to leave the hall, but before doing so I offered to shake the hand of the Labour candidate. His henchmen assumed I was about to hit him and a rather unseemly scuffle took place, the resulting publicity for which probably did my campaign little good. But at least people noticed that there was another candidate.

Worse was to follow. I saw in the *South Wales Evening Post* an advertisement announcing that Aneurin Bevan would address the Labour Party of South Wales in the Elysium Cinema, Swansea, at the weekend. I had last heard him in Oxford in 1954 and this was too good an opportunity to miss. And so, on a wet Sunday evening, as the sole Conservative I snuck in with the hordes of deliriously excited Labour supporters. I took my seat at the rear of the balcony, right at the back of the cinema, and watched the platform party arrive. Aneurin Bevan, by this time a glowing figure of confident celebrity and virtually a national legend, began his speech by introducing the Labour Members of Parliament. And then he turned to the Labour candidate for Gower and said in that almost caressing Welsh way of his, '*And* we have the candidate for Gower here tonight.' Whereupon a voice was heard to proclaim from the back of the balcony, 'You have *both* the candidates for Gower here tonight.' The impact was electric. Nye Bevan hunched over his microphone, stabbed the darkness with a stubby finger and cried, 'Ah, I hear the voice of an Englishman.' Whereupon a thousand Labour voices roared with hysterical laughter. I, too, had to laugh. But it was the end of any attempts I might otherwise have made to elicit publicity from attending Labour meetings.

Elsewhere there was not much encouragement either. One Monday afternoon in my Land Rover I drove into the small mining village of Cwmllynfell at the head of the Swansea Valley and stationed myself in the deserted village square. I began to proclaim the message through the loudspeaker. Slowly at first, but with gathering speed, a sizeable number of people began to appear. For me during that campaign it was almost unprecedented – anyway quite uncharacteristic of the normal reaction. Before I knew what had happened, there were something like a hundred men gathered round the Land Rover, listening unemotionally to the message of Tory prosperity that I was preaching. Eventually I paused, leant over the side of the vehicle and said to the nearest, unsmiling face, 'It's very good of you to come. How is it so many of you happen to be available on this Monday afternoon?' 'Because they closed the bloody pit, boy, two days ago.' It was time to go. I departed Cwmllynfell to search for pastures more promising to my cause. But, of course, there were very few.

I battled until the last hour before the polls closed. In a final forlorn and almost desperate attempt to harvest the vote on polling night, on Thursday, 8 October, I travelled again to the top end of the Swansea Valley, to Ystradgynlais. There was a long queue of voters, waiting with a patient determination outside the polling station to vote. One of them saw me, smiled and said, 'Go home, boy. You've done any good that you can ever do up here.' So it was that I turned for the last time in the campaign down the Swansea Valley for home and bed.

Harold Macmillan had come to speak in the Brangwyn Hall, Swansea, halfway through the campaign. The polls were not looking good but in that avuncular way of his that I was later to come to know so well, he put his hand on my arm and said, 'Don't worry. It will all be all right on the night.' And so, indeed, it was. The Conservative government was returned with an overall majority in the House of Commons of 100. The Gower result was: Ifor Davies 27,441; M. Heseltine 9,837; Dr J. Gwyn Griffiths (Welsh Nationalist) 3,744. I had increased the Tory share of the vote from 21.1 per cent in 1955 to 24 per cent; indeed, the Gower Conservative Association records assert that I increased the Tory vote by 20 per cent but it would be more accurate to record that I only managed a swing of 2.12 per cent to the Conservatives – only marginally up on the national average. I was reckoned to have fought a good campaign. I had made a spirited attack and if the only effect had been to increase the turnout, well, that was an indication of something. At least there had been some interest in what was happening.

If it had not exactly been a baptism of fire, at least I could claim to have come unscathed through four weeks' total immersion in politics. That was more than could be said for my business career at this point. Major Denny now comes back into the story. When Ian and I sold the New Court Hotel and ended our partnership I had moved to a boarding house which Clive Labovitch and I had bought, together with an investment of £4,500 by my mother, just off the Boltons at 29–31 Tregunter Road, SW10. We had subsequently added two more houses at the rear, in Cathcart Road, and turned it into a significant complex of lettings. Of course, all this and my other property developments took a good deal of day-to-day management and supervision – a task (with me away in the Army) that my old colleague at the New Court Hotel, Major Denny, undertook for us. We had also acquired another leasehold property on my original stamping-ground of Clanricarde Gardens, which again came under Denny's management. On my return from the election campaign, I was confronted with a serious shortage of cash in one part of the company's accounts. I compared the rent rolls with the receipts columns in the company books. I checked the bank statements and made up a schedule comparing what should have happened with the record in the company accounts. Clive Labovitch and I summoned Denny to our office, confronted him with the schedule and asked for an explanation. There was none. He made no attempt to deny what he had done. He left at once.

Belatedly, upon inquiry, we discovered that, before he had come to the New Court Hotel some two years earlier, he had been cashiered from the Army for stealing the mess funds. But, because of the way in which he had first come into my life, it had simply never occurred to me to check his references. It was my fault and nobody else's, and it taught me a lesson.

Nevertheless, the cash deficiency was a serious blow. And – due, as I was, to return to Pirbright – there would be no one left to pick up the pieces on that side of the business (Clive's preoccupation was our publishing interests). There was, though, one gleam of hope. Compulsory National Service was just about to come to an end. I got my solicitor to write to the War Office asking whether they really wanted me to return. He cited the problems which had arisen with my business and eventually got a reply saying that, in the circumstances, I would not be recalled.

This outcome, I'm glad to say, confounded the teasing statement made by a left-wing newspaper columnist, Tony Howard, during the election that my colleagues in the officers' mess at Pirbright were so convinced of my defeat that they could hardly contain their excitement at the prospect of my return and listening to my campaign memories. 'Oh Lord, yes,' my adjutant was even quoted as saying in response to a question as to whether I'd be back, 'and we're longing to hear all about it.' That they never got the chance to do so – and that the regimental silver remained unsullied by my no doubt exaggerated tales of political derring-do – is, I suppose, about the one thing I owe to Major Denny.

Chapter 6

BUSINESS AT THE DEEP END

M y parting with Ian Josephs and my going into business with
Clive Labovitch altered the course of my life. By the time
we met again after Oxford – where Clive had been the
founder and co-owner of the weekly student newspaper *Cherwell* (on
which I had served as a director) – he had just bought a vade-mecum
going under the title of *Oxford University What's What* to be published
by a company of his own, Cornmarket Press, which he ran from the top
floor at 1 Lower James Street in Soho above the showrooms belonging
to his family's textile firm, Darley Mills.

Clive and I had bumped into each other once or twice since our
Oxford days. Then one evening in 1957, just after I had returned to
the New Court Hotel from the City, the telephone rang. It was Clive
asking if I would like to hear about a new venture he had embarked
upon. I caught a taxi and went round to his family flat in Prince's Gate,
where he showed me his new guidebook and explained its concept.
It was on sale to, and designed to be read by, all the university
freshmen as they came up to Oxford each October. For the most part,
it consisted of a guide to the city's restaurants, pubs, cinemas and more
important shops. Tucked into the back of it, however, was a section
called the *Directory of Opportunities for Graduates*, a loose-leaf insert
which carried forty pages of display advertising, each page paid for
by one of Britain's larger companies, anxious to attract freshly minted
graduates into their corporate service.

It struck me at once that Clive was sitting on a gold mine without fully realising it. Although the publication had only recently
come under his control, he had failed to spot that it was wrongly
targeted. The corporate advertisers – and they were, most of them,
very distinguished public companies – were paying good money to

advertise to young people who were not going to leave university for at least three years. My immediate reaction was to advise Clive that he should change the formula and turn it into a separate publication to be given away free to all *final-year* students at *every* university in the country. He instantly recognised the commercial possibilities in such a venture and generously asked me – despite the fact that my own business background was then solely in property – to join him. However improbably, that was how I became a publisher.

That same year we brought out a separate edition of *Opportunities for Graduates*. It was a spectacular success, with the advertising jumping from forty pages in the loose-leaf insert Clive had bought only a couple of years earlier to 169 in the product we were now issuing as a hardback book and distributing to students nationwide. And that was only the start of it. Each year the number of advertisers increased by leaps and bounds; so did the advertising rates. We speedily added two companion publications – a *Directory of Opportunities for School Leavers* and a *Directory of Opportunities for Qualified Men*. (This, I fear, was before the days of equal opportunity in the workplace.) By 1961 we had produced Canadian and French editions and were moving into the German market. The overseas editions never prospered, but it was from a particularly rich British golden goose that there came the underlying profit upon which we built much of our subsequent progress and which in the end played a vital role in saving us from the disaster that was to come in 1962.

Cornmarket continued to operate during this period out of the Darley Mills offices in Lower James Street, where I had now established an office for myself as well. And it was from there also that Clive and I started up our own property development company, Bastion Property (later known as the Bastion Group of Companies), which prospered for a time but also ultimately played its part – as we got more ambitious and moved out of London – in what was nearly our commercial downfall. It is difficult now to recapture the drama of the 1950s London property scene. We entered into at least three contracts in the late 1950s and early 1960s – one to buy a deconsecrated church in George Street, W1, another a derelict site in Regent's Park and a third an empty terrace of houses in Pembridge Square, W2 – all of which we had contracted to sell for substantial profits before we had even paid for them in the first place. On another, tiny site, in Queensborough Mews, W2, we built eight houses to an ingenious design by Peter Boston. Each was only eleven feet wide and included a 'cocktail roof' (the *Daily Sketch*'s description, not mine). They sold well, though we managed to lose the anticipated profit by undertaking the building works ourselves. This was a period of tremendous opportunity but it required cool nerves and a willingness to take risky decisions at speed.

At least, however, our property activities brought into my life a lawyer called Charles Corman. It was Clive who originally introduced him to me. He became my solicitor, a lifelong friend and eventually my children's trustee. Charles, a devout Jew, has advised me on innumerable occasions. For his knowledge of the law I am eternally grateful, but much more important than that is my wholehearted admiration for his unfailing and innate sense of what is right and what is wrong.

A telephone call one day from John Dickens, an estate agent in Notting Hill Gate, who had sold our original boarding house in Clanricarde Gardens, told Clive and me that two houses off Kensington High Street – 9 and 11 Stafford Terrace – were available on lease. They had been part of a hostel used for Irish labourers during the war and were in need of restoration. But the potential was obvious. We bought at the asking price and moved to a rapid exchange of contract. So far, so good. I had noticed on my first inspection that the five adjoining properties – numbers 13, 15, 17, 19 and 21 – were in exactly the same state, thus offering a block of seven properties for conversion to flats. I asked John Dickens to inquire of Chestertons, the managing agents, if we could obtain them. He received no encouragement. We completed our original purchase.

Having acquired the leasehold interest of the first two, I decided personally to approach Chestertons. I was encouraged to believe that there would be a reasonable chance of acquiring the other five. Then one day I was invited to meet the then senior partner. To his great regret he had to tell me that they had had to make alternative arrangements about the other five properties. His clinching argument, to explain it all, was that they had discovered that the first two had been acquired by somebody else, making it impossible to split up the block, and they would have to do business with that person. My smile, I fear, had something of the crocodile about it as I explained as civilly as I was able that I was aware of the background but that I was the person who had acquired the other two. There are moments in life to savour. This was one.

To own the lease of seven houses – albeit in some disrepair – in one of London's more fashionable areas, with the opportunity to convert them into twenty flats, felt like the big time. The deal was done. We were to surrender the lease we had bought of the original two properties and enter into a new fifty-eight-year lease for the block. We couldn't go wrong. The future was set. And then the new lease arrived. To my horror I found enshrined in it the clause that no flats could be sold to coloured people. I rang the agents, Chestertons to protest. I explained that I wouldn't enter into a racially prejudiced legal arrangement of this sort. The clause was withdrawn. But I have always felt proud that I was prepared to put principle before financial advantage in what, at that stage, was a spectacularly attractive commercial negotiation.

Chestertons were, however, by now well pleased with us. One day Henry Wells, then a senior partner in the firm (later to become Sir Henry Wells, chairman of Harold Wilson's Land Commission, which was established in 1967 and abolished by the Heath government in 1971), took me to see Hyde Park Gardens, W2, a block of properties they were handling for the Church Commissioners. Anyone who knows London will have passed it time and again – a massive Victorian terrace, bordering the Bayswater Road from Clarendon Place to Brook Street and partially hidden by a well-planted private garden the use of which is restricted to the tenants of the block. It is palatial. The interior matched the scale and quality of the exterior. Henry asked if I would consider taking the block on – at an annual rental of £11,000. I agreed and he promised to let me know. His recommendation to the Church Commissioners, then headed by Sir Malcolm Trustam-Eve, was rejected on the basis, as I understood it, that we were too young. There is no telling how or what we would have done with it, but when I look back, this was 'the one that got away'.

It was Clive again who, back in the spring of 1958, first recruited Lindsay Masters – destined to become for thirty years, while I was active in politics, the effective controller of the business – as advertisement manager of the *Directory of Opportunities for Graduates*.

A former member of the somewhat louche Chelsea set of the 1950s, Lindsay is, quite simply, a phenomenon. The son of artists, he had an awareness of design and a fondness for good writing, neither of which were in evidence in the trade press at the time. He believed that, if the highest standards of design and journalism were applied to the backwater of trade publishing, profits were there to be made. *Campaign* was to be the first of our publications to prove him right. Over the years he developed an appetite for the dry world of comparative management statistics; that would, I believe, have come as something of a surprise to those who knew him in the 1950s and 1960s more as a denizen of Ronnie Scott's jazz club than as the highly successful manager he proved to be.

I sometimes felt that Lindsay could sell anything anywhere. Among his early post-Oxford experiences was a period in Germany. There he worked for Harry Rosancik, a Jewish entrepreneur who had miraculously survived the horrors of Dachau. The job was simple. Lindsay and another man were provided with a suitcase stuffed with lederhosen and helped over the perimeter fence of a local American base, filled to overflowing with GIs and their wives who were loaded with dollars and had nothing to spend them on. Trade was brisk but short lived. The Military Police – known as the snowballs – always caught up with them, bundled them into the nearest jeep and abandoned them a mile or so up the road in the middle of nowhere with apparently a long walk home. Not so. Rosancik would be waiting and on they would go to the next camp and repeat the process. Certainly, the *Directories* prospered mightily while he was responsible for their advertising revenue.

It was in 1959, while I was away on National Service, that Clive told me one day over the telephone that Lindsay had hired a young sales-man to assist him with the *Directories*. Lindsay was earning £800 a year at the time. 'Differentials must be preserved,' he explained, as Simon Tindall was recruited at £400 a year. Simon had left National Service in 1958, joining the advertising agency Greenlys to undertake specific tasks in 1959. The completion of these projects in sight, he was given a week to find another job. Two were offered. Initially he preferred the prospect of becoming personal assistant to Charles Higham, who ran a small agency of the same name with one large account (Dunlop), but, as so often, Lindsay's eloquence won the day.

Simon proved to be an outstanding salesman, although a very different character from Lindsay. Apparently a conventional public school boy, he possesses such an appetite and capacity for work that he has played an invaluable role, latterly as managing director, in developing the business. In his early twenties, he was younger than the rest of us but, as assistant to Lindsay, only one step away from the heart of the company. This position was to change slightly at the end of 1959 after Clive and I bought for £10,000 the magazine *Man About Town*, to which Simon moved with Lindsay at the beginning of 1960, but it altered absolutely after my break with Clive in 1965, from which year on the three of us effectively ran the business.

We had £10,000 to spare in late 1959 thanks to a £30,000 profit we had just made selling the freehold site I have referred to in Regent's Park to Charles Clore and Jack Cotton. *Man About Town* had been launched in 1953 by the owners of the specialist trade magazine *Tailor and Cutter*. It had been conceived as a kind of male *Vogue* and was designed to sell the products of Savile Row and of bespoke tailoring companies generally to what, it was hoped, would be a developing market. For whatever reason, it had not prospered, though we were rash enough to believe – this was, after all, the dawn of the 'swinging Sixties' – that there was a new world out there which we could capture.

With the advantage of hindsight, *Town*, the title which evolved from the original, can be seen in two ways. The first, and more obvious, is that it was a brilliant men's fashion magazine, ahead of its time, pioneering standards of design and photography unfamiliar to the Britain of the early 1960s. (It did this, of course, alongside a similar venture, *Queen*, owned by Jocelyn Stevens – much helped by Mark Boxer – which was aimed more successfully at the enormous and more lucrative women's market.) *Town* never made a penny piece of profit and was eventually closed at the end of 1967. It was, therefore, a commercial failure.

But things were not quite that simple. *Town*'s second, less obvious, but more lasting contribution was the experience it gave us and, to some degree, the reputation it created for us – all combining into a kind of legend which over the 1960s was to enable us to develop from a fledgling business spread over a range of dissimilar activities into a specialist trade and consumer publishing house that has become one of the largest independent companies of its kind in the country. But for *Town*, I am by no means sure that any of this would have happened – and certainly it would not have happened in the way it did. As a magazine it may have enjoyed only a brief but bright life (which eventually had to come to an end under commercial disciplines), but as the vehicle around which we created the team that built the Haymarket Publishing Group of today it was a vital initial throw of the dice.

In the first year of our ownership contributions were written by international names such as Lawrence Durrell, Kingsley Amis, Ray

Bradbury, V. S. Pritchett and Brian Moore, and by the less well known, including Shirley Conran, Alexander Plunket Greene, David Hughes and Anthony Blond. In a sense all this was predictable, if well done. What *was* virtually unprecedented in Britain in the early 1960s was the excitement of the design and the quality of the product. The advertising industry went wild. The copy poured in from the creative hot-shops of the time, such as Collett Dickenson Pearce, anxious to associate their clients' goods with such innovative publishing. Great names from the world of photography, such as Henri Cartier-Bresson, appeared in our pages, but so too did the rising generation. Our art director Tom Wolsey had an eye for talent, unsurpassed for his time. David Bailey, Terence Donovan and Don McCullin all appeared from the earliest issues.

Indeed, briefly, I thought Terry Donovan had snuffed out my potential political career for ever. Greatly daring, I had, as publisher of *Town*, asked for and obtained an interview with Harold Macmillan in Admiralty House, where the Prime Minister was living between 1960 and 1963 while 10 Downing Street was being reconstructed. Terry took an age 'setting up' (as they say in the trade). I became more and more agitated while his assistants changed the angle of the shot, rigged up different lights, switched cameras. How much longer, I could not help wondering, would the PM put up with this? Then without warning Macmillan was up and gone. Not a word, just gone. Despair set in. I could envisage the short, crisp note of complaint from the Chief Whip, Martin Redmayne, through whose good offices I had secured the interview. In my mind's ear I thought I could even hear the famous Macmillan drawl: 'Never let this intolerable young man into my presence again.' But suddenly the Prime Minister was back. 'I thought you might like to see round the house,' he said. 'Just wanted to check it was all right with Lady Dorothy.' It was the first of many meetings during which he extended a number of kindnesses to me.

Yet, despite all our efforts (we also published definitive pieces on Iain Macleod and Enoch Powell, complete with brilliant Scarfe drawings), we never managed to break through to an acceptable share of the 'glossy' market. We printed some 60,000 copies a month but the circulation usually hovered some 20,000 below that. During the latter part of the 1960s it slowly but remorselessly declined.

Editors came and went but none seemed able to staunch the haemorrhage. In 1966 I invited Julian Critchley, who had lost in the 1964 general election the Rochester and Chatham seat he had won in 1959 and failed to win back two years later, to take over the editor's chair. It proved a terrible mistake. We had known each other since childhood and had been the closest of friends since Oxford. Yet nothing could alter the brute, commercial facts. One morning Lindsay came to my office in despair. 'We can't go on like this. The advertisers are demanding audited circulation figures and I can't sell a product that is simply losing all credibility out there. Julian will have to go. I realise how impossible a position this is for you. If you like, I will speak to him myself.' I declined his offer, while appreciating its generosity. 'If anyone's got to do it,' I replied, 'it has to be me.' I walked across to Julian's office and explained the position. He left that day. He was living at the time in a flat at the top of my house. This domestic propinquity necessarily increased the embarrassment, but I still do not see what else I could have done. The bitterness of the ending of our friendship – now happily restored – has nevertheless remained one of the great sadnesses of my life.

The magazine limped on until, in the general sort-out that followed our taking over effective control of the magazine publishing interests of the British Printing Corporation, we closed it down. We could afford to do so by that time because at last we were able to pay in full the printers, paper merchants and others who had stuck with us through all the lean years. The January 1968 edition was to be the last.

Town today is a collector's item. My son Rupert paid £40 for a back number for which we would gratefully have accepted four shillings – less 40 per cent trade discount – in the late 1960s. There is one final aspect of *Town* that I should record. Its launch coincided with the emergence of the *Playboy* empire of Hugh Hefner and his many imitators. Few advertisers at the time would be associated with this type of explicit publishing. Hefner's formula was to package the nudes with quality features and commendable design – for which he charged a high cover price. In the end he achieved such significant circulation figures that the advertisers relented – and he won in terms of both sales and ad revenue. From the earliest days we could tell that to make even a ritual genuflection in the direction of this brand of publishing through the use of titillating photographs or suggestive headlines would have provided us with an immediate 'lift' on the bookstalls. But we turned our faces against that option. I was never required to answer the question whether this was motivated by a sense of personal distaste or by an instinct for survival in the Conservative Party. Either way I didn't feel it was on, and I was determined to keep things that way.

I had better confess that the other magazine we owned in the early 1960s singularly fails to evoke any such fond, if contradictory, memories on my part. I was not the first, nor the last, person to fall for the fallacy that the people of Britain would welcome a news magazine of their own to rival *Time* or *Newsweek*. There is a critical difference between the British and American markets, largely the consequence of geography. Britain has excellent national newspapers available early every morning, seven days a week. America has no equivalent and this opens up a great opportunity for the weekly news magazine. Clive's and my effort to break into this notoriously difficult part of the publishing field was probably a doomed enterprise from the start. In the first place, our eyes lighted on what was already a badly maimed bird with few prospects of successful flight in front of it.

Late in 1961 a group of rather amateur entrepreneurs – including the Prime Minister's son, Maurice Macmillan – had tried to launch a weekly publication called *Topic* to provide the busy British citizen with a kind of summary of the week's events. Ill thought out and under-financed, it was on the point of folding when it fell into the hands of one of the great confidence tricksters of the day, the 'armchair' pig farmer Norman Mascall (he was in reality no more than a sophisticated exponent of pyramid selling). His interest in *Topic* presumably derived from his hope that it would enable him, through its advertising pages, to sell off more and more imaginary sows to gullible souls quite sure that they could breed pigs successfully and lucratively without having to stir themselves from their firesides.

By the spring of 1962, however, as usually happens with snake-oil salesmen, the shadows had begun to draw in and rumours were rife of the imminent collapse of the Mascall empire. At this foolish moment Clive and I resolved to see whether we could not make a success of *Topic*, where others had failed. We entered into discussions with the Rev. Timothy Beaumont, the present Lord Beaumont of Whitley, who we believed had inherited a large sum of money. Tim agreed to join us. We would run the magazine; he would put up £50,000 by way of investment. And so we proceeded to make an offer.

It was an extraordinary experience. Mascall was bust. The wolves were at the door. Yet I watched – mesmerised – as he negotiated with his creditors. I had told them that the only way they could expect to get any money was to sell *Topic* to us. He tried to persuade them that the business was sound, that additional investment was imminent. He had all the characteristics of a rubber ball. Nothing depressed him. He could look them in the eye and lie and lie and lie again. But these creditors were desperate. They had to believe what he told them until all else had failed. And even then, at the very last moment, I remember sitting in the room when Mascall was called out to take a telephone call. He returned to say that he had just heard the excellent news that money was coming from Canada. It was, of course, fiction. In the end the creditors lost patience and in the early summer of 1962 we purchased what was laughingly called the goodwill and title for £10,000.

But Tim Beaumont – who went on to lose a fortune trying to revive Lady Rhondda's faintly feminist weekly *Time & Tide* – had by now had second thoughts. He no longer wanted to be an investor. But, as an honourable man, he felt obligated to us and offered to lend us the money instead. We accepted his loan of £50,000 at a very favourable rate of interest. Tim Beaumont's withdrawal from any direct involvement in the project should have given us the cue for our own exit. We failed to take it. It was one of the greatest mistakes Clive and I ever made, but make it we did.

At the most charitable estimate the next half-year spent running *Topic* symbolised a brave attempt, originating in near chaos. There were no records for the Mascall company. How anyone got paid, if they did get paid while he owned the magazine, I do not know. I simply recall that on the day we acquired the magazine I turned up with a suitcase filled with green pound notes, lined up the staff, asked them what they earned and paid them in cash. That was the only way we could determine what the existing staff cost per week. The payroll was dramatically large, financed by credulous investors who had poured their money into the pig business. Simon Tindall and I, having paid the first week's money, had to face the unenviable task of explaining to a lot of people that there simply were no jobs for them. It was a harrowing experience.

We saved what we could and began the job of trying to produce a weekly news magazine to compete with some of the most professional publications in the world – and knowing we had to do so all the time on a shoestring. Yet in some ways it was exhilarating. We attracted an extraordinary number of very able people. Nicholas Tomalin, who was later killed while working as a correspondent in the Middle East during the Yom Kippur War of 1973, had moved over from *Town* to be editor, leaving Michael Parkinson temporarily in charge of *Town*. The reporting staff consisted of Clive Irving, Jeremy Wallington and Ron Hall – all three of whom, when we eventually closed the magazine, moved over in one day to become the founding 'Insight' team on the *Sunday Times*. There were many others. It was a talented and determined group. But, in retrospect, especially given the economic circumstances of 1962, we never had a chance. The losses were astronomic.

Clive Labovitch and I agreed that it had to close after some twenty issues and so, on 19 December 1962, I spoke to the staff and explained that there was no more money and that that week's issue would have to be the last. We offered to pay everyone until they found other jobs. This offer was, I think, appreciated and from our point of view it proved a shrewd gesture. Put on their mettle, virtually all the staff found themselves new jobs with a speed that reflected their quality (only one journalist, John Izbicki, who finally found a berth on the *Telegraph*, remained on our payroll for some six months).

Shortly after I left the Army, Clive and I acquired 7 Stafford Terrace, next to our existing block, and carved homes for ourselves out of the conversion. I took the first and second floors, creating a maisonette paid for with a 100 per cent £14,000 mortgage. The layout was very striking. There was a large, L-shaped first-floor drawing room, the front half of which I left as a spacious sitting room, while the back half opened out to serve as a hall and kitchen. This area I decorated with dramatic eighteen-inch-square black and white tiles on the floor and huge matching stripes climbing from the tiles up the wall, across the ceiling and down to meet the tiles again on the other side. One wall was floor-to-ceiling pine panelling, which could be concertinaed sideways to reveal the kitchen units. An open staircase rose from the hallway to the bathroom and two bedrooms above. Here I lived, in some style, with Tony Howard. Peter Turton, the husband of the caretaker, added significant tone by acting as our uniformed chauffeur. Ultimately and tactfully, Tony sought pastures new on the appearance of Anne Williams, soon to become my wife.

Indeed, it was from Stafford Terrace that on 31 August 1962 I set off for our wedding, and it was to this quite unsuitable bachelor pad that – after our honeymoon in Greece – we returned to begin our married life before moving to 50 Chepstow Villas, W11, several months later. I had first seen Anne 'across a crowded room' one Saturday evening in early 1961 in an upstairs flat in Notting Hill Gate. Her then boyfriend, Val Schur, was giving one of those packed and smoke-filled parties typical of the time. If the hazy and rather bohemian atmosphere lacked something of the charms of the South Pacific, for me the evening was an enchanted one. Anne was strikingly attractive and I – quite innocent of their relationship – asked our host for an introduction. We never looked back and, ever since, Anne has always been there, a tower of strength and unswervingly loyal.

Anne was the last of five children, and much the youngest, of a London solicitor, William Williams, and his wife Edna. Despite the obvious Welsh connections, Anne's family had made the reverse journey to mine, as they left Wales in the 1860s. With a degree in modern languages from London University, she was, when we met, working for a London art dealer, Andras Kalman, at the Crane Kalman Gallery in Knightsbridge.

By the end of 1962 it wasn't just our magazine publishing business that was in trouble. Our property business had been prospering for years. We had bought and sold sites and we had made money – sometimes considerable sums – developing them. So, when the option came up to buy seventy acres of land with planning permission at Tenterden in Kent, we dreamed the big dream. This was going to be a model development. We were going to build an estate of 126 houses and bungalows which would win the admiration of both the consumer press and the prospective purchasers.

That, at least, was the optimistic mood in which we started off. But it soon vanished. The financial squeeze of July 1962 imposed by Macmillan's Chancellor Selwyn Lloyd was feeding through and by the end of the year the storm cones were already well hoisted. The quarterly interest charges had to be met and everything was going wrong. I still find it difficult to believe there were *any* mistakes that we didn't make. We put show houses in the wrong place, at the far end of the plot, so that prospective buyers had to drive along a road through muddy acres of building site. The communications between Tenterden and London by train were just too distant for that stage of the south-east property boom. The design, for which we had had such high hopes, turned out to impress no one.

There were occasional incidents, of course, on which it is possible to look back with wry amusement. John Dickens, the estate agent, whom I had first met over the sale of the boarding house at 39

Clanricarde Gardens, was keen to handle the sale of the Tenterden houses. Eventually, in the spring of 1963, the day of the launch dawned. The best publishing techniques had been deployed in the glossy brochure. He stood and waited. Nothing sold. He manfully stuck it out for another couple of weekends and then had to explain to us that the market was not as good as we had expected, sales were – to put it mildly – 'sluggish' and he couldn't just go on spending his time waiting for clients that weren't coming. He had a point. It became increasingly clear that, if I didn't take over the selling, no one would. Anne was expecting our first child that summer and Annabel was born on 25 July 1963 in St George's Hospital. I was delighted to be present for the birth. Other fathers used to appear at visiting times with immense bouquets of roses, lilies and other exotica. I remember arriving, sticky and sunburnt, clutching a single teasel picked on the site. And then it was back to Tenterden, desperate for someone to buy our houses. Weekend after weekend I wandered around the site. But nobody came – with one exception.

I had noticed on my visits that always there in the distance was a man watching me. He never said anything. He never came near me. He was just there. On the third weekend he finally approached me. 'How are things?' he asked. 'Very good,' I replied. 'Have you sold any?' 'Oh, we're doing very nicely.' 'It's not the way I see it,' he said, 'and I've been watching. You're in trouble.' 'What's your proposal?' I said. 'Well, what you need is for someone to move into one of these show houses, put the curtains up, break the ice sort of thing. You need a bit of life. Car parked in the drive. You know what I mean.' I did. He offered me £4,000 for a £7,250 house. He proved as good as his word. He did buy, he did move in and he then, of course, had a joint interest with me in selling. That was the way his very impressive deal was going to pay off. Slowly, painfully, the houses sold, but the interest rates on the £70,000 site and the construction costs rose remorselessly and the by now considerable number of completed but empty houses became a frightening burden. We managed to dispose of the undeveloped part of the site but it was years before we finally completed the last house sale.

And that wasn't the end of it either. As I have indicated, we had been buoyed up for several years by our success as property developers in London. After my father died in 1957, my mother had set up in business, trading as Highlight Interior Decorators in Mansel Street, Swansea. The building works had been carried out effectively by

Gordon Rumble. When his son Ron suggested that he work for us in London, starting with the building work on our own developments, it seemed like a way of earning two profits, provided that his father joined us as well. We arranged that his father and he would become equal partners in a new construction business, Bastion Construction. In Swansea the father had certainly been a successful builder and therein lay the basis of my confidence. But he proved to be less than interested in this metropolitan project and the son had very little experience. We saw the development profits eaten up by the losses on the building sites. We agreed that our ways must part.

The problem, inevitably, lay in the existing work to be completed. In place of Ron Rumble we employed a young man from one of the major construction companies who had all the appearance of understanding the business. He was full of confidence. He persuaded us that his salary and that of our own organisation created overheads which could be carried only by a larger construction business than we were currently running. It was a seductive argument and it convinced us that he should tender for public authority contracts. We were overjoyed when he won two contracts to build local authority housing in Stepney. We were moving ahead.

Unfortunately, the price at which we had won the competitive tenders was not only easily the lowest but so low as to be totally unprofitable. We let our new manager go. I decided that I would have to assume responsibility for the completion of the contracts. My faith was pinned on a foreman whom we employed at the time called Billy Parsons. He was a warm-hearted, salt-of-the-earth Cockney – never so happy as when fishing in the Thames on his weekends off, even if he caught only eels. No manager and no entrepreneur, he knew the building business backwards. Billy Parsons and I set out to finish the houses in Stepney, hiring specialist sub-contractors, one after another. We hired the brickies, completed the brickwork, went to the council and got paid. We hired the plumbers and repeated the process. On went the roofs, in went the carpenters, followed by plasterers, more carpenters, electricians and decorators; we finished the contract and got our money. We went way over the contract period, but we delivered the houses and they stand today. The borough surveyors of Stepney Council could not have behaved better. I think they believed we were doing our best, but of course if they had had to bring in fresh contractors they would have faced far larger bills.

To celebrate the final completion of this awesome task, we invited

Billy Parsons and some of his friends down for a day's fishing to Pond Lodge, a cottage in Wiltshire Anne and I had at a peppercorn rent from the Earl of Suffolk. (I had first met Micky Suffolk in a television interview I did with him while working briefly for Associated Rediffusion in the early 1960s, when he had generously offered us this idyllic bolt-hole in the country which helped to sustain my morale through a difficult economic period.) We sent Billy and co. out on to the nearby lake in an ancient pontoon and then watched in horror as it sank lower and lower in the water. Billy couldn't swim. Somehow or other we fished him out, warmed him by the fire, filled him with hot tea and sent him back to London wearing some of my clothes – looking slightly odd as I am six foot two and Billy was five foot four.

All our activities merged into and flowed from each other and by the end of 1962 our cumulative losses vastly exceeded any profits from either the property or the publishing businesses. *Town* – and, to a much greater extent, *Topic* – the construction business and the starting of the Tenterden development had brought us to the edge of the precipice. By the end of that year we faced the collapse of our entire empire. We banked with the National Westminster in Grosvenor Gardens, SW1, and the man in charge there at the time was a temporary manager. He was rather a jovial cove. When we talked about our overdraft, which had by now assumed alarming proportions, I remember him saying: 'Well, it's all dots, really, isn't it?' This might have seemed a helpful attitude in the circumstances in which we found ourselves, but it was hardly one that ensured our ultimate survival.

Eventually, on the morning of 23 December 1962, I went to see him to explain that we were in deep trouble and needed a lot more cash just to keep going. He looked at the evidence and asked why I didn't put the companies into liquidation. I said that I wasn't prepared to do that. I felt a personal responsibility for what had happened and I could not see how anyone could anticipate a political career if they had allowed a company with which they were associated to let its creditors down. If there was any way open to me to struggle through, I was determined to take it. 'Well, this is bigger than me,' he said. 'The only people who can help you now are head office.' I asked him to fix a meeting – quickly.

At five o'clock that afternoon I arrived at the headquarters of the National Westminster Bank in the City to meet a deputy general manager, Sydney Galpin. He listened to what I had to say, questioned me about our plans and asked how much I wanted. 'Eighty-five thousand pounds,' I said. 'And what have you got?' I said, 'I've got a house, a car and a watch.' 'I'll take the lot,' was the substance of his reply. Then he stood up, shook me by the hand and said: 'I'd like to say goodbye. We won't meet again. I'm retiring from the bank today.' I never did see him again, but he undoubtedly saved my business and political careers.

On 28 December, as business resumed after the Christmas break, a visibly shaken successor to Mr Galpin, a Mr Macmillan, summoned me urgently to the bank. It rapidly became apparent to me that we would never have got the money if Galpin had retired a day earlier. But the bank honoured the commitment into which he had entered and which he had, thankfully, recorded before his well-earned retirement. Others too were generous in their support: Tim Beaumont lent us a further £20,000 that bleak Christmas-time. Looking back on it all, it's easy to see the mistakes we made: above all the want of financial control, the lack of a good finance director and the inexperience that let us take on more than was in any way prudent. I have often been struck, in talking to others who have founded successful companies, how frequently they have gone through experiences not dissimilar. I wouldn't wish it on anyone, but you do learn lessons never to be forgotten.

Over the years that were to follow, broadly up until the late 1960s, every creditor was paid off. It was never an easy process and reached the stage where I had a weekly meeting with John Palmer, our new accountant, who would produce a list of the creditors in need of immediate attention. There were three columns on his list: creditors who had sent us solicitors' letters, creditors who had issued writs and creditors who had issued writs fourteen days earlier. We never failed to pay the third column. It was this story, which I have recounted many times in public over the years, which aroused the interest of a less than sober member of an audience when I was President of the Board of Trade in the early 1990s. He informed a journalist that I believed in delaying payment at the expense of my creditors, and the ever voracious press kept the story running for days. My position had been exactly the opposite. I was determined to pay each and every one of those to whom we owed money. If you are wise, you never issue cheques you can't meet. It destroys the confidence essential for trust and thus for survival. Simon Tindall remembers regularly opening the post with me and adding up the incoming cheques in order to determine whom we could pay that day. Whatever the total, we would then produce from beneath the blotting pad an appropriate number of cheques equal in value which could be safely put into the post.

It was a miracle that somehow we pulled through. The underlying profits of the *Directory of Opportunities* series were fundamental, indeed the life-blood in our darkest hour. Those profits increased year by year and enabled us to persuade our creditors to hang on. We never told any creditors anything other than the truth. We never sent out false cheques. If we had to tell people we couldn't pay, we told them. If we said we would put a cheque in the post, we put it in the post.

Slowly we began to climb the hill of recovery. We developed a careers advisory service, called the Graduates' Appointments Register. This was a business which developed out of our *Directory of Opportunities for Qualified Men*. To achieve the necessary circulation we would advertise its availability free to suitably qualified people. We asked them to complete a curriculum vitae and then marketed these details to companies for an annual subscription. The number of companies that wrote 'no coloureds' on their subscription forms told me something of the atmosphere in the employment market at the time.

I picked up another tip in a very simple way. At that time every mother in hospital having a baby – as Anne had been in the summer of 1963 – was presented with a free pack of samples – for example, of powdered milk. The distributors charged the producing companies a fee and made a profitable business out of it. They may still be doing so. It occurred to us that we could build on this idea. We developed a pack of samples to be included along with a gazetteer in every Rootes and Ford motor car. We developed another pack of samples to be given to people moving into new homes. We sent out the assembled packs to milk-delivery companies, who are always among the first to discover new arrivals in any neighbourhood. Neither of these ideas survived as ongoing ventures for very long, but each in its modest way made a small contribution to our balance sheet which was gratefully received.

Another project that failed to make it was *Shoppers' Guide*. We had entered into negotiations in 1962 with the British Standards Institute to take over their languishing publication and inject new life into it. We saw its potential as a competitor to *Which?*, the successful magazine of the Consumers Association. But in the end the project fizzled out and there is little to say about it except that it illustrates our determination to develop the business even in those difficult days and the willingness of responsible organisations to continue working with us.

We were lucky, of course, in that some of our creditors had specific reasons for wanting to go on doing business with us. The printers wanted the magazines they printed to continue publication. The paper merchants had similar motives. As long as they were receiving something on account, they had no more interest in our going into liquidation than we had. Yet there was more to it than that. We had undoubtedly made appalling mistakes. But I think they believed there was a degree of talent and ability which could be harnessed.

There were one or two organisations, for example, which even bought into some of the specialist companies we ran at that time. But, centrally, there also began a chain of events which was to turn Cornmarket Press into the Haymarket Publishing Group of today. The printers of *Town*, Keliher Hudson and Kearns, under the chairmanship of Robert Paterson, were extremely proud of their work, and rightly so. Denis Curtis, our production manager, had achieved with them standards of production which were an immensely valuable advertisement in securing work from other clients. Realising that we were short of money, Robert Paterson invited Clive and myself to lunch one day in 1963 and asked if we would like him to invest in our business. Kelihers would provide the money and we would expand the publishing business, giving them a first crack at the printing. Before the negotiations were completed, Kelihers were purchased by the printers Hazell, Watson and Viney, the chairman there being Geoffrey Crowther, who was also chairman of the *Economist*. Geoffrey, a gnome of a man with a formidable intellect, joined the negotiations and carried them forward to completion. It was he who made the suggestion that the marriage of the two companies led obviously to the amalgam title of Haymarket. Hazell, Watson and Viney owned 40 per cent, Clive and I retaining 60 per cent. Cornmarket's *Directories* remained outside the deal.

This 1964 agreement changed our fortunes, irrevocably and for the better. After the heady days of the late 1950s and the early disasters of 1961 and 1962, we had now signed the deal that led to the establishment of Haymarket alongside Cornmarket, which we kept. The debt repayment and creditor pressure did not immediately go away, but at last we could see light at the end of a very long tunnel. From then on we had access to substantial funds and I set about acquiring businesses. I developed a simple technique. From the directory for the publishing industry, *British Rate and Data*, I extracted the names of the chairmen of magazine companies and then wrote hundreds of letters – suggesting to each that we might prove admirable partners if we worked more closely together. It doesn't sound a very sophisticated approach but it worked. Every year I bought one or more new magazines. And we were now more secure in our new premises at 86–88 Edgware Road.

The first purchase we made – it was one of the most successful – was in response to my first round of such letters. In 1965 I had a cable from Canada signed by one A. E. Morgan. He had created a British medical publishing group which was making £50,000 a year and he had negotiated a deal with Roy Thomson (owner of, among many other publications, the *Sunday Times*) to sell it for £250,000. He was himself an entrepreneur; he loathed the idea of being absorbed into a large company and he said that, if we were prepared to pay him the same sum and let him stay with his publications, then he would sell to us instead. Geoffrey Crowther agreed at once and A. E. Morgan Ltd became the medical division of the Haymarket Publishing Group. In addition to *MIMS* (a monthly listing of pharmaceutical products widely used by the medical profession) and *GP* (a weekly newspaper for doctors) this purchase also brought *Caravan Life* into the fold.

Most other acquisitions were smaller. We bought for a small sum of money a publication called *Amateur Tape Recording* from Vernon Holdings and Partners. It was making very little profit then and there was a debate about whether it was even worth continuing. But Simon Tindall, analysing its advertising, discovered that it was mainly promoting hi-fi products. We decided to convert it into a hi-fi magazine. Today *What Hi-fi?* is the most successful magazine in its field. Again, Anne and I were driving through France on holiday in 1965 and I noticed how many camping sites there were. Within weeks of returning to the United Kingdom we had bought *Practical Camper*.

All these additions, however, were small beer when compared with our bid for the *Manager*, the monthly journal of the British Institute of Management. Here our partnership with Geoffrey Crowther was to prove of inestimable value. It demonstrated, as well, how valuable the reputation of *Town* magazine was proving to be. Word was going round as early as the autumn of 1965 that the *Manager* was potentially available for sub-contract. Roy Thomson was said to be bidding hard for it. It was clear to me that Haymarket by itself could not win this competition. We simply didn't have the stature to persuade an organisation like the BIM to entrust its magazine to us. So I went to Geoffrey Crowther. He agreed to back us, provided that we invited his major shareholder, the *Financial Times*, to join the consortium. It was Hobson's choice. So together the *Financial Times*, the *Economist* and ourselves put in a proposal to take over the *Manager*. Lord Drogheda, chairman of the *Financial Times*, played a critical role in persuading Robert Heller, then business editor of the *Observer*, to become the editor of our proposed magazine in time for its first issue in April 1966. Altogether we had a formidable alignment of talent, but first we had to win the competition.

I remembered a story that Lord Stokes had told me. Donald Stokes was the entrepreneur who had made such a success of the Leyland bus and coach business. He explained how he had won a bus contract in Scandinavia. The specification had been distributed, the bids submitted, together with detailed plans. Six companies from all over Europe were competing. The other five bidders turned up with sketches, blueprints, maps, plans, specifications, to demonstrate the quality of their product. Donald was the last one to meet the committee. 'Gentlemen,' he said, 'if you would be kind enough to follow me, I will show you your bus.' Outside there was a prototype bus that he had built to their specification in every detail. He won the contract.

I persuaded my colleagues that we should try to emulate Donald Stokes. We worked all through one weekend. When we turned up to make our pitch to the British Institute of Management, we were able to put on the table what was to all intents and purposes an issue of the magazine we wanted to produce for them – a glossy ninety-six pages, including a mock interview with the chairman of the Institute and photographs of both him and the director general. To produce a full magazine in such a time-scale was an extraordinary achievement, given the limited technology of the time. We won the contract and the launching of *Management Today* was, of course, a major step forward in the fortunes of Haymarket. Furthermore, the printers who had stayed with us through the *Town* days saw their loyalty pay off. But it was much more than that. It heralded a revolution in the quality of business publishing in this country. We had taken the visual and editorial standards of *Town* and had applied them to business publishing. We couldn't have known it at the time, but over thirty years later you can find copies of Haymarket-inspired magazines all over the world.

We had run out of office space at 86–88 Edgware Road and some time in 1966 I found 30,000 square feet in an old butter-packing warehouse owned by United Dairies about one mile north in the Harrow Road. It was awaiting redevelopment and is today the site of a large hotel. When I discovered it, it had been unoccupied for several years and was in a terrible state: the tramps and pigeons had taken over. With some difficulty I persuaded Simon to move there and take charge of a newly created consumer magazine publishing division. A certain amount of cosmetic treatment was required before I took him to see his new empire. There was a small foreman's office with internal windows overlooking what would make an ideal sales office. But it had been the tramps' loo. Our handyman–builder removed the floorboards and scrubbed the walls the day before Simon's first visit. When he asked why there was no floor in his new office, I told him I wanted to replace it with a superior pine floor commensurate with his new status. He may even have believed me for a time.

Now that he has a warm, clean, carpeted office, Simon remembers the butter-packing warehouse with some nostalgia. When it rained, inadequate drains flooded the ground floor. A small section of the accounts department had to be moved because the pools of water kept blowing their machines. Industrial heaters were provided to keep the staff warm; unfortunately there was only one ring main to support all these heaters and an unsuitable one at that. When the weather was cold, the power circuits in the building also blew. Simon persuaded his team to wear overcoats (while temporary repairs were in hand) and the heaters were turned on and off in rotation, so that everyone was warm for some part of the day. One morning, with a frightful cry, the poor tea lady, while working in her kitchen, simply disappeared from view. She was rescued from the floor below; the kitchen flooring had been rotten.

One of the attractions of the building, for which we paid only £11,000 a year, was its extensive warehouse space, into which we put the circulation department. Our various distributors, to help our recycling policies, would send back unsold copies of our magazines, usually unopened in their original bundles. Simon thought the sight of all these 'unsolds' was so demoralising to his editorial and sales teams that he locked all the connecting doors to prevent them from visiting the circulation department or taking a short cut through the loading bay where all this mountain of paper accumulated.

It was very shortly after our success in winning the British Institute of Management contract that Clive told me that he was uneasy about the direction in which the business was moving and that he felt that the only way he could pursue the publishing career that would really fulfil his ambitions would be to start again on his own.

Years earlier, before either of us had met our future wives, we had agreed that in the event of either of us marrying we would not bring our spouses into the business. Clive had gone on to marry the journalist Penny Perrick, daughter of the well-known *Daily Express* columnist Eve Perrick, and she clearly would have liked an active role in boardroom discussions. We also happened to employ at around this time a rather ingratiating man called Peter Cooper. I got the impression that Clive was coming under pressure from both of them to move out and develop what I imagine was described as a 'real' publishing business. It is impossible to know quite what was in his mind. But Lindsay, Simon and I were clear about our priorities. We were tired of debts, creditors and publications that earned quantities of flattering praise almost in direct proportion to the scale of their losses. We wanted to run a profitable business. Clive enjoyed the feeling of publishing, the look of a well-designed product, the prestige associated with being a publisher.

Yet I was appalled at the prospect of losing Clive. We had been close friends for some twelve years, had shared the excitements and traumas of starting out in business together and we were now about to part. He was a kind, gentle man, something of a dreamer, but with an eye for quality both in people and in the printed page that it would be hard to replicate.

I argued as best I could. I pointed out that I had already earlier that year, 1965, been chosen to stand as the candidate for the safe Tory seat of Tavistock in the West Country and that the election, given the Labour government's tiny majority (Harold Wilson had defeated Alec Douglas-Home, Macmillan's successor, in 1964), could not be long delayed. I would thus almost certainly be an MP in the near future, leaving Clive virtually a free hand to run the business. But it was all to no avail.

On 23 December 1965, all the senior executives of the company were asked to decide whether they wanted to go with Clive or remain with me. The drama unfolded against the background of a large party Anne and I were giving that evening at our home in Chepstow Villas to which they had all been invited, as well as other guests. Simon Tindall told me the next day that, whatever the circumstances, he was remaining with me. Lindsay Masters said that he wanted to come with me too, but he was going to talk to Clive so that at least he knew what was on offer. It was an immense relief to me when, very shortly afterwards, he told me he was staying put. I had retained the loyalty of the two outstanding salesmen in the company. They were essential for the furtherance of the business.

In 1957, when I had joined Clive, we had agreed that, if we ever split up, what we each owned at the beginning would remain under that ownership, but any future developments would be shared equally between us. We had no contract, nothing written down, just a gentlemen's agreement. It is not hard to appreciate that trying to interpret the meaning of that agreement eight years later, after the numerous new ventures I have described, could easily have led to the law courts. There was never any question of that. We agreed that we would list the activities of the business, decide who owned what where we could and then, where we couldn't agree, we would invite our solicitor Charles Corman and our accountant Jimmy Remnant (later Lord Remnant and chairman of Touche, Remnant and Co.) to arbitrate. In each other's presence we would both put our side of the case. We would abide by their decisions. That is what we did. There were very few issues so referred. It took half a morning to resolve them. By the spring of 1966 we had negotiated an amicable separation and parted company, as friends. In essence Clive took with him the *Directory of Opportunities* series. I took our share in the Haymarket Group. We split the outstanding debts and divided our properties by agreement.

Clive was a man I trusted implicitly. Over the ensuing years the press made many attempts to persuade him to criticise me. They all proved totally futile. Sadly, his own fortunes did not flourish. The profits from the *Directory of Opportunities* series were soon overwhelmed by other ventures. By 1973 he was in deep trouble. In my absence from Haymarket as a minister in Ted Heath's government, he approached Lindsay and explained the risk of liquidation he faced. Lindsay, of course, relayed the conversation to me. It was agreed that Haymarket would buy the *Directories* from Clive's company. He had told Lindsay that his bankers, Barings, had assured him that, if the cash from the sale flowed into the company, they would not foreclose. I cannot know the whole picture; I only know what Clive told us. He believed that he had a firm commitment that they would not foreclose. But in the event they did. Clive was so distressed by this development that he tried to commit suicide. Mercifully, he failed in the attempt. I went to the hospital to see him. I walked down a seemingly endless corridor, past his wife, Penny, and Peter Cooper. The two had been instrumental in persuading him to break up our partnership.

The proposal was that Clive should come back to Haymarket as a director. But, in the event, this never happened and he went off again on his own. His remaining business survived, producing small papers for libraries and booksellers, including *Publishing News*. But the truth was that Clive was a dreaming romantic who longed to be in sophisticated, creative publishing and had never been quite content with our network of trade, specialist publications. He was also a marvellously endearing man and, despite all its vicissitudes, my eight-year partnership with him is one of the things I look back on in my life with most pride. He died after heart surgery in 1994 and I was deeply touched to be invited by his son Mark and his daughter Emmy to speak at his memorial service. I concluded my remarks thus: 'He was my friend.'

Clive and I had to all intents and purposes been our own masters, and, despite the enveloping crisis of the debts, had managed to retain at least a controlling interest in all the companies we owned. That remained true after Clive's departure, although I had at that time given Lindsay and Simon my word that when the financial position clarified I would issue them with a significantly larger minority package of the equity than the 5 per cent they held at the time. It was understood, however, that my family would retain control.

In the meantime, Hazell, Watson and Viney had been swallowed first by Purnells and then by the British Printing Corporation (BPC). This conglomerate of printing companies had, as is often the way of things, accumulated a cluster of other small magazine publishing companies, none of which was effectively managed or had anything to compare with the scale or flair of Haymarket. Haymarket was the equal in turnover of all the others added together. In other words, we were about 50 per cent in turnover of BPC's magazine publishing business and, of course, they owned only 40 per cent of Haymarket. They were making no money from their other companies. They needed to rationalise. They asked me whether Haymarket would be prepared to take over the management of the whole group. I agreed with alacrity. One week we were running thirty-six magazines with a staff of 200, the next we had added fourteen more titles and doubled the staff and the turnover. In essence the present Haymarket Publishing Group was now in place. It was an extraordinary piece of good fortune.

At this time the family and I were living at Pamflete on the south coast of Devon in my constituency. One of the BPC directors, John Pollock, who was responsible for agreeing the terms of the deal I have described, came to stay. The actual scene of the negotiations might have appealed to Hitchcock himself. The Erme estuary on the South Devon coast is one of the more spectacular pieces of countryside in that part of England. The little river runs through deep cuttings, down the centre of wide sandbanks, to the sea. The tide, when it comes in, is relatively shallow as there are long sloping beaches. On that Saturday night in 1967 two dinner-jacketed figures walked back and forth, slowly retreating on the edge of the incoming tide, negotiating what proved to be the deal of my life. BPC was to have 60 per cent of the equity; we would be issued with the remaining 40 per cent. We had doubled in size. We had, however, lost control of the company in the process.

Some of BPC's more esoteric titles had to be closed down, and Simon Tindall and I again spent a whole day delivering bad news to old employees. We tried to see each person individually, but as the hours went by we found ourselves forced to see secretaries and others in groups of ten. There is never an easy or pleasant way of going about such a task.

In Praed Street, Paddington, at the top of a very ramshackle building we discovered *Autosport*, then selling a mere 17,000 copies a week. It was transformed by Simon, with the help of a young employee, Simon Taylor, whom he found there and who is now not only one of our directors but also a well-known broadcaster. In even grottier offices, opposite the Old Bailey off Ludgate Hill, Lindsay and I found *World's Press News*, the remarkably old-fashioned parish magazine of Fleet Street. I remember picking up a copy, handing it to him and saying, '*Advertising Age*.' No further words were necessary. He knew exactly what I meant; we were both very familiar with that American giant and the standards it set. A year later he relaunched *World's Press News* as *Campaign*, serving the communications and advertising industries. *Campaign* was the first to recognise that its readers deserved a trade paper equal in quality to the other magazines and newspapers that they read. Lindsay recruited a very young team of journalists, none of whom knew anything about advertising – or often even journalism for that matter – but all of whom had shown that they were good writers. Only the editor, Michael Jackson, who proved to be a brilliant choice, came from Fleet Street. Roland Schenk, an equally brilliant art director, had originally joined us to work on the last issues of *Town* and then on *Management Today*. He gave *Campaign* a look that, as all design should, expressed the character of this revolutionary new creation. The uncompromising nature of the enterprise was demonstrated by the fact that we had recruited eighteen talented young people to compete with *Ad Weekly*'s (the current UK market leader) sleepy six. The magazine that resulted was irreverent and full of energy. Although an instant success, it took the advertising industry a long time to accept that its trade paper was not just a journal of record and a dumping ground for press handouts but an honest and independent observer of the industry. No other trade paper had done this before, and success bred many imitators.

My best stroke of luck as our fortunes improved was coming across in 1969 a copy of the *Accountant*. I first read it while waiting to see the managing director of Gee and Co., which owned it, while cooling my heels in their waiting room. (I was there as a result of another of those letter-writing exercises.) I did not pay much attention to the copy – just to the advertisements – and the first thing I did when I finally got in to see the MD was to congratulate him on the obvious excellence of his sales force in getting classified advertisements into this somewhat old-fashioned professional weekly. 'Oh,' he said somewhat airily, 'we don't have any sales team; it just comes through the post.' I could hardly wait to get back to my own office. When I did, I immediately got hold of Lindsay. 'You won't believe this,' I said, 'but there's this guy just sitting there and every day the money comes rolling in through the post – and his magazine only covers about a quarter of the accountants in the country.' We resolved then and there to start *Accountancy Age*. We launched later that year and sent a copy out free to every chartered accountant in the land. It made a comfortable profit from its very first issue – the only one of our publications for which I could ever make this claim apart from *The Directory of Opportunities for Graduates* a whole decade earlier.

Haymarket was growing apace. We needed new premises. I asked Paul Buckley, one of the brightest young men working for us at the time, to search. He was back in an amazingly short period of time, to say that he had found 21,000 square feet on the sixth floor of Waring and Gillow in Oxford Circus at a rental of £21,000 a year, with no premium. We caught the next taxi and snapped it up. We moved in in the summer of 1967.

In 1974, when I returned to Haymarket after the Tory defeat at the general election, discussions were proceeding to sell this lease for £2 million. The institutional owner (a large City company) wanted to clear the building for redevelopment. Virtually all the other tenants had been bought out. We were in a strong position. I suggested we try for £3 million and telephoned the chairman. 'You are an Arab, Mr Heseltine,' was his response. As I had been listed, albeit inaccurately, in the *Jewish Chronicle* as among the most successful candidates in the Oxford Final Examinations in 1954, this was somewhat disconcerting. We settled for £2.5 million. Such racial discrimination is expensive. It did wonders for our balance sheet and financed our next move, to Regent Street.

In the late 1960s the immensely talented – he knew it – Maurice Saatchi (subsequently of Saatchi & Saatchi fame and later to become Lord Saatchi) joined as my personal assistant. (Lindsay swears he was his.) But far and away the most significant appointment at this time was that of David Fraser as our new finance director. His early days with us were far from shock free. While the worst of the financial crisis was actually over, it couldn't have seemed that way to him.

On his second day at Gillow House representatives of the Inland Revenue arrived to claim seven months' overdue PAYE deductions. When David explained that he had only just arrived in the job and he would look into the matter, they threatened to remove his desk. He eventually satisfied them with a phased programme of repayments. A few days later on arriving at work early, he found bailiffs unscrewing light fittings from the walls. They got paid. Our shortage of cash was aggravated by our failure to collect effectively what we ourselves were owed. David quickly employed a substantial Irishman to ease the cash-flow problems. The Irishman had to go, however, when he returned from a visit to a group of Nigerians whom he had found playing cards in a rundown basement. 'We have no money,' they had told him – but this did not seem sufficient legal justification for the seizure of their passports which ensued.

David did not bear the brunt of these problems entirely alone. Lindsay was buying records one day on a company credit card. The shop assistant accepted the card and disappeared, only to return a few moments later somewhat apologetically and hand it back cut in half on the strict instructions of the credit card company over the telephone.

David introduced a regime – none too soon – which changed our lives. The debts, formerly seeming unassailable cliffs, became low-level hills which we would soon take in our stride. Today Haymarket's management and accounting practices are the equal of any Stock Exchange company. Although I did not know it at the time, David is actually my second cousin – the direct descendant of the marriage of one of the daughters of William Heseltine to a Fraser at the end of the nineteenth century.

Like most small companies, Haymarket was a non-union business. There had been desultory attempts in the 1960s to introduce the National Union of Journalists to our company, but our staff showed no enthusiasm for such a move. As a non-union house, we were able to recruit without the constraints of obtaining an NUJ ticket. We were thus able to attract talented young people otherwise denied access to Fleet Street under the trade union practices of the day.

Then we recruited a young graduate from Oxford, Peter Hillmore (now a journalist with the *Mail on Sunday*). He was lucky with his timing. We had just absorbed BPC magazines, moved offices to Gillow House and were going through a period of great turmoil with constant staff adjustments. We lost a degree of control.

Peter Hillmore came to my office to ask for recognition of the union. The conversation was very short. 'There is no evidence whatsoever that anybody here wants to be a member of the union or even to recognise the union,' I said. 'I think that's probably right,' he said, 'but they *need* a union.' To the best of my knowledge it was the last conversation we had. He persuaded them to strike. We hadn't the financial resources to resist. Our journalists were unionised.

I asked Bob Heller to act on behalf of management. There are always two sides to every story. We were a company that had grown at a significant pace, able to attract the most talented of young journalists, creating and raising standards, in no small measure precisely because we weren't unionised. Into the mix came a newly qualified graduate, prepared to risk the very existence of the company itself. It was a personal strain I could have done without. I have always remained indebted to Bob Heller for coping with the interminable negotiations that ensued. The country went through similar traumas until Rupert Murdoch took on the battle to restore sanity to Fleet Street.

In the end Lindsay acted. After a period of ever deteriorating industrial relations, the journalists arrived one morning to find that the tables had been turned. The doors were locked. Lindsay negotiated the terms of their re-entry through the letterbox. Until the NUJ signed a letter promising to abide by reasonable standards, the doors remained closed. I was in government at the time and have only heard tell of the experience. The letterbox in question was at ground level and the image of the chairman of Haymarket lying on his back, negotiating through that slit in the door with the union representatives on the outside, must surely be worthy of a footnote in the history of the battle to bring the trade unions within the law of the land.

By the end of the 1960s the company was unrecognisable when compared with the bizarre combination of unrelated and often unprofitable activities of the early part of the decade. Some 400 people, mostly in their twenties, were producing magazines that carried respect as leaders in their field. Overall we were profitable. We were on our way. But we were a subsidiary of a publicly quoted giant and had powerful partners in various of our ventures. In 1969 I handed over the responsibilities as managing director to Lindsay, who concentrated on the business and medical publications. Simon was meanwhile engaged in building up our specialist consumer magazines. He had soon launched *What Car?*, another Haymarket formula first which now has its imitators everywhere, in one specialist field after another.

There is no doubt that the opportunity which the BPC deal provided was of incalculable benefit to our growth. The company's turnover was approaching £2.5 million and its profits just over £200,000. We didn't like the subsidiary status we had had to accept, although our personal relationships, particularly with John Pollock, were excellent. But the disciplines of big-company systems were irksome.

To illustrate the point: we had at last secured the services of a first-class finance director in David Fraser. I was clear that we had to keep him. I agreed in late 1969 to increase his annual salary from £3,250 to £4,500 with a two-year contract, having discussed with John Pollock my reasons for doing so. (It was at this time that David first told me of our kinship – although that played no part in the judgement I had made.) Shortly after, I received a stroppy letter from Victor Bishop, the managing director of BPC, suggesting that it would be better to offer David £500 at once and £500 a year later, and pointing out that there were procedures involved in awarding pay increases of this sort and that the rules had to be observed. I replied, explaining why David had to be paid more. I then went on:

> Your letter raises wider issues by implication and it might be as well for you to think of them whilst I am away . . . As Haymarket becomes more important to the overall Corporation profitability, so the greater control you will want. In that scheme of things I am the wrong man and it is better to face this now and part amicably than allow a situation to deteriorate.

BPC appreciated at that moment, I think, that an advance severance notice had been served.

In 1970 I went off to join the newly elected Conservative government as a very junior minister, and Lindsay, with some reluctance, added the chairmanship of the company to his other responsibilities.

The rules relating to ministers' involvement in commercial activities are clearly set out in a guidance note circulated early in the life of a government. They represent common sense and are designed to ensure that ministers do not use their public position for private gain and do nothing that might reasonably cause people to believe that they have so done. Instinctively, I never experienced any difficulty in determining what that meant in practice but, on the belts and braces principle, I always took care to ensure that my permanent secretaries were informed of the full range of Haymarket's activities.

In one instance I interpreted the rules incorrectly and to my disadvantage. Maurice Saatchi left Haymarket to establish with his brother Charles their renowned agency. Lindsay played a significant role in helping to raise the initial finance and invited me to participate. I turned the offer down, believing that such an investment would breach the conventions. It was years later that I discovered that it would have been perfectly proper for me to have taken a small stake in such a business, provided I had no involvement in its activities and gave no advice to its managers.

The issues are more complex when it comes to the restructuring or the purchase or sale of significant holdings in private companies.

It is clear from my letter to Victor Bishop that an edginess had entered into the relationship with BPC by 1969. We were not big-company people and, despite the huge commercial advantage, we were uneasy as a subsidiary of a quoted public company. At one board meeting I saw on the agenda an item, 'Directors' Cars'. I knew that Lindsay had recently acquired a company car but I could not remember, if I had ever known, the details. I passed him a note: 'What sort of car?' 'Mustang' came back the reply. 'Too evocative' I sent back. 'Ford' Lindsay replied. 'Ford' I said and the purchase passed without comment. But, after I had joined the government, Lindsay came to the conclusion that he had simply had enough of the stream of pettifogging inquiries from outside directors – whose magazines we had rescued and whose own business was by then attracting serious and public criticism in the City columns.

This was the backdrop for the final curtain. Before the 1970 election we had been negotiating to purchase two small, unquoted public companies, the *National Newsagent* magazine and *Wine and Spirit* magazine. Before we had entered into contracts, the Corporation informed us that they were no longer in a position to provide the capital (which their contract with us committed them to do) in view of their own financial position. Honourably they agreed that we were free to raise the finances elsewhere, and we decided to proceed in concert with Charterhouse, a City bank with whom we had done business before. This deal, however, was never completed, although the negotiations remained on the table. In the early autumn of 1970 Lindsay and Simon approached other banks in an unsuccessful attempt to raise funds to enable us to make an offer for the BPC holdings in our joint venture. The only offer they received was from Rothschilds and included a shareholding of 'a 5% ride for the executives'. This was not well received.

In early November they reported the position to me. My involvement was essential in view of my family's stake in the company. I called on Dick Strong of Charterhouse and asked if he would obtain the funds for us. By early December he had decided to submit a proposal to his colleagues that they should lead a syndicate to raise the money and enable us to buy out BPC for £1 million and that we would pay off a loan outstanding in the company's books from BPC for £737,000 over two years.

But the situation deteriorated significantly in the third week of December, when I was informed by directors of BPC that, unless they took urgent action to replenish their reserves, they were faced with the appointment of representatives of their debenture holders to the board and the charging of all subsidiaries to the Corporation's debenture. We went to counsel and we were advised that we would win an action to protect our assets, which were totally tied up with a BPC subsidiary. The Corporation themselves decided to offer us the alternative of acquiring their shares along the lines I had already discussed with Charterhouse. They needed the money.

To ensure that I kept within ministerial guidelines, on 23 December I wrote to the Prime Minister Ted Heath setting out the position, saying that Peter Walker as Secretary of State and Sir David Serpell as permanent secretary in the Department of the Environment where I was a junior minister saw no objection but had advised that the matter should be referred to him. I said that I was confident that I could raise the money and that the price was on the low side. I explained that I had to sign the contract that evening and regretted the urgency which had arisen from events outside my control. I had set out the problem on the telephone to the private secretary at No. 10, Robert Armstrong, the evening before and he was therefore able to get back to me the same day, giving me the Prime Minister's agreement to proceed. It was not made a condition, but it was Ted Heath's advice that my shares should be put into a trust and left there as long as I remained a minister.

Events moved to a speedy conclusion thereafter. Control passed back to the founders of our business. I had not yet actually finalised the funding, although negotiations with Charterhouse were well advanced. Charles Corman observed at the time that the worst that could happen was that we would have to sell the company to discharge our obligations to BPC. But that never arose, even as a contingency. By completion on 20 April 1971, Dick Strong, on behalf of Charterhouse, had put together a syndicate. I was able to inform Ted Heath in April 1971 of this satisfactory outcome and confirmed that my shares from now on were to be held in a blind trust.

Included in that final outcome was an important equity scheme for executives, particularly Lindsay and Simon. Inevitably, our new partners wanted an exit strategy. In addition, at the time of the BPC merger I had assured Lindsay and Simon that they could expect to realise the value of their shares as a result of an exit via a public flotation. At that time only two options existed: the disposal of the company or a Stock Exchange quotation. The latter enabled the management to remain in command, while enabling acquisitions to be financed by the issue of shares attractive to vendors, as no capital tax was payable by vendors until the shares themselves were disposed of. So the next stage in the company's development was expected to be a flotation on the Stock Exchange in two or three years' time, in anticipation of which we made much smaller equity arrangements with a handful of our other senior executives, including David. In the meantime, we immediately bought the two public companies for which we had been negotiating.

I have to this day in my possession a draft of 'a scheme to obtain the admission of the whole of the issued share capital (as reorganised) to the Official List of the Stock Exchange', dated September 1973, in the name of Charterhouse Japhet. There is reference to an impact day of 28 November that year, with dealings commencing on Tuesday, 11 December. The company's profits had by now risen to over £700,000, as shown in the last audited accounts, and the flotation would rest on a forecast of £1 million for the current year. But the oil-price hike of the autumn of 1973 was to do untold harm to the Western economies, including ours. For me, on a strictly personal basis, it was one of the luckiest things that could have happened. By early 1974 the Stock Exchange had fallen dramatically and recovery was clearly a very long way ahead. There could be no flotation in such circumstances.

Of course, with the Conservative defeat of February 1974 I thought about returning to Haymarket. Lindsay came to my new home in Wilton Crescent to talk about the role I should play. We looked at all the options, including the possibility that I would resume the chairmanship and that my colleagues would revert to the status which had prevailed when I had left the company in 1970. Lindsay told me he was prepared to go along with this, although it would be a sad decision for him in view of the responsibilities he had carried and the very significant success that had followed. He felt bound to add that it might prove unworkable in practice. I decided to let things be. I became a consultant to the company, leaving my colleagues in the positions in which they had made such a success. It was probably one of the wisest decisions that I have ever made. Our head office was by then in Regent Street, where a room was rapidly made available for me. I moved back and forth between the House of Commons and this new address from which I operated until our election victory in 1979.

Haymarket had prospered. The merger with BPC's other magazine interests in 1967 had lifted the scale of the company. *Accountancy Age* had flourished and, after my departure in 1970, *What Car?* and

Computing added to the company's reputation as a creative publisher of specialist magazines. And it was now agreed by all involved that it would remain a private company.

In early 1976 Dick Strong spelt out the situation to the syndicate partners:

> The present position is that there is little hope of a flotation in the foreseeable future (whose attractions have anyhow diminished) while continued growth by acquisition and new launches currently looks unpromising. This means that a) the syndicate is locked in (there is little chance of a trade investor wishing to buy a minority interest, while the management do not wish to sell control), and b) various management/shareholders have substantial personal debt which they can see little prospect of repaying and is becoming increasingly difficult to service, due to the changes in the tax laws. Thus, as the basis of the original deal has evaporated and new personal requirements have arisen, it appears appropriate (in everybody's interest) to re-negotiate the position.

His paper showed the profits of the company as around £1.75 million at that time.

We were able to negotiate a new deal with the syndicate in 1976, which bought them out – with money provided by them. My family and I now owned over half the company, with the rest of the shares spread among other executives, principally Lindsay and Simon. We had achieved ownership of the company, subject only to a number of joint ventures in subsidiaries. It was a landmark. The Conservatives were, of course, in opposition at this time and I was acting as a consultant to the company. I was much involved in the conclusion of these negotiations. I did not, however, hold an executive post in the company during the five years of opposition and we followed this precedent during my years on the back benches from 1986 to 1990.

It was obvious, after our defeat in the general election of 1997, that I would never hold government office again. I telephoned Lindsay and suggested coffee. Lindsay, Simon and I met in Lindsay's office, by now in Hammersmith. 'You may have noticed that I'm unemployed. I thought I might come back,' I said. 'What would you like to do?' Lindsay asked. The question was more than justified. There were no management vacancies anywhere near the top of the company and it had had a remarkable track record on its journey to becoming one of the largest independent publishing companies in the United Kingdom. Many of the magazines I had helped to acquire or launch in the 1960s were still flourishing, including *Management Today* (where over the years we had bought out the original partners), *Campaign*, *Autosport*, *GP* and *MIMS*, but the company had been transformed in scale and was by now employing nearly a thousand people and earning profits of over £10 million. After some laughter, Lindsay's question was not too difficult to answer. I had always been the entrepreneur in the team, seeking out new developments or acquisitions, and we settled for that. They even agreed that I could have an office of my own, though it took months to materialise. For me, the traditional trauma that follows loss of a government job hardly occurred. I was ill for a short period, but then I was off on a new – or rather renewed – career as a publisher, with a parliamentary constituency to represent, an autobiography to write and an arboretum to tend.

I returned to Haymarket at a particularly exciting moment. The economic inheritance the Conservatives had handed to the Labour government allowed them to deliver domestic economic growth to add to the boom-town American market. Europe and Asia were very soon headed for recovery too and the talk everywhere was of globalisation. Add the electronic revolution and we were on the threshold of a new world in which, if we could get the judgements right, the owners of content and brand names had a head start in an electronic race that was soon to be almost out of control. This was the place for me. My relationship with my old friends in the company needed no formal titular responsibility to restore it.

But in 1999 Lindsay, by now sixty-six, told me that he thought it was time for him to retire from the chairmanship, as he had personal projects to which he wanted to devote his time. We therefore agreed that I would take over my old job again. (I had already, before the election, agreed to buy most of his shares.) I announced the change in a speech at the Mansion House at the conclusion of a dinner which Peter Levene, during his term of office as Lord Mayor, had kindly offered us the chance to hold. I expressed my deep gratitude for all Lindsay had done. For many years he had simply trusted me to deliver a legally binding agreement to buy his shares, for which there was effectively no other purchaser. Beyond the commercial value that he and his colleagues had created, he had played a significant role in giving to British specialist magazine publishing the class, style and quality it enjoys today.

Chapter 7

FINDING A SEAT

My defeat at the hands of the electors of Gower in 1959 was predictable enough but, to keep my hat in the ring, I agreed to be reselected as prospective candidate for the same constituency in 1961. This, of course, was before the storm clouds arose over our business – indeed, so clear did the sky then seem that I had even agreed in June 1960 to become managing director of Bow Group Publications, with special responsibility for *Crossbow*, the Bow Group's quarterly magazine.

Between 1959 and 1961 I gave little time to politics, as business commitments mounted. However, towards the end of 1961 I decided to accept the Tory nomination in the Labour marginal of Coventry North (where the majority against me would be only 1,241 compared with the 17,604 in Gower, whose local Association promptly and decently released me from any obligation to them). I thought, wrongly as it turned out, that Harold Macmillan might hold an early general election in view of his application to sign the Treaty of Rome and join the Common Market. I was not to know that de Gaulle would ruthlessly move to block our entry in January 1963.

Coventry North had been represented since 1945 by an extremely soigné Labour MP called Maurice Edelman. His elder daughter Sonia, by strange coincidence, had been a childhood friend of Anne's. A cultivated man, he was a journalist who also wrote novels, of which *Disraeli in Love* was probably to be the best known. Yet his own political odyssey was a curious one as he moved across the spectrum of opinion in the Labour Party from the far right to the far left – when I first arrived in Coventry he had just called for the resignation of the Labour leader, Hugh Gaitskell, on the ground that he was splitting the party with his support for nuclear weapons. From the outset it was clear, though, that only a national pro-Tory swing – such as Macmillan had enjoyed in 1959 – would bring me victory. But nothing like that materialised in October 1964 and, despite valuable support from Anne (to whom I had become engaged on the day before the selection in November 1961), I lost to Maurice Edelman by 3,530 votes, or rather more than double the margin by which he had scraped in in 1959.

I was disappointed, if only because (like most near-novice candidates) I had probably worked unduly hard in the months running up to the election. I calculated that in the nursing of the seat I had travelled some 13,000 miles up and down the M1 as well as blowing up at least one Jaguar when ferrying Christopher Chataway around as a guest speaker. He himself was standing for Lewisham North at the time (we had been at Oxford together, though we did not get to know each other till later, when he worked on a project with us at Cornmarket Press). My supporters – ranging from my chairman Margaret Birch to my agent Aubrey Nicholls – were a wonderful lot. I only once had cross words with the latter, and that arose out of his anxiety that I might be damaging myself by my insistence on including in a pictorial newspaper advertisement the face of a Sikh bus conductor as among the people who would be voting for me on polling day: I overrode his sense of caution and the web-offset colour ad (complete with the bus conductor) duly went into Woodrow Wyatt's short-lived *Coventry Express*. We circulated a copy of the advertisement to every house in the constituency.

It was a rowdy campaign but never threatening. One old-style barnstorming meeting was held in the police hall, where all three Conservative candidates in the city, Philip Hocking (for the previous five years Member for Coventry South), Ian Gow (later MP for Eastbourne, Margaret Thatcher's PPS when she was Prime Minister and subsequently Minister of Housing before being assassinated by the IRA in 1990) and I, held our own against continuous heckling which had the usual effect of arousing our supporters to energetic reaction.

As well as Anne, who was constantly at my side – we had been married now for two years, and she was enjoying her first election campaign – both my mother and my sister Bubbles turned up to help (and to mind Annabel, who was an energetic toddler), as did thirty members of the staff of Haymarket, who virtually manned half the polling stations on election day. The Prime Minister, Sir Alec Douglas-Home, provided personal support in a major outdoor rally attracting 5,000 people. We hurled ourselves into the fray until exhaustion overwhelmed us. Indeed, exhaustion was responsible for a tragicomic episode – comprehensible perhaps only to those who have actually fought an election. I was half running down a road ahead of Anne when she called me back to meet an elderly lady. I only vaguely heard what the old lady said as I shook her hand warmly. She seemed to be promising me her support. 'Good, good,' I said. 'And what of your husband?' 'He's diseased,' she replied. 'I'm sorry to hear that. I hope he'll be better soon,' I glibly answered. 'No,' she said rather more firmly, 'he's diseased.' I again repeated, rather stupidly, my protestations of goodwill for his future health and only then realised that what she was actually saying was that he was 'deceased'. It was one of those moments when you wish the ground would open up and swallow you whole.

Now, with two honourable defeats at successive general elections behind me, I was anxious to try for a Tory seat. I did not have long to wait. Soon after Harold Wilson's narrow victory at the general election, Sir Henry Studholme, the veteran Conservative MP for Tavistock, announced that he would be retiring at the next election. A letter from the Tavistock Association inviting me for an interview arrived just before Christmas 1964. Anne and I caught the train from Paddington to the West Country on a bleak and cold January day in 1965. I was short-listed, along with the future Tory MP Tim Fortescue and a local man, John Taylor. At a subsequent meeting of the Finance and General Purposes Committee of the Association held on 4 March, the three names were further considered and it was resolved to recommend me as prospective parliamentary candidate to the Association's annual general meeting to be held three weeks later on 26 March.

The West Country had certainly been traditional Tory territory. In the election of 1964 the Conservatives had held all the Cornish and Devon seats, apart from North Devon and Bodmin (where Jeremy Thorpe and Peter Bessell had won for the Liberals). But the writing was on the wall. Jeremy Thorpe had first gained North Devon at the 1959 general election and eighteen months earlier the Torrington by-election had seen Mark Bonham Carter win a spectacular victory for the Liberals, even though a charismatic local farmer, Percy Browne, had won the seat back for the Tories at the general election. The Conservative leadership could see that the party's natural pre-eminence in the area was beginning to crumble. The county squirearchy who had typically represented these seats for the Tories were losing ground to a younger, middle-class, Liberal challenge. Even, I suspect, in my selection the natural instinct for survival, characteristic of the Conservative hold on power throughout the twentieth century, was very much at work.

My predecessor, Sir Henry Studholme, Bart, CVO, belonged to – and was typical of – a certain and admirable English tradition. An Old Etonian, he had married Judith Whitbread of the brewing family and had represented Tavistock in Parliament since 1943. Judy Studholme was an imposing woman and at first somewhat forbidding. But the more we came to know her, the greater grew our respect and, perhaps somewhat to her embarrassment, our affection. Sir Henry had entered politics, so he told me, because 'my wife and my mother felt it was my duty'. He carried that duty out conscientiously and with dignity. But the seat was changing around him. Plymouth hosted an explosion of the property-owning democracy as its hinterland of Plympton and Plymstock absorbed massive new housing estates in the 1950s and 1960s. Henry Studholme continued to serve this community to the best of his ability, but he was part of a passing world and would neither have wished nor been able to change. However, the mood locally was for a significant change. I fitted that mood. I was also much encouraged by the excellent agent, Jim Cobley, who became an ally and briefed me carefully along the way. I suspected that Jim played some part in persuading the more doubtful members of the local Association executive that I was the sort of candidate that they needed to have.

My translation from Coventry was not without its tensions. I then knew nothing of farming. I had virtually no local connections. Perhaps most damagingly of all, it was whispered that I published a rather risqué magazine. Henry and Judy Studholme had generously invited Anne and me to stay with them in their attractive Georgian home, Wembury House, on the South Devon coast for the nights of 25 and 26 March. The rumours were flying. I sat through the day of the AGM in their house listening to the incessant ring of the telephone as ever more anxious calls brought news of growing unrest among the grassroots. There was nothing to be done. I played solitaire on a board thoughtfully provided by Judy Studholme to take my mind off my unpredictable fate.

I myself had no worries about the allegations that I was ignorant of farming or lacked local connections. These are the sort of arguments paraded in virtually every selection process in one form or another and rarely carry much weight. Besides, they weren't choosing someone to run their farms for them; they wanted someone to fight for their interests at Westminster and, to many of them even more important, to fight the Liberals. I could handle those arguments. The rumours about the magazine were harder to overcome, despite the fact that they were groundless. You only have to admit that you own a men's fashion magazine and imaginations run riot. And they did. The situation was far from helped by the front cover of the current issue of *Town*, which had appeared a few days before the critical meeting. By today's standards it would not have merited a sideways glance except as an attractive example of fine design. But in those more inhibited days the bikini-clad, Ursula Andress lookalike – with a diving knife strapped to her naked thigh – was sufficient to set tongues tutting. When eventually the Studholmes escorted us to Tavistock Town Hall that evening, it was packed to overflowing. Over 500 local Association members had turned out. The atmosphere was electric, the stakes absolute. I had the speech ready and well prepared. It went well. They had heard nothing like it. I began by confronting the controversy at the forefront of their minds.

Tonight there is room for discussion. Let there be criticism and frankness because it would be inconceivable that everybody in this room is unanimous without reservation that I am the man for this division. And from some of the things I have heard in the last few days it would be miraculous. So let the questioning be ruthless because this is a serious thing that we do here and something that is not lightly undone.

But at the close of the proceedings let one thing be clear. Whatever is decided here tonight is the will of the Association. Now is the moment of protest; tomorrow there is another job to be done.

And, if I am the man you choose to lead you, as from ten o'clock tonight the battle shall commence.

. . .

I do not share the view that because Tavistock is in the toe of England it can be forgotten. It seems to me that, if that toe is placed firmly enough in the appropriate position, the results might be startling.

There were only a few half-hearted questions and Anne and I left the hall. My apprehension about the outcome was in no way abated by the sight of all the heavy fawn mackintoshes hanging in the corridor, tucked into an unhealthy number of which could be seen the offending magazine cover. It was great for circulation figures but there was nothing great about it for me at that moment.

After my speech, however, the opposition crumbled. An amendment that the question of selection should be referred back to the Finance and General Purposes Committee, proposed by a giant ex-Royal Marine, one Captain H. P. Chichester-Clark, secured only twenty-seven votes. We were called back into the hall to an enthusiastic reception. The next day Anne and I returned to London, but not before she had been told by a group of ladies that they had voted for me only because they liked her hat. Such is politics. Westminster was not far away now. Into our suitcase Judy had slipped the solitaire set, which remains a treasured possession.

On 31 March 1966, the United Kingdom went to the polls. The experience accumulated in Gower and Coventry was put to full use: the design of the election address; meetings in every village; loudspeaker attached to my Land Rover. It was all very different from my predecessor's campaign. But, in general, it passed without incident. Ted Heath, who had succeeded Sir Alec as party leader, addressed a large and supportive open-air meeting in the market place at Tavistock. My mother and Bubbles once again came to help. I recall only one tricky moment. In Lifton, towards the north of the constituency, the locals had turned out to satisfy their curiosity. Question time came. A very elderly farmer, in the broadest Devonian accent, was the first to put his query. I couldn't understand a word of it. I asked if he would mind repeating it. He did repeat it, this time in an even broader Devon accent. The situation was hopeless. I had to tell him so, to the immense delight of the audience.

The Liberals, of course, made much of the fact that I was not a local man and there was a certain concern among my supporters that this argument would carry weight. There is a story of the late Sir Douglas Marshall, the former Conservative MP who lost the Bodmin constituency to Peter Bessell in 1964. It had been a safe Conservative seat but Sir Douglas had not been the most assiduous of constituency representatives, and at a crowded election meeting he had managed to arrive, in a way that was all too familiar to his constituents, rather late. He began his speech by seeking to explain what had delayed him when a voice from the back of the hall interrupted him: 'Where have you been, Sir Douglas?' Sir Douglas began again: 'I was trying to explain to you why I was late.' Halfway through the second time of explaining, the voice interrupted again. 'Where have you been, Sir Douglas?' A by now irritated Sir Douglas began to expostulate. The voice would have none of it. 'Where have you been, Sir Douglas, these last twenty-nine years?'

My principal opponent, Christopher Trethewey, a local business-man and former Liberal agent, launched his campaign under the banner 'One of Us'. He took every opportunity to display his local connections. His picture looked out from posters emblazoned with his 'One of Us' slogan. Some of my more imaginative and enthusiastic supporters dented the appeal of this approach by placing a line of them along the wall of a local cemetery. Whether that helped or not I do not know but on polling day I managed to restore Conservative Tavistock fortunes: my majority was 8,183, compared with the 5,400 achieved by Sir Henry in 1964.

There was one great sadness. In 1964 Anne and I had fought Coventry together, and one of the most rewarding parts of the day, we both agreed, had been the escape late in the evening from the public gaze to talk over and laugh at the little incidents of the previous twelve hours. But in the intervening period Anne had lost a child in mid-pregnancy and, now that she was expecting again, our doctor was insistent that there should be no risks taken this time round. She was kept in London while I fought the campaign alone. The promise I had made her that we would celebrate the victory we both anticipated by an appearance on a prominent balcony overlooking Tavistock's historic town square was never kept. Our second daughter, Alexandra, chose, conveniently, 28 March – just before polling day – to put in a first appearance. The *Daily Mirror* featured mother and daughter. There were still three campaigning days left before the count on the Friday and the follow-up triumphal tour of the constituency to thank the voters. It was some five days after Alexandra was born before I could return to London to see her. It was at the suggestion of Henry Studholme that we gave her the middle name of Victoria – in celebration of my third-time-lucky election victory.

In September 1965 we had rented accommodation in the wing of a house called Sortridge in the village of Horrabridge and we remained there for a year or so. It was an austere stone house, owned by a Wing Commander Smythe, and was much in need of repair, but it housed us while we looked for something else. After the election I heard of a house, Pamflete, on the Flete estate near Holbeton. We were fortunate enough to rent it for £10 a week. Situated on the Erme estuary, it nestled into the hillside leading down to an idyllic part of the south coast of Devon. The bird life was magnificent, a heronry upstream, and access to the beach, where Anne and the children once saw a titanic fight between male swans challenging each other for supremacy. There were enchanting woodland walks, there was a paddock for a pony and the house itself was comfortable, slate-hung, built in the eighteenth century.

The constituency was, of course, gigantic, covering several hundred square miles, including a large part of the ethereally beautiful and unspoilt Dartmoor. Flushed with political success after the election, I bought a fifteen-foot caravan. I would set out on Saturdays with this, my mobile surgery, pausing for quarter-of-an-hour stops around the constituency. This proved a great success – the first time we did it. Small crowds of supporters and enthusiasts turned up at every village; coffee, scones, cakes were laid on; it was quite a party. When I proudly told Chris Chataway, who had lost his own seat of Lewisham North at the same election (he was to be re-elected at a by-election in Chichester three years later), about my new initiative, he shook his head in pity and disbelief. 'You'll never be able to stop doing it, Michael,' he said. I remembered his words months later as I continued to navigate the narrowest Devon lanes with a more or less uncontrollable caravan on the back of my Jaguar – only to wait a quarter of an hour in each village usually entirely alone. The novelty had worn off. Chris Chataway's ominous warning echoed in my ears. We gradually replaced the mobile surgery with announced visits to community halls or to people's front rooms. But three years later, in August 1969, I was still using the caravan for my annual tour of the sixty-seven towns and villages in the constituency.

In its day Tavistock was one of the oldest constituencies in the country and it returned Members of Parliament for a total of 676 years. Indeed, until the reforms of the late nineteenth century it had for some time regularly returned not one but two Members of Parliament. (The electors each had two votes as well; but it should be remembered that as late as 1865 there were only 426 of them out of a population of 9,000. It took the Acts of 1867 and 1884 finally to bring about the general enfranchisement even of male householders.) It had been an area with a strong Whig/Liberal tradition and was in many ways a pocket borough; the Drake family sent one of its members to Westminster no fewer than fourteen times between 1640 and 1734. The first Russell was elected in 1640 and for most of the nineteenth century one of the Tavistock seats was, by convention, in the gift of the Dukes of Bedford, heads of the Russell family, who wielded powerful influence in the area. By that same convention, however, the other seat was generally filled by a representative of local interests – chosen without ducal interference. Tavistock's representatives over the years had included some great men, the most notable of whom were surely John Pym, returned for Tavistock six times between 1624 and his death in 1643 and one of the leaders of the parliamentary opposition to Charles I, and Lord John Russell, who piloted the Great Reform Bill of 1832 through the House of Commons.

But I was to be the last Honourable Member for Tavistock. I fought the seat for the second time in 1970 knowing that it would have disappeared by the time of the next election. My principal opponent on that occasion, the Liberal candidate, was a former Arctic explorer, Himalayan climber and ex-Royal Marine officer, Major Mike Banks. Labour put up Harold Luscombe, a young railwayman from Plymouth. Polling day was to be 18 June and campaigning in early summer through the magic of Devon's countryside was an unforgettable experience. And this time Anne was there to share it with me.

It was also the first election in which I was drawn outside my own patch to work and speak for the party's national campaign, mainly in the Midlands. The national campaign was perceived not to be going well. The polls were gloomy. Halfway through the campaign there was talk that Willie Whitelaw should replace Ted Heath. This was, of course, ludicrous press speculation, but it wasn't the sort of background designed to bolster the morale of the footsoldiers out in the front line. The message of the opinion polls was never, however, reflected on the streets. There things seemed much more optimistic. And so it turned out. Ted Heath was returned with an overall House of Commons majority of thirty-one. My majority in Tavistock this time was 15,449, the biggest the Conservative Party in the constituency had ever enjoyed.

Ironically, I now had to decide what to do about my next seat. In order to keep parliamentary representation broadly in line with population changes, Parliament had established in 1949 a standing Boundary Commission. Independent of party politics, it was charged with proposing the realignment of constituency boundaries roughly every ten years to reflect, for example, the movement of people from inner cities to dormitory suburbs or the creation of new towns. It then became the responsibility of the Home Secretary of the day to put the proposals to Parliament, and the convention was that they were voted through unamended. The Boundary Commission had produced its latest report in March 1969. Its findings were unattractive to Harold Wilson's Labour government. The Home Secretary, Jim Callaghan, laid the necessary orders before the House but Labour MPs were whipped to vote them down – provoking something of a scandal at the time. After the election the new Tory government voted through the recommendations in November 1970. The Tavistock division was to be divided between a new West Devon seat and a third Plymouth seat.

I was asked if I would be interested in applying for either of these. After discussing the matter with Anne, I decided to decline. In the previous two or three years I had become increasingly aware of a growing conflict between my political career on the national stage, my ability to do an effective job as a local Member of Parliament and the demands of a young family. The most extreme example of this had been one August Bank Holiday when, with three children (our son Rupert had been born on 9 July 1967), a nanny, a cat, a dog, a budgerigar in a cage and a bowl of goldfish, we had clambered into our car to head back to London, only to spend ten hours driving the 200 miles from the South Devon coast. Four- or five-hour car journeys were commonplace.

I was also beginning to receive invitations to speak around the country and I wanted to be able to get back home on a Friday night, stay with Anne and the children over the weekend and lead a slightly more normal family life. I decided that I would take my chances in the hope of finding a constituency easier to combine with wider political responsibilities. In many ways I was saddened by this decision. I loved the West Country, I had made good friends there and I enjoyed the opportunity to combine politics with many of the interests – fishing, bird-watching, shooting – that have been a constant part of my life.

The competition for Gower had been less than fierce; Coventry had not selected itself as a likely hunting ground for the high-flyers among Conservative candidates. But I had done well in securing Tavistock soon after the 1964 election and just in time to be one of the few Conservative newcomers in 1966. It was, therefore, with a certain youthful insouciance that I faced the prospect of finding a new constituency.

I discussed the matter with Ian Gilmour, who had been elected at a by-election for Central Norfolk three years before me. His seat was also to disappear. Since we shared very much the same views – though he was a scholarly rather than a practical man – we agreed that it would be unseemly for the two of us to compete. I suggested that, when the first safe constituency came up which attracted him, I would stand back to allow him a clear run. It never occurred to either of us that he might fail. Up came the Ealing Acton constituency, Ian put his name in, but George Young, a future colleague in the Department of the Environment, was chosen. We spoke again. 'It's your turn, Michael,' he said. Mid-Oxfordshire came up. Although suffering from a mild attack of flu, I set off with high hopes, toured the constituency, learnt the local landmarks, familiarised myself with the local industry and turned up for the interview. I wasn't even short-listed. It was no consolation at all that the successful candidate turned out to be so formidable a future government colleague as Douglas Hurd.

Ian and I had a third conversation. 'We're not getting anywhere,' Ian said. 'Next time we had better both go in together.' In early 1972 Mid-Sussex came up. Both Ian and I were short-listed, together with a third, then unknown local candidate, Tim Renton (who subsequently became government Chief Whip, then Minister for the Arts). The usual press comment and speculation took place. I was seen as the favourite and I believed my chances were good. On the day of the final selection in March Ian and I went to Francis Pym, the Chief Whip, and explained that we couldn't be present for the three-line whip at the 6.30 p.m. vote in the House that evening as we had to appear before the selectors of Mid-Sussex. 'I don't give a hoot', Pym said, 'what's happening in Mid-Sussex. You'll be here for the vote.' There is no arguing with a Chief Whip in such a mood. Ian and I sent a message explaining that we would get to Haywards Heath as quickly as we could. Eventually we arrived, nearer to 9 p.m. than the 7 p.m. start of the selection conference for which we had originally been summoned. The upshot was simple: we might as well have saved ourselves the train fares. Tim Renton got the seat and Ian and I withdrew to console ourselves with the knowledge that the government had won the 6.30 p.m. vote with a majority of thirty-seven instead of thirty-five.

But the story did have a happy ending. Ian was shortly thereafter selected for Chesham and Amersham – this time without competition from me (though I had earlier been tempted to enter the lists at

Beaconsfield against a sitting right-wing Tory MP) – and that September I was formally chosen for Henley-on-Thames in succession to one of the first national chairmen of the Young Conservatives, John Hay. After a little humiliation, Ian and I had each secured two of the most attractive Conservative seats in the country. Speaking for myself, it has been a privilege to represent my Henley constituency for more than a quarter of a century. Stretching from the northern suburbs of Reading to Thame to the north-east of Oxford, it embraces not only the market towns of Henley, Goring, Watlington and Thame, but countless villages in highly conserved countryside, including magnificent stretches of the Chilterns and the banks of the Thames itself. My majority has been sustained over the years by one of the best party associations in the country and I enjoyed for many years the unfailing backing of a really first-class agent in Ron Rulten, who knew his job inside out and remained splendidly unflappable whatever the demands or pressures.

Appearing before selection committees again, this time as a junior minister – as I had become when Ted Heath formed his government in June 1970 – was a salutary experience. Over the years you get accustomed to the over-flattering remarks that accompany your appearances as a guest speaker on a party platform. There is a vote of thanks in which the local volunteers are told of your virtues. Everyone is touchingly appreciative of the trouble you've taken to visit them. The language has its own mood music – 'How good of you to come', 'How much we appreciate all you do for us', 'I don't know how you manage to carry the strain'. It's too easy to inhale and almost come to believe all the kind things that are being said. But suddenly, at a selection conference, there you are, standing in front of the self-same people, thirty to fifty of them, unsmiling, examining you up and down, asking hostile questions. 'How do we know we'll ever see you?' 'What will you do for us?' 'Do ministers ever bother with their constituents?' It requires a certain psychological readjustment, a relearning that this is where the power lies. They are the masters. This is democracy in action. Nobody has a freehold in politics.

PART TWO:
1966–1979

Chapter 8

ON TO THE FRONT BENCH

he election of 1966 was a Tory disaster. Harold Wilson had transformed a wafer-thin margin of three before polling day into an overall Commons majority of ninety-seven. It looked very much as if we were in for a long haul before we got back to power. Only ten of the eighty-odd entirely new MPs sat on the Conservative benches; but they included two outstanding intellectuals, John Nott and David Howell, with whom I was to serve in Mrs Thatcher's first government, not to mention the redoubtable Jill Knight, who over the next thirty years was to earn enormous affection as an independent-minded backbencher.

For a young MP, interested in a ministerial career, there is considerable advantage in entering the House of Commons after one's party has suffered a significant defeat. Most of the senior members of the party will have been in opposition before. They know what a thankless task it is. Some will have served in government and now fear that they will never do so again. In 1966, with a majority as large as ninety-seven arrayed against them, they could also have been forgiven for feeling that very few of their contemporaries would ever do so either. The tendency is for such experienced colleagues to drift back to their extra-parliamentary interests in order to replenish the family coffers. Consequently, there are easy opportunities for the energetic young backbencher to make a mark.

Not that initially everything is necessarily plain sailing. Being a new boy in Parliament is unlike any other similar experience. Whether at a new school, as a freshman at university or as a recruit to military service, someone would always explain the form, programme, timetables, duties, rules and regulations – all that sort of thing. But in the House of Commons you arrive, and you are on your own. There are no induction courses. It is presumed that, since you have persuaded people to elect you to represent them, you have some idea of how you intend to fulfil your new-found obligations. Occasionally, a benign older Member will take you aside and show you the geography. In my case, Patrick Jenkin, the young Member for Churchill's old constituency of Wanstead and Woodford, whom I had met only briefly once or twice before, generously took me round the bewildering warren of corridors that is the Palace of Westminster. But that was it.

Once a week a few sheets of photocopied paper arrive to remind you of the following week's business and the times when your presence is either requested (underlined with one line), required (two lines) or demanded (three lines) for a vote and also listing the committees which you are free to attend. The whip, as these instructions are called, will first have been read out to a large gathering of colleagues in Committee Room 14 at 6.00 p.m. on each Thursday evening. No one seems to mind what you do as long as you vote whenever two or three lines appear. I remember feeling disillusioned, if not actually disappointed. I suppose I had expected a more regimental introduction. I was still, however, in executive control of Haymarket and that, together with the constituency, where we had our weekend home, kept me more than busy.

I took my time before risking the plunge into my maiden speech. I delivered it on 14 July 1966, during the debate on the Labour government's Prices and Incomes Bill. If it had any merit, it was owed largely to an old friend of Anne's and mine, John Biffen, a diffident man with deep convictions who had represented Oswestry since a by-election in 1961, and who came round to our home at 50 Chepstow Villas the evening before to advise me on what to say and how to say it. John is a born parliamentarian, as he showed in his six years as Leader of the House spanning the first and second Thatcher administrations, and I was very grateful for his advice.

My maiden speech contained no great rhetorical flourish. It has the virtue, however, of standing the test of time. I argued that broad-based incomes policy would fail in the endless day-to-day decisions of ordinary people to augment their income, that the cure for an overheated economy was to deflate and that, as the government had announced its measures to achieve this, the need for the Bill was already overtaken. The speech argued for an incentive society which delivered the economic growth upon which real improvements in the quality of public service depended. The maximisation of earnings and profits was inherent in such a strategy, as was enhanced competition and the search for denationalisation targets. All that is conventional wisdom today; strange to reflect that Mrs Thatcher never came to regard me as 'one of us'.

What appeared to be the first sign of incipient official recognition came in an approach from Paul Bryan, the Opposition spokesman on broadcasting. The Labour Postmaster General, Ted Short, was steering a bill through the Commons designed, as its long title said, to 'suppress broadcasting from ships, aircraft and certain marine structures'. On buttonholing me Bryan first very tactfully said that he felt that I might be able to help *him*. My sense of expectation and excitement rose. He sensed – he added even more conspiratorially – that I possessed a particular area of expertise which could be of great assistance. Although I was a little bewildered, that sounded encouraging enough. But then came the rabbit punch. Would I, Bryan asked earnestly, take the responsibility for dealing with that part of the Bill covering the activities of *pirate* radio stations? (Pirate radio stations, such as Radio Caroline, used to transmit from ships anchored just outside British territorial waters and were able to reach large parts of the United Kingdom but escape the restrictions of the tightly regulated world of domestic broadcasting. They were a serious headache to the authorities in the late 1960s, though fans of pop music loved them.) Clearly, in terms of reputation, I still had some way to go. Rather limply, I agreed to his request but mercifully managed to extricate myself from this commitment when the first serious alternative opportunity presented itself shortly afterwards.

It was certainly a more promising alternative. Peter Walker, the Conservative MP for Worcester since 1961 and Ted Heath's newly appointed spokesman on Transport, was at thirty-four (only a year older than me) one of the brightest of the Tory frontbench team. That summer of 1966 he asked me if I would organise a tour of the West Country for him during the recess. At the time I hardly knew Peter at all. I had been faintly anxious about some of his views, particularly over Europe (in the original debate over join-ing the Common Market in 1961–2 he had been one of the most active and energetic of the Conservative anti-Europeans). But I was intrigued at the prospect of learning more about high-level politics, which his visit offered. I organised a tour for him in August, during which he was photographed and reported from one end of the

West Country to the other. I had guessed that that was the general idea.

It was, anyway, the beginning of a lasting political friendship which was to stretch over the years, whether we were serving in government or in opposition and even covering those times when one or other of us was in exile. Having left school at fifteen, Peter is one of those rare politicians – I suppose it could be said that I was another – to have created his own business from scratch. A former national chairman of the Young Conservatives, he would in the late 1950s address YC meetings up and down the country, always taking time off from politics on his visits to sell insurance policies, the premium income from which laid the foundations of his personal fortune. He is an entrepreneurial manager of proven ability and an innovative political operator of great skill and flair. It was one of the tragedies of the last Conservative period in power that Mrs Thatcher was never prepared to promote him to a major government post. Indeed, in 1975, she attempted to destroy his career absolutely by refusing to include him in her Shadow Cabinet.

In the event, Peter deemed that 1966 tour of ours a success. On the Sunday night when we returned to London, he invited me for a drink in the flat in Gayfere Street, Westminster, which he shared as an office with two other colleagues, Ian Gilmour and Charlie Morrison. That evening Peter outlined to me his ideas for opposing the plans set out in a White Paper which Barbara Castle, the then Minister for Transport, had laid before Parliament in July. These plans were ultimately to form the basis of the Transport Act of 1968. He invited me to specialise particularly in the urban transport proposals which, when the Bill eventually emerged, accounted for about one-third of it. England's major conurbations were served at the time by municipal bus companies, centred on the local authorities that made up these spreading communities. The local authorities loved these transport undertakings as though they were their own children; prominent councillors chaired the committees; the municipal arms decorated their livery. Mrs Castle threatened to take them over and amalgamate them into conurbation-wide Passenger Transport Authorities. Many of the about-to-be-deprived or – to enter into the language of the time – 'about-to-be-robbed' councils were Tory controlled. This was to be the emotional core of our case. There were also all-embracing proposals to nationalise the private sector bus companies, especially the empire of British Electric Traction (BET). Peter invited me to take up a forward position in the front line of what was to be a classic parliamentary battle of its day.

Mrs Castle's Bill took some time to materialise. It was not until July 1967 that it was announced formally that I was to be the frontbench spokesman on urban transport, though only leaving the back benches when my own subject was under discussion. Fortunately, there were plenty of opportunities for doing that. The Transport Bill took almost a year to get through both Houses of Parliament. We fought it doggedly all the way.

It was a wonderful chance that Peter had given me and I responded to it with enthusiasm. In one way, I was fortunate. In October 1966 I had recruited an attractive and able American graduate of Vassar and Oxford, Eileen Baker, to be my research assistant. She had originally come to work for me to deal with constituency business, but she now moved into the transport field. In those days there were virtually no research assistants in the House of Commons. It was considered a very American practice – and no doubt Eileen's new role merely reinforced that prejudice. But to me she was invaluable. We set out to oppose, line by line, Mrs Castle's vast, 166-clause, 18-schedule, omnibus Bill. Peter Walker's campaign against the Transport Bill was one of the great success stories of the Opposition in that period. It so happened that a good deal of the focus of the committee stage of the Bill* concentrated on the section for which I was responsible. Working under the iron discipline of the committee Whip, Jack Weatherill (a future Speaker of the House of Commons), we sat hour after hour, day and night. I learnt the trench warfare techniques of opposition the hard way.

In Committee Room 10 I found myself face to face with one of the most formidable of the Labour government's ministers, Barbara Castle. She used every known feminine device to secure her way and did so brilliantly – the temper and the tears were equally divided as she brought passion and emotion to those arcane, dry-as-dust sub-clauses. She also possessed that hugely impressive quality in a female Member of the House of Commons: she was always beautifully dressed and immaculately groomed. You never saw Barbara with a hair out of place. She shared the same pride in her appearance which was later to be displayed by Margaret Thatcher – and, indeed, I have sometimes thought that, without the trail blazed by Barbara, Margaret

---

* An outline of parliamentary procedure (including second reading, committee stage, report stage and third reading) can be found at pp. 165–7.

might never have become Prime Minister at all. I am not sure my doughty ministerial opponent over the Transport Bill will necessarily take that as a compliment, but at least it is intended as one.

Outside the House my reputation as a speaker was building. One of the great cheerleaders among the Tory knights, Sir Walter Bromley-Davenport (years before dismissed from the Whips' Office for giving a great kick to a departing diplomat he mistook for an erring Tory MP), approached me one day to say that he had organised a big rally in his constituency at which Quintin Hogg, the Shadow Home Secretary, was due to speak. Rumour had reached him on the grapevine that Quintin was about to cry off. Would I take his place? Walter had not been misinformed, so at the end of that week I travelled with him to his Cheshire constituency of Knutsford. He had not misrepresented the nature of the gathering either. Hundreds of people packed a large hall and there was a general atmosphere of expectation. Then Walter announced that Quintin had not come. Groans arose from the vast throng. Walter tried to do his best for me. He made copious references to youth, the rising generation, the wave of the future. The audience sat stolid, unmoved – I was an interloper. Their initial instinct was to go home. Fortunately, though, my speech went reasonably well. For the first time outside my own constituency I felt I had managed to communicate with a mass audience. Walter, who clearly thought that his own faith in me had been justified, was nothing if not vociferous in his praise afterwards. Few colleagues were spared the tale. Invitations to similar occasions began to flow – though, unlike the sixteen-year-old William Hague, I first spoke at a party conference when I was already thirty-three. I actually opened the Conference on that occasion. It was 1966 and first thing in the morning on the first day. The debate was on transport. My advice to any aspiring politician interested in making an impression at party conference is simple: there are better subjects and no worse time.

On the whole, as a new Member in the House, I kept my nose clean so far as the whips were concerned. In my early years I defied their advice on only two occasions – both, interestingly, had a bearing on racial issues. The first time was over the second reading of the Labour government's Commonwealth Immigrants Bill of 1968, brought in to limit the immigration of Kenyan Asians into this country to 1,500 (plus dependants) a year, despite the fact that those seeking to come held UK passports, whose full validity had been confirmed to them by the Tory government at the time of Kenyan independence in

Our post-war family home: Broughton in Sketty, Swansea, with its two-acre garden, tennis court and greenhouses

My father, Rupert, taken after the war and a picture of my mother in early married life

My sister, 'Bubbles', and myself with our Scottie, Angus, in 1940

My mother and father on a Mediterranean cruise

Preparing to be Minister for Aerospace at the age of eleven

Moser's Hall house photograph taken at Shrewsbury in 1950. I am fifth from the right in the third row just behind the left shoulder of my house-master, A. H. ('Bounce') Phillips

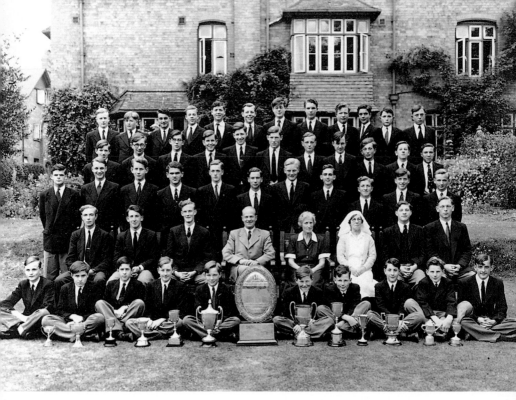

The young undergraduate. A picture taken by Kenny Parker just after I went
up to Pembroke College, Oxford, in October 1951

The Oxford Union Debating
Chamber in Michaelmas Term
1954. Jeremy Isaacs is on my
right and Tony Howard on
my left, with John King-
Farlow in the secretary's chair
(*foreground*)

With Sir Bernard and Lady
Docker at the opening of the
Union's Cellars night-club in
October 1954

Guardsman Heseltine as a member of the Brigade Squad at Caterham in February 1959

In battledress at Mons Officer Cadet School alongside my much-prized Jaguar later in 1959

The aspirant property tycoon. In 1960 with my sister 'Bubbles' outside the property development I had just acquired with Clive Labovitch in Stafford Terrace, London W8.

Clive Labovitch, my business partner for eight years and a kind, gentle man whom I trusted implicitly

1963. The official instruction given in the weekly whip was that all Conservative MPs should support the government Bill. But to me, as to Iain Macleod, the Shadow Chancellor, who at the time wrote an eloquent open letter in the *Spectator* reminding the party of the promise that had been given on its behalf only five years earlier, it was a matter of honour. Anne felt as strongly as I did. On the evening of 27 February 1968, along with thirteen other Conservatives and a smattering of Liberals and left-wing Labour MPs, I proudly followed the Shadow Chancellor into the 'no' lobby, and was to vote against the measure three more times during its hurried progress through the Commons until it finally became law on 1 March 1968.

The second occasion was for me even more intense in that it came shortly after Enoch Powell's notorious 'rivers of blood' speech on Saturday, 20 April 1968. I had been out campaigning against Barbara Castle's Transport Bill that weekend. Unusually for a Conservative in those days, I was speaking the next day – despite its being a Sunday – from a platform in Leeds. I delivered a sharp warning that the party would expect some action to be taken against Powell (to his great credit, Heath dismissed him from the Shadow Cabinet that same evening). My own view at the time was that Powell's purpose was to threaten the government-sponsored Race Relations Bill that was due to have its second reading in the Commons that very week. This particular measure had nothing whatever to do with levels of immigration: it had one simple purpose – to establish by law that no one could act or speak prejudicially about people who had every right to be here in this country and whose sole 'offence' was the colour of their skin. With my earlier experience in the hotel trade and in running a careers advisory service at Haymarket, I had absolutely no doubt that such a bill was necessary – and never more so than after Enoch Powell's speech. I was, therefore, dismayed when the official recommendation came from the Shadow Cabinet (carried against the wishes of the then Shadow Home Secretary, Quintin Hogg) to support a reasoned amendment approving the objectives of the Bill but declining to give it a second reading. Especially in the climate of the times – Powell's speech was to scar the whole racial landscape for at least a generation – this seemed to me quite the wrong signal for the Tories to send out to the country. I was not alone in feeling that. Once again, I was proud to join another Opposition frontbencher, this time our Education spokesman Sir Edward Boyle, in defying the party whip and ostentatiously abstaining when the Opposition amendment was put. By the time of the Bill's third reading three months later the Shadow Cabinet had come round to our view and the party no longer officially opposed what became the 1968 Race Relations Act.

Neither 'rebellion' exactly put my position at hazard, though I was left in little doubt that on each occasion I was not particularly popular with my Association members in Tavistock. (It is a melancholy reflection that the smaller the number of ethnic immigrants in a particular area, the more vehement the opinions expressed about them often are.) On the Saturday evening following Powell's speech I attended the most fearsome local Conservative Association meeting of my entire career. Kitley, a magnificent South Devon home of the Bastard family, was packed. The atmosphere was tense. The meat porters of Smithfield had marched that week in support of Powell; my constituents were with them in spirit. I discussed with my agent what would happen if Powell made a bid to lead the party. We came to a gloomy conclusion. But I suppose I was lucky not to incur the wrath of the Whips' Office. The lesson, I fancy (or perhaps I merely flatter myself), is that where individual stands are taken upon recognisable principle – and not out of opportunistic or simple survival motives – the offence tends to be treated that much more leniently, especially of course when one's views are shared by some of the most respected Conservative parliamentarians of the day. Certainly, there was never any suggestion, so far as I am aware, that I should even be removed from my part-time frontbench responsibilities.

My first four years in the House taught me some more basic house-keeping lessons as well. An MP's salary at the time was a mere £3,250 a year – clearly insufficient in my case to bring up a family, run two homes and maintain a research assistant, to say nothing of a secretary. I became convinced of the need for a proper expense allowance – not necessarily because I wanted to see full-time professional MPs (indeed, I still believe in MPs having other careers) but the 'lobby fodder' system at the time of regular all-night sittings, from which we would all emerge bleary-eyed, seemed to me indefensible. The public regarded it as a farce, too – and not surprisingly since the majority of Members spent most of the next day nodding off in the libraries or fighting a rearguard action against sleep in the Commons bars. Certainly, no one so exposed was in a fit state to do a proper day's work, whether inside the House or outside it. I can remember Lindsay's and Simon's incredulous looks as, exhausted, I tried to justify this salient feature of the democratic process. The pendulum may now have gone too far the other way with the Commons chamber effectively dead from Wednesday evening onwards (and a great deal of the earlier part of the week as well), but I have never felt any nostalgia for a supposed golden age when the division lobbies tyrannised our lives.

Very soon after arriving in Westminster, I also discovered the infinite satisfaction, which any MP will recognise, of taking on the bureaucrats on behalf of an individual constituent, lost in a welter of red tape and officialdom, and securing for him or her proper treatment and justice. However, I almost simultaneously made another decision I have never regretted. In Parliament, as elsewhere in life, it is wise to specialise. It was not difficult to make speeches on more or less any subject by simply reading the briefs sent out by the respective party organisations; but it seemed to me that, if I was to make any real contribution, I should restrict myself to one or two subjects and then take them very seriously.

In 1968 Ted Heath decided to move Peter Walker to be Shadow Minister for Housing and Local Government, and in his place he made Margaret Thatcher the Opposition Transport spokesman. This was my first real contact with Margaret and I was from the start disturbed by the contrast between the success that Peter had had in earning the support of the industry which he shadowed and the confrontational techniques that were later to become so familiar as Margaret rose to power. Possessed of a fine mind and an immense capacity for hard work, she had no trouble in getting on top of her brief – she was, after all, a tax lawyer – and mastering the arguments. But the object of opposition is to build loyalties and support, to persuade and encourage people to believe in you as an alternative to the government of the day. I was dismayed at meetings she held with representatives of the transport sector to have to listen to them being lectured and hectored before they had even had a chance to make their case.

Looking back on my novitiate period in the Commons, I have come to believe that it was probably the most pressurised time of my life. Not only was I undertaking major pieces of Opposition business, with all the intricately detailed work that was required to become familiar with the issues facing the transport industry itself, but I was still chairman and chief executive of the Haymarket Group, which during this time had doubled in size. And I had my family. My third child and my only son, Rupert, had been born in 1967. I had been present at the birth of my first child, Annabel, was campaigning in Tavistock when my second, Alexandra, was born, but had confidently expected to be present again this time. I sat patiently awaiting the call from St George's Hospital, working on papers in our dining room in Chepstow Villas. But Rupert arrived in a hurry. I rushed to the hospital to share Anne's joy, but only after the event. So, with a wife and three growing children, I was now working round the clock, seven days a week. It was becoming increasingly apparent that change was necessary. In 1969 Lindsay Masters became managing director of the Haymarket Group, while I retained the post of chairman.

Margaret remained as Transport spokesman until the autumn of 1969, when she was promoted by Ted Heath to take over the Education Shadow portfolio from Sir Edward Boyle, who was planning to leave politics to become vice-chancellor of Leeds University. Anne and I had decided that autumn to travel round the world: India, Singapore, Thailand, Hong Kong, Japan, across Australia from Perth to Sydney, Hawaii and then home across America via Los Angeles, San Francisco, Washington, New York and Boston. It was a journey of indelible impressions and unforgettable memories across a world that was to shrink and change beyond imagination in the next thirty years. Rather to my surprise, as we headed home, I received an invitation from Ted asking if I would take Margaret's place – though not inviting me to join the Shadow Cabinet. My appointment as a fully fledged frontbench spokesman, rather than an occasional visitor from the back benches, was announced on 30 October 1969. The outstanding piece of Labour government legislation at the time – apart from Dick Crossman's long-promised National Superannuation Bill – was the proposal to nationalise all the major harbour authorities in Britain. The intention, or so Ted told me, was that I should lead the attack upon it. Obligingly, the Labour government had published a White Paper setting out its proposals at the beginning of 1969, so we knew what we were up against. The strategic purpose, the White Paper carefully explained, was that the ten largest ports in Britain – all those handling over five million tons a year – should be transferred to the control of a new National Ports Authority, which would thereby become responsible for 95 per cent of the dock labour force at work in the country.

The Ports Bill, announced in the Queen's Speech of 28 October 1969, proved predictably partisan and doctrinaire. Anyone looking at the ports industry today in this country can readily appreciate that what Labour had in mind was the exact opposite of what was needed in that industry. All our main ports, except for the 'free port' of Felixstowe, were playgrounds of monopolistic unions ruthlessly exploiting their dominant position against the public interest. Over-manning was rife, the quality of management in the private sector indifferent, and especially alarming was the overall loss of traffic to the Continent, where the giant port of Rotterdam was siphoning off our traditional trade. The British shipping industry, once one of the world's leaders, was haemorrhaging.

Rather to my regret, I no longer found myself facing Barbara Castle. She had meanwhile in the reshuffle of the spring of 1968 scaled the heights to become First Secretary of State (not that that did her much good when it came to getting her 1969 trade union reform proposals, outlined in her famous White Paper *In Place of Strife*, past her Cabinet colleagues, let alone the Parliamentary Labour Party). At Transport she had been replaced by Dick Marsh, but he had been sacked at the beginning of October 1969 to make way for Fred Mulley (the Transport Ministry no longer now being in the Cabinet and being required to operate under the general guidance of the new 'Environment' supremo, Tony Crosland). Mulley – later, as Minister of Defence, to be immortalised in a newspaper photograph at an air display fast asleep next to the Queen – was a thoroughly decent, scholarly man who had actually obtained a first in law from a German prisoner-of-war camp. But, unlike Barbara Castle or even Dick Marsh, he was not well versed in parliamentary ring-craft.

I had learnt my trade well under Peter Walker. A general election was not likely to be far off. If I could delay the proceedings sufficiently, there was a chance of Labour and the government not achieving their legislation in that Parliament. They certainly could have done so, if they had taken a grip on the situation from the beginning. But that was not Fred Mulley's style, and his conciliatory approach was my opportunity. We were always prepared to agree a reasonable amount of progress in any one session during the committee stage of the Bill. On our side we never made the mistake of putting down huge numbers of amendments, which simply warns the government that there is a delaying, wrecking exercise in operation. Instead, just a few more amendments would go down every two or three days: just enough to ensure that, although we made progress, we never made enough progress. Fred constantly asked me about an end date to the committee's proceedings. Though I was reassuring about our intention to move forward, I was never quite able to agree the end date.

Fred was advised by Ken Barnett, a deputy secretary in the Ministry of Transport, who could see exactly what I was doing and became increasingly frustrated at the reluctance of his Minister to grasp the danger. There was one wonderful moment when I was negotiating with Fred. Ken became so exasperated with his Minister's performance that he actually intervened in the negotiations to try and achieve the decisions that he knew were vital if the Bill was to be saved.

But Harold Wilson on 18 May called a general election for 18 June, and the Ports Bill, by then just starting its progress through the House of Lords, was nowhere near the statute book. In the general tidying-up process that precedes any election the Opposition holds the cards. Progress is possible only by consent. The Ports Bill – along with the National Superannuation pensions measure – had to be dropped. The strategy had worked. We had won. Since it was the first major piece of government legislation I had been given the prime responsibility for opposing, its failure to get on the statute book was a cause of some satisfaction.

On the whole, exhausting and taxing though it was, I enjoyed my initial years in opposition (I was to experience only one other period of it – 1974–9 – all the way through until 1997). But I already knew that it offered no real substitute for being in government. It was Iain Macleod who once said: 'Being a minister is the only thing worth doing in the whole world.' I am not sure I would go as far as that, but, as the election was called, my hopes were certainly pinned on a Tory victory and getting my feet on a rung of the ministerial ladder.

Chapter 9

FIRST TASTE OF OFFICE

F ollowing Ted Heath's victory in the 1970 election I had hoped to become a minister of state in the government. I had, after all, enjoyed the status of frontbench spokesman on Transport in opposition, and was thus marginally disappointed to find myself made only a parliamentary under-secretary. I was appointed number two to John Peyton, who had been summoned from the back benches to be Minister of Transport.

John Peyton, the MP for Yeovil, who had been very effective in opposition, was at heart a Whig and not a Tory at all. An Old Etonian with a career reaching back to imperial India, he was very much an MP of the old school. He had already served as Parliamentary Under-Secretary at the Ministry of Power under both Macmillan and Sir Alec Douglas-Home between 1962 and 1964. It was rumoured at the time the Heath government was formed that Ted had been minded to make me Minister of Transport but that his deputy leader, Willie Whitelaw, had intervened to secure the job for John – they were, in fact, two birds of the same feather. (But even Willie's pleas could not save John from being passed over by Margaret Thatcher, though he had been on her Opposition front bench, when she came to form her first government in 1979.)

Under the Peyton ministerial regime all meetings of significance would invariably take place under his chairmanship; the junior minister would at least sometimes be invited to attend. However, I had passed the stage in life where I saw my role as sitting in on other people's meetings. I was to find the frustration irksome and this was, of course, exacerbated by the fact that I had been in charge of this area of policy in opposition. But, in politics, you do not get anywhere by sulking. As cheerfully as I could, I thus resigned the chairmanship of Haymarket Publishing, and moved into the Parliamentary Under-Secretary's office in St Christopher House in Southwark.

I remember my first day very clearly. As I walked into my new office, I was entranced by the spectacular view – from the south of the river – of St Paul's Cathedral. I was struck particularly by the coincidence that hanging at home was a watercolour of the same view, painted by my great-great-grandfather, the Victorian artist T. C. Dibdin. I had been given an immense room. I sat down behind an enormous desk, with two empty filing trays and a newspaper which my thoughtful private secretary brought in for me to read. I rang Anne and asked her what she thought I should do. Coffee followed. Peace and quiet reigned. But only briefly.

A file arrived on my desk, inviting me to authorise an investment of £6 million in the electrification of a railway line through the eastern counties. I asked the private secretary to fix a meeting with the managers responsible. Obviously taken aback, he protested with all due courtesy that, if I intended to have meetings every time they asked me to spend £6 million, they would never get any decisions out of me. I had arrived in the public sector. At Haymarket I had been used to authorising personally every petty cash voucher over ten shillings – initially there hadn't been that many ten shillings around. Now I was expected to read the papers and then take a decision to spend £6 million, just like that. I was told I was not there to second-guess the management. Nevertheless, I insisted on the meeting, though I *did* approve the £6 million. A word of advice, not wholly flippant, to any new junior ministers: whatever you do on your first day, do something – preferably something against the advice offered to you. Make yourself a nuisance. The message will soon get round that you're not there to be taken for granted. But remember, too, that the civil servants are usually right. Choose your decision with care. You are on your own. The instructions you give and your reasons for them – or the lack of them – will have been carefully recorded for any subsequent inquiry when things go wrong.

It was shortly after my arrival at the Ministry that I first met Sir Arnold Weinstock. I was responsible for the roads programme. We were installing at the time the now familiar electronic signals which warn of such things as accidents ahead, fog or reductions in speed limits. GEC, of which Arnold was managing director, had won the contract to install this system. It was late, and it wasn't working.

During one of many interminable discussions with officials about what to do about this, I asked who was in charge at GEC. I was given a name – let us call him Blenkinsop. I was clear that Blenkinsop was not in charge; at GEC it was always Weinstock who was in charge. But my civil servants were equally clear that they didn't deal with Weinstock; they had a well-defined relationship with GEC and the man in charge was Blenkinsop. I began to suspect that that was the problem, but for the time being I gave way and instructed them to tell Blenkinsop that the Minister was not satisfied and wanted results. Weeks passed. Yet more meetings took place. Still the system did not work. Eventually I told Sir William Harris, the director general of highways within the Department, to get me Arnold Weinstock on the telephone. This time I meant it. I was put through. I introduced myself as the Parliamentary Under-Secretary, and said, 'Your system doesn't work.' To which Arnold replied, in a way that endeared him to me immediately: 'When can I come to see you?' I was somewhat taken aback. I had not known what to expect but it certainly wasn't this. Ministers don't keep their diaries open on their desks. They have a diary secretary in their outer office who sorts these things out. Regrouping as fast as I could, I suggested 2.30 that afternoon. 'I will be there,' said Arnold.

At 2.30, lined along one side of an enormous conference table, with myself at the head, were all the senior officials in the Department associated with the roads programme. At 2.30 to the minute we heard the approaching tread of many feet and into the room came Arnold, accompanied by an equivalent number of his own staff. He lined them up on the opposite side of the table, and sat down next to me. At the very bottom of the table, the furthest from him, was Blenkinsop. I repeated that their system wasn't working and asked what they were going to do about it. Whereupon, for what seemed an age, Arnold leant forward and cross-examined Blenkinsop in a way that would have done credit to the finest courtroom lawyer. I have seldom seen a man so taken apart in public.

At the end of this fascinating and illuminating example of management in the private sector, Arnold turned to me, told me what he intended to do and said he would ring me at 9.30 the next morning to tell me of progress. In the end I began to weary of his telephone calls. They came regularly, every morning at 9.30, as he reported more and more progress. I once said to him that I was grateful for the trouble he was taking and he used the hackneyed, though still always effective, reply: 'But you are the customer.' We have been firm friends ever since, a friendship which was to stand me in good stead at the time of the Westland crisis some sixteen years later.

Routinely, while at the Ministry of Transport or later at the Department of the Environment, I opened roads. First it was the Westway through Paddington, when John Peyton was unavoidably detained elsewhere. Then there was the M5 in the company of Anne and Alexandra (white fur muff and hat for the occasion, of which she was inordinately proud), when I tried to cut the tape with the inward curve of the dirk presented to me by the proud Scottish contractor. The tape remained intact – to the huge enjoyment of press and spectators. The opening of the M4 extension, this time with Annabel, not Alexandra, in attendance, had a particular significance for me in that it replaced the familiar but interminable route to South Wales with the latest in motorway design. It took only two hours, fifty-nine minutes to ferry gifts for the children of Wales from the Lord Mayor of London to the Lord Mayor of Cardiff – and all within the speed limit. 'WHOOSH' proclaimed the *Evening Standard*. Unhappily, it was not long before a different story appeared, when I was caught speeding at over 100 miles per hour on the same road.

My tenure at the then free-standing Ministry of Transport didn't last long. In October of 1970 a White Paper was published on the reorganisation of the machinery of central government and Ted Heath created the two new super-Ministries: the Department of Trade and Industry and the Department of the Environment. The former combined the Board of Trade, the Department of Industry and the Ministry of Fuel and Power; the latter merged the Ministries of Transport and Public Buildings and Works with the Ministry of Housing and Local Government, and Peter Walker was made its Secretary of State. Under him there were to be three ministers of state: Julian Amery, as Minister for Housing and Construction, Graham Page, as Minister for Local Government and Development, and John Peyton, Minister for Transport Industries – none of whom was in the Cabinet. Beneath these three were the three lowly parliamentary under-secretaries: Eldon Griffiths, Paul Channon and myself.

I had already discussed with Peter my frustrations with John's method of running his part of the Department and proposed that I might find it easier in the circumstances to serve as a junior minister to

Graham Page. Peter was considerate enough to act on my suggestion. Things immediately began to look up. Graham was everyone's idea of a country solicitor, courteous and kindly, infinitely painstaking, portly. He sat behind a desk piled with files through which he would wade laboriously. Nothing was too much trouble but, of course, the detail became the message. It was an ideal situation for me. He delegated significant parts of his responsibility and left me to get on with it. If I wanted advice, he was always approachable and totally supportive of what I set out to do.

He was also a man with a sense of humour. When later on, in the spring of 1973, the government was rocked over a sex scandal by the resignations of Viscount Lambton and Earl Jellicoe, there were rumours that a third minister was involved. Graham Page, it could be said without fear of contradiction, would have been the least likely of any ministerial colleague to be suspected. But it so happened, at the height of the crisis, that he was addressing a large audience of Conservatives in the North of England. He began his speech slowly: 'I am the third Minister.' When the shock had permeated through the audience, he added with the merest trace of a smile, 'to address this conference today.'

Peter Walker was a hands-on politician, but he understood the essential role of delegation. His three ministers of state were from an earlier political tradition and I suspect that two of them, Julian Amery and John Peyton, were resentful of their subordination to Peter as a young rising star in the Tory firmament. I doubt, too, if either wholly approved of Peter's management style. Each working day we met for 'Prayers' at 8.45 a.m. with Peter in the chair and only the seven ministers present. It was not compulsory to attend if you had an appointment out of town, but the meeting became an agenda-setting occasion at which Peter would report upon events and explain what he wanted. We could raise questions, discuss the wider issues affecting the government and generally act as colleagues in charge of a substantial organisation. At the end of each meeting we knew very clearly what was expected of us.

No civil servant was present. No records were ever kept. Although the timing and structure of this management arrangement varies significantly from department to department – at the discretion of the individual Cabinet minister – the morning meeting and delegation to junior ministers is now standard practice. Peter was ahead of the game. He used this process to enhance the role of the junior ministers.

We had each been allocated our own spheres of responsibility and we were effectively working directly to Peter himself.

One of Peter's first priorities was the reorganisation of local government. I had had some experience of the complexities of the issues involved when opposing Barbara Castle's proposals to establish Passenger Transport Authorities, taking power from the individual local authorities in the great metropolitan areas and transferring it to conurbation-wide bodies. I had also come to know a number of Conservative councillors as I travelled the length and breadth of the land on party business. The previous Labour government had commissioned John Redcliffe-Maud to examine the structure of local government in England, which had remained largely unchanged since the nineteenth century. At the time it consisted of some 1,200 different councils organised in a two-tier structure. Each of the forty-five shire counties contained urban and rural district councils. No fewer than seventy-nine larger, free-standing towns enjoyed unitary status as county boroughs and they were fiercely jealous of their independence. Their boundaries tended to be tightly drawn, although of course their influence on the surrounding hinterland was substantial. Many of their more prosperous citizens lived well outside the town or city from which they drew their wealth. In addition London had its own system of boroughs under a London-wide authority, the Greater London Council.

The Redcliffe-Maud Report, published in 1969, advocated the abolition of the county, rural and urban authorities in England and recommended that most of the country should come under a new, single-tier system of unitary authorities. In the largest conurbations, however, it was proposed that there should be a second layer of local government to provide a strategic overview for these burgeoning metropolitan areas. The Conservatives in opposition had been clear that the Redcliffe-Maud proposals were unattractive. They struck at the heart of the self-interest of a myriad of communities, councillors and traditions. Charters granted by King John were threatened. Civic chains and regalia centuries old were to be relegated to the dustbin. The pomp and circumstance of England were at stake – or so it was suggested.

But the party had not been able to work out the detail of any alternative policy. This challenge fell to Peter, and he had been devoting himself to it since the election. By the time I arrived on the scene, his plans were effectively in place; I had played no part in designing the overall strategy. I had much sympathy with the broad thrust of the Redcliffe-Maud Report and am today in favour of unitary authorities. But, even if Peter himself had been so persuaded, such an option did not exist for the Tory government of that time. As was to be demonstrated again over twenty years later, the Conservative Party defended the status quo wherever its councillors were to be found in numbers, and in large parts of England that meant the two-tier, shire county model. Back in the early 1970s Peter had limited choices. He could have left the status quo virtually untouched, maybe amalgamating a few of the smaller authorities at the lower level. But the disadvantage of that was that it would only be a matter of time before the return of another Labour government would lead to an enactment of Redcliffe-Maud unitary plans. So he needed to find an alternative, and that alternative had to be acceptable to the party. The abolition of either tier – the county on the one hand or the urban and rural authorities on the other – and their replacement with a network of single-tier authorities was, in party political terms, a non-starter.

Accordingly, Peter had no realistic choice but a two-tier system. Even then we faced deeply controversial decisions. The free-standing county boroughs were to be incorporated into the two-tier matrix and, final insult, as junior partners to the newly enlarged counties which had previously been their ever present and bitter rivals. Blackpool, Plymouth, Southend and many other independent towns would find themselves subsumed into the likes of Lancashire, Devon and Essex. Hundreds of small rural or town authorities, many of them of great antiquity and local significance, would be reduced to mere shadows of their former glory. This is the stuff of which unholy political rows are made. In order to complete the pattern, Peter also intended to impose a new tier of metropolitan authorities, binding together the numerous county boroughs that made up the great urban sprawl of Liverpool, Manchester, Birmingham, Newcastle, Bristol/Avon, Leeds, Sheffield, South Yorkshire and Humberside. To cap it all, as if this had not already stirred up enough horrors, several historic counties were to be abolished altogether – Rutland, Westmorland and the Yorkshire Ridings – and Herefordshire merged with Worcestershire. The official slide-rules had decreed that local government viability demanded a certain scale. History and tradition were to be snuffed out, leaving a smoke trail of resentment smouldering across the land.

Peter divided the political battlefield between Graham and myself. Was it my imagination that I seemed to have responsibility for those areas where the battle would be the fiercest? I toured the country, facing angry groups of Conservative councillors totally unconvinced of the need for change, implacably opposed to the nature of the reforms proposed and utterly disenchanted with the government they had helped to elect. My experience became a cautionary tale of what can happen to a minister expected to carry through unpopular policies which threaten the self-interest of members of his own party. I was in it up to my neck – jeered out of halls in Blackpool, laughed to scorn in Brighton, as I fought to convince our councillors of the party line. The case for the structural reforms was argued – however unconvincingly to many audiences – on the grounds of efficiency and the need for scale in the face of the unimagined changes that the twentieth century had brought.

The legislation secured, the next battle was even more detailed, local and passionate – not just among councillors but also among rate-payers, all too aware of the consequences of falling on the wrong side of the boundary line between high-spending (urban, Labour) auth-orities and their more considerate and low-spending (suburban/rural, Conservative) neighbours. Peter asked me to conduct a public con-sultation exercise, as provided for in the legislation, in Birmingham, Manchester and Liverpool to determine where the frontiers of the new conurbation authorities should be drawn. I held an open forum in which each local authority was given an opportunity to state publicly its views and preferences in each other's presence. There was only one basic argument. The larger authorities in the centres wanted to extend their boundaries. The smaller authorities outside were determined to preserve their independence. There were many variations on these themes, sometimes cunningly wrapped up. But every speech was a form of municipal nimbyism. People living on the fringes of the great conurbations were particularly angry and bitter at the possible inclusion of their attractive dormitory suburbs in the cities.

Where should the boundaries of, say, Greater Manchester now be drawn, as opposed to where historic local authority lines contained it? I listened to all the interminable arguments. Decisions had to be made. My job was to make them. I chartered a light aircraft and flew around with a map of the area on my knees, to see for myself whether villages were really free-standing rural idylls, as I had been told, or were simply an extension of the urban sprawl into Cheshire, Lancashire or Staffordshire. As I flew over one area after another, I marked the map to indicate the 'ins' and the 'outs'. In this way were the boundaries of the great conurbations redrawn. It would be foolish to pretend that people were satisfied with my judgement and in some cases, particularly Wilmslow in Cheshire on the fringes of Manchester, vehement local opposition developed. The fact is, though, that any objective observation of Manchester today would indicate that Wilmslow has become its prosperous suburb.

Perhaps I had a hidden agenda, the full significance of which was to re-emerge all too clearly a decade later. I had already realised that the people living on the fringes of these cities were, as often as not, the most prosperous and powerful citizens of those communities. Their understandable argument was that they didn't want to pay the higher rates (the old rating system being then still in place) associated with the Labour majorities in the cities. That was a very obvious human reaction. But, if people who are already, by the nature of their business, integral parts of a city simply turn their backs on their fellow citizens as they leave their workplace each evening, it soon becomes a debilitating process. Certainly, it's an attitude in sharp contrast to the motivations of the founding generations – the Victorian city fathers who had presided over those cities and bestowed great wealth upon them. They had been a driving force in their governance and their dynamism.

Admittedly, there may have been a political motive at work, too. Obviously, it helped if, by extending the frontiers, you brought more Conservative voters back into the conurbations. A similar, if reverse, argument appealed to Labour Party councillors, ever anxious to push the municipal boundaries out into the green fields on which to build more council estates – hopefully providing homes for conscientious Labour voters. But in my mind at least these were always subsidiary considerations. I was convinced that local communities needed a social and economic mix and a choice of political leadership. I was, in effect, balancing the political books. I believed this at the time in the early 1970s, but the need for such a philosophy was to become even more abundantly clear when I arrived in Liverpool after the Toxteth riots in the summer of 1981, although the weapons available to me then were financial rather than political.

So I held my nerve and, where I believed that the adjoining village suburbs were part of the conurbation, I put them in. In virtually every case my view prevailed, although after my promotion to be Minister for Aerospace in 1972 the pressure from Wilmslow was such that

Graham Page reversed my decision and took it out. Given that the job had to be done, I still maintain that it was done as effectively as it could have been. Changing such municipal boundaries today would doubtless require the setting of up public inquiries, dragging out the same process endlessly and at great cost. I doubt if the end-result would be much different. But what is indisputable is that, if Graham Page and I had carried out an exercise similar to mine but in the 1990s, we would have been judicially reviewed in every court in the land.

I had lived in London for fifteen years when for the first time I found myself close to the centre of its planning regime. I was already appalled at what was happening – or not happening – on the South Bank of the Thames. This has to be one of the great urban waterscapes of the world. Nobody looking at the developments there could feel anything other than a sense of dismay that we had failed, in one of the world's finest capital cities, to grasp an extraordinary opportunity. Neither the architecture nor the environment lived up to the opportunity that recent history had provided. I became convinced that leaving this matter to a combination of local authorities and slide-rule-driven property developers would never achieve anything other than the lowest common denominator of ghastly modern buildings. I asked one of my senior officials, Ron Brain, who was in charge of housing, to prepare plans for a development corporation to take over responsibility for the reconstruction of the South Bank. He had considerable enthusiasm for the project, but I was moved to the Department of Trade and Industry before I had the chance to submit a proposal to my ministerial colleagues for approval. (On my return to the Department of the Environment in 1979 I called for the papers and the revitalisation and regeneration of East London was put in hand.)

I was bathing our dachshund, Rudi, at our constituency home at Pamflete on the South Devon coast on 7 April 1972 when the telephone rang. I was told that the Prime Minister wished to talk to me. Would I like to be Minister for Aerospace? There was obviously no answer but yes. It was promotion. I would be a minister of state, at the Department of Trade and Industry – though, as virtually my own master, I would be a good deal more independent than many serving in that rank.

The DTI team was headed by John Davies, the former director general of the CBI, who had been promoted as boss of that super-Ministry only a month after being elected to Parliament in 1970 (as one of the indirect consequences of Chancellor Iain Macleod's sudden death that July). Very few examples exist of people who have made a successful leap from outside life directly into the forefront of politics. In my first Parliament I had for a month or two seen Frank Cousins, leader of the Transport and General Workers Union, floundering on the Treasury bench before his resignation over the Wilson government's incomes policy. Like him, John Davies had enjoyed an impressive pre-parliamentary career (before joining the CBI he had come close to the top of the retail side of Shell and BP). But he lacked the political antennae and the cutting edge which come from years of battling through debates in the House of Commons. Essentially a man of committees and quiet, reasoned argument, he failed to inspire or provoke the deep emotions that are inseparable from the front line of politics.

My new job in practice turned out to be Minister for Aerospace *and* Shipping, although the shipping responsibilities were not transferred to me until August. Three months after that, to my great delight, my original mentor Peter Walker moved over from Environment to take charge at the DTI. On a much smaller scale, I had already replicated Peter's management style in my own part of the Department, although with significant adjustments. Cranley Onslow, later to be an old-style and effective Chairman of the 1922 Committee until his defeat by the populist Marcus Fox in 1992, was my Parliamentary Under-Secretary. Cecil Parkinson, elected for Iain Macleod's old seat of Enfield West, became my Parliamentary Private Secretary (PPS). The three of us would meet daily with James Hamilton, the deputy secretary responsible for my part of the Department, the press officer allocated to me, and my private secretary – first Robert Priddle and then, from January 1973, Tony Lane. I had brought civil servants into the morning meeting to help in the process of driving the agenda forward. Of course, party political discussion was denied us in such a forum, but the arrangements worked well enough.

My new agenda was formidable, concentrated largely but not exclusively on the aerospace side of the Department. Before my appointment Rolls-Royce had collapsed and been rescued by the Conservative government, thus bringing to me the policy responsibility for the aero-engine side of its business. Concorde was approaching a critical review point. I was in charge of space policy, the search for a site for London's third airport, the merger of British Overseas Airways Corporation and British European Airways into a single airline and

British Caledonian's battle to survive as a recently created, independent carrier. Hawker Siddeley wanted taxpayers' support to launch a medium-size airliner, the HS146, and Shorts had ambitions to develop their workhorse, the Skyvan, with a new project, the SD3-30

My shipping responsibilities were of a very different order from those of aerospace. The latter centred on a relationship between the public and the private sector that was interventionist to its fingertips. Governments owned, regulated, supported, procured and helped to sell most of the industry's activities and its products. The competition for orders was worldwide. National industrial champions slugged it out in partnership with their governments, against similar overseas groupings. By contrast, the shipping industry was deeply fragmented. The owners were largely private sector, sailing the high seas in search of markets and tax havens, indifferent to the fortunes of any shipyard, unless it was enabled by dint of large subsidies to buy at the lowest price. Certainly, the industry was regulated and the conferences of the worldwide marine organisations were useful, particularly in environmental enhancement, but they were inevitably slow moving.

My third responsibility covered much of the government's research and development activities, including several of the more important government laboratories. Under this umbrella responsibility came a number of individual projects that were briefly to dominate the headlines. One such was the tracked hovercraft, or hovertrain, in Cambridge.

The hovertrain project was run by Tracked Hovercraft, established in 1967 as a wholly owned subsidiary of the government-sponsored National Research and Development Corporation. It was entirely dependent on public funds. The concept was for a commercial high-speed ground transport system: a train powered by a linear induction motor, running without wheels on a cushion of air along specially designed track and projected to reach speeds of 250–300 m.p.h. Its proponents perceived it as a project on the frontiers of modern technology, of dramatic potential and in competition with other rapid-transit systems then being experimented with on the Continent and with British Railways' Advanced Passenger Train being developed at Derby.

I asked the obvious questions. Did the technology have a chance of working? Was there any realistic possibility of somebody – almost certainly the taxpayer – being ready to build the track to carry such a system up and down the country in competition with the existing railways? And, if nobody was prepared to build the track, was there any prospect that the United Kingdom would be able to sell such a design overseas in competition with countries such as France, Germany and Japan which would be able to demonstrate similar rapid-transit systems of their own already in operation? I derived no encouragement from the answers I received to any of these questions.

I was therefore a sceptic, but considerable sums had already been invested and it was my responsibility to explore every opportunity which might give the project a reasonable chance. My officials canvassed the private sector, including Arnold Weinstock at GEC. No commercial partner emerged prepared to invest any of its own money in the project, a firm indication – if I needed one – that my scepticism was justified. I came under increasing pressure to make a decision one way or the other. I could see no market. I had no continuing funds. I could find no partners. It seemed to me that I was faced with the uncomfortable fact that I had no alternative but to close the project down.

I wrote to colleagues to that effect and on Thursday, 8 February 1973, No. 10 minuted back that the Prime Minister had accepted my advice. But nothing in life is ever simple – certainly not in politics. A Parliamentary Question (PQ) had been put down by the Labour MP for the railway town of Swindon, David Stoddart, asking whether the government would make more money available for the project, which I was due to answer on Monday, the 12th. In the meantime, the Commons Select Committee on Science and Technology, under the chairmanship of Airey Neave, had announced at the beginning of that month that it was about to investigate the project. That was a wholly proper thing for it to do, but I was left with an appalling quandary. I was summoned as a principal witness and was due to appear before it on the 14th. My dilemma was to know how to answer the inevitable questions I was going to be asked. To have announced the closure only days before I was due to appear before the Select Committee would inevitably have appeared rather cavalier and an affront to its dignity and responsibilities. On the other hand, you cannot in government simply put the files to one side and hope the problem will go away. I decided to give a holding answer to the PQ (which read: 'The question of the government's providing financial assistance for the continuation of this project is still under consideration. I shall make a statement shortly') and take Airey Neave into my confidence, explaining to him the reality of the position. I told him that the decision had been taken to shut down the project, that I didn't want to embarrass his Committee and that I could delay the announcement but only for a few days. I agreed with him what I would say in evidence so that the Committee would be the first to know. I duly appeared before the Committee on 14 February and told them the project was to close. I also – indeed, that same afternoon – gave a Written Answer in the Commons announcing the decision.

The ensuing furore centred on the holding answer I had given two days earlier. It was alleged that this answer had been misleading, as I had already taken the decision. In practice, of course, it is customary for government decisions – even on crucial matters like devaluation – to be made some time before they can be announced. It is equally the custom for the announcement date to be treated as the decision date, as that is the moment when the government is accountable and committed.

But not on this occasion. When the Report of the Select Committee was finally published on 6 September 1973, during the summer recess, it accused me of 'misleading' the House and declared that my answer to David Stoddart of 12 February had been 'untrue'. The *Evening Standard* that night carried the allegation emblazoned across its front page: 'Untruth! MPs Accuse Minister'. I was speechless with fury at the way I had been treated by the Committee, more than half of whose members were Conservatives. The particular source of my anger was the section of the Report which expressly criticised me for not having informed the Committee or its chairman privately of the main thrust of the 29 January decision before I gave evidence to them on 14 February. This, of course, is precisely what I had done. I can only conclude that Airey Neave had failed to inform his colleagues or steer them away from this unwarranted conclusion. Cecil Parkinson, my PPS, raised the matter with a couple of colleagues on the Committee, who admitted to not having even read the Report that appeared under their name. Cecil has been quoted as saying that various members of the Committee told him: 'We're not after Michael. He's just the junior minister.'

In the meantime, the press had descended on Soundess House, the property we had recently purchased in my new constituency of Henley-on-Thames, notebooks at the ready. They found the children and some of their friends having lunch in the garden. A new family of guineapigs and some baby rabbits were produced. When Anne emerged from the house, she found the reporters sitting there, looking slightly foolish, each with a small furry animal in his lap. All hostility had melted away and the result was a rather endearing series of photographs in the next day's press.

Francis Pym, the government Chief Whip, still felt, however, that – given the Select Committee's strictures – only an apology to the House would meet the case. So, on the first day the Commons returned from the summer recess, I duly apologised for any 'misunderstanding' my reply to the PQ might have caused. I did so with mixed feelings: the decision itself had been right and, if I had delayed the announcing of it for a couple of days, it was only because of my reluctance to offend the Select Committee or embarrass a senior colleague. I should have realised that Airey Neave, subsequently to be Margaret Thatcher's campaign manager, would show no such scruples when it came to embarrassing the government of Ted Heath.

Yet, if the hovercraft affair infuriated me, it was as nothing compared with the permanent headache imposed by the complexities of that other high-profile project, perceived at the time to be at the frontiers of technology: Concorde. I had barely become Aerospace Minister before I was told that I was to take the British prototype of the Anglo-French supersonic airliner project, Concorde 002, overseas for the first time to the Hanover Air Show. Anne and I arrived at Fairford airfield at dawn one day in May 1972 – just two or three weeks after my appointment to the job.

Prototype aircraft have none of the sophisticated polish of the final commercial product. Concorde 002 was a test tube: batteries of computers, wires protruding in every direction, lights flashing, alarms regularly directing vigilant engineers to this or that check in the system and, tucked away at the back, a handful of rather out-of-place airline seats genuflecting to the creature comforts one takes for granted in modern airline travel. Into two of these Anne and I strapped ourselves, doing our best not to reveal to the professional eyes of the British Aircraft Company employees the anxiety we felt. The rattling of metalwork as we rumbled at ever gathering speed down the runway was far from reassuring. The angle of take-off had more to do with a fighter aircraft than a modern civil aeroplane. We were on our way to Hanover. The flight was, of course, subsonic and uneventful. I had come face to face, however, with the project that was to be at the heart of my ministerial life for the next two years.

My other chief memory of the Hanover Air Show in 1972 was that it resulted in my first encounter with the Hawker Harrier Jump Jet. I had had no idea that an aircraft of such versatility existed. It was the thrill of the international air-show circuit, able to take off and land vertically, fly backwards as well as forwards and climb virtually straight up into the air by rotating its engines to suit whatever was required. It was a phenomenon and an enormous achievement of British technological excellence. It was also a show-stopper for the general public, reaching perhaps the zenith of its public relations achievement when a pair of them completed their routine at the Japanese air show some years later and turned to face the Japanese crowd of a quarter of a million people. I would love to have seen it, as the Harriers dipped their noses in a bow to their Japanese audience and a quarter of a million Japanese bowed back.

Concorde had reached a new and critical stage in its life just at the time I became the responsible Minister. The dilemma that confronted me – far more acutely than it had any of my predecessors – was how to reconcile my responsibility to Parliament to present as accurately as I could the latest assessment of the project's costs and prospects with what, in effect, had become a ministerial selling role. They were two very different tasks and often in collision one with the other. The conflict was exacerbated in this instance by the very different perceptions of its future prospects prevailing among the British Aircraft Company team, led by the chairman of their commercial aircraft division, Geoffrey Knight, and the staff of civil servants advising me, headed by the under-secretary at the DTI, Philip Jones. The contrast between these two men could not have been more marked. The former was a tall, debonair, ever enthusiastic salesman who could, in his less serious moments, have played an admirable Bertie Wooster. He was dedicated to the project, believed in it passionately and was never anything but optimistic about the prospects of selling it. His earliest, bullish forecasts were based upon a prospect list across the world of seventy-four options held by sixteen international airlines. Philip Jones, by contrast, was a professional civil servant of the highest order: clever, hard-working and cautious, trained to check and double-check before producing a judgement. He was from the beginning deeply concerned at the lack of control over the costs of the Concorde project and sceptical about the forecast level of sales. I was left in no doubt about his views.

I had no difficulty in reporting appropriately to my colleagues and Parliament on the actual costs of the project. The contracts between the two governments of Britain and France, and between the British Aircraft Company and Sud Aviation, the French-led company, had long since been signed. The process was rolling forward. It was a cost-plus contract with no performance benchmarks or timetable. But the conflict which I faced was between giving official and prudent advice to Parliament and the need to maintain a degree of confidence in the project and its sales team.

I made a clear judgement that, so long as the project was a flagship with the backing of the British government, my task was to give it every support. To have done otherwise would have undermined its prospects and simply provided ammunition for its many critics – including, of course, its subsonic transatlantic competitors. It was not credible for an aerospace minister to separate himself from the sales campaign. Like it or not, I was part of it. Indeed, I can claim to have been the only British Minister who, for a moment at least, appeared to have secured an overseas order on a commercial basis.

In May 1972 BOAC converted five of its eight options for Concorde into firm orders. Air France was expected to follow suit shortly. It was now decided that there should be a major international sales boost and in early June Concorde 002 set out for Australia. By this time the plane had been kitted out at least in part to give an idea of its civil airline fit. Once again, Anne and I left from Fairford. Our first stop was Athens. The stopover there was routine, although the fact that we had to be off the Tarmac before a specified hour, because Concorde was not able to take off when the temperature had reached certain levels, indicated just how marginal was the technology of the time. It had been agreed that I would take the plane as far as Singapore by way of Tehran. After that I would return to resume normal ministerial duties and the Lord Privy Seal, George Jellicoe, would take over for the final leg to Manila, Tokyo and then Australia.

The two big opportunities of my trip were thought to be Tehran and Singapore. The Shah of Iran was seen as a high-prospect purchaser. It was understood that he had a vision of Tehran as a staging post between West and East. He saw Concorde as an important part of the process, if Tehran was seen as a major stopover on its journey both ways. Our strategy was to fly him in the aircraft and hopefully get him to confirm his options to buy. We also needed his agreement to overflying rights. Much of Iran is open desert where the footprint of the sound barrier would have little or no impact. Indeed, it was hoped that the Shah might not be too concerned even if it did.

I was to meet the Shah in the Imperial Pavilion at Tehran airport for a brief introduction to the project, aided by various demonstrator boards, before he joined me for a flight. One of the demonstrator boards set up to be shown to the Shah consisted of a huge map of the world on which capital cities, principal airports and major flying routes were indicated in large, unmissable topography. About ten minutes before the Shah was due someone helpfully pointed out that there was no reference to Tehran on the map. The offending demonstrator board was removed from sight. Crisis averted. The Shah duly arrived. After a quick briefing we set off along the red carpet across the Tarmac to the aircraft itself. During the flight it would be up to me to secure our sales and overflying objectives. I had been carefully prepared for my task.

The take-off was uneventful and we sped heavenwards to the 58,000 feet at which the aircraft is most efficient. However, I had no sooner concluded the initial pleasantries than the Shah, an experienced pilot himself, asked if he could join the test pilot, Brian Trubshaw, in the cockpit. In a second he was gone. I was in despair. There was no other time during our stopover when I could conduct a sales pitch or secure agreements before we were due to leave Tehran for our onward journey to Singapore. But the Shah did not return until we came in to land.

Down the steps we went, heading for the Imperial Pavilion. There were about 200 yards of red carpet between us and the waiting press corps. There was no time left for niceties. I had 200 yards in which to obtain – or not – the objective clearly set for me. I decided to go for it. 'Your Majesty, I hope you enjoyed the flight. I would like to ask you if you would consider purchasing the aircraft?' 'Yes,' he replied. 'I would like two.' So far, so good. 'Your Majesty, we would be grateful for overflying rights across Iran on our journeys to and from the Far East.' 'That would be quite acceptable,' he said.

I had achieved my goal. But the problem was that no one else had heard our conversation. My officials were some way behind me. I had been alone with the occupant of the Peacock Throne. By now we had reached the assembled press corps. The first journalists in the queue were Iranian. The level of questioning focused on such trivia as whether His Majesty had enjoyed the flight, the comfort of the plane and so on. Then a loud voice from somewhere to the rear of the crowd of journalists called out, 'The Times, London, Your Majesty. Are you going to buy the aircraft?' 'Yes,' said the Shah. 'Two.' Another British voice: 'The BBC, London, Your Majesty. Will you give us overflying rights?' 'Yes, I will.' I can never remember before or since a time when the irrepressible determination of the British press to elicit a story and my need for confirmation of the success of government policy so absolutely coincided. I remain to this day grateful to those two journalists – one of whom was David Housego of *The Times* – who cemented the success of our visit to Tehran. Angus MacPherson, the air correspondent of the *Daily Mail*, referred in his piece in the next day's paper to the 'radiant grins' on the faces of Geoffrey Knight, Brian Trubshaw and myself.

In October 1972 Iranair signed a preliminary agreement to purchase two Concordes for delivery in late 1976 or early 1977 with an option on a third. But no firm orders were ever delivered. Six and a half years later the Shah was deposed and for at least two years before that he had come under increasing anti-modernisation political pressure. It was perhaps the closest we got to making an arm's-length sale.

We left Tehran and headed east, first for a quick stopover in Bahrain. Then, as we sped over the Indian Ocean, Robert Priddle, my private secretary, and I were standing chatting to one another in that part of the prototype containing the monitoring equipment and banks of computers, when suddenly the plane literally fell from the sky – and kept falling. One never really remembers the full length of such experiences afterwards, but sufficiently long a period of free fall took place for me to suggest to Robert that we should lie down. Anne was sitting opposite one of a team of mechanics from the accompanying plane which followed us wherever we went, carrying spare parts and tools. Each in turn was being given the experience of a flight in his dream plane. This chap went green as we fell and Anne says she has never seen a seat belt buckled so fast. Finally the plane regained its equilibrium. A few seconds later Brian Trubshaw strolled down the length of the plane with his usual twinkling grin. 'That fooled you, didn't it?' he said to his sheepish, whey-faced passengers. Apparently the weather radar had gone down – it was the only piece of standard equipment on Concorde – and he had hit an undetected air pocket. What conceivable good lying down would have done I fortunately never had to discover.

Later, as we were coming in to land at Bombay, Brian Trubshaw howled in horror: the runway was a sea of humanity, scattering rose petals, waving and cheering. By some miracle we touched ground without inflicting any casualties. Then, after a refuelling stop at

Bangkok, on to Singapore. My brief here was simpler. It was not considered likely that Singapore Airlines would be an initial purchaser but it was important to interest Lee Kuan Yew, then Prime Minister and one of the great controversial giants of the twentieth century, in the project. As I sat over a lunch table alone with this man, discussing the intricacies of British politics, it was difficult to identify him with the left-wing leader who had played the anti-imperialist card to win power in his country. Our conversation ranged widely, revealing his intimate knowledge of and interest in British affairs. The one thing we didn't discuss was Concorde. Approaching the end of the meal, I managed, however, to focus on the main agenda item. The principal objective was to get him to agree to come for a flight, with all the attendant publicity which that would produce. With great courtesy, but very firmly, he declined. My spirits sagged until, with a smile, he turned to me and asked whether I'd be prepared to take his children instead. It gave me great pleasure to escort two of them, Lee Hsien Loong and his sister, Wei Ling, on what proved to be a high-profile conclusion to the visit. Honour was more than satisfied, especially as he did thereafter himself make a tour of the aircraft on the ground. Before that happened, however, I had had to return to London. George Jellicoe took the plane on to Australia. Anne and I met it again on its way back at Toulouse and flew back with it to Heathrow for a final press conference on 1 July 1972.

At the top of our list of prospective purchasers were, of course, the giant American airlines, headed by Pan American and TWA. The citizens of New York had heard of Concorde's noise footprint. Environmentalism was the coming thing. Concorde was not an American project. It was decided that I should visit the New York Port Authority, not only responsible for the quays and services of the harbour activities of the city but also the owners of Kennedy and La Guardia airports, in order to secure agreement to landing rights. The issue had already reached the American courts. The briefs in front of me contained no light at the end of what seemed a series of legal tunnels, each one longer than the last and each with little prospect of success. We were in for a long, hard battle.

In the meantime, as the months passed, cost overruns and increased budgets became the regular routine. Slowly, remorselessly the prospect list of sales dwindled away, one after another. Certainties became prospects, prospects possibilities, possibilities cancellations. We soon faced the likelihood that only the two national flag carriers would be the customers. British Airways then was a chrysalis (BOAC and BEA didn't formally merge until the spring of 1974). Keith Granville was deputy chairman of BOAC at the time, but it was Kenneth Keith, a former vice-chairman of BEA and a shadow director of British Airways, in 1972, who dominated the negotiations. Kenneth was as tough a buccaneering merchant banker as they come. He had me on the ropes. He knew it. I knew it. He had no intention of parting with the airline's money for a project which he knew we had to make available to them on any terms they chose. He suspected that, with the possible exception of Air France, there was not an airline in the world that was going to fly the aircraft and, without a sale to the future British Airways, the prospects were less than zero.

The solution that we eventually found was public dividend capital. This was not a new idea. It was a device originally incorporated in the Labour government's Industrial Expansion Act of 1968. It is a classic example of the public sector at work. The political objective was to claim that the national carrier had bought the aircraft. The national carrier saw no financial prospects of viability, so the public sector provided the money by way of dividend capital, which meant that no interest was chargeable unless the carrier was able to make a profit out of the venture. Of course, the ability of the carrier to make a profit was wholly dependent upon the carrier and its accounting systems.

Kenneth Keith and his negotiating team didn't exactly haggle over the details of the arrangements. There was nothing much for them to haggle over. This was a commercial walkover. And just to rub my nose in the ignominy of the whole thing, when we had agreed the terms Kenneth announced that he wasn't prepared to conclude the arrangements with a minister of state. He insisted that it should be executed by John Davies, the Secretary of State. This was an illuminating example of what ministers of state are paid for. At least I could still claim that I was the only minister ever to have 'sold' a Concorde, although the French government came to much the same sort of arrangement with Air France.

By the autumn of 1973 it was apparent to me that we faced colossal bills, no prospect of even the most remote commercial success, very limited overflying rights and a real possibility that the Americans would develop a supersonic airliner, engaging technologies way beyond anything that we possessed in the European industry. I decided to put the issue to my colleagues. On 14 December 1973, I wrote a minute to the Prime Minister, recommending in effect that we should approach the Americans with a view to securing a partnership for a European–American supersonic airliner and arguing that the money we would save on cancelling the present Concorde programme would go some way towards buying us a ticket on a project that would have, with the Americans on side, a much greater chance of success. The meeting which considered my proposal was held on 20 December and, though what I recommended attracted some support, there was an understandable concern (much emphasised by the Law Officers, who were only too aware of the penalty clauses in the original contract and who advised that, if we broke the treaty, the French would take us to the International Court) as to what the French reaction would be. It was, in fact, extremely unlikely that France would ever have agreed to such a proposal. And there was always the danger that, if we had prevaricated for too long, the American aerospace industry would simply have strung us along, thus increasing our costs and leaving us ultimately with the realisation that we would have to go it alone with France in any case. But I had seen to it that my colleagues had, at least, shared with me the harsh realities of this extraordinary project.

For the record, it is perhaps worth laying out the facts as history has now recorded them. In the end thirteen Concordes were sold – but on the spurious terms outlined above – seven to BOAC and six to Air France, out of a production line of sixteen production models, two prototypes and two pre-production models. Its maiden commercial flight was to Washington DC in May 1976. The development cost of the project to the taxpayers of the United Kingdom and France was £1,126 million (in today's money terms £7.5 billion). The public dividend capital issued to the British airline to enable them to buy their five aircraft was £160 million. In February 1979, following a review of the finances of (by then) British Airways which concluded that the airline could not operate the plane at a profit by any normal commercial standards, the government decided to write off the public dividend capital associated with Concorde. No dividend was ever paid, but in return British Airways agreed to pay the government 80 per cent of future Concorde operational surpluses. This continued until the end of 1983–4 when it was agreed that public in-service support would cease. British Airways paid the government a total of £16.5 million, including payment for the government's stock of spares.

Of course, there are those who say that the technology was of wide benefit to British industry and therefore there were hidden benefits. I tried to make this case in 1973. Sadly, my officials were unable to come up with many serious arguments in support. Indeed, the permanent secretary, Peter Thornton, and Philip Jones were closely questioned by the Public Accounts Committee of the House of Commons at this time and were unable to produce any convincing examples. Concorde relied on yesterday's knowledge. It was brilliantly designed but based too much on technology that was already being overtaken by developments on the other side of the Atlantic and has now long since been left behind by the American aerospace industries. There may be another supersonic airliner. But it will not depend for its success on stretched technologies which, although enabling Britain and France to be the first countries to develop and fly a supersonic civil airliner, were already becoming obsolete almost as they did so.

A submission arrived on my desk one day, asking me to commit £6 million of taxpayers' money to enable a British company involved in the space industry to keep ahead of German and French competition in telecommunications satellite technology. It struck me at once that, if I were to agree to this, the German and French embassies in London would get wind of what was afoot almost before my signature was dry. The cables would flash to Bonn and Paris. Before we knew where we were, their ministers would be all too aware that the British were about to make a quantum leap forward. The Deutschmarks and francs necessary to counter it would flow. It seemed a *Toytown* world compared with the achievements of the Americans and the Russians.

I asked what the total European expenditure on space amounted to, when compared with the Americans. Any one of the European nations was spending at the margin of America but, added together, Europe was spending $574 million a year compared with the American $3.195 billion spent through NASA on civil programmes, not to mention a further $1.47 billion in the Department of Defense budget. Still a huge gap, certainly, but not an irrelevance. If it were possible to devise programmes whereby Europe co-operated with America, then we might be able to secure leading-edge experience and participation on major projects. The Americans traditionally expected partners to contribute equipment and services in kind to their programmes, but I was advised that, once they had agreed to allow such a partner in, they were generous – though not excessively so – in their interpretation of the technology-sharing agreement. Once you were a partner, however junior you might be, you were likely to get more than your pound of technological flesh.

It occurred to me on looking at the evidence that British policy ought to be redirected to persuading Europe to co-ordinate better its civil space activities and to ensure that Britain achieved its ambitions by sharing in what would then be a larger and technologically more sophisticated programme, stripped of the duplication necessary for each of us to reinvent the space equivalent of the wheel. At that time there were two major European organisations, the European Space Research Organisation (ESRO) and the European Launcher Development Organisation (ELDO), and proposals for three major new programmes: a new satellite-launcher rocket (strongly backed by the French), participation in NASA's post-Apollo programme (including the space shuttle and Spacelab, backed by Germany) and a new maritime communications satellite (to become MAROTS). I asked for advice about British priorities. I was told that our industrial objective should be a leading role in the European satellite programmes in general and the communications sector in particular. That was where the strength of our industry lay. However, Britain had pulled out of ELDO after the failure of several attempts to launch the Europa rocket. Although the first stage based on the UK's Blue Streak ICBM had always worked perfectly, we had abandoned this programme some twelve years earlier. ELDO's failures continued for several more years with the Europa 2 launcher, then dominated by the French. Britain was also about to turn down the opportunity to join the post-Apollo programme, in which German industry had a particular interest. I therefore designed a programme which would enable me to go to the Europeans, make an offer that Britain would play a small part in post-Apollo, rejoin the space launcher programme and in return expect a leading role in the European satellite programme. All this was to be conditional upon agreement that Europe merged its disparate organisations into one: a European Space Agency (ESA).

Of course, before I put this programme to the Europeans, I had to secure the agreement of colleagues. This was a good moment to seek such approval. Ted Heath had formally signed the Treaty of Accession to the European Community at the beginning of 1972. The European Communities Bill had worked its way through the House that spring and summer and received royal assent in October. The mood of government policy was to pursue our self-interest in Europe. Here was a tangible proposal that achieved these objectives, as well as enhancing

Britain's industrial prospects. I obtained the agreement of colleagues with two exceptions. The Ministry of Defence argued that creating a single agency in the UK, which I believed was necessary as a prelude to a European agency, was incompatible with our security relationship with the United States. The precise implications were highly classified and I couldn't be expected to share the inner secrets; I had to take it that the Ministry of Defence would not play ball. Mrs Thatcher, as Secretary of State at the Department of Education and Science, was responsible at the time for funding the Science Research Council (SRC). A significant proportion of its grant was already committed to European science programmes, but the SRC was determined to prevent more of its research money being diverted from blue-skies research to industrial support and persuaded Mrs Thatcher to fight its corner. The majority of my colleagues, however, were content for me to proceed, providing the cost remained within my departmental budget and I traded only my own departmental policies with the Europeans.

It is relatively rare, particularly in international politics, for a minister to conceive of a new policy, persuade his colleagues to accept it and actually see the policy come to fruition in government. But in this case that is what happened. There was the usual series of ministerial and official bilaterals with their interplay of national self-interest. Then the final meeting took place in Brussels on 31 July 1973. It lasted well into the night as the predictable last-minute haggling for advantage took place, but the deals were done. Britain agreed to contribute 6.3 per cent to the post-Apollo programme and 2.47 per cent to the new launcher programme (today named Ariane) and secured for the United Kingdom the leadership (at 58.5 per cent of the funding) in a project to give the existing European orbital satellite a maritime purpose. This MAROTS project enabled us to drop our own technological satellite, the GTS, and achieve the same technological benefit at less cost. We also agreed to the merger of ESRO and ELDO and thus the creation of the European Space Agency. A significant negotiating achievement in this context switched the criteria for contribution to the European space programme away from a GDP-based formula to one based on individual national priorities. The target date for the birth of ESA was to be 1 April 1974. (The convention was finally signed on 15 April 1975.) With a certain sense of elation we emerged into the early sun of a Belgian dawn. The European press were waiting. They took one look at the British party and walked up to the distinguished figure of James Hamilton, the senior British official, to inquire: 'Minister, are you pleased with the outcome?' I did my best not to look disconcerted.

I was later, as Secretary of State for Defence, able to revisit the issue. There were no reasons of any substance why Britain could not have a national space organisation and so, when Geoffrey Pattie at the Department of Trade and Industry reminded me of my views in 1973 and asked me in 1985 whether I would bring the defence interests into a British space agency, I readily agreed. A quarter of a century later I was able to discuss the consequences of what I had done for UK industry with Richard White, the executive chairman of Serco, one of our leading space companies. They received their first ever contract from ESA, which provided the launch pad for their subsequent development into a worldwide business covering thirty-five countries. The UK itself became Europe's largest user of space systems – in defence, earth observation, scientific exploration and latterly navigation. In addition, we have successfully exploited the whole field of telecommunications in space. By stimulating competition in Europe, ESA provided a catalyst for industrial development which now enables the UK to participate in space systems for Ariane – the only launcher in the world able to compete with the Americans for the commercial market – while firmly excluding ourselves from the cost overruns so characteristic of projects of this sort.

As Minister for Aerospace and Shipping, my responsibilities also included a range of government research laboratories, which had come under Cabinet Office scrutiny following the appointment in 1970 of Lord Rothschild as director general of Ted Heath's Central Policy Review Staff, a think-tank. His analysis had concluded that it was necessary to create a customer–contractor relationship in government research programmes. 'Customer responsibility' would commission the research projects and monitor progress while 'contractor responsibility' rested with the laboratory, which would bid for funds for projects and carry out any agreed programmes. Requirement boards were proposed to supervise the former responsibility for DTI's government-funded civil applied research.

I had to put this policy into practice. My first innovation was to make sure that half of the requirement boards were under the chairmanship of experienced and successful managers from the private sector. In October 1972 I announced the setting up of six such boards with a budget of some £2 million. Nigel Broackes, chairman of Trafalgar

House Investments, John Atwell, director of the Weir Group, and John Crane, director of Imperial Metal Industries, were to chair three of them. I discussed with my civil servants the prospect of adding to the list Ernie Harrison, already building a formidable reputation at Racal. 'No chance,' they said. 'He's not inclined to divert his energies to the public sector.' I told them to invite him in to see me. Ernie duly appeared in my office and I gave him the hard sell: Britain's future, frontiers of technology, place in history, all of it. He accepted. I was delighted. At the door he turned. 'No, I can't do it.' Every fisherman knows the feeling. I'd hooked the fish and then the line went dead. The rest of the boards I left under the chairmanship of civil servants, my idea being to compare as time went on the public with the private sector performance.

But, in truth, the policy was flawed. Intellectually it had a coherence. Divide the responsibility between choice of project and the allocation of money on the one hand and those in charge of the laboratories on the other and a new creative tension should focus minds on what value the taxpayer was getting from the research. But this apparently neat arrangement failed to understand the relationship which actually existed between the executive management of the research programmes and the departmental civil servants who were responsible for policy advice to ministers. In practice the two were interwoven. When it came to making judgements about where to spend the money, virtually all the money was committed to the staff costs of the public sector laboratories. In order to switch money between one programme and another, unless the switch was between programmes within the same laboratory, there would have to be redundancies. This was quite alien to the assumptions of the public sector. Anyway, the civil servants largely relied on the management of the laboratories to tell them what research was likely to lead to what results. The decision-making process was actually self-feeding. Each of these laboratories would put forward its own programme for continuing research. The system was not suited for any serious attempt to move programmes from the public to the private sector or from one field of endeavour to another. Change was at the margin.

Years later I was able to return to this question, first as Secretary of State for the Environment and then as President of the Board of Trade. The solution which we then adopted was to turn these research bodies into private sector organisations. The effect of this was to cut the knot between the civil service and the managers and, excitingly, to free the managers to pursue contracts wherever the market provided them.

Research and development did not always require decisions at the frontiers of technology. As Minister for Aerospace I agreed to provide launch aid to Shorts in Belfast for the SD3-30, an extension of its existing project, the Skyvan. Skyvan is a phenomenon. Its most ardent fans could not deny that it looks like a box on wheels with a wing across the top. But it is somehow admirable. You still meet it all over the aviation world – a dependable, flying workhorse selling at relatively low prices around the globe.

I went to Belfast in the spring of 1974 to be briefed on both the economic and the political case for this new project. (The issues of Northern Ireland were as acute then as they have remained for most of the years since.) I need not explain that my knowledge of aerodynamics was less than zero. While examining the SD3-30 prototype, I noticed that the hundredth Skyvan, its parent, was on the Tarmac awaiting its first flight. Its most distinguishing feature was a knob on the front of the body above the cockpit. I commented that I found the shape of the fuselage somewhat peculiar. However, the incident passed. The money was duly forthcoming. It was not until years later that I saw an in-service version of the SD3-30 itself. I remarked that when I had last seen its parent, the Skyvan, it had had a knob on the top. 'Oh yes, Minister,' the company's engineers said. 'You objected to the knob, so we took it off.' To think that a minister's casual remark could change the design of an aircraft. So much for my faith in the precision of aerodynamics.

The year 1973 provided a watershed in British foreign policy. On 1 January Britain formally entered the European Economic Community. It so happened that I had taken Anne and the three children – together with my mother and Bubbles – for Christmas to Barbados, where we spent a quite untypical but enjoyable festive season in the Sandy Lane Hotel. Snorkelling and scuba-diving for the first time in the Caribbean, off the beach of one of the most wonderful hotels at that time (this was long before its extension and subsequent rebuilding) was an unforgettable experience.

Early in the New Year the family flew home while I took up an invitation to visit American aerospace companies in and around Los Angeles, including Lockheeds, where Dan Haughton had already presided over the crisis for his company after the collapse of Rolls-Royce, which had threatened to leave his Tristar airliner without an engine.

It had taken a certain resilience on his arrival at Heathrow to answer press inquiries about the future of the project with the words: 'Well, I guess we've got the biggest goddam glider in the world.'

Now I was to be the first Minister from the United Kingdom to visit America after we had formally joined the EEC. I addressed the World Affairs Council there about how I saw Britain's future within Europe:

> For many years I have believed that for Britain and for Europe the arguments led overwhelmingly to the conclusion that such were the resources at the command of the world's major powers that we would find it increasingly difficult to maintain an advanced industrial base unless we moulded together a partnership of nations that in total would be the equal of the competition to which the world will increasingly expose us. The resources of 50 million British people – however proud we may be of what we have achieved – never will in the future match across the spectrum the technologies and capabilities available to you and one or two major powers . . . It has been suggested that Britain could have sought a closer transatlantic association . . . The disparity in size between our two countries would always have frustrated attempts to create such a partnership on a transatlantic basis . . .
>
> I do not for one moment suggest that what we have done has been done for any reason other than our belief that this is the right course for Britain. But European partnership is a beginning, not an end. The creation of a powerful, technologically equipped Community with the integrated resources commensurate with a population of 250 million people in an economically advanced society holds further opportunities. It offers, in my view, a new and more meaningful partnership with you.

I had kept no copy of this speech, or, if I did, it had long since been lost. But I always remembered it. It was not until the height of the Westland crisis thirteen years later that a Foreign Office official, who had heard me deliver it, appeared out of the blue one evening while I was dining in the Harcourt Room in the House of Commons. He thought he knew where he could find a copy. And so he did. I am grateful to him for enabling me to record the consistency of my European views from my earliest days in government.

*   *   *

149

My office at the DTI attracted a continuing flow of the big names of world aerospace. The agenda at such meetings was usually very much project-driven. Someone was always trying to sell you something. Significant among these were George Edwards, chairman of the British Aircraft Corporation, very much a respected grand old man of the industry presiding over the Concorde project, and Arnold Hall, chairman of Hawker Siddeley, a formidable intellect who had first been an academic and had then run the Royal Aircraft Establishment at Farnborough before moving over to Hawkers (one of the two UK airframe companies to emerge from Duncan Sandys' rationalisation of the wartime industry in the 1950s). I agreed on behalf of the government to help him with the launch of the HS146 which, after nationalisation of the industry, was to become the BA146 and still flies under that designation today. Arnold very much dominated his board, as was amply demonstrated by his habit of pausing every so often in the midst of one of his elegantly phrased arguments to glance around the table with the phrase, 'if I carry my colleagues with me'. The glance was enough to ensure that he did. I dined occasionally with these two, along with the redoubtable Arnold Weinstock, ever available to bend his caustic wit to the interests of the company he served. The conversation on these occasions ranged widely over the policy issues concerning their industry.

Responsibility for the shipping industry, as I have already explained, presented very different challenges from those of aerospace. The government's relationship with shipping on the high seas was regulatory and concerned largely with employment, safety and the environment. The other side of the coin, of course, was the shipyards of the United Kingdom and here the government presence was considerable. Both the shipping and shipbuilding industries were on a downward path and no one seemed very much inclined to do anything about it, despite the fact that all the forecasts gloomily predicted a continuing trend in the same direction. My relationship with the Chamber of Shipping was not good. I kept pointing out the deterioration in the statistics but they and I could find no common cause, although at the margin we made some adjustments that reflected their priorities.

I still recall one conversation which left an indelible impression upon me. It spoke volumes about the underlying malaise in the British economy which owed its origins to the punitive tax regimes of Labour's post-war governments. I was talking with Ian Denholm, who at the time was president of the Chamber of Shipping and also running his family shipping line. I was speaking as a minister. I perceived it to be my responsibility to encourage the industry for which I had political responsibility to grow and prosper. I said the sort of things you would expect a minister to say. Ian Denholm kept very quiet for a long time. Then finally he asked if he could explain his position to me. He said he was chairman of a family business which made a small but reasonable profit. He had quite a lot of relatives – aunts, cousins – who were dependent on the income of the business. And at the moment they made enough to satisfy their reasonable demands. What I was asking him to do was to increase the size of the business by expanding its profits to make the business more valuable. What that meant to him was that the confiscatory rates of inheritance and capital taxes would place a burden on those who came after him that they would not be able to meet. They could not know what government would be in power in years to come. 'My responsibility is to my family,' he said. I stopped speaking as a minister. I felt like the businessman that he was. There was nothing I could say. Nigel Lawson changed all that, but some fifteen more years were to pass before his liberating 1988 Budget.

An early responsibility that came with my new office was to wrestle with the proposal to build a third London airport at Foulness on the Essex coast. The pressure on the capital and its environs from the increasing volume of air travel was growing apace. In 1968 Anthony Crosland, the President of the Board of Trade in Harold Wilson's government, had set up the Roskill Committee to study air-traffic growth in Britain and report. When it did so, the Committee concluded that there was a case for a third London airport and recommended a greenfield site near Cublington in Buckinghamshire. The Report was published in 1971, before I was appointed to the Ministry. Heathrow was already the busiest international airport in the world; in the preceding decade it had experienced an average annual increase in the number of passengers of some 10 per cent and in the number of aircraft movements of 6 per cent. At Gatwick the figures were 20 per cent and 9 per cent. Roskill predicted that the new airport would be needed by the early 1980s. But it was one thing to produce a set of statistics to demonstrate the need; it was quite another to persuade any one community that they should fulfil it. Everyone agreed about one thing: it should be somewhere else. There were those who said that we should build up the regional airports of Birmingham, Manchester,

Bristol and elsewhere, particularly as so much of the traffic generated through Heathrow was actually destined for, or originated from, places other than the south-east of England. A number of locations in the south-east itself were also proposed.

It fell to me to visit a variety of sites, including that recommended by Roskill himself at Cublington. We needed a police escort as rumour had it that local objectors had planted a bomb in the ministerial path. This proved an exaggeration but nevertheless revealed the sense of tension that the whole issue provoked. Self-evidently we faced a massive public protest whichever spot was chosen. The threat of congestion, environmental damage, noise and many other objections were unanswerable. Nimbyism as a word didn't exist then. As a sentiment, it was alive and flourishing.

Attention turned to a deserted piece of the Essex coast near Southend. Maplin Sands and Foulness formed part of a coastal strip of sand dunes and shoreline which had been used as a testing ground for high explosives during the Second World War. It was deserted, except of course for birds, including a colony of Brent geese. The site was some forty-five miles from central London, required extensive land reclamation and was virtually inaccessible by road through the East End at that time. In February 1972 a paper by Peter Walker was put before colleagues which recommended one of four possible sites at Foulness, the final choice to be left until after public consultation, particularly in the light of new noise-level figures that had emerged since the Roskill Report. The site ultimately chosen was not the one I preferred, but it was my job to help. My task was to persuade Parliament to legislate in order to bring this project to fulfilment. The Bill was introduced early in 1973 and had its second reading on 8 February. Geoffrey Rippon opened the debate as Secretary of State for the Environment. I wound up. The government won the second-reading vote with a majority of only twenty-three; there were five Tory rebels.

Then in May the Civil Aviation Authority (CAA) published a revised and lowered forecast of growth in air traffic. This appeared to undermine the case for a third London airport by 1980 and it came just at the point when the Maplin Development Bill had finished in committee and was due for its report stage and third reading in the House. Some said the CAA had timed this deliberately. Whatever the truth, more defections were predicted. Geoffrey Rippon and I went to a meeting at No. 10 to discuss the handling of the third-reading debate.

I returned to the Department fully aware of the Prime Minister's strength of purpose. He had insisted categorically that the government must go on because its decision was right; anyone with doubts had been put firmly in his place. So I arranged for the new chairman of the CAA, the former Tory Cabinet Minister John Boyd-Carpenter, to send me a letter which effectively neutralised the Authority's traffic forecasts. This proved a valuable weapon in the House a few days later and we carried the day.

Backbench opposition in itself may not have ended the prospect of a third London airport at Maplin Sands, but the quadrupling of world oil prices soon did. (Tony Crosland, Labour's Environment spokesman, may also have played his own part in laying it to rest by branding the whole scheme – it was initially to include a seaport as well – 'Heathograd'.)

There was, however, one wholly beneficial outcome of the Maplin fiasco. I had chartered a light aircraft to fly from London to Southend to inspect the Maplin site and it was thus that I first saw from the air the full extent of the dereliction of London's East End. Six years later I was able to return to the problem.

My four years' ministerial apprenticeship in Transport, at the Department of the Environment and at Trade and Industry had been – if sometimes frustrating – generally an enriching experience. My work in connection with the reform of local government had taken me from one end of the country to the other and had given me an insight into the workings and structure of municipal England, while two years of responsibility for two great, if contrasting, industries had provided me with experience of international politics and the relationship between governments that was to stay with me for the rest of my parliamentary career. I had also become something of a public figure – certainly it was in this period that the name 'Tarzan' was first coined (obligingly by one of my opponents on the Opposition front bench, Stanley Clinton-Davis, who told the Commons that I reminded him of Johnny Weissmuller, the actor who had played the original role in the Hollywood films – though later Stanley explained that he had meant Lex Barker, another silver-screen Tarzan). As a nickname it stuck for several years but eventually had to serve alongside 'Hezza' – apparently a borrowing from the celebrated footballer's abbreviation 'Gazza' – which has followed me ever since. (Incidentally, that one, I am told, was invented in his journalistic days by Prime Minister Blair's press secretary, Alastair Campbell.)

As a middle-rank minister much preoccupied with the affairs of his own department I had little involvement in the wider issues of government. I was rarely invited to attend Cabinet and then only to participate in discussion of an item which fell within my area of responsibility. Major decisions tend to be taken over the heads of junior ministers. But one memory well away from the Department I do retain. I can still see in my mind's eye Ted Heath (accompanied by a whole posse of Special Branch men) arriving at my fortieth birthday party held at our new London home, 24 Wilton Crescent, Knightsbridge, on 21 March 1973. He appeared to be in buoyant form, and if anyone had suggested to me that evening that he would have lost office for ever and that we would all be back on the Opposition benches in less than a year, I would have treated it as some kind of bad birthday joke. Yet of such twists and turns of fortune is politics made, as we were all to learn on 28 February 1974.

Chapter 10

THE NATIONAL STAGE

B y the time that Ted Heath, as Prime Minister, reluctantly called a general election on 7 February 1974, naming polling day as 28 February (this was the minimum notice permissible), the vultures were starting to gather around his government. A state of emergency had first been declared on 13 November the previous year and then more rigorously extended on 12 December, a three-day week had been introduced for industry from 1 January, electricity cuts were already taking place for domestic consumers on a 'staggered' basis throughout the land and even television (both BBC and ITV) had been forced by government fiat to close down each night at 10.30 p.m.

The occasion for all this was industrial action on the part of the National Union of Mineworkers (NUM) – first (from 12 November) in the shape of an official ban on overtime and then (the product of an NUM executive decision taken on 5 February following a membership ballot) via an all-out strike. But the real cause – and the reason why the government was so vulnerable – lay in the oil crisis in the Middle East. After the Yom Kippur War of 1973, and perhaps partly in retaliation for Israel's victory, the Arab oil-producing states raised the world price of oil four-fold. That not only put an end to the 'dash for growth' policy that Tony Barber at the Treasury had been pursuing; it also widened the doctrinal fissures over the principle and the practical rigidity of our prices and incomes policy within the Conservative Party – a development encouraged as public support declined under economic pressure in late 1973.

Then, almost unbelievably, it seemed that the Prime Minister had been thrown a lifeline. By deliberately putting its own interests above those of the population generally, the NUM had offered to Ted Heath on a plate the rallying cry 'Who governs?' That promised to provide an issue that would enable even the most hard-pressed electors to rise above the economic inconveniences of the time. For weeks – almost certainly for too long – the high command of the party wrestled with what seemed to some of them a dilemma between conscience and expediency (the 1970 Parliament still had eighteen months to run). I was strongly of the view that we should have fought the general election on 7 February, the earliest date we could decently have gone to the country. I believed that the challenge we could then freshly have put before the voters (before they got bored with it, as they seemed to have done by the 28th) was a genuine one – in that sooner or later some government would have to face down the then rampant power of Britain's trade unions. But other counsels (in which the voice of Willie Whitelaw was almost certainly the most influential) prevailed. We waited until the very end of February to take our challenge to the electorate.

In the event the campaign, as I sensed it, seemed to get away to a good start. The 'Who governs?' theme struck a chord. But on the Monday ten days before polling day I remember driving through the streets of Henley in the back of my open Land Rover. Too many people looked away. Too few waved back. The mood had changed. It was too late. When it was all over, we had polled over 300,000 more votes than the Labour Party but, to their evident surprise, they had secured four more seats than we had. The Liberals held the balance. In Henley the Liberal candidate's share of the total poll at more than 30 per cent was higher than I would have liked (it was nearly 20 per cent in the nation at large, and this largely proved our undoing).

After all the results had been declared over that first March weekend of 1974 – and Ted Heath had failed in his effort, made from No. 10, to get Jeremy Thorpe and the Liberals to pitch in with us – I was invited to see him, by then installed in the Leader of the Opposition's room in the Commons. I readily accepted his invitation to join the Shadow Cabinet as Opposition spokesman for Trade and Industry. My opposite number was to be Anthony Wedgwood Benn, now proletarianised as Tony Benn, one of the most formidable parliamentary performers of his time and consequently as stretching an opponent as a new member of the Shadow Cabinet could encounter. I have always considered this a fortunate break in my career. I would be the first to recognise that I very rarely landed a serious punch on the nimble Member for Bristol South-East, but I learnt and developed from him something of the skills that were to stand me in good stead in later years.

*   *   *

The Shadow Cabinet meets weekly on Wednesday at 5.00 p.m. in the Opposition Leader's room in the House of Commons. The first item on the agenda is always the parliamentary business for the following week, which will have been conveyed by the government to the Opposition through the 'usual channels' (meaning the respective Whips' Offices). The Cabinet itself will not be given this information until its Thursday-morning meeting and the House of Commons learns of it by means of a business statement by the Leader of the House after 3.30 on Thursday afternoon. On Wednesday evening the Shadow Cabinet will have discussed this agenda, decided who is to reply to which government ministers in which debates and chosen the subjects which the Opposition itself would like to raise in 'Supply Day' debates. (In the past, Parliament was summoned to vote 'supply' to the Sovereign, as the cost of running the country regularly exceeded the personal revenues of the royal estates. Increasingly, Parliament used these sessions to air grievances and to call the monarch to account. Over the centuries this opportunity has developed into the present practice, whereby on a certain number of days a year the Opposition parties, by convention, choose the subjects which the House will debate. Self-evidently, Oppositions choose subjects of topical interest where the government appears weak and exposed.)

It so happened that I was placed next to Keith Joseph in the Shadow Cabinet. Keith was one of the kindest men I ever met in British politics; he had a brilliant mind, an unswerving integrity and a rigorous commitment to any conclusions that he reached. His highly nervous disposition added a considerable personal strain to the already heavy burden of ministerial life and made him an unsuitable candidate for the top job, as he himself was to be the first to recognise in the autumn of 1974. I remember him particularly in the context of the Shadow Cabinet between the two 1974 elections because every so often he would become engaged in deep disagreement with Ted Heath, still then the leader of the Conservative Party. What you could never question about Keith was the sincerity of his beliefs or the reasonableness with which he put them. My first doubts as to Ted's ability to hold the party together as leader stemmed from the brusqueness and brutality he displayed in the conflicts between the two of them.

I had been an admirer of Ted Heath's from the 1950s. He had accepted my invitation to visit Oxford to address undergraduate

Conservatives and had supported my initial application to become a Conservative candidate. I had formed the belief in listening to him speak in the early 1960s that the future of the Conservative Party lay with this man. I had risked (and almost got) a firm put-down on the part of the retiring Member for Tavistock, Sir Henry Studholme, when during the leadership contest that followed the resignation of Sir Alec Douglas-Home in July 1965 I rang him at his home in South Devon to tell him of the views of his likely successor on who should be the next leader of the Tory Party. Reggie Maudling I remember dismissing, with youthful arrogance, as an amiable enough character but without the bite that seemed essential to give the cutting edge to the radical programme of changes necessary to bring about a British recovery – something that I was sure that Ted Heath possessed. Faced with such brash opinions, Sir Henry, I seem to recall, said nothing but listened in studied silence. I would have done the same in his place.

Of course, Ted never commanded those qualities that would be regarded as essential for the charm-offensive school of politics. But he had a fine record of achievement: a successful wartime soldier, a Chief Whip who showed the toughness and sophistication to hold the party together. He was in the business of change, particularly change in Britain's out-of-date attitudes and its world position. I was proud, along with my mentor Peter Walker, to be identified as a Heathite. If you worked for him, you accepted the package and if you didn't like the monosyllabic manner and often curt rejoinders, too bad. I once complained to Michael Wolff, at that time one of Ted's senior political advisers and thus in continual contact with the leader, about the abruptness of some dismissive remark Ted had made to me. 'Join the club' were the only words of comfort he offered me.

Every leader is on permanent trial. As time passes, the enemies grow in number, rivals emerge and the incumbent becomes the scapegoat for judgements which others shared in but which were not their direct responsibility and which they thus managed to leave behind as they moved on. Inevitably, such pressures erupt in the aftermath of electoral defeat. But, in view of the catastrophic economic events of the late 1970s and the manifest inability of Labour in government to control their union paymasters, there was no reason why Ted should not have led the party back to power in 1979. But to do so he would have had to make some kind of accommodation with those in the party who had reservations about certain of his policies. In particular, he would have had to recognise the inherent pitfalls in the rigidity of a prices and incomes policy. I myself could remember in the past sitting locked in protracted debate over whether one group of workers should be offered a quarter of 1 per cent more than another. In practice, any judgement we made set a target for another group to up the ante. Keith and his supporters wanted a clean break.

But the accommodation required was never Ted's way. The challenge to his leadership, in his view, was bound to come and he would beat it off when it did. From the moment he surrendered to that mood, he was heading down a cul-de-sac that could lead him and the party nowhere. He was, I felt, unnecessarily abrasive and dismissive almost from the beginning of the arguments Keith sought to raise in those increasingly painful Shadow Cabinet meetings. In the end, every party leader, whether in opposition or as Prime Minister, has to be able to assert his or her authority. But the tension any disagreement evoked in Ted soon became apparent. Keith, after all, was raising issues with which some significant sympathy existed around the table. Ted, perhaps sensing this, responded aggressively. I believe that in doing so – for this was too representative of his behaviour – he largely created the conditions for his deposition four months after the October 1974 election.

Labour had won in February by the narrowest of margins. It was obvious a second election would not be long delayed. Harold Wilson used the time to clear out what he would portray as the skeletons in the cupboard and, as he put it, in 'getting Britain back to work' – all this as a prelude to the obvious bid to the electorate to give him a reasonable majority on the simple appeal that he had sorted out the problems and now deserved a real chance. The voters bought it – but only just (his overall majority in October was just three, which Labour was soon to lose through by-elections).

I was again elected for the Henley constituency, the second time in less than a year. My majority on 28 February had been 8,900 over the Liberals. On 10 October the turnout fell but my majority rose. My margin of victory, once more over the Liberals (whose share of the poll declined to just over 26 per cent), was 10,216.

It was now apparent that Ted was bound to face a leadership challenge. His opponents, organised by Airey Neave, were determined on his departure. Rumour and speculation were rife. First Edward du Cann, then Keith Joseph were paraded as potential candidates. But Edward, it was felt, had too controversial a City background. Keith on the other hand agonised over the decision whether to stand or not.

He certainly had to face resistance from his American wife. And there were reservations felt more widely; for all his outstanding virtues, Keith was not perceived – and in my view rightly so – as a leader of a great political party. Then his chances were fatally damaged by a speech he made at Edgbaston nine days after the October general election when he spoke about a decline in family values, ascribing it to an exploding birth rate among those mothers 'least fitted to bring children into the world' and other such ill-judged phrases. The press had a field day and Keith concluded that he was now ruled out of contention.

After the October election Ted had appointed Margaret Thatcher as deputy to Robert Carr, the Shadow Chancellor, and she was given special responsibility to lead the opposition to the Finance Bill – the Bill which gave legal effect to the Budget provisions announced by the Chancellor of the Exchequer, normally in March of each year. But Denis Healey, the Labour Chancellor, had taken to introducing quarterly mini-budgets and the one that November was a panic measure in reaction to the growing crisis in the industrial sector. Healey was proposing cuts in business taxation (having imposed a large tranche of new taxes on business just the previous spring) and a reining-in of some of the subsidies being poured into the nationalised industries. This meant that Margaret was plunged into the thick of the political debate at the very moment when the challenge to Ted's leadership was beginning to gather momentum. There was a high-profile second-reading debate in mid-December. Then in January the Bill moved upstairs to a standing committee. Although only some seventeen or eighteen members of the parliamentary party were members of it, she developed with them a formidable reputation and the word spread among colleagues, who would of course also have seen her clashes with Healey on the floor of the House itself.

By the end of November Ted's opponents had decided that she was their preferred choice and, once she more or less announced her candidature on the 25th via a feature article in the *Daily Mail*, the leadership battle of the winter of 1974–5 began in earnest. In the event Margaret and Hugh Fraser, a romantic Tory who had been Harold Macmillan's Secretary of State for Air, were the two challengers in the opening round of the ensuing contest, conducted under the new rules recommended in the closing weeks of December by a review of the procedure for the election of the leader chaired by Alec Douglas-Home. Willie Whitelaw, out of loyalty to Ted Heath, with whom he had worked so closely, declined to stand. No one can know now what the result would have been if he had been a candidate in the first round. I would certainly have voted for him.

It was apparent to me that Ted could not command the loyalty of the party in a way that was necessary to begin the long fight back. I believed that Margaret Thatcher would be a divisive figure and I had seen nothing about her views up to that time which persuaded me that she had a distinctive approach to politics. It seemed to me that the only option open to me on the first ballot was to abstain, hoping that Willie would come in on the second round and win. I have never regretted the calculation, although of course it proved incorrect. In the first ballot on 4 February 1975 Margaret secured 130 votes to Ted's 119 (Hugh Fraser received 16). Ted Heath stood down and there was a second ballot a week later with Willie, Jim Prior, Geoffrey Howe and John Peyton all standing as well. I argued publicly for Willie and voted for him. But Margaret had, in motor-racing terms, secured the poll position, which saw her an easy overall winner. She received 146 votes to 79 for Willie; Jim Prior and Geoffrey Howe got 19 each and John Peyton 11.

Two days later Margaret appeared before the 1922 Committee and received the acclaim always accorded to a new leader. She made a speech in the usual form, expressing gratitude and promising leadership. She told the assembled colleagues that she would be accessible to all and open to any approaches, which she would welcome, and concluded her remarks with the words: 'And besides, I want to be made a fuss of by a lot of chaps.' Some of them fell for it.

Perhaps because she felt her own position to be far from secure – she had come to office through a 'Peasants' Revolt' and very few of her senior colleagues had voted for her – Margaret started off by making only limited changes to her Shadow Cabinet. Robert Carr, an outstandingly nice man who had served as acting leader in the week between Ted's defeat on the first ballot and Margaret's triumph on the second, departed of his own volition, as did Peter Thomas, a Welsh barrister who had served in the traditionally unenviable position of Chairman of the party in the early and difficult years of government between 1970 and 1972. Geoffrey Rippon, who had always been close to Ted, who had played a prominent part in his doomed campaign to retain the leadership and who had carried the Treaty of Accession to the Common Market through the House of Commons, went too. Geoffrey Howe became Shadow Chancellor of the Exchequer, while Norman Fowler, Norman St John-Stevas and Airey Neave all joined the frontbench team at that time. But the real clue to the new leader's determination to underpin her position came in her two old-stager appointments: incomprehensibly, Reggie Maudling was summoned from the back benches – whither he had gone in the wake of the Poulson affair – to become Shadow Foreign Secretary, while, slightly more understandably (given his 'monetarist' resignation from the Treasury under Harold Macmillan in 1958), Peter Thorneycroft (now a peer) was appointed the new Chairman of the party. Although it would in retrospect have been a most unlikely choice in either case, there had been speculation that either Peter Walker or I might be appointed to Central Office at the time. But, as things worked out, I remember thinking how good Thorneycroft was at the job and how much I could learn from his easy and relaxed approach to media questioning.

Tony Benn in the meantime was enshrining his brave new world in the Industry Bill first introduced to Parliament on 31 January 1975. The principal proposals of the legislation were the establishment of a National Enterprise Board through which public money could be injected into manufacturing industry by 'picking winners' (in its brief history it picked mostly losers) and a network of planning agreements between Britain's major companies and the government, which would also involve the disclosure of company plans to trade unions. There were separate Bills to introduce Scottish and Welsh Development Agencies. I led the opposition to these proposals. The principal argument we deployed in each case was the almost limitless power conveyed to these new agencies of government. Undoubtedly, our criticisms reflected their architect's intention, and our scepticism was shared by the Prime Minister, Harold Wilson, who packed Benn off to the Department of Energy in June of 1975 immediately following the European Referendum in which Benn had played such a conspicuously unsuccessful part in the 'no' campaign.

Wilson had allowed even his senior ministerial colleagues the freedom to speak on either side in the referendum campaign, a piece of political flexibility now largely forgotten but which would have allowed William Hague the prospect of broadening his Shadow Cabinet after his election to the leadership in 1997. The campaign itself was the consequence of Wilson's inability to obtain an agreed approach to our new membership of the European Common Market behind which he could unite his Cabinet and party. There was, however, not a shred of principle in what was simply an opportunistic judgement. Along with my Shadow Cabinet colleagues, I campaigned for a 'yes' vote – and with enthusiasm.

Benn was replaced at the DTI by a former Wilson PPS, Eric Varley, who had no taste for the wilder fantasies of his predecessor and set out to allay some of the worst anxieties, being particularly reluctant to impose planning agreements on company boardrooms (in 1984 he himself left politics to run Coalite). But the irony of his time at the DTI was that Labour effectively defused the political controversy surrounding the Scottish and Welsh Development Agencies by adapting them into roving urban development corporations, a concept which I was to extend to England in the form of English Partnerships nearly twenty years later. (English Partnerships was in turn to be fragmented under Labour after 1997 into regional agencies.)

At the outset of the new Thatcher reign my own position was apparently by no means secure. I was wholly absorbed in the process of opposing Benn's Industry Bill, by then beginning to work its way through the House. But in Margaret's very first week as Leader of the Opposition and on the eve of the second-reading debate on the Bill there was some speculation in the press that she was about to sack Walker, Paul Channon and Heseltine. Putting myself on one side, the quality of Margaret's early judgement was perhaps best reflected in her discovery that she had to bring both Walker and Channon back the moment she formed her government in 1979. If I escaped, the reason was not difficult to find. The sacking itself was due to take place on Tuesday, 18 February. The previous day I had opened for the Opposition against the Benn Bill. Someone may have pointed this out to Margaret; she may also have been reminded that she was about to sack a colleague with whom she had shared a major platform twenty-four hours earlier in Central Hall, Westminster at a mass meeting of 1,000 members of the National Chamber of Trade. Divine intervention, the thought of all that embarrassment, who knows? Anyway, I survived as Shadow Trade and Industry spokesman.

In this post, a few months later, I was to be propelled to the very forefront of the political debate. In its two manifestos in 1974 Labour had pledged to take into public ownership and control shipbuilding, ship-repairing and marine engineering and the aircraft industries. Tony Benn was undoubtedly one of the prime movers behind this particular piece of dogma and had set out its main components in a statement to the House in July 1974. Indeed, one very simple lesson I learnt from Benn at this time was the shameless use of repetition in politics. It is a great mistake to believe that people hear what you say and remember it the first time you say it. Benn had no such illusions. In broadcast after broadcast, on no matter what subject, in the course of those months there would be reference to the Conservative Party's nationalisation of Rolls-Royce. Of course, it was true. We had nationalised Rolls-Royce, not by choice but as a measure of last resort. But by so reminding the political audience of the fact, Benn sought to indicate the reasonableness of his proposals to nationalise the entire aircraft and shipbuilding industries.

In the event, although the Bill itself was finally published on 1 May 1975, it failed to reach its second reading that session because of the pressure on the legislative timetable. By the time it was reintroduced following the Queen's Speech in November 1975, Benn had been moved and it was Eric Varley's responsibility to secure this flagship piece of legislation in the teeth of a dwindling government majority.

The second reading of the Bill took place on 2 December 1975. My position in the Thatcher team was still somewhat precarious. I remember clearly that in Shadow Cabinet on the preceding Wednesday Margaret Thatcher turned to Keith Joseph and suggested that it might be interesting for him to open the debate and that would leave me, as the official spokesman, to wind up (Keith at that time had the policy and research portfolio). In the ordinary course of affairs I would have been the one to open; it was my field of responsibility and a big setpiece House of Commons occasion. After Shadow Cabinet, Keith asked if I could spare him a few moments to discuss the debate. We sat on the benches in the 'no' division lobby, as he asked question after question about the aerospace industry. I did my best to answer. After about ten minutes he said: 'You really care about this industry, don't you? You open the debate. I'll wind up.' That was not the normal coinage of politics. Here was a big, generous man.

Although Harold Wilson's government had secured only a bare majority over all other parties in the October 1974 general election, it frequently achieved much better results in the division lobbies thanks to the opportunist behaviour of the Liberals and other parties. But the government became increasingly at risk when it challenged the

Commons with legislation unacceptable to all the Opposition parties. This Bill came into that category.

The measure was in the classic mould of left-wing dogma. Our opposition was total. The ultimate policy objective would be the return of these industries to the private sector at the earliest opportunity. The ragged case for the government's proposals was significantly worsened by the confiscatory nature of the compensation terms proposed for private shareholders. The basis for the valuation of their stock was by reference to Stock Exchange values chosen when they were artificially low (not least because the companies faced nationalisation at an undisclosed valuation). Here was a Labour Party threatening to buy companies, forcing down the value and then picking them up cheap. This was a precedent of potent danger.

I had been well trained for the task of trench warfare that then characterised opposition to major controversial government proposals. I had not only learnt the tactics of the lengthy committee stage under Peter Walker, but I had also exploited them ruthlessly in destroying the Ports Bill. And there would be opportunities to take the battle out into the wider countryside. I was fortunate, too, in that my number two was the Member for Bridgwater, Tom King. Tom came from very much the same background as me. We shared much the same political philosophy and got on well together. With a fine mind and an appetite for work, he brought with him practical experience in the management of a family business. We began to think of the tactics that we would deploy to secure the longest possible delay, in the hope that the remorseless attrition of lost by-elections would ultimately deny the government its majority. There are very few new tricks in politics. For me this was the Ports Bill all over again. But this time the industries were far larger, the Opposition much more sharply focused and the leading figures in the industry more inclined to fight back. Above all, we learnt early of an unexpected but fundamental difference. It is necessary here to understand the distinction between different categories of legislation and how they are treated in the parliamentary processes.

Government legislation is often preceded by consultative documents known as green papers, although this 'green' stage may be foregone when a full-blown white paper is published, carrying firm proposals of government intent. Neither of these is part of the legislation itself, but the latter and sometimes the former is part of the usual prelude, designed to provoke discussion and controversy and to provide a degree of consultation. The green paper is specifically used to set out a range of options, often with one preferred by the government, but certainly it is far more open as part of the consultative process than the much firmer proposals of a white paper.

The legislation itself consists of a measure in legal form. A bill may start its process either in the House of Commons or in the House of Lords. But the convention is that controversial legislation starts in the Commons. The first stage is formal. The bill is simply read a first time, effectively 'announced', on the floor of the House. Some two weeks or so later there will be a second-reading debate, usually lasting from about 3.30 in the afternoon to 10.00 at night. During this debate, which takes place on the floor of the House, the official spokesmen for government and Opposition will speak for some half to three-quarters of an hour each and the rest of the time is taken by backbenchers or spokesmen of other parties, until the last hour from 9.00 p.m. when two more spokesmen of the main parties will wind up. Occasionally, on matters of wide interest and great controversy, two days are allocated to this process.

The bill is then referred to a standing committee of MPs, anything between sixteen and fifty in number depending on the significance of the bill, and so chosen as to reflect the scale of the government majority in the Commons. At this stage the bill may be considered in infinite detail and any member of the standing committee can put down an amendment, even literally just to change a single word. Endless hours have been devoted to a debate about whether 'will' should be replaced by the more permissive 'may'. The standing committee sits usually on Tuesdays and Thursdays from 10.30 a.m. to 1.00 p.m. but may decide by a majority vote to sit for any period of time, and of course in controversial legislation it has been commonplace for meetings of committees to be extended to afternoon sittings, even continued through the night and sometimes, in extreme cases, for days on end.

The committee stage concluded, one or two days are given up for the findings of the committee to be reported back to the floor of the House. Known as the report stage, it provides an additional opportunity for amendments to be proposed. But these are usually limited in number, being selected by the Speaker to represent new areas of discussion or areas promised for further consideration at the committee stage. Finally, there is – at the end of the report stage – a third-reading debate usually of three hours' duration in which the general contents of the bill may be discussed. At the end of this the bill is given a third reading and referred to the other House, where the process is broadly repeated. Upon the successful conclusion of its passage through both Houses, the bill is sent to the Sovereign for royal assent, upon which it becomes an act of Parliament.

That outlines the route for government bills. It is a cardinal feature of a government bill that it must be general in its application. No piece of government legislation can single out a particular person or company or city for special treatment without the bill being classified as 'hybrid'. Hybridity is determined by the Speaker on advice from the clerks, the legal authorities of the House. If a bill is so classified, then another stage in the process I have described is introduced. The classification of a bill as hybrid gives to aggrieved parties the right to petition Parliament. Devastatingly, from a government's point of view, this removes any time constraints over the passage of the bill. The lawyers take over.

Government legislation must be secured within one session of Parliament. If it fails in that session, the legislative process has to start all over again. So governments will use their majority, including the ability to timetable through a guillotine motion the period available for standing committee or report stage, in order to ensure that they get their legislation. But with hybrid legislation this is not permitted. They are at the mercy of the protracted legal process involved in hearing petitions, calling witnesses from the aggrieved parties, and, of course, Oppositions only too anxious to exploit the complexities of the hybridity process.

Just as we were preparing to do parliamentary battle over the Aircraft and Shipbuilding Industries Bill, a South Wales industrialist, Christopher Bailey, who was chairman of Bristol Channel Ship-repairers, based in Newport, South Wales, approached the Liberals with the suggestion that the Bill was hybrid and that his company had been incorrectly categorised and thus included. The Liberals appear to have quite failed to understand the significance of what they were being told. Either that or they rejected his advice. As a result, Christopher Bailey came to me. I realised at once that, if it were possible to attach the hybrid definition to this legislation, the prospect of its ever reaching the statute books was severely limited. The more protracted the process, the more likely the ravages of by-elections would deny Harold Wilson his majority.

In preparing the list of colleagues I intended to ask to serve on the standing committee with me, I had in mind a number of qualifications. There were, first of all, the professionals: colleagues who had served through earlier battles and who could be relied upon to speak – almost without notice, at significant length, on the most arcane of amendments – and to do so in a way that would avoid the more flagrant examples of filibustering. If they could be amusing as well, that would jolly the whole thing along. But one colleague brought a very different qualification to the process. Robin Maxwell-Hyslop I had known at Oxford when he was an undergraduate at Christ Church and active in the University Conservative Association. He had become a somewhat prickly man, a scourge of bureaucracy and with a terrier-like tenacity. He never let go. When it came to the workings of the House of Commons, he was something of a constitutional expert. He had also come to be feared by civil servants, particularly for his unorthodox approach to the pursuit of information. It was reputed that he used to turn up in their offices, asking to see the contents of filing cabinets – and all this dressed in an open-necked shirt. He was not always – perhaps even not often – right. But he had an extraordinary capacity to pursue remorselessly the detail of a case in which he became interested. I chose him as the man to handle the bone of hybridity. No one was better qualified in the Tory ranks at the time to worry that bone to death. He more than lived up to my expectations and made his reputation in the process.

My earlier experiences in fighting nationalisation legislation – particularly the proposals to nationalise the bus industry in Barbara Castle's 1968 legislation – had taught me that industrialists can be, to put it mildly, fickle in their willingness to die in the trenches for the freedom of their industries. The first rumours of nationalisation provoke fierce resistance by the leaders of the companies threatened. Meetings are organised, protestations of support are forthcoming and the politicians who have to lead the opposition can easily be persuaded that there will be an army marching behind them. It is more than likely that we will never now see another government committed to the principle of nationalisation, in which case my advice belongs only to the history books. But for me a familiar pattern emerged. The initial enthusiasm for resistance, with full attendance at the action committee meetings, begins to give way, as one or two of the principal leaders from the industrial side present their apologies when, for 'urgent commercial reasons', they are unable to attend. The press, previously full of outspoken hostility and criticism, begins to flavour its accounts of the developing battle with references to a steering group or a shadow board of directors for the new nationalised industry. No names at this stage; just private conversations, rumours, nods, winks. The minister in charge of the legislation is obviously anxious to secure some bridgehead in the opposing ranks of industrialists. The plum he or she seeks for their second-reading speech is the announcement of the name of a prominent industrialist who has agreed to be the chairman of the new board to be set up in anticipation that the legislation will successfully complete its passage through Parliament. He or she will try to land the biggest fish possible. If lucky, the Opposition spokesman will get wind of what is afoot. The conversation between the soon-to-be chairman and the Opposition spokesman then takes a predictable line: 'You know I love this industry. I hate what they're doing. But it is important that they have someone who really understands the way the industry works to mitigate the damage they may otherwise do. I know you'll understand, old boy.' The opposition has been dented. The chairman begins recruiting his board. Offers are being made, careers reanalysed. No more action committee meetings are called. Slots in the honours list are already booked. In the end the only people to go on fighting the nationalisation process are your own activists and colleagues in the party. Upon them you can at least rely.

The Aircraft and Shipbuilding Industries Bill was reintroduced on 20 November 1975, and the second reading took place on 2 December. The standing committee sat for fifty-eight sessions between 11 December and 13 May the following spring. At that time Labour's control of the House was precarious. After the death of Maurice Edelman, Labour MP for Coventry North West (and my victorious opponent in 1964) on 14 December 1975, the government had an overall majority of one. The figures seesawed over the next few months, as by-elections came and went. When the MP for Rotherham, Brian O'Malley, died on 6 April, Jim Callaghan, who had now succeeded Harold Wilson as Prime Minister on the latter's sudden and unanticipated retirement, lost his overall majority. The situation deteriorated still further as the session wound its way towards the summer recess.

Slowly then the strategy on which I had embarked unfolded. As the committee stage of the Bill ended, the Labour Party could not command a majority against all the other parties. And the hybridity issue hung over the Bill like the Sword of Damocles.

Christopher Bailey, the South Wales ship-repairer, realised, as we did, the importance of time and was determined to exploit the right to petition for all the delaying opportunity it provided. But it was not on this issue that the first blood was drawn. Success came from the opposite direction. It emerged that a company called Marathon Shipbuilders (UK) on Clydebank had been *left out* of the legislation and Robin Maxwell-Hyslop set out to prove that it should have been included. The essence of his case was that Marathon had built a floating drilling rig, the *Key Victoria*, for the North Sea oil industry which was a 'vessel' within the meaning of the Bill. The government denied that it was such, but Robin was able to demonstrate that the Board of Trade had already insisted that a sister rig of the *Key Victoria* was a vessel and that it had to carry all the safety equipment required as part of the conditions of a licence as such. This gave Robin the rock on which he rested his claim that the Bill was hybrid.

George Thomas, the Speaker of the House of Commons, had to rule on the issue. He could not have enjoyed the responsibility. Elected to the House in 1945 as the Labour Member for Cardiff Central (later West), this rather gaunt bachelor had served in the second Wilson government as Secretary of State for Wales. Doubtless he would have been in sympathy with the purpose of the Bill and appalled at the prospect that his ruling could consign the government's flagship legislation to the dustbin of history. But he was the Speaker, with all the great tradition of that office resting on his shoulders. His duty now was to the House itself, not to the party which had sent him there.

Even now the matter was far from clear. The clerks, in advising him, had not given him the full quotation in the precedent they had put before him, a ruling by Mr Speaker Hylton-Foster in 1962. Again Robin was up to speed. He had – almost unbelievably – remembered the full ruling, which laid down that, if any doubt existed about hybridity, the matter had to be referred to examiners. He copied the text and had it laid under the egg-cup on George Thomas' breakfast tray with a note that read: 'Dear Mr Speaker. *Quod erat demonstrandum.* I claim game, set and match.' Two months before he died in 1997, George confirmed to Robin what the chief clerk, Richard Barlas, had earlier reported, that this was the clinching moment.

On 26 May the Speaker accepted Robin's submission and ruled that the Bill was *prima facie* hybrid. It followed that there would have to be a select-committee stage added to the normal procedures. The government's flagship was heading for the rocks. Immediately Michael Foot, as Leader of the House, announced a procedural motion in effect designed to overrule the Speaker. It is curious how often the greatest self-styled champions of liberty and the constitution prove the most willing to indulge in ruthless suppression of those rights when they conflict with their narrower objectives. The Labour government's motion proposed that 'any Standing Orders relating to Private Business, and consideration of the application of any such Standing Orders, are dispensed with'. It was tabled on 27 May, as was our amendment which was designed to preserve the Speaker's ruling intact.

As the day wore on, the rumours began to circulate that Labour could not muster a majority. In the event of a tied vote, the Speaker, by convention, rules for the status quo and, therefore, if the vote on the government's motion were tied, the Speaker would have to cast his against, thus preserving the existing situation which the government was seeking to change. The prospect, the glittering prize, of destroying the Aircraft and Shipbuilding Industries measure, as I had destroyed the Ports Bill in an earlier Parliament, lay before us. Both sides counted and recounted the names. The situation was complicated by allegations that one of our colleagues, Peter Fry, the Member for Wellingborough, was absent without leave, unpaired, on holiday in Corfu, although he later said that he had been told he was covered before he left.

Most people are familiar with the pairing system in the House of Commons. It is a convenient way of ensuring that those who have urgent business away from Parliament can arrange to 'pair' with a named Member on the opposite side, thus reducing the voting effect on both sides equally. The business managers, the whips, will usually carry out the same exercise for those too ill to attend the House, although the occasional sight of ambulances in Speaker's Court was always an indication of the ruthless determination in extremes to test the physical resources of seriously ill people. (Such Members may, however, be 'nodded through' the division lobby, if seen by whips from both main parties to be physically present within the precincts of the Palace of Westminster.)

By the time of the vote that night, in high tension, it was apparent that the government was in deep trouble. The first vote, on our amendment, was tied. The Speaker therefore cast his vote for the status quo. The government had lost. This alerted them to the very real danger that they would now lose their own substantive motion. The hybridity ruling would have stood. That night the government had agreed a pair for one of its Members, Tom Pendry, himself actually a government whip. This is a gentleman's agreement of honour. Yet

Michael Cocks, the Labour government's Chief Whip in the Commons, encouraged his minion Pendry, who had turned up in the House in spite of being paired, to vote in the government lobby, although Humphrey Atkins, the Opposition Chief Whip, had received Cocks' personal assurance at 9.15 – only three-quarters of an hour before the first division – that Pendry would not vote. The government motion thus secured a majority of just one – Tom Pendry.

The Labour Members of Parliament went berserk. They leapt on to the green benches in the chamber, waving their order papers and singing 'The Red Flag'. *The Times* reported next day that several Members had intervened in the proceedings, some even exchanging blows behind the bar and employing worse-than-barrackroom language. (The bar should not be confused with a place of refreshment; it is merely a defined part of the Commons chamber itself.) It was a moment of history; a serious piece of legislation had secured its passage because the government of the day had cheated.

I watched them from my position behind the Opposition dispatch box. I was acutely aware of the utter helplessness of the parliamentary Opposition, faced with a constitutional abuse of this sort. In the end, the House of Commons can only work because people stick to the rules. The Speaker is their custodian. If the government legislates to overrule the Speaker and does so by breaking its word, then there is no knowing where that process will end. The symbol of the authority of the Commons is the mace and it was the authority of the Commons that had been abused. I picked it up with both hands and offered it to the jeering, ranting rows of Labour MPs. They were celebrating the unconstitutional enactment of legislation for which they had no majority. My critics and enemies have portrayed it as a mad, wild act. Others, including the cartoonist on the front page of the *Sunday Times*, saw it in a very different light. There I was depicted as an heroic figure standing defiantly for the integrity of the House of Commons. Certainly, the mace was never waved. That colouring of the event only arose because the affable Jim Prior, standing alongside me, took hold of my right shoulder, presumably to attract my attention and urge me to replace it on its stand. The effect as I turned was to lower one end of the mace and raise the other. Those who remember the event clearly have told me many times since of the controlled nature of what I did and confirm the great distortions that the reporting of it ensured. Curiously, by good chance, Anne and my daughter Annabel were in the public gallery that night. Anne was horrified by the chaos below.

She and Annabel sat on in the gallery until the House was cleared, then they continued to sit, miserably, outside the Chief Whip's office waiting for me. One of the whips eventually emerged and patted Anne on the shoulder saying, 'Don't you worry. He can survive this if he apologises.' They were eventually asked in by Humphrey Atkins, smiling genially, and offered a much needed drink.

For me, it had been an act of defiance against a constitutional abuse. My response was provocative and theatrical, but the question no one has satisfactorily answered is: at what stage should you protest and in what form? Of the seriousness of the event, however, there can be no doubt. On 29 May the first editorial in *The Times*, after opening remarks deploring the scenes of rowdiness and the effects they had upon the British people, went on:

> Mr Foot's decision to get round the Speaker's ruling must tend to weaken the fabric of convention and consent on which the operation of Parliament depends . . . In the second vote on Thursday night, which the Government won by a majority of one, it seems clear that the Chief Whip decided to cheat . . . This combination of events is a serious reflection on the judgement of the Leader of the House and on the honour of the Chief Whip . . . It at first seemed likely that the Prime Minister did not approve the Chief Whip's action . . . Unfortunately, he has decided to back up his Chief Whip and must share the blame.

The incident, however, was inevitably to become a weapon in the hands of my critics for years to come. Allegations of unreliability and a volatile temperament were frequently paraded in an effort to deny me preferment. Who knows whether they made any real difference? There have been very few incidents in which I took a black and white stand and, as I shall describe, they are curiously linked. They have all had just one thing in common: my opponents had cheated. They had used devices which, as it appeared to me, broke the rules by which our conduct was properly governed. That I will not tolerate. The incident of the mace arose out of the first such occasion. There were to be two more, one perpetrated by Norman Tebbit, the other by Mrs Thatcher herself.

I should in fairness record that many years later Michael Cocks explained to me his side of the story. He believed he was fully justified in putting Tom Pendry through the lobbies as the vote he was entitled to turn out was a matter of numbers, not of names – and he had a minister absent on official business without a pair (though he should have had one). But that was not the view of Humphrey Atkins – Cocks had given him an assurance – and it was certainly not the background against which the events of that evening were seen to have unfolded. There were many on my own side critical of what I had done, although the balance of opinion was that it required only an apology to the House. The House of Commons is civilised in its response to those who apologise and the convention allows you to do so without interruption or questioning. The following day I made a short personal statement of regret for what had occurred and the event of the mace became a footnote in the history books.

Of course, there were practical repercussions. Pairing arrangements were suspended and bipartisan alliances cancelled. An inquiry was held. It found that we were right, of course. However, the government simply organised a repeat of the vote a month later. By this time they had replaced dead Members in by-elections and the government whips did their job thoroughly. A motion to refer the Bill to a select committee (that is, declare it *prima facie* hybrid) was rejected by a majority of fourteen. Labour's cheat had worked.

The delay did take its toll, however. The legislation returned to the Commons for its report stage and third reading which took place over three days, from 27 to 29 July. Second reading in the Lords took place on 28 September. Their Lordships had strong objections to the inclusion of ship-repairing in the Bill and after several government defeats in committee and on report there followed a protracted game of ping-pong with the Commons lasting until the final day of the session on 22 November. Once again the Bill had run out of time. It was reintroduced again in the new session, with the threat of the Parliament Acts (which ensures that the will of the Commons shall prevail over that of the Lords) hanging over it. But by then I had been moved on. The government had this time redrafted the legislation so as to remove – as they hoped – all trace of hybridity. But the combination of Robin Maxwell-Hyslop and Christopher Bailey went back into action and further arguments about hybridity ensued (centred around the Westminster Dredging Company, which had not been included in the list of ship-repairers affected by the Bill). In the end the government had to drop the ship-repairing provisions altogether at the last minute before the Bill finally received its royal assent on 17 March 1977.

I had already made an unambiguous statement about our intention to return the aircraft and shipbuilding industries to the private sector in the standing committee's discussions on the Bill back in May, but I returned to the issue in my party Conference speech in Blackpool in October 1976. I repeated the pledge and made the clearest commitment on behalf of the Conservative Party. But the speech had more permanent significance for me. There was speculation at the time about a reshuffle of the Shadow front bench.

I had first spoken from the platform at a party conference in October 1975. The speech had been well received and earned me a standing ovation late in the afternoon from those delegates who had remained in the hall. The first marker for what was to become something of a conference reputation had been put in place.

The party Conference of 1976 was altogether different. When Harold Wilson had resigned unexpectedly the previous spring and given way to Jim Callaghan, the atmosphere was one of growing economic crisis. As Chancellor of the Exchequer, Denis Healey faced that autumn the ignominy of recourse to the International Monetary Fund. The left-wing tide that was to destroy the Callaghan government and keep Labour out of power for virtually two decades was rising fast. On the morning of my speech interest rates soared to 15 per cent.

I sat up late into the night before working on the speech and I felt in my bones that I had the material to do well. But I could not have known just how well. I only knew that, when I came to my key passage referring to Labour's Conference the week before, I was in full cry: 'The reality lay in Blackpool last week: a one-legged army limping away from the storm they have created. Left, left – left, left, left.' As the audience grasped the significance of the adjustment to the best-known military command of them all, they roared their appreciation. I determined at once to seize the moment. I repeated the words: 'Left, left – left, left, left.' They were ideally cast to catch the mood of euphoria. The speech ended a little later to a prolonged ovation.

No one was going to eject me from the Shadow Cabinet now – though Leaders of the Opposition have other ways of cutting one down. A month later, in November 1976, I was moved from the Trade and Industry portfolio to that of Environment. Mrs Thatcher had apparently been offended by a speech I had made a full ten months before, criticising the Labour government for intervening in industry only to pick losers and thereby implicitly suggesting that the Conservatives were not against intervention altogether.

I had spent two years as a minister under Ted Heath dealing with the interface between Whitehall and the aerospace industry, and presiding over the government's responsibilities for research and development. Every day I had had to take decisions about the level of financial support the government would provide in backing industrial activity in field after field. Indeed, throughout the 1980s and 1990s Conservative ministers, including myself, continued to engage in such activity. You cannot have lived through such an experience and come out mouthing the platitudes of simplistic politics. 'Getting off people's backs', 'tearing up forms' and 'untying the red tape' are great rallying cries for audiences of small businessmen. And with much justification. But it's not the whole story. Where one comes face to face with major industrial sectors, dependent upon government for much of their development underpinning and procurement, engaged in the international search for market places in fierce competition with other similarly interdependent industries, a rather more realistic understanding of what the world is about rapidly sets in. Or that is how matters seemed to the Shadow Secretary of State for Trade and Industry of the time – though evidently not to his more purist, fundamentalist leader.

Perhaps the most open disagreement I had with Margaret Thatcher at around this time arose over the collapse of British Leyland. In March 1975 British Leyland – the only large domestic car manufacturer – faced disintegration. Lord Ryder of the National Enterprise Board recommended that it should be taken into public ownership – and in the end the company was effectively nationalised by July. Margaret Thatcher asked me what my line would be. The government's solution was open to endless criticism. It is difficult to think of a proposal that was less suited to the real problems besetting the British motor industry at the time. I outlined the arguments that I intended to deploy. Margaret urged me to take a different line. 'The company should be put into liquidation and you should argue that case.'

Liquidation, receivership are perfectly legitimate options. Years later I believe I helped to save Leyland Daf (itself a lingering part of the crisis that had continued because the government failed to deal with the problem in 1975) at no cost to the Exchequer through a very successful receivership. But we were not the government. We were in opposition. The idea that a Conservative Party that would be fighting in the next election to win back marginal seats in the West Midlands should have adopted, wholly unnecessarily, a political posture which would have been presented by the Labour Party as closing down vast swathes of British industry was a political misjudgement of the first order. For the government, receivership could well have been a perfectly reasonable option. There could have been time for it to have worked, for the component parts of the business to have been restored under different ownership and for the policy to have justified itself. But for the Opposition to take a position far more extreme than anything that the government of the day was doing (with all the partisan flak that that would entail) would have given a hefty hostage to political fortune. In the West Midlands, that fulcrum of British politics, they would have been unlikely to forgive or forget. I am glad to say that I got my way.

Much good, though, it did me. In the first week of November 1976, just before the opening of the new session, I was summoned to the Leader's room in the House of Commons to be told that she wanted to move me from Trade and Industry to become Shadow Environment spokesman. I made a sufficiently vigorous protest for Margaret to say: 'Well, if you feel that strongly, you'd better stay where you are.' I thought, and hoped, that I had prevailed. But I was called back shortly afterwards to find that the Deputy Leader, Willie Whitelaw, and the Chief Whip, Humphrey Atkins, had joined her. We resumed our conversation. It was made clear that there was no question of my staying with the Trade and Industry portfolio. Reluctantly I agreed to move, making it clear that I would not want the substantive post once we were in government. Obviously, Willie and Humphrey had persuaded Margaret that she couldn't have a member of her Shadow Cabinet refusing to accept her wishes. Looked at from their point of view, I believe they were right and that, in so advising her to take a firm stand with me, they brought the experience of highly sophisticated business managers of the Commons to her aid.

Although I was not wholly satisfied with my new Environment brief, life otherwise at this time was very fulfilling. After some wanderings (including buying a hideous Edwardian house at Nettlebed just outside Henley), in 1977 we had moved into the home of our dreams, Thenford House, just on the Oxfordshire–Northamptonshire border.

The search for our new home had actually begun shortly after my selection as the prospective candidate for Henley, when I had promised to live in or within easy reach of the constituency. We began to comb the estate agents' advertisements in *Country Life*, even taking space in that publication to set out our requirements. We studied ordnance-survey maps and even drove up promising-looking drives in the hope of finding this elusive dream house. There were dangers, of course, in this last process. We risked being stopped and asked our business. We anticipated this risk by having ready the rejoinder that we were looking for a fictitious Mr Wilkins. This device lost its appeal when one day our interrogator asked us to wait a moment while he fetched him.

At last the chance came. In 1975, a friend of ours, Roderick Sargeantson, a Henley estate agent, discovered that a house owned by Jean Summers, widow of the late Sir Spencer Summers, a former colleague of mine in the House of Commons, was likely to be for sale. She was looking for a buyer, although extremely hesitant to put it on the open market. We set off for Thenford, did the best we could to view the house from outside the grounds, crept up the back drive through the stable yard, took one long look and told Roderick we wanted to buy it. Lady Summers, who subsequently became a lasting friend, invited us to lunch. We discovered we knew relatives of the family. She decided that if, with great reluctance, she had to move she would like to sell to someone she thought would care for it. I think she was also attracted by our associations with her late husband. She was to continue to live in a nearby house on the estate for the next twenty years.

We set about restoring, renovating and furnishing it to our own tastes and to the highest standards possible. Over the years, as someone once said, we had always bought our own furniture – and we enjoyed every minute of it. Come to think of it, *someone* always has to buy the furniture. Unless you have ancestors or parents who did it for you, at some stage in life you have to start yourself. The rest of my family still had very good use for what they owned. Anne and I have spent many happy hours combing the junk shops of Portobello Road, wandering from antique shop to antique shop in the Cotswolds, bidding at auctions and searching art galleries together. We do so to this day.

Thenford came with some 400 acres. The woodlands that surrounded the house were in a pretty sad state. The most significant plantings were eighteenth-century beech, most of which were sawn-off stumps of trees long gone or otherwise killed off in the recent drought. Rashly I decided that here was an opportunity to create an arboretum of my own. At the beginning, I owed a great deal to the advice of an

American, Lanning Roper, then the gardening editor of the *Sunday Times*, who – when I rang him to say that I had acquired a garden of some size and wanted his help – at first attempted to brush me off. I was told to ring back in a year – which, to his obvious surprise, I duly did. This time I got a more receptive response. Anne and I became extremely fond of Lanning and, though we had very different temperaments (he always wanted to take things at a slower pace than I did), he, with the considerable help of that great nurseryman Harold Hillier (later Sir Harold), guided me along the first faltering steps in the creation of the Thenford arboretum. Later on – Lanning died of cancer in 1983 – I was to owe as much, if not more, to his successor Roy Lancaster, who had himself worked for Harold Hillier.

Having so large a garden also reawakened my interest in birds, which went back to my childhood in Swansea and to my schooldays at Shrewsbury. One of the first things I did at Thenford was to build an aviary along the outside walls of the kitchen garden and for some years we kept and even bred some of the more exotic species of duck and pheasant there. If I did not quite manage to maintain my initial enthusiasm, however, it was because – as I was soon to discover – creating a garden of trees and shrubs (more constructive, I can't help feeling, than Mr Gladstone's hobby of tree-felling) is a hard taskmistress who brooks no rivals.

The economic situation was moving inexorably from bad to worse. Harold Wilson had done Jim Callaghan no favours in handing the reins to him when he did. But Jim brought a new style to the premiership. Here was an avuncular, somewhat laid-back, reassuring figure – without the deep partisan envy that one associated with Harold Wilson. Jim came from a naval background and one instinctively felt that he was the sort who would stick it out when the going got rough. No one felt that about Wilson. On a personal basis I got to know Jim in an unexpected way. Our second daughter Alexandra had at the age of twelve become aware that a Mr Callaghan was guilty of making disparaging remarks about her father. She increasingly complained about these activities, referring to 'Tut Callyan' – the nearest she could get to mimicking 'That Callaghan' in the accents of a northern soap opera she used to watch. Eventually, unable to contain herself any longer and quite unknown to either of her parents, she wrote to the Prime Minister at 10 Downing Street, complaining about his unacceptable comments about Daddy. The first we knew of this precocious activity was a charming letter from Jim to Alexandra. Years later she met him at a Royal Garden Party and was invited to lunch in the House of Lords – at which he presented her with a copy of his autobiography. He came to a party she gave in 1989 and they still exchange Christmas cards.

My disappointment in finding myself shadowing Environment directly stemmed from the deepening economic crisis the country was facing. Although environmental policy can assume a high profile in opposition at times of relative prosperity, in the bleak circumstances of the mid- and late 1970s the politics of the economy dominated everything. My disappointment was tempered, however, by the recognition that there were two overriding opportunities in the job. Effectively, the task involved a close relationship with local government – and Conservatives everywhere were marching to the sound of guns. Everything was going right for us. During the course of those few years the Conservatives swept into power in local government from one end of England to the other. (My remit for local government did not extend into the other three component parts of the United Kingdom.) The most absolute triumph was the county council elections of 1978. I organised a campaign known as 'Operation Clean-Sweep'. We set out to win every county and we did – with one exception, Durham.

The County of Durham was one of the great Labour fortresses, heavily industrial and scarred with the historic legacy of the coal-mining industry. It is an area where they might as well weigh the Labour votes as count them. I was determined even there to do what I could against the odds. We couldn't for the most part even get candidates to stand as Conservatives. I remember trying to persuade small businessmen that they had nothing to fear, that their businesses would survive, if they only stood by their convictions and articulated their beliefs under the Conservative flag. To no avail. On polling day there were simply not enough Conservative candidates, even if all those we had had been elected, to upset the entrenched Labour majority. Durham kept the red flag flying, but it was the only place that did.

By the 1979 general election the Tories were in control even of the Greater London Council under Sir Horace Cutler. The mood was with us and the tide was flowing. Eventually on 28 March James Callaghan lost a confidence debate in the House of Commons by a single vote and became the first Prime Minister to be forced to go to the country since Ramsay MacDonald in 1924. He had been on the whole a reassuring, relaxed Prime Minister, but the forced timing of the contest could not have been worse for him. The winter of 1978–9 had been a wretched one – with the unions, particularly the public service ones, making life miserable for everyone up and down the land.

In strict terms, resentment against union bully boys did not require specific policy commitments from us. (We were, in fact, very slow in bringing forward our full plans for union reform.) But our promise to make possible the sale of council houses to those who actually lived in them plainly was a policy issue. It is impossible to appreciate the success of Tory policy in the 1980s without an understanding of the significance of the commitment we made in the previous decade to sell, on favourable terms, council properties to their tenants. The first sale of council houses was developed by Conservative councils on a voluntary basis. It was an attractive scheme and, wherever it was put into practice, immediately became very popular with tenants. We were now determined to go further and extend the right to tenants in non-Conservative authorities. National political figures, among them Peter Walker, had long argued for compulsory rights of acquisition, with generous discounts. In fact, the commitment of the Conservative Party to a scheme of compulsory sales backed by legal rights featured for the first time in Ted Heath's election manifesto of October 1974.

That manifesto is particularly interesting in that it contained the pledge to abolish the rates, to introduce fixed-interest mortgages and to sell council houses at a discount to their tenants. Mrs Thatcher was the Shadow Environment spokesman responsible for these promises, although later she claimed that Ted Heath had forced her to adopt the first two. In the climate of 1974 these policies made little impact on the electorate. By the time I became Opposition spokesman for the Environment in 1976, the fixed-interest mortgages had disappeared from sight, but the other two pledges remained. We fleshed out our commitment to the sale of council houses for the 1979 manifesto. The details of the scheme were worked out by the diligent Hugh Rossi, who served as my number two in the Shadow team with responsibility for housing.

The existence of this policy area in my portfolio ensured that I would play a sizeable role in the election. It was agreed that I should open the campaign with a speech in my own constituency making the formal pledge to council-house tenants everywhere. I gave it at the very beginning of the campaign to a packed adoption meeting in Watlington Town Hall on 7 April. The speech is interesting not just for the announcement itself but also for the historical rationale that I set out for it:

> Under the first Conservative Government after the war much of Labour's controls were swept away.
>
> Between 1951 and 1964 nearly four million people bought their own home for the first time . . .
>
> It has proved in virtually every case the wisest decision they ever made.
>
> The average house purchased in 1951 cost £2,000. Today that same house would be worth £16,000.
>
> . . .
>
> These are average figures . . . but they illustrate a trend that has meant for well over half our people a stake in the nation's wealth which is personal, valuable and saleable and which enables parents to leave to their children a help-in-life far larger than those parents had for themselves.
>
> But as house prices rose so those who hadn't bought found themselves further and further away from the ability to buy.
>
> As the capital value of privately owned houses increased, the owners obviously gained or at the very worst were protected from inflation. But in the case of new town or council houses the value increased but the tenants gained nothing.
>
> Their rents rose over the years. In some cases they have more than paid for their houses but they own nothing. And their children look forward to no inheritance.
>
> The Conservative Party can no longer stand back from this growing divide in our nation.

I am not pretending that the council-house sales pledge alone won the 1979 election but – next to the 'winter of discontent' itself – it was, I am sure, the single most important contributory factor. It was Anthony Eden who used to describe 'a property-owning democracy' as the aim of the Conservative Party. By this one policy initiative we did more than anyone else to make that a reality.

PART THREE:
1979–1990

Chapter 11

SECRETARY OF STATE

I was called in on Saturday, 5 May 1979 to see the Prime Minister. The disposition of jobs was taking place in the small upstairs sitting room in No. 10. I passed Francis Pym on my way in; he was looking dejected, having been offered the Ministry of Defence when he had had his heart set on the Foreign Office (which went to Peter Carrington instead). I took a seat and waited to learn my fate. I had been in No. 10 many times before but only as a junior minister in Ted Heath's government. This time it felt quite different. I had no idea what post I would be offered, but that morning such a question was secondary. It was a moment of great excitement, as I was almost certain that I would be offered a Cabinet job, and there is no comparison between the status of a Cabinet minister and the standing of the rest of a department's ministerial team. Over the years I had become increasingly confident that such an attainment might be possible, but this was the threshold of reality. Thirteen years, nine of them in opposition, four as a junior minister, were about to lead to the centre of political power. It seemed a long way from the South Wales of my childhood.

Margaret first offered me the Department of Energy. I expressed the most profound reservations. I had had enough experience, as Minister for Aerospace, of monolithic nationalised industries. I had seen Peter Walker's frustrations, grappling with the problems of that Department when it was part of the DTI back in 1973. The Secretary of State for Energy was eternally sandwiched between the nationalised industries of electricity, gas and coal and their all-too-powerful unions. Faced with my obvious lack of enthusiasm, Margaret said: 'Well, it's difficult to see what else to offer you. We know – because you said so when you took it over in opposition – that you don't want Environment.' I replied that I would much prefer the Department of the Environment to Energy. Thus I became the Secretary of State for the Environment.

The decision taken, I asked if I could influence the choice of my junior ministers. I wanted ministers who were capable of handling the very substantial delegation of responsibility and opportunity which was to be at the heart of my managerial philosophy so long as I was in the Cabinet. Specifically, I asked for Tom King and John Stanley as my ministers of state. Tom, who had been passed over as Secretary of State for Energy despite having held the portfolio for the past three years in opposition, had worked closely with me in shadowing the Department of Industry until 1976. John, tall, fair-haired and with an open face, had been my PPS before moving to work for Mrs Thatcher in the same year. Both were very able and hard-working. I was delighted when the Prime Minister agreed, provided I could persuade John to give up the job he had already been offered at the Ministry of Defence. Hastily, I sought him out and persuaded him to come with me. I found that his instinct to check every last detail himself made him a perfect ministerial foil for me, but he had a creative mind too, evidenced by the comprehensive nature of the housing policies he introduced. (In 1983 he was to move to the Ministry of Defence during my time as Secretary of State there and became Minister for the Armed Forces.) I asked also for Kenneth Baker and Lynda Chalker, but they were both committed elsewhere. Tim Sainsbury joined the team as my PPS. He and I were to work together as colleagues many times over the years to come and have remained friends from that day to this.

Cabinet ministers hold their positions as servants of the Crown. It is an early part of the ritual, on the first such appointment, to kiss hands with the Sovereign, become sworn in as Privy Counsellors and receive the seals of office. A rather raw, excited and nervous group of newly appointed Cabinet ministers attended Buckingham Palace that afternoon to be trained for the Audience: when to bow, which knee to lower to the proffered stool, which hand to kiss, how to navigate into the appropriate line after our turn. It was all very unnerving but, as with all things at the Palace, conducted with extreme professionalism, in no small measure thanks to the Crown equerry to Her Majesty – the presiding officer, so to speak – Lieutenant-Colonel Sir John Miller, my former commanding officer at Pirbright.

If I had initially found little to attract me in shadowing the Department of the Environment (DOE) in opposition, once in office it was an entirely different matter. If ever there was a department designed for a minister, the Department of the Environment was for me. I had, of course, served an apprenticeship of two years there under Peter Walker in the early 1970s. And as Shadow spokesman in the later years of the decade I had established close relations with many of our local leaders and councillors as the tide of Tory fortunes rose in local government. The environment and the heritage brief also reflected my personal interests. To complete the picture, the Department was bound to be at the centre of the political battlefield. In particular our housing policies were certain to provoke bitter controversy. They were to strike at the heart of Labour's concept of how society should be ordered, with an over-reliance on municipal ownership and a union-dominated services culture, where too much began and ended with the 'Corpy' (as I later learnt the Liverpool local authority was called). We were in the business of giving people a chance to run their own lives, of offering them a stake in society, of putting the unions firmly into a legal framework. Incredible as it may seem today, this all spelt big political trouble.

In both personality and style my Labour predecessor, Peter Shore, was a stark contrast to me. He was essentially a don manqué. His style of management was built upon a daily accumulation of paperwork which he would take home with him in a stack of red boxes to study into the small hours. His intellectual turn of mind would stimulate numerous questions which he would then submit to officials the following morning, leading to yet more piles of paper. It was a process that had its own momentum. The workload was formidable but it hadn't much to do with actually taking decisions. To be fair to him, of course, by then the Labour government had a knife-edge Parliamentary majority and was running out of time altogether. But a senior civil servant in the Department of the Environment in 1979 remarked on the irony of moving from a conservative Labour Secretary of State to a radical Tory one.

Towards the end of my time as a junior minister in the Department in the early 1970s, I had extended an invitation to three of the brightest of the younger officials. John Garlick, Terry Heiser and Ken Barnett came to our then home in Wilton Crescent to join me for lunch. I chose more prophetically than I knew. By the spring of 1979, awaiting my arrival as his new political master was Sir John Garlick, now the permanent secretary of the Department. (And, when I returned to the Department once again in November 1990 in John Major's government, Terry Heiser had, one incumbent later, become permanent secretary. As for Ken Barnett, he missed the top job by only one slot, retiring as a deputy secretary in 1980.)

As a new Cabinet minister, one can normally expect a telephone call from the permanent secretary of one's department, the purpose of which – after the normal exchange of courtesies – is to establish one's intended hour of arrival. The new minister is then likely to be met formally at the entrance to the building by the permanent secretary and escorted to his suite. On his new desk will be a set of files, 'which, Secretary of State, you will find helpful for reading yourself into the present agenda of the Department'. I felt we should start as I meant to go on. I rang the Department and asked if Sir John would be good enough to join me on Monday for lunch at the Connaught Hotel, which (as I have shown) has played a significant part in my life from my earliest days in London. It is one of the world's great hotels and both its Grill and Dining Rooms are renowned.

Over lunch I produced an envelope on which I had written down my own agenda for the Department. I wanted no front-line responsibilities for any departmental activities for myself. Everything would be delegated, not just to the ministers of state, in whom I had total confidence, but also to the parliamentary under-secretaries, although I knew them less well. I told Sir John I would be adopting the practice of morning meetings which Peter Walker had established nine years earlier. I intended only to add the departmental Whip to the invitation list.

I also explained my refusal to see my private office used as a training ground for junior civil servants. The role of the private secretary is key to the life of a minister. An effective private secretary ensures that material coming in to the minister is of high quality, timely and of sufficient importance to warrant attention in an overwhelming work-load. The private secretary also sees to it that ministerial decisions are transmitted to the appropriate officials, and acted upon. But the role is deeper than that: the most valuable private secretary understands the real seats of power and influence within a department. He will point the minister to the best route for advice, irrespective of rank, often ignoring the formal organisation charts. He will advise the minister whose judgement to trust. He will send back material – protecting both minister and departmental officials – which is inadequate. He will tell the minister – privately – when junior ministers seem to be getting out of line or when the Whitehall machine is rumbling dissatisfaction. He or she may even cough apologetically before explaining that the minister is overstepping the mark or overreaching himself.

Ensuring an efficient private office is one of the most important steps for a new minister to take. I had discovered this in 1970 as a parliamentary under-secretary, when I had felt myself used as a training ground for young civil servants in their mid-twenties who had no concept of the role and no understanding of my needs. I had demanded – heretically – a more senior person. The then permanent secretary, Sir David Serpell, was a truly fierce old-style mandarin and was appalled at such upstart behaviour. Conventionally in those days, the permanent secretary left his office only to see the Secretary of State. He would never visit the office of a parliamentary under-secretary. As a new minister, albeit a very junior one, I felt it appropriate that he should visit me to discuss the issue. This resulted in a compromise of which the television series *Yes Minister* would have been proud: we met in the corridor, at the top of the marble staircase, between our respective offices and debated the issue there, to the astonishment – I am told – of passing officials. I succeeded in securing a private secretary at least one rank above my entitlement.

In the light of this experience, therefore, in 1979 I sought and received an assurance that whoever became my private secretary would remain with me in that role until I left the Department. I invited Sir John to select the three or four best candidates of the appropriate grade, so that I could choose for myself. He took all this very well. I picked David Edmonds, a rising departmental star with the touch of steel that makes the best sort of private secretary, and he proved an excellent choice. Indeed, in January 1983, when the Prime Minister asked me to go to the Ministry of Defence, I suggested to David that he come with me. He explained his reasons for refusing over the telephone to Tobago: because the Ministry of Defence was a department new to us both, neither of us would know when I was being carved up by the system. I instantly saw his point.

From the beginning at the DOE, I had a clear agenda for much of our policy responsibilities and I had now established their division and delegation. We were set to go. Having freed myself of any front-line tasks, I intended to concentrate not just on helping my colleagues to drive our policy agenda forward but on probing areas of policy, departmental activities and functions which would normally escape ministerial scrutiny. For many in the Department this was a culture shock. I totally rejected the convention that ministers decide on policy and officials execute and administer. I asked John Garlick what management information he received on his desk every Monday morning to check whether the Department was on track to meet its objectives. On hearing the reply 'None,' at least I knew where we stood.

The incoming government was committed to reducing public expenditure and cutting the number of civil servants. Following a Cabinet discussion, we were all invited to explore manpower reductions in our departments of 2.5, 5 and 7.5 per cent. This I had anticipated. I had come to my Department intending to introduce an effective system of managerial control. The process became known as the Management Information System for Ministers (MINIS). It was designed to give ministers a thorough understanding of what each activity of the Department cost by defining each task in detail and allocating the costs of the civil servants involved. No such system had existed before: civil service running costs had traditionally been based on the previous year's out-turn, with a new bid each successive year for extra cash to meet new needs and to adjust for inflationary cost increases. Control of running costs and manpower was thought to be the task of the permanent secretary, not ministers. MINIS of itself was neutral in its effect on staff numbers. It was for ministers to decide if too much or too little was being spent on any particular task. In some areas, for example local government finance and inner cities, we actually increased staffing and resources in my time at the Department. But, predictably, under this detailed scrutiny very soon the opportunities for economies became apparent.

I was particularly fortunate in having Irwin Bellow (created Lord Bellwin to enable him to be a minister in the House of Lords) within my Department. Irwin was one of the best of the Conservative local government leaders. He had run Leeds with a management grip rarely found among elected councillors. His advice to me was clear: 'There's only one way, Michael,' he said, 'that you will control the numbers in this Department and that is for you to control the recruitment.' And that is what I did. Every week I approved which vacancies were to be filled.

But Irwin's method of manpower control, though a vital start, was essentially crude and I had far too high a respect for the civil servants and for the positive role they can play to let the matter rest there. Emancipated by the freedom that the delegation of responsibilities had given me, I wanted to know exactly what the Department was doing, who had authorised what objectives, how the objectives met the priorities of the new government and so on. There's a naivety about these questions to anyone engaged in the private sector. It was not naivety in the public sector. It was the stuff of revolution. I was treading where no minister had trod before.

The assumption commonly made that ministers determined policy and civil servants carried it out might have worked in the small scale of nineteenth-century bureaucracy. But today's ministries are huge. They have an accumulation of functions and responsibilities, the origins of much of which are lost in time. There is no way in which senior civil servants can know what is happening at all times in every part of the Department over which they preside, except in the most general terms. Most careers advance up specialist ladders. The civil service high-flyers who constitute what used to be known as the administrative class make a virtue of the fact that they are generalists who have served at each stage of advancement in their careers in quite a different field of policy. But, although undoubtedly this process widens their perception and gives them a generalist's perspective on policy administration, what it does not do is to give them a depth of expertise in any of the particular responsibilities they hold at any one time. They are, therefore, dependent upon the advice of others.

In 1979 one of the ways used to compensate for this lack of expertise in some specialist and technical hierarchies was to have parallel streams of technically and professionally qualified officials working alongside the administrative-grade officials – who held most of the key jobs. This led to overlapping responsibilities. One of the smaller reforms I introduced was to insist that the person best qualified for the job was put in charge, irrespective of background.

The major discipline in the MINIS process was the personal involvement by the Secretary of State. Initially, I held meetings, lasting about an hour, with each departmental under-secretary. One of the most difficult early meetings was with an under-secretary, responsible for over 150 staff, who believed he had no personal responsibility for understanding the functions of his directorate. His role was not to manage people or resources; it was to advise ministers on policy issues. I expressed incredulity at his definition. Our meeting was polite but tough. He explained that in large parts of his command he had no idea what people did and the concept of output measurement had never played a part in his career. I explained that it would from that moment on. The word soon travelled around the Department that this was serious. The under-secretaries whose meetings came later in the cycle had already got the message.

Once the system was in place, every year we revisited every part of the Department in order to check progress and reassess objectives. I was present at nearly every review. To the credit of the senior officials, despite their initial hostility they co-operated. The results of this method of control were in fact spectacular. When I took over the Department, it employed some 52,500 people, including the Property Services Agency (PSA). By the time I left three years later the numbers had been reduced to 37,500.

Very little of this was as a result of privatisation or hiving off. Two exceptions were the Hydraulics Research Station based at Crowmarsh in my constituency, which was privatised, and that part of the government estate that had earlier been transferred from the Foreign Office to the PSA. Douglas Hurd, then a junior minister at the Foreign Office, put a powerful case to John Stanley for its return to the FCO. He was much aided by the fact that, whenever ministers travelled overseas and stayed in our embassies or high commissions, they were deluged with complaints, not so much by the ambassadors or high commissioners as by their wives – an altogether more resolute breed. Harrowing tales of ill-matching furniture, threadbare curtains, leaking roofs and backed-up drains proved all too much for harassed ministers, well able to defend themselves on the floor of the House of Commons but no match for the more deadly of the species. With barely concealed enthusiasm, we transferred the FCO's share of the PSA back to them.

The civil service went on to develop (and improve) the MINIS methodology. When I returned to the Department in 1990, after an absence of almost eight years, the system was still in place, although it was now being used by officials and not by ministers. It was certainly detailed, time-consuming, laborious. But I had learnt the hard way, as a businessman in the early 1960s, the dangers of not having critical information. It was one of my great disappointments that none of my colleagues, who had actually worked the system with me, ever took it with them to any other department in which they served, although I introduced it in every department over which I presided.

It was all very nearly quite otherwise. Mrs Thatcher had expressed her approval of the way in which my Department was run. In 1981 she decided that I should be invited to No. 10 to give a presentation of MINIS to my Cabinet colleagues, with the idea that the system would be generally applied throughout Whitehall. I was a relatively junior member of the Cabinet and I came from a very different career background from many of my colleagues. The mere notion of the gathering, although I welcomed it, was probably misconceived. The presentation – in the form of a slide show – duly took place. My colleagues sat in a long row with their permanent secretaries seated behind. (They would, of course, have been briefed beforehand by their officials to resist innovation of this sort at any cost.) They listened with bored indifference to the complexity of the additional workload I was suggesting they undertake.

Disaster struck shortly after I had finished speaking. The Prime Minister turned to John Nott, who was at the time battling with serious cost inflation in defence equipment, and asked him what he thought. He replied, with all too evident exasperation, 'Prime Minister, at the Ministry of Defence I am trying to come to terms with an overspend of billions of pounds. Is it seriously suggested that I should spend my time grubbing around, saving ha'pennies in the way that Michael has described?' This was too much for Mrs Thatcher. Her reaction was immediate, hectoring and abusive, striking at the heart of John's perceived managerial inadequacy.

The row that followed marked the end of any prospect of MINIS being adopted throughout Whitehall. So I attempted instead to extend the system by example. I decided to publish the volumes of information which contained a more detailed account of what was happening in a government department than anyone had ever seen before. Here was open government in spadefuls. My hope was that, if I made the information available, first, it would provide a feast of information for the informed observer and, second, the pressure from outside sources to provide similar information for other departments would prove irresistible. In one material way my expectations were fulfilled. I was summoned before the Treasury and Civil Service Committee of the House of Commons, chaired at the time by Sir Edward du Cann. The Committee had become interested in what I was doing at the Department and examined me closely on the subject. It duly reported with a firm recommendation: 'The Management Information System for Ministers (MINIS), or its clear equivalent, should be adopted in all departments and, as appropriate, in other public-sector bodies.'

The Committee's report led to an anodyne reply from the Cabinet

Office. One of my officials was sent on the rounds to explain the workings of MINIS. Nothing more happened. Despite all the clamour for open government and more information, the national press showed no interest whatsoever in what we were doing. Only one journalist, Tony Bevins, then of *The Times*, took the time to acquire the published information, look through it and make reference to it in his column.

Today management skills, effective resource allocation and output measurements have become a central part of the language surrounding the role of permanent secretaries and other senior officials. I doubt, however, if the underlying quality of information justifies the claims that are made for the still limited changes that have taken place.

The 1979 Conservative election manifesto was not a radical document. I remember the drafting sessions and the caution with which every pledge was treated. Beyond the commitment to return the aircraft and shipbuilding industries to the private sector, which I had already promised in the House in the mid-1970s, and a reference to selling shares in the National Freight Corporation, we said of those industries already nationalised only that we wanted to see them 'running more successfully'. The Right-to-Buy was by far the most radical pledge and, as one of the core promises of the election campaign, the legislation to allow the sale of council houses in our first parliamentary session would inevitably command centre-stage. But John Stanley and I had a wider agenda. We set out to address the problems of the nation's housing across both public and private sectors.

The Right-to-Buy was established in the Housing Act 1980, alongside the first ever statutory Tenants' Charter. We certainly encouraged the option of purchase, made even more attractive by council rents which were then rising above the prevailing level of inflation, but initiative after initiative was also taken to introduce a better deal for those who didn't want to buy or couldn't afford to. By tackling inadequate local authority management, setting out best practice on reletting empty properties, improving physical security and involving tenants in the repair and maintenance of their homes and estates, we expanded the numbers of houses available for use. A new Priority Estates project targeted the worst estates. Tenants were granted the right to repair their own property, and council houses in bad condition were offered to prospective purchasers willing to renovate them. More homes were built for the elderly and disabled, while our hostels initiative raised the number of beds available at the most stressed end of the market by well over 3,000.

The private sector housebuilders were encouraged to experiment with low-cost home ownership in urban areas by pressure on local authorities to sell land and by the targeted use of grant. Owners themselves were given every incentive to improve their own homes with the aid of up to 90 per cent grants for basic amenities. This led to a major public investment in the rundown housing stock. New concepts of ownership were introduced under schemes such as shared owner-ship, a radical concept of part-owning, part-renting; starter homes, pioneered by Lawrie Barratt; and homesteading, adopted from the United States, which saw rundown council properties knocked out at basement prices to young people who would restore them themselves. We reversed the spiral of decay in privately rented accommodation set off by the introduction of rent control and statutory tenancy early in the century. Ours was a comprehensive and radical reforming agenda across a wide housing horizon, even though the political spotlight was sharply focused on the Right-to-Buy.

The sale of council houses to their tenants was deeply contro-versial. Labour councils realised and resented the implications of allowing homeowners to become a significant part of the electorate in their hitherto safe municipal baronies. The proposal was of course extremely attractive, and was designed to be so, to the tenants themselves.

The task of preparing the legislation and steering it through its parliamentary stages fell to John Stanley. As the Bill was drafted, he scrutinised it with great care. However, as a belt-and-braces approach, I asked officials to find the sharpest barrister they could and brief him as though he had been retained by an extreme left-wing council with infinite resources and with an absolute determination to break our proposed legislation. His job was to tell us if and how he could do it. These rather over-dramatised instructions would in all substance be precisely how Labour councils would so instruct their legal advisers. We got there before them. Before long, we received word that our *in extremis* lawyer had, indeed, bust our proposed legislation. But, for the same fee, he had also shown us how to close the loophole.

Once the Housing Act reached the statute book, exactly as we had anticipated, Labour councils used every known device to refuse, or at least delay *sine die*, the negotiations with their by now enthusiastic tenants. It is difficult to make a local authority act speedily if it wishes otherwise. Tenants found it hard to get answers to letters, the valuations were slow in coming, surveys were delayed. John Stanley demanded monthly returns indicating the number of applications to buy and the stage that each transaction had reached. The files in the Department became so voluminous and heavy that they had to be wheeled into and out of his office on a trolley for their regular inspection and monitoring.

John understandably became more frustrated as each week passed. Michael Havers, the Attorney General, was closely involved. There was no hint of division between the three of us about the need to act with rigour; but, just as I had felt about the drafting of the legislation itself, so I felt about the implementation of our new default powers. We just did not dare to lose in the courts. If we had, every Labour council in the country would have followed suit. John especially was under growing pressure to act against first one Labour authority, then another, from colleagues in the House, who were in turn being besieged by frustrated tenants. But still we waited. We did not authorise the use of the default powers until Michael Havers advised us that he thought the evidence against one particular authority, Norwich, gave us an overwhelming chance of success. We had been right to wait. When we finally went to court, we won hands down, although we had to fight the matter through to the Court of Appeal.

The political consequences that flowed from the success of this policy were epoch-making. Giving council tenants the right to buy their houses and flats was an exercise in mass compulsory conveyancing that had never been attempted anywhere else in the world before. For the vast majority of tenants who purchased, it was the deal of a lifetime. In the 1987 election campaign I met owners in the South-east who had actually seen their equity increase by £10,000 a year, free of tax, for every year of their ownership. By December 1998 a million and a half families had become owners, providing them with a personal stake in society and an inheritance for their children and bringing about a quiet revolution within the ranks of Britain's property-owning classes. The psychology of this struck a hammer blow at the traditional politics of 'them and us'. We had begun to break up the monolithic local authority estates and to create a less polarised society.

Over the same eighteen years, the sale of council homes brought a total of £24 billion in capital receipts to local authorities in England, much of which was ploughed back into improving the nation's

housing stock. Truly the sale of the century. One of the earliest bene-
ficiaries of this flood of cash was the state of the public finances in the
early 1980s, where central government expenditure was overrunning
forecasts. Local government expenditure, however, was in substantial
surplus, more than balancing Chancellor Geoffrey Howe's Exchequer
books. It drove the government to look with greater ambition at some
of its other activities. It encouraged us to take the decisions that,
beginning with Keith Joseph's plans to privatise what was to become
British Telecom on which he began work in 1979, were to transform
the country's economy in the late 1980s and in the 1990s by returning
– or introducing for the first time – the commanding heights of the
economy to the rigours of the market place.

If ever a policy had been responsible for the dilapidation of much
of our housing stock, it was rent control. Large portions of urban
Britain were simply rotting. Our manifesto had committed us to a
new system of shorthold tenure. Behind the rather dry rhetoric, what
we were promising was the most ambitious reversal of the decline of
the private rented sector since the introduction of rent control earlier
in the century.

Our first change was to introduce 'controlled' rents, whereby the
minuscule rents dating back to First World War rent controls which
had done so much to create the urban slums were replaced by more
realistic rents under the guidance of the local authority.

Next we brought in our promised shortholds. We would have liked
to allow market rents to prevail but, in the hope that we could
persuade the Labour Opposition to accept our proposals, we built
in a concept of 'fair rents', which we adopted from arrangements
passed into law by Harold Wilson's Labour government in the 1960s.
We wanted landlords to be able to let their properties at market
rents for a fixed term under a shorthold lease. At the expiry of
that term and with appropriate notice, the landlord would become
entitled to vacant possession.

There was one immense problem. We could design a lease with
reasonable protections for landlord and tenant. But the Opposition
could easily impose a political veto. All they had to say was that
on election they would restore the old rights of tenure to tenants.
So I invited Roy Hattersley, the Shadow spokesman, to a private
meeting in my office to see if we could reach accord. I offered to
discuss any reasonable safeguard for tenants, but explained that, if

landlords were to be persuaded to let, it would only be by offering them a fixed-term arrangement with the possibility of vacant possession at the end of it. There was, however, no meeting of minds.

We proceeded to legislate anyway but, precisely as we had feared, Labour, in the form of Gerald Kaufman, promised that when they returned to power they would grant security to any shortholder in possession. In the event the consequences were not as dire as we had feared. When our legislation reached the statute books, we still had some years to go before the next election. Landlords opted for the one-year tenancy and the market that emerged heralded the beginnings of a new, healthy, private rented sector in this country for the first time since the First World War. As was to become the familiar pattern, the Labour Party, faced with the evident success of the policy, lifted their veto after the 1983 election.

We also introduced the idea of assured tenancy, to encourage a new market in homes built for rent. Again, this was a first. Landlords were able to let at market rents, offering prospective tenants fixed-term leases. My own experience of letting in the commercial market in the 1950s guided our instructions to officials that the legislation should lay down reasonable terms governing the rights of both landlord and tenant. In essence the package was security of tenure – except on prescribed grounds – in newly built property at market rents. The Labour Party did not resist this proposition, as it added to the housing stock and the tenants enjoyed substantial protection.

These reforms and the later adjustments to them revived the private rented sector in this country, boosting the flexibility of the economy, giving people greater choice and improving the housing stock itself.

I did not see eye to eye with some of my colleagues – particularly John Wheeler and Brandon Rhys Williams, who represented constituents living north of Hyde Park – over the proposals for leasehold enfranchisement. Fred Willey, Minister of State for Housing in Harold Wilson's second Labour government, had introduced leasehold enfranchisement in the Leasehold Reform Act of 1967. Originally, this was aimed at homes of low rateable value in South Wales, but my Conservative colleagues on the standing committee at the time had pressed for and achieved a raising of the enfranchisement ceiling. This meant that occupants of many expensive short-lease London properties could acquire their freehold at effectively confiscatory terms. I could see absolutely no case for legislating to enable one group of relatively rich people to gain at the expense of another group of relatively rich people. I refused to extend the enfranchisement arrangements in the 1980 Act. However, on my return to the Department in 1991 I did agree enfranchisement for high-value housing. There was no intellectual argument for enfranchising houses and not flats and so, under continued pressure from the colleagues from north of Hyde Park, we went on to give a commitment in the 1992 manifesto to enfranchise leases of flats. But I agreed only on the basis that the terms of enfranchisement would ensure that freeholders received the proper value.

It so happened that I myself was in the position of a leaseholder and I later negotiated the acquisition of the freehold of my London home (no longer 24 Wilton Crescent, the lease of which I sold to enable me to buy Thenford, but a house in Chapel Street off Belgrave Square). I was able to satisfy myself – the hard way – that landlords faced with enfranchisement arrangements at least knew that they would be treated equitably.

Our housing reforms were to become an essential part of our wider policies to rebuild our inner cities. So was new home building. The Volume Housebuilders, representing such companies as Barratts, Wimpeys and Christian Salvesen, used to lunch regularly in a central London hotel. At one such lunch, at the Ritz, to which I was invited, their spokesman, Tom Baron of Christian Salvesen, clearly dominated the conversation. A wiry terrier of a man, he threw out ideas like sparks from a firework. He was voluble, argumentative, amusing and one of those characters who are irrepressible in their enthusiasm. There was only one thing for it. I put it to him that, if he knew so much about what government should be doing, why didn't he come and work for me and show us how. It was one of the few occasions in my excellent relationship with him when I actually remember him silent for a moment.

But to my delight he obtained leave of absence and joined the Department as a special adviser. The day he joined I told him that – to be fair to him and everyone else – we needed to decide there and then when he would leave. It would save any future embarrassment. We agreed on six months. He was the first of the special advisers that I brought into government and was a great success. He was followed by Ed Berman, whom I met in an inner-city business and training centre, but I was reshuffled before any very positive results could flow from this appointment. (Special advisers should be expert in a particular field, concentrate on policy relevant to that expertise and work with civil servants rather than with the minister, but with open access to the minister. The special adviser is quite distinct from the political adviser, who is based near to the minister's private office and works closely with the party as well as the department.)

Tom's arrival had coincided with the establishment of the London Docklands Development Corporation (LDDC). (I shall come later to the problems of securing the necessary legislation for this.) He persuaded the Volume Housebuilders to build 2,000 new houses a year for sale in the East End, where there had been virtually nothing built for sale since the end of the Second World War. It was a watershed. The housebuilders moved into alien, Labour-controlled political territory with considerable courage and thus began its transformation from the desolate open spaces and the dreary council estates into the balanced and vibrant community that has now emerged.

The figures speak for themselves. The LDDC's last Report following its demise in March 1998 revealed that the year 2000 would find 100,000 people working in Docklands, many of them in Canary Wharf, which offers some of the finest office space in Europe. Another 100,000 live in the area, many in the 24,000 new homes built there since the start of the 1980s. The LDDC was determined to help local people to own their homes. One of the first new estates, at Beckton, contained over 600 mainly two- or three-bedroom houses with gardens and priced at under £28,000. The Corporation continued to require affordable housing on its land wherever practical. Furthermore first-class communications now give quick access to the motorway network, while the Jubilee Line and the Docklands Light Railway provide a rapid public transport link with the rest of London. The area has its own airport, a major conference centre and the Docklands campus of the University of East London. A clear indication of a world changed beyond recognition is that in 1981 only 25 per cent of 15–16-year-olds stayed on in school; today 75 per cent stay on. (Curiously enough, the last chairman of the LDDC was Sir Michael Pickard, whom I had first met on holiday in Madeira in the early 1960s and who had sat for a time on the Haymarket Board as a director of the British Printing Corporation.)

But new commercial development and the houses of the property-owning democracy were largely still being built on the green fields of suburbia. The small businessman or woman, wanting to expand, would not normally look to convert some dank and clammy archway under a railway bridge, as the more romantic of right-wing theorists wanted us to believe. Instead, he or she would go for a modern industrial or science park, preferably close to a newly built estate of pleasant family houses. The more successful they were, the higher the standards they expected. Not unnaturally, their employees wanted those standards too.

Those who remained in deprived urban areas tended to be the unskilled, the elderly, the dependent, those least able to look after themselves. All too often, local authorities were faced with many problem families, the difficult-to-house cases, the anti-social neighbours. Every Member of Parliament is familiar with the problems. The authorities tended to group these people on to the same estates, thus intensifying the pressures on those who could afford to move out, to do so. To exacerbate the problem, rent control had destroyed the availability of late-Victorian and early-Edwardian houses for rent.

We turned our attention to the redevelopment of unused, often derelict – brownfield – sites. The cost of clearing the detritus of history was often too high to allow any profit on redevelopment, and certainly was far more expensive than new building on the green fields. We made public money available to pay for this negative value. Today public policy remains much as we created it. It may not be possible to avoid all greenfield development, but every effort should be made to contain it.

Tom King looked after our relations with local government, urban policy, the water industry and the environment. For local government the election of the Conservatives brought reality to the phrase, 'the party's over', coined originally by the late Tony Crosland when, as a predecessor of mine as Secretary of State for the Environment, he had attempted to get a grip on its expenditure. Our manifesto at the general election had wisely put reform of the rates as a lower priority than tax reductions: 'cutting income tax must take priority for the time being over abolition of the domestic rating system'. Thus we also admitted that we had no idea how to replace the rates. But the tax cuts had to be paid for and, among other economies, the Cabinet wanted a 3 per cent reduction in local government expenditure. After knee-jerk protest the leaders of the local government associations agreed. 'We always deliver central government targets,' they told us. We accepted their commitment at face value. But the targets they were used to meeting had always been at increased levels of expenditure. We were too easily assured.

Seeking cuts in local government was far from the concerted strategy it seemed. Every year the ritual was embodied in the annual public expenditure review. The Cabinet received a paper from the Treasury in the early summer setting out its expenditure targets for the forthcoming financial year. Cabinet was persuaded to sign up to a global total. The Chief Secretary then got to work to fit individual spending ministers into the preordained pot. Heart-rending, even blood-curdling, accounts of the inevitable consequences were fed to ever ravenous specialist journalists to underpin each minister's resistance. The Department of the Environment was the jam in the sandwich. The Treasury had won the battle for global cuts. The DOE had to whip each local authority into line, while the Department of Education, the Home Office, the Ministry of Transport and other spending departments used every wile to ensure that their local programmes remained intact.

Our colleagues, who controlled so much of local government, certainly didn't like our request for a 3 per cent reduction in their expenditure. However, the great and the good in the Conservative local government hierarchy – Sir Gervas Walker of the Association of County Councils, Sir John Grugeon of the Association of County Councils, Sir Godfrey (Tag) Taylor of the Association of Metropolitan Authorities, Peter Bowness of both the London Boroughs Association and the Association of Metropolitan Authorities, Ian McCallum of the Association of District Councils, and many others – had all fought to elect a Tory government and, if that was the name of the game, so be it. What was left of the Labour Party in local government, under the leadership of Jack Smart of Wakefield, protested with vigour but again pointed to the record of compliance.

What they never took on board was that we wanted a reduction of 3 per cent in their *current* 1979–80 budgets. The financial year had already begun, contracts had been signed, people employed. We wanted cuts in actual spending levels, something few councils had any experience of delivering. Effective management, private sector competition, delivering the same – even better – services with less expenditure all belonged to an unimaginable world. Their officials, every local and national pressure group and much of the media shouted 'amen' to their complaints.

We persevered. The battles were fought trench by trench. By 1983 we had exerted such pressure over local authorities that the numbers employed – which had been rising for decades – had fallen back to levels last seen in 1974. To this must be added Geoffrey Howe's success in reducing inflation from a rising 10 per cent in 1979 to 3.7 per cent in May and June 1983, the lowest rate since 1968. The annual rates bills were no longer a centre of attention.

But the battle with local government was not an easy struggle. It was a battle of attrition. We had few weapons and a resourceful opponent. To any but the professionals the system was shrouded in the mystique of local government finance. Simply put, central government set the level of expenditure it believed local government should spend. By formula these global figures were allocated to each authority according to its 'needs'. (For the cognoscenti, the process by which some of these needs were determined was known as 'multiple regression analysis' – not a formulation for the faint-hearted.) From this resulting figure was deducted a calculation of the amount that the authority could be expected to raise from its own 'resources', that is largely local property taxes. The difference was handed over by way of central government grant.

Of course, the process was pregnant with controversy at every stage. Each authority claimed that its needs were understated and its resources over-calculated. In any case, Labour authorities in particular made things worse by over-spending. We tried to simplify the system by which taxpayers' money was allocated to each authority, by breaking down the allocation process into more clearly understandable categories and figures.

We calculated service by service what an authority needed to spend to deliver a standard level of service. Anyone could understand so much per head for the police service, per child for education, per home for refuse collection. We then deducted what we calculated each authority could raise from the rates and local charges. The difference we paid as grant. It all seemed so rational. In practice, it simply changed the rules of engagement. The battle remained the same. It did, however, give us a weapon in that we were able to suggest how much an authority needed to spend to deliver an adequate level of services. It was one short step from here to targets and another to capping.

The capping debate was led by the Treasury. I was a sceptic; Michael Havers insisted that no system would stand the scrutiny of the courts. Imposing enforceable targets on all or large numbers of authorities would provide a field day for lawyers. A successful challenge by one authority would open a floodgate for the others. In the end Mrs Thatcher prevailed and, after I had moved to the Ministry of Defence in January 1983, a capping commitment was agreed for the 1983 manifesto and introduced in 1984. But it was only ever used in that form on a limited number of the worst-offending authorities.

In our Cabinet discussions I had argued that we should leave authorities the discretion to spend above our targets but only after offering themselves for re-election. My colleagues favoured a local referendum, an idea which I failed to sell to the parliamentary party. The inherent flaw in their idea was that, if a controlling group conducted a referendum and lost, they remained in power and would create mayhem at the government's expense over any cuts they were forced to introduce. Anyway, the backbenchers wouldn't wear it. We had to content ourselves with the abolition of authorities' ability to levy a supplementary rate to meet excess expenditure.

My personal instinct was – and remains – to grant local government considerable freedom to initiate policies and experiment between different ways of delivering services. I like the idea of enabling authorities. Their responsibility should be to make sure that services of quality are delivered, rather than providing them themselves. They will usually be well advised to buy in these services, their quality defined contractually, from outside providers after competitive tendering. It is a question of political philosophy. Is local government to be more an agent than an initiator, carrying out the wishes of an all-powerful central government? Or should it be seen as relatively free to pursue a local agenda, devised by local councillors responsible to a local electorate? I believe we are an over-centralised society with decision-making too tightly controlled by Whitehall.

Tom King and I made a notable breakthrough in this direction in the early days of government by setting local authorities free to move funds from one budget item to another, irrespective of the wishes of central departments, and allowing them to spend half of their capital receipts from council-house sales and as much as they liked of other capital receipts on any capital purpose. After I had left the Department, these figures were progressively lowered so that by 1985–6 the proportion of housing capital receipts available for investment had been reduced to 20 per cent – much to my dismay.

There were, and remain, many – including councillors – who believed in or exploited the myth that pre-1979 local government enjoyed an exhilarating freedom to do its own thing. The more we explored the workings of Whitehall and its relations with local authorities, the more fanciful the notion became. Detailed control over local government was in practice widespread. I once instructed officials to pin up on my wall all the forms required by the Department's housing division before a local housing authority could lay a single brick. Houses not only had to conform to Parker Morris standards, eighty questions had to be answered in meticulous detail before the Department would authorise any building. The size of the room, the pitch of the roof, the colour of the slate, the texture of the brick: all were under Whitehall control, underpinning the reality of centralisation in a way quite unappreciated by councillors or ministers. The same pattern existed across Whitehall.

There were other levers. Just cast a glance at the surge of expenditure that takes place in the month or two before each financial year's end. Any underspend in a department's budget might be seen to prove the case for Treasury cuts. Thus, as the year end approaches, officials search out potential underspend. The telephone calls begin. The regional offices get to work. No experienced local officials are going to quarrel lightly with civil servants in their sponsoring department when, once every twelve months, it may have goodies to dispense. This is the real world of central power. It has one awful, conformist consequence. What should be the very essence of local autonomy – freedom, experimentation, excitement, competitive achievement – is snuffed out by these deadening processes. Yet it doesn't suit anybody to reveal how it works, let alone complain about its consequences.

It was this culture that Tom, John and I set out to challenge and reverse. Much of the suffocating detail, particularly within our Department, was scrapped. The Parker Morris housing controls went. The detailed forms were dramatically reduced. Our Urban Programme came increasingly to rely on local initiative and public–private partnerships, which ultimately led in the early 1990s to City Challenge and later Michael Howard's City Pride.

With increased freedom we demanded increased accountability. Authorities now had to publish much fuller information about the costs and quality of their services. Their Direct Labour Organisations (DLOs) were to keep proper accounts and to be opened up to competition from the private sector. Their land, classified as unused or derelict, had to be placed on a register so that the private sector and councillors were made aware of the hidden resources tucked away, unused and unexploited. We were accused of excessive centralism. We were simply ensuring that local people were properly informed about the councils they elected.

But the most ambitious innovation of them all came in 1982 with the establishment of the Audit Commission, charged with auditing local authority accounts. Private sector auditors were appointed to enhance the experience of the District Audit staff, which the Commission absorbed. A wealth of comparative information, benchmarking the cost and quality of each service that authorities provided, was published. I tried to achieve this reform in 1979. It was the only serious battle that I lost in those first six months of government. Incomprehensibly, it was resisted on behalf of the Treasury by Nigel Lawson (then Financial Secretary), who argued that he was waiting for some obscure report. I won in the second year. I invited John Banham, a partner at McKinsey and Co., to be its first Controller. Authority by authority, service by service, for the first time it was possible to compare individual councils and their performance. The work of the Audit Commission continues to this day and, with its value-for-money audits, it is able to identify potential savings if best practice is adopted. In the six years to the end of October 1998, for example, such savings could have amounted to £443 million, of which £219 million were actually achieved.

In 1979 we faced the worst of all worlds. Inflation was rising fast; government was cutting the percentage of central taxpayers' grant support to local authorities, which were in turn actually increasing their budgets. The outcry from ratepayers was intense, particularly in Labour areas, where many of the Labour voters were protected by social security subsidies of one form or another, leaving more prosperous Conservative voters at the mercy of their political opponents. Widows living alone in large family houses were the most exposed of all.

But by the end of 1982, with the downward pressure on expenditure, increased income from higher council house rents and a big reduction in inflation, the issue of the rates had begun to fade from public concern and we had effectively rejected the option of abolition. There is no such thing as a popular tax, however, and for most people it remained true that the annual rates bill was one of the highest bills they received. The more visible the tax, the more unpopular it is likely to be.

It was always easier to define the problem than find a solution. Peter

Walker had looked at the issue comprehensively in the early 1970s, when I was his junior minister, and had concluded then that there were no easy or attractive alternatives. Mrs Thatcher complained that she had been bounced by Ted Heath when, as Shadow Secretary of State for the Environment in the run-up to the second election of 1974, she committed the party to abolishing the rating system. But she produced no alternative. I took over responsibility for this portfolio in 1976. Still no alternative had been identified. Nor had I produced one by 1979. Indeed, I was under no pressure to do so. Our 1979 manifesto drew back from the October 1974 commitment. We concentrated on the altogether more straightforward issue of reducing income tax.

Immediately after the 1979 election officials in the DOE raised with me the need for a reassessment of the property valuations upon which the rating system rested. I think it was Iain Macleod who once said that no government that carried out a rating revaluation had ever been re-elected. But intellectually the need to revalue was self-evident. The last revaluation had taken place in 1973 and house prices had doubled since then. To tidy bureaucratic minds it was time for an update. But I was doubtful. I went to see Mrs Thatcher. Her response was immediate and simple. 'We're not doing it, Michael,' she said. I was much relieved and returned to my Department to face down the civil servants. My colleague in the Scottish Office, George Younger, took powers to delay the mandatory review in Scotland for two years. Tom King and I turned our attention to the long-term future of the rates.

A local income tax – arguably the most coherent of options – would simply mean that, as we lowered income tax nationally, local Labour authorities would push up the tax locally. Local sales taxes made little sense in the tight geography of this country, where local boundaries are not readily identifiable and where, in any case, the worst effects would be felt by local businesses, already indignant about the burden of the business rates. A poll tax had attractions in that it would ensure that voters identified much more clearly the consequences of voting for high-spending – invariably Labour – authorities, and it would also reflect the number of occupants enjoying local services in a given property. But it would be difficult to collect and quite impossible to persuade a fair-minded electorate that the richest and the poorest alike should pay the same towards what was effectively a local tax system. Each alternative we examined had its merits and demerits. Every conceivable idea was explored, including the option of transferring the cost of a major service, education, to the national taxpayer, which would have seriously lowered the bills but would also have reduced the responsibilities of local authorities.

Tom and I saw virtually every member of the parliamentary party. There was a blocking minority against each option. We concluded that the real villain in the rating system was not the rates themselves but inflation. If ordinary people knew approximately what their bill was likely to be from year to year and increases were small, there was little trouble. A discount to reflect single-person occupation could answer the most frequently voiced criticism of single people and particularly widows living alone. Our Green Paper, published in December 1981, concluded: 'Probably none of the possible new sources of local revenue could be used on its own as a complete replacement for domestic rates.' The debate went to the Cabinet itself. The outcome was a decision to leave the rating system in place. The question was reviewed again by Willie Whitelaw, who stood by our judgement to leave well alone. It was the right decision, as the ensuing election campaign proved. After the election, however, Mrs Thatcher – faced anew with the prospect of revaluations – instructed Patrick Jenkin to re-examine the issue. But it was her agreement that George Younger should conduct a revaluation in Scotland that led, on publication of the figures, to an explosion of protest there, and to all the devastating consequences that were to follow when the poll tax was introduced.

But I must step back. The defeat of inflation had been achieved at a heavy price. Unemployment had soared to levels reminiscent of the 1930s. The repercussions were at their most acute in Britain's impoverished inner cities and in the overspill communities created by slum clearances. There was widespread debate and growing concern, but no one in government foresaw the ferocity of what was to happen in the summer of 1981.

Chapter 12

'It Took a Riot'

Peter Shore, my predecessor at the Department of the Environment, had seen how important it was to help those living in the worst urban areas. He had extracted from the Treasury some £47 million for an Urban Programme which was distributed to the most hard-pressed authorities as a top-up to their existing housing, transport, education and environmental programmes.

I accepted that it was possible to prop up these communities by increasing the flow of public money, but that didn't address the fundamental issue of concentrated poverty. We needed to attack the root causes of the problem. The teenagers with the skills, the young would-be homeowners, the aspiring entrepreneurs, the strong, all those with the resources to choose, had to be persuaded to stay – even to come back, live and invest – close to the areas of deprivation. It was necessary to tackle the infrastructure problems, to improve dramatically the quality of the public services and to create an environment to persuade people that it was in their own interests to live and work there. In other words, one had to 'enable' these communities to compete for their place in the sun.

Peter had established partnership committees, each chaired by a minister, to monitor his initiative towards deprived areas. He chaired the Liverpool partnership himself. I took it over. I told the local authorities there that they would still receive the Urban Grant but that a condition of this from now on would be that they would have to discuss the use they made of the money with the local Chamber of Commerce, as representative of the private sector. I cannot pretend that I regarded the Chamber of Commerce as the ideal vehicle, but it was the only vehicle available.

It was a culture shift and was to have profound effects. This early initiative moved rapidly to the next stage. We encouraged local authorities to approach the private sector to determine what they might add by way of private expenditure if Urban Grant led the way. The private housebuilders offered to build houses for sale on land cleared at public expense. The concept of gearing emerged, enabling us to attract additional private money as a consequence of the public grant itself.

The focus even of my early time in Liverpool was naturally the city itself. But my activities spread well outside the city boundaries. During a visit to the Pilkington glass company in St Helen's not long after the 1979 election, I first met Bill Humphrey, a senior manager at the firm who had established an enterprise agency. Operating, by design, from a backstairs, rundown office, owned and financed by that great paternalistic and international company, he offered advice to local people on how to create new small businesses in a bid to counter the rising level of local unemployment – much of it caused by Pilkington's own battle for survival. Drawing on information from the local authority and local employers, he could identify vacant premises with appropriate planning permission, set up the basic books of account and provide the necessary encouragement to give confidence to those starting out on their own for the first time.

There were similar experiments elsewhere. We determined to encourage their spread nationwide. Tom King organised a conference at Sunningdale which led to the founding in 1981 with thirty member companies of Business in the Community. Sir Alastair Pilkington became chairman and David Sieff deputy chairman. We seconded Tony Pelling, a civil servant in the Department, to act as chief executive. Creating a partnership of business, central and local government, voluntary bodies and trade unions, it began to set up a network of enterprise agencies and reached its first target of establishing one in every substantial town within two years. From there it has grown and over the years has played a vital role in creating many, many thousands of new businesses and jobs.

Another national organisation which has flourished after an early initiative of the time is Groundwork. It was first conceived to bring together volunteers to tackle that awful urban fringe of post-industrial blight – litter-strewn streets, neglected fields despoiled by overuse, a general seediness – which so often characterises the frontier between town and country. I went off with enthusiasm to the original presentation, was horrified by the top-heavy paid 'volunteers' that it was

Tory candidate for the
safe Labour seat of
Gower in 1959 –
not many voters
responded either. I
was, in fact, not hitch-
hiking but trying to
demonstrate what the
Government had done
for South Wales by
building a modern
steelworks

Campaigning in
Coventry North in
1964. Desperate for
publicity!

I married Anne Williams at Holy Trinity, Brompton, on 31 August 1962

Apprentice to the publishing trade: early days of *About Town* (soon to be simply *Town*)

(BELOW) Pond Lodge on the Earl of Suffolk's estate in Wiltshire. Our first country home, an idyllic bolt-hole, an escape from financial pressures and our first garden. To clear the ground, we knocked down thirteen sheds

The family man. In the garden of our London home at Chepstow Villas in 1967.
Annabel stands on her own two feet, I hold Alexandra, while Rupert is in his
mother's arms

Ted Heath, as Leader of the Opposition, visits the Haymarket stand at a magazine exhibition in 1967. I seem already to have developed a talent for looking straight at the camera

Meeting Zhou Enlai on my first visit to China in 1973, joining Peter Walker on a successful trade delegation there. It was a country that I was eventually to get to know well

Showing HM the Queen
over Concorde. Behind
me is Sir George Edwards,
chairman of the British
Aircraft Corporation

The *Sunday Times*
reconstruction of the Mace
incident of May 1976. A
defiant gesture against a
Labour rabble – but not
everyone saw it that way

Arriving at the House of Commons with Anne the day after the incident with the Mace, 1976

(BELOW) Thenford House, the dream home we finally moved into in 1977

proposed our grant should finance and exchanged a few sharp words. The proposals were substantially revised and the first Groundwork Trust was established on Merseyside in 1981. My old friend from the House of Commons, Christopher Chataway, was to be a future chairman of the national Foundation, and today there are forty-three such trusts in England, Wales and Northern Ireland, and helping with regeneration of urban fringes remains a key part of its work. But it has also expanded into areas such as crime prevention among young people, environmental programmes in schools, green job creation and assistance with environmental impact assessment for companies large and small.

Within a mile of Liverpool's city centre were a thousand acres of decaying, toxic waste, dumped over the decades to fester as a monument to the pollution of a bygone day and occupying a great waterfront site with no prospect of regeneration. It was, incidentally, within a mile of Toxteth, with its alienated population and high unemployment. Add to the mounds of waste the rotting warehouses of a port industry apparently in terminal decline, the great architectural triumph of the Albert Docks an empty ruin then threatened with demolition, and you get the feel of Liverpool's prospects at that time – as bleak as a winter's day. 'You can't go in there, sir,' they said, as I peered through the rotting doorways of the old Dock Traffic Office. 'It's too dangerous. It's not safe.' (It's now the Liverpool headquarters of Granada Television.)

I have already described my first involvement with the concept of an Urban Development Corporation while I was serving in the Department of the Environment under Peter Walker in the early 1970s. I had been appalled at the nondescript, piecemeal development of the South Bank of the Thames and I had asked officials to explore the concept of a development corporation to take responsibility for land assembly and planning.

Later, as Minister for Aerospace with responsibility for the third London airport project on the Foulness mudflats off the Essex coast, I had found myself in a small plane, heading in that direction by way of London's East End. My indignation at what was happening on the South Bank was as nothing compared to my reaction to the immense tracts of dereliction I now observed. The rotting docks – long since abandoned for the deep-water harbours able to take modern container ships downstream – the crumbling infrastructure that had once supported their thriving industry and vast expanses of polluted land left behind by modern technology and enhanced environmentalism. The place was a tip: 6,000 acres of forgotten wasteland. But this was not the responsibility of the Department of Trade and Industry where I was then based. Anyway, we were defeated in 1974 and life moved on.

It was not until 1979 that I remembered the coincidence of these two experiences. The concept of an Urban Development Corporation (UDC) was on the envelope I had given to my new permanent secretary, Sir John Garlick. I inquired about the whereabouts of the earlier work that Ron Brain and I had undertaken. To my surprise, they dug out the proposals, but much of the official advice was strongly opposed to such an assault on the powers of local government. Every manner of argument was paraded against my conviction that little was likely to happen without the dynamic and resource of government action coupled with private sector commitment. What was obviously intended as the quietus to my plans was delivered when I was warned that, as I proposed only to use the powers I envisaged in London, that would mean that the legislation would be categorised as 'hybrid'. That, it was carefully explained to me (overlooking my experience on the Aircraft and Shipbuilding Industries Bill), was because I was not seeking to take general powers enabling Parliament to designate sites generally throughout England and Wales; instead I was proposing to use only London as a laboratory for my scheme. Reinforced by my observations in a trip over the East End in a helicopter with John Stanley, I was determined to fight on.

I asked officials what was the second worst area of urban dereliction after London's East End. The reply was unequivocal: the banks of the Mersey as it ran through Liverpool. I decided then and there that we should take general powers and designate two specific sites for the first experiment. I had won the initial skirmish. All that was left was to obtain the consent of ministerial colleagues. Officials in the Treasury and the Department of Industry were opposed and went to work on Geoffrey Howe and Keith Joseph. It fell to Margaret Thatcher to sort out the impasse. The three of us were summoned to No. 10. I was deeply concerned at this confrontation. I could see no easy way in which my bid for such powers and the money to exercise them could succeed against the combined opposition of two of the most powerful colleagues in government.

In advance of the meeting I consulted Reg Prentice, the new Tory Member for Daventry and Minister of State in the Department of

Health and Social Security who had formerly represented East Ham as a Labour MP for twenty years. He understood my dilemma, and came up with an inspired idea for solving it. 'Tell the PM they're all communists down there,' he suggested.

The evening arrived and the four of us sat together at No. 10. Keith explained that this was not an interventionist government and that the market should be allowed to take its course without us sending so misleading a signal about the nature of our policies. Geoffrey argued that my scheme would lead to enhanced demands for public expenditure. My turn came. I expressed great support for the rigour of their arguments, pledged total commitment to the government's economic strategy, offered to keep the expenditure within my existing budget and moved to my final point. 'If we don't act as I propose, nothing will happen. The land is in public ownership, much of it is polluted and the whole place is in thrall to extreme left-wing councils that Reg Prentice tells me are almost certainly controlled by the communists.' I had lit the blue touch paper. The rocket took off. I won. The Urban Development Corporations, which were to change the face of great stretches of inner-city Britain, were born. I had begun the process of reviving the inner cities from which the New Towns built in the post-war years had attracted so many people and so much economic activity.

Our plans to set up the first UDCs met further resistance from a predictable quarter: the local authorities. I didn't blame them. Their cosy monopolies and the assumption of inevitable decline to which they had become accustomed were to suffer a profound shock. In London I had originally identified land to be designated in seven boroughs, including two on the South Bank at Greenwich and Lewisham. In the event I settled for 5,500 acres, largely to the north of the river. The Greenwich site was to remain untouched for another fifteen years, until as Deputy Prime Minister I negotiated its transfer to English Partnerships as home for the Millennium Dome.

Vociferous opposition also greeted my proposals to take over 1,000 acres along the Mersey and to establish a second UDC in Liverpool. Unbelievable as it may now seem, the Conservatives had won control of Merseyside County Council. It was led by Sir Kenneth Thompson, a former Tory junior minister and until 1964 MP for Liverpool Walton, and he and his colleagues had been developing plans to make the regeneration of the Mersey waterfront their major initiative. Who could fail to understand their frustration when the focus of their plans was whisked away, so to speak, under their very noses. My decision was right in that it brought both money and executive coherence to the project, but that was not the way it seemed to the Council. They had already instructed Dr Richard Foster, the new local director of museums, to look for a site near the river for a major maritime museum and in 1980 the first tentative exhibition attracted over 60,000 people to the former Pilotage Building on Mann Island. This encouraging start was the foundation on which the argument for a much larger project was based. We incorporated this into the UDC plans for the Albert Dock.

The leader of Liverpool District Council, when we launched the UDC, was a former national president of the Liberal Party, Sir Trevor Jones (widely known in his own party as 'Jones the Vote', in recognition of his success in running various Liberal by-election campaigns). He was not popular among most local Conservatives, with whom he had inevitably crossed swords in the past, but he became a significant source of strength and support to me.

As with our approach to housing, itself a vital part of our urban programme, Tom King and I comprehensively reviewed policy towards urban areas and began to set it within an essentially Tory philosophy. We had seen the large-scale hoarding of land in the hands of the public sector. We acted to ensure the publication of 365 registers listing all sites of any size that could be available for alternative use. Derelict Land Grant that Peter Walker had introduced in the early 1970s to attack rural dereliction – chiefly the product of coal and mineral extraction – was classified more widely as available for use in the reclamation of derelict urban sites. Expenditure on such clearance rose from £22 million in 1979 to nearly £60 million by 1982. Geoffrey Howe's Enterprise Zones were established to attract investment to areas of acute unemployment. The Urban Programme we inherited from Peter Shore was changed in emphasis and scale and was extended to some forty authorities.

Thus, by the spring of 1981, our commitment to urban regeneration was set. The Urban Development Corporations were up and running in London – under the leadership of Nigel Broackes, the chairman of Trafalgar House, with Bob Mellish, the former Labour Minister of Housing and government Chief Whip, as deputy chairman – and in Liverpool – under the chairmanship of Leslie Young, the chairman of J. Bibby and Sons, with Sir Kenneth Thompson, my initial opponent, as deputy chairman. The membership of the UDC boards had been carefully chosen to balance the need for private, entrepreneurial experience with the legitimate interests of local government. It had taken a Tory government to begin to tackle the worst areas of urban decay. The council tenants were buying their homes, the Volume Housebuilders were starting to build private sector homes in the inner cities. The building societies, encouraged by Clive Thornton of the Abbey National, were changing their approach to red-lining – a process whereby mortgages had simply not been available in certain areas red-lined on their maps. It requires no imagination to understand what sort of areas these were, but without mortgages the local inhabitants had little prospect of any reversal of their predicament. Slowly but steadily the culture of the enterprise system was being forcibly injected into the attitudes of local government towards the spending of public money. The policies were right, the philosophy essentially Tory.

Then the whole thing appeared to blow up in that long hot summer of 1981.

The troubles had begun with the riots in Brixton over Easter. In July the rioting was more widespread: in South London, in Southall, in Moss Side in Manchester, in Birmingham, Preston, Wolverhampton, Hull and to a lesser extent in other cities around the country. But among the very worst was that which took place over a period of a week or more in Toxteth, Liverpool 8.

There are many ways to react to such disturbing circumstances. No Conservative government could fail to support the forces of law and order in the face of such a challenge. Predictably, the voices of the left sought explanations and alibis, forgetful in the newly found freedom of opposition of the role of extremists in undermining Jim Callaghan's government. It was perhaps not sufficiently emphasised at the time how limited were the numbers of people actually involved and how dramatic the impact caused by the magnification of the headlines. If there was a moment when Enoch Powell's dread forecast in his 'rivers of blood' speech might have assumed a hideous reality, this surely was it.

The harsh (though ultimately vindicated) economic policies pursued by Geoffrey Howe had led by mid-1981 to unemployment approaching three million; bankruptcies and receiverships were widespread. The miners in early 1981 had won their first confrontation with the new government. Labour was moving left. Roy Jenkins, David Owen, Shirley Williams and Bill Rodgers in March that year had abandoned Labour's sinking ship to break the mould – as they believed – of British politics. (I regarded this then – and still do – as a major political misjudgement. I always believed Labour would eventually recover. They would have hastened the process more effectively within the party than they ever did outside it and perhaps have shared in the opportunities thus created.) Now scores of youths had taken to the streets. Petrol bombs had been thrown and buildings burnt. Yet this was no mass uprising. The vast majority of people of all colours and races stayed at home and shuddered.

Already uneasy about the short-term social effects of the policies being pursued by the Treasury, I was alarmed by the suddenness and extent of these manifestations of arson and violence. I was unwilling to accept the all-too-easy assertions that saw such outbreaks either in stark terms of disgruntled troublemakers on the one hand or police intolerance on the other. There was a political menace in the relatively small-scale disturbances which no responsible government could ignore. We had not expected this to happen and it was a warning. Next time the scale might not be so limited. Besides, I felt that I bore much of the responsibility. I had been Secretary of State for two years. I had chosen to take a particular interest in Liverpool. I asked Mrs Thatcher to allow me to spend some two to three weeks away from day-to-day departmental duties while I concentrated on Merseyside. My ministers of state, Tom King and John Stanley, were well able to run the show in Whitehall. I intended to find out what had gone wrong in a way that no Cabinet minister had ever been allowed – or perhaps ever asked – to do before.

Mrs Thatcher agreed to my suggestion. Willie Whitelaw, the Home Secretary, seemed more wary. He sent Tim Raison, his Minister of State, to accompany me and watch over his Department's interest in police matters – a decision I welcomed, not simply in order to avoid the dangers of misreporting from Liverpool back to the centre but because Tim was a man with a real interest in the problems with which we were grappling. I was fortunate also in having with me my Parliamentary Private Secretary, Tim Sainsbury. The three of us, together with attendant officials, took up residence in the Atlantic Tower Hotel. I was booked into the Port of Liverpool suite on the sixteenth floor and for two and a half weeks this was to be my home. My office during the day was in the Liver Building, the headquarters of the newly established Merseyside Urban Development Corporation.

Alone, every night, when the meetings were over and the pressure was off, I would stand with a glass of wine, looking out at the magnificent view over the river and ask myself what had gone wrong for this great English city. The Mersey, its lifeblood, flowed as majestically as ever down from the hills. Its monumental Georgian and Victorian buildings, created with such pride and at such cost by the city fathers of a century and more earlier, still dominated the skyline. The Liver Building itself, the epicentre of a trading system that had reached out to the four corners of the earth, stood defiant and from my perspective very alone. The port had serviced an empire and sourced a world trade. From Liverpool's docks its ships had plied the seven seas. The quays had been the last stopping place for thousands of fellow countrymen and women and for Europeans of all nations heading for the New World and the gateway for millions of Irish labourers attracted by work on the railways and canals of England. High above it all loomed the two great cathedrals of Rome and Canterbury, then wedded together in the brotherhood of the Roman Catholic Archbishop Derek Worlock and the Anglican Bishop David Sheppard.

In truth, everything had gone wrong. I had constantly been struck by the number of people I met in everyday life who were born and brought up in Liverpool but who had long since left it. The seagoing trade had transferred, principally to Europe but also to the southern English ports, much of this switch, though not all, encouraged by internecine warfare between generally incompetent management and consistently belligerent dock unions. The city had lost too many of its leaders and much of its way. Toxteth, a tiny microcosm in terms of location and population, became a very misleading symbol, though still a symptom of a spreading disease.

Toxteth differs from most other areas of immigration in that the black population there is in considerable measure made up of people whose ancestors first came to Liverpool in the nineteenth century. There is a local mythology which says that they arrived as part of the slave trade. But this is unlikely, at least in any significant numbers. Slaves were carried in Liverpool ships certainly, but not to Britain. They sailed directly from Africa to the West Indies and the southern states of America. Most of the earliest black settlers in Liverpool probably arrived from the west coast of Africa as able seamen, cooks, stewards, firemen – all part of the port's thriving shipping industry. The American writer Herman Melville observed them in the 1830s and contrasted their position with that of blacks in the United States in the same period: 'In Liverpool indeed the Negro steps with a prouder pace, and lifts his head like a man; for here, no such exaggerated feeling exists in respect to him, as in America.'* It is their descendants who are the heart of Toxteth's black population, but they have been added to in this century by substantial further recruitment of sailors from all parts of the Empire and the Commonwealth during the two world wars and, of course, by the unlimited immigration from Africa, the West Indies and the Indian sub-continent that prevailed until 1962.

I was soon to discover the danger of accepting 'black' as an umbrella word covering numerous races and apparently binding together many parts of the human race that are not white. No such bonding exists. People whose origins lie in different parts of Africa, the West Indies, the Indian sub-continent or elsewhere in Asia have little, if anything, in common. Certainly, they don't see themselves as one homogeneous group. But it suited the spokesmen of the largely Afro-Caribbean activists to widen the community of protest. The word 'black' served their purpose and associated them with the ever more influential 'black', African-originated American protest groups. The Toxteth blacks were largely of Afro-Caribbean descent, but Asian and Chinese communities added significantly to the local ethnic mix.

Close to the city centre, a few hundred yards from the Mersey, lay this isolated community. It embraced many thousands of people, living either in rundown nineteenth-century terraced housing or post-war, low-quality council accommodation. In Toxteth, the boarded-up properties, the empty, derelict, rubbish-strewn sites and the pervading street-corner atmosphere of hopelessness were proof of the long-term decline of the wider city. The middle and professional classes, who had once inhabited this part of Liverpool, had long moved out to a more salubrious suburbia. Employment in the docks remained but on a much reduced scale, and what work there was demanded the skill to operate ever more sophisticated equipment. To make matters worse, the area was red-lined by the insurance industry, making it

---

* Herman Melville, *Redburn*; quoted in Tony Lane, *Liverpool: Gateway of Empire* (Lawrence & Wishart, 1987), p. 117.

effectively impossible to get cover against the high risks of burglary and vandalism.

Among the commonest allegations made against politicians is that they never listen. That allegation indeed greeted my arrival in the city. I responded in the only way that seemed credible at the time. 'I have come to listen,' I said. And for the first few days, that carried the audience. But not for long. Very shortly, and inevitably, the allegation turned to questioning. 'What are you going to do?' I knew that, if I spent anything like the two to three weeks I had anticipated in the city, I would not be able to leave having merely thanked them for being so articulate. But nor was there any question of a quick handout or conspicuous expenditure. From my first day I made clear the terms of reference guiding my visit. On the evening of 20 July, my first night there, I organised a meeting of the local community groups in Toxteth. I arrived at the venue, the local YMCA. A small group of journalists and a television camera were waiting at the door. One of the journalists whispered to me: 'They're going to walk out.' I saw at once the next day's headline: 'Heseltine snubbed in Liverpool'. That would be the story. The journalist had not specified who 'they' were. It wasn't long before I found out.

I made a few opening remarks. I explained that I had come to listen. I had plenty of time. I would talk to everyone. I made no promises but I made no preconditions either. With varying degrees of articulateness and persuasiveness, a number of people, representing a wide range of local organisations, put their complaints to me. Then, after a few remarks aimed specifically at the journalists' notebooks, a group I understood to represent the black community of Toxteth walked out. The meeting itself continued until everybody had had their say, but the focus of interest had moved outside. The press were waiting. I knew the only questions that mattered would concentrate on my reaction to the race issue. This was perceived to be the root cause of Liverpool's problems. It wasn't, of course. It was a violent and dramatic symptom, not the problem itself, which stemmed from the long-term structural and economic decline of the city under a local leadership quite unable to rise to the challenge of events.

They asked what I had thought of the protest. I replied that it seemed a pity that those who claimed that no one ever listened to them seemed so indifferent to the opportunity now that it so plainly existed. Then the trap was sprung. 'They say they will only talk to you again if you go to them.' In an instant decision, I shrugged my shoulders and said: 'Fine. That's okay by me. Where and when?' We were now in uncharted territory. With the exception of the riots in Notting Hill in the summer of 1958, there hadn't been any such inner-city riots of any significance in my lifetime. No Cabinet minister had come face to face with such a community in circumstances of this sort before.

I had been fully briefed by Special Branch about the problems facing the Toxteth community. There were many ties which held this community – or parts of the community – together: colour and racial bonds, of course, although a substantial proportion of the residents were white; but also a shared feeling of hopelessness born of low attainment and encouraged by the inevitability that anyone who had actually prospered would have long since moved away; a sense of grievance against the police and a belief that even a home address in Toxteth was a certain barrier to employment. But there was something else. Toxteth was the centre of numerous criminal activities. Many of the most powerful people in the area at the time were deep into drugs, prostitution and protection rackets. All of this was the real world of Toxteth. This was the world with which I had to come face to face.

Of course, it would have been congenial to meet people within the community who didn't have these associations. There were many such people, quite untainted by criminal activities and resentful of their presence. But none of those people would have come forward without the tacit agreement of the power-brokers. Their lives simply would not have been worth it. The community proposed their own representatives. And, again, the power-brokers had a veto: speak to those they approved of or speak to no one. The choice was that simple.

The second meeting was arranged by my private office by telephone with the Afro-Caribbean leaders of the self-styled Liverpool 8 Defence Committee. We were escorted to it by armed policemen. We arrived at the door of a building in Princes Street, the Charles Wootton Centre, which was used by local community groups. It was made clear that only my political colleagues, my officials and I could attend the meeting. The police had to remain outside. They did (with the exception of one Special Branch constable, who handed his gun in a brown envelope to my private secretary and surreptitiously took his place) and the rest of us went in. We descended into a basement room, sat with our backs to the window, as far from the door as it was possible to be. The room was packed. Some of those present had cuts and bruises sustained in recent events. I would be the first to admit that it was the most demanding meeting I have ever chaired. It was not ill-tempered, just extremely brittle. Afterwards we all agreed we had felt as though we were sitting on a powder keg. The wrong gesture, the wrong remark and the whole thing could have exploded.

The meeting lasted for something approaching two hours. Slowly but surely, the tension subsided. The same issues came up time and again. I explained once more that I was there to listen, hopefully to understand, as a senior representative of a government that took their concerns seriously. That was why I was sitting there. The visit was unprecedented. The very repetitiveness of the questions and, therefore, of the answers had its own dampening effect, as, I think, did my repeated request that they should suggest solutions.

When we had been at it for just short of two hours, I noticed that first one, then another, of the leaders was leaving the room. I became deeply anxious about what was going on. There was no point in allowing them the opportunity to plan another initiative or to feed a hostile spin to the waiting press. So I explained how constructive the meeting had been, referred to the prospects of further talks and led my colleagues out. But we never discovered the significance, if any, of the departing leaders. They gave no indication. Our departure was without incident. We uttered a few words to the press and called it a day. We held further meetings on future days but of an altogether more relaxed nature. It would be an exaggeration to suggest that we had established more than a formal relationship, but a door had been opened, through which we were to pay many visits to local community centres, youth clubs, training workshops. In that sense the meeting I have described was a small breakthrough. It created a line of direct communication. And it led to subsequent initiatives in Toxteth which have proved beneficial.

Not all our initiatives were to prove successful, however. At the height of the riots the local National Westminster Bank had been burned down. Much to the credit of the bank, they decided to rebuild it. Some time later they invited me to open it. I asked if they intended to employ anybody from the black community. They said they hadn't thought of that. I made it a condition of my attendance that there were some black employees. They took on two and some months later I officially opened the bank. Progress, I hoped. Many years later I attended a dinner in Liverpool where my neighbour turned to me. 'I don't think you remember me. I've been waiting to run into you for a long time,' he said and introduced himself as the manager of the bank I had opened in Toxteth. I immediately said that that had been a welcome initiative and I hoped that all had gone well. He demurred, and reminded me of my condition for opening the bank. 'Yes,' I said. 'How did they get on?' 'Well, one of them stole a thousand pounds and the other held up one of our customers with a shotgun.' I hope he has forgiven me for smiling as I remarked: 'You must try harder.'

There were, of course, constant allegations of police harassment of the black community. The police knew that crime of every sort was organised by the powerful and ruthless gang leaders operating from Toxteth. They knew that the community was cowed into a posture of non-co-operation and sullen antagonism. There were examples of conspicuous wealth for which there could be no legitimate explanation. But relations between the police and the community were virtually non-existent. Even if the police had seriously tried to foster them, the peer pressure exerted within the community would soon have deterred any such 'Uncle Toms'. The idea that members of the community might join the police and help fight the endemic crime was simply inconceivable. That's how it seemed to the police force of Chief Constable Ken Oxford when I visited their headquarters in the centre of the city.

For the local youth the world seemed quite different. All around, crime and its associated drug business offered the easiest way out of the hopelessness of the situation they perceived themselves to be in. The streets were their playground and the police an alien presence – white, outsiders, the enemy. And at night, when the personal radio alerted the local police patrol to a snatched bag or a mugged pedestrian, 'some black youth running up Parliament Street' would become the prelude to a stop and search of every young black in the area. Time and again they would be questioned for no apparent reason, simply because they were part of the anonymous group of local kids that could be identified by only one distinguishing characteristic: they were black.

These were near irreconcilable views. But we had to try. Day after day we walked the streets of Liverpool. A hectic series of visits here, consultations there, we travelled hither and thither in a blaze of publicity. 'Why do you waste your time there – with them?' I was asked time and again by Conservative sympathisers in the prosperous suburbs. 'There are no votes for us.' But within days a pattern clearly emerged. Put simply, this was a city without leadership. It was this void that it was hoped I could fill. It was almost as though, subconsciously, people were waiting for it to happen. The offers of help were widespread. The apparent goodwill for a new direction was expressed on all sides.

And yet there was so little time. I was there for a matter of days. Besides, it would be positively undesirable for ministers from central government to try to assume responsibility for the running of the great cities of our country, or any other local authority for that matter. It had never been that way and excessive centralism would be administratively and physically undesirable even if attainable. But I perceived that I could, perhaps, above all else, try to restore some sense of confidence to the city. For that to happen, I had to show that things were possible, that new ideas could be developed and be successful. I had to create exemplars, in the hope that, once precedents were set, others would take up the running and build on them. I had to convince that a 'can do' attitude was possible and practical in Liverpool as elsewhere.

How to get this message across? We had to do it in a way that would attract attention and focus minds. I decided to go to the heart of the matter. I asked David Edmonds, my principal private secretary, to ring the chairmen of the fifteen largest financial institutions and banks in the country. My message was very clear: Liverpool might seem a long way away to them but, if Liverpool could burn, so could other cities. And as the cities burned, their assets would go up in smoke as well. So this was not just my problem, or the government's problem. It was their problem too. I wanted to show them Liverpool as I had come to see it in the previous few days.

The response was one of amazement that a Secretary of State's private secretary should be telephoning from Liverpool to invite the chairmen of Britain's most distinguished private sector companies to travel on a bus around some of the most underprivileged neighbourhoods in the United Kingdom. Amazement and hesitation. But a few of the braver spirits agreed straight away. David reported to me every day on his progress. First one, then three, then five. The numbers built up and what could have been a public-relations disaster of an empty bus – except for the Secretary of State, his colleagues and his wife – began to look as if it might be made to work. The breakthrough came when David received a telephone call from the secretary to the chairman of a financial institution who had not been invited. 'I understand that some of my chairman's colleagues have been asked to tour Liverpool with the Secretary of State,' an anxious voice said. 'My chairman was wondering if there had been some mistake and whether a letter for him had not gone astray.' The bus was full.

At the end of the tour I took them back to the Adelphi Hotel for tea and invited them to sit while I gave them my impressions of what had gone wrong and what had to be put right. I explained the absence of leadership and the consequence of the branch-office syndrome: where once there had been great head-offices of north-western companies, there were now simply small local branches, often of giant City of London institutions. 'I need your help,' I said. Thirty pairs of eyes hastily turned to the floor, fearful that the advice they would all have been given before they left London – that I would be after their money – was about to be proved right. I told them I wanted no money. What I wanted was for each of them to agree to second to my Department for a period one of their ablest young executives to help me discover what could be done that would be commercially viable and socially desirable to help restore the confidence of the city. I said that I believed that whatever lessons we could learn from this experiment would be of value far beyond Liverpool, because its problems were the problems of urban deprivation everywhere. A dozen companies lent me some of their best young recruits and they, together with civil servants not just from my Department but also from Employment and from Trade and Industry, made up the Financial Institutions Group with which I worked for the next fifteen months. Among them was Colette Bowe, a young civil servant in the DTI, herself a Liverpudlian, who was to feature so prominently in the Westland affair four years later.

As the days passed, it became more and more clear to me that there were projects that should have, in the main, long since been undertaken and that now lay within my capability to launch. At the end of my two and a half weeks I called a press conference. I was able to list thirteen initiatives. They included a town-planning brief to restore the Anglican Cathedral precinct, a scheme for the provision of community workshops for small firms, a government grant of £1 million for sporting facilities (to be matched by private money), a management training scheme for the young unemployed at two separate centres and – the one that caught the headlines – the establishment of a Tate Gallery of the North on the old Albert Dock site.

In fairness I should make it clear that this last owed little to me. I was presented with it as an idea just as I was concluding my list.

I was attracted by it but took some persuading that so exciting a project could have emerged, so to speak, out of the blue at the last moment. But I was told that Alan Bowness of the Tate had already been investigating the possibility for about a year and that it was sufficiently likely to get the necessary backing to merit inclusion in the list of initiatives. I am delighted that today it is flourishing and has exceeded its sponsors' – and certainly my own – expectations.

But a list of initiatives was not enough. They had to be driven forward. I realised that to turn promise into performance I would have to take a continuing personal interest and I needed a team. A bright civil servant in the Department of the Environment, Eric Sorensen – who had been Peter Shore's private secretary before I took over – was put in charge of the Liverpool office and he became, effectively, the chief executive of the programme upon which we had embarked. A local task force, seconded from Liverpool employers, gave him the resources to keep up the pressure. And, until January 1983, when I left the DOE for the Ministry of Defence, I visited Liverpool usually once a week.

Upon my arrival in the city each week, usually on a Thursday night, we would have a working dinner in restaurants carefully chosen for their cuisine, during which Eric would produce for me a loose-leaf notebook. Every project had its page, with notes on progress to date and instructions issued. We would go through each one, updating on what had been achieved and determining what, if anything, needed to be done to add momentum. The next day would be spent discussing new initiatives, visiting the work on the ground and keeping in touch with local people.

Effectively I was in charge of a Merseyside Task Force, with Eric as local executive. The organisation he created became the prototype for the Government Offices for the Regions more than a decade later. And the Financial Institutions Group helped develop a number of ideas, among them Urban Development Grant (later City Grant) to attract the private sector into joint inner-city projects, the promotion of business development in inner-city areas by the banks and a private-sector-funded development company specialising in the inner city, later known as Inner City Enterprise.

There were many other initiatives. During my original stay in Liverpool I had visited neighbouring boroughs, all of them facing as acute social challenges as the city itself – from which so many of their inhabitants had been rehoused. Jim Lloyd, the Labour leader of

Knowsley Council, took me on a tour of the Cantril Farm housing estate, a classic post-war concrete jungle, badly designed and poorly built with nine tower blocks, deck-access maisonettes and a derelict shopping centre on top of a vast underground car park. A third of the properties were empty and – as Jim put it to me – left as it was, in another ten years the last one out would turn off the lights. They had tried everything they could think of to encourage people to live there and nothing worked, he said. Could I help? I agreed to try but asked for his assurance that there would be no doctrinal opposition to whatever proposal I came up with. 'We have no alternative,' was his realistic, if despairing, reply.

The solution we devised was the Stockbridge Village Trust, a pioneer in the harnessing of private sector finance to provide good social housing. With Tom Baron in the driving seat, we persuaded the Abbey National Building Society and Barclays Bank to provide the millions needed to attempt the rescue, along with funding from Knowsley Council, the Housing Corporation and the DOE. Tom effectively became the chief executive of the Trust, to which the property was transferred. The remodelling began. Slowly, the worst of the concrete jungle was torn down and replaced. Lawrie Barratt courageously built additional houses for sale to add an element of choice and diversity to the by now legal Right-to-Buy on the estate itself. The queue to get out became a queue to get in. What had once been a dismal, monolithic public sector housing estate, known locally as 'Cannibal Farm', is now a decent, multi-tenure modern estate with its own waiting list.

And there was Wavertree. I have been particularly impressed by the progress there. I launched this scheme as a model in December 1981, with four equal partners: Plessey, English Estates and both Merseyside and Liverpool Councils. The result has been to transform the derelict land I first saw in 1981 into the hugely successful Wavertree Technology Park. By the completion of Phase II, £11 million in grant had levered in six times that amount in private sector investment and some 2,700 jobs had been created.

Last but by no means least was the Garden Festival. Liverpool was to be the first to benefit from a decision taken soon after the election to introduce this idea to Britain. First suggested to me while in opposition by Philip Goodhart, the Member of Parliament for Beckenham, garden festivals had originally been developed on the Continent to restore parts of war-damaged cities to useful activity. The concept was simple. Use public money to eliminate dereliction, and green the area to produce a high-quality environment. Stage a festival of attractions for six months and then sell the much improved site for redevelopment. We organised a national competition, offering public money for the reclamation of significant derelict sites, providing the local authority was able to persuade us of private sector commitment. The two best entries came from Liverpool and Stoke. The Stoke case was very powerful. They had a marvellous site consisting of old colliery workings and their proposals were imaginative and convincing. The Liverpool proposals covered part of the Merseyside Development Corporation (MDC) area and included the worst of the waterfront toxic wasteland. I decided in Liverpool's favour but promised Stoke that they would have the second festival two years later.

The initial reaction was very mixed. 'Give us jobs, not trees' was the word on the streets of Toxteth. In the event, the site was restored, and the Garden Festival was opened in the summer of 1984. Over three million visitors came – and the early targets set by Basil Bean, the energetic chief executive of the MDC, were exceeded.

One unfortunate but very human consequence of the success of the Garden Festival was that the critics, who had been vociferous in their opposition, now became equally vociferous in demanding its retention. Parts were subsequently developed for housing. But the original idea of creating a site which would bring a new economic infrastructure to the heart of the city was forgotten. In reality the nature and scale of the toxicity limited any potential after-use.

My fondest memories of Liverpool in the early 1980s are of its people. They were – and are – wonderfully irrepressible. In some ways, of course, their very irrepressibility has made them their own worst enemy. They have a spontaneous wit and a capacity for uproarious comment. Their instant sense of humour at least in part explains a certain ill-discipline that makes them difficult to organise in manufacturing industries but brilliant in the creative world of entertainment and other service industries. The children certainly had a charm of their own. Wherever I went, they followed, as though I was the Pied Piper himself. In that inimitable accent, some asked for my autograph. I later discovered that it had a market value of fifty pence a time back at school. My heart went out to them. I resolved that the least I could do was to try and enable them to grow up in a more optimistic Liverpool than the one I found in that troubled summer of 1981. One of my most gratifying moments came when I was invited back to Merseyside in

July of 1990 to be awarded an honorary degree by Liverpool University for a contribution to urban renaissance which I hope had provided at least some of that much needed optimism.

Upon returning to London in August 1981, with the help of officials and ministerial colleagues, I wrote to the Prime Minister and Cabinet colleagues. I gave my paper the title which embodied the phrase most frequently heard during those two and a half weeks. 'It took a riot', they all said, 'to bring you here and to make government listen.' Well, that was true, but we were the first government ever to listen so attentively and to act so positively. 'It Took a Riot' was never officially published. It had been marked 'Strictly confidential' and each copy was numbered. But a version of it was leaked and appeared in *The Times* within days of its being circulated. It set out a six-part strategy, though I fear I could not persuade Mrs Thatcher to accept all of it. For the record, its conclusions were these:

The economic and social decline evident in Merseyside, and other conurbations, requires a new priority for these areas in our policies.

A continued ministerial commitment to Merseyside is required for a specific period of, say, one year.

A single regional office is needed in Liverpool comprising the main departments concerned with economic development. Similar arrangements should be adopted for other conurbations.

Our industrial, regional and training policies should be reassessed within the new context and administered with flexibility.

As part of this, we should involve the private sector and the financial institutions to a far greater degree than hitherto.

The future of the metropolitan counties and the GLC should be examined quickly.

Substantial additional public resources should be directed to Merseyside and other hard-pressed urban areas to create jobs on worthwhile schemes.

Today such policies by and large command all-party support. But it was to be a Conservative government over the next few years that forced through the necessary changes. And, if I failed to get agreement to my recommendations straight away, I had one consolation. Just before the 1981 party Conference, the Prime Minister announced that I would continue to act as 'Minister for Merseyside' – something that

I went on doing, supported by my admirable task force, for the whole of the next year and a half.

As ill luck would have it, the Liverpool crisis coincided with the beginnings of the public expenditure review in the summer of 1981 and the Cabinet upheaval which that provoked. The divisions within the Cabinet were characterised at the time as divisions between 'wets' and 'drys' and, in so far as I was associated at all with either camp, I would have been listed with the former. This did not, though, reflect the case I argued.

Certainly I argued against the Treasury, but from a standpoint that was essentially my own. I could see the inadequate levels of infrastructure expenditure associated with so many essential public services: roads, schools, inner-city policy and water provision. The last Labour government had cut into much of this capital investment, following the IMF crisis of 1976, and I was convinced that the economic recovery – in which I believed – required not only private sector investment but also the essential public investment upon which so much private investment depends. I could see the burgeoning appetite for public sector consumption and, as a consequence, a softer option for politicians was to make even more cuts in public sector capital programmes. Added to this, it was my Department that was responsible for the enormous cash flow that council house sales and local authority asset disposal were delivering to the public finances.

But, of course, at that time there was no serious attempt to distinguish between capital and current expenditure in the public sector. It was all simply grist to the Treasury's mill. I fought to increase public sector capital programmes. I argued that this would create jobs, stimulate private investment and reflect the fact that so much cash was flowing as a result of the sale of capital assets. I was pushing through large increases in local authority and housing association rents, thus cutting current expenditure on subsidy, and I was also in favour of reducing mortgage interest tax relief (MITR), as a further saving to the Treasury. The taxpayer was already gaining from income tax reductions and, in practice, MITR had the effect of pushing up house prices.

In a meeting of the Cabinet that July, Mrs Thatcher lost the argument for further retrenchment to a coalition of critics. She retaliated with a September reshuffle. When the Cabinet reassembled after the summer recess, the cast – with Lord Soames, Ian Gilmour and Mark Carlisle gone (and Jim Prior banished to Northern Ireland) – was significantly different. The appointments of Nigel Lawson, Norman Tebbit and Cecil Parkinson tipped the balance in the Cabinet in favour of the right wing and ensured that it was extremely unlikely that she would lose on a major issue again.

But for me there was always another audience. The Tory Party Conference was due to meet in October 1981 and expectations were rising that I would produce 'one of those speeches'. I was determined that I would tell the story of that summer the way it was. I was proud of what I had to say and was helped by the fact that the initiatives that I had taken were very largely designed to restore private sector opportunity, enterprise and confidence in areas far too long stifled by local authority culture and practice.

But it was the race issue which dominated my thought as I prepared the speech. I do not remember any speech in my public life over which I anguished so long and so hard. I was as aware as anyone of the Powellite undercurrents that existed, not just in the Conservative Party but throughout British society. I personally had no truck with such an approach, but how was I to handle this explosive issue and still make clear the message I wanted to convey? I drafted and redrafted. With each draft the words became fewer, the meaning clearer. I worked late into the night until, at about half-past two, I finally decided that – whatever the consequences, whatever the risk – I would express what I wanted to say in the shortest, most unambiguous sentences. No one in the hall, or any wider audience, would have the slightest doubt about where I stood on the issue of race relations. As a member of a Conservative government, there were things that had to be said.

The speech itself seemed to be going all right but, as I delivered it, my mind was focused ahead, waiting for the crucial passage, unsure of the reaction or consequences it might provoke. I set the issue in context: 'In our generation we must show the same courage and vision as the leaders whose memories we so frequently applaud. We talk of equality of opportunity. What do those words actually mean in the inner cities today? What do they mean to the black communities? We now have large immigrant communities in British cities.'

I now came to the words over which I had anguished for so long:

Let this party's position be absolutely clear.
They are British.
They live here.

They vote here.

However tight the immigration legislation – and in everyone's interests they should be tight – there will be a large black community in this country tomorrow, just as there is today. There are no schemes of significant repatriation that have any moral, social or political credibility.

I will and I do condemn the handful of blacks who rioted. But I condemn just as strongly the whites who rioted alongside them. I totally support the police in their brave and unenviable task of restoring stability to our society.

But the rioters were a tiny section of the black and white populations, the overwhelming majority of whom deplore the riots as vehemently as we do. But the fact remains that of those black communities, who stand for the same values I have described, far too many – our people – know that the education they obtain, the jobs they are offered and the careers that are opened to them do not match up to the finest traditions upon which we pride ourselves.

As soon as I got to the words 'They are British', the audience began to cheer. Six words later they were on their feet to give me a standing ovation halfway through the speech. I have never felt closer to the Conservative Party or prouder of that underlying sense of fairness and decency which I believe to be at the heart of its history and its philosophy. The speech itself ended to wild applause. David Dimbleby, the BBC commentator reporting the event, remarked that it was as though I had picked up the Tory Party, shaken it and put it down where I wanted it to be. I could not have asked for more.

On reflection, I think that the divisions between 'wets' and 'drys' in the early 1980s have been magnified beyond the substance. In fact I never heard of any formal grouping of the so-called 'wets' and never attended any meeting of such a group, however unco-ordinated or loose it might have been. The nature of Cabinet government encourages conflict. Ministers are briefed to defend their corner. Spending departments are always ranged against the Treasury. There were inevitably divisions but they were exaggerated by leaks and briefings, with the result that the dialogue was conducted largely in the headlines of the national press.

Certainly, there were debates in Cabinet, carried on against a deteriorating economic situation and rising unemployment. I was often struck by the drama attributed to those debates when I read about them. It generally far exceeded the reality of the discussions themselves. The debate – and the reporting of it – had more to do with people's perceptions and Mrs Thatcher's style of management than with any critical division over the policies themselves.

I had been brought up to believe that one listened to what one's colleagues had to say before intervening. In particular, I deferred to members of the opposite sex. Yet I learnt quickly that it was all too easy to find one's arguments cut off in midstream by prime ministerial interruption, to have the case one wished to deploy hijacked by premature conclusions and often hectoring interventions. One either gave in to it or one learnt to fight back. Hard experience taught me to wait until Mrs Thatcher paused for breath and then I began again – and again – and again – until I was satisfied that what I had to say had been clearly heard. It was wearying, but those who shrank from it soon found themselves marginalised in the endless power struggle of Cabinet life. Those who were still around in the late 1980s told me it became a great deal worse after the middle of the decade, when some of the older, more formidable members of the Cabinet had left or been sacked and Mrs Thatcher came to dominate her colleagues in a way that was simply unhealthy.

Where there was no doubt about the pernicious effect of the division into 'wets' and 'drys', however, was in the parliamentary party. Under the leadership of the Member of Parliament for Reigate, George Gardiner, a former provincial journalist, a group organised itself into the 92 Group of Tory backbenchers. (It was named not after the general election of that year – that had not yet taken place – but after the number of the flat in which it first met.) They saw themselves as the Thatcher Praetorian Guard. They organised slates of candidates for party committees. They held regular meetings. They marched into the Chief Whip's office to demand policy changes. They became a party within a party. The success of this exercise led, of course, to an unbalancing of the parliamentary party and a degree of personal bitterness on the back benches which I had never known before.

But in my Department I felt at home, exposed to criticism though we often were. The Department of the Environment in the early 1980s remained as Ted Heath had created it, perhaps the greatest protector of our heritage and the natural environment in our history. Its quangos spanned an immense range of responsibilities. In theory many of the powers necessary for the protection of these sensitive areas rested directly with the Secretary of State himself. The legislation is always quite clear. 'The Secretary of State may . . .' 'The Secretary of State shall . . .' That is what Parliament enacts. The real world is different. Consultation, official advice, the threat of judicial review, simply the scale of the numbers of decisions that have to be taken – all ensure that many decisions are taken by officials in the name of the Secretary of State. The vast majority never cross the desk of a minister. Ministers usually lay down rules, which means that if the rules are to be infringed they wish to be consulted. They rely on officials to ensure that if, in addition to these defined areas, other decisions might be politically sensitive they are referred upwards. But, by delegating responsibility widely to my colleagues, I ensured that many fewer decisions were left unscrutinised by a political eye.

In addition to the jumbo Local Government, Planning and Land Act, Tom King steered the Wildlife and Countryside Act 1981, the Town and Country Planning (Minerals) Act 1981 and the Water Act of 1981 to the statute book. He was a warm and friendly colleague but with that invaluable quality of telling you tough truths to your face. He once gently chided me, 'You'll find, Michael, that "I" is not the only word in the English language. You could try an occasional "we".'

Nevertheless, I was particularly proud of the Wildlife and Countryside Act, which gave government the power to designate environmentally important sites as SSSIs (Sites of Special Scientific Interest) and put them into the care of the Nature Conservancy Council. It also significantly extended protection of wild birds, wild animals and wild plants. I had invited the then chief executive of the Royal Society for the Protection of Birds into my office, put my credentials on the table and asked what the RSPB would like from the government. 'If I may say so,' I said, 'you are unlikely ever to find a minister more sympathetic than me.' Whether we got it wholly right, I have subsequently wondered, however, as I count the Canada geese and ponder the plague of magpies. This explosion in the magpie population may ironically have done more harm to the migrant warblers than was ever done by egg collectors. But ministers do not actively seek embarrassment. The RSPB has more than a million members.

Every minister faces the endless carping of the media in its relentless search for headlines. On one occasion I attempted a counter-attack. I invited the environmental correspondents of the national press to my office and, somewhat to their surprise, asked them to imagine that they were sitting on my side of the table as Secretary of State. It was a singularly unfruitful exercise, there being virtually no positive suggestions about what should be done, with one exception. 'Why don't you reintroduce architectural competitions?' I was asked. The practice had been widespread in the nineteenth century and had been used in the mid-1830s to select Barry and Pugin to design the present Houses of Parliament. But it had since fallen into disuse. I liked the idea and decided to revive the practice.

Open competitions can lead to large volumes of nugatory work and obvious expense for the losers. This problem can be met only partly by having limited competitions among nominated architects. But I was anxious to stimulate and liberate a new generation in the profession.

The most famous competition of the period was undoubtedly that for the National Gallery extension at the north-west corner of Trafalgar Square. The Gallery needed more space but had not the money to fund any new development on its own. John Stanley proposed a solution whereby a composite building would offer commercial office space as well as new hanging space for pictures. With that as the object we organised a design-and-build competition. My preferred choice did not find favour with the National Gallery. Nor, famously, did the subsequent preference – for which I had no responsibility – gain the approval of His Royal Highness the Prince of Wales. But at least our endeavours laid the foundations for the Sainsbury family's gift of the magnificent new wing. One more derelict site had gone.

With Geoffrey Finsberg's help we restored the Palace of Westminster, but only after bits of it fell off, mercifully killing no one in the process. I saved Billingsgate from the property developers, and we also managed, at John Stanley's initiative, to open up the Cabinet War Rooms to the public. The key had simply been turned in the lock once the war was over. Everything was still there: files, maps, furniture – all left as commonplace reminders of momentous events. It has now become an outpost of the Imperial War Museum and has proved extremely popular with both domestic and foreign visitors.

I killed more quangos than any other minister, but where appropriate as an act of effective management, I created new ones. If a task has to remain in the public sector, it is arguable that greater accountability and effectiveness can be achieved in a free-standing quango than is possible when the same activity is lost to sight as a small part of a large government department. One of my officials, Maurice Mendoza, suggested that we should put together the Ancient Monuments Board and the Historic Buildings Council for England and turn them into a free-standing organisation, the Historic Buildings and Monuments Commission for England, later simply known as English Heritage. He had already persuaded the leading figures at that time, Dame Jennifer Jenkins, chairman of the Historic Buildings Council, and Sir Arthur Drew, her opposite number at the Ancient Monuments Board, of the merits of his idea. I was delighted to move my quango-count down by consent. I pondered long and hard over the obvious and sensible idea that we should include the Royal Commission on the Historical Monuments of England, the chairman of which was Lord Adeane, a former private secretary to the Queen. I decided that this was an historic building too far and that the Palace was best left undisturbed. Edward (Lord) Montagu of Beaulieu became the first chairman of the new body, a post he held for some ten years, and he helped it achieve a well-respected start. Jocelyn Stevens, who made an admirable successor when I appointed him in 1992, saw to it that the task was completed and the further merger took place in 1999. I should have kept my nerve at the beginning.

As a general rule, questions get disposed of in Cabinet after one exposure of the arguments. Very rarely do matters get referred back a second time and hardly ever three times. That was not the case with the Queen Elizabeth II Conference Centre. The Broad Sanctuary site directly across Victoria Street from Westminster Abbey had remained derelict since a German bombing raid forty years earlier. As will have become evident by now, I have a thing about derelict sites and particularly about derelict sites so close to the heart of London. This one was a real eyesore. Word got round that there was a proposal to build a conference centre not just to attract high-security government business, but also to meet a demand for a suitable location for prestigious international conferences. The government wrestled with the familiar arguments. If there was a need for a conference centre, why didn't the private sector provide it? It would send quite the wrong signal for the government to indulge in such conspicuous public expenditure. And, anyway, there was no money for the public sector to build it.

There is one specific factor about arguments of this sort. Every Cabinet minister understands them and has views on them. The proposal went to Cabinet for the first time. The Treasury and the Prime Minister were implacably opposed. It is conceivable that the combination of Peter Carrington and I arguing together heightened the tension. I supported the need for the building but offered to find private finance. The Cabinet refused to kill the project but agreed that it could proceed only with private funding. I found backers, but approval was again deferred because the Treasury didn't like the terms. At the final meeting the Treasury, so fearful of the private financing of a public building a decade or more before the Private Finance Initiative became Treasury orthodoxy, agreed to finance the whole thing rather than establish a precedent. The villain in Mrs Thatcher's eyes was John Nott, usually one of her 'trusties' on economic matters. On this occasion, as Secretary for Trade, he broke ranks and the Carrington–Heseltine axis prevailed by one voice. The Queen Elizabeth II Conference Centre opened in 1986. By then I had left the government and used occasionally wryly to contemplate it in all its Xanadu glory as quixotic proof that where there is a will, there is a way.

I spent three and a half years at Environment between 1979 and 1983. For the first time I had run a major government department. It had been hugely exciting, not least because it involved daily exposure to the intellectual firepower of our civil service. It was always a privilege just to enjoy the debate, over a bewildering range of options, in the context of myriad issues and unrelenting pressure. The political battles in which I was engaged at the DOE were at the centre of Britain's domestic transformation in the early 1980s. Another historic battle, against the seemingly irreversible advance of communism worldwide, was entering its final phases. It was to this front line that I was now moved.

Chapter 13

COLD WAR HOT SEAT

A nne and I spent the morning of Thursday, 6 January 1983 bird-watching in the forests of Tobago – we had taken a short break after Christmas – and we went back to our hotel before lunch to find a message to ring No. 10; Tony Dawe from the *Daily Express* had somehow materialised as well and had been awaiting our return with what patience he could muster. I held him at bay, called Downing Street and was put through straight to Mrs Thatcher. She invited me to become Secretary of State for Defence and – unlike the last occasion when she had proposed a Cabinet post for me – this time I accepted with alacrity. By now the Falklands War was seven months behind us but, even in times of peace, it is a job which ranks as one of the more responsible Cabinet posts.

As Secretary of State for Defence, you are answerable for the safety and welfare of the men and women of Britain's armed forces, beyond argument among the most professional in the world. You are trusted with a high level of security clearance and some of the most sensitive secrets of modern government, involving foreign allies and opponents alike. You may not always share the judgements of the Foreign Office but the closer the working relationship that exists between the two departments, the more effective policy-making is likely to be in key areas of interest to the United Kingdom across the globe. Some of your decisions will affect the fighting power of the British armed forces for perhaps twenty years or more. In any period of conflict you carry life and death responsibility for those who serve in Her Majesty's forces. I felt privileged to have been offered the job and appreciated the Prime Minister's confidence in me – never dreaming that within three years Mrs Thatcher's closest advisers would portray me as a character whom it would have been a gross act of political irresponsibility to have put in charge of a corner shop, let alone British defence interests. In the three years, almost to the day, that I was to serve as the political head of the Ministry of Defence (MOD), I found myself at the forefront of events, not merely of the election campaign of 1983 but of one of the most testing international confrontations of modern times.

The world of defence is, on the surface, a world of panoply and pageantry. A Secretary of State for Defence is exposed to much ceremonial. Honour guards become part of your everyday life. That is easily understandable. Every political system accords a special significance to its military personnel. The British military system is essentially hierarchical and deferential. Each member knows his or her place and immediately defers to superior rank: private soldiers to corporals, corporals to sergeants, sergeants to lieutenants, lieutenants to captains, majors to colonels and brigadiers to generals. Orders are given and obeyed. The word of the Chief of the Defence Staff is a command. In this order of things the Secretary of State takes his place close to the top of the heap, and the respect for the office demands the accord of military recognition and ceremony. In addition, between friendly armed forces around the world there is a mutual esteem, as of members of a club recognising each other's status and position. Hence the honour guards, the bands, the red carpets.

I had been brought up by my father to admire the military way of life and, although my own experience of it in National Service had been so brief, I felt a deep respect throughout my time at the MOD for the servicemen and women with whom I came into day-to-day contact, some with experience of combat going back to the end of the Second World War and many others who had been exposed to great danger since, not least, of course, in the then very recent recapture of the Falkland Islands. One can never know how one would have fared in their place. But such people never needed to ask themselves questions of that sort; they had served their country and done so with honour.

Routinely I visited British forces stationed at home and overseas. Such visits carry their own hazards. I grew to suspect that there was a competitive element between the three services to see which one could expose me to the most gruelling physical activity. It was quite difficult to emerge unscathed from the physical indignity of trying to perform – in front of such professional eyes – tasks that to them were routine and commonplace, but which for me combined genuine apprehension with the prospect of physical incompetence.

It wasn't too bad firing a machine gun at a distant target. No one really expected you to hit it. But there was an element of the absurd about the Secretary of State for Defence who, given his height of six foot two inches, simply found it impossible to get his other leg into the driving seat in the turret of a tank. Even more amusing – for the spectators – I once hung on the end of a rope in the North Sea, beneath a Royal Navy helicopter, desperately hoping that the submarine at which I was being aimed down below would stop rolling long enough for me to land on the deck and clamber down the conning tower. Of course, common sense told me that the sailors would not let me come to any harm. The Royal Navy would never risk the loss of face. But life seems less certain swinging up there in the wind, halfway between sky and sea.

Then it was the RAF's turn. Although an amateur ornithologist, I was still taken aback when a smart young squadron leader appeared one day in my office to ask if I would like to fly the Hawk. Recovering rapidly, I realised that the Hawk in question was one of the most effective aircraft in the Royal Air Force, extensively used for training fast-jet pilots prior to their conversion to front-line units. There is no way in which, as Secretary of State, you can do anything other than smile as enthusiastic an acceptance as you can manage. I had rather forgotten this fleeting encounter when the squadron leader reappeared in my office some weeks later, explaining that he had come to check a few facts about my impending visit to RAF Valley in Anglesey. 'Perhaps you'd be kind enough to come and sit over here, Secretary of State,' he said, taking an upright chair and placing it against the wall. He placed my legs firmly so that thigh and calf were at right angles to each other and produced a tape measure with which he proceeded to measure from the front of my kneecap to the wall behind me. I inquired, in as inconsequential a tone of voice as I could muster, what he was doing. 'Oh, it's nothing, Secretary of State,' he said. 'I'm just checking for the ejector seat.'

There was no going back. The day eventually dawned. I discarded my everyday, familiar, comfortable clothes and was kitted out to look like a fighter pilot. A thorough briefing on the aircraft, its characteristics and performance, a short walk across the tarmac and we were hurtling skywards. The squadron leader was in the front seat of the cockpit. I was close behind. We had been flying for ten minutes or so when a voice over the intercom told me that I had 'control'. That was very far from the way I saw it. We landed about half an hour later at St Athan, Cardiff. It had been – how shall I put it? – an exhilarating experience. I was certainly in no fit state, however, to field the first question lobbed at me from the waiting pack of journalists: 'Can we have your comments on the recent upsurge in support for the Welsh Nationalists, Secretary of State?' I suspect my answer fell somewhat short of the standards I would like to think I normally maintained.

The Ministry of Defence shares with the Foreign Office the distinction of having a structure unlike that of any other department in Whitehall. Most government departments are designed as a narrowing pyramid, with a permanent secretary and a handful of deputy secretaries at the top. But the FCO and the MOD have so wide a spread of senior personnel that their pyramids have an apex that is almost flat.

The Ministry at that time employed 10,000 civil servants in its headquarters, alongside whom worked the top military staffs. Outside the Ministry itself, of course, there were tens of thousands more civil servants and the great bulk of the armed forces, from the commanding officers of senior rank down to the newest raw recruit, wherever British servicemen and women were stationed. I was fortunate in my permanent secretary, Clive Whitmore, a civil servant in the top flight with the calibre to have been Cabinet secretary. A man with an easy charm and a ready smile, he had been Margaret Thatcher's private secretary in No. 10 before his promotion to the Ministry of Defence a short time before my arrival. I also inherited from John Nott a first-class private secretary in the tousle-haired Richard Mottram, already reputed to be heading for the permanent secretary's seat. Peter Blaker – a friend from Oxford when, as President of the Union, he had first invited me to make a speech 'on the paper' – and John Stanley, who later moved over from the DOE, were in turn Minister of State for the Armed Forces. There was, in addition, the Procurement Executive, under the ministerial responsibility during my time first of Geoffrey Pattie, then of Adam Butler, and lastly Norman Lamont (the future Chancellor of the Exchequer) and with its own permanent under-secretary, which was responsible for specifying and procuring military equipment. Add to this organisations such as Royal Ordnance, the Royal Dockyards and the Research Establishments and in total I was responsible for some 530,000 military and civilian personnel.

Tim Sainsbury came with me from the Department of the Environment as my Parliamentary Private Secretary, but was soon promoted to the Whips' Office and his place was taken by Keith Hampson, who had previously served as PPS to Tom King during our time together at the DOE. Keith had great sympathy with the brand of Conservatism he believed I stood for. Too easily misrepresented as the 'left' or 'wet' wing, his concern was that the party should never forget or ignore its one-nation credentials. He was in complete accord with radical policies of change, if they had as their purpose the advance of what he termed 'caring' capitalism. His academic mind brought a power of analysis to politics that could sometimes lead him too far from his more conventional colleagues. Keith proved a good friend to me over the years; his help was always generous and of great value. I was sorry when personal problems led to his resignation in 1984.

I do not recall ever being given any indication of what was expected of me on being appointed to any political job. The briefest of personal meetings with the Prime Minister or Leader of the Opposition – perhaps only a telephone call from the Chief Whip – is designed solely to find out if one is prepared to accept the post. That established, the conversation is rapidly concluded. (The appointee to fill the next vacancy is usually already waiting at the door.) It must remain, therefore, a matter of conjecture as to why Mrs Thatcher promoted me at this time. It was not simply to play a significant role in the battle against the Campaign for Nuclear Disarmament (CND) and in the forthcoming election, although that was, I believe, part of the explanation. But even in that long-distance call to Tobago she said I was to remain in the Ministry after the election. The longer-term and most likely reason was the impression that my management approach had made on her across the range of policy and administrative issues that made up the Department of the Environment.

John Nott's relationship with No. 10 had deteriorated significantly after his promotion in 1981 from Trade Secretary to Defence. He had faced three huge problems: an inflation in the cost of defence equipment well above the national level; a defence review in which the Royal Navy had been the principal casualty, with all the bitter internal controversy that had provoked; and, overshadowing his last nine months, the Falklands War itself. Inevitably, the outbreak of the war led to a search for scapegoats. Some argued that it was John, rather than Peter Carrington, the Foreign Secretary, who should have resigned. Critics pointed to the 1981 Defence Review which had recommended the withdrawal of HMS *Endurance* from the South Atlantic and the proposed sale to Australia of HMS *Invincible*, one of our two new aircraft carriers. Fairly or unfairly, both decisions were seen as having sent quite the wrong signals to the Argentine junta. And John had not done well in winding up for the government in the original Falklands debate on Saturday, 3 April 1982 – the day after the capture of the island's governor, Sir Rex Hunt, and the surrender of Port Stanley. I was, of course, informed on these issues only as a member of the Cabinet (not of the Cabinet committee that dealt with foreign policy and defence). But I discussed the matter some time later with my former colleague Nicholas Ridley.

Nick was one of the few who could genuinely be said in the period of opposition up to 1979 to have argued a radical right-wing agenda. He held clear, coherent views which he was more than able enough to articulate and pursue. Later as a Cabinet minister he was to impress civil servants for just those reasons. By way of background, he was the younger son of a landed family and had been brought up on a magnificent estate north of Newcastle. The genes of his maternal grandfather Edwin Lutyens must surely have strongly influenced Nick's talent as a watercolourist and his ability to design and build around his Cotswold manor a water garden of great charm and interest. Politically we were miles apart, but I knew Nick well and liked him. Our mutual interest in gardening drew us together – much to the surprise of his officials after I had gone to the back benches in 1986, when from time to time they had to take delivery at Marsham Street of various pots of young trees arriving from me in transit on their way to Nick's country garden.

But over dinner one night some years later Nick explained the background to the Argentinian invasion of the Falklands. He had been extremely bitter when in 1979 he found himself, as he felt, banished to a remote corner of the Foreign and Commonwealth Office where, among his responsibilities, he was in charge of the Falkland Islands. The subsequent events are well established in the public domain. He had discussed among other things a deal with the Argentinians that could, if the islanders agreed, set out a framework for the long-term relationship of the islands with the mainland. On 2 December 1980 in a statement to the Commons Nick said that he proposed to explore either a way of freezing the dispute for a period or – and this is where the trouble lay – exchanging the title of sovereignty against a long lease of the islands back to Her Majesty's Government, the so-called lease-back arrangement. However, there was an immediate and quite unanticipated explosion on the Tory back benches, led by the redoubtable Sir Bernard Braine. Bernard suggested that the option of yielding on sovereignty and a lease-back undermined a perfectly valid title in international law. Julian Amery pronounced the statement 'profoundly disturbing'; Viscount Cranborne, at the time MP for Dorset South, spoke of 'grave disquiet' at a proposal to 'surrender sovereignty'; John Farr expressed 'intense dissatisfaction'. The consequence was that the government was forced to abandon the terms which Nick had been authorised to negotiate.

It was in this context that the Argentinian leader, General Galtieri, so misread the likely reaction to an invasion of the islands. He calculated that Mrs Thatcher would never seek to recover by force, with the horrendous risks involved, territory over which she had been prepared to negotiate a deal – even though she had been unable to conclude it. It was a fatal misjudgement which totally failed to anticipate the reaction of both the Prime Minister and the Cabinet. Neither could the General have anticipated the reaction of the Royal Navy, which, in the formidable personage of the First Sea Lord, Admiral Sir Henry Leach, saw the chance to argue that the fleet should sail but not if its destroyer and frigate force were to suffer the indignities consequent on the conclusions of the latest Defence Review.

I admired Mrs Thatcher's conduct of the Falklands War, although I was not myself a member of the inner War Cabinet. The military advice to the full Cabinet was clear. We had the capability to dispatch a task force which could ensure the recapture of the islands. What it was not within their power to predict, except within a wide range of probability, was the scale of the casualties. The government rightly accepted this advice. It was not an easy decision; to go to war never is. But the subsequent military success was of the highest order and mercifully the number of casualties was close to the lowest forecast.

Whatever the Prime Minister's purpose in promoting me to the Defence portfolio, she cannot have been unmindful of the approaching election. The Cold War was entering a new and, as it turned out, decisive phase. The Soviet Union had devised a new-generation, medium-range, nuclear-armed rocket, the SS20. Its launchers could be moved around on trucks, thus giving it a high degree of mobility and therefore undetectability. It was capable of targeting western Europe and the United Kingdom and constituted a new and heightened threat to NATO security, as the Russians began its deployment in the late 1970s. The Western alliance determined to respond to this escalation of the Cold War by the deployment in turn of both the American Pershing II rockets (though not in the UK) and their nuclear-armed cruise missiles, themselves capable of targeting the Soviet Union from land bases in NATO Europe and enjoying the same undetectability as a consequence of the road-based mobility of their launchers. We had agreed that these missiles could be based in Britain. At around the same time we had decided to modernise our own independent nuclear deterrent housed in Polaris submarines, and replace it with a more powerful and technologically advanced system incorporated into Trident submarines, to be built in Barrow-in-Furness. The appropriate contracts were entered into to acquire the necessary American technology.

The decision to base cruise missiles in this country as part of the NATO response to the Soviet threat had provoked the usual left-wing storm of reaction in which the Labour Party played its characteristic role, opposing the strategy and encouraging protest. This was despite the fact that Labour in power had actually modernised our Polaris missiles with the Chevaline programme and dealt with their left wing by the simple device of not telling either them or anyone else what they were doing. But Labour were now back in opposition and the old veteran of the Aldermaston marches, Michael Foot, was their leader. By so undermining the effective implementation of our defence policy, they threatened its very credibility and in this they were enthusiastically assisted by their colleagues and allies in CND. Hardly noticed at first under the shadow of the Falklands War, by the time of my appointment to the Ministry there was seen to be a growing threat to the political will of the country to maintain a credible defence strategy within the NATO alliance. CND were back on the streets.

Only two days after my appointment to the MOD, a letter arrived at the Ministry from the 'chair' of CND, Joan Ruddock (later to be both a Labour MP and a junior minister). She was an ideal choice for the leading role in CND: intelligent, smart and good-looking. If anyone was to articulate effectively the inherent fears which so many share of the menace of nuclear devastation, she was the person to do it.

Her letter challenged me to a public debate on the issues in quasi-flattering tones – 'It has been reported that you have been appointed largely because of your "oratorial capacity" and your "popular appeal". It is, of course, a great compliment to CND and the peace movement that a senior Cabinet appointment should be made with anti-CND propaganda as the primary concern. On our side, we feel that our campaign against cruise and Trident have the support of the majority of the nation – hence the recent government concern over the growth of the peace movement.' Saucily, she encouraged me to keep up with my grassroots contacts, 'so that you will learn for yourself why people from all walks of life joined this campaign'.

Her invitation may have sounded innocent enough, but it was, of course, the oldest political trick in the book. Challengers always have everything to gain and nothing to lose from trying to put themselves on a level with their entrenched opponents – in this case a Secretary of State in a democratically elected British government. Conversely, I had nothing to gain and everything to lose. I was new to the job. I had no background knowledge of the complexities of nuclear weapons or of the science that surrounds them. I was a sitting duck.

If I had done the debate well, the best I could have hoped for would have been: 'You'd expect him to, wouldn't you?' Yet, confronted by an attractive woman, explaining to me that I couldn't really be expected to understand the legitimate fears of women everywhere and also to appreciate the appalling civilian consequences inherent in the nuclear threat, I was highly unlikely to emerge a clear winner. I resolved, therefore, to have nothing to do with her proposal. But how to turn down the invitation without immediately provoking the propaganda response that I was too frightened to take Mrs Ruddock on in public debate?

Happily, fate and fortune were on my side. I had, in 1982, while I was still at the Department for the Environment, accepted an invitation to address a meeting of the West Berkshire Conservative Association at Newbury town hall, two miles from Greenham Common, on 7 February 1983. By that time, of course, Greenham Common – the intended host airfield for the American cruise missiles when they arrived – was already being picketed by numbers of women associated with CND and living in indescribable squalor. I decided that I would use the occasion of a speech to a Conservative audience to reply to Joan Ruddock's letter, refusing her challenge and setting out the government's case.

Anne and I set out for Newbury. Our arrival there revealed the nature of the peace movement. The protesters descended on the car. The police immediately surrounded me, I'm afraid leaving Anne very much to look after herself. About a dozen policemen formed a human wedge slowly edging its way through the seething crowd. We headed towards the town hall. Such was the weight and pressure that the police began to bend and give way. I was deeply fearful that I would be crushed. I had one knee on the ground and was using all my strength to help the police before the wedge managed to reassert itself and deliver me into the waiting arms of the local Conservative chairman. Meanwhile, Anne had nipped into the back of the hall with a plainclothes woman police constable.

My refusal to debate with CND received extensive coverage in the broadsheet newspapers, but of course, as a result of the mob behaviour with which they had greeted my arrival, the whole perception of the peace movement also changed. Joan Ruddock's friendly, sympathetic face vanished from the public gaze, replaced by a harsher world that the media rapidly turned into a vivid reality. Looking back, I think that Newbury was probably the turning point in the battle against CND. If they had behaved, as their younger followers did some time later, when the students at Durham University simply greeted my arrival in silence, lining the street with quiet, well-behaved people, each holding a single lighted candle, then it might have been different. But at Newbury they did quite the reverse and the image they created there, and were to go on creating across the campuses of British universities and in demonstrations when senior members of the government appeared, succeeded in alienating moderate opinion and inflaming the Conservative Party's enthusiasm to defeat them.

I had a number of encounters with the women of Greenham Common and not just in Berkshire. The *Guardian* regularly invites Secretaries of State to appear before its entire editorial board and team of journalists. Questions are asked, statements made and lunch with the editor and his senior colleagues caps a stimulating morning. I attended such a lunch. Word of my visit must have been 'conveyed' in advance; I arrived to find two unilateralist women staging a protest inside the newspaper's building by lying across the threshold of the room I had to enter. It was not exactly my life that I was asked to take into my hands as I made the hazardous step. The natural queasiness of the *Guardian* editorial team at the prospect of the women having to be physically ejected was more than compensated for by the Guards sergeants in the Royal Corps of Commissionaires who thankfully dealt with the duo in the manner one would expect from so intrepid a service.

I decided that, as part of my briefing, I would see the anti-nuclear films that had done so much to fuel the hostility to these weapons. In my office I looked at an American film on the aftermath of nuclear attack. Then, one Saturday afternoon, I sat at home at Thenford watching for several hours as reel after reel portrayed the horrific consequences should either side decide to incinerate Europe. At the end I knew that I had a job to do. Whatever the horrors portrayed, the essential fact remained: Soviet nuclear weapons were targeted on Western cities. Nuclear blackmail was just as unacceptable in the early evening as it had been in the early afternoon. We had to win the argument and turn the tide. We needed to recover the political high-ground.

There wasn't much time. A general election was not far away. By the end of 1981 the government's fortunes had begun to recover with improving economic trends. The rise in our popularity was helped by the victory in the South Atlantic. But by early 1983 – with Roy Jenkins' newly founded SDP now the joker in the pack – there was still ground to recapture before the government could be sure of re-election. It was obvious that, just as I had been at the forefront of the battle for council tenant enfranchisement during the 1979 election campaign, so was I going to be at the centre of the 1983 campaign as well – though this time arguing the case for an effective defence policy within NATO. The continuing effectiveness of the strategy of the whole Western alliance was at risk. We established within the Ministry of Defence a small group of politicians backed up by a unit of civil servants known as Defence Secretariat 19 (DS19) to develop the arguments in support of NATO's plans.

The initial challenge was to redefine the nature of the debate. Close examination of the opinion polls proved invaluable. Public opinion inclined against nuclear weapons and showed no enthusiasm for either Tomahawk cruise missiles or Britain's Trident, but, if other questions were asked, a very different picture emerged. If, instead of nuclear disarmament, the public were invited to give their views on the concept of one-sided disarmament, they rejected it overwhelmingly. From that moment on, nuclear disarmament was banished as part of departmental vocabulary. From then on, the forces of the peace movement were the one-sided disarmers. Similarly, although talk of Tomahawk and Trident provoked negative reactions, when asked if Britain should give up its own independent deterrent, public opinion was far more open to persuasion. Trident was dropped from the vocabulary. Britain's independent deterrent took its place. I embarked on a series of speaking engagements up and down the country.

It is impossible today to recapture the mood on the university campuses or, indeed, the atmosphere of the public meetings of that time. However daunting the mobs of demonstrators might be, the police would usually ask me if I minded breaking through to the already assembled audiences of Conservatives incarcerated in various halls. I always insisted that my job was to make a speech setting out the causes in which I believed and that I wished to go in, though if the police had ever advised me that it was too dangerous and that I should abandon a meeting I would not have asked them to act against their professional judgement. But I cannot remember any occasion on which they failed to gain access for me. It was often formidable, sometimes frightening, but it always had its up side. The most amateur of public speakers had a gift of a speech to make once he had been delivered safely to the waiting Conservative audience. 'The voice of the mobs on the street will never silence the voice of freedom' was not a difficult theme upon which to expand one's arguments.

Few of the demonstrations were intended to end in violence, though eggs and tomatoes were considered fair game. I can recall only one occasion when a brick narrowly missed me, to break a window just behind where I was standing. I remember with much greater pleasure the egg heading straight towards me; I ducked, and was able to relish the spectacle of a bull's-eye it scored on one of the demonstrators immediately behind me. There was the custard pie in Leeds, which I managed to punch before it hit my face, but not quickly enough to identify the perpetrator, who was recovered some moments later by a healthy squad of rugby players and paraded for identification, which regrettably I was unable to provide. He, I suspect, had a lucky escape. Anne was less lucky at Winchester, where we were bound for the local Conservatives' Annual Dinner. A flurry of eggs aimed at me hit her instead, ruining her dress. Not my most popular moment.

How serious accidents and perhaps worse did not follow from that period is little short of miraculous. I remember leaving the Cambridge Union by a side door and being bundled into a police car that accelerated fast up the narrow street. At the far end of the street, round the corner, came a mother holding a little child in her outside hand and swinging the child far out from the pavement into the road. The police car missed the child by inches. Of course, the protest movement would have blamed the police, but the entire responsibility lay with the mother who was prepared to play so lightly with her child's safety.

Easter weekend fell at the very beginning of April in 1983 and had been chosen, somewhat obviously, by the protest groups for a major demonstration at Greenham Common. Their plans were well known and were designed to attract the maximum public sympathy. The idea was simple: they would circle the base at Greenham Common with women, peacefully holding hands. I was deeply preoccupied by the symbolism of this. If they did it well, they would be likely to receive saturation coverage from the British media for the whole of the Easter weekend. Their spokesmen would be given extra air-time and they would have a propaganda coup.

I believed it was my responsibility to counter this. I felt that I would be at a distinct disadvantage, however, if all I could do was to appear in some television studio, reacting to their dominance of the headlines. No one was able to come up with an effective idea that would give me the initiative and leave CND having to react to it. I remember being extremely worried about this dilemma, but perhaps at the time I did not fully appreciate just how concerned in my sub-conscious I was. Then one morning, quite vividly, but while still asleep, I saw what I had to do. I woke up about 6.30 a.m., instantly wide awake. The strategy was clear.

On 31 March, the Thursday before Easter and the day before the demonstration at Greenham Common was to begin, Anne and I went to Berlin. I visited the British troops, toured the Wall, looked at the Russian troops and stared into that no-man's land between West and East with its mines and machine guns. We returned to Heathrow as the Greenham demonstration was getting under way. The national press was waiting, in large numbers. I delivered my message: I had seen the real peace-keepers, the men and women of the British forces who every day were risking their lives in defence of the peace and the freedom which allowed others to march in protest over Easter weekend. CND's demonstration proceeded but it made little impact on public opinion. It had been put into the context in which it belonged.

The next challenge was to reveal the true composition and motives of the peace movement. I asked Peter Blaker, as Minister of State in the MOD, to conduct a thorough analysis of the personalities and funding involved. It was not long before he was able to produce evidence that a majority of the CND council was drawn from left-wing organisations. I decided that this information should enter the public debate. On 22 April 1983, I sent a letter to all Tory MPs and candidates in marginal seats giving biographical details of the communists, Marxists and socialists in the CND movement and alerting them to CND's decision to challenge Conservative candidates in marginal seats in the forthcoming election. I wrote:

> Many people attracted to the peace movement will just not want to believe that behind the carefully tuned phrases about peace lies the calculating political professionalism of full-time socialists and communists. Many people will feel betrayed and insulted by so overt a party political decision by CND . . . We must ensure that the British people do not vote against this country's ability to defend itself without knowing about the real motives and purpose of the peace movement. They march in the name of peace. Ask them where their journey ends.

I used the same theme as the basis of a speech in Exeter the next day, in which I warned that, for its extremists, CND's purpose 'was to argue the cause of the Soviet Union at the expense of the free societies of the West'. Both letter and speech attracted widespread attention and provoked the fury of the leaders of CND. Only one person named threatened libel proceedings, Roger Spiller, a vice-chair of CND and a white-collar union official, but he eventually dropped his action. Throughout we were meticulous that no information was used that was not in the public domain. The allegations by an ex-MI5 junior officer, Cathy Massiter, that the Security Service collected information for this purpose were untrue.

Mrs Thatcher called the general election on 9 May and it took place a month later, on 9 June. By that time, far from being an asset to the Labour Party, the peace movement had become a serious liability, but Labour found themselves too deeply committed to pull back. In truth, with a few honourable exceptions like Roy Hattersley and Gerald Kaufman, they believed in the CND cause. An intervention to the same effect by Jim Callaghan – by then no longer Labour leader – was also particularly helpful to the government. Labour were not just led by people committed to a non-nuclear policy; they had compounded that misjudgement by threatening major cuts in the defence budget. We were able not only to argue the strategic defence case but also to point to the lost jobs that would flow from the cuts in conventional expenditure. We listed the constituencies with major defence contractors and suggested the scale of unemployment that could follow. During the election campaign, I visited Barrow-in-Furness, a seat that in virtually any circumstances ought to be won by the Labour Party but which was the home of Vickers Shipbuilding and Engineering, under contract to manufacture the Trident submarines. In one of the great upsets of the 1983 election the Tory candidate, Cecil Franks, won it by 4,577 votes. In the country at large we increased our majority from 44 to 144, with my own margin of victory in a redrawn Henley reaching nearly 14,000.

I had already been told by Mrs Thatcher, when she appointed me at the beginning of the year, that I would be going back to the Ministry of Defence after the election, in the event of a Conservative victory. So I did. The victory itself had denied the protest groups the prospect of any constitutional route to power. Democracy had spoken.

But that was not the sort of thing to discourage the hard left. The next stage of the battle would be to oppose the deployment of cruise missiles themselves. It had been determined from the beginning that there would be two bases for cruise missiles. Greenham was one. The second was at RAF Molesworth, a disused base in the Huntingdon constituency of John Major. The one essentail difference between Greenham Common and Molesworth was that the latter had no fence around it. It had an eight-mile perimeter and thus was a gift to anybody wishing to disrupt its effective use. If we began to build a fence, however, the protest groups would simply lie down in front of the construction equipment, and do so every yard of the way.

I held a meeting in the Ministry with my principal advisers. 'I want to build a fence overnight,' was my simple request. 'Quite impossible,' they said. Various estimates were submitted to me; they were all in terms of months, not hours. I remembered Tom Baron from our time together in the Department of the Environment. I invited him to a second meeting. Tom had been a private in the Royal Engineers during the war – not quite in the league of the top brass around that table in the MOD. His advice was straightforward enough. There was no way a permanent fence of the kind envisaged was possible in less than a month. The only solution was to get the Sappers to erect between dusk and dawn a three-coil, razor-wire fence around the airfield so that the contractors could erect their fence inside the wire, free from harassment. He had found the solution. The course was set.

Every manner of subterfuge was employed. Vast orders for barbed wire were placed – notionally to be dispatched to the Falkland Islands. Leave was cancelled for various services under the pretext of some wholly fictional routine exercise. Contractors were engaged for a project which bore no resemblance in time or location to the reality (their senior management was sworn to secrecy). The fifth of February 1985 arrived. That night we were to move, but not before the nation had gone to bed, by which time the morning newspapers would have been printed, the last television and radio news programmes effectively off the air and the protest groups safely abed. Nothing was to happen until 11 p.m. We feared that, if the 10 p.m. news bulletins, whether on television or the radio, had carried any hint of our plans, the protest groups would have been at Molesworth within an hour.

The day advanced. Tension mounted in the Ministry. At about 3.00 p.m. a telephone call to my press office from a local Cambridge newspaper inquired about the military and other movements in their area. Fortunately, the anodyne reply they received satisfied them and we heard no more from them. Nothing was yet happening at Molesworth itself, but large numbers of people and mountains of kit were being moved to assembly points within reach.

By eleven o'clock that evening our luck had held. The exercise entered its last decisive stage and by early the next morning it was virtually complete. The eight-mile perimeter had been secured and was defensible. I followed events on a screen monitor in the MOD until 4.00 a.m. when I set off by helicopter for the base to congratulate the people concerned on a quite remarkable achievement. As I walked from the helicopter in the cold, grey morning air, there was the lightest of drizzles. An accommodating wing commander took off his flak jacket and put it round my shoulders. 'You'll get wet, Secretary of State,' he said. I hardly noticed, such was the excitement of the achievement. But, for the media, the flak jacket was the message. If there had been a single CND body lying in the way of that fence, it would have been a front-page story, but the factor of surprise and the meticulous organisation that led to securing that fence in a night was lost to sight, as the focus of attention was on the Secretary of State apparently masquerading as a soldier leading his troops. The demonstrators eventually arrived, and fussed around at some deconsecrated church ruin in an attempt to gain a symbolic spot in the public presentation. They were welcome to it. We had achieved our objective.

There is a footnote to this history. The project to build that fence at Molesworth was one of the largest ever undertaken by the Royal Engineers. The single largest was the crossing of the Rhine some forty years earlier. On that occasion, there was present one Private Tom Baron.

But the story was far from over. The essence of cruise missiles was their invulnerability to pre-emptive attack. Mounted on large vehicles, they could be deployed by road many miles away from their home base very quickly and were thus virtually untraceable. It had been one thing to fly the first cruise missiles into Greenham Common, protected by its perimeter fence. It was going to be quite another to get the vehicles carrying them actually out on to the roads, free to travel to their operational positions. The women of Greenham Common were well aware of our dilemma and were determined to block the exit.

Of course, in the end we could have deployed whatever police presence was necessary to secure passage, but there was always a risk that the resulting confrontation would lead to casualties and escalate the trouble still further. We decided instead on a subterfuge which was perhaps so obvious that, surprisingly, it worked. The cruise missiles had arrived with much publicity on 14 November 1983. It became known that the first 'road test' exercise was scheduled for the evening of 8 March 1984. During the day we made ostentatious arrangements to suggest our intention to use the main gates at the base. Towards the allotted hour the demonstrators gathered in force. We organised a large police presence in order to make clear our ability to ensure effective deployment through the crowds. The scene was set. Expectations rose. Then we sent the missiles out by a side entrance. There was no trouble. To this day I am amazed that we got away with such a simple device. Cruise missiles had been deployed for the first time. We had shown it could be done, and the propaganda victory was ours. We had relatively little difficulty thereafter.

The United Kingdom had honoured its pledge to the NATO alliance. We had provided a base for the modernisation of NATO's nuclear deterrent and we were modernising the British deterrent. The consequence of our decision, along with some of our European allies, to support the American response to the deployment of the Soviet SS20s was to persuade President Brezhnev that the West would counter any military enhancement that the Soviets might make. This reality led directly to the Intermediate-Range Nuclear Forces (INF) Treaty of 1987, whereby the SS20s were withdrawn from Eastern Europe to the Soviet Union and cruise missiles to the United States. For the Soviet Union the cost of the economic burden involved in its defence policy was crippling. The next generation of Soviet leaders had learnt the lesson. The West would respond to any threat, and remain united in doing so. Their realistic appreciation of this and the action that followed ended the Cold War, and led to the break-up of the Soviet Union and the restoration of freedom to central Europe. Every inch of the way down that road was opposed at home by the British Labour Party in the House of Commons and, often, on the streets of Britain as well.

In addition, together with our German colleagues, particularly Manfred Woerner, we had resisted the French attempt at about this time to reactivate the Western European Union (WEU). Of all the foreign ministers with whom I worked, I formed the closest personal relationship with Manfred – I liked his directness. He and I were both suspicious of France's intentions in this regard. We believed, as did our governments, that the rock of Western security rested on the NATO alliance. If France was genuinely interested in enhancing European security, there was an obvious step for it to take and that was to re-engage with the NATO military structure from which it had opted out some twenty years earlier. Any non-NATO initiative by France had all the hallmarks of its latent anti-Americanism, and I was determined we would not have any association with that.

In general, therefore, no closer bonds bound together any two members of the alliance than those between Britain and the United States. But there was one major policy divergence between us – though it was largely determined above my head.

I attended a NATO meeting in Portugal on 22–23 March 1983, during which I had the customary bilateral discussion with the US Secretary of Defense, Caspar Weinberger. I got on well with Cap, an acute lawyer, despite a continuing disagreement about the desirability of breakfast meetings (to me, an essentially unEnglish practice). I returned to my office in London later on the 23rd and was more than a little surprised to receive a telephone call from him towards the end of the afternoon in which he told me that the Americans were just about to announce the development of a Strategic Defense Initiative (SDI, and which, after the George Lucas film, became popularly known as 'Star Wars'). President Reagan made his famous speech launching the project without any early consultation with either his allies or, some say, even most of his Cabinet. I was concerned at this escalation in the confrontation between the superpowers.

The issues that arose from SDI were complex and ranged far beyond the questions of cost and workability. Would the Soviet Union respond by escalating a new phase of the arms race in space? It was argued that they were already conducting research with just this aim in view. What would such an initiative do to the already agreed Anti-Ballistic Missile Treaty and to other arms-control negotiations then in progress? Again, it was argued that the Russians were already in breach of the existing treaty with their development of their radar system capability at Krasnoyarsk. The official advice to me from the Ministry was that this American accusation was based on less than rock-solid evidence. It is possible that the Americans were right, but officials were cautious. More difficult still were the questions surrounding the possible success of the technological leap. Suppose it did work. Would American behaviour towards the Soviet Union, and so the risk of war in Europe, change if the US itself was defended by impenetrable weaponry? What if the Soviet Union succeeded in developing such a system in turn, which might then neutralise the British and French independent deterrents?

All these issues and many others were discussed at a Chequers seminar, ostensibly on the subject of NATO, in October 1984. From that meeting there emerged the stance with which Mrs Thatcher went to Washington in late December and drew up with President Reagan the Camp David Accord, a four-point agreement – largely drafted by the British – which set out clearly the need for a proper balance between the policies of SDI research and of continuing arms-control negotiations. Geoffrey Howe and I accompanied her on a subsequent visit to Washington in February 1985, the occasion on which she addressed, to great effect, both Houses of Congress. She received a standing ovation for her speech, although it should be recorded that Senator Edward Kennedy, in a conspicuous example of bad manners, remained firmly in his seat, near to my own.

On that occasion we went on to lunch with President Reagan at the White House, and there discussed the defence aspects of the Western alliance. In her memoirs Mrs Thatcher records the inhibitions she felt at Geoffrey's and my presence at that lunch. One can only suppose that, without two witnesses from the Chequers meeting, her natural instincts would have inclined to the rather more simplistic views of the President's own perspective. But we had been cautioned by his staff before lunch that SDI was not a subject upon which the President wished to dwell. I did raise a few questions, but the discussions were perfunctory. A decision had already been taken and the expenditure of some $30 billion was committed to the advance research programme.

For this country – and indeed many others – another very real anxiety associated with SDI was the technology transfer that such a dramatic, horizon-stretching development would deliver to American hi-tech companies. The research necessary to prove the feasibility of such a system would push the knowledge and capability of these companies beyond the present technological frontiers. Such advance and the spin-offs that would flow from it would give a competitive advantage in the next generation of both civil and military products which would be quite beyond the industrial base of any other nation to equal.

I was fortunate to have a vivid illustration of this. One day US General James Abrahamson, the Director of the SDI programme, came to visit me in the Ministry. He explained its virtues from a military point of view. He went on to discuss the technological advantages that would flow to the United Kingdom if it joined the programme. 'I would be willing to commit today $100,000', he said, 'to back the research being conducted at Heriot-Watt University.' It was clear to me that this conversation was being repeated all across the world. He knew exactly where the leading-edge technological development was taking place and he was systematically offering to establish partnerships in every field. The consequence in aggregate was obvious: that in one major defence initiative America would have acquired a partnership with the best brains and the best technological advances in the world in each of these vital industrial sectors.

Of course, Heriot-Watt would have gained. Once partnerships were struck, the Americans were generous in bankrolling them. They did not count on a pound-for-pound basis what they were prepared to spend and compare it with our level of expenditure. Undoubtedly, Heriot-Watt would have been the richer for that particular partnership. For them, that was the attraction of it. But the aggregate of all these partnerships across the world would represent a technology transfer to the United States staggering in its scope, and such a wealth of technological excellence would strengthen the American industrial base, sharpening its competitive edge, and inevitably be turned into products offered on the world's markets with which our companies had to compete. And this process was all to be financed by American taxpayers. Hence my caution – which I think some elements in the Pentagon (though not General Abrahamson) eventually came to understand. In the end we joined up, but I did my best to ensure that Britain derived the maximum benefits from the deal.

The United States signed collaboration agreements in support of SDI with countries across the world. West Germany, Israel and Italy signed in 1986 and Japan in 1987, but ours was the first in late 1985. I agreed with Cap Weinberger that the contract should include a flow of one billion dollars' expenditure in the UK. If, as was inevitable, we were to sign, I also believed that we should try to obtain for our companies access to the wider technologies involved rather than simply in those areas where we were already ahead. However, the procurement systems of the Pentagon and the enthusiastic monitoring of Congressional committees provided an apparently inflexible set of disciplines which, or so it was claimed, prevented non-competitive assurances of this sort. I didn't believe a word of it. If it had suited American interests, ways would have been found. In the event, my colleagues had no stomach for a confrontation over such an issue.

To the best of my knowledge no account has ever been kept of the cumulative value of SDI to this country in terms either of total spend or of technological transfer. I made inquiries in 1999 and was told that 'the MOD does not maintain a central or comprehensive record of all contracts let by the US Government with UK industry and universities under the Strategic Defense Initiative'. I pressed further and elicited the following information about contracts awarded to British research facilities:

> As with contracts established directly with British companies, no central or comprehensive record is maintained. It is believed, however, that most research has been undertaken on a Government to Government basis under an arrangement known as Letters of Offer and Acceptance (LOAs) . . . The total value of LOAs entered into since 1985 is approximately $150M. While expenditure on an annual basis is not available in detail, work commenced at approximately $2M per annum in 1986, building to $12M over a seven-year period, then falling away to some $5M currently.

These figures should be seen against a background of a projected £30 billion spend in the decade after the programme was launched. The views of John Pike, a space-policy analyst at the Federation of American Scientists in Washington, as reported in the *Financial Times* in March 1987, are revealing: 'While Britain had plenty of good ideas that could be contributed to technical studies, Mr Pike believed most UK companies lacked the technical expertise to work on the aspects of Star Wars which involved development of hardware for operational systems.' This, of course, was the Catch-22 situation I had hoped to circumvent.

The only serious rift between the American Defense Secretary and myself arose over the invasion of Grenada. On 19 October 1983 a pro-Soviet military coup had overthrown the government of this independent Commonwealth country and there was widespread speculation in the British press that the Americans, concerned as ever about their own backyard in the Caribbean, were contemplating invasion. Four days later, on Sunday the 23rd, the headquarters of the US Marines in Beirut was bombed and over 200 Americans killed. The two events were not related, but the understandable anger of the American people at this outrage undoubtedly spurred the US administration to do some flag-waving closer to home. Mrs Thatcher pressed the case for restraint and the Foreign Office received assurances from the State Department that the US intended to proceed with caution. On Monday, 24 October, Geoffrey Howe (as Foreign Secretary) made a statement in the House of Commons saying that we were 'in the closest possible touch with the US and Caribbean governments' and that there was 'no reason to think that American intervention is likely'. 'I know of no such intention,' he said.

But the situation deteriorated dramatically that evening when first one, then a second, tele-letter arrived at No. 10 and it became clear that President Reagan was, indeed, preparing to intervene. Geoffrey and I joined Mrs Thatcher in the little upstairs drawing room at No. 10 to discuss the situation. A reply was dispatched with the utmost urgency in the early hours of Tuesday morning. It was clear that speed was essential and the only solution was for the Prime Minister to talk to President Reagan. Geoffrey and I were present during the conversation, although, of course, we could hear only her side of the exchanges. But the message was plain enough. While agreeing to consider the British arguments, Reagan apparently added the ominous words: 'We are already at zero.' In fact, as it later transpired, he had given the final order some two hours earlier. Indeed, he had taken the decision to mount such an operation the previous Saturday morning. In the early hours of Tuesday, 25 October, American troops landed on the island. The British press erupted. Geoffrey had to make a second statement to the House that afternoon, and the next day there was a full-scale emergency debate.

I was indignant. I took a folder of the more humiliating headlines from our newspapers with me to the Montebello meeting of the NATO Nuclear Planning Group at the end of that week and remonstrated with Cap Weinberger himself. I produced the cuttings and said that in my view this was an unforgivable way to treat one of America's closest and most reliable allies. I explained that it was only US 'misinformation' that had led to Geoffrey's having to eat his words in the Commons and observed with as much restraint as I could muster that the whole episode amounted to a very inadequate return for all the loyalty that Mrs Thatcher's government – including its Foreign and Defence Secretaries – had demonstrated in the execution of American-led and -inspired NATO policies.

It was not an easy moment, but I have never regretted the frankness with which I spoke. With hindsight, however, I may have embarrassed Cap more than I intended, since it later emerged that the chief proponent of the invasion policy was George Shultz at the State Department, and Cap himself had expressed misgivings within the administration. Shultz had believed in the need to seize 'a window of opportunity' and 'fire a shot heard round the world', while Cap had argued strongly for a more cautious approach. The State Department had good cause, therefore, not to stir up one of Cap's natural allies in the days leading up to the invasion. Mrs Thatcher was kept in the dark and Geoffrey was left to twist in the wind.

Chapter 14

MANAGING THE MOD

M rs Thatcher had put me in the Ministry of Defence in the first place in part to enable me to bring to bear on that vast department a management style that she had admired in the DOE. Its present structure largely reflected the changes introduced by Harold Macmillan as Prime Minister, supported by Peter Thorneycroft and Lord Mountbatten. Earl Mountbatten of Burma had become the first Chief of the Defence Staff in 1959. Previously the post had rotated between the single service Chiefs of Staff, one of whom would act as chairman of their committee but each of whom had responsibility for their own policy staff. As Supreme Commander of the Allied forces in South-east Asia in 1945, Lord Mountbatten had become convinced that modern warfare demanded a unification of the command structure of the three services. He was initially appointed Chief of the Defence Staff for three years, but his term was extended for another two years to allow him to oversee in 1962–3 the preparation of a white paper (published in July 1963) which led to the setting up of a single, unified and Whitehall centralised MOD. The actual change took place in the dying months of the Alec Douglas-Home government on 1 April 1964. The restructuring did not go as far as Mountbatten would have liked; the MOD was a loose federation and the command structures were insufficiently integrated. From the moment I arrived, I was determined to try and complete the task that Macmillan and Mountbatten had started.

In 1979, when the Conservatives returned to power, the organisational framework of the Ministry was simple. There were five main groupings: Central Staff, the staffs of each of the services, Navy, Army and Air Force, and a Procurement Executive. Each of the military sides had its own policy-making and command departments and a junior minister to represent it. The Chief of the Defence Staff was in theoretical overall charge but in an advisory and not an executive role. The position of the Secretary of State was invidious. In any controversy his three junior, service-linked ministers would put the conflicting views of the particular service he represented. The Secretary of State thus spent much of his time arbitrating between his colleagues and was deprived of a sense of collective purpose and the ability to delegate that I believe essential in the successful administration of a large organisation. To make matters worse, each of the services had an umbilical link not only with the defence correspondents of the major newspapers but with their distinguished former Chiefs, many of whom were safely ensconced in the House of Lords. A large number of senior Conservative backbenchers at that time had served in the Second World War and rightly treasured their loyalties to their old regiment or service. Change was nobody's ally. Any Secretary of State who embarked upon the process of reform was heading for trouble. Even the Palace itself could not fail to be aware of the furore such controversy provokes.

I was materially assisted in the task upon which I was embarked, however, by an earlier experience of Mrs Thatcher's while John Nott was still Secretary of State. In 1981 Keith Speed, the junior minister for the Navy, had made a speech in his constituency, in effect disowning the conclusions of that year's Defence Review even before it was published. This infuriated the Prime Minister, who was not at all mollified to discover that John Nott, Speed's boss, did not want him sacked, believing that the best solution would be to move him sideways in the next reshuffle. (Mrs Thatcher went ahead and sacked him anyway, but the episode did nothing to improve her relationship with her then Secretary of State.) At this point she decided – rightly – that having three junior ministers, each responsible for one of the three services, made the position of the Secretary of State impossible. Thus, before I arrived, the position had been changed. A Minister for the Armed Services was given overall responsibility for the three services with a junior minister to support him, while the pattern was repeated with a further two ministers responsible for procurement. This was a big step towards cross-service co-ordination. Left unchallenged, however, was the fundamental separation of power between the services.

There was a general recognition that I was going to be interested in the structure and management of the Ministry. One of the first conversations I had with my new permanent secretary, Clive Whitmore, was about the MINIS system. I told him I wanted to introduce it to the MOD. He said he had guessed as much. I added that I wanted an organogram – setting out the chains of responsibility and demonstrating who was answerable to whom – to show how the whole place was organised. I pinned the resulting chart, when eventually it had been designed and prepared, to a green-baize-covered board I had had fixed to one wall of my room in the Ministry.

It took some time to familiarise myself with the existing structure and to understand the politics of it. I engaged in many discussions with senior officers and civil servants and with growing clarity I began to develop a picture in my mind of the way forward. Of particular interest to me were the views of many of the rank of colonel and below who had formed the Falklands task force, and their experience and conviction were decisive in persuading me of the direction of change. The culture of the more senior officers was one of dismissive criticism, particularly reinforced by reference to the experiences of the Canadians who had 'purple-ised' (as it was known) their armed forces. This experiment, which had included a single armed-forces uniform, had succeeded in undermining the service loyalties, so vital to military life. I had no intention of making the same mistake, but, despite my reassurances, there was no way of persuading the top brass that unification was needed. I thus faced a lonely decision. If any change was to be made at all, it would have to be done by imposition. That meant that I needed, first, the PM's support and, secondly, a clear blueprint to put it into effect. I went to see Mrs Thatcher in No. 10, outlined to her what I had in mind and said that it would be quite impossible to carry this thing through if she had any doubts, and unless she supported me through the row which was wholly predictable. She gave me that assurance and I drew up my plans. On an aircraft bringing me back from Kuwait, I sketched out the structure I wanted. During the flight, in an RAF VC10, my private secretary Richard Mottram and I drew up the proposed outline of a unified structure for the Ministry of Defence.

It was essential to preserve the loyalties that underpin and bind together the whole British service structure. I believed that the position of the Chief of the Defence Staff had to be changed from chairman of a committee to that of the person clearly responsible for providing military advice to the government and for the conduct of military operations. It was vital to preserve as well, as far as possible, the integrity and prestige of the individual service Chiefs: the Chief of the Naval Staff, the Chief of the General Staff and the Chief of the Air Staff. Yet at the same time they had to be made accountable and answerable to the Chief of the Defence Staff. That was the first major step.

The second was that the policy work of the individual services had to be combined into a single policy unit for all three. Instead of each service working out its own strategy and putting up often incompatible or conflicting policy and spending proposals, representatives of the three services would have to work together to produce agreed papers – or, if not agreed, then at least papers where disputes had, however reluctantly, been settled or where the options were clearly set out for all to understand. That meant removing the single-service policy staffs from each of the service Chiefs and centralising them under a new, four-star appointment: the Vice-Chief of the Defence Staff. Procurement had already been so centralised, under the Procurement Executive, in earlier reforms.

The plan was clear. I then had to take one of the most controversial, but most unavoidable, decisions that ever faced me as Secretary of State. The way of modern government is consultation, with a range of proposals leading to a conclusion. I knew that any sign of weakness on my part, any private sharing of my ideas with the military, would have been a disaster. Particularly was this the case with the Chief of the Defence Staff, Field Marshal Sir Edwin ('Dwin') Bramall. No Secretary of State could have asked for a more loyal or experienced military adviser than I found in Dwin. He had served under Montgomery at the end of the Second World War and by repute had been an officer marked out for the top from his earliest days as a light infantryman in the Green Jackets. He had been on Mountbatten's staff in the MOD in the mid-1960s and so had some background in these streamlining issues. He was deeply hurt that I didn't consult him about my plans and I pondered long and hard before I took that decision. Not just for my sake and the sake of the policies, but also for his, I decided that the least undesirable way forward was to present him with a *fait accompli*. To have done other than that would either have required him to keep the information confidential, opening him up to charges of betrayal by his fellow military officers, or have made him feel compelled to consult them and in that case the process would have unravelled at bewildering speed.

The first he knew of my plans was when they had been drawn up in a near final form which was not for serious negotiation. The row was as predicted. The ultimate challenge came in a letter from the Chiefs; it was a reasoned and balanced critique of my proposals, acknowledging that they had some merit and, indeed, in some ways that they had advantages. But the last paragraph contained the killer punch with words to the effect that, while seeing the virtues of what was proposed and recognising that there might be advantages in peacetime, they did not believe the structure would work in war conditions. I held my position. From the start I had always believed that the Chiefs would exercise their constitutional right to appeal over my head to the Prime Minister. But, of course, I already knew what her views were. Mrs Thatcher stood her ground, as she had promised she would. The changes went through.

British forces have been on active service on several occasions since those reforms were introduced. The Gulf War was probably as close to 'war conditions' as any and the reaction there to the new system was very positive. I have never heard it seriously criticised. Indeed, I believe that it is seen now as a model upon which to base the structure of the armed services, preserving the traditional loyalties but recognising the interrelationships of the three services in any foreseeable active conditions.

All recent Prime Ministers have to a degree felt let down by the system. They all seek to get their hands more firmly on the levers of power. Indecisive ministers, inert civil servants are characterised as the grit in the works, slowing and impeding the peaceful introduction of the required revolution. Centralisation in Downing Street becomes the solution. Among the early manifestations of this desire on Mrs Thatcher's part was the appointment in late 1982 of Sir Anthony Parsons, a distinguished career member of the Foreign Office and Britain's ambassador to the United Nations during the Falklands War, as her personal foreign policy adviser. These centralising instincts or their resulting actions are generally ill judged. In our system of government they end in tears. First, the system entrusts power to the departments of Whitehall and elsewhere. Confuse that responsibility and their ability to disengage is mighty. Secondly, the Prime Minister can not only undermine the authority of colleagues as a consequence but may all too easily become engaged in and therefore responsible for far too much of the detail of administration. Prime Ministers must be good butchers. It's not always easy to wash blood off hands steeped in the slaughter process.

But there is another particular danger in the appointment of personal advisers of this kind for any Secretary of State. Any minister who wishes to impose his or her will on a department is likely to meet opposition. When a minister makes proposals to colleagues, that is his or her responsibility. Nothing is more aggravating than in a Cabinet committee, or in the Cabinet itself, to find oneself in a debate with a seconded official from one's own department. You will not have seen the briefing papers that such an official has provided for the Prime Minister. Arguments which you thought you had resolved within your department are recycled. There is an uncomfortable feeling that disgruntled officials from your own department may have gone behind your back.

It was, therefore, with some concern that I learnt that the next ministry on the Prime Minister's hit list was mine. A bright official, Roger Jackling, who went on well after my time to be the second permanent under-secretary at the MOD, was – at the Prime Minister's direction – to be moved across Whitehall from the MOD to No. 10. I was frankly apprehensive of the trouble that this could cause but, of course, was in no position to block Mrs Thatcher's decision. I simply issued an instruction, through my permanent secretary, that the Prime Minister was to receive any briefing that Roger Jackling wished to give her on any subject of interest to the Department. However, any briefing of Roger Jackling by my officials was to take place only with the knowledge and approval of my private secretary. Jackling was back in the Department within a matter of months.

John Nott's Defence Review had established the strategic policy framework for the immediate future. I was not, therefore, concerned with a further Defence Review. I was interested, however, within the resources available to me, in moving as many servicemen and -women as possible into front-line fighting capability at the expense of the rear echelons. John Stanier, the Chief of the General Staff, and I worked together on an exercise known as Lean Look. I did a deal with him whereby the more he cut the support staffs, the more personnel he could switch to the front line. He turned up one day to present his findings, dressed in full military rig, sword drawn, as he marched into the Secretary of State's office with his presentation boards. The British Army of the Rhine and other Army units gained some 4,000 posts.

The military side of the Ministry had its own culture. Years before the final decisions had to be made, the likeliest successors to the top jobs were pencilled into what was known as the 'Top Plot' in order to ensure that such potential high-flyers were posted to receive the widest experience. Secretaries of State were invited to indicate, after receiving appropriate advice, who was likely to become the head of the individual services or, ultimately, Chief of the Defence Staff. In the latter case, the presumption historically had been that the three services would take it in turn. John Nott had determined that the government would no longer follow this practice. It fell to me to implement the change when I decided that the best candidate to succeed Dwin Bramall was Admiral of the Fleet Sir John Fieldhouse, who had been Commander-in-Chief Fleet during the Falklands War. I have no doubt it was the right decision.

John Nott had had to grapple with the Ministry's procurement budget in the acutely difficult circumstances of high and rising inflation. The economic background had now eased. But establishing control over the long-term costing, which guided the planning and matching to available resources of the entire defence programme, including all the activities of the Ministry, the services and their procurement programmes, remained one of my more formidable challenges. The long-term costing was literally a ten-year programme, showing year by year how every part of the likely budget would be spent. In essence, it was a perfectly reasonable system. Everybody had some idea when, for example, a particular piece of equipment was likely to be in service and thus could plan for it. But the process had, in a sense, been sanctified. Any minister seeking to establish the availability of cash would be presented with the long-term costing showing that for ten years ahead there was no cash. Everything was already spoken for. This defence mechanism was, I think, more a front-line trench in the annual war of attrition with the Treasury than a denial of ministerial choice. But it conveniently served both purposes. 'We've spent our money, Secretary of State. If you want something different, you go and ask the Treasury for the cash.' Thus had the Ministry of Defence learnt to protect itself from the annual ravages of the Treasury and the spending round. Any cut led at once to an unacceptable degradation of our military capability. The long-term costing was as much a weapon of war as a tool of financial discipline.

To any manager with the remotest idea of the real world the idea of this rectangular slab of ten-year expenditure was nonsense. I asked the obvious question: I asked them to show me how much of this expenditure had actually been authorised by ministers and contractually committed. I knew what the answer had to be – that beyond the first two or three years hardly any of the expenditure had been contracted. In practice there were vast, uncommitted amounts of money. The Ministry was expert at moving programmes about within this discretionary element. Contracts slipped, new requirements emerged, mistakes had to be rectified, weapon systems gold-plated. If money suddenly needed to be found, gaps in the programme were wonderfully and miraculously discovered. But when the Treasury or their own ministers called, the shutters were up.

Thus there were three ways to cut the procurement budget. The first was simply to answer the question: 'Which weapon system would you like us to cancel, Secretary of State?' Only the foolhardy were taken down that road. The second was to move the programme to the right, as the process was known; the third to manage the costs of the programme with greater effectiveness.

I had much stimulating debate over the second method. If you moved the whole programme so that in eleven years you bought what you had previously budgeted to buy in ten years, you could look to something like a 10 per cent reduction in procurement expenditure in any one year. As most procurement programmes slipped anyway by reason of technological failure, add-ons to existing designs or changing priorities, this was not the harsh decision it seemed. But this analysis was deeply unpopular when I expressed it within the Ministry.

The third means of controlling the budget was to grip the contractual process and introduce competition. I had been immensely impressed with the work that Tom Baron had done in the Department of the Environment. Here was a special adviser with expert knowledge who worked alongside civil servants, was respected by them and contributed very much to the formulation of housing policy. This precedent led me, on my arrival at the Ministry of Defence, to look around for the brightest young industrialist who might be persuaded to turn from poacher to gamekeeper and help control procurement. The name of Peter Levene soon surfaced. He had developed a publicly quoted company, United Scientific Holdings, which procured either by manufacture or purchase military equipment that was then sold across the world.

We lunched together at Wiltons, the Jermyn Street fish restaurant.

I asked him, on the strength of that lunch, whether he would consider coming to the Ministry as my special adviser. He is a man of outstanding ability, with a rare talent not only to see the heart of a problem but to persuade people to accept his solution for it. We were to work together in many different guises over the next fifteen years and today Peter (now Lord Levene) is a director of the Haymarket Publishing Group and one of my children's trustees. He added to his already formidable reputation in proving to be one of the most successful Lord Mayors of London in 1998–9.

In 1983 we set out to transform the MOD's approach to procurement. One of the most admirable of the traditions of the British armed services is their understanding of the need to preserve and enhance an excellent working relationship from the front line to the top of the command structure. It is the philosophy of the weakest link in the chain and they are expert in ensuring that everything is done to make that weakest link as strong as possible. Their man-management philosophy is a major contributor to the morale and excellence of their fighting capability. They are, so to speak, all in it together or, as the Royal Navy put it, 'all of one company'. It was one of the sharpest contrasts between the British forces in the Falklands and the Argentines, as illustrated when I visited the islands and was shown the difference between the rations for the Argentine officers and those for their men. In the British Army they all got the same – which, incidentally, is the best way to ensure that the troops are well fed.

Yet this sense of being all in it together is not one that should be automatically transferred to govern the relationship between the military and industry. Customers and contractors need to work closely together but they are not partners. The natural consequence of the Ministry's culture was the guaranteed 'cost-plus contract', of which the most notorious example was the Ferranti scandal which the House of Commons Public Accounts Committee unearthed in the early 1960s. There were seldom any penalty clauses and, even if there were, it was often difficult to enforce them. If things went wrong, the cost of putting them right would be borne by the Ministry. Too often extras were required and the Ministry would have to pay, as it would for the delays that were inevitably part of the process. It was a one-way ratcheting-up process, maintained at the taxpayers' expense. Industry liked it.

I lost no time indicating that this approach had to change, that we would move to competitive procurement and that cost-plus was in future to be the exception rather than the rule. The deputy under-secretary for defence procurement, Kenneth MacDonald, persisted in arguing for the current system. It led to the only time I can remember when, having had three meetings on the specific issue, covering the same ground again and again, I said in exasperation that I was not prepared to discuss the matter any further. I was now going to dictate the policy. I set a ceiling of £250,000 above which there would be competitive tendering for all contracts.

It was impossible, of course, to change the culture overnight. One of the larger procurement projects which the Ministry had to determine while I was there was the updating of the airborne early-warning system. One of my predecessors had had to choose between AWACS, the existing American system, and the GEC-designed Nimrod to be carried on converted Comets. A decision had been taken to place a contract with GEC. But the radar contract had long been in trouble. The cost overruns were substantial. The specifications had been changed during the contract. The technology was not passing its test trials satisfactorily. The Air Force, and latterly I myself, discussed the matter with Jim Prior and Arnold Weinstock, the chairman and chief executive of GEC.

It was the old type of MOD cost-plus contract. There were no effective sanctions that we could apply. The only option available was to cancel the contract and procure from the Americans. This was not a trouble-free option. Critics would decry the wilful destruction of our radar capability – an important part of the industrial defence base. Constituency Members of Parliament would join the protest and the media would exploit the arguments for all they were worth. All this must be judged against a background wherein the company were adamant in assuring us that they would be able to deliver the project. I was moving reluctantly to the conclusion that the contract would have to be cancelled, but I had not finally resolved the matter.

My resignation at the beginning of 1986 preceded any final decision. The moment that my successor, George Younger, arrived in the Department the papers were put before him. Just as I had done, he clearly did everything possible to save this important high technology for British industry. It took another year before, in December 1986, he announced the cancellation of the contract. Arnold Weinstock was, predictably, enraged and, although years later I tried very hard to assure him that I would almost certainly have taken the same decision and that it was a decision strongly advocated by the Procurement

Executive and the Air Force, he was never wholly convinced that it was anything other than a price that he paid for the remarkable support he gave me over Westland. In fairness to George Younger and to the military establishment in the Ministry of Defence, I don't believe that their judgement was influenced one way or the other by Westland.

When Peter Levene joined me, he was still active as chairman of his company and I therefore asked him as his prime task to tackle the situation in the dockyards, since this was entirely divorced from his commercial interests. Ever since the time of Samuel Pepys, who was Secretary to the Admiralty, the Royal Navy had always had problems with the naval dockyards. Even earlier, in 1662 when he was deputy to the Earl of Sandwich as clerk in the Privy Seal Office, Pepys had written: 'But, good God, what a deal of company was there from both yards to help to do it, when half the company would have done it as well; but I see it is impossible for the King to have things done as cheap as other men.' Over-manning, late delivery of refits and repairs and massive cost overruns remained endemic in the late twentieth century. Peter visited the two dockyards at Devonport and Rosyth, and then proposed to me that we should adopt a practice from the United States known as GOCO (Government Owned, Contractor Operated). Today it is more simply termed contractorisation.

The plan had the benefit of simplicity, and the senior admirals on the Admiralty Board, led by the then First Sea Lord, Admiral Sir John Fieldhouse, urged me to go ahead. The Dockyards Services Bill was introduced in Parliament. Then, somewhat to our surprise, during the House of Lords consideration of the Bill, the trade unions – who had been making all sorts of threats of action – persuaded Lord Denning to propose an amendment which would give them the right to go to the High Court before any dockyard transfer could take place, if they felt they had not been properly and fully consulted. With the parliamentary summer recess looming, we gave way. The unions then decided that they had no need to take part in consultation meetings with officials. Instead they took us to court, where they were soundly defeated. We had prevailed. The transfer took place. Over-manning was dramatically reduced. Delivery on time was significantly improved. The taxpayer and the Royal Navy achieved better value for money. Several years later both the Navy and the Ministry of Defence were sufficiently comfortable with the commercial operation of the yards that they were finally privatised. The battle was slowly being won; we went on to other successes, including the sale of Royal Ordnance.

After Peter had been with me for six months, we realised that there was a huge job still to do and I formed the impression that he would like to stay. The appropriate position for him, of course, was to become chief executive of the Procurement Executive, but for that to happen he had to become a civil servant. I consulted Mrs Thatcher, who was persuaded by my argument that we would never take a grip on this extraordinary cash flow unless we had someone with experience of procurement and a deep knowledge of the defence industry working on our side. She agreed that he was the man for the job. Then we hit the buffers of civil service procedure. The rules demanded open competition for such an appointment. The rules themselves are sensible and are designed to prevent the politicisation of the service. But in this case the attitude was absurd. There was no one inside the civil service with a fraction of Peter's experience and I suspected that the obstacles put up were simply delaying tactics in the hope that the appointment would never be made. It didn't help that Peter was also to be paid more than the civil service scale would allow. Clive Whitmore supported my proposal to recruit Peter and persuaded the Cabinet secretary, Sir Robert Armstrong, to go along with it. But the Civil Service Commissioners were so concerned that it might contravene the Order-in-Council which provided the legal basis for their processes that the First Civil Service Commissioner, Dennis Trevelyan, took the matter to the Prime Minister and, I believe, threatened resignation. I doubt if he has ever forgotten the peremptory way in which his complaints were dismissed. Peter became the chief of defence procurement on 18 March 1985. Such was his contribution that he was to remain within or close to government for the rest of our time in office – twelve years in all.

Procurement is not simply a case of buying the right equipment for the armed forces. The procurement programme greatly affects the direction and scale of a modern industrial economy's technological development. It accounts for a hefty proportion of publicly funded research and development. Time and again it throws up judgements involving choice between particular weapons or equipment where one of the candidates is manufactured in the UK – perhaps has been funded throughout its development by the British taxpayer – and the alternatives are overseas products, again taxpayer-financed.

Only the naive believe that the theories of the classic market place are the driving influence.

I came to the Defence Ministry twelve years after the collapse of Rolls-Royce. As Minister for Aerospace I had been responsible for that rescued company between 1972 and 1974 and was very familiar therefore with the background. In the 1960s the company had decided to commit its private sector resources to the development of an engine, the RB211, to power the new generation of long-distance jets. Without access to this market, Rolls-Royce had no future. The problem was that there was no military requirement in the UK to fund the development costs. Exactly the opposite situation existed in America. General Electric had developed a civilian derivative – the CF6 – of a US military engine, the development costs of which had been met by the Pentagon. Rolls-Royce decided in effect to compete with the US taxpayer.

Incidentally, any of those who criticise the rescue in 1971 of Rolls-Royce have to face the fact that it now not only serves Britain's defence requirements but powers one-third of the world's civil airliners. Without the Heath government's intervention it would today be at best a branch of one of its American competitors.

At the same time and as I have already described, as Minister for Aerospace I had helped to create the European Space Agency. I cite these two experiences to indicate that in procurement one could never escape the American dilemma. The American defence and space budget was dramatically larger than that of the whole of Europe, let alone each individual nation. Almost invariably, when a procurement requirement arose, there would be an existing American system. It worked, was available and was probably cheaper than any equivalent we could produce, given the economies of scale available to the Americans and given that we would have to reincur the research and development costs that the American taxpayer had already borne. But the process of buying American, logically extended, would leave Britain with no research and design capability in the defence field at all. Our military industrial base would rapidly become mere sub-contractors. We would have little to offer to the vast international market place for defence products and the European stake in defence would thus be dramatically reduced, adding to the already existing pressures to relegate defence spending lower among Europe's political priorities – an outcome that is far from either European or American interests. No government has been prepared to contemplate such a posture, although the Treasury constantly pushed us in that direction.

Shortly after I arrived at the Ministry in January 1983, I had to address the subject of a new fighter aircraft for the RAF to replace both Phantoms and Jaguars. The project was at the earliest stages, where it is rare for a minister to play an active role in exploring the options. But I knew that at the same time the Germans needed to replace their Phantom jets and the French their Mirage and I was told that they were considering collaboration on a next-generation fighter aircraft – without us. We in turn had to decide whether to buy American or to produce our own aircraft.

I was appalled at this prospect. My first bilateral meeting with Charles Hernu, the French Minister of Defence, had been set up in Paris as a get-to-know-you occasion and covered a range of subjects, but he responded positively to my proposal that the fighter-aircraft requirement should be met by Anglo-French-German collaboration. In due course there was a trilateral meeting involving him and myself and Manfred Woerner, the German Federal Republic Defence Minister, and the three of us agreed to try and take such a project forward. British industry, the Royal Air Force and I patiently negotiated to create a scheme involving Britain. Italy and Spain joined the discussions as well. Our operational requirements were all based on the same Soviet threat. It made sense to have a trans-European project, the costs of developing which would be shared by five nations.

As we negotiated our way into the project, the emphasis changed: it was now how to keep the French in. They faced much the same dilemma as we did. They had a military all-round capability in airframes, avionics and aero-engines. In that context they were the only European power to match our defence industrial base. Their fighter-aircraft manufacturer, Dassault, had enjoyed considerable export success with their Mirage aircraft and were deeply apprehensive of the effect of a transnational pooling of expertise. They had their own project, Rafale, a lighter aircraft designed with carrier-based operations in mind. Once it became clear that we had negotiated British Aerospace and Rolls-Royce into the club, the interest of the French began to drift. I did everything I could to persuade them to stay in. As it grew evident that British and French industrial aspirations could not be reconciled and that what was by then a five-nation project was teetering on the brink of collapse, I got into an RAF plane late one afternoon and went to see Manfred Woerner.

He gave dinner to me and my officials in his residence in the Federal Ministry of Defence and I persuaded him that Germany should stick with us. After returning to England, I received a message that Manfred had been invited to meet President Mitterrand. The deal was now hanging by a thread. I rang the Prime Minister to ask her to use her influence to get me in to see the President of France as well. She tried, but he refused to see me.

Of course, one never knows the precise calculations that lie behind the policy arguments deployed by other, particularly foreign, ministers. Years later, I was to talk to François Heisbourg, who had been Charles Hernu's *chef de cabinet* at the time, about whether or not there was a genuine chance that we could have persuaded the French to remain in the project. He told me that for the first few months of the dialogue the possibility was decidedly there. But slowly the window closed. Perhaps the defining moment had come in a private conversation I had with Hernu in which he offered me a compromise. If I would give Dassault the lead on the airframe, he would give Rolls-Royce the lead on the aero-engines, and the avionics could be parcelled out between us. This was not a deal that I could do. Probably it was not a deal that he could do. The enormous influence held by the Dassault company through its founder Marcel Dassault and his son Serge, who were, between them, always determined to maintain their perceived pre-eminence in fighter aircraft, could well have been the crucial factor in France's decision to go it alone. (It should be borne in mind that the French engine company, SNECMA, at the time had no engine of their own with which to compete with Rolls-Royce. SNECMA had an agreement with the American firm GE and would have had to offer their GE404 engine.)

In the event, France went its own way, and ultimately we concluded a four-nation, £20-billion partnership to develop the European Fighter Aircraft (EFA) – far and away the biggest industrial deal that Britain had ever done. I am convinced to this day that there were many in France who regretted their inability to come to terms with us. The long-term future of the project itself was to remain a matter of continuing debate for several years, as the Germans faced not only costs that were inevitably larger than had been anticipated but, more particularly, the changed perception of the Soviet threat. Yet, despite all the speculation, on 26 November 1997 the Bundestag finally gave its approval to the production contract.

The process of negotiating such international deals can be exhausting. I do not share with some colleagues the ability to survive on little sleep. I'm an eight-hours-a-night man. As Clive Whitmore and Richard Mottram accompanied me round Europe, they found it increasingly difficult to get me up at the often ludicrous hours demanded by the need to return to a busy schedule back in London. One hotel manager in Madrid actually had to smash down the hotel bedroom door to bring the Secretary of State back to consciousness.

Collaborative defence procurement was the background to much of the dialogue that was developing at that time in Europe. At ministerial conferences, we would genuflect towards the need for additional co-operation. Accords were reached, programmes were discussed and progress took place at a snail's pace. In reality, as long as there are self-standing national industrial champions, each trying to win in competition against the others, real European co-operation will advance no more quickly.

Our policy was clear, however. In the Defence White Paper of 1985 our commitment to a European defence industrial strategy was set out. Traditionally, the Defence Secretary presents the annual Defence White Paper in draft to his colleagues in Cabinet just before publication. I remember this particular Cabinet meeting well. The documents were voluminous and I will not insult my colleagues if I say that I doubt if anyone had read them. I was mildly surprised at that Cabinet, therefore, when the Prime Minister turned to me and said: 'What is all this stuff about defence co-operation in Europe?' Fortunately, I knew what answer to give. 'It is the government's policy, Prime Minister,' I replied. In point of fact, the Eurogroup meeting of Defence Ministers dated back to 1968 and the Independent European Programme Group had been created in the 1970s.

Mrs Thatcher would not have had time to read the White Paper herself. Somebody would have framed that question for her and briefed her on it. She let the matter pass that day. It was government policy and that was that – for the time being. But the question was an indication of troubles to come.

Before my commitment to a European procurement policy was to reach its epic climax in 1986, there occurred one other significant event – centring on Norman Tebbit. Norman represented an important constituency of the Conservative Party. Hard, with a sharp wit and sharper tongue, he articulated the basic instincts present to an extent in us all but most closely associated with Essex man.

In 1984 Norman was Secretary of State for Trade and Industry and, as such, had responsibility for the British shipbuilding industry. In the MOD the procurement policies were my direct responsibility. At this time the Royal Navy wished to invite tenders for two Type 22 frigates. The competition was between Cammell Laird Shipbuilders on Merseyside and Swan Hunter on Tyneside, both yards being owned by British Shipbuilders, a nationalised company (set up following the passage of Labour's nationalisation Bill back in 1977, the Bill in which I had led for the Opposition) sponsored by Norman's Department.

The stakes were high. Both yards were short of work and whichever lost the competition faced the risk of closure. Cammell I knew well from my time on Merseyside. They were certainly in trouble; work was far advanced on HMS *Edinburgh*, a Type 42 destroyer (Anne had broken the traditional bottle of champagne over the bow of the *Edinburgh* at the formal launch ceremony in April 1983) and a jack-up rig for the British Gas Corporation. There was no prospect of much in the way of new orders. But within government the proper procedures were followed, tenders were submitted and the matter moved towards the award of contracts. In the normal way, the order would have gone to Cammell because they had submitted a lower price for the two ships than Swan.

However, before any decision had been made, a group of some fifty workers occupied both HMS *Edinburgh* and the British Gas rig in the Cammell yard, in protest against the inevitable large-scale redundancies that the completion of those two projects would precipitate. In addition, picket lines were formed at the shipyard gates in sympathy with the occupation. The company sought help from the courts on two occasions, the second being an application for contempt of the first order, thus involving the police in an exercise to remove the offending workers. In the end twenty gave up, while twenty-seven were defeated by lack of food and water and were imprisoned. These events were played out against the backdrop of the miners' strike and all the tensions it provoked. The vast majority of Cammell's 2,500-strong workforce faced down the picket lines with police protection and gave no support to the handful of militant colleagues. But, because of the disruption, it was decided by a Cabinet committee that we had to look again at the tenders for the two frigates and we decided in all the circumstances to re-run the competition.

I was perfectly content. Quite unbeknown to me or my Department, however, Norman Tebbit informed Graham Day of British Shipbuilders that Cammell would be invited to bid for only one ship, while Swan could proceed as before and bid for both. This was effectively the end of Cammell's chances. All the overheads of the yard would have had to be loaded on to the cost of building one frigate while Swan could divide theirs between the two.

When I heard what had happened, I telephoned Michael Murden, the managing director of Cammell, to ask why he had thrown away the chance to win in such a fashion and why, this second time round, they had failed to comply with the Department's tender request. And thus it was that I discovered that Graham Day had telephoned Dr Peter Milne, Cammell's chairman, who had then instructed Michael Murden to limit his bid to one ship. The yard had no choice but to comply; the instructions had come direct from head office. But they were extremely worried about the implications.

In January 1985, when the matter went back to Cabinet, I said that this had been an infringement of my tendering procedures and that Tebbit had deliberately fixed the rules in order to ensure that Swan won. This was a cheat which I could not accept. After discussion the Prime Minister concluded that Swan had won. I said there and then that I would not accept that decision. Another minister had interfered in my tendering procedures and had simply determined the death of the company that had won the original competition. The matter was left unresolved at the end of Cabinet. However, immediately thereafter, before I had even got back to the MOD, Mrs Thatcher had instructed Robert Armstrong, as secretary of the Cabinet, to find a solution. He had telephoned my permanent secretary, Clive Whitmore, to tell him that there had been a major disagreement, that the Prime Minister wanted it sorted out in a way which I could accept and that we had until three o'clock that afternoon to do so. As he hung up, I entered Clive's office to be told what Armstrong had said. In the next two hours the Department put together a proposal which was eventually the basis of the way forward. Swan would get one Type 22 order and Cammell the other, but, to keep Swan happy, they should be told that they would receive the first order for the proposed new class of frigate, the Type 23. (In the event the order was never placed.) The Prime Minister accepted this.

I was seen as having fought for Cammell because of my former relationship with Liverpool. This was not the case. If Cammell had lost on the first round, I would not have intervened on their behalf. I intervened – if that is the right word – only because I was not prepared to see such a flagrant disregard of the proper conduct of government between colleagues. The significance of the event is twofold: first, it was precisely such an abuse that forced me to leave the government in 1986; in addition, at the beginning of the Westland saga, when I could see the way in which events were being manipulated, I said to Charles Powell, the Prime Minister's private secretary, that he should perhaps be aware that I felt as strongly about what was happening in the case of Westland as I had done over the saga of the frigates. I have no doubt that this message reached its destination. I will come back to that story.

On Wednesday, 10 October 1984 I wound up the party Conference defence debate just before lunch. By now my Conference speeches had become a part of Conference ritual. The party activists responded with enthusiasm, colleagues less so, while the journalists had fun with the headlines. Indeed, the oft expressed view by this time was that I had the pre-lunch Wednesday slot because, as I was speaking, the BBC Conference report was replaced by a pre-school playgroup pro-gramme. The speech was, however, well received. I left the platform after a rousing ovation, and made my way to the exit where my car was waiting to begin my journey to a NATO conference in Italy. Anne and I had already checked out of the Grand Hotel in Brighton, where we had spent the previous night. As we left through the revolving doors, Tony Berry was coming in with Sarah, his wife. I had first got to know Tony when we had both served on the marathon Transport Bill committee in the late 1960s and we had spent many long hours together planning the Opposition campaign against that particular piece of legislation. His last words to us as we left that October lunchtime were: 'What a shame we will miss our regular Conference dinner together.' A few hours later he was one of those killed by the IRA bomb which destroyed so much of the Grand Hotel, leaving Sarah a tragically young widow.

I was stunned when I was told the horrific news the following morning in Italy. The consequences for the Tebbits, John Wakeham, Sarah Berry and many others were hard even to begin to imagine and were a brutal reminder of the fragility of our day-to-day assumptions. Geoffrey and Elspeth Howe had taken over our room in the hotel and were unhurt, although the ceiling of their bathroom came down in the blast.

I have described some part of the human tragedy. The enormity of the event politically was the determination of the IRA to try and assassinate the British Prime Minister and most of her Cabinet. By a miracle they failed. The Conference carried on. The government carried on. It was business as usual: Britain at its best.

Shortly after I became Defence Secretary, allegations were made that Mrs Thatcher had issued instructions during the Falklands War to sink the Argentine cruiser *General Belgrano* while that ship – far from menacing the British naval forces, as had been understood at the time – was actually steaming for her home port. It was even said that the sinking was a calculated piece of provocation, quite unnecessarily executed. It was claimed that the Prime Minister herself had known that the *Belgrano* had already turned away from confrontation. These were serious allegations and were immediately pursued with pertinacity by the Labour MP for Linlithgow, Tam Dalyell, that epitome of the awkward squad who has an infuriating habit of often being right.

It was my responsibility, as Defence Secretary, to respond on behalf of the government, although at that stage I had no personal knowledge of the details that had led to Mrs Thatcher's decision. The first meeting to consider what reply we would make to the by now official complaint from Denzil Davies, the Shadow Cabinet Defence spokesman, took place on Friday, 30 March 1984. It was a very high-level gathering, attended by, among others, my deputy, the Minister for the Armed Forces John Stanley; the permanent under-secretary of the Department, Sir Clive Whitmore; the First Sea Lord, Admiral Sir John Fieldhouse; and my principal private secretary, Richard Mottram. The meeting lasted for what I was told was for me a remarkably long time – nearly three hours – and we convened again on the evening of Sunday 1 April (minus Sir John Fieldhouse, who had meanwhile had to fly to America, but with additional intelligence chiefs present as well). We were trying to hammer out the text of a letter that could be sent by the Prime Minister to Denzil Davies (he had originally written to her) setting out the whole *Belgrano* story while protecting national security. To that purpose an assistant secretary within the Department had earlier that month been asked by Richard Mottram to put together from the contemporary records (including intelligence sources) a detailed chronology of the events that had led to the sinking; this document was later to become known as the 'crown jewels'. At the time of the Friday and Sunday meetings in my office I hardly noticed its author; sitting quietly towards the back of the room was the thirty-eight-year-old Clive Ponting, the head of the DS5 division in the Department and already awarded the OBE for his work within the Ministry. If he had had something to say, this would have been the obvious moment.

With the exception of Ponting, as later became clear, there was no doubt in the minds of all those who participated in those discussions that Mrs Thatcher had been right to issue the orders she did. She did not know that the *Belgrano* had changed course when she gave the instructions to torpedo her. (Even if she had known, it would still have been a perfectly justifiable decision to take.) Complex examination of detail about the times at which messages were sent, the time gaps separating the South Atlantic from the United Kingdom, the inevitable delays before the submarine could surface and receive messages, were all to be the subject of the most exhaustive scrutiny. My overwhelming impression of those early meetings remains one of surprise that here were the principal characters who had given Mrs Thatcher very clear advice to sink the *Belgrano*, and yet on many of the details so soon after the event they were arguing among themselves. I remember thinking at the time that here was as closely recorded and as recent an historic event as any that students could be asked to study and yet there was disagreement. It raised in my mind some obvious questions about the ability of learned professors, writing about a moment in history hundreds of years later with the sketchiest of information in their possession, to understand the events and the motives of those who moulded them with the clarity found in the average history book.

The very complexity of the issues of time and place provided a field day for the media and Opposition politicians, and those who had tried to suggest that the sinking of the *Belgrano* had been a deliberate act designed to wreck the May 1982 peace plan devised by Peru showed no sign of going away. No sooner had I got Downing Street approval for the draft of the letter to be sent to Denzil Davies than I had to turn my attention to yet another communication from Tam Dalyell.

As is normal practice, this letter had been referred to officials for a draft reply. The official responsible, Clive Ponting, drafted a dismissive response, which I didn't use. Less than a month later he sent an anonymous typed note to Dalyell urging him to press on with his inquiries and even suggesting forms of words that he, Dalyell, might like to use to put down parliamentary questions on the Commons order paper. Ponting, of course, knew that he would be the official responsible for drafting the replies for my approval to those questions. That was clearly highly unprofessional conduct. It was to take Ponting down a slippery slope that was to end in July with his leaking to Dalyell an internal minute and a rejected second letter he had drafted but which had never been sent. The documents were enclosed in a plain envelope, but this time the name and address had been carefully typed on his own home typewriter.

Tam Dalyell quite properly and promptly passed the papers which he had been sent to the Conservative chairman of the all-party Commons Foreign Affairs Select Committee, Sir Anthony Kershaw, who saw to it that both documents were back inside the MOD within ten days. It did not take the Ministry police long to trace the leak and establish the source. By the afternoon of Friday, 10 August – less than a month after he had sent the confidential material to Dalyell – they were able to confront Ponting in his office and, after some prevarication on his part, extract a confession from him.

I was informed by Sir Euan Broadbent, the second permanent secretary in the MOD, that he was referring the case to the appropriate authorities. I had no part in the decision to prosecute Ponting under the Official Secrets Act; although I had my own views on the need to do so, it was entirely a matter for the Director of Public Prosecutions and the Attorney General. They, however, appeared to share my own sense of outrage. The prosecution was launched and by the middle of October 1984 Ponting had been committed for trial at the Old Bailey.

The case had to wait its turn in the list, so the trial did not start until 28 January 1985. It went on for a fortnight and, since I was not called as a witness, I had no occasion to appear in court, although naturally I followed the proceedings with professional interest. Nothing particularly new or surprising seemed to emerge, which made the denouement when it came all the more startling

On Monday, 11 February, I had been invited to join the Prime Minister for lunch, along with a small number of other colleagues in the government, for a routine discussion. As the lunch came to an end and we rose to leave, an official from Mrs Thatcher's private office came into the dining room to announce that the jury had acquitted Ponting and had even awarded him costs. I realised at once that I was going to have to appear in the House of Commons to defend our position.

It fell to the Attorney General, given the jury's verdict, to make the initial statement straight away. Then, a week later, on 18 February, I stood up in the Commons to move a government motion insisting that the sinking of the *Belgrano* had been 'a necessary and legitimate action in the Falklands campaign' and equally firmly maintaining that 'the protection of our armed forces must be the prime consideration in deciding how far matters of national security and the conduct of military operations can be disclosed'. It was, I think, the most difficult speech I had ever had to make in the House. It was certainly the longest, lasting for an hour and twelve minutes. But I had warned the House about that at the outset, declaring that there was no alternative to making a 'lengthy and detailed speech on what is an important issue involving the rights of Parliament and the duties of ministers'. I did not say so, but the matter also involved the honour of Mrs Thatcher, and her reputation was in a real sense in my hands.

I rose just after 3.30 p.m. Not surprisingly, the chamber was packed. But you always know when you are carrying the House with you and I sensed fairly early on, partly as a result of a succession of foolish Opposition interruptions which I was able easily to crush, that I was winning. The challenge before me – in effect seeking to demonstrate that the verdict of a British jury had been not only wrong but perverse – was also much complicated by the fact that the truth required revelations of matters of high-security classification, the disclosure of which could, if handled clumsily, not only damage relations with other countries but also expose capabilities for intelligence-gathering that would be highly prejudicial to British overseas interests.

Fortunately, it was widely agreed that I won the argument. One abiding memory I have is of watching David Owen (like Anthony Eden, a charmer in public but a martinet to his officials), who had entered the chamber clutching voluminous texts and notes in support of what he had plainly planned as a devastating speech, slipping away in silence after I sat down. My opposite number on the Opposition front bench, Denzil Davies, in a sense fared worse. He had to speak. But, as you would expect from an articulate Welshman, it was sound knockabout stuff, even if his own side seemed to sense, after my revelations about Ponting's conduct, that it was all somehow irrelevant.

One other clear memory is the intensity of the bitterness his civil service colleagues felt against Ponting. Several of them were intimately involved in the preparation of my speech, and they took to the task with relish. So far as they were concerned, he had broken every ethic and principle in which the best of the British civil service believes. Through their own sense of what is right and wrong in the conduct of public affairs, rather than out of any political loyalty towards the government of the day, they were out to get him. So, I have to admit, was I.

My most devastating revelation was, I suppose, that Ponting had been leaking draft questions to Tam Dalyell, knowing full well that, if those questions were tabled, he was the one within the Ministry who would be asked to supply the draft answers, and that he then used those answers to encourage Dalyell in his pursuit of Mrs Thatcher. In the light of that, there was nothing really that the Opposition could say. I was not surprised when subsequently the all-party Foreign Affairs Select Committee by a majority gave the government a clean bill of health over the whole episode. I had decided to trust them with access – within the privacy of the Ministry – to the document known as the 'crown jewels'. That trust was never betrayed.

My only other close connection with the Falklands was the responsibility for building their airport. Self-evidently, we could accept no risk that the Argentines would try an invasion for a second time. To station a sufficiently strong garrison on the islands permanently would involve prodigious cost. The alternative was rapid reinforcement. That meant air transportation. The only aircraft that we possessed at the time of the Falklands War that could be used for regular transportation was the RAF Hercules. One of the workhorses of the world's defence forces, this very reliable but lumbering plane was used essentially for the movement of personnel and equipment and had to be capable of landing in limited circumstances. The Falklands provided circumstances of extreme limitations.

My first visit to the Falklands, in January 1984, was via a VC10 to Ascension Island and thereafter, for 3,500 nautical miles over the next thirteen and a half hours, by Hercules to Port Stanley. The RAF treated their Secretary of State with style. The journalists on board were curtained off in the back of the fuselage, while we were served an excellent dinner on card tables covered with white tablecloths and provided with silver cutlery. The Hercules hadn't the range to complete the journey on its existing fuel tanks so I experienced my first air-to-air refuelling. Not only the RAF crew on the flight deck but a total of thirteen of us, including a BBC television camera crew and reporter, all watched as our aircraft connected up with another Hercules tanker. Just as well.

I was in the Falklands for three days. We toured many of the battlefields, now restored to a stillness and serenity which made it nearly impossible to relate to the battle scenes of only a few months before. I was deeply moved as I laid a wreath to the Welsh Guards who had died in the liberation under the command of my friend and former colleague from Caterham and Pirbright, Colonel Johnny Ricketts. The living conditions of the British troops were very tough. The military had rightly ensured that the length of any tour of duty was limited, but even that must have been strain enough in the forbidding climate of the Falklands.

Our return journey was very different from the outward one. We reached RAF Brize Norton in Oxfordshire after a record-breaking flight in a Nimrod of seventeen hours and fifteen minutes, with three air-to-air refuellings. I was even allowed to fly the aircraft part of the way, and managed to keep her reasonably steady within a margin of 1,000 feet either way of the prescribed height of 30,000 feet.

Once a decision had been taken to maintain a limited military presence in the islands, it was clear that the Hercules would not provide a credible means of rapid reinforcement. Rapid reinforcement meant big aircraft and big aircraft meant an expensive airfield. The plans that were put forward by the Ministry and the Property Services Agency, in conjunction with a Laing–Mowlem–Amey Roadstone Construction joint venture, envisaged an initial runway of 8,500 feet in length (with a second of 5,000 feet to follow a year later). This is over a mile and a half long and not that far short of the length of the runways at Heathrow at between 12,000 and 13,000 feet. Heathrow, however, is one of the busiest airports in the world, while the military landing strip on the Falklands serves only seven flights a month. But there was no choice, and the contract for the main runway was delivered to time – no mean achievement given the logistics of such an operation at such a distance in such a climate.

I was to return to the Falklands, with Anne, sixteen months later. The RAF Tristar inaugural flight took us, via Ascension Island, all the way in about eighteen hours. We touched down at Port Stanley, where we were greeted for the only time in my political career by a governor, in full imperial fig, white plumes and all, in the form of the redoubtable Sir Rex Hunt. Mount Pleasant Airport was duly opened by Prince Andrew, a serving Royal Naval officer based in the Falklands at the time, on 12 May 1985.

For the keen bird-watcher the Falklands provided unforgettable memories of a different kind. A helicopter landed us on Beauchêne, south of the main island and at that time quite inaccessible from the sea. It was home to nothing except birds – including 600,000 rock-hopper penguins and 400,000 black-browed albatross. The island was carpeted with birds, except for one thirty-yard-wide diagonal strip, running perhaps fifty yards from one side of the island to the other. This was the birdport – a landing and take-off strip for the albatross. They would waddle slowly but majestically to one end and flap off westwards, slowly gathering height and soaring into the sky. As one took off, another would come coasting in to land. The rock-hoppers had learnt over the centuries to keep well clear of this ornithological Heathrow of the South Atlantic.

In my travels as Secretary of State for Defence, I found a disproportionately large number of fellow twitchers: at the top of the Foreign Office, in British embassies around the world and among the overseas commands of our armed services. There is an explanation for this. Bird-watching is a worldwide hobby. It is more than understandable that people whose job moves them around the world should develop a hobby they can pursue no matter how remote their posting.

In the early 1980s Saudi Arabia decided to modernise its air-defence capability. American sensitivities about its relationship with Israel were a formidable barrier to US arms sales to the Kingdom. A window was thus open for the sale of the Tornado, a three-nation, multi-role combat aircraft of high capability, produced – under the leadership of British Aerospace – by the industries of the UK, Germany and Italy. Competition inevitably came from France, but we were well placed.

As Defence Secretary, I once again found myself as part of the sales team. The Ministry has its own large and sophisticated marketing organisation, usually headed by a secondee from British industry. During my time it was James Blyth and then Colin Chandler.

The 1985 contract for the sale of the Tornados was in itself huge: 132 aircraft to be purchased at a price of £4 billion – some of which was to be paid in oil. But everyone knew it was only the beginning. It was to lead on to the much larger Al-Yamamah contract which was signed the following year, after I had left the Department, and a follow-on contract in 1988 which together could be measured in tens of billions of pounds and thousands of jobs.

The ministerial role – as I saw it – involved policy clearance for the sale of such sophisticated technology to so sensitive an area, agreement to divert aircraft scheduled for delivery to the RAF to meet the tight timetable, acceptance of the oil in part settlement (Peter Walker was far from pleased; his Energy Department was not consulted) and, inevitably, the ministerial visits to the Kingdom, where we were royally received – literally.

The House of Saud rules with a rod of iron. The vast reserves of oil have financed the building of a modern state by a ruling family that came in from the desert at the turn of the last century. Their ways are not always ours, but no one can deny their extraordinary commitment to quality as one drives along the great carriageways and passes the massive buildings designed by the world's leading architects. They have built and are building an infrastructure for the new century. Their attitude to the role of women, their methods of punishment and their rigid system of censorship are not compatible with the standards of our democratic societies and it is not a country where you want to be out of step with authority. Within those constraints the transformation of education, health and general living standards has been remarkable.

Ministers keep well away from commercial negotiations, which are fought out with no holds barred by the giant industrial companies that bestraddle the commercial world. I walked the royal corridors, and sat in audience with the King and Prince Sultan, the Defence Minister and one of the King's brothers. There was much ritual, well-established courtesies, talk of bustard hunting, an introduction to some magnificent falcons and numerous banquets. Mrs Thatcher played her part in the process. We won the contract. In September 1985 I signed what was then the largest contract ever won by British industry.

Britain enjoys significant relationships throughout the Middle East that stretch back in origin to our imperial past but have been enhanced in the very different circumstances of today. During the protracted civil war in the Lebanon we had agreed in the summer of 1982 to take part, with the Americans, French and Italians, in a peace-keeping exercise following the Israeli invasion of the country and the later massacres of the Palestinians in the refugee camps around Beirut. We had decided to keep our detachment small, believing that as such it could perform its patrolling and guarding duties effectively while provoking less of a challenge to local militia. In the event, we deployed about 120 men from the Queen's Dragoon Guards. One of our tasks was to provide a guard around a disused bank in which peace talks between the two sides were taking place. But the peace-keeping efforts of the four nations were to prove of no avail. It was only a matter of time before the peace-keeping forces were themselves at risk. The French suffered heavy casualties when their base was blown up by a suicide lorry bomb. Another suicide mission in October 1983 blew up the headquarters of the US Marines in Beirut (and our ambassador, David Meyers, who happened to be visiting at the time). Over 200 lost their lives.

It was a time of great anxiety for all those who took part and had to live with an ever present threat around them. One morning I remember I was standing talking to Mrs Thatcher in the corridors of 10 Downing Street on my way into a meeting when an official approached us to tell us that Druze Militia were putting down shells a hundred yards to the right of the British barracks in Beirut. I was appalled. We were there guarding their negotiators and they were now laying down explosives next to our building. I insisted on telephoning Walid Jumblatt, the Druze leader, at once to protest. (In her memoirs, Mrs Thatcher wrongly suggests that this was her idea.) Officials rapidly located him in Amman, the capital of Jordan. 'Get him on the phone,' I said. Almost unbelievably quickly I was connected. I explained who I was and protested vehemently that he was deliberately risking British lives in a quite unforgivable use of military force, when we were there purely to protect him and his peace negotiators from exactly the sort of behaviour to which he was now subjecting us. He assured me that he had already ordered a ceasefire at noon. As justification for his actions, he then made reference to some conference concerning Israel which had taken place in London and of which he disapproved.

Just before Christmas 1983 I decided to visit our troops. In the early 1960s Denis Curtis, the production director of Cornmarket – later Haymarket – Publications, had taken a holiday in Beirut. He described to me in glowing terms its prosperity and excitement. It was then a model of harmony and entrepreneurial flair, one of the world's honeypots. People speculated wistfully as to why the Northern Irish couldn't learn the multiracial, multicultural lessons of the Lebanon. By the time I went there, Beirut had been flattened. The British Embassy was embunkered for fear of attack. We drove from the airport through streets many of whose buildings had been reduced to piles of rubble. It was a terrifying example of what racial and ethnic hatreds, once unleashed, can lead to.

Our detachment was stationed in what was about as conspicuous a landmark as remained in that devastated city, a tall, narrow tower that would have been the obvious target if one was indulging in a military training exercise. You simply couldn't have missed. We flew in by helicopter from Cyprus, made a heavily guarded tour of inspection and departed as we had come. Just above the rooftops we stared down into the ruins, as though our hostile glares might of themselves act as a deterrent to the shoulder-launched missiles we knew only too well were down there. Our tension lifted the moment we flew out over the open sea, and rather over-excited chatter broke the silence as we tucked into some champagne and Christmas cake thoughtfully provided by the RAF to tide us over on our journey back.

All our efforts to provide a background of stability in the Lebanon proved futile. The men were in constant danger. Finally, in February 1984, the Lebanese government collapsed and President Reagan decided to pull his troops out. No one else was prepared to stay behind; we did the same. The peace-keeping mission had failed.

As Defence Secretary, and in my capacity as chairman of the Commonwealth War Graves Commission, I was in attendance on the Queen for the commemoration of the fortieth anniversary of the Normandy landings later that same year. The day began with the Queen as the guest of the local municipality of Caen. Only the French could have designed a programme for such a day which included a visit to the tomb of William the Conqueror, the last foreign invader to have conquered England.

As I was waiting for the Queen to return from lunch, I watched countless British visitors standing quietly, talking in subdued tones behind a half-circle of rope around a swathe of neatly cut grass. I noticed two elderly gentlemen deep in conversation, walked over and made a trite opening remark. 'You've obviously come over together for the ceremony,' I said. A broad Welsh accent softly replied: 'No, no, boy. We last met on that beach forty years ago today.' It was a profoundly moving moment. I looked away.

Later that afternoon saw the Allies, including Presidents Reagan and Mitterrand, on Utah Beach where the Americans had faced the fiercest German resistance in 1944. After the Allied commemorations, the British moved to the little town of Arromanches, which had been the scene of British landings. The centre of the town was built as a hollow square: three sides of buildings and on the fourth the seafront. The innermost side of the square was separated from the two wings by access roads. The parade entered from the left, passed the saluting base and departed on the right. No one who was there will ever forget the experience. I described it four months later to the Tory Party Conference of October 1984:

> Into that village square there marched the men and women of the British forces – soldiers, sailors and airmen in their sixties and their seventies. We could not see them coming and we could not see them go, but suddenly they were there. They held the centre of the stage, just as they had once before. No one knew how many there were. No one knew for how long they would march. They just kept coming, a British people: clerks, farmers, factory workers, miners, dockers, drivers, officers and men. Some were crippled, some were blind and some were helped along. They were ordinary people who had done an extraordinary thing. In no sense were they of a political party. They were of all parties from all places. A country united in the common belief in freedom and tolerance. They were the British. With their allies they had come to right a great wrong. They had done so at great cost.

Of a quite different character, of course, were the great commemoration celebrations in 1985 on the fortieth anniversary of VE Day. Anne and I visited Copenhagen, where candles flickered in every window. We stood in the Grande Place/Grand Platz in Brussels, where the fighting troops of a dozen different nations that had taken part in the liberation paraded in alphabetical order. Almost last – and in strange contrast to all the others – came the contingent from the United Kingdom comprising my old unit, the Prince of Wales Company of the Welsh Guards. The casual observer from another planet would have been bemused. Who were these almost *Toytown* soldiers in their bearskins and tunics? The more discerning would have spotted that at their head was once again Sir John Miller, my former commanding officer, who as a major had led the Company as one of the first units into the city in 1944.

The men and women who served in the Pacific and wear the Burma Star have long felt that they fought in a forgotten war. It was three months after the capitulation of Nazi Germany that the bombing of Hiroshima and Nagasaki ended the war in the Pacific. I well remember standing with the Duke of Kent and the Chief of the Defence Staff, Field Marshal Lord Bramall, in the heat of Remembrance Sunday 1985 before the Kranji War Memorial, Singapore, as prayers were offered by the priests of the Muslim, Buddhist, Christian, Hindu, Jewish, Sikh and Zoroastrian religions, and being moved beyond measure by the sight of the graves of so many men and women from the imperial forces, of so many creeds and races, who had sacrificed so much in our common cause.

I had discovered that there had never been an organised visit for the British widows of those who had died there. I determined to rectify this sad omission. I shall never forget the sight of those elderly ladies, mostly in their sixties, some in their seventies, searching the cemetery for the gravestones of their loved ones who had died so long ago. A most welcome but wholly unanticipated development from this initiative was the creation of Remembrance Travel. We had invited the Royal British Legion to undertake the organisation of the initial tour on our behalf and at our expense. Out of this experience, Colonel Piers Storie-Pugh MBE, TD conceived the idea of developing a commercial service to take relatives and sympathisers to battlefields around the world and stretching back to the First World War. It flourishes to this day.

I pocketed a stone from the Irrawaddy river to take back to an elderly friend of mine whose brother had died as Orde Wingate's Chindits fought their way across to help in the liberation of Burma. And in a commemorative service in Rangoon Cathedral I read out those familiar yet haunting words: 'At the going down of the sun and in the morning / We will remember them.'

These commemorations helped me to stand back from the day-to-day controversies over policy at the MOD and to understand the ultimate role of this great department of state. But such controversies could not be escaped. Even as I stood by the Irrawaddy contemplating one Chindit's sacrifice, the financial difficulties of a British helicopter manufacturer had already started to give the procurement dilemma dramatic form.

Chapter 15

'A VERY GOOD RESIGNATION'

The Westland affair did not break all at once. It grew from a cloud no bigger than a man's hand into what proved to be the most powerful storm of my political life.

The policy background to Westland, as Britain's only manufacturer of helicopters, was clearly enshrined in government policy. The Independent European Programme Group had been created in the 1970s and in 1978 the then Labour government had signed a policy document on helicopter procurement with France, Germany and Italy, setting out the principles on which they would co-operate and establishing that each country would make appropriate efforts to procure European-built helicopters. This policy had been accepted and reinforced in the wider context of defence procurement when the government led by Mrs Thatcher set out in its Defence White Paper – the statement on defence estimates – in 1985 the importance of Europe coming together in order to provide the basis of a more equal partnership in defence matters with the Americans within the NATO alliance. Indeed, as I have already recounted, Mrs Thatcher herself had raised a query about the specific paragraph in that White Paper when I presented it to Cabinet in the customary way. She had asked me, as Defence Secretary, why this forthright statement of European co-operation appeared in the document and I had explained, as any of my predecessors would have done, that this was British policy as I had inherited it and as I believed it to be. She had let the matter go in that Cabinet, and the White Paper was published as drafted by my Department.

My commitment to closer European integration was wholly consistent, therefore, with government policy. The reader will have followed my experiences in the establishment of the European Space Agency under Ted Heath and in the decision to develop the European Fighter Aircraft in concert with our German, Italian and Spanish allies while I was at the MOD. In order to secure what was then the largest contract that Britain had ever negotiated, I had overturned a Franco-German initiative that would have left Britain in a go-it-alone position and at risk of being marginalised in the European procurement of fighter aircraft.

As I have already explained, there was a constant tension – for me and for all other incumbents of the Ministry of Defence – in the field of defence procurement. This was an area where the government was continually faced with the need to decide between purchasing a project that had been developed by British industry at taxpayers' expense or cutting its losses and moving to a prudent and often successful alternative that was available on commercial terms from an American company. Of course, the commercial terms were the marginal costs of production for a project that had itself been developed by the American taxpayer through the procurement policies of the Pentagon. It was self-evident that for the British taxpayer to compete with the American taxpayer in the field of high technology, via the chosen instruments of their respective industrial bases, was a hazardous exercise which in the early 1970s had led directly to the bankruptcy of Rolls-Royce engines.

The dilemma presented by Westland was, therefore, a familiar one to me. As the Secretary of State for Defence, I was not responsible for the sponsorship of the company. That lay with the Department of Trade and Industry, where Leon Brittan was the Secretary of State. But, equally, I was intensely preoccupied with the company's future; not only was it our sole manufacturer of helicopters, it also provided a significant outlet for products such as Rolls-Royce engines in the helicopters that were purchased by the Royal Navy and the RAF. The arguments assumed a familiar pattern. Westland was in severe financial difficulties, with all the implications which that had for our industrial defence base.

Coincidentally, the Americans had got wind of a procurement requirement by the British Army for a battlefield helicopter capable of moving troop contingents rapidly from place to place. They had a product – the Black Hawk, manufactured by Sikorsky – that had seen extensive service and which they believed fitted the specification. The Ministry of Defence advice to me was clear, however. They had carefully considered the Black Hawk helicopter and had no intention of purchasing it. In the view of the armed forces it did not meet their operational requirements. I played no part at all in the formulation of this advice, although of course its existence in the background was to play a crucial role in what was to follow.

Equally, I was faced with a dilemma familiar to any minister in Whitehall. I was, in my defence role, concerned about the future of Westland, but the policy towards the company was the responsibility of another Department. Shorn of its official phraseology, what this actually meant was that, if anybody's departmental budget was going to be called upon to give support to the company, it was the DTI's and not that of the Ministry of Defence. The DTI had, in fact, the pole position as the sponsoring Department.

Superficially, this jockeying on each side could easily be seen as a trivial manifestation of Whitehall in-fighting. In a sense that was no doubt what it was, but there are practical grounds that make such posturing inevitable. First of all, any minister with experience knows that, if a department wants something sufficiently, it can invariably find ways of providing the money. I shall never forget the 'strapped-for-cash' atmosphere within the Ministry of Defence, which disappeared overnight when three civil airliners came on to the market cheaply. The money was promptly found with no apparent difficulty.

For the truth is that government departments, if only by reason of the pressure of the system, must always appear short of cash. Any hint of available resources and the minister's position at the annual public expenditure round is cut from under him when the Treasury indulges in its regular marauding exercises. Equally, officials in one's department – who know the ropes – have no time for a Secretary of State who wanders around Whitehall giving away what they earnestly believe to be *their* money to other departments which could well afford this or that project on their own but whose interests are better defended by a more aggressive political master. Issues of this sort are the daily bread and butter of the political world. Westland has to be fitted into that context. The company was in trouble. It was the job of the Secretary of State for Trade and Industry to sort it out, even if that meant the Treasury stumping up the extra cash.

Consistent with that position, however, I tried to help. In June 1985 I devised a scheme by which my Department would accelerate procurement of needed helicopters in order to provide relief for the company's cash-flow problems. This idea of mine was turned down at a meeting chaired by Mrs Thatcher. I made no complaint. It was open to the criticism that it didn't solve the Westland problem, even if it did buy time. I mention it merely to make the point that I was the only one to make any positive suggestions at all to help. I refute the charge – made later – that I took no interest in the Westland situation before it was too late. I did more than any other minister to try to help the company before my colleagues were forced to do likewise in the more extreme circumstances that were to develop.

In October 1985 I also directed the accounting officer of my Department to release some £6 million to the company that had been held up. The Department had feared that to hand over this cash might have been unwise, if the company subsequently had to go into liquidation and been unable to meet any claims from the MOD. I consciously bent the rules in view of the urgency and seriousness of the situation.

Leon Brittan, as has since become abundantly clear, was a European by instinct and conviction. We all knew it then. He was fully aware that Westland would not survive as an independent entity. He knew that the American firm Sikorsky were interested in buying the company, under a deal that would see Westland producing the Black Hawk. But he wanted a choice, especially one that would help Westland within the European family of helicopter manufacturers. He had written a minute to the Prime Minister, circulated to colleagues in the usual fashion, on 4 October 1985, recommending the need to explore the European option.

That same autumn, as I have recounted, I led a mission to the Pacific to commemorate the end of the war forty years earlier. By the time I came back it was obvious that Leon was not making progress in his quest, and at a meeting I had with him in his office I asked whether he would like me to help. He welcomed the suggestion. I believed, and I think he accepted, that my relationships with the defence ministers of Europe were far closer than his and he knew of the role that I had played in achieving the successful conclusion of the European Fighter Aircraft with very largely the same cast of ministerial characters that would be involved in any deliberations about helicopter procurement.

Sir John Cuckney, the suave and persuasive chairman of Westland, had in the meantime approached Sikorsky, a subsidiary of the giant American company United Technologies Corporation (UTC). There was nothing novel in such an approach. Peter Levene from my Department had also talked to them as the crisis developed during the summer. I realised that it would be necessary to establish Westland's position before I carried out the agreement I had reached with Leon Brittan. I therefore invited Cuckney to my office in the Ministry of Defence on 26 November, where in the company of my private secretary, Richard Mottram, we discussed the matter frankly. He explained the attractions of Sikorsky to Westland but did not rule out other options, providing that they had as much to offer. But he said that he did not have the management or the time himself to explore these issues. He welcomed my proposal that I should help. Thus it is clear I acted only in agreement with both the company and with my colleague Leon Brittan. I was not prepared to become involved in discussions with my European colleagues except on a basis of good faith and, therefore, the clearance of my intervention with Brittan and Cuckney was an essential prelude to my doing so.

Events then moved quickly. It so happened that I met my German opposite number, Manfred Woerner, on 27 November in another context. I put the position to him frankly and explained the time imperative. It was agreed that the national armaments directors (NADs) of the United Kingdom, Germany, Italy and France, should meet at the end of that week, together with the helicopter companies which were to form the European consortium, Aérospatiale, Agusta and MBB. All three companies came. Westland, though invited, did not attend. Without doubt the national armaments directors would have been aware of the developing problems of Westland. They would also have been aware of, and probably participated in, an ongoing dialogue about the rationalisation of the European industry. Virtually everybody involved in the aerospace industry at the time knew of the desirability of creating companies of a size that could be serious competitors or partners with the Americans. But, of course, it was easy to theorise and very difficult to find volunteers when it came to taking second place in any proposed rationalisation.

The NADs appreciated the urgency and, perhaps to the surprise of many, concluded an outline agreement that the needs of the countries concerned for three helicopter classes – 13 tonne, 8–9 tonne and light attack – should be covered solely in the future by helicopters designed and built in Europe. They agreed also to complete the rationalisation of their requirements, carrying out the objectives which had first been set out in 1978. I immediately gave a copy of this agreement to Sir John Cuckney, who responded that arrangements of the sort now set out in this agreement would preclude an arrangement with Sikorsky, whose products did not fit the European definition.*

We were now faced with a clear choice. On the one hand, there was the Sikorsky deal, to which Fiat of Italy had not surprisingly added their name, as Gianni Agnelli, Fiat's chairman, was a director of UTC, Sikorsky's parent company. On the other hand, a serious European proposal was emerging which had the prospect of being backed by either or both British Aerospace and GEC. Did the British government wish to consider a serious alternative to Sikorsky in the form of a European co-operative venture? The agreement reached by the NADs had to be put to colleagues collectively. Two meetings took place on 4 and 5 December. They were informal meetings of the ministers most intimately involved and were chaired by Mrs Thatcher. No one seriously believed, as Margaret Thatcher argues, that there was an urgent need to overrule the NADs agreement. It was the basis of a proposal which could stand alongside the Sikorsky offer.

The matter to be resolved was very simple. Should the Europeans be given the chance to have their proposals fully and openly considered as an alternative to Sikorsky's? Self-evidently, I argued that case. My opponents wanted to close off the option raised by the NADs' agreement. Mrs Thatcher supported this latter view. Most colleagues supported me. Her most bitter anger at these two meetings was reserved for Norman Tebbit, the party Chairman at the time, and certainly someone normally perceived as 'one of us'. He sat alongside me and resolutely defended the option of considering both alternatives. Mrs Thatcher grew more and more ill-tempered in her attempts to convert him to her point of view. I had never seen such naked anger betrayed in such a forum. She was losing the argument, and at the hands of her usually loyal supporters. Norman displayed no emotion but quietly repeated the arguments. Exasperated, Mrs Thatcher declared that she would call a meeting of the Economic Committee of the Cabinet, over which she assumed she would prevail.

The Prime Minister's distrust of our European partners was common knowledge, particularly to those of us exposed to the colourful language with which personalities and proposals were regularly

---

* This hard and fast view was later to be challenged by the Defence Select Committee in its Fourth Report, *Westland plc: The Government's Decision-Making*, Session 1985–6, p. xxiii, para. 64.

dismissed. What none of us knew was that, as Sikorsky's battle for Westland began to intensify, she received a telephone call from General Alexander Haig, acting as senior adviser to UTC, Sikorsky's parent company. Al Haig had been the American Secretary of State under Ronald Reagan at the time of the Falklands War and he claimed credit for the decision to provide radar cover from American AWACs (the airborne early-warning system) for British forces in the South Atlantic during the conflict. He had been president and chief operating officer at UTC 1979–81, and after leaving the Reagan administration in 1982 he had returned to UTC; as he graphically put it years later, 'I called in my markers.' Such a claimed obligation was never revealed to the ministerial colleagues involved in the consideration of the issues at the time. Certainly, I knew nothing of it.

The meeting of E(A), the principal sub-committee of the Economic Committee of the Cabinet, took place in the afternoon of Monday, 9 December. In order to enhance the prospects of her stance being endorsed, Mrs Thatcher took the unusual step of inviting Sir John Cuckney to attend the meeting so that colleagues would have the opportunity to hear his case first hand and to cross-examine him on the implications of delay. In the event, matters had moved on. Two of Britain's leading defence contractors had decided to respond to the NADs' opportunity. I informed the committee that I believed there would be a British-led alternative solution within a few days, knowing as I did that British Aerospace and GEC were now working seriously on proposals of their own to join the European bid. The committee meeting was orderly and articulate and the arguments were fully explored. John Cuckney, whose background in government service doubtless persuaded Mrs Thatcher that he was an appropriate person to be present at a Cabinet committee, made his statement, answered questions and left the meeting. Overwhelmingly colleagues argued that I should be given until Friday in order to present a proper alternative. Perhaps the most telling argument, to which neither the Prime Minister nor Cuckney could provide an answer, was that I was asking for only four days. I was seeking no more than a proper consideration of alternatives. I made it clear that, if there were no viable alternative, I would support the Sikorsky option *faute de mieux*.

Mrs Thatcher was furious at her inability to win after three runs round the course. Eventually, she brought the deliberations to an intemperate conclusion with the words: 'Very well. We shall meet at three o'clock on Friday, after the Stock Exchange has closed, to consider the matter further.' She and her supporters have since argued that there was never any intention for there to be such a subsequent meeting. This allegation does not bear scrutiny.

First of all, the Cabinet Office, which arranges meetings of this sort, put in train the process of setting it up the very next day, Tuesday, 10 December. The various ministers' offices were contacted to discuss their availability. It has been argued that there was a misunderstanding, that officials were acting simply on a contingency basis. Again, this argument cannot stand closer examination. On what basis would civil servants have begun such a round-robin of telephone calls? There is only one answer. The minutes of Cabinet or of a Cabinet committee are not written at the time of the meeting but after it has been concluded. At the meeting itself civil servants from the Cabinet Office make copious notes in notebooks issued for precisely this purpose. These records are far more detailed than the minutes of the Cabinet or its sub-committees.

It was my extreme good fortune that the permanent secretary of my Department at the time was Sir Clive Whitmore (who, as I have indicated, had been Mrs Thatcher's private secretary at No. 10 before his dramatic promotion to the Ministry of Defence). Immediately whispers began to be heard that the Friday meeting was to be cancelled, he went to the Cabinet Office and asked that the notebooks of the civil servants who had attended the Monday meeting should be checked. Every one of them had recorded the same remark by Mrs Thatcher. There is not the slightest doubt whatever that another meeting was intended and that is why preparations were made – and that it was then expressly cancelled. Mrs Thatcher had lost three times. There was to be no risk of a fourth occasion.

But, of course, this meant that there was then no opportunity for further collective discussion. Colleagues would not be able to make a judgement about the rival merits of the two alternatives. British Aerospace and perhaps GEC were to be denied the chance to put their case to the government of their country. My fellow defence ministers in the NATO alliance would draw their own conclusions about the nature of the assurances I had been authorised to give them. As Secretary of State for Defence, I was to be denied the right of every Cabinet minister that his or her voice should be heard by immediate colleagues.

The Prime Minister refused on the Thursday – 12 December – to allow a discussion in full Cabinet. I insisted that the Cabinet secretary should record my protest in the Cabinet minutes. When they were circulated, however, there was no reference to any discussion about Westland and consequently no record of my protest. I complained directly to the Cabinet secretary, Sir Robert Armstrong, who admitted that there had been an error which he agreed to rectify. I can remember no omission of this sort during nearly twenty years of life as a minister. An addendum was issued. But again this did not record my protest.

After my resignation and as a response to the statement I made at the time, I received a letter from Sir Robert setting out the position as he had seen it. He told me he had decided, in view of the especially sensitive record of the discussion on Westland in Cabinet on 12 December, that it would be better not to include a full account in the minutes but had instead instructed that a brief summary record be included in the minutes as circulated. But due to a misunderstanding in his office, which he said he regretted, the summary had not been so included.

He had not realised this until a week later when, in 10 Downing Street just before the next Cabinet meeting, I had told him that the minutes were wrong. It was this that had prompted him to ask questions of his private office and thus discover the omission. He did then circulate the addendum, but, as I have already observed, it failed to record the essence of my complaint, which was that the meeting promised for the Friday to discuss my proposals on behalf of the Anglo-European consortium had been cancelled.

I did in fact write to Sir Robert on 24 December saying I still wanted a word with him about the minutes. But in the event I never discussed the matter with him again until I told him just before the 9 January 1986 Cabinet that the record was still incomplete. I could have pressed harder and insisted on a new draft just after Christmas, but the way events were unfolding had pushed the matter down my list of priorities.

On Friday, 13 December the board of Westland Helicopters – determined to consolidate the Sikorsky position as far as lay within their powers – approved the Sikorsky deal, and the same day they dismissed the proposals put forward by the European consortium, which by this stage included British Aerospace. The issue by now was attracting increasing concern in the defence establishment. The officers of the backbench Conservative Defence Committee, without any prompting from me, put out a statement supporting the approach

I was taking. The all-party House of Commons Defence Select Committee, following a telephone call from my private secretary, invited me to a private meeting on 18 December and, helpfully, put out a statement that day saying that the defence implications of the Westland issue merited further consideration.

Cabinet met again on Thursday, 19 December. I knew that British Aerospace and GEC were very close to concluding their formal arrangements, but on that Thursday morning they had not yet actually done so. There was therefore no discussion of the merits of the potential choice that would be on offer. I told my colleagues that I believed that very shortly we would face a different situation. I would be forced to answer questions about the potential procurement policies of my Ministry. It was agreed that I should answer them, giving the same information to any inquiries. In the meantime the Cabinet concluded three things: Westland should be left to make their own decision in the best interests of the company and their employees; ministers would not lobby for either option; and major issues of defence procurement were for collective discussion. Taken at face value, it was possible to live with these words, but in reality these conclusions were a sham. The Westland board believed they could put only one deal – Sikorsky – to shareholders. In the event they had to put both, but subsequent events prevented any effective shareholder involvement, which made a mockery of 'letting Westland decide'.

Mrs Thatcher and by now Leon Brittan were actively helping Sir John Cuckney in his determination to enter into a deal with Sikorsky that would involve the manufacture of Black Hawk helicopters. Years later I learnt quite by chance, at a private dinner, that Gianni Agnelli, the chairman of Fiat, had visited No. 10 at this time, anxious to establish that his role as a partner of UTC was not offending government policy. I knew nothing of this visit and still know nothing of what he was told. I am only disappointed that my efforts to establish his side of the story have proved unsuccessful – because, he has explained, 'I can't remember details so long ago.' I had been no less actively engaged in putting together an alternative option, with the acquiescence of Sir John and the original encouragement of Leon. Ministers most involved were deeply committed and actively supporting one project or another.

The next day, Friday, 20 December, the predictions I had made in Cabinet were proved right, as the British–European consortium announced its plans in the form of an offer to Westland which was widely described as superior to the Sikorsky–Fiat alternative. But this proposal was rejected out of hand by the Westland board.

The position now was clear. With the Christmas recess fast approaching, I once again tried to secure proper consideration by my colleagues of these matters. This request was refused by the Prime Minister. Relations between No. 10 and myself had obviously reached a point at which it was becoming difficult to see a way through the impasse. I did not seek to involve my colleagues in the storm that was brewing, although I was increasingly dismayed at what could only be considered the breakdown in the conduct of government. One day, as I sat in the Ministry of Defence, I thought I would try one more initiative to bring matters back to an even keel. I asked my private secretary to get either Quintin Hailsham (the Lord Chancellor) or Willie Whitelaw (our Leader in the House of Lords) on the telephone, my intention being to see if they could help to restore a proper decision-making process. Quintin, I discovered, was in America, while Willie was out playing his beloved golf. The moment passed, though I had never placed great faith in the possibility of success from such a quarter. I did, however, make one further try. On 23 December I rang Sir John Cuckney at his home in Kent and offered to drive over to see him on Christmas Eve to sort matters out. But this initiative served only to irritate him, since (unknown to me) his wife had recently come out of hospital after an operation and he did not wish to have their Christmas disturbed.

Anne and I had originally arranged to take our now grown-up children on a visit to Nepal over the Christmas recess to explore that magnificent country. We had been much looking forward to it. As the crisis developed, I realised the dilemma I faced. To be abroad at a critical stage in the saga that was unfolding would have been to abandon all those who shared the objectives I believed important. In my absence it was impossible to foretell what might have been done to advance the Sikorsky cause. I believed it was my responsibility to stay. Anne loyally insisted that she would remain as well and so I cancelled our two tickets. Our two daughters and son went, however, and hugely enjoyed the experience. It is impossible to know how my life would have turned out if I had chosen the peaks and precipices of Nepal over the peaks and precipices of British politics.

On Christmas Eve officials in the Procurement Executive of the

MOD wrote to Lloyds Merchant Bank, on my instructions and following an inquiry from the bank, who were acting as advisers to the European consortium. The letter set out the implications of an American tie-up, against a background where British procurement policy for defence equipment emphasised the need for co-operation between European companies. The issue was clear-cut. The agreement reached by the NADs had made it plain that only by joining the European consortium would Westland be able to take on the British share of European collaborative projects.

On 30 December Sir John, having received a copy of the MOD letter to Lloyds, wrote to the Prime Minister to seek clarification of the policy. He asked whether Westland would still be considered under the terms of the NADs' agreement a European company if a minority shareholding was held by a group from a NATO country outside Europe (that is, America). In the normal course of events my Department would have been asked to draft the response. Instead, Mrs Thatcher's private secretary sketched out the line the Prime Minister intended to take and sent it to the Department of Trade and Industry, asking for a draft reply to be submitted by 4.00 p.m. the following day.

I received my copy of the draft letter on the morning of that day, the 31st, and I immediately pointed out that these were matters within my ministerial responsibility and that the line which the Prime Minister proposed to take was materially misleading. I insisted that the draft be referred to the Law Officers. My Department worked up a fuller and more accurate reply. The Solicitor General, Paddy Mayhew (deputising for the Attorney General, Sir Michael Havers, who was recovering from massive heart surgery, which had kept him away from the office for many weeks), came over to the MOD and I showed him what I believed to be the relevant papers. He supported my view, advising that, while my draft could be shortened in order to protect the government from liability (if it could be shown that the letter was misleading), it was, as I had argued, necessary to include in the Prime Minister's reply reference to the attitudes of other governments and companies. Eventually, a line with which we could all live was agreed and the text finally appeared at about 10.00 p.m. on New Year's Eve. Anne and I had been having supper with Paddy Mayhew in a Chancery Lane restaurant when a telephone call from No. 10 cleared it with me. I had succeeded in ensuring that Mrs Thatcher's letter now contained the words: 'In this connection you should be aware of indications from European governments and companies that they currently take the view that a number of projects in which Westlands are expecting to participate in co-operation with other European companies may be lost to Westland if the United Technologies/Fiat proposals are accepted.' This tried to preserve a balance between the American and the European offers, but she was furious that I had prevented her from giving the clear answer that Cuckney wanted. The letter was sent to Westland on 1 January 1986.

Paddy Mayhew's conduct throughout this matter was exemplary. We had known each other since Oxford days, where he had been President of the Union in my second year, and he has always brought the highest standards of conviction and integrity to the deliberations of government and of the Conservative Party. He was later to say of his involvement in the Westland affair that it was like being the family solicitor to both the Montagues and the Capulets.

I was keeping in close touch with the European consortium through their advisers at Lloyds, and with directors of British Aerospace and GEC. The status of Westland as a European company was of obvious interest to them and I agreed that, if they wrote to me, I would reply setting out more fully the position as I saw it. In a further letter of 3 January to David Horne, the managing director of Lloyds Merchant Bank, I answered three questions he had put to me. I reiterated the fact that the MOD had no requirement for the Black Hawk helicopter. I said there were no examples of Westland exporting any helicopter that was not part of the inventory of the British services. And I gave instances of the indications from European governments and companies that Westland might lose out if the UTC/Sikorsky/Fiat proposals were accepted. I copied this to Sir John Cuckney. The contents of my letter were reported in the national press the next day, Saturday the 4th. But there was nothing confidential in anything I had written and the fact that Lloyds made public use of this letter was hardly surprising, as it contained information relevant to the debate.

Mrs Thatcher was even more furious. She discussed my letter with Leon Brittan. She made no attempt to contact me but left him in no doubt that he should take the matter up with Paddy Mayhew, whom she wanted to write a letter to me alleging material inaccuracy in my text. She determined that, just as I had prevented her from sending a misleading letter, she would now force me to retract. What had been sauce for the goose should be sauce for the gander. Her problem was that what I had said was accurate. Paddy's letter, when it came, said only that he had not by then seen sufficient evidence to substantiate all my statements. Sir Michael Havers was later questioned in the House of Commons about Mrs Thatcher's involvement in the subsequent leak and specifically about whether she had spoken to Paddy over the weekend. He replied that she had not. But he had been asked the wrong question. She had made her wishes known via Leon.

The first thing I knew of any concern was a telephone call I received from Paddy on Saturday night at home in Oxfordshire. He told me that he had just been contacted by Leon and explained the background to his, Paddy's, concern. He indicated the nature of a letter which I could expect to receive from him first thing on Monday morning, 6 January, after he had checked the documents in his office. It was not until its actual arrival that Monday morning, however, that I was able to appreciate what had happened. His letter did not baldly accuse me of sending out a letter that contained 'material inaccuracies'. What he said was that, 'on the basis of the information contained in the documents to which I have referred, which I emphasise are all that I have seen, the sentence in your letter to Mr Horne does in my opinion contain material inaccuracies in the respects I have mentioned and I therefore must advise that you write again to Mr Horne correcting those inaccuracies'. As soon as I received his letter, which he had perfectly properly copied to No. 10, I spoke to him on the telephone and said I quite understood why he had written it but it caused me no concern because I could let him have accounts of various conversations I had had with my European counterparts which would provide sufficient additional evidence that would more than justify the points that I had made. He could not have been aware of these, but I would – and did – write back immediately setting out the nature of the evidence I had.

None of this should have become the stuff of newspaper headlines; it ought to have been dealt with in the ordinary way of ministerial correspondence. I believed I had a perfectly satisfactory answer to Paddy's points and had begun drafting my official response. Yet within two hours of his letter arriving in my office, that single highly selective phrase, 'material inaccuracies', was leaked. I was appalled when I heard this. In the event, it transpired that Charles Powell, the highly influential private secretary in the Prime Minister's Private Office responsible for foreign affairs and defence, had telephoned John Mogg, Leon Brittan's private secretary; then, after Leon had been reached during his lunch, the matter was passed to those with the press contacts and expertise: Bernard Ingham in No. 10 and Colette Bowe, chief press officer at the DTI. I quickly asked for and obtained a copy of the Press Association's tapes. These tapes, under the name of Chris Moncrieff, their senior political correspondent, featured neither the letter nor any substantial part of it. The leaks they contained were a handful of phrases, including those two words presented misleadingly out of context. Chris Moncrieff could not have known that he was being fed so partial a story. And my early experience of working with Colette over many months during my time as Minister for Merseyside left me in no doubt that she would not willingly have leaked a law officer's letter, which by convention is always confidential, to harm me.

What seems beyond any doubt is that those on the Prime Minister's staff – and answerable directly to her in No. 10 – were responsible for encouraging the leaking of a selective and misleading quotation from one of the two Law Officers of the Crown in order to discredit a senior colleague. Miss Bowe was the reluctant intermediary. I was later gratified to learn that the Attorney General, Sir Michael Havers, newly back from convalescence, had demanded in the strongest terms an inquiry into so gross a breach of the normal conventions of confidentiality and apparently of the Official Secrets Act. If it weren't forthcoming, he had threatened to put the police into No. 10 to conduct one – a brave stand for one who hoped to become Lord Chancellor. Paddy's own views of the matter were doubtless much influenced by the recent prosecution of a junior official, Sarah Tisdall, with the consent of the Attorney General, and her conviction for a breach of that same Act. Sir Michael got his inquiry. And he did become Lord Chancellor.

I completed and sent my reply to Paddy's letter on Monday, 6 January, the same day that I had received it. There was no further attempt to query the points that I had made and I accordingly wrote further to Lloyds Merchant Bank, telling them that my original answer to them needed no correction. To the best of my knowledge Paddy Mayhew's letter was never actually leaked in full. At the time there was some shoddy excuse that the Westland board needed to know the contents of the Solicitor General's letter before a press conference they were holding later that day, but in fact Westland's advisers decided it was a 'cheap point' and it was not used. This excuse becomes even more threadbare against the revelation by the Defence Select Committee in its subsequent inquiry that further parts of Paddy's letter were disclosed after the original telephone call by Miss Bowe. As the Committee's report says: 'Their only purpose can have been further to discredit Mr Heseltine.'* The full letter was only published some months later, with the leaked passages italicised, as part of the evidence following the Defence Select Committee's subsequent inquiry.

I dined that same evening – Monday the 6th – with Clive Whitmore, my permanent secretary, who had been a tower of strength throughout these difficult weeks. We discussed frankly how events might unfold and my view that night was that somehow or other we would muddle through Thursday's Cabinet, despite the breakdown in good government relations that had taken place. He accepted my judgement. I remember adding that I thought the worst that could happen was that I would resign and that the next leader of the Conservative Party would bring me back. But I did not think then that the issue would come to resignation.

Paddy responded to my letter the next day, recognising that I was entitled to rely on the extra evidence – largely of numerous conversations with my fellow European defence ministers – which I possessed and which he had not previously known of. In the circumstances he did not feel he could form a judgement himself about these conversations, but recognised that it was my responsibility to satisfy myself about the statements I had made. His letter was copied to the Prime Minister and colleagues, and received no further comment. This may have been in part because in the same letter he set out his forthright views about the leak itself.

Wednesday, 8 January, the eve of the fateful Cabinet meeting, arrived. My mood had shifted since Monday but only marginally. It was increasingly clear just how serious British Aerospace and GEC were in their endeavours to put together a European consortium. Certainly, I was encouraging them. In the early days of the deliberation on alternatives, Mrs Thatcher may have argued to colleagues that it should be left to the shareholders to determine Westland's future; but the rules had been materially changed. Indeed, on this very day Leon Brittan called Sir Raymond Lygo, the chief executive of British Aerospace, into his office. Ray Lygo was to react with fury at this meeting. He believed Leon Brittan to have told him – in the presence of

---

* Fourth Report from the Defence Select Committee, Session 1985–6, *Westland plc: The Government's Decision-Making*, p. xlix, para. 165.

officials and Geoffrey Pattie, the number two as Minister of State at the DTI – that the American aircraft company, McDonnell Douglas, had been on the telephone warning that British Aerospace's involvement in the European bid was not doing their interests any good in America and that, as the role of British Aerospace in this context was incompatible with the national interest, they should withdraw from the consortium. There was no collective authority for such a request. There had been no discussion that gave any indication of the undesirability of British Aerospace and GEC partnering Westland. Neither was my Department consulted.

Before I left the office that evening I again discussed the prospects with Clive Whitmore. He sensed that the atmosphere had tensed over the past two days, and was less certain now of the outcome. Anne remembers that we had dinner together on the 8th and discussed the next day's Cabinet. My doubts may have increased but I did not share her conviction that I would have no alternative but to resign.

I remained reasonably optimistic until some way into the Cabinet meeting itself the next morning. There was a discussion, not about the substantive issue but about the bad public image that the row was creating. It was, indeed, now arousing considerable public interest. Mrs Thatcher proposed that all questions to do with Westland should be referred to the Cabinet secretary for prior clearance before being answered. I was prepared to go along with this proposal, provided that it applied to questions that related to the relative merits of the rival bids or to unresolved issues of *future* policy. But I also asked for confirmation that I could not be expected, in dealing with *established* policy or statements that had already been made, to profess an inability to give again answers that I had already given in public. The answer was that *all* questions had to be submitted to the Cabinet secretary.

It was, of course, a trap. The press would immediately have been briefed that I had been silenced. They would have asked me questions which – the day before, the week before, the month before – I had answered clearly and accurately, only to be told on this latest occasion that I needed to check with the Cabinet secretary that this was still the right answer. They would have made the most of it and they would have been encouraged every step of the way by the destabilising briefing processes from No. 10 with which every member of the government was all too familiar.

If I needed any evidence to support my judgement that this strategy had been carefully thought out in advance, that evidence surfaced when Mrs Thatcher, in Cabinet, produced from her *handbag* a small piece of paper upon which the conclusions of the meeting were already written. Prime Ministers usually sum up meetings orally, drawing on drafts in the form of alternative sets of words in a briefing folder provided by Cabinet Office officials for the various alternative conclusions they have anticipated. A scrap of paper produced from a handbag could only be the product of some political discussion with close confidants and advisers. This is what she now read out. One or two colleagues, including Peter Walker, tried to find a way through. But their efforts led nowhere. I could not accept such a gagging order. I folded my papers, rose from my chair and left the room. There was no drama. No storm. No scene of any kind.

There have been many accounts of my departure from the Cabinet that Thursday morning. They are coloured very much by the approach individual colleagues adopted to the issue in general and to me in particular. However, history may be helped by the recollection of Christopher Mallaby (later Sir Christopher and our ambassador first to Germany and then to France). He was one of the Cabinet Office notetakers on this occasion. He remembers the events clearly: I said 'Then I must leave this Cabinet.' He watched as I then stood up, calmly, and walked without haste from the room. Not everyone left behind was sure that I had resigned. But they were to know for certain a few minutes later when my comments to a journalist in Downing Street were relayed back to them.

I walked alone through the corridors of No. 10 and out into Downing Street. I crossed to a single waiting camera and made the simple announcement that I had resigned and would make a full statement later that day. I then walked the short distance along Downing Street, across Whitehall and into the Ministry, where I had served with such pride for three years. I had left behind me prestige and influence, and now faced an unpredictable future. But every instinct told me that what I had done was right. I would never have felt confident in my own integrity if I had remained seated at the Cabinet table. (The last Minister to resign halfway through a Cabinet had been Joseph Chamberlain over the issue of imperial preference in 1903 – though, rather differently from me, he had 'fixed' the announcement of his departure with A. J. Balfour, the Prime Minister, beforehand.)

The first thing I did on my return to my desk was to pick up the telephone to tell Anne the news. To my astonishment she knew already. Apparently, Chris Moncrieff had called her from the press gallery a few minutes earlier and asked for me. 'Surely you haven't forgotten it's Cabinet day, Chris,' Anne replied. 'Then you don't know,' he said and told her the news. Her stunned 'Oh my God' became a newspaper 'saying of the week'.

There then followed an afternoon for which I doubt there is any precedent. I needed to make a statement. There had been no prior preparation. I started with a blank sheet of paper. From eleven o'clock to four o'clock I worked at my desk, with all the resources of the Ministry of Defence checking the facts, typing the text and organising the press conference that was to be held in the Concourse Hall in the Ministry. My already appointed successor, George Younger, with great tact and understanding had telephoned to ask at what time it would be convenient for him to come and take over his job as Secretary of State. He made no protest when it was suggested that six o'clock would be a good time and no attempt was made to prevent me using the facilities of the Ministry for what turned out to be a momentous press conference. The permanent secretary sat at my side, as I made my statement five hours after I had left the government. Whatever the constitutional curiosities of the situation, I cannot overstate the gratitude I continue to feel to so many in the Ministry of Defence for their support in such difficult circumstances. The text of my statement was reproduced in full in, among other newspapers, the *Daily Telegraph* the following day and is included as an appendix to this book.

Of course, all resignations are controversial and usually traumatic, unless they are seen as the gentle ending to a distinguished career by mutual agreement. Otherwise the analysts invariably look for the hidden motive, for the well-judged timing providing the launch-pad for future advance. There was much press speculation along these lines. But the lead editorial in *The Times* the next day, 10 January, would in many ways be difficult to improve upon from my point of view. Headed 'A Very Good Resignation', it comes as close as any newspaper of such authority ever would to supporting what a rebel minister had done.

I believe to this day that the paper was right in its overall judgement, but I have to say that some of its speculation was ill founded. There was no calculation of advancement. I certainly did have an inner confidence that it would not be the end of my career. But I went because I believed that what Mrs Thatcher had done was an affront to the standards of government in which I profoundly believed. You cannot allow progress by cheating and, if ever you start down that road, it will not be long before cheating and sharp practice become the norm. There has to be a line that no one should cross. And if that was the judgement that propelled me out into Downing Street on 9 January, events that were to follow more than vindicated my view.

Of course, there are 'might have beens'. If I had persisted, would that telephone call to Willie Whitelaw before Christmas have made a difference? He was interviewed years later, for an instalment of the BBC series, *The Thatcher Years*, screened in October 1993. I do not need to add to his words. Speaking of me, he said: 'It would have been better if there had been more discussion – he'd been able – he'd – well, put it this way – that he could have felt that he'd been able to put his case strongly to Cabinet. He always felt he'd been denied that. And I think it was perhaps – looking back on it – a pity that he always appeared to feel that. And I think to some extent he *had* been denied it.' He might have added that it is impossible to think of any other country on earth where a defence contractor would be sold to a foreign purchaser with the government refusing even to allow a discussion about the merits of an alternative solution, led by two of its own leading national companies.

Mrs Thatcher herself said, when she went to the House of Commons for the debate that the Opposition precipitated on the Westland issue on 25 January 1986, that she was not sure whether she would return to No. 10 as Prime Minister. I have never understood her doubts; if her side of the story was accurate, she had nothing to fear. But, of course, her advisers were frightened that I was out to bring her down. This thought had simply never crossed my mind.

John Wakeham, the Chief Whip at the time, who must be regarded as one of the most sophisticated fixers in the political game, approached me about the speech that inevitably I would make in the House to explain my resignation. I said I had no intention of escalating the row or exploiting the divisions. I had, however, one condition. I wanted it accepted that the Prime Minister should not make a speech attacking me and what I'd done. She had to accept a personal responsibility for things that had gone wrong. I agreed with John a form of words that she would use in the House of Commons. I still have the note from him confirming our agreement. Referring first to the leak of the

Solicitor General's letter she said in her statement, 'I deeply regret that this was done without reference to the Solicitor General. Indeed, with hindsight, it is clear that this was one, and doubtless there were others, of a number of matters which could have been handled better, and that too I regret.' I had explained that, if she said that, she would have no trouble from me on the floor of the House. In a brief speech following hers that day I responded:

> I heard the Prime Minister clearly say that she deeply regretted the fact that the letter from my Rt Hon. and Learned Friend the Solicitor General had been leaked. She went on to say that a number of other matters could have been handled better and she regretted that too. I think that that is a difficult and a very brave thing for a Prime Minister to say in such circumstances. I could not have asked for words other than those that my Rt Hon. Friend the Prime Minister used.

The fact that Mrs Thatcher accepted the use of those words – which she knew I had dictated – indicates the degree of anxiety she felt about the whole affair. In the event, there was a minor hiccup even in this arrangement. John Wakeham had believed that I had agreed that, if she used these words, I would intervene, as soon as she had done so, with some encouragingly supportive remarks. Apparently, he told me years later, there was some consternation when I remained woodenly in place, and he feared that I might be about to go back on the deal. That is not my style. I had understood that my part of the bargain would be concluded when I rose to speak myself. So, indeed, it was.

My speech, in the circumstances, was a modest success, attracting murmurs of approval from various parts of the parliamentary party. I deliberately emphasised the words which showed that I had no intention of pursuing a vendetta. I kept the speech brief and crafted it with some care to ensure that I remained as on side with my colleagues as the prevailing atmosphere would permit. As a final point, I turned my attention to the Labour Party – never, I had found, the hardest target to attack. I sat down to a mixture of relief and also to a surprisingly sympathetic reception from the benches around me.

From that moment on I never sought to raise the Prime Minister's behaviour in the Westland affair again while she remained in that office. Press inquiries were either brushed aside or dealt with in the fewest possible words: 'I have said all I have to say on the subject.' I voted with the government in all the votes that the Labour

Opposition subsequently engineered on Westland. I was encouraged through the lobbies, along with the rest of the parliamentary party, under the ever present eye of the whips. 'Don't worry, Michael,' said one of them, Peter Lloyd. 'We'll do the same for you when you're leader of the party.'

The findings of the leak inquiry, which was set up under the Cabinet secretary at the time to explore the circumstances in which the selected extracts from the Solicitor General's letter were leaked, have never been made public. But Colette Bowe herself refused initially to give evidence to the Armstrong inquiry on the ground that what she said might be used in further proceedings. She requested immunity from such an eventuality. The nature of her involvement in the leak itself may be deduced, however, from Sir Michael Havers' reply on 3 February 1986 (see that day's Hansard, col. 15), when he said: 'When I was asked to grant immunity because the girl – the information officer – was refusing to give evidence unless she had immunity and her evidence was uniquely important in the pursuance of the inquiry, *I was told enough* to make it clear to me that under no circumstances would I have prosecuted her in any event' (emphasis mine).

As the fateful Cabinet meeting of 9 January approached, the battle for control of Westland entered a decisive stage. The two sides had both made offers for the company. The Sikorsky deal was in aggregate worth £72.2 million. The board of Westland had met on 30 December to consider an improved rival bid from the Europeans valued at £73.1 million. *The Times* reported on Tuesday, 31 December a board decision to pass on the European offer to its shareholders but to withhold a recommendation as to which offer it supported until the company had received a reply to the letter it had sent to Mrs Thatcher. That reply was sent the next day and, in the event, again as reported in *The Times* on 7 January, the board decided to recommend a revised Sikorsky bid of £74 million, which had been submitted on the 6th.

The *Daily Telegraph* gratifyingly recognised the role I had played and summarised the situation fairly in its editorial entitled 'Westland's Choice' on 7 January:

It is easy to pick holes in the actions and motivations of most of the participants. An orgy of charge and counter-charge will be of little benefit to Westland, its shareholders or its workers. They are best served by a cool examination of the respective merits of the two bids.

If nothing else, Mr Heseltine's intervention has forced Sikorsky to increase its bid. The American company is now offering more money, more man-hours of work and a higher proportion of development and engineering work than before. Its offer will be the only one put to shareholders at present. If they accept this offer, and with it the principle of free market forces in this sector, the shareholders should at least be aware of the thinking behind the other bid: that long-term European co-operation is the only way to prevent American monopoly of the arms supply market. Whatever the final outcome, and whatever may have happened in recent months, that is argument enough for allowing the European consortium a fair and equal position as a bidder.

Of course, my resignation on the 9th was not the end of the Westland saga. Indeed, the date can be seen as a pivotal moment in this affair in more ways than one. Quite unbeknown to me, on that same day, Alan Bristow, the owner of Bristow Helicopters (an operating rather than manufacturing company) and a former Westland chief test pilot, had entered the market. Bristow is a twentieth-century buccaneer. He had built his own helicopter company from scratch, serving the worldwide oil and gas industries, including in the North Sea. He was a well-known character in the industry, knew the business backwards and during the summer of 1985 had mounted his own takeover bid for Westland, only to withdraw when it materialised that the company's financial problems were considerably greater than he could possibly have known when his bid was launched. He had the ambition to play a significant managerial role in the manufacture of helicopters, about which he was an acknowledged expert. Indeed, he had been summoned by Mrs Thatcher to discuss the problems facing Westland when he was preparing his abortive bid. He now sought to increase the shareholding he had retained from the previous summer and bought more Westland shares at 109 pence a share. Over the next few days he went on buying. By the end of that period he controlled 17 per cent of the company and had invested a further £6 million.

Now that I was a backbencher, I was determined to give what support I could to the European consortium. The shareholders of Westland had before them two alternative offers. One was the Sikorsky bid, recommended by their board of directors under Sir John Cuckney's chairmanship. The other was that put forward by David Horne of Lloyds Merchant Bank on behalf of the British Aerospace, GEC and

European consortium. Sir John and his colleagues needed a meeting of the company's shareholders in order to secure – and the rules required a 75 per cent majority – a special resolution to restructure the company to allow their preferred Sikorsky deal to proceed. The date was set for 14 January.

Alan Bristow's emergence as owner of a large stake in the company threatened their prospects of success. Worse still were the rumours that other large shareholders were attracted to the European case. A block of just under 5 per cent held by United Scientific Holdings (USH), under the chairmanship of the former permanent secretary of the Ministry of Defence, Sir Frank Cooper (and a company which had been built up by Peter Levene before I persuaded him to come into the MOD), was committed. Robert Fleming Merchant Bank held 9 per cent. I attended a meeting on Friday, 10 January with Ray Lygo and two members of the Fleming board at which we learnt that they too were about to opt for the European proposal and not to move in the direction that Cuckney and his colleagues wanted.

There then followed a series of events and meetings that were to lead to a Stock Exchange inquiry, which in turn would conclude that there was a need for an investigation by the Department of Trade and Industry.

The Westland camp met on Friday, 10 January – to contemplate their deteriorating prospects. It fell to Peter Wilmot Sitwell, a partner in the stockbrokers Rowe & Pitman, to attempt to redress the balance. He had to find shares to buy and someone to buy them. He failed to reach Bristow but on Sunday managed to contact John Emley, head of UK equity at Robert Fleming. He was quoted a price of 125 pence per share – a substantial advance on the 109 pence Bristow had paid in the market three days earlier. It remained necessary to find someone to pay such a price. James (Lord) Hanson, knighted by Harold Wilson in 1976 and ennobled by Mrs Thatcher in 1983, was the chosen instrument. Together with his colleague Gordon White, he had built up an international conglomerate with powerful American interests but he had (twice) refused to become involved in Westland when approached by both Alan Bristow and Sir Basil Blackwell, then chief executive of the company, earlier in 1985.

On that Sunday night, subject to confirmation the following day, Hanson agreed to purchase the Fleming shares for £7 million. Sir John Cuckney had not been present at the meeting where it was decided to seek Lord Hanson's assistance. Up until this moment it could be argued that the market would determine the fate of Westland. Certainly, nothing illegal had happened, even if events had moved in a way no member of the Cabinet had contemplated. As Hanson's partner Sir Gordon White was quoted as saying at the time, the motivation for the Hanson intervention was part political. That is not illegal.

As these events unfolded, the day of the approaching meeting of the shareholders, 14 January, drew closer. It was still far from obvious that Sir John could secure the 75 per cent majority necessary. The meeting was postponed on the ground that the Connaught Rooms were 'too small' to contain the large number of shareholders who, it was suggested, were likely to come. The meeting was refixed for Friday, 17 January, in the Royal Albert Hall, which had a seating capacity of 4,500.

On 16 January, the day before the Albert Hall meeting, Alan Bristow was invited by Hubert Faure, the senior executive vice-president of UTC, to meet him at 3.30 p.m. at Claridge's Hotel. When he arrived he found that Cuckney had also made arrangements to meet Faure that afternoon and that Sir Gordon White, Hanson's partner, had similarly agreed to meet Cuckney. As to the coincidence of these events, one can only speculate. What no one challenges is that all four men ended up in the same room at the same meeting later that afternoon. The substance of the conversations is disputed. Bristow told me that he was offered 135 pence a share. I subsequently wrote to the chairman of the Stock Exchange questioning how the chairman of a company who had recommended that his shareholders should accept a valuation of 65 pence a share so recently could be present in negotiations only weeks later at which one shareholder was offered just over double that sum. Cuckney, when challenged later, said that he had left the meeting before the offers were made. I have never understood how either White or Faure believed that they had the authority to offer to buy shares on behalf of Westland. What cannot be disputed is that the offer was made. Later that same evening Faure rang Bristow from Westland's London head office to confirm it. This conversation was overheard by Sir Frank Cooper, chairman of USH. I reported this to the Stock Exchange when I gave evidence to their investigation in February, although at the time I referred to Sir Frank not by name but only as a person of 'impeccable repute'.

Alan Bristow himself was to record attempts to persuade him to change sides. He rang me early the next morning when I happened to be with my daughter Alexandra in the kitchen of our home in London. I asked her to listen in to the conversation in which he relayed his indignation. He referred not only to the Claridge's meeting but to two earlier ones as well. Apparently, the hotelier Lord Forte had telephoned him on 13 January in an attempt to persuade him to vote for the Sikorsky bid. He had refused, but the next day he had been invited to 56 Park Lane where Forte had wasted no time in asking what could be done to change his mind. In the course of this conversation, Forte had said it was about time Alan was publicly recognised for his services. Alan made it clear that the only thing that would change his mind was a British government commitment to buying the Black Hawk, without which he had no faith in its export potential. His account of the meeting is that Lord Forte then telephoned No. 10 and was put through to Denis Thatcher, whom he invited round on the ground that he believed he had the solution to the Westland affair. When fifteen minutes later Denis Thatcher was shown into the Park Lane offices, it was suggested that Bristow wait outside. After a brief ten minutes Lord Forte had to report that the Prime Minister's husband had refused to have anything to do with such an improper proposal. Alan was incensed at the crudity of the tactics he believed were being deployed against him.

The matter of public preferment did not rest there. On 16 January Alan Bristow received a telephone call from Lord King, whom he had known for many years and whom he knew to have close links with the Conservative Party. A meeting was fixed for that day at Cleveland House, King Street, the headquarters of Babcock and Wilcox, of which Lord King was chairman. At that meeting Alan explained again his scepticism about the Sikorsky deal based on the prospects for the Black Hawk, for which he had been clearly told by his contacts at the MOD there was no likelihood of an order. He records that King made a firm offer of a knighthood if he changed sides. King also undertook to buy his shares at a price Bristow calculated would show him a personal profit in excess of £2 million and to secure him an immediate directorship of Westland, with the prospect, a year or so later when the dust had settled, of the chairmanship of the company. Alan had left this meeting to keep his appointment with Faure at Claridge's.

It has to be said that even matters of this seriousness can have their lighter moments. Lord Fanshawe (formerly Anthony Royle, Tory MP for Richmond, Surrey, and at one time a junior Foreign Office minister) had a role on the periphery as a member of the board of Westland. It was put to him that he was one of those who had been involved in offering Bristow a knighthood. Tony had certainly played a part in trying to persuade Alan Bristow but he denied making any offer on Mrs Thatcher's behalf, and said: 'There was obviously a misunderstanding. What may have been offered to him was a night out.'

In the event, the postponed shareholders' meeting took place at the Royal Albert Hall on Friday, 17 January. It attracted only about 500 people – which would have been well within the capacity of the Connaught Rooms. The vote, too, failed to deliver Cuckney his desired result. The Sikorsky camp received 65.2 per cent of the poll, short of the required 75 per cent. The next device had to be a reworking of the original scheme into such a form that a simple majority would secure its success.

That same week, I received a letter from a member of the public dated 13 January. In simple, stark sentences it set out an account of one small shareholder's experience of what had been going on behind the scenes:

> As one who has followed the fast-moving events at Westland with great interest, I was disturbed to hear today of the manner in which Westland is treating at least one of its shareholders. Whilst I realise that you may be fully aware of this, I would not like it to remain unknown.
>
> The mother of a colleague of mine holds several hundred shares in Westland. She decided to vote, by post, for the European solution. Since then she has received 3 telephone calls from Westland or their agents, attempting to persuade her to change her mind. Despite the fact that she is over 70 years old, this might be regarded as just about within the bounds of decency.
>
> What I regard as unacceptable is the fact that her voting paper has been returned with a plea for her to reconsider her decision. She was told (on the basis that the meeting was to *have* taken place on Tuesday 14th, morning) that she could deliver her new voting paper to any number of 'convenient' points by the morning of Tuesday 14th.

But the game was about to assume an even more bizarre character.*

---

* The events are graphically set out in the book, *Not with Honour*, by the journalists Magnus Linklater and David Leigh (Sphere Books, London, 1986).

Within a matter of days Sikorsky, having first reversed its original decision to enter the market by selling the shares it had acquired (believing that their action might have been judged illegal), now re-entered the market, apparently reassured about the legal implications of doing so. The Prudential sold its 4.4 per cent at 151 pence a share, followed by Prolific Unit Trust, whose 2.3 per cent raised Sikorsky's stake to 6.7 per cent. Subsequently they reached the maximum permitted at 9.9 per cent. (Under Stock Exchange rules Sikorsky had been warned several times that no one with a *material* interest in an *extraordinary* general meeting could buy more than 10 per cent of the company concerned.)

Rupert Murdoch's associated company TNT (Australia's largest transport group) added to his interest in Sikorsky as a non-executive director of its parent company, UTC, by purchasing up to the permitted maximum of just under 5 per cent. (The law at the time required a person to make disclosure to a public company if he became interested in 5 per cent or more of any class of its voting share capital; in other words, no undeclared holdings above 5 per cent were allowed.)

Unknown to any but those involved and leading members of the Stock Exchange a number of nominees now rapidly accumulated blocs of shares on behalf of a range of overseas buyers, who preserved their own anonymity by remaining within the 5 per cent limit.

Meanwhile David Horne, acting on behalf of the three European companies within his consortium, decided to make a public offering for 12.63 million shares (21 per cent of the company) at 130 pence per share. This was apparently the first time the small shareholders had had a chance to gain from the remarkable windfall that had now dropped into the laps of those who only a few weeks before had owned a near bankrupt company. But the offer was a failure. I can only guess at what had happened in the meantime.

But the guess is not uninformed. Nicholas Goodison, the chairman of the Stock Exchange, had become increasingly concerned at reports reaching him of all the activity in the Westland shares. On 4 February he invited Peter Wills, a partner in the stockbrokers Sheppard & Chase, and a former deputy chairman of the Exchange, to chair an investigation into whether Stock Exchange rules had been infringed and to report generally. I asked for an interview with the inquiry team and was invited to appear before them on 11 February. I declared my ignorance of both the law and the Stock Exchange code of practice, and added that in my layman's judgement there had been a number of occurrences which needed explaining.

I expressed concern about the delay of the shareholders' meeting on grounds which had the effect of allowing more time to influence the result. I was concerned that there were buyers targeting those shares which were likely to support the Europeans. And, third, I raised the question of the possible involvement of the chairman of Westland in negotiations concerning large shareholders where prices for shares were on offer very different to the 65 pence a share he had recommended to the majority of ordinary shareholders.

Peter Wills questioned me about each of my concerns in turn, putting to me the context in which the other side might seek to justify its position. Then, some little way into the meeting, a draft press release was produced which the Stock Exchange intended to release later that day. This revealed that, as at that date, 20.33 per cent of the total issued share capital of Westland was now in the hands of nominee owners, registered overseas. The minutes of the meeting record my reaction: 'I don't know who they are. You don't. It's a scandal.' When asked if I had any knowledge of European dealings in shares behind nominee names, I was able to say that I did not.

At the second shareholders' meeting the next day, 12 February (this time back in the Connaught Rooms), Sir John confirmed that 20.33 per cent of the company was in the hands of six mystery shareholders. He also read out the names of four holding companies appearing on the company's register but said he did not know who the beneficial shareholders were.

By this time, the Sikorsky–Fiat deal had been duly recast so that its approval would require only a 50 per cent majority. When it came to the vote this time round, the necessary resolution secured 67.8 per cent. Cuckney and his board had delivered Westland to Sikorsky. Sikorsky itself, Hanson, Rupert Murdoch and a range of unknown and invisible owners whose identities were intentionally concealed behind a façade of foreign banks, holding companies and anonymous clients' accounts had been of some assistance.

Readers may wonder if the Cabinet, in taking the view that the matter should be left for Westland itself to determine, had it in mind that the decision-making process would be conducted in such a manner. We shall never know; they have never expressed an opinion. Perhaps even more important is the question whether a significant defence contractor should be made subject to ownership decisions in this way. I do not believe that any other government of a nation of our standing would have stood by, tacitly supporting events which were both plain to see and scandalous.

Matters did not rest there, however. The Stock Exchange inquiry was still due to report and there were two investigations under way by the Select Committees on Defence and on Trade and Industry.

The Stock Exchange inquiry was helped in one respect in that Peter Wills and his colleagues had known early on in their investigations the names of the nominee accounts. What they did not know, and had no means of establishing, was the reality behind the nominees. They were also concerned about the legal risks they might run if their report was too direct in its allegations that a concert party had been in place. Under the 1985 Companies Act, where there existed an agreement between parties to acquire shares in another company (a concert party), each member of that party was required to treat his interest in the company as including the interests of all the other concert party members, so the obligation to inform the company of a large shareholding could not be avoided by acquiring the shares indirectly or in concert. It was an offence under Section 210(3) of the Act to breach any of the disclosure obligations, with a maximum penalty of two years' imprisonment, an unlimited fine or both. However, concert parties are notoriously difficult to prove even when arranged within British jurisdiction: evidence is unlikely to be found simply lying around. The task becomes well nigh impossible when the transactions take place abroad.

The Stock Exchange Report was published on 18 April. It concluded:

The Committee are satisfied that Members of The Stock Exchange, in difficult circumstances, acted in accordance with established practices and took full account of the interests of their clients where no precedent was available for guidance.

The Committee concluded that a two-tier market of the type that operated during the period is acceptable provided that all participants are aware of it and it is widely published, which was not the case during the period in question. They therefore recommend that the availability of different prices which may result from special conditions regarding votes should be formalised.

The Committee also recommend that the guidelines for open market purchases should be reviewed to make the Market more efficient to a wider clientele in future situations, and that guidelines be provided on dealing in shares with proxies attached to them.

The Committee also recommend that it should be a positive requirement that only a declared beneficial owner could vote at a special
meeting. The Committee believe that it is essential that there should
be changes in the law so that notwithstanding the absence of any
relevant provision in its articles, a company should have the power
to disenfranchise shares which are registered in nominee names but
where the ultimate beneficiary is not disclosed.

The Committee were unable to determine on the basis of the
evidence available whether there was an undisclosed concert party
in existence. In these circumstances, they cannot comment on whether
there has been any contravention of Section 204 of the Companies Act
1985. The Committee concluded that the Department of Trade and
Industry, which is responsible for enforcing the Companies Act, should
make further enquiries on this matter and that information arising from
The Stock Exchange's enquiry should be passed to the D.T.I.

The Committee accepted that the decision to change the venue of the
meeting from the Connaught Rooms was reasonable in view of the
number of Westland shareholders.

Michael Mates, a member of the Defence Select Committee and
about to become my closest colleague, sent me a copy of this report
on 1 May, commenting: 'The Stock Exchange's "hand-wringing" over
this deplorable story does them no credit.'

On 7 May Peter Wills, called to give evidence to the Trade and
Industry Select Committee and protected now by parliamentary privilege, was more forthright. When asked about the share deals, he
replied: 'Yes, it screams concert party at me.' Sir John Cuckney
described the support of the anonymous shareholders to the Committee in rather different terms. It was a 'fan club', he said.

When the report of the Defence Select Committee, chaired by the
former Tory Cabinet Minister Sir Humphrey Atkins, was published
on 23 July 1986, it quoted the Stock Exchange Special Committee's
observation that its 'credulity was sufficiently strained to be sceptical
as to the absence of a concert party of some sort'. The Defence
Committee stated: 'Nevertheless, it is unacceptable that the future of a
public company important to the defence interests of the United Kingdom should be decided on the votes of anonymous shareholders.' The
Committee recognised the right of Westland, as a private company, to
take their decisions in the light of their own commercial judgement.
But, while believing that the Sikorsky deal was likely to meet the

commercial needs of the company and do little damage in itself to European helicopter procurement, they went on to conclude on the substantive issue that 'an association with the European consortium might in the long term have better served the broader defence interests of the United Kingdom'.*

When the all-party Trade and Industry Select Committee, under the chairmanship of Kenneth Warren, the Conservative MP for Hastings and Rye, finally published its report in February the following year, it concluded *inter alia*:

> We therefore entertain substantial suspicions, which, however, fall short of proof, that a 'concert party' operated to purchase Westland plc's shares for locations outside the UK Government's jurisdiction. We consider that the public interest demands a high degree of transparency in share dealings involving a public limited company and this, of course, is especially so in the case of a company involved in defence contracts. The Westland case has demonstrated the inadequacy of the Stock Exchange rules to deal with this matter effectively and accordingly we recommend that the Government should introduce early legislation to require prompt disclosure of the identity of those controlling the voting rights in the shares.†

I wrote to the permanent secretary at the DTI on 11 October 1999 as follows: 'I would be grateful to know what action your Department took in pursuance of the recommendation of the Stock Exchange, following its examination of the movement of shares in Westland Ltd, as set out in the statement by the Council of the Stock Exchange issued on 18th April 1986, and what conclusions the Department's inspectors reached.'

The following is the reply I received: 'After due consideration of the Report of the Stock Exchange the then Secretary of State decided not to appoint inspectors under Section 442 of the Companies Act 1985 to investigate the membership of Westland plc. This decision was reviewed and reaffirmed after receipt of the report of the Trade and Industry Committee in February 1987.'

Anyone familiar with the working of Whitehall knows the form.

---

* Third Report from the Defence Select Committee, Session 1985–6, *The Defence Implications of the Future of Westland plc*, pp. xxxiv, xxxv and xliii.
† Second Report from the Trade and Industry Committee, Session 1986–7, *Westland plc*, p. ix, para. 20.

A recommendation to investigate a criminal offence, however it originated, would go in the first instance to officials. Such a suggestion, if it took the form of a letter from the Stock Exchange or a select committee report, might well be sent to the office of the Secretary of State, but the private office would refer it straight to the appropriate part of the Department for advice. A minister invariably first becomes involved when on his or her desk a file appears, to which could be attached a suitable reply already drafted. The file will contain officials' advice as to the appropriate way forward. It is inconceivable that a recommendation to launch a criminal investigation would be rejected by a politician without waiting for official advice. It would be improper and would attract immediate intervention by the permanent secretary.

In the Westland case the desirability or otherwise of an investigation was correctly referred to the Investigations Division at the DTI, headed at that time by Andrew Duguid. His advice, when it came, would have set out the arguments for and against, quite properly including the risk that the results of any investigation could be inconclusive and that in the process the inquiry might stir up matters that were embarrassing. The balance of his advice was not to proceed with an investigation. However, as one would expect of a wide-awake permanent secretary, by this time Sir Brian Hayes, the papers would pass his desk. Sir Brian was not satisfied that the advice was right and therefore wrote a dissenting note arguing that an investigation should proceed. Paul Channon was Secretary of State, having replaced Leon Brittan in January. He decided to accept Duguid's advice and the matter ended there.

As a result of the Stock Exchange and Select Committee investigations, on 11 May 1987 Paul Channon announced sixteen changes to the existing Stock Exchange regulations, the effect of which was to leave the extra-legal status of the Takeover Panel intact, while providing for it to have a closer relationship with the financial regulators. There was to be consultation over proposed changes in the law, many of which were enacted in the late 1980s.

The central fact remains, however, that the effect of Paul's decision was that the allegations surrounding the possibility of a concert party were never officially investigated and that allegations of criminality remain, to this day, unanswered. One day someone will talk. We shall then learn on whose behalf Mauricio de Castro of Los Angeles, Marc A. Odermatt of Palma de Mallorca, Guillermo Schiess of Uruguay and a Mr Hoffman of Liechtenstein (on two separate accounts) acquired over three days in early February 1986 some 15 per cent of Westland shares. A letter addressed to me at the House of Commons, London, or, as is the way these days, sent via e-mail to mrdh@haynet.com would suffice.

The Westland affair cost Leon Brittan his parliamentary career. I never personally regarded Leon as a key player in the events as they unfolded. His credibility as a European-minded politician was never in doubt. He found himself dragged along by a plot-line devised by Sir John Cuckney on the one hand and myself on the other. Leon had to go along with the clearly expressed intentions of Mrs Thatcher, working closely with Sir John Cuckney, or join my side of the argument with all the high political risks which that entailed. Leon was essentially a cerebral politician of great ability but with no power base in the House of Commons. I have always believed he became enmeshed in a process for which he had little enthusiasm and some distaste.

His actual downfall occurred over what was almost an irrelevancy, as a result of a question I asked, during a statement he made in the House on 13 January, about the arrival of a letter from British Aerospace, the dispatch of which I had heard about from Sir Raymond Lygo. Leon gave the House the impression that he had not received this letter, when in fact it was already in the hands of his Department. But the oversight, trivial in itself and, I have no doubt, unintended, caused a significant number of Tory backbenchers – led by Peter Tapsell – to call for his head. I am convinced that Downing Street saw him as a convenient scapegoat. One day history will answer the questions that Leon felt unable to answer in the face of persistent questioning by the Defence Select Committee.

The Defence Select Committee was, of course, all-party, although it had a Conservative chairman in Humphrey Atkins and a Conservative majority. Humphrey, a former Chief Whip, was close to the Prime Minister and his first instinct was to try to avoid conducting any inquiry at all. He invited the Committee to drinks at his flat off Smith Square, Westminster, and put forward three options: first, that the matter was not for the Defence Committee and was better left to the Trade and Industry Select Committee; second, that any inquiry should be in private; and, third, that if conducted in public it should be focused narrowly on the leak and be dealt with in a day or two. To a man his colleagues rejected all three. Humphrey's position was not helped by the fact that earlier on, when Mrs Thatcher was asked if there should be an official inquiry, she had accepted John

Wakeham's advice that there was no need on the basis that it would be properly dealt with by the Select Committee. She did not on that occasion specify which committee, perhaps assuming that, with Conservative majorities, party loyalty would suffice. Unfortunately for Mrs Thatcher at least two of the Tory members, Keith Speed and Winston Churchill, on the Defence Select Committee had been sacked by her and that a third, Michael Mates, had been one of Willie Whitelaw's more outspoken supporters in the leadership contest. Michael Marshall, too, was deemed suspect in view of his declared interest as a consultant to British Aerospace. Cuckney's furious protestations about his membership were rejected after consideration by the Committee, who believed Michael had properly declared his interest.

The Defence Committee wished to question the officials most closely involved and to see copies both of the minute Leon Brittan had sent to colleagues on 4 October (in which he supported the need for a European option) and of the record of a meeting that had taken place between Cuckney and Brittan on 17 October. Mrs Thatcher initially refused both requests. The Committee were incensed and eventually forced agreement that Sir Humphrey Atkins, as their chairman, and their senior Opposition member, Dr John Gilbert, could read the documents in private. My version of their contents stood: no one challenged my evidence that Leon Brittan had recommended a European option. Those parts of the documents that Humphrey and John Gilbert considered material were subsequently officially submitted to the Committee and published with their evidence. The device used to prevent officials appearing took the form of the Cabinet secretary himself, Sir Robert Armstrong. It was argued that, as he had already interviewed all the people concerned during the leak inquiry, he could now answer on their behalf. But the officials concerned had not seen his report. They were simply told that they would not appear, although Colette Bowe herself was entirely happy to do so in order to clear her name of guilt by association, about which she felt strongly. Officials acquiesced in this instruction, but only after taking the advice of departmental solicitors.

Sir Robert duly appeared – after a dress rehearsal had been conducted in the Cabinet Office at which officials played the parts of the various Committee members and interrogated him as they believed the Committee might. An observer at the Committee hearing noted his extreme nervousness. He was told he would be called back for a second time, and given a list of thirty-six questions in respect of which the Committee were not satisfied with his answers and wished for further information. Many of these had been deliberately drafted to demonstrate that he couldn't possibly answer them from first-hand knowledge. He was due to appear for the second time on 5 March at 7.30 p.m. Late on 4 March a reply from the Cabinet Office produced the additional information required. The presumption that this would prove too late for the Committee to be properly briefed for Sir Robert's appearance on the 5th proved unwarranted. The Committee Clerk had still been in the office when the papers arrived, and he sat until the small hours ensuring that his Committee members would be fully briefed to go the next morning.

In the way of things, every base motive is attributed to those who challenge established authority. Jim Callaghan offered me a stark warning of what the future held when he spoke about my resignation in the Commons debate on Westland on 15 January: 'The decision to resign is not an easy one to make. It means parting with friends and colleagues. It means that whispers and slanders and untruths will be told about the person who has resigned. When a person resigns, he will be told that he has weakened the party and it will undoubtedly be said that he is fulfilling some long-range ambition. I am sure that it is an agonising decision.'*

Certainly, it was from the issues of the Westland affair that my critics labelled me anti-American. Nothing could be further from the truth. I had from my earliest political days recognised the vital significance of the Atlantic Alliance to Britain and Europe, and nobody detected any latent anti-Americanism in the battle that I had fought a year or two earlier against CND to bring American weapons to our shores to take their place in the defence of the Alliance.

There are those who simply refuse to accept the intellectual judgement that to be pro-European is not to be anti-American. Indeed, in the post-war world it was President Eisenhower who was among the first great American leaders to indicate to the United Kingdom that it should seek its destiny in closer co-ordination with the fledgling European movement – a consistent theme of the State Department ever since. A remark that I have always treasured, even allowing for the niceties of the professional diplomat, was uttered by Charles Price, the American ambassador to the Court of St James's at the time

* Hansard, 15 January 1986, col. 1108.

of Westland. He was a kind man and the sort of friend you like to have in times of trouble. He said to me one day when we were alone: 'If I had been you, in your position, I'd have done the same.' And Anne recalls standing in the central lobby of the House waiting for me, not long after I had resigned. Old friends passed by, averting their eyes, but Charles walked straight over to her and enveloped her in a great big bear-hug. She said it changed the attitude of many of those fair-weather 'friends' around her.

One final comment in the same context. No part of the British establishment works more closely with the United States within the NATO alliance than the Ministry of Defence. I never sought to enlist the support of members of the armed services for the policy that I pursued towards Westland. I have no doubt that there were those who disagreed with me and that there was controversy within the Ministry. But what I clearly remember is that there was no one leaking or briefing against me from the higher levels of the armed forces and I have never read any criticism from those quarters as the years have passed. I hope I do not make too great a claim to believe that in that collective loyalty there was a degree of respect for the stand that I took.

Events now, of course, have moved on in the years that have since elapsed. The EH101 helicopter, an Anglo–Italian project my Department had helped to finance, proved the success I had forecast. The Ministry of Defence steadfastly refused, under successive Secretaries of State, to buy the Black Hawk helicopter.

On 13 December 1985, Sir John Cuckney had written to Margaret Thatcher expressing the view that, as she had taken a direct interest in the fortunes of Westland, he would among other points ask that the UK government refrain from issuing a statement 'to the effect that HMG will never purchase the Black Hawk'. She replied on 17 December: 'So far as Black Hawk is concerned, as United Technologies are aware, there is currently no Ministry of Defence requirement for these and no provision in the defence budget to buy Black Hawk or any comparable helicopter.' This reply did not tell the whole story. It failed to mention that the Ministry had recently examined such a requirement. The army had looked in 1985 at a Staff Target (AST 404) for a light support helicopter. The choice was considered to be between the Westland W30, Aérospatiale's Super Puma and the Black Hawk, then being offered by Shorts of Belfast on behalf of

Sikorsky. Although the Staff Target was put in abeyance later that same year, the advice to me, which I had made public, had been that there was no prospect of a Black Hawk purchase.

In any case Cuckney should have had no doubt that basing his case on that helicopter's prospects had – to put it mildly – a certain fragility about it. Yet two days later Westland had sent to my private secretary, Richard Mottram, a copy of a press release issued that day by Lazard explaining why the board of Westland had supported UTC and Fiat, based on the strength of UTC's existing world-class helicopter, the Black Hawk, rather than an offer from the European partners which, 'whatever its long-term political attraction, was distinctly deficient of commercial offers'. The press release went on to state: 'In the view of the Directors it is the outstanding helicopter in its class in the world today and the right to manufacture and sell the Black Hawk . . . will strengthen the Company's helicopter division.' While recognising the lack of a current MOD requirement, the board expressed the view that such a requirement would emerge and that in any case there was a considerable potential for exports over the next fifteen years.

On 12 February 1986, the day of the second shareholders' meeting, when Sikorsky effectively gained control of the company, Robert Zincone, president of Sikorsky Aircraft, wrote to Westland's employees to reinforce the message and, quite honourably, made clear the motivation of his company. 'When Westland approached us,' he said, 'we reached the conclusion that an investment associated with a Black Hawk licence would, in fact, make sense. A Westland-manufactured Black Hawk should be a winning competitor in Europe, as well as in the areas of the Middle East and Far East, where Westland has traditionally had strong ties.' Sikorsky was clearly calculating that, once it was in partnership with Westland, the political and employment arguments would turn the MOD round – or ensure that it was overruled in Cabinet.

Westland continued to present this delusion. In their annual report for that year the board explained that the Black Hawk had enabled a gap to be filled in their present range. The prospect of a Rolls-Royce engine was added to the domestic mix and a demonstrator aircraft was promised for the new year. The hope was expressed that the Ministry would buy the Black Hawk should such a requirement arise.

The position of the Ministry remained clear. It still had no intention of buying the Black Hawk. On 9 April 1987 my successor as Secretary of State, George Younger, made a statement in the House about the future defence requirement for support helicopters. He declared (inconsistently with Mrs Thatcher's letter of 17 December 1985) that the choice in meeting the requirement for a large helicopter capable of lifting a platoon – that is, some thirty men and their equipment – lay between additional Chinooks, made by America's Boeing, and a utility version of the Anglo-Italian EH101. Westland were told that the latter was the Ministry's preferred choice and that the government did not intend to proceed with an alternative European collaborative project, the NH90, which was designed to meet this specification, in view of its preference for the EH101. George was questioned at the time about the Black Hawk. He replied that he had been told by Westland that even if there were an order for it, it would not produce any work for the company for about five years.*

The game was up. Sikorsky's bid to sell Black Hawk to the Ministry of Defence was not just dead – it had never seriously been alive – but the prospect itself was now buried. No prototype of the helicopter was ever flown in the UK, although a single kit was assembled from American parts.

The bail-out now began. One small holding of 1.38 per cent of the Westland shares purchased between 3 and 5 February 1986 was sold on 26 January 1987 – before George's announcement. All the shares bought by the mystery buyers were sold by April 1988. The sale of Hanson's shares was announced on 3 October 1988. He had done nothing illegal in purchasing them. The following year he put it rather quaintly in an interview he gave to Dominic Lawson for the *Spectator*: 'Let's look at the facts, shall we? We are in the helicopter business. We were trying to get a deal with Sikorsky, to be their agents in another part of the world. Now, if I had imagined that two Cabinet ministers would have resigned over a tin-pot company in the West of England, I would never have gone near it with a barge-pole.'

In April 1994 Sikorsky sold its shares in Westland to GKN, the giant UK engineering company. On 17 April 1998 *The Times* front page ran the story that GKN was to merge Westland with Agusta, the helicopter arm of Italy's Finmeccania, to create the world's second largest helicopter group in a major step to rationalise the European defence industrial base.

If John Cuckney's original claims about Sikorsky's intentions had been true, if there had been considerable potential for exports over

* Hansard, 9 April 1987, col. 475.

the next fifteen years, why then did they pull out after only eight? According to the defence specialists Jane's Information Group, in 1999 Black Hawks were operating or on order in Turkey (103 helicopters), Australia (35), Saudi Arabia (22), Israel (15), Jordan (9), Japan (6), Brunei (4) and Egypt (2). Another 50 were sold in Central and South America and 116 in Korea – mostly for local assembly, and with a further 70 under consideration. That's over 400 helicopters. Not one has been built in the UK. But, as the president of Sikorsky said in his letter to the Westland employees (which I have quoted above), the deal on offer had always been that, as well as Europe, Westland could exploit those export markets 'in the areas of the Middle East and Far East, where Westland has *traditionally* had strong ties' (emphasis mine). No Black Hawks have been sold in Europe (unless you count Turkey, and that was always going to be an American market). Australia, Saudi Arabia, Jordan, Brunei – those might have been considered traditional Westland export targets, but produced no more than seventy sales.

Whichever way you argue it, the Westland judgement was flawed. Orders of this number, spread over several years, would never have justified Sikorsky's opening a second production line in the UK. Already by 1986 the prospects for volume export sales from America looked bleak. The only rationale for Westland's move that makes sense was to achieve the underpinning of a substantial MOD order. But there had never been any serious prospect of that, as I had told them and as Mrs Thatcher had confirmed.

I have been asked many times whether I regretted what I did. My answer is to be found in the Hansard report on the Westland debate on 15 January 1986, when I concluded my speech thus: 'I was with great pride Secretary of State for Defence in Her Majesty's Government. There are special responsibilities in that job and one of them is a conviction in one's capacity to do whatever one believes to be right and against all pressures. With great regret, but no doubt, I left the Government.' I have never had a shred of hesitation in concluding that what I did was right. Indeed, for me, it was the only thing I could have done.

I saw many good people broken by the Downing Street machine. I had observed the techniques of character assassination: the drip, drip of carefully planted, unattributable stories that were fed into the public domain, as colleagues became marked as somehow 'semi-detached' or not 'one of us'. I had been right to insist upon collective decision on the substantive issue, which had been denied me. I had been right about the procurement issue, as perceived by the British armed forces. And I had been right about the need for Europe to get its act together, to form trans-European companies big enough to make worthwhile partners with their North American equivalents and thus to strengthen the European pillar of the NATO alliance and the alliance itself.

The *Times* leader at the time of my resignation, to which I have already referred, concluded: 'The Prime Minister's mode of government was more widely tolerable when her administration had a sense of urgency – to control the unions, to bring down inflation, to win the Falklands war. It is less acceptable if the momentum is seen to be slowing down. It is an issue which will last.' It was, as the paper said, 'a very good resignation'.

Chapter 16

'SAY NOT THE STRUGGLE NAUGHT AVAILETH'

M uch telling of the same sad tale has enshrined the tragedy of the fallen Minister in the public mind: a career in ruins; an uncertain future; the car and driver a thing of the past; the adrenalin of the red boxes and constant media attention cut off at source; a forlorn, lonely figure standing at the Members' Entrance of the House of Commons, waiting for a taxi.

My experience was quite different. 'Are you coming with me, Andy?' I asked my driver. Andy Gregory had worked for me in the Ministry of Defence for the previous ten months. His arrival heralded the beginning of a relationship that remains unbroken, as he followed me in and out of government over the next fifteen years. He possesses that shrewd appreciation of the inside world of politics often found within the Government Car Service but heightened in his case as he became the conduit between me and many members of the Westminster lobby of political journalists. I once, only half in jest, suggested he should write his biography and provided the title: 'Me and Michael Heseltine'. Just as valuable, he gave me the gossip circulating among the other drivers. On that Thursday afternoon he took his career in his hands. 'Yes,' he said. Together we departed for the private sector, taking with us the government armoured car and the Special Branch guardians. It was all very gentlemanly. I was given three weeks to purchase my own new Jaguar and bid goodbye to the men who had so faithfully watched over me.

Meanwhile, they accompanied me wherever I went and that included all my constituency functions, which continued unabated despite the dramas of the preceding few weeks. It had not been an easy time for my Association and I was grateful for their forbearance and support. The chairman of a Conservative Association pays a heavy price for the privilege, even at the best of times. The job demands leadership with tact. The followers are all volunteers. Attendance at endless wine-and-cheese parties is *de rigueur*. There are also occasional branch dinners. There are sometimes surprises. The wife of my chairman opened the exchange with her neighbour at one such event conversationally enough: 'What branch do you come from?' 'Special' was not the reply she had been expecting.

The Westland affair continued to make headlines, of course, for several weeks after my departure from the Ministry of Defence. Indeed, the pressures were to continue unabated, as the saga unfolded. The most immediate issue was where to set up shop. It so happened that our daughter Alexandra was living in the basement flat of our home in Chapel Street, at the back of which was a mock-medieval hall which had been constructed in the 1890s to house a collection of armour. This became the new base of operations.

Sackloads of letters arrived, with which Anne and Alexandra battled – dividing them into piles of pro and anti. Christopher Morgan, a public relations consultant whom I had first got to know when he had been advising Lloyds Merchant Bank over the bid for Westland, provided secretarial support. I was lucky to discover that Eileen Strathnaver (formerly Eileen Baker), my original research assistant from the late 1960s, was available to help – for a couple of months, she said. (She has been with me ever since.)

It was clear that my departure from the government had provoked not only the inevitable hostility and charges of disloyalty but also an equally powerful surge of support from disenchanted Conservatives who wanted to signal their appreciation of someone they believed had stood up for his convictions. Certainly, there were letters from Conservative associations cancelling speaking engagements. But for every cancelled engagement there were three or four new invitations to take its place. I had no need to organise a programme of visits or to seek opportunities to speak. The demand was immediate and continued unabated until my return to government at the end of 1990.

It is easy to be flattered by the invitations that come pouring in; it is important to put them in context. All over the country there are people charged with finding speakers for this or that occasion. If they can land the latest name on the circuit and give their event a boost, then they will have more than discharged their responsibilities. There is a never ending cycle of such annual events. In truth you can fill a maximum of only fourteen mealtime engagements a week and I always kept a considerable part of the weekend free for family and home. But within a relatively short period I found myself making up to a dozen speeches a week. It rapidly became clear that survival, at least in the public eye, would not be a problem.

The response to such speeches was generally gratifying, even if the consequence was almost invariably simply to add an ever larger number of invitations to the pile. There were exceptions, however. I was invited to deliver the Linacre Lecture by Sir Bryan Cartledge, our recently retired ambassador to the Soviet Union and the new Principal of Linacre College in Oxford. I spent some considerable time preparing a full text. The traffic was appalling and I was late arriving. I found not just a packed lecture theatre but an overflow hall equally crammed. Bryan introduced me generously, praising the work I had done as Secretary of State for the Environment and stressing the particular significance of environmental policies to this audience, whose concern could be judged by its size. I have seldom wished so fervently to be elsewhere – and a very long way away elsewhere – as slowly it began to dawn on me that my speech, a robust articulation of the defence and nuclear policies of the NATO alliance, was undoubtedly not what this audience had assembled to hear. There was only one thing for it: profuse apologies and a pause while half the audience walked out.

Expressions of solidarity came not just from members of the public. Very shortly I was to find myself the focus of backbench discontent in the House of Commons. There is always an underlying element of frustration among a section of any parliamentary party, for the most obvious of reasons. There are the sacked, the more senior who have never been promoted and the more junior weighed down with the thought that they never will be. There are those backing both sides and others who are simply in a hurry. There are also the more sympathetic figures who merely feel disconnected from the current position of the party. The longer a party is in office, the larger this body of potential protest grows. The unifying and uplifting spirit of early victory has been slowly eaten into by every manner of frustration and bitterness. For many, a new start under a new leader is the only hope of restored fortune or of too-long-denied fulfilment.

My relationship with the media changed overnight. In government, up until the Westland saga, I had tended to remain distant from and suspicious of the press and broadcast journalists. I did not feel at home with its world of in-fighting and bitchery, its climate of unattributed quotation and the supine tameness with which all newspapers would print, and news programmes broadcast, the self-seeking leak. I remember once sitting in the corridors just outside a Conservative Party Conference in Blackpool, discussing this reluctance of mine with Adam Raphael, the political editor of the *Observer* at the time. I had used every opportunity the media offered in the years in Opposition between 1974 and 1979, but in office I had taken a very different view. (Indeed, so reticent was I reputed to be that it worked to my advantage when I began to talk so openly about the issues of Westland before my resignation. Journalists recognised a different approach and took it seriously.) Adam had listened to my account and then concluded the conversation prophetically. 'Very interesting,' he said, 'but one day you will need us, Michael.' He could not have made a more accurate forecast. Indeed, on the day after my resignation I lunched – I hasten to say by long prearrangement – at the *Observer* and two days after that the main article on its leader page appeared under my byline. From 1986 on, the media were the vehicle of my survival. Let me say thank you.

Of course, it was a two-way pursuit of self-interest. Harold Wilson is reputed to have been deeply mortified by his treatment as Prime Minister at the hands of the political correspondents whom he had deluded himself in the heady days of Opposition into believing were his friends. It is a great mistake for any politician to believe that the pack of lobby journalists will be constrained by bonds of personal loyalty. They have a job to do. That job involves talking to people in all parties and of all persuasions within those parties. They have to compete, like all the other specialist correspondents, for space in the newspaper or for slots in the programme for which they work. Their job is to get the stories and to get them first. If they believe that you have something that will enliven their column or move the agenda on, they will be all over you. The very same people will hatchet you if the going gets rough or the smell of blood is in the air. They may not always do it under their own bylines. They can feed the story to a colleague on the same newspaper or hide their more vicious comments under a pseudonym. The process is predictable. Expect no mercy.

But for journalists, for the time being, I was 'news'. I was the nearest thing to an opposition within the party that Mrs Thatcher faced. There was great danger in this for me. I had not set out to end Mrs Thatcher's premiership. What she had done over Westland was wrong. She had behaved in a way quite incompatible with my understanding of the

The London Docklands as I first knew them on becoming Secretary of State for the Environment in May 1979

On the streets of Liverpool in August 1981. I never lost my admiration for the sheer *joie de vivre* of young Liverpudlians

"That chain will have to go!"

My plans for cutting back on local authority expenditure caused widespread indignation

"So you thought the film was realistic, Mr Heseltine?"

The BBC decided to show Peter Watkins's 20-year old drama-documentary *The War Game* during my time as Secretary of State for Defence

At the Tory Party Conference 1977: 'left left, left left left'

The perils of being
Defence Secretary

RAF Molesworth: fenced in a night

Paying tribute at the Welsh Guards Memorial at Goose Green in the Falklands on my first visit there in 1983

With US Defense Secretary, Cap Weinberger – an engaging colleague though we differed on the desirability of breakfast meetings

My loneliest hour: coming out of the Cabinet to announce my resignation as Defence Secretary over the Westland affair on 9 January 1986

A clutch of Defence Secretaries. Nine former holders of the office that I held from 1983 to 1986. Front row (*from left to right*): Fred Mulley, Peter Carrington, Peter Thorneycroft in wheelchair, Roy Mason, George Younger, Francis Pym. Back row (*from left to right*): Ian Gilmour, Tom King and myself rights and responsibilities of a Prime Minister under our constitution. I knew, too, that if I had stayed in the Cabinet in those circumstances I would have gone the way of so many previous colleagues who had tried to stand up to her. Remorselessly, by demotion via reshuffle and through the insidious undermining technique of Bernard Ingham and the press office at Downing Street, my reputation and power base would have been eroded until, with both safely destroyed, I would have found myself pushed out altogether. Yet I was not trying to raise any flag of revolt: standing up for one's convictions is very different to undermining the position of a Prime Minister. I was not in that line of business, although clearly there would be no return to government office for me as long as Mrs Thatcher remained in No. 10. But there was no serious or substantial constituency of revolt at this time and, of course, she had still to win the 1987 election.

I determined that I would not become a backbench jack-of-all-trades, carping on the touchlines of power, seeking any opportunity to embarrass my former colleagues. I would stick to the political subjects in which I had had experience and argue for those Conservative policies in which I strongly believed. It was only a short step from forming this judgement to deciding to write a book setting out those beliefs.

Publishers had besieged me immediately after my resignation. But it soon became apparent that their principal interest was I that should do a carve-up job on the government which I had so recently left. I was not prepared to provide any such text. I was willing to write a personal credo, based on experience and on my own ideas. I accepted an offer from Hutchinson and three months after leaving government I had signed a contract to produce such a book by the spring of 1987. It was to be called *Where There's a Will*. (The obvious sequel, *There's a Way*, was never to be written.)

It was not long before the pressures on the back-room office in the basement of Chapel Street became intense, as the daily flow of letters, interviews, articles and speeches increased. The jamming-up of the domestic telephones and all manner of associated nuisance imposed unacceptable strains on our home life. Anne set out to find us more suitable accommodation. With the help of our solicitor Charles Corman and his contacts with John Brodie, the senior partner of J. E. & E. Levy, she discovered a two-room suite of offices on the sixth floor of 25 Victoria Street, within convenient distance of the House of Commons. Eileen and I – a two-person task force – moved in.

My newly re-established relationship with Haymarket ensured my financial independence – a very material fact during those long years fighting for survival in the political wilderness. I still remember the twinge of embarrassment I felt at the time when I received a letter from an old-age pensioner, shortly after I had negotiated with Lindsay my substantial increase in income. She congratulated me on the integrity of my stand, which meant I was 'giving up all that salary' from government as a Cabinet minister.

During the course of the Defence Select Committee inquiries into the Westland affair, I became friendly with one of its Conservative members, Michael Mates. A former regular soldier, he held views very similar to mine on European co-operation and, not surprisingly, had taken a particular interest in defence policy. His advice and support was to prove of immense value in the nearly five years I spent on the back benches. Keith Hampson, who had resigned in 1984 after being my PPS for two years, also came back into my life, offering his assistance unstintingly in coping with the workload of writing, speaking, issuing press releases and undertaking all the other myriad tasks that modern political life demands. Over the next five years these two colleagues were the closest supporters I had in the House of Commons.

As my initial isolation diminished later on, some colleagues commented adversely on the extent of my reliance on just two backbench Members of Parliament. 'What you need, Michael, is for senior members of the party to come out in your support,' they said. This is to misunderstand completely the tribal instincts of the party in the House of Commons. I understood them even more clearly as I witnessed John Redwood's activities after his resignation from John Major's government in 1995. It is relatively easy to become the focal point of discontent and frustration – some of it inevitably rather 'oddball' – but there is another side to the coin. Those on the ladders of promotion, serving in Mrs Thatcher's government, had no interest at all in being associated with so obvious an epicentre of discontent as myself. They would have been all too aware of the 'drip, drip' of prejudice emanating from No. 10, attributing to me every manner of underhand motive or uncontrolled behaviour. Who could be expected, then, to prejudice their own prospects by too close an association with me?

It goes further than that. Again, I recall the Redwood phenomenon. As a backbencher, you have a very great degree of freedom to express views that do not strictly coincide with the decisions that the government has taken. Virtually every decision of government is controversial within the government itself. Battles are fought, sometimes bitterly, in order to reach the compromise which becomes the 'line to take'. As a backbencher, I was free to support the government view, while making the point that it might easily have reached a slightly different decision. This 'slightly different decision' I advocated would, naturally, often reflect the alternative view – with which I agreed – of those who had argued precisely that case and lost in the dialectic processes of Cabinet government.

But this, in turn, gave rise to two potential sources of tension. There were the people who had won the argument in government and who saw your criticisms as a challenge to the consensus that they had achieved. And there were the others who had lost and resented your exercising the freedom to express a view in which they believed but were no longer able to put forward. Both camps, inevitably, saw me as an outsider.

Inevitably, too, there is a ministerial club. Its members live under the same disciplines, work under the same pressures. They drive themselves with an arduous, stretching commitment to furthering their careers beneath the common umbrella of government. It is a disciplined business, constantly scrutinised for indiscretion and constrained by the frustrations of collective responsibility. Watching one of their former colleagues free to roam the corridors of power and exploit the op-ed pages of Fleet Street was undoubtedly an irritating experience. It was quite unthinkable that they could be openly associated with me.

Conversely, the number of backbench colleagues interested in talking about the possibility of a change of leader slowly began to grow. I was only too aware of the dangers this too posed. To have encouraged the idea that I was working to remove Mrs Thatcher would, first, have intensified the already unacceptable level of poisonous briefings from Downing Street, and, secondly, would have fanned the flames of criticism among the voluntary footsoldiers of the party – for whom loyalty was one of the cardinal virtues but who were, nevertheless, increasingly looking to me as a legitimate successor.

The challenge, therefore, was to stay sufficiently close to the mainstream of the party, rigorously to attack the Labour Opposition and to couch what criticisms I felt I had to make in language that was emollient and constructive. *Where There's a Will* was designed against this set of criteria. It had, above all else, to be a book in which experience was combined with ideas. It should not alienate the Conservative Party itself nor provide too ready a source of ammunition for our political enemies. In truth, in the years after I returned to office, it was constantly used as a source of criticism of the government of which I had become a member. But at the time the book received a better reception than I could have dared to hope. It hit the bestseller lists for a number of weeks, and it was well reviewed and commented upon in the national press – although I have to admit we played a part in that since, when the time came for the book to be published, we took the trouble to offer literary editors not only early review copies but suggestions for suitably conspicuous reviewers as well. Thus Alec Home reviewed it in *The Times*, Peter Walker in the *Independent* and the future proposer of my nomination for the leadership, Neil Macfarlane, in the *Daily Express*.

Writing my first book did not come easily to me. I read only with reluctance and I could never have contemplated such a task as a serious project without the help of a number of people. Michael Mates and Keith Hampson were indefatigable, as were Eileen and Praveen Moman, the experienced new researcher I had taken on. But the principal credit for whatever literary merit the project possessed has to go to Julian Haviland, the former political editor of ITN and *The Times*, who took my ideas and language and turned them into publishable prose.

As I re-read the book today, it is with some satisfaction that I find many of its proposals have now been adopted directly or effectively. Privatisation has been extended far beyond the economic commanding heights into every nook and cranny of the public sector. It has not been, as was so widely believed in the 1960s, socialism that was irreversible, but enlightened capitalism. Mortgage interest tax relief has rightly been ended, while housing subsidies have been switched away from fabric-destroying rent control to targeted personal allowances. England got its development agency, English Partnerships, to match those of Scotland and Wales (although the Blair government subsequently broke it up into regional agencies). The unemployed are increasingly exposed to the rigour of the sort of workfare I advocated: exchanging time and effort in return for state support. The competitiveness agenda has changed the nature of Whitehall's approach to intervention. Competitive bidding is now an integral part of local government funding.

The year after the publication of *Where There's a Will*, George Weidenfeld suggested that I should write another book, this time about Europe. There were two time-bombs ticking away under Mrs Thatcher's later years as Prime Minister. The first was Europe, the second the poll tax. Of course, she had allies in government who supported her attitudes towards Europe but it would be pointless to disguise the deep convictions held by those on the other side of the argument, including some of her more important colleagues. A popular book, setting British self-interest in the context of a closer and wider Europe, appealed to me at once. The title of the book said it all: *The Challenge of Europe: Can Britain Win?* I had spent enough of my political life on the European stage to know that that was precisely the approach of all our European partners. The idea that the Germans, the French, the Italians or any of the other member states saw the European process as a surrender of national sovereignty or a sacrifice of their national self-interest to faceless Brussels bureaucrats bore no credibility for anyone who had participated in the interminable meetings in which the politicians from each nation state fought for their share of the action. They simply believed that within Europe there were wider opportunities, greater than those that, as individual nation states, they could achieve alone. I agreed with them then, and still do.

The team who had made *Where There's a Will* set to work to produce the European book. It appeared in the spring of 1989 and, again, it achieved the bestseller lists. It also won the Bentinck Prize, established in 1972 in memory of the late Baron Adolphe Bentinck, Dutch diplomat and former ambassador to Britain, and awarded annually to a book deemed to be 'an important contribution to the building of Europe, the cause of peace, or the fight against fanaticism'. It was a clear indication to Europhile Members of Parliament and to a wider constituency of my long-term commitment to the beliefs they shared with me.

My career seemed to be taking a literary turn. Shortly after the completion of *The Challenge of Europe* I was approached by William Rees-Mogg with the suggestion that I should write a book about Japan for Sidgwick & Jackson. I entered into a contract to do so, began my researches and learnt a great deal about that country. But events overtook the project and I refunded the advance upon returning to government. I've always thought it was fortunate that things worked out this way. I had a good title: *Mightier Than the Sword: A Study of Japanese Economic Imperialism*. But I fear the judgements that I might have included would not have stood the test of the Asian collapse that was to follow. I was not alone in failing to read those particular tea leaves.

I did, however, find time to write a pamphlet with the assistance of Professor Richard Layard of the London School of Economics, entitled *Unemployment: No Time for Ostriches*. I addressed the issue in terms of the obligations that fell both upon the state and upon the unemployed themselves. My analysis was simple: 'Rapidly we are coming to accept that a cash dispersal system to ameliorate hardship is not enough . . . So the debate has to be about what work, at what rate of pay and with what rights of refusal by the individuals concerned. And the objective should be clearly stated: it is to find work for, and to train to work, people without it. The purpose is to find employment – not finance unemployment.' My proposals were prophetic: to 'design in Britain a concept of "Community Benefit" linking service and employment to our unemployment benefit provision'. I was to return to the theme as a member of John Major's government after 1990.

Equally radical were my ideas to change the emphasis of local government funding. Unaware at the time that a year later I would be back in the Department of the Environment with responsibility for local government, on the evening of 26 October 1989 I spelt out in a speech my proposals that local authorities should produce corporate plans and engage in a competitive bidding process to secure the funding necessary to implement them from central government. It would be a condition of their success that they attracted a wide degree of support from their local communities, including where appropriate private sector investment.

The impact on the media of this speech was less than zero. This was not altogether surprising in the circumstances since, as I was delivering it, Nigel Lawson was resigning as Chancellor of the Exchequer.

In general I continued to stick to the subjects I knew. Defence and the field of environmental policy were two of my special subjects. I had for instance myself experienced the exposure that Nick Ridley, as Secretary of State for the Environment from May 1986 until the summer of 1989, faced over the proposals to build ever more houses on the green fields of southern England. Nick remained a countryman by instinct and background. He would have had no natural inclination to cover the green fields with ever larger housing estates. Thus he would have felt nothing but resentment at my comments in an open letter which I sent to him on 13 March 1988. I linked the widespread anxiety of the home counties – 'Wherever I drive in southern England today, the place is being torn up and torn apart' – to another theme to which I was committed. 'You will detect in this *cri de coeur* the urgent need to extend the urban programme of the government to reclaim desolate and derelict land in the run-down Northern and Midlands towns and cities to which development should be attracted.'

Nick's successor was Chris Patten, who served as Secretary of State for the Environment in 1989–90 and was as committed to the job as any politician could be. I knew only too well the tension that exists between the Department of the Environment and the Treasury, fearful of any expenditure commitment, and between the DOE and the Department of Trade and Industry, anxious to keep any 'do-gooding' regulation off the backs of British companies. Chris, by virtue of his office and by personal conviction, would have wished to pursue – and, indeed, did so with great effect – what broadly could be called a 'green agenda'. But, time and again, I was able to come up with ideas, probably very close to what he himself would have liked to do, but for which he had not secured the consent of colleagues or which he had seen watered down by them.

The process was simple. One of the more successful political lobbyists in the environmental world was Tom Burke, at that time running the pressure group, the Green Alliance. He was expert in the policy, was politically astute and had a perceptive understanding of the workings of Whitehall. His technique was straightforward and effective. He talked to all political parties. Indeed, he wrote speeches for all political parties. Without ever pursuing an extremist agenda, he suggested what broadly could be regarded as incremental advances to each in turn. If the Tory government took a new environmental initiative, Tom would brief the Labour and Liberal spokesmen on what the next move ought to be. The consequence, of course, was that there was always unfinished business and he was always moving the agenda on. He was good enough to incorporate me in this process and so, as Chris was pushing 'the art of the possible' frontiers within Whitehall, I was making statements from the back benches pushing 'the art of the possible' just another step further. This is not the way to endear yourself to your former colleagues.

Whatever the over-arching importance of the European question in the later years of Mrs Thatcher's government, it was the poll tax that was to turn out to have the more explosive consequences in the short term. There had been no resistance in Cabinet in 1982 when I set out my view, as Secretary of State for the Environment, that a poll tax was unacceptable as an alternative to the rates. Curiously enough, it was the next item on the agenda to be taken by Cabinet on the day I resigned in January 1986. There is no point in speculating now about what the outcome of the dialogue in that Cabinet might have been if I had remained to support the Chancellor, Nigel Lawson, in his opposition to it. Realistically, it is probably safe to assume that Mrs Thatcher would still have got her way.

I faced a significant hurdle when the government announced the legislation to introduce the poll tax into Scotland in advance of the 1987 election. I decided to vote with the government, rationalising to myself that we would fight the battle again in England after the election and, having destroyed the poll tax in England, that would necessarily lead to its repeal in Scotland. My resolve to vote for it on this occasion is not a decision of which I am particularly proud; but it was *realpolitik*. I was deeply concerned not to highlight my distance from the government on this issue, with all the embarrassment that might cause during the election campaign.

As it happened, I was only once asked a question about the poll tax at any major speaking engagement during the campaign. One night at a large public meeting in Manchester, I was asked a straight question which left little room for manoeuvre. Suddenly, there was a loud explosion of unknown cause in the street outside. The audience's attention was distracted for just long enough. When calm was restored, no one seemed to notice when I simply asked 'Next question?'

The election campaign itself proved something of a success in the survival stakes. I was overwhelmed by invitations, sometimes passed through Central Office, to speak in constituencies from one end of the country to the other. I undertook a national tour, visiting some 108 parliamentary constituencies in three and a half weeks. I avoided any critical headlines; no colleague suffered any embarrassment from my presence. Much more positively, colleagues saw and noted the size of the audiences and the warmth of the reception. I also devised a rather novel visual aid to illustrate the point. No campaign at constituency level is today complete without the sticker, emblazoning the candidate's name on the lapel – or wherever – of anyone who comes within reach of enthusiastic canvassers. At the beginning, I wore my own rosette. First one label and then another was stuck on to it, until I ended up with a roundel consisting of 87 different constituency candidates' names – a gimmick undoubtedly, but the larger it got, the clearer the message became.

My now enlarged team in Victoria Street operated an early version of the modern rapid-response unit. Christopher Morgan arranged to cover the early-morning party political press conferences and relay to me the key issues of the day. Long before the official press releases were out or the media had finished their reports, I had my own contribution to whatever story was running. Journalists, often crowded into the back of the Jaguar, were somewhat surprised, if not impressed, at my support system. We even experimented with a mobile fax machine, but, since this was still the early days of the information technology revolution, it never managed to work very well.

Polling day was Thursday, 11 June. Mrs Thatcher swept back to power with an historic third successive victory, an overall majority in the House of Commons of 101 and a majority over Labour of 146. I felt I had contributed in some small measure to the success of the campaign. In Henley I was returned with an increased turnout, an increased majority and an increased share of the vote – all very gratifying in the circumstances.

Almost immediately after the election Mrs Thatcher's popularity began to wane. The journey was downhill from then on. She was losing her grip on the parliamentary party. There was talk of her era coming to an end, and very few of the commentators speculating on the party's future failed also to speculate that I might be a part of it. Opinion polls began to measure the most popular Conservative challenger and, therefore, possible successor. In the way of things, the odd 'what if' article speculated about the next leader after the 'leaderene' had gone. My name had featured in earlier times, never as favourite, but often as second to Kenneth Baker (serving during this period first as Secretary of State for Education and subsequently as Chancellor of the Duchy of Lancaster). Now the references became more frequent. The journalists who wrote these pieces were not in any way committed to a change. They simply thrived on the bloodsport element of it all.

By 1987 Mrs Thatcher had been in power for eight years. Two more years would see her tenth anniversary. She would be sixty-five in October 1990. Her place in history was assured, even if there was still room to debate exactly what that place was. The Cold War was coming to an end, Britain's economy was significantly restored to health and she had played a powerful role in designing the structure of the

European single market, despite her initial resistance and instinctive distrust. It would have been the sensible time to allow an orderly transition to a successor. But that was neither her style nor her intention.

With hindsight it is easy to see how the plot unravelled. Within the high command of the party itself deep divisions were opening up over Europe. A growing panic was to spread through the parliamentary party and many of their activist supporters at the electoral consequences of the poll tax. Her inability to reach accommodation with two of her most powerful Cabinet colleagues provoked personal dramas not dissimilar to my own nearly four years earlier and led to the resignations of first Nigel Lawson and then Geoffrey Howe. (I have often been asked to what extent I had kept in touch with them when I was on the back benches. The answer, quite simply, is: not at all.)

In September 1988 Mrs Thatcher delivered her controversial Bruges speech. Undoubtedly its language expressed her personal convictions and deeply felt emotions about our whole European involvement. It was as though she was getting off her chest all the frustration she clearly felt as, despite herself, she had been forced time and time again to come to terms with our European partners. For all the rhetoric of sovereignty and nationhood, by her agreement to the documents that were to be enshrined in the Single European Act she transferred more sovereignty to the European Community (as it was then known) than anyone has done before or since. She could see no other way to protect our national self-interest against the inevitability that, with or without us, the Europeans were going to institutionalise and legalise the framework of what was – and would remain – our largest home market. She couldn't contemplate a re-run of the Common Agricultural Policy, when we had opted out and let others fix the rules which later we had broadly to accept. That could not be allowed to happen to Britain's manufacturing and service economy. She hated it. But she did it. In the real world there was no alternative.

The Bruges speech was designed to draw a line in the sand, or to erect a kind of political Maginot Line to prevent any further advance of what she saw as socialist European centralism. The speech attracted enthusiastic support from her like-minded colleagues and admirers. It sent a chill of despair down the spines of many others. She had divided the Tory Party and unleashed the hounds that were to eat away at the vitals of party unity from then on – to no discernible political benefit.

Her antipathy to Jacques Delors – socialist, French and now the chief European bureaucrat – was further fuelled in the spring of 1989 by the publication of the Delors Plan, which set out a programme for the next stages in economic and monetary union – leading ultimately to a single currency, an independent central bank, a common monetary policy and ever closer co-operation on economic policy generally. Nothing could have been better designed to feed the fears of the Prime Minister and her most ardent supporters that Europe was a conspiracy and that one of its targets was the sovereignty of Britain.

By her tenth anniversary, on 3 May 1989 – which she celebrated by giving Labour their first by-election gain in years – it was beginning to seem unlikely that she would stay on until the next election. In the summer her dismissive treatment of Geoffrey Howe and his principled defence of Britain's pursuit of our self-interest in Europe led her to replace him at the Foreign Office with John Major, Chief Secretary at the Treasury. Geoffrey and Nigel Lawson had threatened resignation if she did not agree that Britain should join the Exchange Rate Mechanism (ERM) of the European Monetary System (EMS). She had given in at the Madrid Summit in June but Geoffrey had been moved thereafter. With reluctance he accepted the post of Leader of the House of Commons and Lord President of the Council, to which he persuaded her to add the title of Deputy Prime Minister. This apparent promotion was promptly put into context by Bernard Ingham; *The Times* reported him on 26 July as having made No. 10's view clear to the lobby that 'the title of Deputy Prime Minister is a "courtesy". They doubt if he [Sir Geoffrey] will take over the running of the government in her absence.' Geoffrey's friends on the Europhile side of the party were furious.

This drama was hardly out of the headlines before Nigel Lawson resigned as Chancellor of the Exchequer. Mrs Thatcher had reappointed Sir Alan Walters as her personal economic adviser in No. 10 in May, against Nigel's wishes. As I had so clearly foreseen when Defence Secretary, the creation of an alternative source of expertise and advice for the Prime Minister is always fraught with tension in the British system of government. Walters was known to be taking a line on economic policy in contradiction to that of the Chancellor. The media made a meal of it, rapidly disseminating Walters' critical views of the EMS as he expressed them both in writing and at private lunches in the City. Nigel's position became impossible. Something was bound to give. He was right to go. In his resignation speech to the House of

Commons on 31 October his words had a certain familiarity for anyone who took the trouble to read what I had said in similar circumstances nearly four years before. This is what he said: 'For our system of Cabinet government to work effectively, the Prime Minister of the day must appoint ministers that he or she trusts and then leave them to carry out the policy. When differences of view emerge, as they are bound to do from time to time, they should be resolved privately and, whenever appropriate, collectively.'

I regretted deeply Nigel's going. I had listened to him deliver his Budget on 11 March 1988 with growing excitement. The changes he announced – reducing the standard rate of income tax to 25 pence and the top rate to 40 pence in the pound – represented in my view one of the critical economic decisions of the last half-century. It is impossible to overstate the damage that the Attlee government of 1945–50 did to this country's economic prospects. It nationalised the Bank of England, thus allowing politicians to let the currency drift in line with Britain's ineffective industrial performance. It nationalised the commanding heights of the economy, thus protecting great swathes of industry from effective competition while denying them a role in world markets. And – perhaps worst of all – it imposed a punitive and confiscatory level of taxation on the capital of the very people who should, if they had been allowed to save, have been investing in the new small businesses of the future. Nigel's Budget finally transformed the prospects for this latter group of citizens. An explosion of new enterprise followed. Tax avoidance ceased to be the principal topic of conversation at middle-class dinner tables and there was a new morality, as people felt that the tax bills they were being asked to pay were no longer grossly unfair and began to stick more closely to the rules.

For me it was not just the reduction in tax rates. It was the inheritance provisions which at last allowed family businesses to pass from one generation to another, freed of the previous burden of tax which had meant that first-generation businesses were invariably floated on the Stock Exchange or sold to publicly quoted companies. This had been one of my themes in *Where There's a Will*. Now all that would no longer be necessary. All the advantages of encouraging owners to invest for the longer term and giving them the incentive and resource to do so were now built into the system. Today it has improved even further, but to Nigel must go the credit for a revolution in the generation of new private and entrepreneurial wealth.

With Nigel's resignation, John Major now went back to the Treasury (after only thirteen and a half weeks as Foreign Secretary), this time as Chancellor. Douglas Hurd took his place at the Foreign Office. While it is true that many colleagues had become unhappy with Nigel's policies, nevertheless there was now widespread unease at Mrs Thatcher's conduct of her government with the damaging explosions to which it could lead. The Conservative backbench 1922 Committee fired a warning shot urging her to end the feuding and adopt a more collective style of decision-making in Cabinet. The *Daily Telegraph* on the day after Nigel's resignation speech reported one Cabinet minister, Ken Baker, as saying, on leaving No. 10 after a meeting, that the 1922 Committee had called on the Prime Minister 'to get her act together'. The report made it clear that he fully supported this demand.

The turmoil inside the government was watched with growing dismay by the Europhile wing of the parliamentary party and in particular by Sir Anthony Meyer, MP for Clwyd North West, an ex-Foreign Office diplomat and a man of strong European convictions. In November he stood – as under the then rules he was entitled to do – for the leadership of the party as a challenge to Mrs Thatcher. There was never the slightest chance that he would win; he was universally described as a 'stalking horse'. The only interest was in the number of votes that in a secret ballot he could attract. George Younger was a good choice as Mrs Thatcher's campaign manager. Widely trusted and respected, he provided exactly the right degree of reassurance that the job demanded. At no time during this contest did I have any personal contact with Anthony. He had asked Keith Hampson if his challenge would hurt my prospects and Keith had told him no – but on his own authority, not mine. In the event Anthony's challenge persuaded some sixty colleagues to vote for him or abstain. In the vote itself I abstained 'in person', walking along the committee corridor but failing to enter the room where the ballot was taking place.

But the sixty were only the tip of the iceberg. Another sixty told George Younger that, while they would vote for Margaret this time, he should not count on their loyalty if another challenge was mounted a year hence. Anthony had delivered a clear message. No one appears to have taken it sufficiently seriously. On 27 November Peter Morrison, a close confidant of the Prime Minister, told a Young Conservative audience that Mrs Thatcher believed she would need five terms of office to achieve her purpose. That thought certainly galvanised the troops but not, I fear, as Peter had intended.

My own battle for political survival began to change emphasis. The growing number of those prepared to come out in my support, the decline in Mrs Thatcher's own personal poll ratings and some further truly ghastly by-election results all combined to provide an atmosphere in which I moved from possible to probable successor. I worked hard and loyally during the Euro election campaign of the summer of 1989. Its dismal outcome (thirty-two Conservative seats as compared with forty-five Labour ones) seemed to demonstrate just how ill judged the consistently anti-Brussels note adopted by Central Office in its campaign publicity had been. If I had to select a moment when I was forced to recognise just how widely I had come to be seen as 'the king over the water', it arrived when I learnt that the BBC flagship current affairs programme, *Panorama*, was that October of 1989 proposing to devote the whole of its pre-Tory Conference edition to a film concentrating on me. Even so, I thought it a bit excessive when Michael Mates presented me with a nesting box for my collection of ducks, bearing the slogan 'Thenford les Deux Eglises' (General de Gaulle had retired to his home at Colombey les Deux Eglises in the early 1950s to await his recall to become President of France).

By the spring of 1990 reports that Mrs Thatcher might be going to step down began to circulate. On 9 March Geoffrey Howe had to deny that the Cabinet had discussed her resignation the previous day. Two days later three Sunday newspapers ran polls taken among Tory MPs about her future. All showed that about a quarter of the parliamentary party wanted her to go before the next election (anything up to two years away). *The Times* on Monday the 12th went on to point to the dangers inherent in any challenge from me: 'it is impossible to see how he could stand against Mrs Thatcher without grievously splitting the Party – which would probably deliver victory to Labour at the next election'.

This call for unity ignored the fact that the party was already split. I had consistently stated that I could foresee no circumstances in which I would challenge Mrs Thatcher. It was her supporters who were raising the spectre, in order themselves to attack it. Their case was not helped by a report in the same edition of *The Times* that I had not been invited to help in the Mid-Staffordshire by-election. The sensitivity of Central Office to my absence was sufficient to ensure that an invitation was issued to me that same day and I was in Mid-Staffs addressing two meetings two days later. The by-election itself was a disaster, with a Tory majority of 14,654 being converted into a Labour majority of 9,449. Ten days later Ken Baker (appointed party Chairman in January) sought to pull the party out of its panic: 'The lesson is clear. Talk of a leadership election, the canvassing of candidates openly or surreptitiously, when there is no vacancy, and there will be no vacancy, is welcomed only by our opponents. I say to you: let this idle chatter cease. We have serious work to do.'

Ken certainly did his fair share of that work in the municipal elections in May. We contrived only to hold on to our London 'flagships' of Westminster and Wandsworth while Labour won 300 seats and control of eleven councils, but he was famously able to declare that these were 'remarkable results' which 'wiped out allegations that the Prime Minister's leadership has been fatally undermined'. Ken was extremely effective in that he had won the propaganda battle. Once again, I ruled out a challenge to Mrs Thatcher on the BBC's *Question Time*. The press followed Ken's line and savaged me. The *Independent on Sunday* got the flavour with its 'Willing to Wound, Afraid to Strike' front-page attack. Talk of leadership challenges began to fade.

Then, as had Galtieri in 1982, so Saddam Hussein at the beginning of August reinforced Mrs Thatcher's rescue. Iraqi forces occupied Kuwait. She was back on the world stage. She was still vulnerable, but not removable. Or so it appeared.

But we were losing the electoral war. The truth was that the poll tax was beginning to gnaw at our vitals – not just in industrial areas but in rural ones too. I had opposed the poll tax legislation for England with what I thought one of my better speeches on the Bill's second reading in December 1987 and, when it came to its committee stage in May 1988, I was proud to give my support to the 'banding' amendment put down by Michael Mates, which at least tried to introduce a degree of fairness into its operation. But the government would have none of it and, when the Bill eventually reached the statute book, it was still in its original crude, regressive form, equating – as I said in my speech in the House against it – 'in the eyes of the tax collector, the rich and the poor, the slum dweller and the landed aristocrat, the elderly pensioners living on their limited savings and the most successful of today's entrepreneurs'. My forecast that it would become identified as a 'Tory tax' was abundantly fulfilled, in the local government elections and in the by-elections at Mid-Staffordshire in March and

Eastbourne in October when the voters handed the seats (fortunately, on a temporary basis) to Labour and the Liberal Democrats respectively.

The party Conference of 1990 at Bournemouth was a notably gloomy affair, with Nick Ridley (whom even Mrs Thatcher had had to remove from the government after his passionate anti-German outburst in the *Spectator* in July) and I competing with each other over the issue of the Tories and Europe. We held identically timed fringe meetings. Each was well attended and they reinforced the already evident warnings of the geological fault line that was developing within the party over Europe. More solid and damaging evidence was to appear before the month was out.

Mrs Thatcher attended the Rome Council of Ministers over the weekend of 27 and 28 October, where Jacques Delors, as President of the European Commission, outlined his view of the next stage of European development. Michael Buerk read the BBC news headlines that Sunday evening: 'Britain has been left isolated as the rest of Europe sets a timetable for economic unity. Mrs Thatcher tells the other European leaders they are living in "cloud cuckoo land".' He went on to report the leaders' discussion about the introduction of a single currency and a European central bank; Britain was alone in dissenting.

On her return Mrs Thatcher made the expected statement in the House of Commons reporting the outcome of the Council and, evidently proud of the stance she had taken, replied to a question from Neil Kinnock, the Leader of the Opposition, about her response to the three principle points at issue with the now famously defiant answer: 'No! No! No!' I had had no contact with Geoffrey Howe and was not in the House to gauge for myself the impact of this stance upon him.

On the afternoon of Thursday, 1 November 1990, I set off to fulfil a speaking engagement for David Willetts, prospective parliamentary candidate for the Havant constituency (the sitting Tory Member, Ian Lloyd, was due to stand down at the next election). My very first intimation that something was up had been a glimpse of a newspaper placard in Portsmouth. I arrived at the hotel to be greeted by a journalist from the *Portsmouth News*, asking for my comments on Geoffrey Howe's resignation. I refused to make any until I had personally telephoned London to establish the facts. My only comment to the reporter after that was: 'I think it's serious. He is the Deputy Prime Minister. He is a man of great eminence and distinction.' Inevitably I was asked if this influenced my intentions.

I replied as I had done so often: 'I have made my position clear about that. I will not be part of that process.' But I have to say that my mind was not much on the speech I made that night. I realised that events were now unfolding, inconveniently, unpredictably and probably uncontrollably.

That same night Geoffrey, through his Parliamentary Private Secretary David Harris, made it clear that he would not stand for the leadership. On my return to London I contacted Geoffrey and told him that I did not believe his undoubtedly courageous decision had materially altered my own position.

Anne and I were anyway due to leave that weekend for a long-planned trip to the Middle East, where I had been invited to meet both King Hussein of Jordan and Yitzhak Shamir, the Prime Minister of Israel. (Such invitations were another sign of my increasingly high profile; six weeks earlier I had been asked to Germany to meet and talk to Chancellor Kohl.) I did not see, with the Commons in recess, that there was much I could do. Michael Mates and I sat in the drawing room at home in Chapel Street late that evening and anguished over the options. The party was in crisis and I was bound to be followed and bombarded with questions wherever I went. There was no opportunity for me to give full, in-depth interviews. We decided that I would use the time-honoured device (as Geoffrey Howe himself had done recently) of an open letter to my constituency chairman, Peter Owen, to be released to the Sunday newspapers for publication on 4 November. I discussed the idea with Peter in advance and cleared the draft with him. Its tone was critical without being in any way confrontational, but writing it and arranging for its publication turned out to be a mistake. If you go away, you necessarily lose control of the situation and, sure enough, from his bunker in No. 10 Bernard Ingham promptly emerged to announce that: 'Whenever we're in difficulty, he lights the fuse and retires to a safe distance.'

The story ran in all the daily papers on Monday the 5th. The proverbial government sources had once again been in touch with *The Times*. Mrs Thatcher was understood to have told colleagues that she regarded me as 'glamour without substance' and that she believed I would 'pursue an industrial policy more interventionist than that favoured by Tony Benn'. Those were not quite the qualifications one might have expected of a colleague she had appointed Defence Secretary and were in some contrast to the statement I issued from

Tel Aviv when I had seen the papers the next day: 'I have made my position clear . . . I think that Mrs Thatcher will lead the Conservative Party into the next election and that the Conservative Party will win it.'

I now found myself at the eye of a storm. From every quarter I was the object of advice. In the editorial column on Monday morning *The Times* did its best for her. The most famous passage was, I believe, directly inspired by Bernard Ingham in No. 10: 'The attempt by Mr Heseltine to demoralise her into resignation, so that he can avoid the odium of abandoning his pledge not to stand against her, will not work. In the event of a stalking horse standing, she will fight and certainly win. Mr Heseltine is at present merely helping the Conservatives to lose the next election. He should put up or shut up.' But the newspaper went on to say that, if the situation proved to be too serious for a stalking-horse candidate, 'This means that Mr Heseltine must abandon his promise and stand in a first ballot. He will almost certainly be beaten, thus strengthening Mrs Thatcher's hand for a clear run to the next election. But he will have made his point and she, her party workers must hope, will have taken the message to heart.' It was not the kind of counsel designed to leave one with much room for manoeuvre.

The allegations were preposterous. Mrs Thatcher was at war with a significant section of the parliamentary party over Europe, she had become a hate figure in large parts of the country as a consequence of her determination to impose the poll tax and she was losing by-elections on a fearful scale. This feeling of loathing was acute in my own constituency in South Oxfordshire, where small agricultural cottages often house three or four adults and families were receiving poll tax demands larger than any bill they had ever known in their lives. To suggest that I was attempting to demoralise her was to circumnavigate the abyss she was facing with astonishing journalistic dexterity. The challenge to 'put up or shut up' was a mistake. It raised the game. Colleagues began not only to see a certain inevitability but at the same time to wonder if I was man enough for it.

In the meantime Mrs Thatcher had announced the timing of the annual election procedures if anyone wished to challenge her for the leadership, as the party rules at that time provided. The lists would open on Thursday, 8 November, close a week later and any necessary ballot would take place on 20 November.

*   *   *

The one thing I had not anticipated when I wrote my original letter to my Henley officers was that there would be a reply. Clearly many conversations took place within the Association over Sunday and Monday, 4 and 5 November, and my chairman, Peter Owen, came under pressure from Ken Thornber, the Conservative Wessex Area chairman. The upshot of all this activity was that a meeting was held at Peter's home on Monday evening. Present were eight of the senior officers of the local Conservative Association, including the president Raymond Monbiot. The media soon had a clever label: the 'Henley eight'. Also in attendance were the Central Office area agent, Donald Stringer, and the recently appointed constituency agent, Tom Morrison.

Raymond Monbiot came with his own draft reply already prepared. I can only report the meeting based on accounts subsequently given to me. The simple truth appears to be that the officers were deeply and equally divided. Monbiot and three others were in favour of or prepared to go along with what would have amounted to a rebuke for me and an emphatic declaration of support for Mrs Thatcher. The rest queried whether any reply was needed at all, public or private, and only agreed to one in the end on Donald Stringer's firm advice that a reply was necessary and on the basis that it was supportive of me and bland in its tone. This they believed the ultimately agreed draft to be. It was read to me over the telephone to Israel and then released to the papers.

There was, therefore, a furious reaction locally when Monbiot was reported in the national press on Wednesday of that week as making comments such as: 'there was dissatisfaction that they had not had time to discuss Mr Heseltine's letter before he flew to the Middle East', 'By writing his open letter, then flying off, Michael left us to field the flak' and 'Michael is given to outbursts. His timing could have been better.' Monbiot was also quoted in the press as saying that the Association's reply had been written to emphasise their support for the leadership. Again, this was not the agreed position.

The local vice-chairman, Maggie Pullen, wrote on 10 November to Monbiot. Her opening words were: 'I am writing to you to put on record my dissatisfaction at the outcome of our meeting on Monday evening and the ensuing repercussions. I feel that we have been misled and totally misrepresented and not only by the press!'

She went on: 'Firstly, I agreed with Cecil [Cecil White, an Associ-ation vice-president] that it was unnecessary to reply openly to Michael's letter; you however, with the Central Office Agent and our own agent, assured us it was the common and correct way to respond primarily for "getting the press off our backs". (Something which it abysmally failed to do.)'

Cecil White himself sent a letter the next day to Donald Stringer. He wrote that, while he had enthusiastically supported Mrs Thatcher from her earliest days, he had now concluded that 'There is just enough time to win with a new leader and I believe there are about four current and ex-ministers who could do this when Mrs Thatcher cannot.' He also protested to Stringer that 'The tone of our meeting and the content of our reply were seriously misrepresented to and in the press and on the BBC in my opinion.'

Inevitably, the deep feelings of resentment aroused by the press handling of what my supporters believed to have been a private meeting reflected diverging views of what had happened. Monbiot argued that he had been targeted by the media, although he apologised for what he termed his 'transgression' in going beyond the confines of the letter in the way he had provided certain quotations to the national press. Monbiot's essential case was that by departing for the Middle East I had left a vacuum and that all he had done was to fill it. The fault, he argued, was mine.

The presidency of a Conservative association is an honorific post. The role requires the occupant to attend at the AGM to take the chair while the chairman and senior officers are elected. The Association itself is represented by its chairman. How the president came to find his home under siege, with TV cameras on the lawn, reporters and constant telephone calls, is a matter of conjecture. Certainly, after serving first as chairman and then as president of the Henley Association, Monbiot saw his future political career as advancing up the ladder of the National Union, the central powerhouse of the voluntary side of the party organisation. He went on to serve as Wessex Area chairman, continued to maintain his close ties with Central Office and carried through to the glittering prize of chairing the party Conference in 2000. And who knows what next: perhaps a knighthood or something even better.

The presence of the Central Office area agent, Donald Stringer, at the meeting actually worked to my advantage. It had been sufficiently extraordinary to find him there to provoke in people's minds the thought that here was some plot by the powers-that-be in the party to set me up, although years later Donald assured me that this was not the case.

More difficult for my critics was the behaviour of my new agent, Tom Morrison, who had taken up his post only some five weeks before. A week after the letter and the row that followed, he rang his successor as the agent for Putney, Sue Howat. Referring to me, he proclaimed: 'I've stitched him up, haven't I?' He then went on to explain how he and Monbiot had arranged the Association's reply and the press coverage of it. Unfortunately for him, Morrison was not aware that Sue Howat shared a mutual friend with Nick Kent, who was working at that time as a research assistant for Michael Mates. The mutual friend informed Nick Kent of Morrison's conversation and Nick rang Sue Howat to confirm it. But Morrison wasn't being particularly careful with his claimed coup anyway. He had much the same conversation with Sir Paul Beresford, the New Zealander who had achieved such remarkable results as Tory leader of the London Borough of Wandsworth (and went on to be elected in 1992 as MP for Croydon Central).

Meanwhile Anne and I had returned to London on the evening of Wednesday, 7 November. That same day Geoffrey Howe announced his intention to make a formal resignation speech in the House of Commons 'in the next few days'. On Thursday the Bradford North by-election took place. It was a Labour marginal but they held it comfortably; the Conservative vote fell by 22.8 per cent.

The following weekend, on the afternoon of Sunday, 11 November, I attended another meeting at Peter Owen's house. This time there was no representative of Central Office in attendance. The proceedings culminated with an unequivocal statement that the Association's original reply to my open letter had not been intended in any way as a criticism of what I had written; it went on to add that I retained 'their full confidence and support as their Member of Parliament'. Peter Owen himself issued the statement and delivered a copy to Morrison for wider dissemination. The press saw it as an endorsement of me and interpreted it therefore as a repudiation of Mrs Thatcher. Monbiot telephoned Owen the next morning, urging him to speak to the press and explain that this was not the intention. Owen replied that he had not spoken to the press after the first meeting and he had no intention of doing so after the second. Somehow the contrast between the outcome of these two successive meetings reinforced my suspicion that a bungled 'dirty tricks' exercise by the higher powers had been attempted while I was abroad. I was grateful to have got back in time to regain control of the situation. But the events left long-lasting bitterness in my local Association.

Nor did we succeed in damping down the fevered headlines in the press. Indeed, ever since Geoffrey Howe's resignation had opened the floodgates of speculation, the drama had been escalating rapidly. Article after article had appeared in the national dailies second-guessing my intentions, prefiguring Geoffrey's anticipated speech in the House, weighing up the chances of various candidates in a leadership contest, analysing who might support whom. The press was in a fine old feeding frenzy and a seemingly never ending stream of words poured from the mighty pens of Fleet Street.

In one edition of *The Times* alone, on Monday, 12 November, there ran a headline claiming, 'King [Tom King, Defence Secretary] Plays the Gulf Card to Help Thatcher' over the name of Richard Ford, its political correspondent. The political editor, Robin Oakley, was hard at it. He wrote a lengthy column headed 'Conflicting advice for Heseltine as deadline nears', a profile of me entitled 'An advocate of caring Conservatism with a gung-ho image' and in a smaller piece mused that 'Support for a challenge could come from pool of MPs who feel unloved.' Matthew Parris devoted a column to suggesting that MPs could stand for the leadership without revealing their identities, while, rather pathetically, Ronald Butt argued for Mrs Thatcher to remain under the headline 'Give her time to go in peace'. But the message was black and white in the concluding words of *The Times* editorial headed 'Heseltine Must Stand': 'The leadership issue has to be resolved. The country needs to know whether Mrs Thatcher does or does not retain sufficient Party support to remain a strong prime minister. If she does not, she must go. In the immediate future there is only one serious challenger. If Mr Heseltine fails to throw his cap into the ring, he will thoroughly deserve to have it stuffed down his throat.'

Of course, the coverage in *The Times* was reflected throughout Fleet Street – free as ever with its advice and opinion. On the same day, 'PM may lose, ministers say', Anthony Bevins reported in the *Independent*, while its editorial was entitled, 'Cometh the hour, cometh the man' and went on to state: 'Therefore, largely as a result of ill-judged sniping and sneering from the Prime Minister's supporters, Mr Heseltine has to put up or shut up. [There was that phrase again.] He seems to be moving inexorably towards the former position and should do so without embarrassment.' The *Daily Express* would have none of it. 'Back off now, Mr Heseltine,' its first leader cried, advising that I was in danger of being bounced by my supporters into a contest which would end in defeat for me and ultimately for the Tories. But it also took a whole page to proclaim: 'Howe in the spotlight as calls grow for challenge'. The *Daily Mail* set out Tom King's concern about the effect of a challenge on the morale of our troops in the Gulf, but its big story was the backing I had received from my local Association, angry at what they felt had been a set-up by Conservative Central Office over their reply to my open letter. The *Telegraph* reported Tom King as believing that a challenge would give comfort to Saddam Hussein, while the *Evening Standard* had a very different conflict in mind when it informed its readers under a banner headline that 'The Councils of War Meet'. The *Guardian* announced that 'Heseltine weighs up the ballot risks', but the *Sun* was clear that 'Heseltine is ready to stand'.

The headlines in the broadsheets and the tabloids were echoed throughout the broadcast media. Each day, each news bulletin, each pundit was breathless with excitement. And they only reflected the turmoil that was going on in the House of Commons itself.

I was still declining to stand. But it was becoming an increasingly difficult position to hold. And then Geoffrey stood up in the House.

On Tuesday, 13 November I returned from a visit to Hamburg at two o'clock in the afternoon, leaving me just enough time to get back to the House of Commons for Geoffrey's memorable resignation speech.

Geoffrey stood up in the House at 4.19 p.m. The immediate impact of his speech, not least on Mrs Thatcher, has been well recorded. It was electric. His concluding words – 'The time has come for others to consider their own response to the tragic conflict of loyalties with which I have myself wrestled for perhaps too long' – presented the unavoidable challenge. As I walked the few yards from my seat below the gangway on the government benches on my way out, I passed the former government Chief Whip Michael Jopling at the entrance to the chamber. 'What the heck do I do now?' I said. 'You do nothing,' he replied. 'You'll be Leader of the Opposition within eighteen months.' 'But I don't *want* to be Leader of the Opposition,' I replied, and oddly enough that continued to be my feeling right up to 3 May 1997.

I had stated innumerable times that I could not see myself challenging Mrs Thatcher and that was genuinely my view. Obviously,

I had become the centre of attention whenever discussion focused on Margaret's departure. But it had always seemed clear to me that my prospects would be incomparably better if the party brought about that departure without any precipitant action on my part. I had been more than content to wait.

Geoffrey's decision to resign had been as much of a shock to me as it had been to everyone else. I had had no idea what was in his mind, even though I had witnessed the treatment handed out to him years before in Cabinet. Yet his resignation and his speech, when they came, were like a call to the colours. He had taken a principled stand on the issues in which I believed and spoken for the sort of Conservative Party of which I was proud to be a member.

Of course, there was an option to stay put. But there was also a tide running and it was almost out of control. 'Have you got the balls for it?' the irrepressible Tory MP David Evans asked me. It reflected a view that, to quote Alexander Pope – as the *Independent on Sunday* already had – I was 'willing to wound, and yet afraid to strike'. We did not quite reach the stage where accusations of cowardice were added to the formidable list of charges of which the Thatcherite press had long since found me guilty. But we had reached a critical moment of decision. The pressure for a challenge was now acute and, realistically, I knew I was the only person with the necessary stature to do it. Fifteen hours after Geoffrey had sat down, following the most devastating speech heard in the Commons since that of Nigel Birch in the Profumo debate of June 1963, I gave a press conference outside my home in Chapel Street, coupling the announcement of my decision to stand with a commitment to abolish the poll tax. Before me stood a massive gathering of journalists and photographers, many of them balancing precariously on portable folding ladders. I remember a tremendous feeling of relief as I made my statement. I was out on my own now, free of the inevitable evasion and temporising that the growing crisis of recent weeks had forced on me. What I told the press was this:

> I have said many times that I could not foresee the circumstances in which I would allow myself to be nominated to challenge Mrs Thatcher for the leadership of the Conservative Party.
>
> The past few days have been tumultuous for my party. The Deputy Prime Minister, Sir Geoffrey Howe, has resigned. The reasons he gave to the House of Commons yesterday cannot be dissociated from my

own resignation four years ago and the more recent departure of the then Chancellor, Nigel Lawson.

In essence, the Prime Minister holds views on Europe behind which she has not been able to maintain a united Cabinet. This damages the proper pursuit of British self-interest in Europe.

The Conservatives have been driven into third place in Bradford, an industrial city which has unavoidable comparisons with other constituencies essential to the future re-election of a Conservative government.

The opinion polls now say that I am best placed to recover those people who have indicated that without a change of leader they will not vote Conservative at the next general election.

More than 100 of my parliamentary colleagues have urged me to stand and promised me their support. None of this could I have foreseen, but neither can I ignore the conclusion.

I am persuaded that I would now have a better prospect than Mrs Thatcher of leading the Conservatives to a fourth electoral victory and prevent the ultimate calamity of a Labour government.

I have accordingly informed the Chief Whip, Tim Renton, and the chairman of the 1922 Committee, Cranley Onslow, that I intend to let my name go forward.

A significant consequence of my election as leader would be an immediate and fundamental review of the poll tax which I believe to be important for the revival of government fortunes. Finally, let me say that Mrs Thatcher's outstanding contribution to the politics of our times is not in question. It has been remarkable.

The issue now, however, is how best to protect what we have all achieved under her leadership and advance under a Conservative government to meet the already daunting challenges of the 1990s.

My decision cannot have come as a thunderclap of surprise to anyone – indeed, I had been pre-empted that very morning by a splash story in the *Independent* written by Anthony Bevins. But even so resourceful a journalist as Bevins would hardly claim to have been the beneficiary of second sight. The truth was that the opinion polls had constantly placed me either top or second to any other conceivable successor and the degree of support from colleagues in the House of Commons had continued to grow apace. Eventually, Michael Mates and I had begun to record the approaches that were made either directly to me or indirectly through Michael or Keith Hampson. By the time I decided to stand, we were able to predict with remarkable accuracy the number of votes that we could expect to receive. Some we got wrong. Others never declared their hand. But by and large the first-round total of 152 was very close to the list we had been keeping in Victoria Street. (Michael and Eileen had calculated in advance of the result that I would get 151 votes. When the result was declared, I turned to them and said, 'Can't you two get anything right?' A joke, but not very gracious in the circumstances.)

We had avoided meticulously over the years any attempt to create an organisation or team in the House of Commons. Time and again colleagues would approach me with offers of help. But the answer was always the same: 'There is no organisation. The only help you can give me is to let me know of any colleague who feels the same way as you do.' Any deviation from this policy would have been known to the government Whips' Office within hours. I cannot prove that among my confidants there was anyone deliberately planted by the whips to tell them what we were up to, but I would not be astonished to learn they had a pretty good idea of the various informal consultations that had been taking place.

There were very few exceptions to the rule. Dennis Walters, the MP for Westbury, certainly approached me, and indicated a growing support for me. I attended a few meetings at his home in Chelsea at which David Mellor, a minister of state at the Home Office and then Minister for the Arts, promised backing. In the event, David switched to John Major in the second round, having – honourably – explained to me that John was a close personal friend. Tony Durant, a member of the Whips' Office, had confided in me at a meeting I attended in his constituency that he was committed to my support and we lunched once or twice at Wiltons, where he briefed me on the unfolding scene.

Perhaps the most bizarre approach was the meeting in Victoria Street in which Bill Cash came to ask if I would consider making him a minister of state at the Foreign Office in the government he believed I would shortly form. I made him no such promise and certainly would not have made him a minister. Interestingly, though, I discussed this matter with John Major years later, who had had a similar approach from Bill Cash and reached a similar judgement.

So we simply remembered what people had said to us. The only comprehensive record that existed was a colour-coded chart on a pinboard, safely stowed out of sight behind a curtain in my own office in Victoria Street. Even this only came into existence in the early months of 1990, as the anticipation of change began to build to serious proportions.

I knew, of course, from the outset that I would have negligible support from within the Cabinet. Mrs Thatcher made them take a collective oath – virtually in blood – not to vote for me. The only one who escaped was the Secretary of State for Wales, David Hunt, who happened to be in Tokyo at the time. He was approached there on the telephone by Mrs Thatcher, who explained what the Cabinet had agreed and sought his assurance that he would follow suit. David replied that he regretted he was unable to comply as he had already promised his support to me. 'You must go back to Michael and ask him to release you,' he was instructed. David put his dilemma to me on the telephone. 'I'm very sorry, David,' I replied. 'I can't agree to that.' 'Thank you,' he said. It was a brave decision he reported back.

Understandably there were strong feelings. Teresa Gorman, the MP for Billericay, publicly threatened to leave the party if I was elected. On reflection this might not have worked against me. Yet I did find some valuable support within the government. David Hunt brought with him his two colleagues in the Welsh Office, Sir Wyn Roberts and Ian Grist, to give me a clean sweep of that Department. I was particularly grateful to David Trippier who, as Deputy Chairman of the party, also came out for me – an act that must have taken some courage, given the atmosphere prevailing at Central Office.

Sir Neil Macfarlane, by now on the back benches but who had worked with me as Minister for Sport at the Department of the Environment, was my proposer, and my nomination papers were seconded by my old Oxford contemporary, the veteran backbencher Sir Peter Tapsell, probably the most talented member of the Conservative Party in the House of Commons never to hold public office. He did some very effective work on my behalf on television over the following few days.

A large part of the battle was to be fought out on the airwaves and in the media. I tended to concentrate on the mainline current affairs programmes and the big Sunday-morning interviews. Mrs Thatcher conducted most of her campaign in the newspapers, giving increasingly strident interviews to the *Sunday Telegraph*, the *Sunday Times* and *The Times*. I did not, incidentally, do badly in terms of press support myself, receiving the endorsement among Sunday papers alone of the *Observer*, the *Independent on Sunday*, the *Correspondent* and, perhaps even more remarkably, the *Mail on Sunday* and the *Sunday Times*. Andrew Neil, the latter's editor, had personally rebuffed Rupert Murdoch's attempt to dissuade him from his determination to support me. (The Prime Minister, by contrast, had to be content with the *News of the World*, the *Sunday Express* and the *Sunday Telegraph*.)

It had been Mrs Thatcher's choice that the election should take place as quickly as it did, in fact a mere six days after my announcement that I would stand. (Even before my hat was in the ring, she had arranged with the chairman of the 1922 Committee, Sir Cranley Onslow, that the annual period in which nominations could be received against her should be reduced by two weeks. By getting my papers for the first ballot in by noon on 14 November I had beaten the deadline by just twenty-four hours.) I can only surmise that she was influenced by the knowledge that she was due on 18, 19 and 20 November to be in Paris for a conference on security and co-operation in Europe and wanted the whole business finished by the time she returned.

Once again, George Younger acted as her campaign manager. It did not appear to us that his heart was in it. He would not have needed any reminding of the warnings he had received a year before that many of the Prime Minister's earlier supporters were not to be relied upon in a second challenge. Her team operated out of Lord McAlpine's house in Great College Street and included John Moore, Norman Tebbit, Mark Lennox-Boyd, Gerry Neale and Peter Morrison, her PPS. Inevitably I had the time to devote to my campaign which Mrs Thatcher, as Prime Minister, could not have contemplated. But, that said, there was evidence of a certain complacency. Senior ministers were encouraged to put the Prime Minister's case for her. John Major, confined to bed with acute toothache, put out a press statement; so did Ken Baker. Mrs Thatcher herself suggested that abolishing the poll tax would lead to increases in the rate of income tax, but I was able to point to the forecast economic growth figures from John Major as Chancellor, which could over time generate the resources without such increases being necessary.

She was to up the ante as far as her attack on me was concerned in an interview she gave to Simon Jenkins, the editor of *The Times*, which appeared on 19 November, the day before the first vote. 'If you read Michael's book, you'll find it's more akin to some of the Labour Party policies: intervention, corporatism, everything that pulled us down.' She went on: 'Look, you've seen the crumbling of the more extreme forms of that philosophy in the Soviet Union.' That sort of rant might well have enthused her more ardent admirers, but to many it simply made her look silly. For me it was a godsend. (I should just add that the contents of this interview caused us no surprise – they were leaked to us by someone in No. 10 the previous Friday. I never knew who.)

Not all the interventions by ministers worked out quite as planned. Douglas Hurd on a visit to Yorkshire on a speaking engagement was asked if he would stand in a leadership election. A journalist reported what he thought had been said. 'Under no circumstances then will you stand?' 'Against her,' Douglas responded. Predictably, the next day's papers were full of stories of another possible candidate. But the most significant aspect of this event was a passage in Douglas' speech. 'When this contest is over, the Prime Minister and the Cabinet will want to consider how to draw the threads of our policy on Europe together unmistakably, and rally the party and the country behind us.' This was seen as a warning to the Prime Minister that she would have to take the views of the Cabinet more seriously in future.

My campaign was conducted with the most rudimentary organisation. Based on my Victoria Street offices, with an overspill in Michael Mates' House of Commons room in Norman Shaw North, we had a limited number of helpers. I canvassed colleagues with the assistance of Michael Mates, Keith Hampson and William Powell (who was to become my PPS on my return to government). I toured the television studios while press releases and articles were drafted by Keith and two researchers, James de Candole in Victoria Street and Nick Kent in Norman Shaw North. We were short of telephone lines and Eileen struggled to deal with a positive torrent of media requests.

I visited Scotland to speak at a rally for the Paisley by-election campaign in support of the Conservative candidate on the Thursday before the House of Commons poll. It was a meeting that could have been specially designed by my team. Held in an old-fashioned music hall with tiered balconies and a substantial stage, it was packed to the rafters. Friend and foe alike recreated the atmosphere of turn-of-the-last-century electioneering. I was in my element. The electronics did me proud. The next day *The Times* published a MORI poll showing that my leadership of the party would give the Tories a ten-point lead. The weekend saw this result confirmed by three more polls.

Mrs Thatcher was in Paris, however, when Peter Morrison brought her the news on 20 November, the day of the vote, that he believed she would win by 238 votes to 80. In the event the votes cast – 204 votes for her and 152 for me – meant that she had failed to clear the hurdle required under the rules of having an absolute majority plus a 15 per cent 'surcharge' of those entitled to vote. She had, in fact, missed fulfilling that qualification by just four votes. But that was hardly the point. What was universally noted was that, after eleven years in office, she was able to command the loyalty of only just over half of the Parliamentary Conservative Party and that at least two-fifths of them now preferred another leader. To anyone with the faintest knowledge of how Westminster politics work, her position was manifestly untenable. It says much for Mrs Thatcher's capacity for self-delusion that at first she stubbornly refused to recognise that fact. I watched on television, along with millions of others, as she strode down the steps of the British Embassy in Paris just after 6 p.m. to announce her intention to fight through to a second ballot. In doing so, she alienated many of her Cabinet colleagues, who had believed she would consult them before announcing her decision, if the first ballot failed to give her a clear lead.

George Younger decided not to continue as the Prime Minister's campaign manager. John Wakeham was asked to take charge and he set about the task of building a new team. He turned first to Richard Ryder and Tristan Garel-Jones, both with extensive past experience in the Whips' Office and at the time the Paymaster General and a minister of state at the Foreign Office respectively. Both of them had helped to organise Mrs Thatcher's defence against Anthony Meyer's challenge a year earlier. They met in Tristan's room in the House of Commons. John explained that he had now been appointed campaign manager and asked if they would join with him.

Tristan said he thought it would be difficult for Mrs Thatcher to win and set out a number of points that would need to be addressed if she was to have any chance. The poll tax should go. All personal attacks on me by both Mrs Thatcher and her supporters should cease and I should be brought back into the Cabinet. Richard said he would be prepared to help but first he wanted a meeting with the Prime Minister to explain his views on the necessary alterations to both the style and the substance of her campaign. He wanted to put the points to her personally and not through an intermediary. Neither was approached again by her team.

Not content with her statement in Paris she reiterated it the next afternoon outside No. 10 – 'I fight on, I fight to win' – before going first to the Commons and then to the Palace to acquaint the Queen of her intentions. I have no doubt myself that at the time she believed what she said – and, if I made an error, it lay in thinking that her Cabinet colleagues would not be able to get her to change her mind. I knew, of course, of the pressure on her to stand down, but through Wednesday night there remained, it appeared to me, a real chance that she would indeed fight on. In fact, having consulted the Cabinet one by one, she had decided late that night that the game was up. Several of them would have supported me on the second round. It was not until early the next morning as I was on my way to London Zoo to plant a tree that Eileen telephoned me in the car to tell me that the jungle drums had relayed to her that the Prime Minister had decided to withdraw from the contest. Apparently my response was: 'She hasn't!' I went ahead with the engagement – it was for the benefit of schoolchildren – but I have seldom performed any public role with my mind more abstracted elsewhere.

Fortunately, the planting of a tree is for me a fairly familiar process and I do not think my demeanour gave me away. For I had realised the moment I heard the news that my prospects of reaching No. 10 had for the moment come to an end – if what Enoch Powell once called the 'golden ball' had ever been in my hands, it had fallen on to the floor of my Jaguar that morning at about ten to nine. I had never had the slightest doubt that in a head-to-head second ballot contest with Margaret Thatcher I would win – the assurances we had already received from MPs defecting from her cause provided the proof of that. But now other candidates would come in and I, as the notional front-runner, would inevitably become their target. I had once over lunch in February 1986 encapsulated my position to the *New Society* journalist David Lipsey: 'He who wields the knife never wears the crown.' I had thought at the time that I was repeating a well-known quotation. I now find that it is attributed in the *Oxford Dictionary of Political Quotations* to me. I am amused by my early and uncharacteristic flash of modesty. It turned out to be a prophetic, if injudicious, comment.

To defeat her in open combat was one thing; to be held account-able for making her quit the field was quite another (even if the real responsibility was not mine but that of her own Cabinet colleagues). Michael Mates, who unluckily for me was away in the Persian Gulf for most of the second week of the contest, takes the view that if I had had a single rival rather than two – in the formidable persons of the Chancellor John Major and the Foreign Secretary Douglas Hurd – I could still have won. But I am by no means convinced of that and my own feeling is that my hope of being Mrs Thatcher's successor vanished when she resolved to give up the contest.

However, I had to be seen to be trying. One added disappointment was, I suppose, Tom King, the Secretary of State for Defence. We had worked together in opposition and we had been very close at the start of the Thatcher government when we worked side by side in remarkable harmony at the Department of the Environment. I had believed that, if the moment ever came when I ran for the leadership, Tom would play a leading part in my team. On Mrs Thatcher's departure I immediately telephoned him, in the hope that he would propose me for the second ballot. He told me he was supporting Douglas Hurd, with whom, as Foreign Secretary, he had developed a close relationship. The timing of the contest was difficult for Tom, coming as it did in the middle of planning for the Gulf War; he had legitimate concerns about the effect on troop morale of a complete change at the top.

Two of the more surprising of my lost supporters were my ex-PPS Cecil Parkinson and Norman Lamont. I had kept in touch with Cecil during the wilderness years. He had never wavered in his assurances that he thought I should succeed Mrs Thatcher. We dined together regularly. On the day Mrs Thatcher resigned, he telephoned me in great agitation. I took the call in my outer office, where it was overheard by others. 'People are saying you have committed regicide,' he said. I am told I was heard to say: 'Reggie who?' But he was clearly deeply distressed. I caught up with him later in the corridors of the Commons, where he explained that 'in the circumstances' it was not possible for him to back me.

In Norman Lamont's autobiography he claims that, although friendly towards me, he had always made clear that my European views were a barrier to his support. I have no recollection of such a conversation taking place. He continually offered encouragement and, indeed, he told me after the meeting of the so-called Blue Chip dining club at the height of the crisis following the first ballot that he had tried to interest them in my candidature, a claim he repeats in his autobiography. It was, he said, only when he had failed to do so that he heard the call to lead the Major team. This is flatly contradicted in John's own book, which has Norman canvassing for him well before the contest itself. Tristan Garel-Jones complained to John on the afternoon of Thursday, 15 November that he had been canvassed by Norman on John's behalf and that he regarded this as improper. This was before the result of the first ballot was known – indeed, before the nominations had taken place.

I have reflected on this in the light of Norman's conversation with me at the time of my resignation from the government some five years earlier, when he told me that he had considered offering his own resignation as well. I had had to balance this against the rather contrary reports I was receiving at the time – particularly from Michael Mates, whom I first got to know when he came to my office in the MOD to warn me of the very close relationship that Norman continued to maintain with those with whom he had formerly worked at Leon Brittan's Department of Trade and Industry. But then such is politics – well, for some.

One abiding memory of the second phase of the leadership contest is the dramatic change of atmosphere that followed Mrs Thatcher's departure. The personal relations between John, Douglas and me were relaxed and friendly. It was as though the poison had been let out of the system. If I had won, I would have hoped that they would both have remained in their positions. Douglas knew that was my view.

In the last week, although we went through all the motions – photo-opportunities, newspaper articles, TV interviews and all the rest – I found it increasingly difficult to buoy myself up. There was little realistic hope of victory. We had stopped making the kind of headway that we had done in the two days that immediately followed the first ballot result. Central Office had gone to work in a big way for John Major. It was some compensation, however, that both John and Douglas recognised too the liability the poll tax had become and gave pledges that committed them to a full-scale review. Mrs Thatcher had regarded the community charge, as she always called it, as the flagship of her government programme. Certainly, the captain went down with the ship.

There was no denying, however, that I sensed that even some of those upon whose support we had counted were stealing away. Our final throw was the announcement, timed for the Sunday papers on 25 November, that Geoffrey Howe, Nigel Lawson and Lord Carrington had all come out in my favour; both Geoffrey and Nigel had been anxious to help, and would have come back to the forefront of political life if I had formed an administration. But the association of their names with mine as the lead story in the *Sunday Times* rammed home the linkage of the three of us – all of us having departed from Mrs Thatcher's government in very dramatic and public circumstances – and that undoubtedly accelerated the drift of support among Tory colleagues and supporters.

Up until that time my most powerful card had been my public support, showing I could bring back lost votes to the party. But even this card now disappeared, as John Major drew level with me in the polls. Few seemed to notice that I still remained significantly ahead among those Labour and Liberal voters whom we had to win over, but John's lead among Conservatives now balanced that advantage out.

By the evening of Tuesday, 27 November I was fully prepared for the result. I waited at Chapel Street with Anne and the children, Michael and Eileen. The street was under siege; there were reporters and cameras everywhere and neighbours crowded on to their balconies. A telephone call from Keith Hampson at the House of Commons within a minute of the result being declared told me that John Major had secured 185 votes, I had 131 and Douglas Hurd 56. Once again the ballot had failed to produce the kind of outcome envisaged by the 1922 Committee's rules, as even now John did not have an overall majority. But he was so close to it that there was plainly no purpose in going on. At the most optimistic calculation we thought that Douglas' votes might split two to one to me. This was not enough and it ignored the bandwagon effect which John's lead would precipitate. Anne and I immediately went out on to our front steps to congratulate the victor and announce my withdrawal from the contest (Douglas did the same from the Foreign Office shortly afterwards). The Conservative Party had settled its leadership for the next six and a half years.

There was a series of votes in the House that night. I had to face my colleagues, many of whom were elated that I had been denied the premiership which I had wrested from Mrs Thatcher. Some were magnanimous – Teresa Gorman kissed me in the smoking room. But a significant minority, who had devoted themselves to my cause, shared my deep sense of disappointment. They were invited to join me in Committee Room J so that I could express my thanks for their efforts. This was the most emotional moment of the whole leadership challenge. I put the bravest face on it I could. I might not have won, but Mrs Thatcher's departure had appeared to ease the tension in the party, and John Major showed every indication of restoring a fairer and more attractive balance in the inevitable conflicts that make up the agenda of a national party. I took an optimistic note and read, with tears in my eyes, the poem by Arthur Hugh Clough which Eileen had given to me earlier in the evening:

> Say not the struggle naught availeth,
>   The labour and the wounds are vain,
> The enemy faints not, nor faileth,
>   And as things have been, things remain.
>
> If hopes were dupes, fears may be liars;
>   It may be, in yon smoke concealed,
> Your comrades chase e'en now the fliers,
>   And, but for you, possess the field.
>
> For while the tired waves, vainly breaking,
>   Seem here no painful inch to gain,
> Far back, through creeks and inlets making,
>   Comes silent, flooding in, the main,
>
> And not by eastern windows only,
>   When daylight comes, comes in the light,
> In front, the sun climbs slow, how slowly,
>   But westward, look, the land is bright.

There are, inevitably, the 'what ifs?' What if I had done nothing in the autumn of 1990? Suppose I had faced down the 'Put up or shut up' editorial in *The Times* and done neither. There would have been some loss of street cred with my more enthusiastic supporters but perhaps a more than compensating gain among Thatcher's less committed followers when she lost the 1992 election, as she almost certainly would have. We are back to Michael Jopling's advice and my reaction to it. I did not want the Conservatives to lose the next election. I did not want to be Leader of the Opposition. I did not want to see a largely unreconstructed Labour Party gain power, with all the ensuing prejudice and risk to everything that we had achieved. My friends now say that that's all very well but Labour would have enjoyed only their characteristic one-term parliamentary majority before losing again after the exchange rate fiasco, another Labour devaluation and amid peak post-war unemployment. If only

I had held back, the prize would have been mine, they claim: a short few years in which to consolidate the party on the Opposition benches and then a head-to-head with Neil Kinnock and an election victory. The timing fits, of course, with the subsequent benign economic circumstances which did so much to shore up New Labour. But, without John Major's and Ken Clarke's influence, who believes that the economic inheritance would have been as it became? And who would have looked after the party, with what consequences, after my heart attack in 1993?

An intriguing suggestion was put to me years later: that I should have withdrawn after the first ballot. Mrs Thatcher could not long have survived and might well, in the face of backbench pressure, have felt obliged to bring me back into the Cabinet. I would thus have regained a place at the heart of government and have immeasurably strengthened my prospects when she departed. But this option was never considered when it might have proved attractive – at the time.

All this is idle speculation, however, and neither then nor since has it occupied much of my time. I have never been one for introspection, rationalisation or self-pity. There is always another mountain top.

PART FOUR:
1990–1997

Chapter 17

BACK TO ENVIRONMENT

S hortly after I had conceded victory to John Major the telephone rang in Chapel Street. 'Come and join us,' he said, and it was arranged that we should meet the next morning.

In the meantime I heard whispers in the House of Commons that I was to be offered the Home Office. I recalled sitting as an undergraduate in 1954 at a Conservative Association meeting in the Oxford Union alongside an idol of my youth, Iain Macleod. During dinner later that evening he had asked me what great office of state I would like to hold if I ever came within reach of such an opportunity. 'The Home Office,' I had innocently replied. 'The graveyard of politics,' was his crushing rejoinder. The phrase remained with me for the thirty-five years and more that were to pass before my youthful dream confronted the prospect of its being fulfilled.

I had by then already changed my mind anyway. I have been extremely fortunate in that every ministerial job that I have held has been broadly consistent with issues and opportunities that were of personal interest to me. I was never asked to serve in Social Security or at the Department of Health. This is in no way to deny the importance of the policy areas for which these two departments are responsible. It is more about my own experiences and aptitudes, which have always been heavily inclined to the industrial and commercial world or to issues of national security, the environment and heritage. I had never been attracted by the Treasury which – beyond the prodigious workload it imposes on its ministers – always seemed to me to be rather more preoccupied with finding reasons why things can't happen than with encouraging them to happen (which has always been my natural instinct). Fundamentally, I suppose, it is all a matter of style and temperament. I have been lucky in that I was always put where the opportunities seemed to reflect my personality.

The Home Office is undoubtedly one of the great offices of state. Ministers there confront some of the most intractable problems of modern society, including of course the never ending battle against crime and the insidious spread of drugs. But it is a lawyer's paradise. The problems may have solutions but these are much easier to articulate than to achieve. More often, in the harsh light of day, the over-simplicity of political platitudes comes face to face with complicated reality. (I was to confront just such an issue, concerning rough sleepers, in the Department of the Environment.) Warned by Michael Mates that the Home Office was the senior job most likely to be available, therefore, I let it be known in short, crisp sentences that nobody was going to send me there.

The next morning, on 28 November, John and I met in the upstairs study of No. 10 and we discussed what role I could play. He made it clear that the Chancellorship was not on offer; it had already gone to Norman Lamont. This did not upset me. It was not a job I coveted. What I really wanted was the Department of Trade and Industry. His reaction was immediate: 'Yes, but not until after the next general election.' The election itself could not be far away, and I was sensitive to the presentational difficulties that he would face with the unreconstructed, anti-interventionist sections of the Parliamentary Conservative Party if I were to move into that Department at once and displace Peter Lilley. We settled for the Department of the Environment.

So at the end of November 1990 I was back in Marsham Street and another permanent secretary, Sir Terry Heiser, received his version of the by now familiar back-of-the-envelope the morning I arrived. When I left two years later he gave me what he called a half-term report on progress as he judged it. I will come back to this.

I was fortunate to be able to bring into the Department with me, as my political adviser, Eileen Strathnaver, who had run my office in Victoria Street since 1986. She was now able to focus her very considerable abilities on the day-to-day business of a large government department, as well as acting as liaison with the party organisation. To her credit she never became part of the back-biting, intrigue and petty rivalries that can so often characterise political advisers, most of them would-be politicians in their own right and seeking to climb the political ladder from student politics to research department to political aide to parliamentary candidate – accumulating views on everything along the way but with actual experience of very little. Terry Heiser reminded me shortly after my return of a conversation we had had years earlier. 'Why don't you have political advisers?' he had asked. 'I do,' I had replied. 'They are called ministers.' Eileen was to be the only exception.

I was also lucky in my first year to recruit Tom Burke – the highly sophisticated environmental lobbyist whom I had come especially to admire in my years outside government. I put it to him that he had spent his life pointing politicians in the direction he believed environmental policies should go and challenged him to become a special adviser and put his shoulder to the wheel. He knew his subject backwards, rapidly won the confidence of the environmental correspondents and was a great success – indeed, he stayed on under two further Secretaries of State after I had left. I hope he will not misunderstand it if I say he also proved wholly trustworthy – a compliment not easy to earn for a man whose life and friends had been centred in the world of environmental politics.

For me, of course, going back to those huge ugly tower blocks in Marsham Street felt something like the return of the native. I had already served in the department twice before, as Parliamentary Under-Secretary from 1970 to 1972 and as Secretary of State from 1979 to early 1983. In modern politics it is extremely rare for a politician to head a department twice, with a gap at another ministry (in my case Defence) in between – in fact, the only other Tory to have done so in post-war politics was David (Viscount) Eccles, who between 1954 and 1962 was twice Minister of Education (he served as President of the Board of Trade in between). But I was pleased by the opportunity and I could not deny there was a certain justice in it – from the beginning I had campaigned for the leadership on the platform that the poll tax had to go. Both John and Douglas had been forced in their campaigns to hold out the prospect of a similar change but without my clear commitment there can be no absolute certainty that the Conservative government would have repealed one of the most inequitable pieces of legislation the party in power has ever introduced. That became one of my prime tasks.

There were many other familiar responsibilities. Chris Patten, whom I succeeded at the DOE (he became the new party Chairman), had been an extremely effective Secretary of State and I was particularly enthusiastic to build on the environmental policies he had been pursuing. And nothing could give me greater satisfaction than to renew my responsibility for the London Docklands Development Corporation, in whose territory, after various alarums and excursions, the massive development at Canary Wharf eventually found its way to a viable future. I welcomed, too, the opportunity to return to some of the issues governing the structure of local government. I had spent much time on the back benches thinking about the problems of the urban agenda and how to take it forward. And I was determined to create within England a replica of the success of the Scottish and Welsh Development Agencies.

But, by way of prologue, let me first reflect upon the government I had joined and the new colleagues with whom I was now to be associated. When I joined the Cabinet for the first time in 1979, around the table were politicians who had made the headlines for most of my political life: Quintin Hailsham was Lord Chancellor and had been a candidate for leadership of the party nearly two decades earlier; Christopher Soames and Peter Thorneycroft had served in Harold Macmillan's government in the late 1950s and early 1960s; Peter Carrington and Willie Whitelaw had had distinguished careers in the Guards Armoured Brigade in the Second World War and were now respected national figures. There were others, of course, younger and less well known. But around the table sat representatives of a heavyweight generation. Not all of them survived through to my voluntary departure in 1986, but the process was gradual and my first memories of entering the Cabinet in 1979 were always there to give a sepia tint to the picture I retained in my mind.

When I came back in 1990, those giants were gone. No longer was I looking at a table around which sat a generation senior to mine and who seemed to bring a certain ballast to politics. I say this with no disrespect to my new colleagues of 1990 and in no way as a qualitative judgement on their abilities. But, whereas the first time I sat round the Cabinet table I was looking up to a generation older and more experienced than mine, now I was looking down to a generation younger and less experienced. It was a curious feeling, reflective of the last year of school or one's final few terms at university or perhaps of life itself – as one grows older, yesterday's personalities become memories, while at the same time one slowly grows apart from the generation coming along behind.

Effectively, I had been gone from government for five years. My battle for political survival had been conducted from the back benches, during which time – in reshuffle after reshuffle – younger colleagues had climbed the ladders of promotion. I hardly knew them. They had never worked with me in government. Their minds had been focused on their ministerial responsibilities. They had been on the inside track. I had certainly not been.

Of the twenty-one members of John Major's 1990 Cabinet only two – Norman Lamont and Tom King – had ever served in a government department with me and thus knew something of me. The rest thought, however, that they knew me only too well. Month after month, year after year, they had read in the national press other people's views about what I did, what I believed in, what motives drove me on. Mrs Thatcher had had many friends and supporters and, if 'rid me of this turbulent priest' were never words that actually passed her lips, there were those both in Downing Street and outside it ready to sentence me to death by a thousand cuts. I had been the outcast of politics, warily watched and guardedly marked lest I felt tempted to get up to what they saw as mischief. Why should any of them have risked their good names with No. 10 by too close an association with someone whose motives were thought to be so suspect?

There had been one conspicuous exception to this general pattern of reserve. Ken Clarke, as a minister in the DTI, had heard of my reputation in Liverpool and in typically robust fashion invited me in 1988 to accompany him on an official tour of the city to visit projects, by this time matured, which had formed part of my original Merseyside initiative. In the world outside politics that may appear a small gesture; but in the hothouse of Westminster it was a brave one, if only because these things seldom pass unnoticed – least of all by those who like to function as whips' 'narks'.

It was from an even younger Conservative generation than Ken that John Major came. He had been elected to the Commons only in 1979, a full thirteen years after I had arrived and when I was already a Cabinet minister: my relationship with him thus had been restricted to a handful of encounters. We had liaised closely over my plans as Defence Secretary to secure the perimeter of Molesworth airfield in early 1985, because the air base lay in his constituency. But I can recall no further encounters with him until the late 1980s. His rise to prominence had been meteoric and he was, down to his fingertips, a professional. I had observed the skill and tenacity with which he 'worked' the lobbies. He was engaged in making friends in the parliamentary party.

When a division is called in the House of Commons, some eight minutes or so passes while in each of the 'aye' and 'no' lobbies Members mingle and chat, as they slowly make their way to the tellers' counter and the exit point. The overwhelming majority of Members move steadily through at a measured pace, exchanging the occasional remark with colleagues, but eyes fixed on their voting duty. Ministers tend to hang back, as do the party whips. It all has something of the atmosphere of a Middle East bazaar or an eighteenth-century London coffee-house. Information is exchanged, jokes shared, gossip passed on. It is, in effect, a great bonding session, a sort of non-physical pressing of the flesh. Ambition thrives here. One keeps in touch, barters compliments and hopes no doubt to be observed mingling with those possessing real power. (I should not make too much of the intimacy of the voting lobbies: I had exchanged only one remark with Mrs Thatcher since my resignation, and that had occurred one evening when I stood back to allow her precedence so that she could pass through the lobby door ahead of me. I had murmured, 'Prime Minister,' and she had replied in one word and with the slightest incline of the head, 'Michael.')

John Major entered the Cabinet a year after I had left it. At my invitation, we dined one night – in early September 1989 – at the Stafford Hotel off St James's. Our conversation covered the usual horizon of contemporary events and gossip; the only remark I remember of any significance was my prediction that, if anything happened to destroy her relationship with Nigel Lawson at the Treasury, Mrs Thatcher would immediately bring John back from the Foreign Office, no matter how brief a time he had spent there. This forecast proved surprisingly accurate.

I had hoped in those early days that we could develop the cordial relationship that I felt had been generated during that dinner. But it was not to be. My subsequent invitations to get together again were all rejected. Presumably, this was a product of John's natural caution. In November 1990 I have no doubt he fully appreciated just how controversial for some – including for Mrs Thatcher, who never forgave him for it – his decision to invite me to join his Cabinet would be. It was bound to be contentious with the Thatcherites; but at the same time, being the acute politician he is, he would have realised that, if he wished to heal the wounds in the Conservative Party, he could not ignore the scale of support that I enjoyed, not just in the parliamentary party but in the country at large. In any case, as things worked out, the judgement that I had expressed to Clive Whitmore, my permanent secretary at the MOD, in that fateful second week of 1986 had been proved right. I had returned to office at precisely the point when a new leader had replaced Mrs Thatcher.

From that point on my relationship with John was cordial, but for several years after I sensed that there was an attitude of suspicion prevalent among his closest advisers in No. 10. Perhaps wariness is a more accurate description of their mood. I was being carefully watched. Their fears were quite unnecessary. But I could understand, in the climate that had developed from 1986 to 1990, why they felt as they did. It did not unduly bother me. I believed that events would allay the suspicions and in this, again, I believe I was right. John was to prove more than generous when, years later, he described our relationship thus:

> In later years I was to find out that crises were meat and drink to Michael. He loved them . . . I remember striding down a corridor, when there were some 50 disasters going on around us, and Michael smiling happily and saying: 'Isn't it fun.' The pace of events, the drama of politics, whether good or bad, filled him with excitement, and he loved it; this is the core of the Heseltine personality.
>
> Another of Michael's qualities which I gradually came to recognise was that when the chips are down he is absolutely loyal and 100% supportive. Other people may have wanted to duck away from shot and shell, but Michael would get in and fight . . . As Deputy Prime Minister he never failed me.*

At the DOE I was particularly fortunate in that, as one of my Ministers of State, I had Sir George Young, who was responsible for the housing side of the Department's activities. George – one of the few ministerial colleagues I had who was taller than me – had acquired a wide and well-deserved reputation among people not normally associated with the Conservative Party as a deeply concerned MP who well understood the complexities and frustrations of many of the more intractable social problems of our time. Together we took the housing revolution a stage or two further.

No one can now seriously question the success of the Right-to-Buy policy in spreading ownership, but tenants of municipal flats

* John Major, *The Autobiography* (HarperCollins, 1999), pp. 207–8.

– as opposed to tenants of houses – were understandably concerned about the maintenance costs of common parts (which had tended to be strewn with graffiti and litter) and about the proposed service charges. We opted to transfer such estates out of the public sector into what effectively were housing co-operatives, a version of Nick Ridley's Housing Action Trusts, later replaced by Large-Scale Voluntary Transfer, a policy of transferring all of a local authority's housing estates to a housing trust: in both cases tenant support was secured by referendum. In order to help develop a long-term local housing strategy, we also decided to abandon formula-based funding and instead to invite housing authorities to submit plans and proposals, to canvass their tenants' views and generally compete for our support. Both initiatives aroused fierce controversy, but they rapidly proved their worth. No less effective was the far-ranging report by Dame Jennifer Jenkins into the future of London's Royal Parks, for which George also deserves the credit.

George's very considerable reputation was at its most evident in his dealings with the charities concerned with rough sleepers on the streets of London. I was personally appalled that in one of the world's great capital cities, within a stone's throw of Trafalgar Square and throughout central London, night after night, huddled in the doorways of locked shops or empty alleyways were these drop-outs from conventional society. There were at the time anything up to 2,000 rough sleepers on any one night on the streets of London. George and I discussed the matter very frankly. I wanted results and my instinct was to ask the police why they did not use their powers to prevent this nightly accumulation of human misery and failure.

But here the real world crowded in. The advice to me was that the police didn't want to do it. There weren't enough shelters to take these people, let alone more permanent accommodation. If they were brought before the magistrates, the magistrates would let them go. The media would relish it. Every pressure group would exploit the harrowing scenes of policemen confronting vagrants, to the delight of the television camera crews and photographers. The best to be hoped for would be to move them on; the worst would be nightly clashes with no solution. And then there was the killer argument: if the police were involved in this way, there would be no co-operation from the voluntary sector, who alone possessed the skills any solutions demanded.

George offered me a better way, lower profile, slower but more likely to work. He asked if he could recruit one of the most experienced leaders of the charities involved in the field to help sort out the problem. He stressed that we would have to create more hostels and provide services to transport these rough sleepers from the streets to the shelters – and that it would all take time. He persuaded Nick Hardwick, then chief executive of the Centrepoint shelter (later he was to run the Refugee Council), to join us as special adviser on rough sleepers for a period of six months.

On more than one occasion George and I went down to the Strand and the Bull Ring next to Waterloo and talked through the problems with some of the street people ourselves. A co-ordinating group involving the police, the voluntary services and officials worked hard to target the worst areas. We committed £90 million to a comprehensive programme involving outreach workers and training schemes, as well as the construction of shelters, hostels and move-on accommodation. Some ideas were simple but brilliant: mobile phones enabled charity workers to call ahead to hostels (often some distance from central London) to ensure there was a bed before setting off in their vans to deliver another old boy. Pets were a difficulty because most hostels would not accept them. We identified a couple that would. Inveterate alcoholics proved the most intractable problem. Manchester had led the way in experimenting with a 'wet' hostel; we set one up in London too. Night after night my driver Andy and I would go from Trafalgar Square past Charing Cross and up the Strand, and for a frustratingly long time the situation on the streets hardly seemed to change. But slowly, and with especial success in Lincoln's Inn Fields, the numbers began at last to fall. Over the ensuing months they dropped steadily and in our time together we reduced the numbers on the streets of central London by two-thirds. Many of the remaining simply rejected all offers of accommodation and help. But we were now able to start to tackle the situation outside London.

As so often with these acute social problems, the issues themselves are complex. There is no stereotype rough sleeper, but the research we originated tended to divide the problem into two broad categories of people. There were the young. For some of them it had become a way of life; with outstretched hand and empty cap, there were pickings to be had. Others worked the passing crowds until they dwindled with the advancing night, whereupon the 'beggars' went home. They did have homes to go to. There were the young girls, persuaded by the rashness of youth (or some man) to leave home for the bright lights of the capital city – only to find themselves homeless on the streets within weeks. I found difficulty in feeling a great deal of sympathy for many of these young people, although I recognised that, if I had known the individual circumstances which led them to leave home, I might have seen things differently. Most of them appeared fit and healthy although there was the ever present menace of drugs, an all-too-common ingredient in the noxious cocktail called poverty. But they were the tiny exception to the overwhelming majority of young people who worked for a living and retained the disciplines of self-support and self-respect.

At the other end of the spectrum were the human breakdowns, the real dossers, the meths drinkers, the alcoholics, the broken wrecks of human life. Wrapped in layer upon layer of ancient clothing, shambling, possessionless or with their supermarket trolleys laden with waste paper and accumulated rubbish, often filthy, distrustful of authority, they were the ghosts of men and women who had once been ordinary human beings just like everyone else. Heaven alone knows what takes a person to such ends, what breaks the will or crushes the human spirit. An already existing problem had been exacerbated by our policy of closing down the long-term-care psychiatric hospitals and introducing care in the community. This was a good policy and worked well for most of the former patients. No one was released from one of the secure hospitals with nowhere to go. There was, however, a tiny minority who simply 'walked'. They used their new freedom to leave the sheltered accommodation to which they had been moved and, of their own volition, take to the streets.

Among this community, as in any other, there are standards and those at the extreme of social unacceptability often find themselves ejected from the hostels where, because of drink or behaviour, their presence proves unacceptable to their colleagues. We sought a chink of light that would encourage this hard core to a more ordered way of life. We arranged interviews. It has to be said that, if there were any reply at all, it was as likely to be a stream of abuse and invective as a constructive response. But we knew that any attempt to put right what had so evidently gone hopelessly wrong was a long-term process. George and I conducted a continual dialogue about the issues week after week in that year and a half that I was in the Department. Taken altogether, however, he had undoubtedly been right in the advice he had given me about tackling the problems of rough sleepers.

I mention just one last example of the complexities of the problems with which we were confronted. I was walking through King's Cross station on my way north one day when I noticed a relatively young man, say thirty years old, dressed in an assortment of old clothes and rags who appeared to have taken up residence in a corner of the station. To my inquiry as to why the police failed to act, I was told that the man had Aids and that he had threatened that anyone who approached him would be bitten. Of course, one should never give in to blackmail of this sort, but where was the police sergeant who was going to order a young constable to take that kind of risk?

The person who faced the most acute trauma of loyalty in the changeover to the new administration in 1990 was Michael Portillo. Here was the man who, a matter of only six weeks before Mrs Thatcher's resignation, had stood in front of the Tory Party Conference in Bournemouth defending the poll tax with all his considerable talent and ability. This was the acolyte who had forced his way into No. 10 on the critical eve of her departure to beg her to stay. By the next throw of the political dice he now found himself the Minister of State to the assassin himself and, worse still, he was the chosen instrument to trump that central card in the Thatcherite hand: the poll tax. An olive branch of some substance was plainly required.

I invited him to lunch in an Italian bistro in Westminster. It was an uncomfortable meal. I could understand how he felt. Usually there are two sides to every story, but he could have no comprehension of or sympathy with mine. I did my best to establish the sort of relationship I always sought with my ministerial colleagues in the departments over which I presided; but, try as I might, I would not say that the temperature rose much above freezing on that first encounter.

However, Michael was to work with me as Minister of State in the DOE until the general election of 1992 and during that time he diligently carried through the legislation to replace the poll tax with the council tax. He executed the policies associated with my vision of urban renaissance – which was essentially based on a public–private sector partnership. Looking back, I cannot today remember a single area of policy over which we significantly disagreed; nor can I remember any example where any criticisms he may have had of me ever materialised in a public forum. Indeed, when I asked him for his comments on a list of our achievements together in the Department in preparation for the Conservatives' 1992 manifesto, he replied, 'Looks very good.' Needless to say, I agreed. A senior civil servant told me long after the 1997 election that he had been struck with the obvious respect we accorded to each other's views, despite the gap in age and experience. Indeed, towards the end of our time together journalists were beginning to write of a 'dream ticket' consisting of Heseltine and Portillo. Later on, of course, we were to disagree in the interminable wrangles over Europe. This is the fault-line that runs through the bed-rock of the Conservative Party and, if anti-Europeanism is all that Thatcherism amounts to, then it is true that Michael Portillo and I belong to different wings of the party. But, as so often in my political life, I found that in practice the things which unite ministers as colleagues are incomparably more important than those which divide them. This was the case with what became my close working relationship with Michael.

The poll tax had threatened the Conservative Party with disaster. As the more conscientious reader may recall, I had left the government before it was approved by the Cabinet in 1986 but well before that, in the early 1980s, I had been deeply engaged in an analysis of replacement schemes for the rating system, as a result of which the Cabinet collectively had come to the view that there was no sensible alternative to the rates, or at least something very like them. Yet now, as I discovered, it is one thing to commit oneself to abolishing a tax; it is quite another to find a plausible alternative. This, however, was my initial responsibility. I had effectively killed the poll tax and now I had to find a substitute acceptable to the broad mass of the Parliamentary Conservative Party.

There were two fundamental flaws in the concept of the poll tax. The first lay in the real difficulty of collecting it, as people moved, refused to register or engaged in one form of defiance after another. The second was its inherent unfairness. It bore down with equal weight on rich and poor alike. In the Tory shires the prosperous landowner paid the same as the impecunious tenant. In central London the multimillionaire was levied at the identical rate as his daily help living a few blocks but an economic world away. It offended against an inherent sense of justice and fair play. Whatever efforts were made to explain it, no one could be expected to understand how, for instance, I – living, as I did, in one of the most affluent neighbourhoods of London – was paying a fraction of the sum demanded for some appalling tenement flat in a Labour borough just the other side of the river. And when you throw into the pot the intricacies of the central government grant-distribution mechanism, and add to that the Treasury's determination to lower the overall level of grant itself, you have all the conditions for political trauma. That trauma did not merely surface in traditional areas of agitation, like Glasgow or Lambeth or Trafalgar Square. Across the home counties and even in the broad acres of remote areas like Shropshire good Tory voters packed protest meetings as they had never done before. Members of Parliament were being deluged with letters. So was the Department – a redoubtable civil servant named Bob Treacher had the unenviable task of replying to them and for months was barely visible at his desk over the top of mountains of 'red jackets' (each incoming letter from a member of the public received a red file cover).

The moment I was appointed to the Department, the Opposition moved in on the poll tax. They announced a supply day debate, obviously hoping to embarrass me should I appear to defend the indefensible. But in fact the initiative was with me. I was determined that the tax should go, but in all fairness to my colleagues I had no blueprint for its replacement. John, in his first days as Prime Minister, agreed that I could announce a review of local government, encompassing finance, structure and management. He also agreed to my using a specific form of words in respect of the poll tax: that, as to its replacement, 'nothing's ruled in and nothing ruled out'. It became something of a mantra for the next few months.

I decided to invite the Opposition parties to participate in the search for an alternative. Labour rejected my offer out of hand; but the Liberal Democrats, the Welsh Nationalists and others made contributions to the debate. It was one thing, however, to collect views from the Opposition parties: I was still the one who had to recommend what to put in the poll tax's place. On 30 January 1991 I found myself scheduled to attend a conference of OECD Environment Ministers in Paris, together with my bright and alert principal private secretary, Phillip Ward. It was a two-day conference and mind-blowingly boring. I had recently returned from Kuwait, where the results of the Iraqi invasion had wreaked havoc with the oilfields and the resulting pollution was appalling – and I was trying to persuade the ministers of the world's most prosperous countries that we should establish a contingency facility to which we would all contribute and which would have resources, equipment and trained personnel on call to enable it to react to future environmental crises of this sort. Ministers were closeted in one room, officials separated off in a *salle d'écoute* from which Phillip heard me proclaim that I thought the collective reaction of the meeting to my proposal was 'pathetic'. (The early response –

or lack of it – to the floods in Mozambique in 2000 shows how little progress was made in the intervening decade.)

At the end of the first day I said to Phillip that I had had enough, and the next morning we settled into the residence of our ambassador to the OECD, John Gray. We had time on our hands before our flight was scheduled to depart for London. I took a piece of paper and sketched out the ideas that were to become known later as the council tax.

We would, in effect, revert to a property-based tax, dividing the nation's homes into five bands (this subsequently became eight), valuing them in categories and using the same government grant-distribution mechanism. The effect would be that those living in the more expensive properties would pay significantly more than people at the bottom of the scale. I added to this a single person's discount, thus addressing one of the most glaring criticisms of the old rating system: the unfair burden it placed on widows and single people living alone. My ideas were fleshed out into formal proposals which were then put to No. 10.

The usual comings and goings took place. Several colleagues fought a tough rearguard action to preserve what they argued was the virtue of accountability built into the concept of the poll tax. Sarah Hogg, head of the Prime Minister's Policy Unit, was insistent that there should be a cut-off point, so that the value categories did not continue on and up beyond a certain threshold. I regarded this as no more than a minor adjustment to the system, and by and large the ideas that I had put forward were prepared for legislation.

John Major himself presided over many of the discussions that ensued, making no substantive objections. Where he did make a decisive intervention, one that must be considered an important part of the success of the ensuing council tax, was in a meeting with Norman Lamont and myself. He recognised the damage that the Treasury had done over the years in reducing the percentage of central support for local government and thus forcing up first the rates and subsequently the poll tax. He believed that a necessary commitment to the success of the council tax was a substantial increase in central government support for local government expenditure. Norman and I disagreed with him about the scale of the increase that he proposed. I took the view that this was just another example of escalating revenue expenditure, which I knew from long experience would lead to compensating capital reductions in the ensuing public expenditure round. But in the end John's view prevailed and the level of local funding for local government expenditure was reduced. In the interim we announced a flat-rate reduction in all poll tax bills as a holding measure while the new council tax was legislated for. The 'Big Bertha' (Chris Patten's phrase) of a 2½ per cent increase in value added tax was rolled out to fund the gesture and, to the Treasury's surprise, the markets accepted it. John was right to recognise that simply changing the system would not prove enough, unless the change ensured that there were no substantial losers around to drown out any muted appreciation from the gainers.

Michael Portillo steered the ensuing legislation through its lengthy committee stage in the House with skill and precision, and by the general election in 1992 the poll tax had been consigned to the dustbin of history. One final obstacle failed to come to anything; it had been argued that it would not be possible to value the nation's housing stock at the speed the exercise required. 'The district valuers' offices can't possibly cope,' I was told by my officials. I insisted that they get the private sector surveyors and estate agents in to help and give every householder a right of appeal to the district valuer. This worked and the obstacle was overcome.

I vividly recall one particular moment in all the weeks of protracted discussions about the poll tax. I was just about to begin a routine meeting to discuss the issue with Sarah Hogg in her room on the first floor at No. 10, when the IRA mortared the building from a site in Whitehall a couple of hundred yards away. It was in a sense all over before it started. We heard a loud bang, then the sound of doors opening and corridors filling with people, with voices pitched higher than normal. Everyone moved downstairs where things felt a bit more secure. Mercifully no one was hurt, though there were one or two close calls. The damage, such as it was, was localised and behind closed doors. My comment to Sarah when we reconvened our examination of the poll tax was: 'I knew this was an explosive issue, but . . .'

There was another perceived threat to homeowners during this time. The recession of John's first years, as Norman Lamont and he grappled with rising levels of inflation, struck at the heart of our support. The heady days of rising property prices and freely available mortgages, at ever more indefensible multiples of not one breadwinner's salary but two, had gone. Sale boards everywhere advertised not just the availability of individual properties, but, by their number and the ever lengthening time of their display, the existence of a recession.

'This house is for sale' is one thing. 'This house has been for sale for months and, like all the others in this and many other streets, no one is buying it' is quite another.

The politics of the property-owning democracy had come temporarily unstuck. Negative equity became a chilling reality, as a growing number of new owners found themselves with mortgages larger than the falling value of their homes. For many, of course, this could be seen as a short-term phenomenon that the all too familiar inflation of past decades would sort out, provided that is that they kept their jobs and their salaries intact. But many were losing their jobs. Instead of two breadwinners, in a growing number of families there was only one and sometimes not even that. The battle was to persuade the mortgage lenders to hold off on foreclosure and agree more lenient terms. Many did so, at least until the housing recovery gave them a better chance of getting their money back. But not all would and not all could. Some owners faced with monthly instalments beyond their new circumstances simply put the keys in the letterbox and disappeared.

Norman Lamont was not at his best in dealing with the Council of Mortgage Lenders. His low flashpoint was considered not to assist the delicate art of persuasion in which the government was engaged. I was drafted in to smooth the discussions along as I was responsible for housing policy. Slowly the crisis passed, but, with the poll tax on the one hand and negative equity on the other, Labour was not the only party facing a double whammy around that time.

So the council tax replaced the poll tax and, despite the gloomy forebodings of a hostile homeowner reaction in the Tory suburbs, nothing of the sort surfaced. The general election victory in 1992 could never have been achieved without repeal of the poll tax. But that in itself, while a vital part, was not the whole of my agenda.

I wanted to exploit the opportunity provided by the council tax legislation. I had the agreement of my colleagues that we should look at the much broader context of local government in a wide-ranging review. At an informal meeting of senior colleagues in No. 10 in the first few days of John Major's government, I had outlined my idea of making local authorities compete for some part of central government funds, and I was determined to use my time back in the Department to give practical effect to this. In addition, though with some difficulty, my colleagues had accepted that we should look again at the structure and particularly at the management of local authorities. In April 1991 we published two additional consultative documents, alongside that on local government finance – one on the national structure of local government and one on its internal management, including proposals for directly elected mayors.

I was determined to have another go at the structure of local government which we had established back in 1971. I had already changed it significantly in the early 1980s. Originally, there had been two tiers in the metropolitan areas with massive conurbation-wide authorities interspersed between local and central government. I had persuaded the Cabinet to get rid of these conurbation authorities together with the GLC. And in 1988 Norman Tebbit and I had formed an unlikely alliance to pressure the government to dismiss in a similar fashion the Inner London Education Authority by leading a backbench assault on a reluctant government front bench. But I now wished to remove another whole tier of local government, and encourage – as far as I was able – the establishment of unitary authorities.

I was acutely aware of the unpopularity which we had endured during the last major reform of local government some twenty years earlier. The effective way in 1991 to have achieved our objective would have been simply to abolish the districts and transfer their functions straight to the counties. This would then have left the counties in much the same position as the London and metropolitan borough councils, which were already unitary authorities. However, I did not believe there was a ghost of a chance of persuading the parliamentary party to accept a reform which would be fiercely resisted by many of their most active supporters on the district councils. The only viable way forward I could see was to establish a commission with powers to examine the situation area by area and then to make individually tailored proposals. I believed that we might prevail, if the battle to change could be a series of local skirmishes as opposed to a national big bang. I recognised there were weaknesses in this approach, but in practice it was the only measure that stood any chance of getting on to the statute book. My English colleagues could see trouble ahead. They expressed considerable reluctance but I managed to get the legislative authority for it. Ian Lang as Secretary of State in Scotland and David Hunt as Secretary of State for Wales had few Tory councillors to worry about. In Scotland and Wales they took powers to abolish a tier of local government, laid down the new structure by legislation and met little resistance. To this day no one is arguing to bring back the unlamented authorities there.

The legislation for England remains on the statute book. But progress has been slower and more disappointing than I expected. Area after area has fought to preserve the status quo. John Gummer, who took over at the DOE in mid-1993, was left with a dwindling parliamentary majority and a growing series of local rows. In the end, however, a number of cities, such as Nottingham, Southampton, Plymouth and Bristol, have gained control over their own destinies and traditional areas such as Rutland and the Isle of Wight have been restored. (These had been merged, to their deep regret, under our earlier reforms.) By reliable reckoning there were, by the beginning of the new millennium, well over forty 'all-purpose authorities' as well as the London and metropolitan boroughs. But there is still more to be done. One day someone will return to this battleground and, with luck, the legislation I put on the statute books will provide them with all the tools they need.

I was at the same time determined to enhance local enterprise and initiative at the expense of Whitehall and to encourage much more effective local partnership, both within the public sector and in the professional relationships between the public and the private sectors. I was committed not merely to intensifying our attack on urban deprivation but also to rewarding those authorities that brought the most effective dynamism and determination to the task.

There were two essential prongs to the attack. The first was to create effective regional offices and to make them multi-disciplinary as opposed to just a series of individual outposts of some central government departments. The second was to build even further on the distribution of taxpayers' money by competition which I had developed in the Urban Programme some ten years earlier and was now introducing into housing policy as well.

I was lucky in one material respect in the advancement of my plans. Since my earlier experience as Secretary of State in the Department of the Environment a succession of new Cabinet ministers had followed me through the Department, either as junior ministers or as Secretaries of State, and they had experienced for themselves the galvanising effect of allocating funds in the Urban Programme on the basis that, for every pound of public money, additional private cash was added. Treasury ministers, too, had found this augmentation of public expenditure attractive. Self-evidently, this meant that more money was spent in urban areas. More profoundly in the longer term, it made Labour councillors work with the private sector. Relationships of frozen hostility became partnerships, if not friendships.

Against this background of experience, my plans for extending this approach by moving away from specific sites to a much larger concept based on whole deprived communities appealed to colleagues. And they went hand in hand with my proposals, which appeared in our 1992 election manifesto, to merge the regional offices of the Departments of the Environment, of Transport, of Trade and Industry and of Employment into one multi-disciplinary regional office (just as I had originally done in Liverpool). In order to persuade my colleagues – and get their consent to place in a common fund parts of their individual departmental budgets – I was only too happy to agree to share out the lead responsibility in these new regional offices among officials from the contributing departments. The new arrangements came into existence in 1994. I think today that being the head of one of these regional offices is one of the most exciting tasks Whitehall has to offer. The officials concerned responded magnificently to the opportunity to advise, not just about whether a road went here or there or whether this or that environmental scheme was advantageous, but about the needs of the localities in which they were based on a much more strategic and comprehensive basis.

While we were planning the regional offices we were preparing to launch City Challenge. We invited certain local authorities whose areas contained deprived urban populations to submit in competitive bids their plans as to what they would do if central government gave them £35 million over a period of five years. Their schemes would have to cover not just the strategy but detailed proposals for achieving the objectives. Crucially, they had to produce evidence that their ideas were endorsed by the people in the communities concerned and by those, such as the chief constable or the local head teachers, without whose support implementation would be meaningless. We also wanted to know exactly what commitments the private sector would make to add to this flow of public funds.

The results were predictable. The Labour Party reacted with hostility, hurling accusations of gerrymandering, pork barrels, political fixing and all the rest. But one of the charms of local government is that in the end it has a simple understanding of the financial imperative. If councillors perceive an enlightened self-interest on behalf of their community, then they go for it regardless of party politics. Whatever the hullabaloo and the press headlines, if there is some money available, you can be pretty sure that local government won't be far behind. We said that out of the fifteen authorities invited to bid, only ten would win. Ministers would listen to each presentation personally and would determine the winners and losers. It was essential to the success of the scheme, in my view, that the presentations should be in public, with the local press invited to listen as the local councillors submitted their bid. In the event, City Challenge exceeded our highest expectations. Indeed, six authorities not on our original list of fifteen were so attracted by the idea that they submitted plans anyway. In tribute to their enthusiasm and initiative two of the 'rogue' bidders were asked to make presentations to ministers, and I increased the number of winners from ten to eleven. We announced them in July 1991 and at the same time we also declared our intention to launch a second round in which all fifty-seven Urban Programme authorities would be invited to bid.

Many imaginative schemes were inspired by the City Challenge competition. Perhaps the most striking was the redevelopment of the Hulme estate in Manchester, a sprawling concrete jungle just a mile from the city centre. Once notorious for its rundown estates, high levels of unemployment and crime, it has been transformed by a dynamic partnership between the public authorities and the private sector, led and inspired by Sir Alan Cockshaw, chairman of AMEC. I myself judged the Birmingham bid in the first round. It was presented by the then leader of the council, Dick Knowles, an entertaining old Labour war-horse who treated me to a monologue on their plans to tackle crime. When he had finished, I asked him one simple question: 'What does the Chief Constable think?' The Chief Constable hadn't been consulted. Birmingham lost – but not on the second round.

There was little downside to City Challenge – the ritualistic reaction of the losers received short shrift from their local papers. Much the most encouraging sign was their determination that next year they would be winners. More to the point, they received guidance from the Department on how to improve their bids and resubmit for round two. They looked hard at what they had got wrong and at what the winners had got right, and this trading up of quality gave the second round an added thrust. And making one authority compete with another had the result of drawing the public and private sectors into the most effective working arrangements that had been seen in modern times. It made the departments within local authorities work together for strategies that were born essentially of local circumstances and needs, and it refocused the minds of local officials on what they had to do in their areas of responsibility to improve standards, which they were expected to spell out and quantify in advance. And under City Challenge no bid was credible if the local people themselves had not been involved in its preparation. It was a culture shift, as it had been deliberately designed to be.

On my return to Marsham Street in 1990 I found myself again responsible for the London Docklands Development Corporation. In 1986, Paul Reichmann, who had achieved spectacular property deals in Canada and America through his company Olympia and York, had turned his attention to London. A deeply conservative and orthodox Jew, he spoke so quietly that it was always something of a strain to hear what he was saying. He was infinitely courteous and in all my dealings with him displayed a patience which was exemplary. He had approached the LDDC with a proposal to build Canary Wharf, a development on a scale without modern precedent. Perhaps the Grosvenors' Belgravia 200 years before had displayed a similar vision and boldness. Paul foresaw the need for the giant trading floors of the financial world, now consolidating and centralising on London, and realised that soon there would no longer be sites in London sufficiently commanding to interest these enormously profitable companies. He wanted to build a scheme of high architectural quality and on a scale commensurate with his vision. He was undoubtedly attracted by the financial incentives created by Geoffrey Howe's Enterprise Zone.

He was made welcome and, as part of the deal to attract him, the government agreed to extend the London public transport system – ultimately by way of the Jubilee Line and in the interim by the Docklands Light Railway (DLR) – out to this part of East London. For Paul the two projects went hand in hand; Canary Wharf without effective lines of communication would, as a concept, be dead in the water. It was not so dramatic the other way. There would still have been a demand for the Jubilee Line, although it was never scheduled to show an economic return. But the coming of Canary Wharf would be a major shot in the arm for its potential revenues.

Shortly after I returned to the DOE Paul Reichmann asked to see me. His message was simple. He had committed astronomic sums of money to make Canary Wharf the success it undoubtedly could be. But he had done so on the basis that the government would deliver the transport. He was now faced with an economic recession as deep as anything we had seen since the war, the DLR wasn't working and there was no prospect of the Underground line being completed anything like to schedule. I had great sympathy. If this had been the private sector, it would have ended in court and the failure to deliver the Jubilee Line would have been difficult to defend. But the public sector has an indifference all its own. Canary Wharf was now going into receivership. I believed that to a large extent this was the government's fault. How could one let office space in buildings, however prestigious, if people couldn't get there?

I was determined we should deliver on our promises. First, we had to wrest control of the DLR project away from London Transport, which was done almost over the dead body of its chairman. In the event John Major announced the change of ownership in his speech to the Lord Mayor's Banquet in November 1991, and Peter Levene was brought in immediately in order to ensure viable delivery of the link. Michael Portillo and I rode out on the DLR with Peter the next day to take over and install him as chairman. We were accompanied by the press and, indeed, my press office had advised against the journey, in case the train broke down. It used to do so regularly – but on this occasion it didn't.

This was to be one of my first encounters with the management of London Underground. I learnt that their capacity to deliver projects on time and in working order was severely limited. This experience was to stand me in good stead and helped me eventually to persuade the Labour government to bring in, first, Peter Levene and then the giant American engineering firm Bechtel when the same old troubles re-emerged with the Jubilee Line extension to the Greenwich Dome site some five or six years later.

A second tenure at the Department of the Environment also gave me the opportunity to catch up with the wider development in London's East End, which I had first initiated in 1979. My vision was to build on the success of the London Docklands Development Corporation by stimulating development out into the East Thames corridor. On the advice of Terry Heiser, I recruited Professor Peter Hall, a left-of-centre but internationally renowned expert on urban planning, as a special adviser to the Department. I was determined to combine the development with high qualities of environmental protection. His personal politics never affected his contribution, and I valued the benefits we gained from the range of his knowledge and his stimulating grasp of the issues. Following his inspiration we invited all the local authorities from both banks of the eastern stretches of the Thames to a meeting in the Department. The idea was to get them to start thinking about working together in a co-ordinated fashion towards the regeneration of their area. We had limited success; some councils were more enthusiastic than others, and they were all determined to preserve their share of the action. But it was a start.

A strategy for East London could not be effectively developed solely within the Department. I maintained a close interest in other departmental policies which might frustrate my ambition to nudge the opportunities forward. Rumours reached me that Malcolm Rifkind, at that time Secretary of State for Transport, was to back a British Rail preference that the Channel Tunnel Rail Link should go south of the Thames into Waterloo. The route had been protected by British Rail for some time, as a consequence of which they had already bought up many of the affected houses along the way. I asked to be invited to the meeting in the Department of Transport at which these plans were unfolded. I argued that this was a wasted opportunity. If we sent the rail link north of the Thames and included a stop at Stratford, it could help to rejuvenate that rundown and poverty-stricken part of East London. And, critically, it would join the Channel Tunnel Rail Link to routes to the Midlands and the North. The Department of Transport and British Rail were horrified at this proposal, but fortunately the world-renowned firm of civil engineers, Ove Arup, had come forward with just such a plan. The matter was ultimately referred for arbitration by the Prime Minister. I was delighted when the arguments that I had advanced for a wider strategy of regeneration coupled with the rail link appealed to him, as they had to me. I announced the decision at the party Conference in 1991.

It had always been my intention that the Urban Development Corporations, which I had invented in 1979, would have a limited life. Their task completed, the land and its development would be transferred back to the local authorities from which they had originally been removed. There were still serious areas of dereliction crying out for such treatment. But I was now able to conduct another crusade, long part of my agenda.

UDCs are designed to relate to large areas of dereliction, comprised of hundreds if not thousands of acres. By definition they are rigid in that their boundaries are designated and their powers closely defined. In Scotland and Wales development agencies had been introduced by the Labour government back in 1975, with much more general powers that were originally intended for industrial support for ailing businesses but were later transformed into the environment-enhancing and infrastructure-creating agencies which helped transform some of those countries' worst areas. I had long believed that England needed the same flexible approach. The Treasury saw it as another drain down which public money would rapidly flow – and the dread word 'intervention' lurked just under the surface of the political debate.

I wanted an agency able to acquire land and restore it in partnership with the private sector. I was forced – at the insistence of Ken Clarke, who was deeply involved in drafting the manifesto for the 1992 election – to accept that this new agency was to be restricted in its activities to urban areas. Ken was supported in this by Peter Lilley, who as Secretary of State for Trade and Industry was the sponsor of English Estates, an interventionist quango of government that, as its name implies, was able to provide and manage industrial and commercial sites and premises in England. I had failed to persuade Peter to transfer English Estates to the Department of the Environment, which would have made much more sense. Actually, I was pretty relaxed about this refusal on his part because I knew what my colleagues did not – that, all being well, within weeks I would be in charge of the DTI. One of the first decisions I intended to take would be to hand over English Estates to my successor at the DOE, who would be responsible for enacting the legislation to which I had now ensured that we were committed. I judged that, once that transfer had taken place, the scope of the proposed legislation would have to be widened in order to allow the new agency to operate in rural areas as well. With, I hope, not too knowing a smile on my face I therefore accepted my colleagues' restraints, confident that their lifespan would prove limited. Events were to unfold in exactly that way. English Partnerships was established, able to act anywhere throughout England – just as the Scottish and Welsh equivalents had with such success for eighteen years – although the Blair government later divided it up into regional bodies.

My predecessor, Chris Patten, had been an outstanding Environment Secretary. I inherited from him David Trippier as my third Minister of State. They had worked together on the environmental responsibilities of the Department. David, as Deputy Chairman of the party, had boldly supported me in the leadership election and his infectious enthusiasm for his work made friends for us wherever he went, including the numerous overseas tours he undertook on my behalf. Together Chris and David had produced a White Paper, *This Common Inheritance*, comprehensive and detailed, outlining the range of the government's environmental policy. I decided to build on this by turning it into a regular event, equivalent to an annual report in the private sector. The effect of this would be to set targets and to report systematically against them. It also had the virtue of dragooning Whitehall at large into a collective approach to green issues by adding each department's policies to the collective ambition. Our first-year report detailed over 400 measures already taken towards the White Paper's goals and listed over 400 commitments to further action. It was to be followed by two more reports issued successively by the next two Secretaries of State at the Department, Michael Howard and John Gummer. The whole exercise was designed as an example of open government and to keep Whitehall, ministers and officials up to the mark. Indeed, it was joined-up government in practice – long before New Labour coined the phrase. Later I was to use the same technique with the competitiveness agenda in the Department of Trade and Industry.

Tom Burke's influence in helping me to achieve our environmental objectives can be easily detected in the Shell Lecture which I delivered at the Royal Society for the Arts (RSA) on 7 May 1991 under the title, 'The Environment Business'. It set out the context: how over the past decade the nature of public concern had changed. In the early 1980s the public had expected those in authority to protect the environment. By the beginning of the 1990s they wanted to play more of a role themselves. The green consumer, eco-labelling, green politics, green auditing and green investors had all emerged, alongside a significant increase in the size and influence of green quangos.

It was clear to me that, where once policy initiatives had been largely reactive, this had given way to an increased emphasis on prevention. The precautionary principle and the concept that the polluter should pay now underlay our approach. Particularly welcome was the changing attitude of and towards industry. I believed that it was now generally recognised that partnership held more promise than confrontation. Leading companies cared for their reputation and were often managed by people with a deep concern for the quality of life that affected them and their workforce as much as everyone else. There were also huge opportunities developing for environmentally friendly products on the one hand and for companies which cleared past dereliction on the other. I wanted British industry to be in on the ground floor of both.

Sir Crispin Tickell, recently retired as our ambassador to the United Nations and the driving force behind John Major's policy initiative on sustainable development a couple of years later, made a well-remarked speech at about this time in which he said: 'People have become rich making a mess over the last two hundred years. In my judgement, they could become richer clearing it up over the next two hundred.' In my own, rather more prosaic language I had reminded my audience at the RSA of the Victorian adage: 'Where there's muck, there's brass.'

I was convinced that industry would respond to a closer working relationship. The government already had in place policies for Integrated Pollution Control and Environmental Impact Assessments, to tackle some of the most damaging effects of industry on the environment, and in the latter case we were committed to extending their scope. It now made sense for us to work together to meet the environmental challenges ahead. Peter Lilley, as Secretary of State for Trade and Industry, and I had already announced in April the establishment of a new Advisory Committee on Business and the Environment (ACBE) and had been delighted to secure the services of John Collins, the chairman of Shell UK, to lead it. In its subsequent reports and recommendations it was to prove a model arrangement for bringing first-hand and first-class practical experience into the policy formation of government.

As Minister for Liverpool I had been horrified at how the Mersey had degraded, effectively, into an open sewer and I had put in place the 'Clean Up the Mersey' campaign. The concept had been a simple one: we would attack from the source to the sea, until the Mersey became an environmental asset attracting industries that needed clean water, residents committed to caring about the quality of life and visitors looking for beaches safe for their families to use. Less than a decade later it was still too early to expect dramatic improvements. (The reader can understand my excitement, however, at the headline in the *Mail on Sunday* on 14 May 2000: 'Across the Mersey by ferry, a dolphin is swimming' – a clear indication of progress.) Responsibility for water quality in general was scattered around Whitehall. The National Rivers Authority controlled our rivers, Her Majesty's Inspectorate of

Pollution had statutory responsibilities for regulating emissions from industry into land, water and air in the policy known as Integrated Pollution Control, while the Minister of Agriculture, Fisheries and Food dealt with coastal protection. What was needed was a unified Environment Agency. Chris Patten had first floated the idea back in 1989. But John Gummer, as Minister of Agriculture, was adamant that no part of his empire was to be severed from his control and in the end it took a prime ministerial intervention to persuade John to go along with the view that colleagues had reached. The Environment Agency was born. Lord (John) De Ramsey became the first chairman after the passage of the Environment Act of 1995. Ironically John Gummer himself was the one to see it through to completion when he became Secretary of State for the Environment in the reshuffle following Norman Lamont's departure from the government in late May 1993. Such is the roulette wheel of politics.

Environmental policy had, of course, by the 1990s moved on to the international stage. The most crucial event in the environmental calendar at this time was the upcoming Rio Earth Summit and with it the need to agree a climate-change convention. The consequences of global warming – the expansion of the world's great deserts, the melting of the polar ice-cap, the rising level of the oceans, famine and population movements – provided the new agenda. Sir Crispin Tickell was forecasting a migration of many millions of people forced from their homes by rising sea levels. An international response to this crisis was sought at Rio, whereby each country would accept targets to limit the damage to the environment to which its economy contributed. John Major was the first leader of a Western power to commit himself to attend the conference. The Americans at the beginning were lukewarm about being represented at the highest level. Our lead exerted pressure on Washington and, when June 1992 arrived, both President Bush and John Major were present. And, indeed, they both signed the Convention on Climate Change. The targets were modest: 'to return emissions of carbon dioxide to 1990 levels by 2000'. Few countries were to achieve even this, though the United Kingdom would.

I continued, of course, with the annual MINIS exercise, which I had first introduced into the Department some ten years earlier. But beyond that I gave much time to considering how effectively to manage a large government department alongside my interest in the management of public bodies more widely. On one occasion I invited a group of senior industrialists to share their experience with me. At a dinner at the Queen Elizabeth II Conference Centre, Allen Sheppard, chairman of Grand Metropolitan, Sir Adrian Cadbury, recently retired as chairman of Cadbury Schweppes and Richard Greenbury, chairman of Marks and Spencers, among others, discussed with me what similarities and differences there were between their world and mine. The similarities proved elusive. The role of the Treasury kept cropping up in the dialogue. At the end Allen summed up their feeling: 'We think our businesses are so different from yours that we cannot offer any insights into the right way to manage government, but none of us can understand why you allow the finance director to run the company.'

I found the heritage side of the Department's responsibilities especially rewarding, and one project in particular. Somerset House is one of the least noticed architectural treasures of London. Largely obscured by the giant plane trees of the Embankment on its south side and hidden behind its arched approach from the Strand to the north, few trespassed into the grandeur of this extraordinary eighteenth-century courtyard with its rectangular, stone-faced elevation enclosing a grand piazza of which any capital city would be proud. I became aware of this masterpiece during my first tenure in the Department of the Environment, where as the Minister responsible for the government estate I presided over the early negotiations to move the Courtauld Institute into the northern block of the building. Built on the site of Protector Somerset's sixteenth-century house and later worked upon at various times by Inigo Jones and John Webb, most of the present structure was built by Sir William Chambers who, from 1776, created the first ever purpose-built government building, and it had originally housed the Navy Office, a miscellany of Revenue offices, the Royal Academy and the Learned Societies. From the first moment that I crossed the threshold, I had a vision that here London could acquire a great cultural centre for public enjoyment. It called out for galleries, collections, exhibitions and, in the right weather, open-air performances and other such activities. Others had had a similar vision, particularly Simon Jenkins when back in the late 1970s he was editor of the *Evening Standard*. Quite independently we had, each in our way, determined to campaign for a change of user and it had been most gratifying when, in June 1990, the transferred art collection of the Courtauld Gallery was officially opened by Queen Elizabeth the Queen Mother to great public acclaim.

This event and my early recollections attracted me back to the subject. One side of the rectangle was not sufficient to meet my aspirations for the building. In modern times this elegant structure was home to the Inland Revenue and various legal departments under the responsibility of the Lord Chancellor's office. I decided to call on the Lord Chancellor, James Mackay, and the Chancellor of the Exchequer, Norman Lamont.

Lord Mackay of Clashfern is, above all, a public figure who gives the lie to those who see politicians as cynical opportunists, only in it for what they can get out of it. The Conservative Lord Chancellor since 1987, he was not only a public servant of the highest integrity but a courtly, polite and gentle man with a twinkle in his eye. He did not immediately accede to my request that his lawyers and their minions should find alternative accommodation, but he promised to consult and consider. He was eventually persuaded and he kept his word, although not without resourceful support from Peter Levene, who three to four years later, while working alongside me in the Cabinet Office, helped to find them a new home.

Norman Lamont similarly gave me the assurance I wanted – that, if other accommodation could be found, the Inland Revenue would move from their historic home. Progress, however, was interminably slow. Eventually in 1997 it was agreed that the whole property would be transferred to a trust in the public sector and I invited my former ministerial colleague, Tim Sainsbury, a distinguished and most generous member of that illustrious and prodigiously generous family, to be its first chairman. But the Inland Revenue fought back (there must have been a moment when I took my eye off the ball) and on the basis that they would pay an annual rent to the trust – it needed income – they negotiated a lease. To this day they are still there, despite heated scenes from time to time following the 1997 general election between myself and the chairman of the Board of the Inland Revenue, Nicholas Montagu.

The work of conversion, however, has proceeded apace. A major advance followed the intervention by Lord (Jacob) Rothschild, who by chance had come across Arthur Gilbert (later to become Sir Arthur), a self-made Jewish East-Ender who had emigrated to the United States and made a fortune in property development in California. He had amassed two quite remarkable collections, one of gold and silver boxes decorated with jewels of bewildering variety and the other of miniature mosaics. His relationship with the intended recipient of his collection, the Los Angeles County Museum, had deteriorated. Jacob saw the opportunity and struck. The south block of Somerset House is, as a result, now the home of the Gilbert Collection, and one of Britain's most successful expatriates knows that the treasures he collected over the years will form a lasting tribute to his generosity to his native land. Anne and I attended the official opening in April 2000 with quiet satisfaction.

The battle is not yet wholly won. I left the job three-quarters done, even though the struggle spanned my time not only at the DOE but at the DTI and as Deputy Prime Minister in the Cabinet Office as well. One day another politician will get the Inland Revenue out.

I have always been proud of the relationship I developed with Liverpool over my years in government. Whatever I may have achieved in the inner cities, it is Liverpool that is most frequently linked with my name. In the event, however, it is probably Manchester with which I have been engaged on more occasions and on more significant projects. Tom King and I had sorted out a way forward for the G-MEX centre there in the early 1980s. And in my second term at the DOE my departmental responsibilities meant that I visited Manchester more than Liverpool. I was in the front line over Manchester's Olympic bid, which, although unsuccessful, saw the building of the new sports arena, the Velodrome and an Olympic-standard swimming pool, all of which undoubtedly helped to secure the Commonwealth Games 2002 for the city. The rebirth of Hulme and the regeneration of the city's centre, including the new concert hall (and, of course, my involvement in its later, comprehensive redevelopment following the IRA bomb in the summer of 1996), were each in its way projects of historic significance and lasting value.

My last public act as Secretary of State for the Environment was a visit to Manchester – on the day the 1992 election was called – to announce that the government was going to allow the building of the new concert hall to go ahead. A photo-call had been arranged at which I was to conduct a section of the Hallé Orchestra. This had seemed a good idea when it was originally suggested to me by my able and experienced chief press officer, David MacDonald, and it only dawned on me at the last moment that I hadn't the foggiest idea how to go about it. Fortunately, Robert Key, a junior minister in my Department and a man of considerable musical ability in his own right, was able to give me a crash course in the basics, although I am certain that whatever musicality the resulting sound contained was due to the professionalism of the orchestra rather than the arm-wavings of its mercifully temporary conductor.

The flight to Manchester that day had been notable for the fact that it contained not only the boxer Henry Cooper and his brother but also the Leader of the Opposition, Neil Kinnock. The only difference was that he had waited in the VIP suite while we sweated it out in the transfer bus along with everyone else. A little foretaste of the style of the election campaign which was about to come?

John Major became Prime Minister in November 1990. Within the constitutional framework he had some eighteen months to go before he had to face an election. In October we had trailed Labour by sixteen points in the polls. The figure halved to eight points in November, reflecting the prospect of a change in the leadership, but with the poll tax seeping like poison through Tory support, inflation running at over 9 per cent and nearly one and three-quarter millions unemployed, John faced a massive task. Seventeen months later on the morning of Friday, 10 April he was returned to office with an overall majority of twenty-one; more people had voted Conservative than the party or any other party had ever previously achieved. The public liked him. He was no platform orator. But it was felt – and he certainly felt it himself – that his fortunes in the election turned when he mounted a soap box in Luton and argued back, detail by detail, against the allegations thrown at him by the hecklers in the crowd. Here he was on his own territory and he exploited it, rightly, for all it was worth.

The campaign itself had been long delayed, the simplest explanation being that there were no grounds for believing that it was winnable at an earlier date, with the possible exception of the immediate aftermath of the Gulf War, but John was reluctant to use that as a springboard for a 'khaki' election. (It has to be said that, had I been elected Tory leader rather than John, in November 1990, I would have wanted to go to the country virtually straight away. It seemed to me that it would have been the best option to unite the party behind me. Mrs Thatcher's supporters would have been less than enthusiastic at the start, but the prospect of a Labour government would have done wonders in curing their initial hesitancy.)

No Prime Minister relishes the prospect of going down to the wire, with all escape routes cut off and the Opposition as certain of the election date as the government itself. The 1992 election campaign was uphill all the way, with a continual flow of adverse opinion polls which reached a nadir when they gave Labour a seven-point lead. On the Wednesday of the penultimate week, Labour overreacted and organised a rally in Sheffield that displayed an exuberant triumphalism that frightened off many voters. Our propaganda campaign lost no opportunity to rub home the familiar and twin threats of tax and interest rate increases – party Chairman Chris Patten's famous 'double whammy'.

No member of the team comes anywhere near the prominence of the Prime Minister in an election campaign. That said, I received more than my fair share of exposure, travelling in the familiar and exhausting routine that I had got to know so well over twenty-five years. My audiences were large and generally well disposed. The preceding winter I had had a less than enthusiastic response at the Conservative Central Council following the departure of Mrs Thatcher and the press had portrayed this as a rebuff. The truth was rather different. I had remembered Central Council meetings as very *piano* affairs. My speech had been ill prepared. I had had no hot lunch – a vital part of my sustenance, as every constituency agent who has ever organised a tour for me will confirm. I had abandoned my original text after the first few pages but completely misjudged the occasion. The nature of the Central Council had changed during my five backbench years. I completely cocked it up.

However, despite some speculation to the contrary, in October 1991 my first party Conference speech after my return to government had seen my reputation with the wider membership of the party restored to its former status. I had known better than to take my audience for granted that time. I had fun with Labour's emblem of a red rose and the well-known song from the Lionel Bart musical *Oliver*, 'Who will buy my sweet red roses?' Neil Kinnock was naturally cast as the Artful Dodger, but, perhaps less convincingly, I awarded the role of Fagin to the then Shadow Chancellor John Smith, who, in the light of his tax plans, I even had singing: 'You gotta pick a pocket or two.' The speech anyway went down well enough with the Conference audience and I recycled it at a rally in Battersea during the election campaign itself.

When, during the campaign, the tide began to turn in our favour, I am not sure all of us realised it: the national polls continued to be discouraging and it was the reports flooding in from the thousands of party workers – the canvassers on the doorsteps – that gave the first hint that things were beginning to come our way. My anxiety all along had been the sluggish state of the economy and the consequent absence in this election of the 'feel-good factor'.

On our side we had, of course, the fear factor – fear of change, of the unknown. Indeed, perhaps not the unknown. Real and vivid memories of Labour in power were legion. Although he is credited with initiating the reforming journey to new Labour that John Smith and Tony Blair were to conclude, Neil Kinnock personally looked and sounded the old familiar brand: truly a Welsh Valleys boyo, with plenty of form stretching deep into his past. Neil Kinnock negotiating with Chancellor Kohl, working closely with President Bush, speaking up for Britain's defence interests? No, it was not credible. He had too much baggage: too much wind and not enough sail to take advantage of it.

All too credible, on the other hand, was Chris Patten's brilliant 'double whammy'. Aimed at the jugular of the Shadow Chancellor, John Smith, the country was told with increasing vehemence that both taxes and prices were sure to rise under Labour. Sadly for him, but joyfully for us, John Smith played into our hands by calculating incorrectly the effect of his policies on national insurance. The press were persuaded that this tax for higher earners would certainly rise.

Labour also saw their attack on our handling of the NHS in the so-called 'war of Jennifer's ear' turn decisively against them after what had seemed at first a serious breakthrough. When they first released the story, the public were treated to allegations of scandalous irresponsibility in the medical treatment meted out to a young girl from Kent. But it deteriorated rapidly into a family brawl with the child's father saying one thing and her mother and grandfather – who both turned out to be lifelong Tory supporters and in the grandfather's case thrice Tory mayor of Faversham – quite another. The precise effect of all these headlines upon the voters is impossible to calculate. Suffice it to say that we were materially helped throughout the campaign by the Labour Party themselves.

I spoke across the country during the campaign, including at a well-attended meeting for Chris Patten in Bath. That occasion was followed by a sad but unforgettable dinner with my friend the distinguished columnist Peter Jenkins and his wife Polly Toynbee, when Peter explained to Anne and myself something of the lung condition that afflicted him and which within three months was to lead to his untimely death. (I was very touched to be invited by

Polly to give an address at his memorial service in St Margaret's, Westminster, the following October.)

I always spend polling day in my constituency, which during recent elections had seen relatively little of its Conservative candidate in person during the rest of the campaign. But frequent appearances, as part of the national campaign, on radio, television and in the press meant that I was not entirely out of sight to the voters in the Henley division. My home base was held secure by a long-time member of the voluntary party, Maggie Pullen, who during the election acted as the agent for Henley. She was a former vice-chairman and chairman of my Association, and was to become chairman again in the latter half of the 1990s and president in 2000. To each of her innumerable roles she has devoted herself with exceptional energy and enthusiasm.

On polling day our programme is invariably the same. Anne sets off in one direction to tour our committee rooms, where volunteers monitor activity at the nearby polling stations, at the doors of which yet more volunteers collect details of the actual voters. I set off as well, but in the reverse direction. This allows us to coincide midway for lunch together and to compare notes. The evening always drags out a bit. But the tension mounts. On this occasion the exit polls were encouraging. The early indications were for an upset for the pollsters. The last pre-election polls had shown Labour with a wafer-thin lead. Both ITN and the BBC organised their own limited polls in selected constituencies on the day, which indicated a close race. They ignored the nationwide surveys which they had also conducted and which showed a convincing Conservative lead. Even when the early results bore out these more optimistic (from our point of view) national findings, the broadcast media were slow to recognise that we were going to win.

Swings are usually consistent to within a point or two. This enabled Peter Snow to start leaping about with his swingometer within minutes of the first declaration. David Amess held Basildon early on. Eileen, who had accompanied us to my count at the Icknield School in Watlington, said that that was it; we had won. I advised a bit more patience. But so it proved to be.

John had secured an unprecedented fourth consecutive victory for the Conservative Party, albeit with a slim overall majority of twenty-one. He had delivered us another five years in office. The reforms of the 1980s were to continue uninterrupted well into the 1990s. We had the chance to consolidate what had been put in place, to privatise industries previously left untouched and to bequeath to our ultimate successors the most benign economic circumstances of modern times. But John was to get few thanks for his pains – least of all from Europhobe members of our own party in Parliament, some of whose seats he had saved through his own personal exertions.

For the third and last time I left the Department of the Environment. I always left with sadness, but this time there was one unusual feature. I have never heard of another minister being graded for his performance by his permanent secretary. I took with me as I left a progress report which Terry had written in the August of the previous year as he had double-checked back on the envelope which I had presented to him on my first day in 1990.

Of course, the esteem of one's officials, particularly the permanent secretary, is built into the information-gathering process which advances, retards or terminates careers in government. Prime Ministers need to know who can deliver and who can't, and many channels of information are available to them. Personal observation, the judgement of colleagues, the flavour of the press, the siftings of the whips are all weighed in the balance. As sophisticated a college as the top mandarins of Whitehall have long since learnt how, after a deprecating cough, to feed the view of officials into the process. But it is one thing to pass on an oral opinion behind the back; it is quite another to hand over personally a written score sheet. I laughed at the effrontery of it, although secretly I was touched by the strength of the relationship which made it possible.

For my work in replacing the poll tax I earned A+ and the same accolade was accorded to the advisers I had brought into the Department. I was given an E for being in charge when my previous private secretary, David Edmonds, left to become chief executive of the Housing Corporation, although what I was supposed to do to deter an official seeking to enhance his career outside the Department I still don't know. Our local government reforms, paving the way for unitary authorities and the introduction of competitive bidding for funds joined the Housing Action Trusts as worthy of alpha grades. At the other end of the scale I scored only gamma/delta over land release and the privatisation of the Property Services Agency. (I might have scored better here if the report had been written six months later at the end of my stay, by which time what was left of the PSA was privatised.) Elsewhere, a scattering of beta performances led to the overall performance assessment:

> Michael Heseltine performed with his usual will and energy. Probably took on too much; on the other hand, he may in practice have achieved more than he would have done if he had set out more cautiously to do less. Once again, inspired his civil servants to follow him towards the sunlit uplands, which however for some were obscured by the dust and smoke of battle.

I was awarded the overall mark of B+/A–. Charmingly, his assessment of me was followed by an assessment of himself: 'Terry Heiser did his best to keep his Secretary of State in sight – but had to run hard.' He awarded himself only gamma+. That was certainly a ludicrous underestimation.

With the election over, I was, I believed, leaving the Department in Marsham Street for the last time. I also believed that everyone else would shortly be leaving it as well. Renowned for their awful appearance (although the recipient of an award when first constructed), the three towers were, by the 1990s, showing serious signs of premature ageing. Green netting had had to be draped around the parapets to prevent masonry falling on pedestrians far below. We had had to bring in technicians who abseiled all over the buildings to check for signs of decay. I was advised that any long-term repair costs were likely to be prohibitive. There were no friends inside or outside of the towers and I had little difficulty and much support for the proposition that they should come down. I secured agreement from my colleagues, including the Treasury. I held a press conference on the terrace of the north tower in February 1992 and managed to enthral a passing crocodile of schoolboys with the prospect of a very big bang in the near future.

The only piece of the jigsaw missing was a suitable building to which to move. The atmosphere of favourable approval for my idea changed dramatically when it became known that I was talking about a most attractive offer from Peter Levene to locate the Department at Canary Wharf – at, I think, £13 per foot. Terry Heiser manfully held the line as colleagues, not just in his Department but more widely across Whitehall, discovered the risk that a substantial part of officialdom could be moved to Docklands. Every minister, every official could find, and did find, common cause against so obvious a threat of banishment into outer darkness. Terry alone argued that the DOE should go. But official resistance was determined. There was little difficulty in persuading Michael Howard, my successor after the election, to look elsewhere. His successor in turn, John Gummer, devoted much effort to preparing a masterplan for the site but, although the Department has now moved (though no further away than Victoria Street in Westminster), a decade and more after I secured agreement for its demolition, 'Marsham Towers' was still standing. I frequently wondered over the years whether it wouldn't fall down before the government ever got around to giving the go-ahead to knock it down.

Chapter 18

THE COMPETITIVENESS AGENDA

M y experience in business and politics provided the background to my ambition to be Secretary of State for Trade and Industry. I not only wanted the job, I wanted to hold it long enough to change the culture of the Department and possibly of a wider constituency as well.

Occasionally, a Cabinet minister with an entrepreneurial background has held the Trade and Industry post – Peter Walker and David Young are examples, but there aren't many. The DTI for the majority of incumbents is just another job and not a very important one at that. It has been treated as little more than a staging post to higher things, if the luck held. Sometimes, of course, the luck did not hold. In the twenty years between 1979 and 1999 there were seventeen incumbents, allowing for the years at the beginning of the period when the trade and industry portfolios had each had a separate Cabinet minister. Some were there only for the briefest of times; Cecil Parkinson, Leon Brittan and Peter Mandelson were all in the post for less than five months. I stayed for three of those twenty years, from 1992 to 1995, and thus set a record.

The government had had a strategy in the 1980s to raise Britain's national performance by returning the commanding heights of the economy – many of which Attlee had nationalised after the war – to the private sector; by bringing the trade unions within the rule of law; by cutting taxes; by reducing bureaucracy; by improving the workings of markets through deregulation and competition policy; and by controlling inflation. This was a critically important programme, and no one was more committed to the strategy than I was, but a moment's reflection reveals that, although the DTI had had an

415

important role to play – particularly in the privatisation of British Steel and the deregulation of the telecommunications industry – it was not in the driving seat. Instead the Treasury was central, although other departments such as Employment, Energy, Defence, Agriculture, Health and the territorial departments all sponsored or otherwise influenced significant industries.

I had differed from the orthodox Conservative thinking of the 1980s in that I didn't believe that even so ambitious an agenda as this was enough. Of course I was for it, but I knew that in the international growth tables at that time Britain was not being overtaken so much by the lean, low-tax, low-cost Asian economies – the so-called Asian Tigers. The economies of equivalent size that were really winning in world markets and growing faster over the years than Britain were the high-taxed, high-wage-cost, public-sector-partnering economies of western Europe, which had achieved their improved living standards and paid for their growing social costs by rising productivity and an obsession with quality. I believed that national economic success required, therefore, a broader agenda, embracing education, training, standards, design, marketing and a constructive relationship between public and private sector. No one should – although many did – construe this as a soft touch. The competition policy Peter Levene and I drove through the Ministry of Defence had saved the defence budget millions of pounds. But, even so, this was an unpalatable message. It struck at the heart of Treasury hostility to any attempt at such a dialogue with industry. It was inconsistent with the proprietor-led ethos of our larger-circulation newspapers. It sat uncomfortably with the simplistic agenda of tearing up forms, getting off businessmen's backs, cutting taxes and promoting competition and free trade which was the cure-all agenda so often to be found in political speeches.

There was something missing. It was this gap that I sought to fill with a comprehensive competitiveness agenda. I knew how long it would take to introduce a culture change of this sort. That was why I wanted to remain in post long enough to achieve my purpose. In the three years from 1992 we virtually completed the privatisation programme, leaving only the Royal Mail as a significant mountain yet to climb – and that was not for want of trying. While strongly supporting the macroeconomic policies that John Major, Norman Lamont and Ken Clarke were following, however, I also set out to turn the spotlight on microeconomic issues by addressing the supply side of the economy and its weaknesses. Industrial and commercial success was not the product of a few important, headline-grabbing policies. Success in the real world needed attention to detail in every aspect. In too much of Britain's public and private sector performance this was lacking. There was too little understanding of just how far down the international league the country had slipped. It seemed to me that part of the challenge to change direction was to explain frankly what had happened. If businesses were to seek solutions, they had first to understand the problems. In the event the pursuit of our objectives was to take four clear directions: the competitiveness agenda, embracing public and private sectors; a positive approach to sponsorship; a sharper export support service; and a massive reorganisation of the services that support small businesses.

No minister enjoys a clear run to pursue his policy objectives. When Harold Macmillan said that the greatest difficulty for any politician lay in 'Events, dear boy, events,' he was stating a fact of life. During my tenure at the DTI events came thick and fast: the coal crisis, Matrix Churchill, the Pergau Dam affair, the collapse of Lloyd's, the receivership of Leyland Daf and the rising tide of sleaze, much of it directly concerned with my areas of responsibility. Collectively, as a government, we had to face the trauma and tragedy following the disintegration of Yugoslavia and the outbreak of civil war which ensued. Both the military and the humanitarian issues were highly complex and there were some very difficult decisions to be taken. But I am in no doubt that Britain made a critical contribution to the international peace-keeping force and also in our response to the refugee crisis. Then in the middle of my time in the Department there occurred what for me and my family was the most worrying event of them all: my heart attack.

To add to all this, John Major's majority slowly ebbed away, while the Eurosceptic forces remorselessly undermined his public credibility – highlighted by the crisis of the Maastricht Treaty to give effect to European proposals to extend the social contract and introduce a single currency (to both of which John had brilliantly negotiated an opt-out) and catastrophically by the ERM débâcle. My own prospects were a constant topic of speculation, as John's hold on the premiership was threatened by a combination of Fleet Street editors, political critics and opinion polls reflecting dwindling support for the party. But let me begin at the beginning.

John Major's victory in 1992 was not only great news for the party, it was a resounding triumph for him personally. Sadly, however, Chris

Patten lost his seat at Bath. His responsibilities as party Chairman in Smith Square had placed him at considerable disadvantage in fighting his own constituency, where the Liberals, who had been stalking the seat for years, threw everything into the contest. Chris lost by 3,768 votes. One of the more shaming episodes of election night was the way in which his result was cheered as a 'Tory gain' at one of the private celebration parties, attended by Margaret Thatcher, held within a hundred yards of Central Office.

The loss of so formidable a figure – he would have become Chancellor in place of Norman Lamont had he survived – was bad enough. I was dismayed to discover that, after Chris's defeat, John Major had straight away virtually agreed with him that he should go to Hong Kong as Britain's last Governor. I tried to intervene, but the die seemed already cast. I expressed strong reservations to Chris and even came up with the suggestion that he should join the government as one of a new class of life peers appointed to sit for one Parliament only, at the end of which they should have the opportunity to stand for the Commons again. This would have enabled him to hold a place in the government without prejudicing his future career. But it was all to no avail; his mind was made up and he was determined to go. Chris's departure, not just from Parliament but from the domestic political scene, was (to borrow his own phrase) a 'double whammy' which the Conservative Party could ill afford.

So far as my own position was concerned, when I saw the Prime Minister in No. 10 on the Saturday after the election, I reminded him of the agreement we had reached in 1990 about the Department of Trade and Industry. John had forgotten the conversation, but no matter. He was content. In justification of the proposed pecking order for the new Cabinet, in which figures such as Ken Clarke (Home Secretary), Norman Lamont (Chancellor) and Douglas Hurd (Foreign Secretary) all appeared above me, he quite reasonably pointed out that back in 1990 I had already made it clear that I was not interested in the Home Office. My interest was to raise the profile and relevance of the DTI as a great office of state. So I asked if I could not go under the name – as my predecessors all had done until 1970 – of President of the Board of Trade, an historic title reaching back to 1786, when Lord Hawkesbury (later the Earl of Liverpool) first took the office. John was amused and saw no objection. I knew the change of title (with its suggestion of transatlantic delusions of grandeur) would send journalists into orbit and that a good deal of merriment would be had at my expense. I thought that would be rather fun, adding a bit of spice to the routine of politics. A fresh name for its political head would refocus attention on the Department. In that cause I was prepared to risk any number of jeers.

'What is our strategy?' was one of the first questions I asked my civil servants at my new headquarters in Ashdown House, near Westminster Cathedral in Victoria Street. 'We're not allowed to use that word, President,' came the shattering reply. I suppose I could have consoled myself with the reflection that, given the rapidity with which my predecessors had come and gone, it would have made scant difference even if the DTI civil servants had possessed a strategy, since between one occupant and the next they would hardly have had time to implement it. I was clear that I was there to help British companies win. And by British company I meant any company operating in the United Kingdom. One of my aims was to mould the Department so that it provided the best back-up for those companies that could be devised. Our comprehensive agenda would be set out in a new competitiveness White Paper, while we pushed ever more fiercely forward with the existing policies of privatisation and deregulation.

I had spent thirteen years in major government departments. I knew that in practice, whatever they may say, ministers are involved in decisions affecting the climate and circumstances in which companies operate every day of every year. As purchaser, regulator, standard-setter, subsidiser, owner, tax-raiser and sometimes as marketeer, the government of Britain and every similar country is in there, taking decisions, consciously or (worse) unconsciously, which profoundly affect the wealth-creating conditions of the nation.

Sadly, I was all too well aware that for a hundred years or more Britain's relative performance had been steadily failing to keep pace with those of competing economies. I believed that there was nothing God-given in such relative decline. It was up to us to analyse the world as it is, and then decide where we could help to achieve improvement and enhance effectiveness. 'You are an interventionist,' came the accusing cry, as though merely uttering that dread word was sufficient deterrent to require no intellectual rationalisation. Indeed, I was and am. How could I be anything else? I had been responsible for the roads programme, for space policies, for the airlines, for the aircraft and ship-ping industries, for the ports infrastructure, for government research programmes directly assisting British companies or the universities upon which many companies depend, for the defence procurement budget, for the housing and construction industries, for the water industry, for the purchasing programmes of local government. Was it seriously suggested that, in the myriad of decisions I took, I never thought about what was good for Britain, for its companies, for its wealth-creating process? Were the countless millions of pounds spent encouraging companies to locate here merely a haphazard scattering of government largesse, divorced from any strategy?

My approach demanded an agenda – a competitiveness agenda. At the beginning I faced much scepticism and a large credibility gap. When I announced my ideas to the industrial correspondents, Roland Gribben, an old Fleet Street hand employed by the *Daily Telegraph*, asked me if I could give him just three headline statements to sum up my proposals. I told him that that was precisely what I wouldn't do. If I had chosen three, and he had reported them fairly and accurately, the net result would have been that his readers believed the problem had nothing to do with them, unless they happened to be directly affected by one of the three chosen headlines. I believed part of my task was to persuade the people that each and every one of them had a role to play in improving Britain's performance. I wanted a culture change across both the public and private sectors, in which millions of people identified their enhanced efforts as a contribution towards Britain's national performance. This was a rather more complicated message than Roland Gribben was prepared to convey to his readers, as his subsequent reporting revealed.

I set up a competitiveness unit under Dr Bob Dobbie in the Department of Trade and Industry, and I invited them to draw up a list of all those factors in both the public and the private sectors that affected our national performance. I told them I intended to publish this data and to report openly on Britain's standing against the rest of the world. The official advice inclined towards a narrowing of the agenda, arguing that twelve factors could cover the ground sufficiently, but I refused. I wanted a wide-ranging, comprehensive survey, although I agreed that twelve factors should be at the heart of our message. I likened the competitiveness agenda to an imposing organ in a cathedral where you can get music by playing on a few of the bigger stops but to achieve great music you have to have all the stops in the right position at the right time. I wanted a strategy that would ensure that a thousand stops were in place – and in the right place. Sir Peter Gregson, the permanent secretary, supported me and played a crucial part in getting officials in the DTI and in other departments to focus on the reasons behind both our competitive successes and, too often, our failures.

We had to change attitudes. We had to replace the traditional (and insular) British and government view that 'we are doing fine' with a realistic appraisal of the nation's strengths, weaknesses and relative performance against others. Over the next five years Bob Dobbie and his team did a magnificent job, with total dedication, developing a creative understanding of a complex subject and skill in the arts of argument and persuasion, often – particularly in the early days – in the face of entrenched resistance. Slowly the concept of national competitiveness became accepted in both the public and private sectors. With a workable definition of GDP per head at purchasing power parities as the most reliable single measure of national competitiveness, productivity became recognised as the test and indicator of our success.

An understanding of the drift and seriousness of our problem was needed as much inside government as outside it. We created in the Competitiveness Division in the DTI a mixed public–private sector team that had credibility in Whitehall and in the wider world. To persuade Whitehall to co-operate in the first Competitiveness White Paper was a serious achievement. The process of writing successive annual White Papers drew together officials throughout government, just as it drew together ministers through the Cabinet committee structure. This network was continued under the Blair administration and many others, including the United States, Canada, Germany, France, the Netherlands, Ireland, Sweden, Japan and Singapore, have undertaken similar exercises. After our first publication, my departmental colleagues and I travelled up and down the country to sell its message to British business – and a wider audience. We were well received.

I needed the DTI's structure to reflect and drive the agenda. Before I could design such a structure, however, I had to know how the DTI was presently organised. It was back to MINIS and organograms. The Department of Trade and the Department of Industry had originally been soldered together by Ted Heath in 1970. It had included the Department of Energy as well but that had been split off into a separate department during the energy crisis in the winter of 1973–4, and the Trade and Industry portfolios were divided again after the general election in 1974. Mrs Thatcher brought these two back together again in 1983 and then in 1992, as I arrived, John Major returned the Department of Energy to the DTI as well. Fortunately for me, Sir Peter Gregson, who had been permanent secretary at Energy, had moved across to become the permanent secretary at the DTI in 1989, thus considerably easing the load.

The Department sponsored a bewildering range of commercial and manufacturing industries. The old DTI industries ranged from the motor industry, with the British companies in a permanent atmosphere of crisis, to small industries such as ceramics, printing, stainless-steel cutlery, electrical components and the like. No resources were devoted to these. The former Department of Energy's industries – coal, gas, electricity, nuclear power – had separate baronies within the re-amalgamated Department, staffed by high-quality civil servants.

As Secretary of State, Nicholas Ridley had forbidden the use of the word 'sponsorship'. I now told the permanent secretary that I wanted to change this approach. We would interest ourselves in the industries we sponsored – and say so. The first task was for officials to understand their sectors. They had to examine what was happening in those industries across the world and understand the competitive forces at work. I instructed that a 'SWOT' analysis – of the strengths, weaknesses, opportunities, threats – be undertaken for each of them. I wanted to know how Britain was performing, where its companies were strong and where weak. In other words, I was asking for a quite different approach from that which had existed before, where civil servants simply reacted to the submissions made to them by the companies themselves. My approach was a seismic shock to the Department, but slowly and with relish I watched attitudes change. For the first time for most DTI civil servants, ministers had set out clear objectives; they knew what we were trying to achieve and that we were determined to go for it.

A new cadre of officials familiarised themselves with specific industries. A high-profile example of how we worked was the help given to British fashion. The Department had provided nominal support to the British Fashion Council, but effectively there had been no serious attempt to back the companies engaged in this creative and publicity-hungry industry. We were asked for more money to augment the contribution that Vidal Sassoon personally provided in addition to sponsoring London Fashion Week. But money alone did not appear to be the problem. A wider commitment was needed. The trick was to find the right person to lead it. Richard Needham suggested Clinton Silver, the newly retired deputy chairman and joint managing director of Marks and Spencer. It was an inspired choice. He knew the industry well and enjoyed its respect. Sights were raised and my officials played their full part in talking up the opportunities. We battled with Paris and Milan for a better slot in the spring and autumn show timetables. I approached the Princess of Wales. She agreed to attend a launch ceremony at Lancaster House. Journalists from all over the world and a new wave of buyers headed for London. London Fashion Week entered into a period of prolonged expansion.

The Department sponsored the insurance industry, while also acting as its regulator. In practice we interpreted our role as essentially one of regulation. There were, however, legitimate grounds for criticism of the performance of the industry. Once perceived as a jewel in the City of London's crown, slowly like so much of Britain's industrial and commercial capability, it was being bought up by overseas companies. I persuaded several of the larger companies to second to the Department young, aspiring managers to analyse what was wrong and how to put it right. The separate cultures of government and industry were brought together. At one memorable evening in Lancaster House a report was produced by this joint team, in many ways very critical of the industry. Indignant chairmen rose to protest at this extraordinary example of ministers condoning the selling short of Britain's expertise. I was able to tell them that it wasn't ministers or officials who were responsible; it was the people they had seconded to me. The relationships of the Department and the industry improved dramatically from then on.

But, if I had had to imagine what Macmillan's 'events' might be in the insurance world, it would have been difficult to devise happenings more dramatic than the threat to the insurance market following the IRA bomb in the City or the collapse of Lloyd's. The pressure on the Department in both instances was considerable.

Late in 1992 a bomb caused large-scale damage to the Baltic Exchange building in the City. In consequence, commercial property owners checked the adequacy of their cover while the insurance industry calculated the potential cost of a sustained IRA bombing campaign in Britain. With great skill officials helped to devise a plan to provide a government back-up guarantee to support the reinsurance industry, which could not as it stood cover the scale of risk involved.

Lloyd's had carefully protected its self-regulatory status at one remove from the DTI, but we were required to approve its balance sheet at the end of every summer. We had to know what was going on, understand the business and monitor the consequences for Lloyd's of huge losses arising particularly from hurricane damage and asbestos claims. The situation became further complicated when it was alleged that Lloyd's had issued misleading information to its members in its projected figures in the early 1980s, when it was said already to have been aware of the seriousness of the asbestos time-bomb. In consequence members were now refusing to pay up.

In 1993 David Rowland was brought in as chairman – from the Sedgwick Group, where he had served first as chief executive and then as chairman – to retrieve the situation. The approval of the Department for any rescue plan was essential, however. It was important for ministers and officials to preserve their independence of judgement, without which their decisions would be open to judicial review. That said, thousands of people faced bankruptcy or, at the least, the loss of a large part of their personal fortune under the unlimited-liability responsibilities that membership of Lloyd's involved. Over the years it had come to be seen as a sure-fire thing and members had grown used to the cheques rolling in, often sustaining a way of life that would have been impossible without them. (I had never joined myself, although friends had often urged me to do so. I was never prepared to risk the unlimited nature of the guarantee required.) In the meantime many serious allegations were current and Britain's national prestige and the reputation of the City were at stake.

Approval of the balance sheet in the summer of 1994 was a close-run thing and there began a series of lengthy meetings in the Department as the process of restructuring progressed. A team of officials led by Jonathan Spencer and his number two, Richard Hobbs, did a tremendous job as the complex negotiations proceeded. There was the ever present possibility that the dissident names would not accept the new deal. When in 1995 I became Deputy Prime Minister I retained my overall responsibilities in this area, as my successor at the DTI, Ian Lang, was himself a Lloyd's name and had, therefore, to rule himself out on the ground that there was a conflict of interest. Anthony Nelson, at that time Minister of State for Trade at the DTI, dealt with the day-to-day management. In the end a rescue scheme was devised whereby the claims were to be quantified and new, corporate members attracted to keep the business going by means of a new company,

Equitas. After seeking legal advice and a little extra accountancy advice, I authorised the new structure. Nearly all the names signed up to it and Lloyd's could begin to rebuild its reputation.

I also looked at the support we were giving to exports. In the Ministry of Defence, some 700 military and civilian employees in the Defence Export Services Organisation support Britain's defence industries in export markets across the world. The defence industries are among the country's most successful exporters. In contrast, in the DTI we had about 100 officials sponsoring a vast range of industries. But here MINIS was at its most effective.

The old Department of Trade, part of my inheritance, was a free-trader's paradise. Here was the high altar of non-intervention. Bring down the barriers to trade, they believed, and all would be well. Officials were organised into regional groupings, dividing the world into neatly ordered packages. So far, so good. But the moment you had the detailed organisation clearly set out on a piece of paper in front of you, it hit you between the eyes that the people responsible for each market place were not only responsible for supporting British exporters; they also sat on innumerable committees, meeting in the capital cities of the world, negotiating every manner of treaty, communiqué and proposal. I did not doubt their energy or ability to fight for Britain's national interest, but it was instantly apparent that this was where they spent much of their time – negotiating in committee. You can't do this and at the same time get out and visit companies or investigate market places.

The effect of this jumble of responsibilities was that the support for exporting companies from the DTI was minimal, although by this time some of the Foreign Office embassies were beginning to raise their game. The answer was obvious. We divided the trade side of the Department into two. Tim Sainsbury retained responsibility for trade policy, including the Uruguay Round of GATT (the wide-ranging international treaty on the rules governing world trade), while Richard Needham became Minister of State for Trade concentrating on international trade and export promotion. Tim directed the officials responsible for the conduct of trade negotiations, for the Trade Councils and their time-consuming agenda. Richard, as well as being the sixth Earl of Kilmorey (he doesn't use this Irish title) and a self-made businessman, had spent seven years as a minister in Northern Ireland helping to rebuild Belfast and the economy of Ulster. He is a natural-born salesman with indefatigable energy and irrepressible enthusiasm. He set up eighty individual country units in the Department, one for each of Britain's principal export markets. Within each unit were the people responsible for helping existing and potential exporters. Some of what they did had plenty of precedents: organising missions, supporting exhibitions, trade shows and conferences and disseminating market information on a wide scale. But we were looking for a much more pro-active role and we needed experienced people.

With so many desks to fill to staff up the trade promotion side of the Department, Peter Gregson was having to look to relatively young and inexperienced officials. I decided to ask our exporting companies to help. It was in one respect a propitious moment. The economy was in difficulties. Downsizing was the order of the day. Tiers of managers were being made redundant. I announced at the party Conference in October 1992 our intention to recruit 100 men and women seconded from the private sector to work alongside civil servants as export promoters. Richard Needham and I wrote to over 200 of Britain's leading companies and asked them to lend us one of their managers for at least twelve months. Their first task would be to put together individual market plans with the support of local embassies and the officials in the DTI. They would then identify particular contracts and opportunities that were available and contact British companies to encourage them to 'go for it'. The experiment became a considerable success. Today there are still at any given time between eighty and a hundred private sector secondees operating as export promoters within the Department. They now come for two years, although some have stayed three, four, even five years. Through their activities, the DTI, the FCO and business are brought together to target commercial opportunities around the world.

The Department was at the time deeply engaged in the Uruguay Round of GATT. Yet the credit for moving Europe towards the successful outcome which was secured in the GATT talks must lie principally with Leon Brittan, the senior British Commissioner in Brussels responsible for negotiating on behalf of the European Community. This was Europe working as it was intended to work. The French, characteristically, were unenthusiastic and often obdurate, but pressure from their Community partners kept them in the game. Within the regimes of the European Union the United Kingdom undoubtedly had an influence in achieving what proved to be a satisfactory conclusion, and Tim travelled to Marrakesh in April 1994 to sign the final treaty on behalf of Her Majesty's Government.

Perhaps the dominant position of the European Commission in negotiating trade matters had, however, dulled the sense of reality within the Department. The theoretical pursuit of the ideal, much encouraged by some of my predecessors, had removed the DTI's gaze from the practical hurdles that we faced. I was amazed at the reaction when, in order to focus upon reality and allow a shaft of light to pierce the shadows of real-world protectionism, I asked the policy division for a list of the protectionist practices of Britain's principal trading partners. This was clearly regarded as being totally off-side. In the end, after repeated attempts, I became so indignant at what was either the refusal or the inability of officials to produce this information that I gave them a fixed time-scale for delivery and told them that, if I did not get what I wanted, I would call for a report from outside consultants. That achieved the necessary result. Inevitably, as I knew would be the case, all of Britain's principal partners, including the United States, had restrictive practices embedded deep in their ethos. It simply hadn't occurred to my officials that, given the responsibility of the European Commission for the negotiations, they would be far better employed rigorously seeking to expose these practices and then, through diplomatic and other channels, bringing pressure to bear to see that they were ended. Tim Sainsbury tells the story of his return late one evening, after a protracted Trade Council session, to the residence of Sir John Kerr, then our ambassador and UK permanent representative to the European Union. There Tim found the Foreign Secretary, Douglas Hurd, enjoying a late-night drink with Sir John. 'How did it go?' Douglas inquired. 'The usual story,' was Tim's reply: 'eleven against one.' Only seconds elapsed before Douglas' response: 'Oh, so the French were isolated, were they?' Bull's eye.

The fourth leg of the strategy was to enhance the support available to thousands of small and medium-sized companies that constitute so much of the nation's wealth-creating capability. Britain's best companies are the equal of anything in the world. Whether they happen to be the large go-getters or the entrepreneurial small, they are to be found in every corner of the global economy, winning orders for themselves and their shareholders to the immense benefit of the national economy. But, again, our analysis showed that the national weakness lay in the tail of under-performers, a tail that was far longer than in the case of other equivalent economies. How could we reach this under-performing majority?

I had long thought that the most sensible way to tackle this deficiency in the British structure was to work through the chambers of commerce. But here we were fighting an uphill battle. With a few conspicuous exceptions, the existing chambers were no match for their better-resourced European counterparts. Most of these latter enjoyed public law status which meant that all companies had to join, and thus pay a subscription to, their local chamber. In this way the private sector on the Continent financed a range of services of a quite different scale and quality to anything available to British companies. Across the great trading centres of the world you would find powerful German or French chambers representing their exporters to an extent Britain could not begin to match. In most of those markets, particularly German and often French exports easily surpassed the UK performance.

In the early 1980s I had argued that our plans to provide a new training service should be organised through the chambers, thus enabling them to recruit people of a quality that would raise standards, not just in training but in a range of services beneficial to Britain's companies. I lost the argument in Cabinet. A strengthened Manpower Services Commission (MSC) was set up, headed at the start of his public career by Mrs Thatcher's 'problem-solving' discovery, David Young.

Nothing lasts for long in the public sector, however. By the late 1980s, when I was on the back benches, the government reviewed its child's progress. The MSC was seen as too statist and bureaucratic. 'We must bring in the private sector' was the cry. The Training and Enterprise Councils (TECs) were born out of the MSC, and brought in a quality of private sector support and management that had hitherto been absent. Once the TECs were in existence, however, we had two local organisations competing for the attention of local companies, as there was no co-ordination with the chambers. This overlapping and confusing pattern did not stop there. Indeed, in the early 1980s, I had myself played a role in creating a third – the growing network of enterprise agencies. In many cases, local authorities had also moved into the field of providing advisory services and support for small companies, as had the DTI itself, and there were numerous services funded by various European Community programmes. To make matters worse, some of the TECs were about to move into the business of recruiting individual members, thus intensifying the rivalry with the chambers.

The argument had come full circle. The question I faced was simple: how did we create a single, effective support service for British companies? It was quite apparent that two things were needed. First, the TECs and chambers needed to come together to create a one-stop shop for small businesses and, secondly, the quality of the support service available to businesses up and down the country had to be greatly improved. By good fortune, responsibility for small firms had been transferred from the Employment Department to the DTI and we inherited a budget of some £30 million a year earmarked for this purpose. In addition, we had £60 million from the DTI's consultancy support schemes. Here was the glue with which to stick together a new, properly organised and unified back-up organisation. Business Link was born.

We now had to persuade as many as possible of the local players – the TECs, the chambers, the local authorities and the enterprise agencies – to co-locate and provide a centrally managed service. We offered to include certain of the Department's regional and export services through this same local network. From the start we received powerful support from the national umbrella organisations representing their local offspring. We used the £90 million budget available to offer financial help to provide business advisers, export consultants, IT specialists and – by breaking up the old London-based Design Council service – design engineers. A key innovation was the introduction of Personal Business Advisers, a 'general practitioner' service to help small firms identify what assistance they needed and then to ensure that they got a tailored package of specialist support to address their individual needs. Under the energetic leadership, significantly, of David Grayson from Business in the Community – which I had been instrumental in creating twelve years before – and Jim Reid, an official seconded to the DTI from the Employment Department, the task of persuasion began throughout England.

We set the ambitious target of opening within two years 200 Business Links, covering the whole of England and based in all the main centres of population. With one exception, we achieved that target. From the outset we made certain that the brand was carefully controlled to ensure an acceptable level of service and co-location before its award. We insisted that all the proposals were scrutinised by a national Assessment Panel, involving all the relevant national agencies, but also including experienced business people. If the proposal wasn't good enough, it didn't get through – no matter how hard the lobbying from vested interests – and some had to come back three or even four times before they learnt that lesson.

Undoubtedly there was always going to be room for improvement. Results varied depending particularly on the quality of the individual Business Advisers. Benefits flowed more clearly where the old rivalries, largely fuelled by more backward chambers, were forgotten. Despite the clearest instructions to the contrary, IT compatibility throughout the system was less than it should have been.

Incidentally, this illustrated a common problem. We were constantly criticised for too prescriptive and centralised an approach. But often, the moment we relaxed the broad standards we had set, local standards, far from showing the initiative about which we were so frequently told, simply relapsed to the levels we had sought to replace. Too many people were too ready to accept a 'first-stop shop' approach, seeing Business Links as mere signposting agencies which left the status quo unchanged, rather than taking up the more daunting challenge of creating the consumer-focused and co-located one-stop shop which was what small businesses wanted and we were determined they should have.

The overall response was impressive, however, and we made much progress. Before I left the DTI in the early summer of 1995 – during the course of just one year of full operation – the number of inquiries received by the network of Business Links each week had risen from an initial 1,000 to 3,000. The demand was clearly there; by the end of the decade inquiries were running at 8,000 a week – some 400,000 a year. In the second quarter of 1999–2000 one in four of all companies employing between 10 and 200 people used Business Links, an increase of 18 per cent over the corresponding period a year earlier.

The quality of the service has steadily improved. We created a robust system which to this day has kept pace with technological changes and rapidly developing means of communication quite beyond our perspective in the early 1990s. The mergers have continued, although the Blair government decided to abolish the TECs and establish Learning and Skills Councils instead. And they may have changed the name, but New Labour's Small Business Service is very much Business Links as we created them, so much so that Business Links will continue to be the brand under which the services of the new Small Business Service will be promoted.

In my three years there a very different DTI was created, with strategic direction, a sense of purpose and a commitment to quality. We were there to serve the best interests of Britain's companies. Yes, we *were* interventionist. So why be mealy-mouthed about it? At the party Conference of October 1992 I decided that I would risk a small joke at the expense of the theoreticians within my own party. There was no room for compromise. I crafted words which were to echo around the political debate, just as I had intended they should: 'If I have to intervene to help British companies, like the French government helps French companies, or the German government helps German companies, or the Japanese government helps Japanese companies, then I tell you I'll intervene before breakfast, before lunch, before tea and before dinner. And I'll get up the next morning and I'll start all over again.' The conference cheered the sentiment to the rafters.

It also did something for morale. For that Brighton party Conference followed almost immediately on the heels of 'Black Wednesday' – 16 September – when the government had been forced to pull out of the European Exchange Rate Mechanism (ERM), and spirits were distinctly low. I had been summoned on Black Wednesday, along with Douglas Hurd, Ken Clarke and the Chief Whip, Richard Ryder, to join the Prime Minister and the Chancellor, Norman Lamont, at the first of two crisis meetings held that day. I have no doubt that one reason for the presence of the Foreign Secretary, the Home Secretary and the President of the Board of Trade was that we should all – in Ken Clarke's vivid phrase – 'dip our hands in the blood'. Certainly, I had had no briefing on the purpose of that first emergency meeting, held just after 1 p.m. at No. 10, and had not realised until I arrived just how serious the crisis for the pound was. John Major and Norman Lamont were under the most intense pressure; for me there had been no such build-up.

Norman presented the background and set out what he thought to be the options facing us. If he had said firmly that in his view there was no choice and that he could not accept responsibility as Chancellor for anything other than an immediate decision to withdraw from the ERM, I (and the others) could not have resisted. But that is not the way the situation was put to us. What we were presented with were alternatives. I was well aware that in the early days of the ERM the French had twice realigned within the rules. Norman himself later told me that he would have considered taking such a route if the French had been prepared to join us. But they weren't – and to do it by ourselves would inevitably have been presented as a devaluation. He regarded that as unthinkable.

At that tense lunchtime meeting I therefore opted – along with Ken and Douglas – for the 'tough it out' approach. This involved dramatic but, as it turned out, quite ineffective hikes in interest rates. It was nevertheless the preferred option that everyone present had agreed. We believed it important to show to our European partners that we had exhausted every alternative remedy before unilaterally suspending our membership of the ERM. We met again, this time at 5.00 p.m. in Admiralty House, then used in tandem with No. 10, which was under repair following the IRA mortar attack. It was clear that our effort to defend the pound against the speculators had failed. We agreed to Norman's recommendation that we should leave the ERM forthwith. Norman – inevitably in a somewhat battered state – made the announcement from the inner courtyard of the Treasury (the first time, as he ruefully remarks in his memoirs, that an important policy announcement had ever been made from such a location). The effect on the public of this sudden economic policy U-turn was catastrophic – indeed, it has been argued that the Major government was electorally doomed from then on. The Eurosceptic wing of the party and their allies in Fleet Street derived a massive uplift in confidence which underpinned the civil war into which they were plunging the Conservatives with increasing bitterness.

We tried, of course, to rally the troops. The 1992 party Conference started on a pretty low note, but, despite the divisively destructive efforts of Margaret Thatcher in a newspaper article and Norman Tebbit on the conference floor (both fulminating against the Maastricht Treaty), things had cheered up a bit by the end. In his winding-up speech John Major succeeded in raising the spirits of the party faithful by aiming a positive injunction to declare war on red tape at me, Tarzan. 'Come on, Michael,' he cried. 'Out with your club. On with your loincloth. Swing into action.' It was a popular line. All of us warm to the anticipation of a cool breeze of freedom as hapless civil servants and local government officials lose their ability to frustrate, impede, deny, obfuscate and generally grit up the works. Would that real life was so simple. Regulations, after all, are there because ministers put them there. Government's response to food scares, safety concerns, planning controversies, environmental degradation, water pollution, fraud, exploitation, City scandals, consumer rip-offs, tragic accidents – in summary, the edifice of a civilised society – is built on regulation.

The political option is more modest than the grabbing headlines devised by ingenious sub-editors. I knew it. I was not about to expose the government to the devastating charge of a cavalier approach to the health and safety of the nation.

But, that said, there are always regulations that have outlived their purpose and others that are over-zealous in their scope and inflexibility. I decided that the best way forward was to employ poachers as gamekeepers – to put those who had complained most vociferously about the burden of red tape in charge of the deregulation exercise. I invited Lord Sainsbury of Preston Candover, the recently retired chief executive of his family grocery business, to lead a task force and recruit members widely from the private sector. He did so with great enthusiasm and no little success. Pub-opening times were extended, building societies were given more freedom to compete with banks and hundreds of other changes followed across every department, each of which had their own minister in charge of tackling red tape. I asked Neil Hamilton, my Parliamentary Under-Secretary for Consumer and Corporate Affairs in the DTI, to assume political responsibility, a role which he performed with relish. It led to his greatest political triumph, which came when he received a rapturous ovation for his speech at the party Conference the following year as he energetically ripped great piles of paper forms into shreds. It also led us to an embarrassing rebuff during the passage of the massive Deregulation and Contracting-Out Bill through Parliament, when Tim Sainsbury had to go down to the House of Commons at report stage, accept defeat and withdraw the provisions (which too many of our colleagues would not accept) designed to deregulate local authority control over local markets, which Neil had been so determined to force through.

After about six months in office, I had in place the new departmental structure and answers to the many questions about the new ministerial approach. It was time to test the reaction of the parliamentary party. In the autumn of 1992, I asked my new, energetic and astute PPS, Richard Ottaway, to invite every Conservative backbench MP to come to a presentation. We did the same for the non-Cabinet ministers in the government. No Tory MP was left in any doubt about precisely what we were doing and why. The meetings, by and large, were well attended and produced very little policy criticism. I can't say that all those who came would themselves have taken the same steps, but, faced with the logic of what they heard, the cliché-ridden debate about interventionism had been replaced by a practical programme involving minimal government money but a high degree of intervention aimed at raising performance in companies and public administration. We also invited Richard Lambert, the editor of the *Financial Times*, and his colleagues to a presentation in the DTI. Their reaction was immediate and encouraging and the strategy received massive coverage in that paper. However, the DTI was responsible for only a fraction of the policy involved. Using my co-ordinating role achieved via the annual Competitiveness White Papers, I set out to persuade other colleagues to adopt a similar approach in their departments, which I continued to do when I moved over to the Cabinet Office as Deputy Prime Minister.

In my opening year at the DTI, I was to be given the sharpest of all reminders of Harold Macmillan's 'events'. I had hardly crossed the threshold of the Department before anxious officials asked for a meeting about the coal industry. They had a simple message. During Margaret Thatcher's last year in office the electricity industry had been privatised. As part of the run-up to that process, the nationalised electricity industry had concluded five-year contracts with the nationalised coal industry to supply sixty-five million tonnes of coal to the generating stations. Theoretically the coal industry had those five years in which to reduce costs and downsize, to reflect whatever it believed the commercial market for its coal would be at that future date. By the time the contracts ran out, the electricity industry would be in private hands. Another general election would have come and gone. Alternative power producers, direct competitors for the provision of energy, were already in private hands and were applying for, or in receipt of, licences to build new generating stations fired by North Sea gas. But in 1989 this was all a long way ahead. Someone else could pick up the pieces.

The 1992 election was now over. Those pieces lay scattered on my desk. The facts were stark. The coal contracts ran out in March 1993. The power stations had stocks of coal so large that it was difficult to find anywhere to store more. The pits themselves were surrounded by piles of coal for which there was no market. Yet every day they produced more, at a unit cost far above the world market price. This was being funded by taxpayers to the tune of £50 million a month. Some of the independent power producers' original planning

The BBC's flagship programme *Panorama* comes to Thenford. Its post-
Thatcherism edition (with me as its centrepiece) eventually went out on the eve
of the party conference in 1989

I announce my challenge for the leadership of the Conservative Party on the steps of my London home, 14 November 1990

" HE LOOKED SO FORLORN. I SAID HE COULD SLEEP AT NUMBER TEN AND PRETEND FOR JUST ONE NIGHT. "

Two cruel cartoons. The first by Mac in the *Daily Mail* speaks for itself. The second, by Peter Brookes in *The Times*, commemorates an assault on me in the Commons by Gordon Brown in which he announced: 'The tiger that was once the king of the jungle is now just a fireside rug'

Geoffrey Howe and his wife Elspeth together with Norma and John Major joined Anne and me at the constituency association dinner in 1999 marking my 25 years as Henley's MP

My turn to celebrate: lunching with my old friend Lord Levene, during his
highly successful year (1998–99) as Lord Mayor of London

Dressed for different parts:
the flat-capped country-
man at work in his
arboretum and (*below*) as
President of the Board of
Trade on a North Sea oil
rig

In November 1995, John Major had to be away for the annual Remembrance Sunday Service at the Cenotaph. I took his place, not entirely to the approval of the baleful figure behind my left shoulder – indeed, Margaret Thatcher had complained to John about my stepping into the role at all

Surprisingly cheerful after my first interview following my heart attack in 1993. Asked what I proposed to do, I replied 'Make trouble'.

Engraving the labels to identify the trees in my constantly growing arboretum

The long, reflective view. Walking with Dominic the dachshund and Hamish the West Highland at Thenford

permissions had now been converted into operating gas-fired power stations, delivering far cheaper power to British homes and industry than almost all the coal-burning stations could match – and there were more on the way (the 'dash for gas', as journalists nicknamed it). In addition, there was a real and growing concern about the environmental impact of sulphur emissions from coal-burning stations. The electricity-generating industry itself was now privatised. Officials, after careful inquiry of the generators, advised that when the five-year contracts ended in a few months' time any new contracts offered to British Coal (as the National Coal Board had become in 1986) would see demand reduced from the current sixty-five million tonnes to forty or less a year. The consequences of this dramatic reduction in demand would, in the absence of increased subsidy, be the closure of a large number of pits. 'What would you like us to do?' my officials asked. There were only two options. Either we had to persuade the generators to buy more coal than forecast or we had to preside over a massive pit-closure programme.

It is usual in negotiations to have some cards in your hand. As we opened discussions with the generators, the only card we possessed was the worst card of all. It was the card of bluff. However much we might have talked of looking for tough options, John Baker, chief executive of National Power, and Ed Wallis, chief executive of the rival PowerGen, knew there were none. A quick telephone call to the Treasury would have told them that there was no subsidy forthcoming. Any colleague in the House of Commons would have informed them that there was no legislation that a Conservative government could conceivably pass that would prejudice their unassailable position. It was not so much a case of our being between a rock and a hard place. Both the rock and the hard place were lying directly across our path.

The generators' case was unanswerable. They could purchase coal on the world market considerably more cheaply than from British Coal. They could produce electricity more cheaply and more cleanly from gas than from coal. They had coal stocks in their balance sheets of a value indefensibly against their companies' interests. They had a fiduciary responsibility to run the companies on behalf of the shareholders effectively and efficiently. They were offering to buy coal to the maximum extent that prudence permitted. Any costs we imposed on them would adversely affect the competitiveness of British industry, which would have to pay. And, in addition, the electricity regulator was already consulting with a view to bringing about a reduction in the generators' charges.

The end of the journey was unavoidable and totally predictable. The decision centred on three issues: which pits to close, when and at what cost? In all of this Tim Eggar, as the Minister for Energy, bore the brunt of the detailed analysis. He did it with considerable skill and applied himself with great diligence to the thankless task. There was some flexibility in the answer to the question: which pits? There were those near the end of their natural life span that presented themselves for early closure. There were those that were the least economic. There were those where the cost of extending the life involved investment that could not be justified. British Coal's analysis was carefully checked by the Department under Tim's supervision. The one factor to which all arguments ultimately returned was the size of any likely contracts with the power generators. In the absence of a serious export market, this fixed the volume of coal output for which there was any demand. Several months passed as we tried to negotiate so-called supplementary contracts with the generators' teams, led by John Baker and Ed Wallis of National Power and PowerGen. We also explored alternative markets with British Gas. But the track record of nationalised industries in winning new markets was sufficiently poor for me to have little confidence in this idea. And it was clear that any extra contracts with the generators meant taxpayer subsidy.

In the meantime, by midsummer 1992 a list of thirty-one pits proposed for closure by British Coal had been drawn up and presented to ministers. If ever there was a leak waiting to happen, this was it. Tim Sainsbury's responsibilities within the Department included regional policy and in this capacity he wrote on 1 September to Michael Portillo, Chief Secretary to the Treasury (he had been promoted there after the general election), with copies sent to various colleagues, including Gillian Shephard at the Department of Employment, listing the threatened pits and asking for financial support to pay off redundant miners, and ameliorate the social and economic consequences in the coal communities.

Inevitably, the letter was leaked to Arthur Scargill of the NUM, who in turn gave it to the press. On 18 September the *Guardian* reprinted it in full. But not on the front page – that was still taken up with the fall-out following our withdrawal from the ERM two days earlier. Considering the furore that attended the subsequent closure announcement itself, this leak caused few waves. All summer there had been speculative – but remarkably accurate – pieces about the future prospects for the industry. No one seemed greatly surprised, therefore, by the contents of our leaked letter then or in follow-up stories over the next few weeks. On 22 September the *Guardian* again ran a story by its labour editor, Keith Harper, which said: 'Delegates from 75 coal mining areas were told last night that the industry was on the brink of "a disaster" following last week's revelations in the *Guardian* that the Government is to shut 30 pits and sack 25,000 miners as soon as possible. Stephen Fothergill, director of the Coalfield Communities Campaign, said he feared that industry could be making "its last stand". Speaking on the eve of its annual conference in Doncaster, he went on: "If this speculation is true, the industry is facing a disaster and could end up so small, it will be trivial."' The industry knew what was coming and so did the media – but no national uproar ensued.

But there was one other consequence of the leak. Unless the government was prepared to subsidise coal production for which there was no market, the moment any of the listed pits were closed we would be asked about the others. The further down the list we moved, the more inevitable the closure of the rest would be seen to be. We were boxed in.

Throughout the spring, summer and early autumn of 1992 we had conducted protracted negotiations with the Treasury over the compensation terms to be offered to the redundant miners; but Michael Portillo proved obdurate and refused to acknowledge the need for any special treatment. We failed to resolve the disagreement with the Treasury at a meeting which John Major chaired in the summer. This inconclusive outcome reflected the view that when the announcement was made it would not prove that difficult to handle and that British Coal were overstating the necessary level of redundancy pay. Indeed, from all the endless, frustrating correspondence with the Treasury about the redundancy terms for the miners, one phrase sticks vividly in my mind: the Chancellor Norman Lamont's cold declaration that, whatever else happened, 'The lights would not go out.' So the summer months had passed. Eventually, John Major resolved the dispute and the terms of compensation were finally agreed at a meeting he chaired on 23 September. The Treasury insisted that the expenditure be incurred before the end of the following March – the end of the financial year.

The only issues then outstanding were how and exactly when. We had very little choice over timing, but we did not anticipate the reaction itself. The announcement had, of course, to come from British Coal, the nationalised company running the pits. Their view was that the sooner, the better. I too believed, once the course was set, that it was best to proceed quickly. The costs were mounting. It had been possible to defend holding off an announcement as long as we were fighting for better terms but, now we had them, it was up to us to act. In the practice of modern government there was also the ever present risk of further leaks. And I wanted to end the uncertainty with which the miners and their families had been living for so long. Only when they knew the worst could they begin to rebuild their futures. What escaped us was just how bruised public opinion had become as a result of the national humiliation over the ERM exit; the last thing it needed was another such blow. Nevertheless, we provided just that. And we failed to take account of the deeply felt emotional bond with the mining communities on the part of middle England.

On Tuesday, 13 October, the week following the party Conference and before Parliament had returned, British Coal announced a pro-gramme of closure for thirty-one of the remaining fifty deep mines with the loss of 30,000 jobs. To make and announce this decision was their statutory responsibility. I had a different one: to announce the redundancy terms and any financial package the government would make available to ameliorate the impact of their decision. The clear advice was to preserve this distinction, however much of a sham that was in dealing with a nationalised industry every day in the closest touch with officials in my Department. On the same day, therefore, but at a separate press conference I announced a £1 billion package, mostly for redundancy payments but also to help with retraining programmes, job-creation schemes and regeneration proposals for the mining communities.

It was a dreadful moment for all concerned – indeed at my own press conference there were some officials with tears in their eyes. For myself, I knew that I could not let my heart rule my head. Worse was to come. Without any advance knowledge on my part, British Coal's announcement included the statement that the first pits would close at the end of that very week. Of course, for this and every other manifestation of insensitivity, the blame was put squarely on the government. The consequence was uproar on all sides. I have to say this only served to reinforce my doubts about the ability of nationalised industries to attract first-class management.

To add to our difficulties, the National Union of Mineworkers immediately and successfully applied to the courts for judicial review, joining me as co-defendant because it was alleged that I had acted in collusion with British Coal. The accusation was that British Coal had short-circuited the official colliery review procedure: this was a process which had been agreed years before with the NUM to explore every avenue before a pit was actually shut down. In practice the system had been short-circuited for many months effectively without protest. (Two months later, however, the High Court found in the NUM's favour.) It was also alleged that British Coal had failed to notify the Department of Employment of the intended redundancies as they were legally required to do. I have always remained puzzled by this last. It was reported widely in the press at the time that Gillian Shephard was incensed that she had known nothing of the proposals. Yet Tim Sainsbury's letter of 1 September – the letter which leaked – had been copied to her, with the details of the pits due to close. It is inconceivable to me that a letter of such moment was not brought to the Employment Secretary's attention by her officials or that the subsequent leak had not attracted that Department's notice. But the challenge stood. In practice, of course, the Department of Employment knew what was going on. The mistake lay in that British Coal had not carried out the formal procedures laid down for notification of redundancies in such cases.

The public reaction to the announcements was immediate and immense. The middle classes marched with the miners. Indeed, the middle classes appeared to feel even more strongly than the miners themselves, although within the mining communities, which had long since sensed the writing on the wall, there was much resentment. This was especially true of the Union of Democratic Mineworkers, the breakaway union largely based in Nottinghamshire whose courage in crossing the NUM picket lines in 1984–5 had been crucial to the government's victory in that strike. They believed that they had been given assurances about their future by the government at that time and felt badly let down. Their leader, Roy Lynk, staged his own personal sit-in in protest for several days 1,200 feet underground at Silverhill pit in Nottinghamshire.

The package on offer was reasonably generous: individual miners could receive £23,000 each, provided they took redundancy as the

Treasury had insisted in the financial year 1992–3 – in other words, within the next five months. After that, the terms were to be withdrawn. Over the following months large numbers did leave the industry voluntarily, just as British Coal had predicted they would. The underground workers were much sought after as employees. They are valued for their skill and experience in working in tough, dangerous conditions. The very nature of the working conditions has taught them a loyalty to each other, a sense of team-work and yet a self-reliance that is transferable to many other jobs. It was no surprise to me at all that the overwhelming majority of them were able to find work within a reasonable period in industries that offered a more acceptable way of life than those found in Britain's deep mines. The above-ground workers and those connected with supplying services to the collieries, however, had a tougher time, as we had feared.

The reaction of our MPs to the two announcements reflected the anger of their constituents and the newspaper headlines. I was summoned to No. 10 on the evening of Sunday, 18 October for a meeting with John Major, other colleagues including Norman Lamont, and a host of officials. There was an emergency Cabinet on Monday, 19 October. The atmosphere in Cabinet was distinctly frigid. In the event, it was agreed that we would review twenty-one of the threatened pits and that the Treasury would provide more money for the mining communities. I was faced inevitably with the need to make a ministerial statement in the House of Commons later that day – the first day that MPs were back from the summer recess.

In the House that afternoon I set out the substance of the previous week's announcements – that thirty-one pits needed to close over the next five months with the potential loss of 30,000 jobs. The generators had still not signed new contracts, although I had originally hoped that British Coal would have concluded them before the summer recess. I was still not able, therefore, to give any details. I said that I regretted that I had not made my initial announcement to the House. I then modified the terms of the original announcement. No pits would be closed immediately. Only ten pits would be earmarked for early closure – and then only after the statutory period of consultation. Redundancies would be voluntary. No other pits would close except by agreement. In the meantime, there would be an extra £165 million of help for the coalfield communities and Peter Walker would act as co-ordinator and facilitator to implement our programme. Finally, I assured the House that there would be an opportunity to debate the issues and that there would be a three-month period of widespread consultations.

Later that evening I was roughed up at a packed meeting of the 1922 Committee. Its chairman, Sir Marcus Fox, Member for the Yorkshire constituency of Shipley, had already given frequent television and radio interviews in which he expressed colleagues' displeasure. The gist of his message had been that the closures were 'unacceptable'.

The Opposition inevitably went for an emergency debate, which took place on Wednesday, 21 October. The miners had organised a march on London and a mass lobby of Parliament that day, and such was the concern of the police that Eileen and I had to be driven down to the House in a Special Branch car for the debate. In my speech I clarified the closure process that British Coal now planned. They would consult over the future of each of the twenty-one pits, and do so without prejudice to the outcome. Any threatened pit would be maintained in a condition where it could be reopened, if the consultation led to the conclusion that it should be. I promised a thorough review of the remaining ten pits as well and I told the House that the government would publish a White Paper setting out our findings in the context of our wider energy policy, including the implications for employment. I welcomed the announcement by the Trade and Industry Select Committee that they were to investigate the market for coal.

The government's overall majority of twenty-one did not permit a large-scale revolt. Winston Churchill and a number of colleagues had already formed themselves into an unofficial 'friends of the miners' lobby. I have rarely felt so alone. There was talk of a censure motion. In the event, the government secured a majority of thirteen in the ten o'clock vote that night. We had survived the worst of the crisis. We had gained time, during which we could bring home to colleagues – and to the country at large – the unavoidable nature of the problem we faced. I held interminable meetings with Winston, the two Wintertons – Nicholas and Ann, the husband-and-wife team from adjoining Cheshire constituencies – Elizabeth Peacock *et al.* in an attempt to win them back on side. Their lack of knowledge of the mining industry and its predicament was astounding in all the circumstances. The only thing missing was a way out. Tim Eggar spent weeks trying to find acceptable alternative options, but the generators would not agree to buy more coal at prices British Coal could live with.

Then, incredibly, Richard Caborn, the Labour chairman of the Trade and Industry Select Committee, threw the government a lifeline. I doubt if it was his intention. After a hasty examination of the circumstances and after calling me as the principal witness, the Committee reported at the end of January. That the Report would be critical was inevitable. What was far from inevitable was that they would come forward with their own proposals. But they did, and the fact that these proposals came from an all-party committee on which sat Labour Members with mining constituencies was an unexpected bonus when later I had to face Labour frontbench attempts to reignite the issue. This outcome had in part been facilitated, however, by the Department's commissioning of a series of expert reports on markets, pit life expectancy and the scale of viable coal reserves, which were published just before the Committee published theirs. Several of these independent advisers had been summoned to give evidence to the Select Committee and, indeed, that had been one of our intentions. None produced ammunition for the critics.

The Committee's key proposal was that the government should provide a subsidy to enable British Coal to cut its prices under certain conditions and thus allow the generators to purchase quantities of coal in excess of their fixed contracts for forty million tonnes in 1993-4 and thirty million tonnes in each following year until 1997-8 – at the price of imported coal. I knew that the generators would not in practice take up any significant extra tonnage; they had no demand for it. But I saw that the Report could provide a way through. I went to the House of Commons, praised the foresight of the Select Committee, agreed in significant measure to accept the proposals and promised to report back.

The outcome was in all practical senses what I had originally announced. A large number of working miners had taken the redundancy terms on offer and left the industry. My colleagues on the back benches had come to terms with what was happening. Time had served to replace the initial shocked reaction with a degree of acceptance of harsh reality. Given the circumstances, there was simply no alternative. From that day to this nobody has come forward with a credible rival set of options that I could have pursued. What I said at the time was true. Overall closures have taken place on the scale we anticipated. The long-overdue rationalisation of the industry *had* to happen. But, as I write today, seventeen major deep mines are still operating in this country, and coal still accounts for 29 per cent of national electricity generation. The false prophecies of the Opposition spokesman Robin Cook that we would see wholesale closure of the industry have proved to be no more than the overblown rhetoric he should have known them to be at the time.

The preparation of the White Paper, announcing the results of our review, was finally concluded in March 1993, after a midnight meeting with John Baker and Ed Wallis of the two generators, who had now agreed the contract quantities they were prepared to take. The full text was finally cleared at about two o'clock in the middle of the night. Floppy discs were entrusted to two motorcyclists – two, in case one crashed – waiting outside the DTI, engines revving and ready to go to deliver to the printers somewhere up the M1.

On the day of the publication of the White Paper I made a statement in the House about the outcome of the whole review of energy policy, which was well received on the government benches. I spelt out our proposals. The generous redundancy terms were to be extended to the end of the calendar year. We offered a subsidy for British Coal if it helped develop new markets, promised that no pit would close without first being offered to the private sector, the gas and electricity-generating sector (which provided cheap electricity and supported a large number of jobs) would remain unchanged but coal would continue to be the most important fuel for electricity generation, and, finally, we increased investment in clean-coal technology and announced additional funding of up to £200 million for the regeneration package for mining areas. A few days later there was a full-scale debate, which proved a rather uninspiring repetition of the earlier occasion.

In the meantime we had decided to go for full privatisation via a trade sale. I had already announced the intention to privatise in my 1992 party Conference speech and an early paving bill – preparing the way for subsequent legislation – had originally been introduced into the House even before that (in May 1992) but subsequently withdrawn. During the autumn crisis we had been told repeatedly and very firmly by Richard Budge and others that there was an additional market for coal. At some point during one of the innumerable meetings at the DTI in which we agonised over the future of the different pits, I said: 'Aren't we missing a trick here?' The trick was to let the private coal companies put their money where their mouth was. We decided to let them bid for *all* the remaining pits, thus proving their confidence in the market potential for coal That is what we did.

In the following session of Parliament, Tim Eggar secured the privatisation legislation, working with Rothschilds as the main advisers. It was a superb achievement. That, and the privatisation of the nuclear industry in 1996, accomplished two of the most difficult and controversial privatisations of them all. The deep-mine industry in England was divided into five packages of pits to which were also allocated their financially more attractive open-cast neighbours. Bids were invited. Richard Budge's company, R.J.B. Mining, purchased the main three, with the industries in Scotland and Wales being sold separately. In Wales there was a miners' buy-out of Tower Colliery. No one would have believed ten years earlier that the nationalised industry whose union had brought down the Tory government in 1974, forced Mrs Thatcher to retreat in 1981 and fought and lost in a titanic re-run in 1985 would be just another private sector industry so few years later.

The coal crisis was not without domestic incident. We woke one day at Thenford to find a couple of tonnes of coal dumped in the drive. Our farm equipment easily shifted it but the disposal was trickier. I told the police we would give it to an old peoples' home. 'Oh no,' they said; 'we might trace the owners.' 'Okay,' I agreed, 'I'll wait a bit before giving it away'. That wouldn't do either. 'No, you must keep it. If it's stolen, it might be needed as evidence'. Eventually it was auctioned off locally and the proceeds went to charity. Meanwhile some 'miners' began to 'dig for coal' in a field behind the house. The police rightly played this down, certain the novelty would wear off once the press lost interest. What they didn't know was that our 'miners' were Labour councillors from Hammersmith. I was grateful to an alert Tory councillor who spotted her opposite numbers in a press photo and blew their cover.

There is no doubt that mistakes were made over coal. Mistakes were made in misjudging the public mood both in its preparedness for the announcement and following on from the ERM crisis. There is no doubt either that, if Norman Lamont and Michael Portillo at the Treasury had not simply dug in when the problem was first put to them, the closures would have taken place within an earlier and more orderly programme which would almost certainly have cost less than, in the event, it did. If ever there was a case of locking the stable door after the pit-pony had bolted, this was it.

Matrix Churchill was a small engineering company manufacturing machine tools in Coventry in the West Midlands. In the autumn of 1992 three of the company's senior executives, Paul Henderson,

Trevor Abraham and Peter Allen, were due in court on charges of export controls offences. It was alleged that they had deceived the government over the intended use of some lathes exported to Iraq and for which they had sought export licences.

In preparing the case for trial the government's lawyers were required to disclose relevant documents to the defence. In some cases, however, disclosure of sensitive documents may cause damage of an unacceptable nature either to the national interest or to personal security. Put at its most extreme, intelligence reports may include information that could severely prejudice our diplomatic relations with other countries or details of agents, disclosure of which could endanger their lives. Self-evidently, special arrangements have to exist to enable a fair trial to take place without unacceptable damage being done to the country or its employees.

The means to implement these protections lies in the issuing of Public Interest Immunity Certificates (PIIs), which have been used by governments of both parties over the years. They designate which papers in the bundles prepared for a trial should not be disclosed to the defence or in open court *unless* the judge specifically so orders in the interests of a fair trial. PIIs have to be signed by ministers and at that time took the form of a written statement that the documents cited in the certificate, having been read by the minister, either had contents which it would be against the public interest to disclose or belonged to a class of documents which ought to be withheld. A 'class' of documents was deemed to include all documents that might reveal the identity of informants or which related to the operations or personnel of the intelligence or security services and, in addition, those relating to policy-making within government departments. This last group, known as 'advice to ministers', is the most difficult to defend. But the convention is clear. Ministers are responsible for their judgements. The advice they receive from officials is confidential.

I was quite unaware of this background when in early September 1992, in the routine course of business, a file appeared in the in-tray on my desk. It advised me that I would shortly be invited to sign an additional PII certificate to one already signed the previous year by my predecessor at the DTI, Peter Lilley, in respect of certain documents. Five further documents not covered by Peter's certificate now required one from me. But in addition the one I was invited to sign was to include all those documents already covered by Peter's certificate.

A PII certificate only makes a *claim* for immunity. It is the judge's ultimate responsibility to make the final determination as to whether all or any part of a document is to be revealed to the defence. When a judge insists on disclosure, the government has the ultimate option of dropping a case, if it feels that disclosure would be so damaging as not to justify the prosecution. In this case a bevy of officials from my own Department and the Law Officers' offices urged me to sign.

Every alarm bell started ringing. I was profoundly uneasy. I am no lawyer but it was clear to me that there had been a security relationship with Matrix Churchill. I couldn't understand why the prosecution was concentrating on the allegation that the defendants had lied in the information they had submitted in pursuit of their export licence and not on the offence of actually exporting proscribed goods themselves, unless – as I suspected – there had been officially at least an awareness that something was going on. And I felt uneasy at the vehemence with which I was being pressed to sign the certificate, which seemed to me not to reflect the normal detachment with which officials present advice. The more they argued, the more concerned I became that here was an example of Whitehall protecting its own. The ultimate charge against the defendants was that they had breached the sanctions regime by breaking the arms embargo on Iraq. Yet I had read in the documents before me that members of the intelligence services had actually visited the company. I believed this supported my suspicion that they must have been aware of what was going on. The more I looked through the files, the more appalled I was. You can see it: my sidelining of the submission grew more vehement and fierce, as I progressed through the text. What it was telling me was that, as I subsequently told the Scott Inquiry, 'everyone knew'. Yet a criminal trial was impending. It was clear to me that no trial could be fair that denied the defence the sort of evidence that I was reading. There was no way I was going to sign anything that prejudiced the chances of these papers being made available. At the heart of the matter I believed that some of the documents before me were material to the defence. I wanted the judge to know that was my view.

Yet it was simply not possible to read through every page of every one of the great welter of files – the pile was a foot high – which were put in front of me and about which I was asked to make detailed and specific judgements. I knew nothing about the background of the trial and it was simply impossible to devote the necessary time to the scrutiny of every single page of those voluminous files that the seriousness of the situation demanded, if I was going to give any blanket assurances about their contents. I certainly wasn't going to give any such assurances without having done so. Indeed, I was so suspicious about the whole procedure that I took the file to show John Major. He didn't say much but he didn't need to; the look of concern on his face mirrored mine. The outcome of that was that the Cabinet secretary, Sir Robin Butler, appeared in my office in the twinkling of an eye to talk the issues through with me.

Confronted with my clearly expressed reservations, officials had drawn to my attention a law report of the judgement by Lord Justice Bingham (later Lord Chief Justice) delivered in the *Makanjuola* case on appeal in 1989. It was not the easiest judgement to understand but it set out the rules governing the PII procedure and included a sentence, 'the ultimate judge of where the balance of public interest lies is not in him [the Minister] but the Court'. As I later told the Inquiry, that was 'the clinching part as far as I was concerned'. In the end, I signed but I did everything I could to ensure that in doing so I drew to the judge's attention my very real concerns that the three men should not be denied the papers they needed for their defence. Nick Lyell, the Attorney General, had been at pains to point out the legal requirement upon me to sign a PII but agreed that the words of the certificate in front of me could be redrafted to reflect my disquiet.

My certificate was in consequence different to those signed at that time by Ken Clarke in the Home Office, Malcolm Rifkind in the MOD and Tristan Garel-Jones in the Foreign Office – all in relation to the same case. No one should read anything into that, although the press tried to. My three colleagues were signing in respect of different documents emanating from their own departments. None of us had met together to discuss the handling of the documents before us. After signing my modified certificate, I asked that they be informed of what I had done and told that I had refused to sign the original draft certificate. I also put a clear request in writing to the Attorney General's office that the judge should be made aware of my reservations and opinions and was assured that he would be.

In the event that assurance was never satisfied. As Sir Richard Scott subsequently concluded in the Report of his findings following his Inquiry, Alan Moses QC, the prosecutor, 'was not made aware of Mr Heseltine's opinion that the DTI documents ought to be disclosed to the defendants'.* If counsel did not know, he was in no position to alert the judge.

---

* *Report of the Inquiry into the Export of Defence Equipment and Dual-Use Goods to Iraq and Related Prosecutions* (5 vols, HMSO, 1996), vol. 3, p. 1364.

The account of all this hit the headlines when the trial itself collapsed in November 1992 because Alan Clark, the ex-MP and former DTI Minister, changed his testimony. I was appalled that I, along with others, was now being accused of trying to withhold information, of a cover-up, of being willing to see innocent men go to jail, as the press would have it. All this was precisely what I had refused to do. I explained my position at length and under detailed cross-examination on the *Newsnight* programme on BBC2. It made not a blind bit of difference. From the heavyweight commentators, such as Lord Rees-Mogg, down to the usual Fleet Street rabble the lies were repeated and repeated. There was no protection for ministers.

That same month John Major appointed Sir Richard Scott to conduct an examination into the wider question of the whole 'arms to Iraq' affair and whether or not the export conditions had been changed without notifying Parliament. Until that examination was concluded, we had to sit and take whatever the Opposition and the press dished out to us. Robin Cook, the Shadow Trade and Industry spokesman, took particular delight in constantly repeating for the next three years the wholly misleading phrase 'gagging orders' to describe PII certificates. He knew full well that we could not reply until Sir Richard concluded his investigation. Indeed, we were the ones who were gagged.

In the event, the Inquiry ultimately revealed the truth of my position as I have recorded it here. Sir Richard was generous in referring to me in his Report, which was finally published in February 1996: 'It is plain from Mr Heseltine's written and oral evidence that he had formed the view that the documents ought to be disclosed for use by the defence and that he expected the Court so to be informed.' In conclusion, he said: 'Mr Heseltine's reluctance to sign the PII Certificate in case he thereby deprived the defendants of access to material documents evidenced an instinct for the requirements of justice that was fully justified and corresponded, in my opinion, with the legal principles correctly understood.'*

The publication of the Report, or rather the long delay before its publication, caused further headaches for the government, however. It is frequently the fate of an administration to live under the shadow of an inquiry which it has itself created – and that was certainly our experience with the Scott investigation. I doubt if anyone at the start

---

* *Report of the Inquiry into the Export of Defence Equipment and Dual-Use Goods to Iraq and Related Prosecutions* vol. 3, pp. 1386, 1537.

thought that Sir Richard Scott would take as long as he did to conduct his hearings (mostly in public) and to produce his Report. It took over three years – which we had had to endure in silence – before it was finally published and the government was able to make its own comments on the learned judge's findings. In delivering the Commons statement on the result of the Inquiry on behalf of the government Ian Lang, my successor at the DTI, did extremely well and we were able to survive even a bravura performance from the shadow Foreign Secretary, Robin Cook. One week later we squeezed home by one vote on a full-dress censure motion put down by the Opposition.

By the time the Scott Inquiry reported I had become Deputy Prime Minister. I had also kept the press cuttings. I took legal opinion as to the advisability of suing a number of newspapers for libel. The redoubtable George Carman QC was consulted. To my dismay, he told me that it is not enough for a minister to show that what has been said about him is untrue. He has also to prove that it was said with malice. On that latter count there was no way I could make progress in the courts of law. Politics is a rough old game.

It was quite soon after the 1992 general election that Edward Leigh, a junior minister with me in the DTI and a right-winger who had, however, long since expressed personal support for me, suggested one morning that I should privatise the Post Office. I told him I had considerable reservations. He pressed his case. The more I listened, the more persuaded I became.

The Post Office consisted at the time of about 800 Crown Post Offices, known as the 'Crowns'. These are the big, high-street Royal Mail post offices where one can draw a pension or children's allowance, post letters or parcels, pay bills, invest in savings accounts, renew television and vehicle licences – as well as buy stamps. In addition, there were some 19,000 post offices in corner shops and newsagents – and sometimes front rooms – in the vast majority of towns and villages in the land. It is these which attract particular public affection. You can carry out almost all of the same transactions in these local post offices, but they are privately owned. If you buy a copy of *Exchange and Mart*, you will find numbers of them there advertised for sale. They are often an integral part of community life, the place where young mothers, pensioners and others meet as they draw their weekly entitlement, post a letter, pay the gas bill and then spend a bit in the shop alongside. Such post offices were already 'privatised'.

What Edward was proposing was the privatisation of the Royal Mail, together with its wholly owned subsidiary, Parcelforce. It is this service which delivers letters and packages from one end of the country to the other, in some places twice a day, for a common tariff regardless of distance.

Few people stop to think about the importance of letters in their lives. Most of the missives that come through the post nowadays are junk mail, catalogues, brochures and other promotional material, bills or greetings cards. Whether a bill comes on a Monday or a Tuesday or a Christmas card at the beginning or the end of a week is a matter of little consequence. With telegrams long since a thing of the past, no one any longer relied on the Post Office for urgent messages. The business in which Royal Mail was engaged was changing rapidly. Its services were being undermined by fax machines, e-mail and courier services provided by a myriad of private sector contractors. Under Treasury restrictions Royal Mail couldn't expand overseas directly or in alliance with partners. Nor could it meet the growing competition by entering the world of electronic communications itself. It didn't help that, in the great Royal Mail sorting offices, the bad old world of restrictive practices and over-manning still flourished.

We received strong support at the time from the management of the Royal Mail, led by Michael Heron, the chairman, and Bill Cockburn, the chief executive, although of course the unions argued vociferously for the status quo. Colin Baker, general secretary of the National Federation of Sub-Postmasters, was unswerving in his support for our proposals. Consultants and analysts revealed, particularly in the large metropolitan sorting offices, a situation even worse than such a sceptic of public sector activity as myself could have anticipated. The postal services represented a major cost to businesses and our job was to pursue efficiency as part of our competitiveness agenda. There was no magic charm in maintaining public ownership. We had received offers from reputable private sector companies like TNT to provide the same service. Edward Leigh had won his case.

I put forward the proposal. John Major was anxious, not in any way about the merits of the case, but about the politics (even Margaret Thatcher had once famously said that there was no question of privatising the Royal Mail). Richard Ryder, the Chief Whip, was deeply pessimistic. But the Treasury, in the form of Ken Clarke, was characteristically bullish about anything that raised money. We eventually agreed that I could publish a consultative paper, which

I duly did. The controversy raged on; the Opposition were stirring mightily. I outlined the proposals in my party Conference speech in October 1994, holding up a copy of *Exchange and Mart* to emphasise that sub-post offices were already in the hands of the private sector. I added a cautionary warning about buying a second-hand post office from Robin Cook. The speech was warmly received. It was agreed that in the company of one of the whips, Simon Burns, I could consult the parliamentary party to see if, despite the fragility of our majority, we had a chance of getting the necessary legislation through.

In the end, we were down to about nine hard-core opponents. Sitting with Simon in a committee room on the lower-ground floor of the Commons, I faced a bizarre coalition of the ultra-left of the party, led by Hugh Dykes; the ultra-right of the party, in the form of Rhodes Boyson and Jim Pawsey, and in addition the two Wintertons, who had detected, as they had a knack of doing, a populist cause waiting for a voice. We had to report to the Cabinet that there was still entrenched opposition. Hugh Dykes and his colleagues were prepared to compromise; if we sold only a minority stake in the Royal Mail, they would go along with it. But there was no moving the hard right.

There is an element of artificiality about a consultation of this sort. It is one thing for colleagues to say that they will vote against their government in the cool calm of a Commons committee room, supported by several like-minded friends. It is quite another actually to vote in that way in a division, when the government's reputation and possibly its survival hangs by your decision. What would you say to your constituents when you got home that weekend, if your vote had brought down the government? But we could not create artificially the atmosphere of intense pressure that the whips, colleagues, events and circumstance can bring to bear at ten o'clock on the night of a second-reading vote.

My consultation process failed to guarantee a majority. I offered to take my chances anyway, knowing full well that I would have to resign if I failed. John Major, ever cautious and already besieged by splits in the parliamentary party, shrank from such a high-profile throw of the dice. Given the problems that he, the government and the party were facing, I had no difficulty in accepting that decision, though for me it will always remain a missed opportunity. Over the years I had been responsible for council house sales and for privatising the coal and nuclear industries, the Stationery Office and numerous smaller public services, but this would have been the jewel in the crown.

Chapter 19

THE HAND OF FATE

By the summer of 1993, with the loss of the Newbury by-election in May and the removal of Norman Lamont from the Treasury already behind us, the new Major government had been in power for a year. Anne and I decided to take advantage of a free weekend in June to visit Venice. We booked into the Cipriani Hotel. I was to stay until Monday morning and then head off for a ministerial visit to Germany, leaving Anne behind to visit the Biennale art festival. The Cipriani is a superb hotel. Located on the Giudecca and approached only by the hotel's own water-taxis, it offers wonderful food in the most tranquil of settings, with lovely gardens and a magnificent swimming pool. On Saturday we set out to find the vantage point from which Canaletto had painted a picture of the church of SS Giovanni e Paolo, the Scuola di San Marco and the famous equestrian statue of Colleone. Eventually, after many false turns, we discovered a small alleyway between two buildings through which a cobbled street only a yard wide ran to the edge of a canal. It was here we thought that Canaletto must have sat to paint the picture that hangs in our home. We were discussing the location and admiring the perspective, when a voice alongside us said helpfully: 'No, it was not from here. When the Queen's picture was exhibited in Venice, they tried to find the viewpoint, but he invented it.' (Canaletto often painted several versions of a favourite view for Grand Tourists.)

The next day, Sunday, we went to an exhibition of early Spanish paintings in a gallery alongside San Giorgio Maggiore. I felt a little tired afterwards, so we returned to the Cipriani for a swim. Much to her surprise, Anne overtook me as we swam a length; my arms felt heavy but it never occurred to me that there was anything to be concerned about. Later, we dined in Harry's Bar, and afterwards had to run for our water-taxi back to the hotel. I felt sluggish, and hardly made it. We went to bed. For many years, if I had drunk a quantity of white wine, I had taken an Alka-Seltzer, which I had found to be a perfect cure for heartburn. But that night it failed to work. I remember lying in bed, wide awake, increasingly preoccupied with the thought that I would find it very difficult to carry my own dispatch case and the red box on my journey the next day. About one o'clock in the morning I got out of bed to take another Alka-Seltzer. Shortly after that I realised that something was more seriously adrift. By this time Anne was awake. I asked her to call a doctor.

Anne spoke to the night porter, who asked some amazingly pertinent questions. He then came up to our room, and said that he had already called for a water ambulance, as the doctor lived on the other side of the lagoon and would take too long getting to the hotel at low tide. He told Anne that he had some basic first-aid knowledge, and had dealt only a few months earlier with another heart-attack victim – her first confirmation of what she already suspected was wrong. When the ambulance arrived, a wonderfully archaic wicker bathchair was produced to wheel me through the moonlit gardens down to the water. In a way it was a mercy it all happened at night. The busy canals, normally thronged with vaporetti and gondolas, were empty. We motored through unimpeded.

We arrived on the quay beside the Ospedale Civile, which was housed in the old Scuola di San Marco which we had visited only the day before. Once inside, we were in a sequence of courtyards and cloisters. Anne recalls being horrified – 'I could not believe they would know how to treat Michael here.' To her relief, through an archway we soon reached the stark building of the ultra-modern cardiac unit. Built only a year before, it had become the northern Italian base for EU cardiac research and was headed up by the eminent specialist Professore Caturelli.

A young Italian doctor gave me a quick examination, expressed the most self-evident relief on being told that I didn't smoke and sent me on my way to a cell-like room, the only window of which was some ten feet above the floor level. Since by now I was in a distinctly woozy state, that did not really bother me, but for Anne it must have been awful. I was anxious that she should have some moral support, so I suggested that she telephone Alistair and Romilly McAlpine (Baron McAlpine had been Treasurer and Deputy Chairman of the Conservative Party), who live in Venice and whom we had met the day before at the Cipriani. Romilly was very kind, lent a mobile phone that proved a godsend and even sat with me so that Anne could get some breakfast. She did this in the café outside with Alistair, the victim of a heart attack himself – though a much more serious one than mine. He was both consoling and buoyant.

Our two daughters, Annabel and Alexandra, flew out shortly after Anne had contacted them and the three of them made sure that I was never alone. The hospital imposed strict visiting hours. This constant family attention tested the administration somewhat, but without it I would never have been washed or had a pee, until finally the hospital tracked down a superb male nurse who spoke English. But Rupert, our son, probably had the hardest task. He stayed at home to make arrangements for my return – a lonely business which he discharged most sympathetically and effectively.

Two doctors, our GP and a long-standing friend of forty years, Richard Rossdale, together with the consultant heart physician he had recommended, Peter Mills, flew out later that day. They were totally confident that the attention and care I was receiving was quite the best and did not come out again until the following Friday to help ferry me home.

For Anne, the main problem was the press. The journalists, whom she could not help thinking of as vultures, descended almost at once. This normally quiet hospital didn't know what had hit it, and it certainly wasn't geared up to keeping the paparazzi at bay. They arrived on my floor, by means of a lift normally reserved for stretcher cases, and were narrowly prevented by Anne and the nursing staff from pushing their way into the intensive-care unit. She angrily rejected the request for 'just one picture of your husband sitting up in bed' but eventually did a deal whereby she would give one television interview – with Michael Brunson of ITN – in return for the camera crews and journalists allowing me to leave the hospital for the helicopter quietly and without fuss, and with just one prearranged photo-opportunity.

The time had come to go. I offered to pay but they would not hear of it. 'We have a Health Service,' they proudly explained, 'just like you.' I felt reasonably comfortable as I was loaded into a wheelchair, pinned a huge blue rosette on my white dressing gown – never a photo-opportunity knowingly undersold – and was wheeled towards the point at which the photograph was to be taken.

All went well. I put on my best campaigning smile and, the

photograph taken, was wheeled out of sight to the waiting helicopter. It so happened that one of the drugs that I had been given as a routine reaction to the loss of the end of an artery, which I had suffered, had as a side-effect the encouragement of gout. My right foot had become extremely painful as a consequence. It was necessary for me to step from the wheelchair up the steps of the helicopter. In the process of doing so, as I put my right foot on the ground, the pain was fierce and caused me to double up. This need not have mattered (except to me) had it not been for the fact that a host of paparazzi were perched along the ruined wall around the garden in which the helicopter was located. The next day pictures of this crippled, crumpled figure, apparently struck down and bent double by his recent heart attack, adorned the front pages of the London newspapers.

The journey home was uneventful. Thanks to the far-sightedness of the excellent head of my press office, Jean Caines, I was able to fly into RAF Northolt and go straight to the Harley Street Clinic. The next stage of the game was an angiogram, in which a local anaesthetic to the groin precedes the injection of a telescope into the heart, thus enabling the audience of doctors and anaesthetists to examine on a computer screen the inner secrets of your very life. As I lay there in the operating theatre, the anaesthetist cheerily told me I had the arteries of a man of forty and invited me to take a look. I confess I had no particular desire to see the inside of my heart, no matter what condition it was in. My judgement then was that there are things in life it is better not to see or know. But I relented the next time I had an angiogram and gazed at my heart beating away three feet above my head.

But the news appeared good and, after a second opinion from a leading cardiac surgeon, it was confirmed that I could look forward to a full recovery with a return to an active political life. The process of recovery was simple enough: sitting up, getting up, a few hours in the sun at the hospital before a period of convalescence at home in the country. I was not one to participate in the exchange of experiences that characterises hospital or clinic life. I remember sitting out one day in the sun with a newspaper deliberately held in front of me to fend off any attempts at idle chitchat, when a sympathetic voice said: 'How are you getting on, then?' Without lowering the newspaper, I answered: 'Very well. They say I will make a full recovery.' 'That's what they told me five years ago,' the now lugubrious-sounding voice replied. This did not strike me as a profitable conversation and I ostentatiously returned to studying my paper.

I spent a peaceful summer at home, an experience unknown in my adult life, gradually benefiting from the fresh air – with the aid of a golf-cart – and eventually enjoying the opportunity of working lightly in the garden, which since our acquisition of Thenford in 1977 had played so central a part in my life. John and Norma Major came to visit me on a Sunday in July and I attended the party Conference at Blackpool in October. I decided, however, against attempting a speech, if only to prevent it from being seen as something very different to what they had come to expect. Tim Sainsbury, as Minister of State for Industry, made the speech. But I was able to appear on the platform. It turned out to be the only time in my life when I have received a standing ovation for keeping quiet and letting someone else do the talking. I responded with a display of what used to be known as 'physical jerks'; 'fit as a fiddle' was the mute message. Norman Fowler, the party Chairman and one of my supporters in the leadership election, organised a giant 'welcome back' card.

In October after the party Conference I returned full-time to the Department of Trade and Industry, which Tim Sainsbury had in my four-month absence run with great care and efficiency. In particular, he had presided over a difficult redrawing of the map delineating the areas eligible for European regional funds. I felt considerable trepidation. Although I was now fully recovered and rested, it is one thing to cope with the relaxed comfort of a Northamptonshire home and garden, quite another to face the unremitting pressure of Cabinet life. I had returned to find that the government's position, in parliamentary terms, was deteriorating seriously.

The Maastricht Bill had reached the statute book in July, although not without plenty of alarums and excursions along the way. I had played a critical part at a crucial moment. Perhaps over-scrupulously, after the disaster of the Danish referendum repudiating the Treaty in the summer of 1992, the decision had been taken to suspend the Commons' consideration of Britain's own Maastricht ratification Bill. When the House came back after the summer recess, one of the first pieces of business was what became known as the Maastricht 'paving Bill', designed to jolt back into action – via an ersatz repeat of the second reading – the stalled legislation on the Treaty. This 'paving' debate took place on 4 November 1992; the Prime Minister opened for the government and Douglas Hurd, as Foreign Secretary, was due to wind up. It was a day of high tension. We knew that the vote would be uncomfortably close. Some time after 8 p.m. I went into the Whips' Office to get the latest intelligence. Richard Ryder, the Chief Whip, gloomily told me that there was still uncertainty over a number of colleagues, a list of whom he held in his hand. We faced defeat by one or two votes. The Prime Minister was dining in Room D (the smallest of the four dining rooms reserved for Members of Parliament and their guests); I interrupted his dinner and we returned to the Whips' Office. Richard repeated to him what he had told me.

I knew some of the doubters pretty well and asked John's permission to put a proposal individually to each of them which might secure their support. I proposed to offer that the third reading, and therefore the final Commons vote on the ratification of the Treaty, would not take place until the Danes had voted in their second referendum, scheduled for the following spring. John agreed.

We had both, however, failed to take one thing into consideration. Douglas Hurd was already sitting on the Treasury bench listening to Jack Cunningham's wind-up speech for the Opposition and by 9.30 p.m. (in less than twenty minutes' time) would be on his feet delivering his own reply. The question was how to apprise him of the seriousness of the situation and of the proposed concession. I went into the chamber, sat down beside him and tried to convey to him the danger we were in. I outlined the gist of what I was about to do. But he was concentrating on the debate and I am not sure that he took on board much of what I said – and anyway I had little time left to bring the sheep back into the fold. I spoke to Gerry Vaughan briefly, but the last prospective rebel to whom I talked was Michael Cartiss; indeed, I was spotted from the press gallery having an animated conversation with him on the floor of the House even after the vote had been called. Luckily I prevailed and, encouraged by a prime ministerial arm around his shoulder, he walked alongside John Major into the government lobby that night, helping to give us a majority of just three.

I returned to the whips' room, just off the Members' lobby, where I was offered a triumphant glass of champagne – only to be told that it was my own. When the world is falling apart, the whips are there to pick up the pieces. At the height of the reaction to the pit-closures announcement two weeks before they had played a vital role in helping to bring the parliamentary party back on side. After the critical vote I had sent Richard Ryder a case of champagne as a gesture of appreciation. I little thought that I would be sharing it with them when the case was opened.

That was not, though, the end of the story. The next morning Michael Cartiss told the newspapers about the deal I had put to him, on the promise of which he had changed his mind. Douglas, who had not really taken in what I had whispered to him the previous night, was not amused. A rather frosty conversation took place later that day in the Cabinet Room at No. 10, where I had been summoned to join a meeting between the Prime Minister and Foreign Secretary – at which, before I arrived, the latter had clearly been giving vent to his indignation at having this kind of deal done behind his back.

My relations with Douglas, my constituency neighbour in Oxfordshire, generally were as good as any I had with my Cabinet colleagues. A man of great integrity and fine intellect, he was one of the very few ministers who, although no great orator, made speeches at party conferences which were worth listening to, not just for their elegance and style but for their content. We only really differed on one policy issue. He tended to adopt a tougher line with the People's Republic of China – where in May 1995, in my last months as President of the Board of Trade, I took 130 industrialists on a successful export mission – than I would have done. But here, no doubt, he was influenced, as the Prime Minister certainly was, by his feeling of loyalty to Chris Patten who, as Governor of Hong Kong, had become involved in a confrontation with Beijing, with all the risks that spelt for our trading prospects in that vast market of 1.2 billion people.

I had been a member of Margaret Thatcher's Cabinet committee which determined the policy, as we concluded the 1984 agreement that was to lead to the 1997 handover of Hong Kong. I stated at the time that I believed the conclusion of that agreement opened the way for an improvement in our relations with China and to establishing confidence in Hong Kong's long-term future. Of course, I understood the arguments for introducing just before the handover the new democratic structure that Chris proposed. But how could one expect the Chinese to accept such a unilateral approach so shortly before 1997? We had governed Hong Kong for long enough to introduce a democratic constitution if we had believed it necessary or desirable. Perhaps it was to our discredit that we had not, but deathbed repentance, however genuine, looked very different when viewed from Beijing. Anyway, we had not done so. So what was the case for this last-minute change of heart? It could only be that we wished to create restraints for the mainland government which we had not suffered under ourselves. If that implied a lack of trust in Chinese willingness to abide by the 1984 agreement, well, the Chinese could work that out for themselves. If we didn't agree the changes with the Chinese, they would simply remove them – which is what they did, but not before much suspicion about our motives had been aroused.

I sometimes got the feeling, when these matters were discussed in Cabinet committee, that any decisions had already been pre-empted by the close personal contacts that existed between the Foreign Secretary and the Prime Minister on the one side and the Governor of Hong Kong on the other. Ignoring the severe loss of his exceptional talents to the Conservative Party, the story of Chris's governorship illustrates, I believe, the dangers and complications inherent for any Prime Minister in appointing a personal friend to so sensitive an official post.

I was to return to China as Deputy Prime Minister in May 1996 with a second trade mission, this time including 280 executives from British companies. We were well received first by Vice-Premier Li Lanqing, who had been to lunch at Thenford during an earlier visit to Britain, and then by President Jiang Zemin, who had just returned from a visit to South Africa. We met at Zhu Hai. The meeting was memorable in that after the first three-quarters of an hour – longer than the expected thirty minutes – the President said: 'Now the official visit is over. Let us talk in English.' For the next half-hour, in fluent English, he described the scale and complexity he and his government faced in transforming his enormous and diverse country from its largely peasant rural or low-skill urban economy into one that could hold its own in the twenty-first century. No political leadership had ever faced so substantial a task, to be undertaken at such a pace, in all human history. The city in which we met was evidence of the strategy: an immense airport, massive roadways, impressive infrastructure of every kind – way beyond any existing demand from the local population. It was a city built for a time that had not yet dawned.

Latterly, much of my time at the DTI was taken up with trying to shore up the position of the government – though the press, of course, would cynically have had it appear otherwise. Among our many problems a particularly virulent virus was spreading through the body politic: sleaze.

I remember one thing above all others of the Profumo affair of the early 1960s. It was the incomprehension of Harold Macmillan that Profumo could lie not only to his colleagues but to the House of Commons. Of course, such a reaction opens Macmillan up to the charge of naivety, but that is to oversimplify. The House of Commons is a club and, for all its deep and sometimes bitter rivalries, the very proximity and intimacy of life there, the long hours and the shared duties create a greater bond. Put simply: we are members of the House of Commons and few are not humbled by and respectful of the privilege. It is easy to feel ties of trust. Accusations of sleaze and corruption threatened all this.

As President of the Board of Trade, I found myself called upon to exercise a degree of judgement over three senior members of the Conservative Party, two of them ministers (indeed, one of them serving in the Cabinet with me): Jeffrey Archer, Jonathan Aitken and Neil Hamilton.

Jeffrey Archer I had never believed was reliable. I recall him approaching me one night in the division lobbies in the 1970s (when he was, briefly, the Member for Louth) and telling me that one day he would like to be a member of my government. The implied flattery was, I assumed, part of an approach widely scattered on the off-chance that one of the seeds would produce fruit. There was something about him that I did not trust and in this I disagreed with John Major, who felt that Archer might be silly and make mistakes but was not dishonest. I took a harsher view, but it was based more on instinct than on evidence.

Allegations that he had engaged in insider share dealing were reported to the DTI for investigation. It was alleged that he had information available to him, as a result of his wife Mary's position as a director of Anglia Television, that alerted him to an impending takeover. The DTI procedures in such cases leave the Secretary of State with no more than a presiding role over a well-oiled machine. Whatever investigations appear appropriate are conducted by inspectors, who are themselves recommended to the Secretary of State by the responsible section of the Department. Such investigations are by tradition and long practice confidential.

In Jeffrey Archer's case it was not that simple. I was told one afternoon that *The Times* intended to reveal the following day that an investigation was under way. Normally the Department's response would have been neither to confirm nor to deny an investigation

– there had only ever been one exception back in the late 1980s. This is a sensible way to proceed. Wild and wholly unsubstantiated allegations can be made against innocent people. Such allegations may be speedily dismissed, but each has to be properly examined. It is perfectly reasonable to protect those so accused by this simple formula.

I did not believe such protection would suffice in this case. *The Times* was going to print the story. There were only two alternatives for me, given that the investigation could not be denied. I could stick to the formula. If I had, the national press would have accused me of covering up for a senior member of the party. The only alternative was to admit the fact, although I knew I would be accused of foul play by Jeffrey Archer's friends. I decided that the balance of the argument lay in confirming that the matter had been referred to the Department, where it was proceeding along routine and well-established lines. I do not believe that Archer's position was in any way worsened by what I did. Any other route would have led to intense criticism, not just of me but of the government as a whole. In the event the inspectors, having considered all the evidence, recommended that we should not take the matter any further, and I accepted their advice.

Jonathan Aitken was altogether a more sophisticated operator. Few arrive on the political scene blessed with more talents. Possessed of elegant good looks, a cosmopolitan charm and a fine mind, he was as much at home in the writing of his much praised biography of Richard Nixon as he was in defending the Eurosceptic cause in response to Ted Heath at the Tory Party Conference. He moved easily and gracefully along the corridors of power and he possessed the qualities to find distinction at the end of them. He was easy to get along with. As Chief Secretary to the Treasury from 1994 his task was to screw my Department's budget as close to the floorboards as he could. But at the end of the day we had a private arrangement that, if a particularly attractive inward investment opportunity needed an extra grant to facilitate its agreement, I could always go back to him. He was a man with whom one could do business. Unfortunately, others felt the same and there arose a series of allegations about his business relationships, especially in the Middle East.

The arms-to-Iraq scandal had led to the controversy over PII certificates and the establishment of the Scott Inquiry. Not surprisingly, it had also left DTI ministers more than a little sensitive to the possibility that there might be other, similar cases concealed in the woodwork.

In the spring of 1995 Ian Taylor, the junior DTI Minister in charge of trade policy at the time, drew to my attention his concern over answers he had received when he had asked about the Department's knowledge of the background to certain export licences issued in the late 1980s. At the heart of his concern was a company called BMARC, of which – when he was a backbencher – Jonathan Aitken had been a non-executive director. It was alleged that the company had at that time been exporting arms to Iran via Singapore.

Parliamentary questions about BMARC had been tabled by the Labour MP Brian Wilson, and they were for the DTI to answer. Neither Ian nor I was fully satisfied with the draft answers submitted to us by the Department. We required further information. Our subsequent probings raised some doubts about the handling of documentation in support of export licence applications and of intelligence reports and showed that earlier MOD answers to two related questions had been inaccurate. It was clear that we had no alternative but to inform the House of Commons at the earliest moment of the information that had now come to light and that, in doing so, it was unavoidable that Jonathan would be questioned since there were already accusations in the press about his links with the company. I was not prepared to countenance either delay or the suggestion that a Cabinet colleague was, in some way, being protected from a full and proper investigation by virtue of his position. Jonathan has since suggested in his autobiography, *Pride and Perjury*, that I had a hidden agenda. This charge is groundless. I was determined that Parliament should be told the truth. I had to accept that, in order that no hint of scandal should attach to the government, Jonathan would have to undergo an intense scrutiny.

I cleared my course of action with the Prime Minister, and made an oral statement to the House on 13 June. This seemed the best means by which to inform Parliament of the information we had so far discovered. It meant that I could be questioned there and then, thus minimising the risk of any accusation of a cover-up or of concealing the facts. I wanted the matter fully investigated. I announced that all the information we had available had been passed to Customs and Excise for them to determine whether any offences had been committed. In addition, I offered to co-operate with the Trade and Industry Select Committee, if it was minded to undertake its own speedy investigation. As it was an all-party committee under a Labour chairman, any charge that we might be trying to hush this matter up would look ridiculous. My advice to Jonathan at the time was that, if he was innocent, he should weather the storm; I believed that to have been the best counsel available in the difficult circumstances in which he found himself. But his career ended in tears. He resigned some two weeks later, following a continual barrage of media attention.

In the meantime the Committee responded to my initiative and Jonathan later testified before them. His explanation that he knew nothing of any illegal activities was accepted in their report. He took the *Guardian* to court for libel but the case collapsed and subsequently in early 1999 he stood trial himself for perjury and attempting to pervert the course of justice, and was found guilty.

It was important that he served time in prison; it was typical of his resilience that he carried the experience with no little dignity. At the time of my challenge to Mrs Thatcher in 1990, Jonathan was not a supporter of mine. My European views were quite unacceptable to him but he treated my endeavours with great courtesy, even sending me, attendant upon my defeat, a copy of Kipling's famous verse 'If', which begins: 'If you can keep your head when all about you are losing theirs', and ends, 'you'll be a man, my son'. I looked at it hard on the day he was sent to prison in 1999, but decided against sending it back to him.

Neil Hamilton had proved an effective junior minister. His political instincts placed him firmly on the right-wing of the party but, as so often in my experience, this had been of little relevance in the day-to-day conduct of departmental affairs. He had prepared a significant update of competition policy, which was approved in Cabinet committee and was designed to replace the existing presumptions upon which competition policy was based with a regime much more familiar among our European partners than in Britain. But in the event we did not succeed in getting a slot in the legislative timetable and the legislation was never enacted.

Inevitably, a Secretary of State does not always accept the advice of his junior colleagues but I remember few examples of this with Neil. On specific competition policy references, attempts were made to suggest that under my regime competition policy changed. There is no truth in this. In practice I took relatively few important decisions and almost invariably agreed with the advice I received via Neil from officials.

Neil had been my junior minister for two and a half years when, just after the party Conference in October 1994, allegations began to circulate that he and a junior minister at the Northern Ireland Office, Tim Smith, had been in receipt of payments by the owner of Harrods, Mohammed Al-Fayed, some years earlier when they had both been on the back benches. Tim admitted receiving payment for asking questions on Al-Fayed's behalf in the mid-1980s and resigned immediately. Neil flatly denied any such charge. The Prime Minister asked Sir Robin Butler as secretary of the Cabinet to investigate a series of allegations about a number of colleagues, including Neil, which were being made by Al-Fayed. These had been relayed to John a few weeks earlier in a bizarre attempt to coerce the government over the publication of a DTI report on the takeover of Harrods. Brian Hitchen, editor of the *Sunday Express*, found himself acting as go-between. John absolutely refused to do any deal, but naturally enough the allegations had to be checked. As a result, Robin had spoken to Neil, who assured him that he had received no money from Al-Fayed. I pointed out, however, that we should also ensure that Neil had had no financial relationship with anybody or any organisation that could be associated with Al-Fayed.

I agreed that I would put that specific point to Neil and I spoke to him on the telephone. I was satisfied by the answer I received and I duly reported to Robin Butler, who recorded our conclusions in a note for the record. It subsequently emerged, however, that Neil had been retained as a consultant by Ian Greer, a parliamentary lobbyist with connections to Al-Fayed. Neil was to say that he believed there had been a misunderstanding about the meaning of my question with the consequence that his answer related only to what he thought I had meant. His understanding had differed from mine. There can be no way of reconciling such a difference of interpretation. But Tim Smith had already resigned and, as the storm around Neil blew and other allegations against him came to our attention involving a Mobil Oil consultancy fee, it was agreed that the Chief Whip, Richard Ryder, and I should talk to him. His situation had become untenable. I remember well what I said to him: that there was no evidence to support the accusations made against him and that we all respected the fundamental principle of justice that he was innocent until proven guilty. But, as the Minister responsible for the good conduct of corporate governance, it no longer seemed possible for him to exercise such a responsibility, which demanded the highest standards of integrity and probity, while his position was day by day undermined by sensational headlines. Neil again protested his innocence and expressed deep resentment at the injustice of trial by headline, but accepted the logic of what Richard and I had had to say to him. He resigned then and there. His ministerial career appeared over. But he enjoyed strong support from a substantial body of the party activists in his Tatton constituency and there was a running battle within his divided Association up to and including the general election a year and a half later, when he lost the seat to the independent Martin Bell, 'the man in the white suit'. Neil continued with his determination to clear his name by various legal means but, over two years later, his case was to be delivered its final quietus by his own unwise libel action in the High Court.

Many others contributed to the allegations that so enmeshed John Major's government. John could be forgiven for feeling that the fates dealt him a marked deck of cards when he inherited a party and a government destined to be sucked down in an uncontrollable whirlpool of sleaze. One colleague after another was to be exposed by the relentless attention of the national press. Several of the events sensationalised with such disastrous consequences for the good reputation of the Tory Party and the government it formed had taken place before he ever became Prime Minister. Frequently such allegations as appeared were half denied by the colleagues in question. But the cumulative effect was devastating.

In the summer prior to the allegations against Neil and Tim, the *Sunday Times* decided to try and trap certain MPs by arranging for so-called 'businessmen' to offer payment in return for the tabling of parliamentary questions. Two colleagues, David Tredinnick and Graham Riddick, fell for it and paid a heavy but legitimate price. Then came the allegations against Neil and Tim. What these two episodes demonstrated was that, despite the existence of the Register of Members' Interests, there was a grey area surrounding the relationship between Members of Parliament and outside organisations, legitimately or otherwise pursuing their own interests whether through the offices of parliamentary lobbyists or by directly retaining MPs as paid consultants. So, at the end of October, John announced his decision to invite Lord Nolan to lead an inquiry with clear terms of reference: 'To examine current concerns about standards of conduct of all holders of public office, including arrangements relating to financial and commercial activities, and make recommendations as to any changes in present arrangements which might be required to ensure the highest standards of probity in public life'.

John's intentions in all this could not have been more honourable, but the subsequent Nolan Report and the select committee recommendations which followed proved yet another rod with which the party could beat his back. The Tory back benches regarded Nolan's recommendations on disclosure as a slur on their collective integrity; a select committee tried to mitigate these and thus placate the worst of this sense of outrage; and the Opposition played the issue for all it was worth – helped by ever more sleaze allegations emerging in the press. The upshot of the resulting sound and fury was that on a free vote the House of Commons, with the help of twenty Tory defectors, defeated the government's preferred option, which had incorporated the Select Committee's recommendations, and adopted the Nolan Report instead. It has to be said, too, that Labour, when they came to office, found to their own cost that questions of cash payments and of the influence of paid consultants on government decision-making are not quite so cut and dried as they made out in opposition.

More lurid headlines began to impact on one of the government's most successful policies. Despite the unquestionable and incalculable benefits to the national economy of the privatisation programme, there was always a whiff of easy pickings for a privileged few associated with it. The frustrations of the left at the evident success of the policy made them ever hungry to undermine its credibility or to portray it as a rip-off of the legitimate assets of the state. The press were ready and willing to become accomplices. The controversy centred on the nature of the contracts awarded to former public sector managers following the transfer of their businesses to the private sector. It should be stressed that this was all totally within the law. There was no misconduct and a clear distinction must be drawn between these matters and the issues of private misconduct which arose from the behaviour of a small number of parliamentary colleagues. The question was whether the rules should be changed, not whether anyone had broken them.

The issue itself became personalised by the case of Cedric Brown, the chief executive of British Gas. In November 1994 the *Sunday Times* reported that his salary was to increase by 75 per cent. Other cases were rapidly added to the tabloid press rogues' gallery, particularly from the newly privatised water companies. By and large the public sector grossly underpays its senior executives, but they have virtual job security for life and an index-linked pension to go with it. Transfer to the private sector, if it meant anything, involved uncertainty, risk, genuine accountability and, above all, the need to recruit top-class managers at open-market rates. But you can't run a privatised business paying yesterday's low public sector pay rates to the existing, formerly publicly employed executives and at the same time recruit new colleagues from the private sector at similar levels of seniority but at higher market rates. So a massive post-privatisation adjustment took place. The newly privatised executives signed up deals for themselves commensurate with their new status. In particular, they obtained stock options which, when realised, produced substantial capital gains, as the companies' balance sheets rapidly improved, often in a way quite unanticipated at the time of privatisation.

Of course, some weren't worth these enhanced packages. A high proportion of these executives soon found themselves jobless, but with the cash from their recently negotiated and now terminated contracts. As many of these gains were quantified as part of a compensation package on dismissal from office, it is easy to see why the charge grew that they were being rewarded for failure. Government was powerless in retrospect to prevent these arrangements in what were now private sector companies, but the criticism was nonetheless intense and damaging.

I could see no course of retrospective action open to government that was either practical or desirable. But in order to try and deflect some of the criticism and particularly to look for a means of avoiding future outcry, I invited Sir Richard Greenbury, chairman and chief executive of Marks and Spencer, to examine the issues involved in remuneration packages and good governance more widely, not just in the newly privatised sector, and to make recommendations. He had experienced the problem for himself as chairman of the Remuneration Committee of British Gas where, on privatisation, they had increased salaries significantly, but had outlawed share options for three years after flotation. He was joined on the new committee by some of Britain's leading industrialists, including David Simon of BP, Sir Iain Vallance of British Telecom, Sir Michael Angus of Whitbread and Boots, and Sir Denys Henderson of ICI. The press immediately labelled them 'fat cats' – unfairly in my view, given their positions as heads of some of Europe's leading companies and their comparatively modest salaries by UK corporate standards of the day. But it became a popular catchphrase which began to affect the private sector more widely. (The irony, of course, was that at the same time the public were more than prepared to see pop stars and footballers paid far greater sums.)

The Committee was an attempt to find answers through City self-restraint rather than legislation. I think in the end Rick Greenbury deeply regretted accepting the job. He was harshly treated by the Select Committee, but his scorn was reserved for the press, who exposed him to the sort of treatment politicians though not business-men have come to expect, and even invaded the privacy of his home and children. His recommendations made good sense, but the problem had been much exacerbated by the one-off adjustment as industries moved from the state sector to the private. That adjustment, one way or another, was bound to happen, yet we paid a high political price for it. It added to the general atmosphere of 'sleaze' that was already undermining the good reputation that people are entitled to expect of their government.

This growing atmosphere of public cynicism towards the privatisation revolution in no way diminished my enthusiasm or undermined my own conviction of the desirability of the process. I privatised more organisations than any other minister, stretching from the council houses back in the early 1980s to the decisions which led finally to the sale of the nuclear generators. I doubt if even the most determined and doctrinal of Tories, of which I was one (where privatisation was concerned), seriously contemplated such a disposal programme at the beginning of the journey in 1979.

The government had included the nuclear generators in its original privatisation package for the electricity industry in the late 1980s but had withdrawn them from the deal when their inclusion threatened delay. Tim Eggar and I now met the leaders of the industry to search for a way forward. The problem was how to separate the modern nuclear power stations, for which there was a market, from the older, limited-life stations, the cost of the cleaning of which meant that they were actually liabilities. We needed to do this against the background of suspicion and controversy which surrounds this particular industry. Our discussions persuaded us, however, that the problems were less formidable than supposed, provided we had the will to do it. The safety card was played against us; it was said that it would require eighteen months for the Nuclear Inspectorate to issue the necessary safety certificates and thus privatisation could not be achieved before the election. The argument was preposterous. The plants were already up and running. Either they were safe or they were not. The nuclear physics involved, the stations themselves, the safety procedures and the management were not to change. We obtained the certificates in three months. And following the legislation one more commanding height became just another company.

My intention at the DTI had always been to enhance its role but not its size. Every agency was put under a spotlight. My preference was always to move them into the private sector or to engage them in commercially disciplined partnerships. The onus was on them to prove that they had to remain within the public sector. Companies House, the Patent Office, the Insolvency Service and the Radiocommunications Agency – none of these had any enthusiasm for such change but change there was to be. However, even I could not have anticipated just what it was to mean for the Radiocommunications Agency, when, following a joint report by NERA and Smith Associates, Ian Taylor, whose departmental responsibilities included Science and Technology, suggested for inclusion in our Competitiveness White Paper in 1996 a proposal to exploit the potential value of the radio spectrum. I was at first concerned that this would lead to a charging structure which might be seen as a backdoor stealth-tax on industry and also that that most loquacious of pressure groups, the London black-taxi drivers, would react against the potential increase in their two-way radio costs. I was finally persuaded and, having enlisted the backing of Ken Clarke at the Treasury, together we overcame a hesitant No. 10. The proposal to auction the spectrum appeared in our 1997 manifesto, with my strong backing as Deputy PM (I had by now moved to the Cabinet Office). We had believed it would raise between £1 billion and £1.5 billion. Three years later the Labour government landed a windfall of over £22 billion. I should point out, however, that over twenty years the Treasury receipts from corporation tax will be £6.6 billion less, as the initial cost is tax deductible. (In the event the two-way radio costs of London's black taxis have not increased; so many of them share each channel that the cost in most cases has actually fallen.)

My attention focused in turn on the government research laboratories which the Department sponsored. Our policy was to separate our interests as customer from the laboratories' status as contractors. I supported this policy although I recalled my earlier experiences over the Rothschild recommendations in 1972. We proceeded to privatise the National Engineering Laboratory in Glasgow, the Atomic Energy Authority laboratories at Harwell and the Laboratory of the Government Chemist (LGC), although I failed to get Michael

Howard to agree to merge the Home Office's forensic laboratory in London with the LGC as part of the package. The National Physics Laboratory (NPL) at Teddington in London was provided with commercial management under contract. That left the Warren Springs Laboratory in Hertfordshire, which undertook environmental work but whose facilities were only half used.

Without my foreknowledge a press release was issued stating that an offer from the pharmaceutical company Glaxo had been accepted for the sale of the Warren Springs site, thus providing £30 million to enable the laboratory to rebuild its facilities near by. As soon as this announcement was brought to my attention, I was deeply suspicious. I was told that the new laboratory represented the best value of the available options. I decided to appoint outside consultants. PA Consulting Group duly presented their findings, which concluded that there would be £45 million of savings if the Warren Springs scientists were transferred to Harwell and that the science would not suffer and might actually benefit from such a merger. Officials did not contest the findings. I had previously been told it was all too late, yet we discovered that no contracts had been exchanged. Warren Springs moved to Harwell and on into the private sector.

Before I returned in October 1993 to full-time work at the DTI following my heart attack, Tim Eggar rang me at Thenford to discuss the appointment of a new director general of Ofgas, the regulator for the gas industry. I very much relied on his judgement, and Clare Spottiswoode, from a private sector background, was chosen. Together, we were determined to introduce competition into the gas industry.

British Gas enjoyed a virtual monopoly of supply even after privatisation. The problems were formidable, particularly as no new entrant into the field would duplicate the national network of pipes that delivered gas to its customers. Tim Eggar and the new regulator came up with a plan to leave the monopoly in gas transportation in place, regulated as a monopoly, while allowing private sector companies to compete in the selling of the gas itself. We were promised – and subsequently saw achieved – substantial reductions in prices, thus benefiting the individual customer and industrial users alike. We wanted to ensure that Britain's international competitive strength remained unimpaired. Again, experience has justified the care we took, as has the maintenance of standards of safety and reliability, both of which featured high on our list of priorities. Britain's gas industry today is a world model. None of this would have proved possible without Tim Eggar's political skill and industrial acumen in giving the lead that he did. It has to be said in passing that he was marginally helped by the row over Cedric Brown's salary, which in some measure undermined the support among MPs for British Gas in their efforts to avoid the break-up he subsequently steered through the Commons in what became the Gas Act 1995.

Politically, the government's position was becoming, if anything, more serious – at least in the polls. Speculative undercurrents were washing about again in the Members' lobby, in the tea rooms and in the press gallery.

John Major's easy victory against Douglas Hurd and myself in the leadership election of 1990 and his outstanding triumph in the general election a year and a half later should have ended any further speculation about his leadership in general and my prospects in such a context in particular. But they had not. When I returned to full-time activity as a minister following my heart attack, the coal crisis of a year earlier was fading and I was now given a generous reception by colleagues whenever I spoke in the House. The divisions over Europe continued to besiege John and the leadership question rumbled on, aided and abetted by the endless stirrings in the media.

In early 1994 my PPS, Richard Ottaway, was quoted in *The Times* as saying that 'If there was a vacancy Michael would consider his position.' In the hothouse of politics this was enough to fuel speculation about my intentions once more. As the opinion polls turned sour and as we faced local and European elections which my colleagues feared would be a rout, Richard became the conduit through which messages of support were once again sent. In February the *Sunday Times* listed six possible successors should John be challenged. I scraped on to the list at 20–1 against. But new bets the following day shortened the odds at William Hill to 7–1. My appearance before the Scott Inquiry provoked articles in *The Times*, the *Daily Mail* and the *Sun* suggesting I could yet take over the leadership before the next election. By March Richard believed that any vacancy would be filled by either Ken Clarke or myself. John was continuously at the receiving end of adverse press comment, which he was finding increasingly difficult to bear. I told him simply not to read it. But such advice ran counter to his character. He was a man who had to know.

My problem was by now abundantly clear. I had had long experience of living in the media eye as a potential candidate for the
leadership of the party. The interminable polls had begun quoting
odds against my name back in the early 1980s, when I ran second
to Francis Pym. This was followed by a period when I trailed behind
Kenneth Baker, which in turn gave way to the fevered speculation in
the period leading up to the downfall of Mrs Thatcher. Now I was
seeing it all over again, this time with Ken Clarke in pole position. No
one can pretend to be unaffected by such coverage. It is not sought but
it is, after all, your career that is being analysed and foretold. Of course,
I listened to what Richard had to tell me but never with any serious
belief that it would lead anywhere. In addition, I was determined to
give no encouragement of any sort to the speculation, and was anxious
that Richard did not do so either. It may be quite impossible to stop
the chatter. It is quite another matter to encourage it. This I would
not do.

The pressure on John increased, particularly from the Eurosceptics
on our own benches. The European Union was intending to admit four
new members at this time: Austria, Sweden, Finland and Norway. It
was proposed that at the same time the number of votes needed to
form a 'blocking minority' in European decision-making be increased,
making it easier for a majority to overrule resistance. The Cabinet was
unanimous in supporting John's determination to resist this proposal,
which was underpinned by official advice that we had many allies,
including France and Germany. The Eurosceptics exaggerated the
issue out of all proportion, with a little help from the press. In the
event our European allies all melted away and Douglas Hurd had an
extremely difficult time at the Ioannina meeting of foreign ministers
in Greece. John reluctantly had to agree with his advice to accept a
compromise. His ensuing statement in the House was listened to in
near silence, though the Eurosceptic Tony Marlow felt compelled to
call on him to resign.

By late April Richard Ottaway had started to come under fire. John
came close to accusing him of openly canvassing my prospects. Archie
Hamilton (who had retired from his position as Minister of State for
the Armed Forces the previous year but was completely loyal to
John) so accused him to his face. Andrew Mitchell, a junior whip,
told him he had been rumbled. Graham Bright, the Prime Minister's
PPS, let Richard know that he was not enhancing his own career by
his advocacy of my position. Richard put out a statement, printed in

The Times on 27 April, denying the allegations and pledging loyalty to the Prime Minister. Inevitably, no one believed him. They all thought they knew better.

In early May, William Rees-Mogg was writing in *The Times* that John should hand over to me and become Foreign Secretary. Richard continued to keep me fully apprised of the gossip – that was his job. I remained quite relaxed whichever way events unfolded. I would do all I could to help John, do nothing to undermine or encourage others to undermine him and get on with my job at the Department. Anything I could have said about the matter would only have added to the headlines and fuelled speculation further.

Then on 12 May, during the usual early morning ministers' meeting with my colleagues in the DTI, my ever vigilant private secretary Peter Smith came in, carrying a single piece of paper which he handed to me in silence. 'Oh no,' was my reaction as I read the note, which told me that John Smith, the leader of the Labour Party, had died of a second heart attack. This was sad news indeed. I cannot claim to have been a friend of John's but, like many Tory MPs, I had developed a great affection for him. He was a warm and generous man. He had suffered an earlier heart attack in 1987 and had been one of the first to write to me when I was in hospital the previous summer – a sympathetic and encouraging letter. Now his death just a year later, at the age of fifty-six, was a great shock and tragedy. He had been a brilliant Commons debater and from the Opposition's point of view had made a lot of mileage out of the Maastricht Bill – although, having been one of the original sixty-nine pro-European Labour rebels back in 1971, he still possessed a root commitment to Europe. Not for one moment did I ever doubt the sincerity of his convictions, although they in good measure differed from mine. He had an open smile not far below the surface of his political wit. We crossed swords across the dispatch box and we both gave of our best, but each time I attempted to shower scorn and sarcasm upon him the look on his face was more that of a teacher awarding marks for performance than of an embittered opponent deeply offended by the enemy's attack.

By lunchtime my parliamentary enemies were briefing the press about the implications of John's death for my own future. Life in the jungle of politics moves with ruthless speed.

As a mark of respect the government postponed controversy in the House and delayed some business at the request of the Opposition, including the publication of our first Competitiveness White Paper.

None of this was a mere superficial gesture. I had been due to make a political speech to an audience of party activists the night John died. I simply couldn't do it. The words wouldn't come. The party points seemed empty and unbecoming. There is something above the battle that binds us together. I am glad I reacted the way I did. It told me something about how much my time in the House of Commons meant to me.

Following John Smith's death, the momentum for a change of leadership of the Tory Party that had taken such hold that spring subsided like a pricked balloon. Within a matter of weeks the focus of attention had shifted. Suggestions now began appearing regularly that I should become Chairman of the party; who inspired these and for what motives I have never been entirely certain.

Events drifted on through the summer and the party Conference. The government's problems continued unabated. Our Eurosceptics had by no means given up once we had got the Maastricht legislation through – indeed, as late as November 1994, eight Tory MPs abstained on a three-line whip requiring them to vote against a Labour amendment to the European Communities (Finance) Bill. I fully supported the Prime Minister in his insistence that the government regard the passage of this Bill (which, again, involved treaty obligations) as a matter of confidence. I backed his determination to resign and precipitate a general election if he failed to get it through. That threat did not deter the eight hard-core rebels who, on 28 November, the fourth anniversary of John Major's accession to the premiership, ostentatiously sat out the division. The whip was duly withdrawn, while another Tory MP, Richard Body, voluntarily resigned it in sympathy. We had seen this rebellion coming and I had been present at an earlier discussion of the proposal to withdraw the whip at a small dinner at No. 10, and strongly endorsed it. However, these nine 'whipless ones', as they came to call themselves, attracted a good deal of sympathy and were accorded continual coverage in the media. They were portrayed as victims whereas they were, in fact, the agents of their own fate. As John Major recounts in his autobiography, he came under increasing pressure to bring them back from sympathisers in the Cabinet and on the back benches, including members of the 1922 Committee executive, not least Marcus Fox, its chairman. Richard Ryder warned him of the risk he ran and John felt bitterly let down when these warnings proved more than justified. Far from the new mood of unity and harmony he had been given to expect if and when they were reinstated, he was faced with triumphalist statements given to the nation's press on College Green. Such leading figures as Teresa Gorman, Christopher Gill and Tony Marlow went on to use their time to regroup and emerge as 'whippers-in' for John Redwood's leadership campaign against the Prime Minister the following summer.

But as a result of all the dramatic developments of November 1994 the tension was again approaching fever pitch. Rumours reached Richard Ottaway that the right wing were collecting signatures to mount a challenge to John. Richard came down to Thenford to bring me up to date. I told him I had lived with this sort of speculation since 1986 and at times longed to escape from it. I was constantly asked the same question over and over again, *ad nauseam*, about my leadership ambitions. I always answered categorically that I would never stand against John Major. But the pressure was now back where it had been before John Smith's death.

By the second week in December the Conservatives were trailing Labour by thirty-nine points, the largest gap since polls began. John Major fully appreciated the acute nature of the position, both for himself and for the party. He could only wait for the evident economic recovery to turn the government's fortunes. I constantly told him that our prospects would revive only if people's real disposable income had been improving for at least twelve months before polling day. There was still time, if only just.

What little patience I had had with the backbench leaders of the Eurosceptics had long since disappeared. My instinct now was to take them on. Richard and Michael Mates tried to persuade me that I needed to moderate my position. The party in the House wanted it. My continued hostility could only damage me personally should any contest develop. It was important in the coming weeks, they argued, that whatever move were made to try and bring the Eurosceptics back into the fold I should not seem too distant from it.

Anne and I saw in the New Year of 1995 in Kenya, with family and friends. On my return Richard told me that he foresaw a risk that I would be approached by backbenchers urging me to suggest to John that he should step aside. I made it clear that I would not even contemplate such a suggestion. In the meantime Michael Mates was deeply concerned later that month to learn that I was working on a high-profile, pro-European speech with all the stops full open. Regardless of any personal considerations, its drafting was in practice rather more a way of venting my frustration over what was happening to opinion in the party. I couldn't have made the speech within the bounds of collective responsibility. In the end, Eileen saw to it that all copies were shredded – except one. I had enjoyed writing it and was determined that one day I would make it. Let me set out a few of its concluding paragraphs. I would not in the light of subsequent events rewrite them:

> When Mrs Thatcher signed the Single European Act, she encouraged and stimulated a set of economic processes that were bound inevitably to affect the lives and practices of every citizen in the land.
>
> No Prime Minister in her position could have responsibly taken any other decision. Any more in his time could John Major at Maastricht.
>
> But once the floodgates of economic advance were opened, as night follows day there would be demand for political control.
>
> And this is the nub. Individual control according to the self-interest of twelve, or now fifteen, nation states is not control at all.
>
> You cannot maintain acceptance for a market place without rules.
>
> You cannot have rules that are unpoliced. You cannot police rules effectively without a court.
>
> Inevitably the process of politics leads to the language of compromise. How far should the process go? At what pace and when? What balance should be struck between national competence, pride and expertise and the encroachments of less cosy, less familiar, less accountable, supra-national authorities? No one can define answers to these questions. No answer can be blessed with immortality. Should you build a democratic structure there to control the supra-national authorities? How do you do that without undermining the national parliaments? This is the stuff of politics. But the most uncomfortable question of all is how do you influence those decisions as seems right at the time, if you are not even at the conference table that takes them?
>
> Draw a line in the sand? Sands have been known to shift.
>
> Build the fortifications of a Maginot Line? Someone found a way round.

The arrival of spring brought no change in our fortunes. Richard was still continually being approached with messages of support and, by the end of March, offers of backing from two prominent right-wingers, David Evans and Alan Duncan. Richard told them both I would do no deal. In early April, Michael Fabricant reported conversations he had

had with David English, the editor-in-chief of the *Daily Mail* and the *Mail on Sunday* and on another occasion with Rupert Murdoch. Both were now doubting if they would support John in a general election but told him they would back me for leader, if a contest developed. And so it went on: more offers of support, more press speculation, more advice.

But the contest when it did develop – occasioned by John's bomb-shell resignation as leader of the Conservative Party – came as a total surprise to me. One night in early June 1995 I had walked out with him from the House of Commons chamber after a ten o'clock vote. I asked if I could have a moment or two of his time to discuss some routine matter of business. He invited me to join him for a drink in his room behind the Speaker's chair. When we had disposed of my departmental business, he changed the subject and said that he had been thinking for some time about how to involve me more closely in the running of the government.

We had already had an earlier discussion about the possibility that I might become Chairman of the party. About a year before he had invited me to join him for a talk in the garden of No. 10, and asked me if I would do the job. At the time I had expressed an unwillingness to give up the DTI and said that I did not believe it was possible to combine the two roles – as even Mrs Thatcher had been forced to recognise when one of her latterday favourites, David (Lord) Young, had wanted to try. John seemed to accept the case I made and did not raise the chairmanship with me again.

Now, on this subsequent occasion, the Prime Minister began by making some highly flattering comments about the contribution he felt sure I could make in some new, undefined role. He told me about a memorandum he had received from David Hunt, who, as Chancellor of the Duchy of Lancaster, was a member of the Chief Whip's No. 12 Committee tasked with overseeing the presentation of policy, which David himself co-ordinated. David's memo had concluded that he did not have sufficient clout within the government to draw together or control the numerous currents of activity in the way the job demanded. He was consequently more than willing to stand aside for someone who did. John and I explored together what this might mean in specific terms. This was the first time that the possibility that I could become Deputy Prime Minister was raised. But it was the second occasion that the suggestion had been put to me that the government would benefit if I became more closely involved at the centre. In a way it no doubt reflected just how gravely John regarded not merely our problems with the electorate (we had now lost three safe Tory seats – Newbury, Christchurch and Eastleigh – at by-elections to the Liberal Democrats) but, even more crucially, the difficulties we faced in managing an increasingly recalcitrant party in the Commons. However, I think it also reflected a growing sense of trust that our time together had engendered.

John asked whether, if I were to be appointed Deputy Prime Minister, I would expect precedence even over the Lord Chancellor, at that time next to the Prime Minister himself at the top of the Cabinet pecking order. I replied firmly that, if the job were to be done effectively, that was the authority it would require. We agreed that we would both think about it. The broaching of the matter was a total surprise to me, although before mentioning it to me John had obviously been turning it over in his own mind – and, I afterwards discovered, had discussed it with at least Douglas Hurd, if not with other colleagues, whose judgement he valued. However, I left his office in the House late that evening with no agreed timetable or initiative by which matters would be taken further. We had explored the territory and each understood what any decision to proceed would involve for both of us; but there was no commitment on either side that any such arrangement would be entered into. Some have suggested that this was simply an exercise to cast a fly over me. Others have said that in most of life, but especially in politics, it is worth a search for the hidden motive. But I did not then and do not now believe that. And subsequent events argue against it.

Two or three weeks later, on 22 June, just before Cabinet I was again alone with John, this time in No. 10, talking over government business. I had discussed our earlier conversation with Anne, whose feeling was that I should react positively, although her preferred option would have been for me to go to the Foreign Office (I did not at that stage know that Douglas would be leaving it; he didn't announce his resignation until 23 June). No one questions the illustrious nature of the Foreign Office, but I was very much aware that it would not provide the base from which I would be able to undertake the role that John seemed to have in mind for me. We were facing a general election in less than two years and elections are essentially about home, not foreign, politics. As our routine discussion that morning concluded, I brought up our earlier conversation: 'By the way, I have thought about the discussions we had that evening in your office—' He interrupted by saying: 'Well, interesting that you should raise that issue, but there has been another development that I would like to talk to you about.' He then outlined to me his continuing frustrations with the behaviour of certain colleagues and the endless speculation that surrounded his future and that of the government in what was, by now, a largely hostile press. He told me he was seriously considering resigning as leader of the party and putting himself up for re-election. He asked my opinion of such a strategy. I was amazed.

I had always tried to be frank with him. My immediate reaction was to say that it was extremely difficult for me to advise him since I could be the principal beneficiary if anything were to go wrong with the strategy. It was difficult to give dispassionate advice about a situation in which potentially I had such a considerable personal stake. That was my first reaction and at least it had the merit of being honest. But after a moment's thought I went on to tell him that I thought the strategy was sound and courageous – and, with its substantial element of surprise, stood a real chance of silencing the critics. John thanked me for the advice, adding that he recognised that there was a downside and that it could go badly wrong but still felt that the present situation could not be allowed to continue. That afternoon at five o'clock he held his famous press conference in the garden at No. 10 and took the world by surprise.

There has, of course, been much speculation about whether or not a deal was reached between us. I explicitly reject any such suggestion. John never sought to extract from me any sort of understanding that I would not enter the contest which he now proposed. He had made no attempt between our first meeting and that in the Cabinet Room to see how my mind was moving on the initial option he had put to me. He had not even waited to hear what conclusion I had reached over the suggestion that I might become Deputy Prime Minister. He may have personally reached a judgement that I would not enter the lists. He may have calculated that I would accept the Deputy Premiership. I cannot know what was in his mind. I do know, however, that he never sought to establish these facts before he told me of his new plan. I prefer to believe that he judged that the strength of the relationship that had developed between us meant that I would not stand against him. It never occurred to me to do so. He had treated me well. I had been part of every serious decision and discussion – with the possible exception of his painstaking work for peace in Northern Ireland – that he had undertaken as Prime Minister.

In fact we did discuss Northern Ireland together too. He told me one Sunday night over dinner in No. 10 of his planned initiative, to try once again – in concert with the Irish Taoiseach Albert Reynolds – to find a solution to the impasse over Northern Ireland. I said it demonstrated real courage and that I had only one piece of advice: he should prepare his exit strategy. I could understand the community of interest which might, with skill and patience, draw the British government and that of the Republic together. I could understand that Gerry Adams might be tiring of the endless excuses for wanton violence his position forced him to make and that he might trade it for some share of legitimate power and a much enhanced prospect at the ballot box. All that I could see. What I could not see were the arguments which would persuade the young activists to give up their weapons. They enjoyed power in their community based on cruelty and fear. I could not see them exchanging this to enable others to indulge in the inevitable compromises and fudges of democratic life.

John and I had fought the last election together on a manifesto which I had played a full part in designing. He had done as good a job of leading the country and the party as anyone could in all the circumstances, so there could be no ground other than that of naked ambition to challenge him for the leadership. Of course, as the resulting contest moved through its early stages, I was asked by many colleagues what I wanted them to do. I answered invariably that it was a matter for them but that I would be voting for the Prime Minister. I have not the slightest doubt that, if I had given a different answer, it could well have influenced those who sought my views. I have equally no doubt that any such advice from me which appeared to be prejudicial to the Prime Minister's prospects of re-election would have been known to the lobby within minutes of my uttering it. I never gave it and in the light of the subsequent revelations in John Major's autobiography that he had set himself a minimum target of 215 votes (a total which he managed to exceed by just three), it is perhaps ironic to reflect that the votes cast by myself and just two of my possible supporters must have been critical to his re-election.

Those twelve days between John's bombshell announcement and the declaration of the result on Tuesday, 4 July were a political nightmare. I knew, as did everyone else, that, if John's gamble failed, the spotlight would swing immediately on to me. Of course I would have entered the subsequent contest with a high hope of winning it. But for the best part of two weeks I intended to maintain my commitment to John and to do all I could to ensure that none of my supporters did anything that could be interpreted as acting on my behalf in a way inconsistent with the position I had taken. The press didn't help. Michael Mates was reported by the *Evening Standard* to have been seen stalking the lobbies and claiming 120 people ready to wield the dagger. Michael was in fact in America at the time. Ray Whitney was accused of holding a meeting of my supporters who had decided to vote for John Redwood in the first round. Ray was in bed with flu at the time. So it went on.

As rumour chased rumour around Westminster, I talked them through with Richard. Was Michael Portillo going to stand? Would John Major pack it in and nominate Gillian Shephard as his successor? In the event his only challenger was John Redwood, who stepped down as Secretary of State for Wales. I maintained my position. Richard reported faithfully. Eileen responded to all telephone calls in a completely non-committal fashion and then relayed the messages to me. We had no plans and I refused to permit even the most tentative arrangements. No banks of telephones were going to be installed at some convenient address on my behalf at this stage.

On the day of the vote itself, we held no meeting of ministers in the Department. Richard Ottaway came to see me at 9.15 a.m. in my room and we discussed for an hour or so what we would do if John's gamble failed. I told Richard that I would place the responsibility for my campaign in his hands. I was fully aware that we would be crossing the starting line way behind other colleagues and certainly we had not got in place any of the physical back-up that such a campaign demands. Our knowledge of our colleagues' preferences was restricted purely to those who had personally volunteered their support. Even this did not provide a concrete base; I later discovered in conversation with John that he had in the odd case received the same message from some of the same colleagues. I reiterated my intention to vote for John and knew Richard would so report to anyone who asked.

Shortly after this meeting John asked me to come to No. 10, where we sat in the Cabinet Room alone. Obviously, neither of us knew how the events of the day would unfold. Our conversation centred round the job of Deputy Prime Minister and the responsibilities that would go with it. John gave me the choice of combining it with my existing position or moving to the Cabinet Office, but after discussing it we both agreed that a physical presence close to No. 10 was the better. He said he wanted me to take over the chairmanship of a number of

Cabinet committees and to set up a new co-ordinating committee to draw together the presentation of government policy and move us on to an election footing.

We talked for perhaps an hour or so, although my failure to emerge for over two hours provided the insatiable appetite of the waiting press pack in Downing Street with fodder enough for every manner of alleged plot or deal. There was no deal. There was no talk of a deal. There was no need for a deal. I had made clear my support for John and later that day I gave him my vote. I had no contact with any alleged supporters after my meeting with John and to this day I have no idea at what time of day any of them voted. So much for the story that I delivered them to John *en bloc* that afternoon.

I voted late in the afternoon. Aware that, if anything went wrong for John, I could be blamed, I made a point of ensuring that the scrutineers saw where I put my cross on the ballot paper and then waited for the results in front of a television set in the House of Commons. It was a close-run thing. John's own calculation of votes was exceeded by a hairbreadth. His team, headed by Ian Lang and Robert Cranborne, made a great success of the spin. Eager colleagues streamed from the Palace of Westminster on to College Green to proclaim the triumph. It worked, demonstrating the inherent wisdom of Churchill's famous dictum that a majority of one was enough. I had not allowed my expectations over the previous few years to rise very high. They therefore never had far to fall. Yet I was now to be Deputy Prime Minister, at the very heart of government, in the number-two position in the Cabinet.

That same day, before the result was announced and while the waiting press assumed I remained in protracted negotiations with John, I had left him after an hour or so to go through the connecting door in No. 10 and discuss my new position with Sir Robin Butler, the secretary to the Cabinet, in the Cabinet Office at 70 Whitehall. He and I talked over how things would work out and the logistics for the job that it was likely that I would assume. Much fun was later made over the huge office that I was in the event given. Fleet Street had it that it was the size of a squash court, then a tennis court; I awaited the first breathless comparison with a football pitch. Whether it was cause and effect I cannot know, but when I went to see Sir Robin I was shown into his office, which had to be one of the best offices inside government – palatial, panelled, it is precisely what you would expect the head of the civil service to achieve. After all, ministers come and go but the civil service remains. Over a cup of coffee, as I sat on his elegant sofa, I told him the apocryphal story of Duncan Sandys, who had years before become Minister of Housing. He had been greeted by the permanent secretary of that Ministry, who showed him round the offices and indicated the one that he thought would be right for the newly arrived Minister. They had then repaired to the permanent secretary's office for coffee. Duncan asked, apparently innocently: 'Whose office is this?' The permanent secretary replied, 'Mine, Minister.' 'Good, it'll do,' Duncan had said. Robin perhaps got the message. I was awarded a very large conference room on the third floor of 70 Whitehall as my office – with a security pass for the connecting door into No. 10 itself.

Rumours soon flew about extravagant redecoration, extensive refurbishment – troublemakers seemed to be thinking of a figure and then doubling it. The truth was more prosaic. There was no redecoration. The pictures came from the government store. The furniture was no match for the grandeur of that eighteenth-century room. Second-hand sofas, somewhat frayed around the edges from previous use, were so low and deep that those shorter than the tallest of us had to deploy all their ingenuity to extract themselves after a meeting. Some of my colleagues learnt to seek the higher chairs.

There is a footnote to this story. The day of the general election in 1997 came and went. The next day Robin Butler saw to it that my office was dismantled and restored to a conference room, so that by the time the new government was appointed all trace of the Deputy Prime Minister's imperial eyrie had been removed and any hint of this unwelcome intrusion into the ordered workings of Whitehall destroyed. It was as though I had never been.

Chapter 20

DEPUTY PRIME MINISTER

O nce I had accepted John Major's invitation to become his deputy, it immediately became clear to me that the most crucial aspect of the job would be my relationship with the Prime Minister himself. Inevitably, Fleet Street and its host of political commentators would try to find the thinnest wafer of difference between us on any subject. I determined that they would never succeed.

This was not as easy as it sounds. John's arrival in No. 10 had been achieved not only by his abilities and qualities but also because a number of MPs who voted for him were hostile to me. In his autobiography he very fairly acknowledges this: 'The depth of my support came for both positive and negative reasons . . . The negative reason was that I was not Michael Heseltine but was the person best placed to defeat him.'* My detractors were still lying in wait, and I knew full well that my every move would be watched, reported upon and interpreted in the worst light.

To make the job work, I had to act with his authority. It was vital that ministerial colleagues and their officials knew that there was no point in going behind my back or indeed over my head direct to the Prime Minister – if only because I would have been there first and would never have acted without his clear support. It was fundamental in my view that on no occasion should John find himself in a position where he had to overrule me. In the two years that we worked so closely together he never did.

My relationship with other Cabinet colleagues was altogether more complex. They were varied and sometimes contrasting characters:

* John Major, *The Autobiography* (HarperCollins, 1999), p. 189.

485

many of them relaxed and easy to work with, others less so. Such 'big beasts' – to borrow Chris Patten's phrase – did not lightly surrender territory and were ever watchful of their authority and status. I had nothing but respect for such feelings. After all, I had sometimes shared precisely that attitude myself. I remembered vividly my resentment in the first half of the 1980s at earlier centralist aspirations on the part of No. 10 and how, as Secretary of State for both the Environment and Defence, I had resisted them.

Now it was my responsibility to be what the Labour government would later, rather unwisely, call the 'enforcer'. Of course, I had the authority of greater seniority than that possessed by either Jack Cunningham or Mo Mowlam, the two Cabinet ministers successively appointed by Tony Blair to secure 'joined-up' government from the vantage point of being Minister for the Cabinet Office and Chancellor of the Duchy of Lancaster; but my job – like theirs – was to find the compromises that are part of the daily Whitehall ritual. Very early on I decided, so far as such an attitude was compatible with making progress, to conceal whatever stick I might possess and to rely on the carrot of persuasion.

It is possible that in years to come others may tell a different tale; but I believe that the stance I adopted worked well. If any credit was going, I was content for colleagues to enjoy it. My task was to sort out those problems with which I was charged and to push forward the government's agenda – or sometimes, perhaps more wilfully, to put particular emphasis on an aspect of policy to which I personally was committed. But, if I look back with some satisfaction that things worked as they did, there were certainly exceptions which showed just how easily it could all have gone very badly wrong.

Immediately my appointment was announced Robert Cranborne, a former right-wing MP for Dorset South but since 1994 our leader in the House of Lords, simply disappeared. Nobody seemed to want to talk to me about it. I became aware of uneasy silences when I came into a room, even of slightly guilty, averted glances. It was plain that something was up but it took time to discover what it was. Apparently, this scion of the Cecil family had been so incensed at my being made Deputy Prime Minister that he had retired to his country seat in Dorset and threatened to sever all connection with the government of which (as Lord Privy Seal) he was a senior member. Fortunately, John Major proved just as capable of dealing with such a fit of petulance as Harold Macmillan had been in face of similar behaviour on the part of Robert's grandfather in 1957 (though 'Bobbity' Salisbury did actually fulfil his threat and walk out of the government). Robert eventually reappeared and for the next twenty months we worked together on a number of difficult issues in which his House played a pivotal role. It proved to be a constructive and harmonious relationship, at least as far as I was concerned.

My judgement about the need to be scrupulous over the susceptibilities of colleagues – and the attendant risks of failing to do so – could not have been more vividly exemplified than in the overreaction of Michael Howard, the Home Secretary, to an incident which took place within a few days of my appointment. Early one morning, very much in the margins of a discussion in the Cabinet Office, I had expressed an interest to Sir Robin Butler, the Cabinet secretary, in exploring the possibilities – post-Cold War – of making use of the security and intelligence services in the fight against domestic organised crime. Robin suggested that I should be briefed on the matter. I had given it no further thought when I returned to my office later that day to find waiting for me there a selection of very senior officials, including the permanent secretary from the Home Office and the directors of both MI5 and MI6. They were eager to talk through the difficulties involved in my suggestion. With hindsight, I suppose I could have sent them away at once, but there were no decisions to be taken and I was simply familiarising myself with the subject, about which I had scant knowledge. So I listened carefully to what they had to say. Unfortunately, my fellow Welshman Michael Howard, on hearing about this meeting, blew his top. His reaction may have been extreme, but what I had done was exactly the opposite of the resolve I had formed as to how my role should be played. It was an early lesson. Yet I still have to say that most colleagues would have accepted my apologies and explanation in a more generous spirit and with a rather better grace than Michael managed.

Curiously enough, considering the pressure under which senior politicians live and the pace with which business must be got through, the exchanges between Cabinet colleagues tend to be remarkably good-tempered. Often the differences of view are real and genuine. Every day there are winners and losers. But such is the kaleidoscope of interests involved that a pattern of mutual tolerance gradually emerges. There is, of course, a good reason for this: in the morning you may find yourself at loggerheads with a particular colleague but then arguing passionately on his or her side on a different issue that same afternoon. And it has to be said that John Major was entitled to a great deal of the credit for the improved atmosphere, particularly in Cabinet. In contrast to the Thatcher years, everyone was allowed their say. Arguments were countered by reason and not interrupted or shouted down. Personal abuse and raised voices were never part of the currency. There may have been occasional and very human lapses even on John's part – but they always took place in circumstances which he had every reason to believe were private.

Moving to the Cabinet Office, I was especially fortunate in that I was able to take with me a team with whom I had worked for a considerable time. My always focused and unflappable principal private secretary, Mark Gibson, came from the DTI. Eileen Strathnaver, who had worked for me consistently since 1986, continued in her role as political adviser. Alan Kemp, a bright ex-MOD civil servant, who had gone into the private sector and worked with me part-time as a special adviser on a variety of privatisation and competitiveness issues at the DTI, now came on board full-time. In addition I enjoyed full access to Sir Peter Levene, who was the efficiency adviser to the Prime Minister but in day-to-day terms very much a part of the group of people upon whom I relied.

The immediate task that faced me was to recruit a press officer and spokesman. I decided to canvass the idea with various journalists I knew well, including Stewart Steven, editor of the *Evening Standard*, Max Hastings, then editor of the *Daily Telegraph*, and Philip Stephens, who was about to become associate editor of the *Financial Times*. It was probably unrealistic to think that any of them would sacrifice their careers to come to work in Whitehall. But so convinced was I of the importance of the job that I even sought to tempt my former PA from Haymarket in the 1960s, Maurice Saatchi – but the king of advertising men wouldn't bite either. In the end, I was extremely fortunate that a career Foreign Office official, Mike Horne, who had recently completed a highly successful job co-ordinating the media handling for the commemorations of the fiftieth anniversary of the end of the Second World War, accepted the post. He joined me in the summer of 1995 and remained until the general election was called in the spring of 1997.

The Cabinet Office at 70 Whitehall was home to a glorious confusion of responsibilities. It contains, of course, some of the highest-flyers of Whitehall, often on secondment from their parent departments.

These are the officials who organise the committees, often broker the compromises which enable conclusions to be reached at official level before ministers meet, take the notes at the meetings and prepare the minutes afterwards. It is they who skilfully draft the likely conclusions to every meeting long before the meeting itself takes place, prudently providing alternatives in anticipation of the possible swing of debate. Few of those who reach the top of the Whitehall tree have not passed a significant period of their time in the Cabinet Office. But otherwise it was a bran tub – an accumulation of central government activities that did not fit easily into any of the other departments and all incorporated into the Office of Public Services (the OPS) under the day-to-day supervision of a minister with the splendid title of the Chancellor of the Duchy of Lancaster. The OPS had up until the summer of 1995 been the OPSS, but the second 'S', which stood for science, moved to the DTI just as I moved to 70 Whitehall. I strongly supported the relocation, which reinforced an enhanced role for the DTI by increasing its influence on the government's research and development policies and priorities.

Once again, I introduced MINIS to establish what was going on in this rabbit warren of offices and myriad of agencies. I found out that I presided over, among other things, Her Majesty's Stationery Office (HMSO), with its publishing empire of government publications and parliamentary papers including Hansard; the Civil Service College at Sunningdale; the Recruitment and Assessment Services Agency, which ran the boards that tested and selected recruits to the higher ranks of the civil and diplomatic service; the Chessington Computer Centre, which ran the civil service payroll and pensions; the Central Computer Telecommunications Agency (CCTA), the government centre for information systems; the Central Office of Information (COI), which ran the government's media campaigns; the Buying Agency, which purchased everything from furniture to paperclips for government departments; the Property Advisers to the Civil Estate (PACE), which was what was left of the old Property Holdings/PSA; the Occupational Health Agency; the Whitehall messenger service security staff; and the Government Car Service – that is, all those drivers who take ministers to and fro, and have direct access to the most senior members of the Cabinet whenever they have a grievance (as I soon discovered when I tried to privatise them).

There was no evidence that ministers had ever subjected this miscellany of activities to critical scrutiny. What were we doing all these things for? Why did the public sector need to provide services of this sort? Within a very short period of time we had a list of candidates for privatisation. Just as he had in the DTI, Alan Kemp acted as the front-line infantry, probing and skirmishing to find the facts and to push the process forward relentlessly. I was particularly fortunate in having as Chancellor of the Duchy my fellow Cabinet Minister in the same Department, Roger Freeman, a professional accountant and investment banker highly competent in administration. He was the very exemplar of a safe pair of hands and could be relied upon to throw himself into any challenge we faced, whether it was the complexities of a privatisation or the crisis over BSE.

When I arrived at the Cabinet Office it employed 5,846 officials directly or through associated organisations. Two years later the number was 2,975. By the time I left, we had transferred to the private sector HMSO, the Chessington Computer Centre, the Occupational Health Agency and the Recruitment and Assessment Services Agency. The CCTA and the COI had been refocused and streamlined beyond recognition with the help of private sector managers brought in for the purpose. Working with Douglas Hogg, the Minister of Agriculture, to overcome the opposition of his permanent secretary, Richard Packer, and other officials, we also privatised ADAS (the Agricultural Development Advisory Service).

Most of the Cabinet Office privatisations attracted little attention. Not so that of Her Majesty's Stationery Office. HMSO was a microcosm of everything that is wrong with state-owned companies. It was grossly over-manned and hopelessly inefficient, as transferring it to the private sector so amply demonstrated. However, it had the contract to print Hansard, the daily record of proceedings in Parliament, and thus found little difficulty in finding supporters prepared to argue that, if anything were to go wrong, the process of government would come to a juddering halt. We faced a simple choice. We could put in new management, give them time to sort out the mess and then maximise the sale proceeds by establishing a profit record, but only after incurring massive redundancy costs on the way. (The taxpaying reader may be interested to know that civil service redundancy terms are such that the average cost of making a civil servant redundant during our efficiency drive, of which my efforts were just a part, was well over £50,000 a head. Little wonder ministers are sometimes loath to take on their bureaucracies.) This would mean that privatisation would not take place in that Parliament.

The alternative was to accept the existence of the hidden redundancy costs and transfer these in the form of a reduced purchase price to a commercial buyer. This had the virtue that at least the privatisation would be achieved and overdue changes accelerated. We chose this second option. When I became responsible for the Cabinet Office, the Stationery Office employed over two and a half thousand people. Its total operating losses for the twenty-one months leading up to its privatisation in 1996 had been £50.1 million. In 1998 the privatised group employed about a thousand fewer and declared operating profits of £18.3 million. Crucial to the speedy delivery of this and the remainder of the Cabinet Office privatisation programme was Margaret Bloom, an assistant secretary seconded to us from the DTI, whose determination to carry out clear ministerial policy was far from popular with her senior colleagues. But, despite the risks to her career, she never flinched.

Within the Cabinet Office I was able to hasten the reform of the civil service. First, I wished to address the fact that senior civil servants' pay was falling significantly behind that of their peers in the private sector. Second, I believed that, despite the findings of the Report of the Fulton Commission as long ago as the late 1960s, Whitehall remained too insular in its approach to moving people from one department to another. Much virtue was claimed for the policy of moving officials widely across a single department in order to broaden their experience. I believed the same argument should be extended away from the culture of one department by moving officials more widely around Whitehall. I also wanted to see a higher proportion of commercially, technically or scientifically qualified men and women recruited in the market place to serve as officials inside government.

I had, however, to recognise the validity of Robin Butler's arguments that these were very difficult objectives to achieve when the number of officials was being reduced as a consequence of the efficiency gains upon which the government was insisting. Good-quality officials were entitled to expect promotion. It would be very much the same in any large public company. It could do nothing but harm to morale if every time a senior post came up it was filled from outside the civil service. Given the rate at which senior posts were disappearing, there was irrefutable logic in Robin's position. But we were able to agree targets that, over a period, would move the civil service in the direction that I sought.

Where I clashed with Robin was over my proposal to privatise the

Civil Service College at Sunningdale. Set up as a result of a recommendation of the Fulton Commission a quarter of a century before, the Civil Service College is housed in a large, mostly purpose-built set of buildings nestling in well-landscaped grounds in Berkshire. Not long before, the civil servant in charge of the college, Marianne Neville-Rolfe, had proposed that it be transferred to the private sector. She had been moved to become regional director of the Government Office in the North-West before I arrived at the Cabinet Office. I quickly came to the same conclusion as she had. I had several reasons for doing so. First, I didn't think that the existing training of officials raised them to the standards of management that ought to be on offer. Second, it was virtually a closed shop for government officials. The courses for fast streamers at a senior level are joint public-private sector, but I believed that all management training should be multi-disciplinary, mixing people from public and private sectors and thus securing a cultural fusion, working to the advantage of both. Third, I wanted to attract more overseas students, with all the benefits in terms of future influence and understanding which that could create. As the leading country in so many public sector reforms – privatisation, deregulation, market testing, next-step agencies, the public finance initiative and a wide variety of public-private sector partnerships – we had a unique opportunity to spread our experience and earn revenues from the many countries around the world which were following our lead. The courses of the official training centre of the British civil service, which had pioneered these reforms, would be highly marketable. Those were the positive reasons. In addition, the college was losing increasing amounts of money, because shrinking departments were doing less training and more of what they did was in-house, as they sought to avoid the high costs charged at Sunningdale for residential courses. Something had to be done if the subsidy was not to rise and standards fall.

It was as though I was splitting asunder the tablets of stone. Robin Butler was implacably opposed. One of the arguments that was put to me was that there was already a healthy flow of foreign cash arising from the number of students that came from abroad, thus indicating that one of my objectives was already secured. It was only when I asked the second question about who paid for these students that I discovered that every one of them was paid for by the British aid programme – in other words, by our taxes. But the least defensible of Robin's reactions was when I asked him to canvass the opinions of his fellow permanent secretaries. Instead he sent them a letter containing three reasons which, he suggested, they might want to use to argue against my proposals. His main argument, which must have influenced his overall view of working with the private sector, was that, if the college was privatised, it would need to be profitable and would therefore cost more for the client departments. He could not accept that privatisation could lead to greater efficiency and thus savings. We normally got on well enough, but his letter struck me as an extraordinary interpretation of the proper constitutional function of officials charged with carrying out the wishes of the elected government of the day.

In accordance, therefore, with the guidelines I had set myself, I resolved to discuss the matter with John Major. I explained the problem, told him what I thought was the right way forward and asked whether he would support me if I took on the Cabinet secretary. His reply was unequivocal: 'Michael, if I have to choose between the Deputy Prime Minister and the Cabinet secretary, I will choose the Deputy Prime Minister.' This was the assurance I needed, but I never put it to the test. In the context of the problems with which we were grappling, it was too small a battle to fight to the death. In that sense I made the right decision. In every other, it was the wrong one. Let no one ever naively think that officials strive assiduously to serve the elected government of the day, when they believe that that government is wrong. It may be so in theory but it is far removed from the practice, especially when they perceive civil service interests to be at stake.

I had brought with me from the DTI the Competitiveness Unit under Bob Dobbie. We had already produced two annual Competitiveness White Papers. We were now engaged on a third. In order to spread the message among my Cabinet colleagues, upon appointment as Deputy Prime Minister I presented each of them with a copy of Correlli Barnett's latest book, *The Lost Victory*, which had just been published. A sequel to his earlier work, *The Audit of War*, the sad tale of Britain's pre-war and wartime decline, *The Lost Victory* is a chilling analysis of how in field after field, through ignorance or neglect, in the decades of post-war economic recovery we had remorselessly slipped down the international league tables. People themselves were better off in absolute terms and did not, therefore, sufficiently perceive that the country itself was drifting into decline when compared to similar advanced countries else-where.

Nowhere was this more obvious than in education, which our White Papers identified as a key factor of competitiveness. Historians will point to a relative decline in the output of our schools and universities, measured over the last hundred years or more, compared with competitor economies. I was faced with more immediate and pressing consequences. For example, leaders of the pharmaceutical industry were telling me that they would have to move their research facilities to the United States because they couldn't recruit sufficient graduates with the training and expertise they needed for sophisti-cated research. The statistics backed the widely expressed complaint that the quality of the product was simply not good enough. The 'product' in this instance was, of course, our children – upon whom our future depended. In the 1980s and early 1990s the Conservative government had taken the first vital steps to expose the shortcomings. Ken Clarke, when Secretary of State for Education, had established an inspectorate to look more critically at the performance of individual schools. There were already inspectors employed by the Department within HM Inspectorate, but it was too easy for them to develop a cosy relationship in the discharge of their responsibilities. In the relevant Cabinet committee at the time, therefore, I suggested that this new inspectorate should be independent of his Department. The subsequent appointment of Christopher Woodhead in 1994 unleashed a ceaseless flow of venom against his activities, revealing only too well just how entrenched are the vested interests that militate against the improvements that we were seeking.

In 1994 Gillian Shephard, Ken's successor bar one at the Department, introduced the power to send 'hit squads' into failing schools and, in the last resort, take them over from local authority control. I much regret that we hardly used this power, although Brian Mawhinney, the Chairman of the party, and I did everything we could to urge Gillian to do so. In fairness it must be recorded that Gillian was in a 'no-win' situation. John Patten, her immediate predecessor, had become extremely unpopular by pushing forward reforms with which much of the educational establishment strongly disagreed. He had been right but paid a high personal price when he lost his job in the July 1994 reshuffle. Gillian herself had been a teacher and saw it as an important part of her remit to cool the temperature and heal the wounds in the run-up to the next election. After the July 1995 reshuffle, she also faced the challenge of crafting together the two very different cultures of the Departments of Education and Employment. The amalgamation of the responsibilities of these two departments was very much part of our competitiveness agenda and I had urged the merger on John Major. It remains my conviction, however, that we will never grasp the nettle of our under-performing schools until we insist that those who run them risk losing their jobs if they fail to perform. The Conservative reforms revealed clearly, school by school, where the problems lay and created the legislative means to address them. But we did not take the next logical step.

My commitment to annual Competitiveness White Papers was not without its problems. Ken Clarke, now Chancellor, and I argued about the validity of the international comparative statistics themselves. Far from accepting that Britain was way down a particular league table, Ken would attack the legitimacy of the international comparisons. His political judgement coincided with the self-interest of the Treasury, which knows from long experience that to acknowledge a problem only encourages ministers to come up with expensive solutions. The mandarins there have a simple answer: never admit to the problem.

It was not only the Competitiveness Unit that moved with me to 70 Whitehall. So did the deregulation team, headed by Lucy Neville-Rolfe (sister of Marianne, the former head of the Civil Service College). John Sainsbury was by now anxious to shed his responsibilities as head of that task force after some three years in the job. I invited Francis Maude to take his place. I had served in the Shadow Cabinet with his father Angus in the late 1970s and, of course, had known Francis as a junior ministerial colleague when he was Financial Secretary to the Treasury before he lost his seat in the 1992 election. Here was a man profoundly committed to removing unnecessary restrictions on commercial freedom. To the right within the party and with a commercial background with the merchant bankers Morgan Stanley, he had every qualification for the job.

I myself chaired a committee of junior ministers, responsible department by department for deregulation across much of Whitehall. Each of these had his or her own agenda but, within the constraints of the initiative itself, steady progress was made. Francis, though, was intent on securing a major breakthrough. He developed the radical idea of merging the two apparently parallel systems governing national insurance contributions and PAYE tax deductions. The former was administered by the Department of Social Security and the latter by the Treasury. Francis invited Peter Wyman of Price Waterhouse to draw up proposals which would leave business with one system, not two, within which to act as unpaid tax collectors. It was an eminently sensible proposal and Peter Wyman demonstrated, despite officials' objections, how the desired result could be achieved. Ken Clarke and Peter Lilley dug their toes in, however, reflecting the traditional Whitehall instinct to defend turf. Eventually, agreement was reached, although it required the deliberations of a Cabinet committee to enable me to secure a collective judgement against my two reluctant colleagues. In the event, we didn't complete the task, as the integration processes were overtaken by the election. The new Labour government, however, announced its intention to proceed with the plans that we left behind.

Francis argued as well for the use of what were known as sunset clauses wherever possible in new legislation. This meant that, after a prescribed period, the legislation or regulation in question would expire, thus forcing ministers and ultimately Parliament to consider its justification afresh. I was a sceptic. The idea sounded attractive but in practice I believed it would simply increase the parliamentary workload, reintroducing the bulk of perfectly sensible regulations.

As an ambitious and talented politician, Francis was anxious to play whatever part he could in the workings of government while he was himself out of Parliament. I was sympathetic. But Robin Butler rightly pointed out that Francis's attendance at my Ministerial Committee on the Co-ordination and Presentation of Government Policy (EDCP) would be quite outside the normal conventions – he being neither a member of the government, a party official nor a civil servant. I had to explain this to an understandably exasperated Francis.

EDCP met every morning at 8.30 in my office. It included Brian Mawhinney, as Chairman of the party; Alastair Goodlad, the Chief Whip; Tony Newton, Lord President and Leader in the Commons; my old critic, Robert Cranborne, Lord Privy Seal and Leader in the Lords; Roger Freeman, Chancellor of the Duchy of Lancaster and my number two; David Willetts, Parliamentary Secretary and latterly Paymaster General (both these jobs were based in the OPS); my PPS Richard Ottaway (subsequently Seb Coe and then Nigel Waterstone); and the Prime Minister's two PPSs, John Ward and Ian McColl. Also in attendance were civil servants and party staff, including the Prime Minister's principal private secretary and his chief press officer, my and the party Chairman's press officers, the head of Central Office

Research Department, Howell James and Eileen Strathnaver, the political advisers from No. 10 and the Cabinet Office, Mark Gibson, my principal private secretary, and two officials provided by the Cabinet Office to act as secretariat.

It was this somewhat unwieldy body which was charged with countering the remorseless waves of attack to which the government was subjected from 1995 onwards by Labour's formidable election machine. I have raised many a merry laugh in the post-election period when, asked to address audiences of senior management, I have begun by saying: 'It is good of you to listen to my advice on matters to do with marketing, coming so soon, as I do, after being charged with the responsibility to secure the re-election of John Major's government.' Self-evidently our endeavours failed.

No doubt great academic treatises will eventually be written on the effectiveness of the spin-doctor and all the sophisticated techniques of modern news management by governments. My view, however, is simpler. When the dice roll against you, there is little you can do. Even powerful governments – and by 1995 we were certainly not that in terms of our parliamentary majority – are impotent to divert a sustained flood of adverse events, all breaking against a background of economic uncertainty and national frustration.

The tide of what came to be known as 'sleaze' first lapped about the government's feet with the entrapment of the Heritage Secretary David Mellor and the exposure in the *People* of his affair with an actress in the summer of 1992. After that the waters never seemed to recede. By the time I came on the scene with my regular meetings of EDCP in 70 Whitehall, the high-water mark may have passed, but I was often reminded of my early days on the Gower coast, watching the waves crash relentlessly against the pebble-strewn beach. Now they kept coming, and the seventh – generally after the weekend – was usually a big one. The Opposition spin-doctors, like agile surfers, could ride the crest of these waves until they crashed against the shore. The pebbles on the beach were churned into mayhem.

The Labour Party had established a rapid-response unit in its headquarters at Millbank, just beyond the Palace of Westminster. It enjoyed the luxury of being free to say whatever it liked, without the need to undertake detailed checking of policy, precedent and programmes first, and often even without reference to the Shadow Cabinet spokesmen responsible. No such luxury is remotely possible in government. Statements and press releases have to be checked, circulated, co-ordinated and collectively agreed. Failure to do so would run the risk not only of the personal hostility of colleagues but of the very real danger of cock-up compounding confusion. In addition to that, the Opposition rapid-response unit was in full-time session, under senior political direction. My political colleagues and I had demanding government departments to run and over-full daily diaries. Once EDCP broke up each morning and we returned to our departmental duties, simply getting back in touch frequently presented a formidable problem.

Meanwhile, the rituals of parliamentary life continued to be played out each week in the House of Commons. Modern technology may have greatly diminished the traditional role of a deputy prime minister, certainly from the days when Churchill would often be virtually incommunicado on the high seas while Attlee stood in for him. Prime ministers today may be out of the country but they are never out of touch. Their office in No. 10 is able to make immediate contact with the private secretary travelling with the Prime Minister wherever they are in the world. Although the deputy is nominally in charge while the Prime Minister is away, it was very rare that the substance of this transfer of responsibility ever mattered in the conduct of policy.

Yet, however ubiquitous the age of the mobile, the fax, the e-mail and the internet makes prime ministers, no one has yet found a way to beam them back to appear in virtual reality in the House of Commons. Prime Minister's Questions (PMQs) – at that time, before the arrival of Tony Blair, two quarter-of-an-hour slots from 3.15 to 3.30 every Tuesday and Thursday afternoon – is an awesome experience. Behind the courtesy of parliamentary convention the Prime Minister can be asked, without notice, about any subject under the sun. There is a sporting chance, but no guarantee, that questions from his or her own side will be sympathetic: 'May I congratulate my Rt Hon. Friend . . .' 'Has my Rt Hon. Friend heard the good news that . . .'. But even here embittered and frustrated colleagues have a way of turning the knife, as John Major frequently found with Nick Budgen's informed and critical questioning from a Eurosceptic standpoint. Most questions are carefully prepared beforehand. A few are made known to the Prime Minister by sympathetic backbenchers before he even reaches the chamber. From the other side of the House there is no mercy. The object of the exercise is to trap or catch out the Prime Minister. The simple, one-sentence question is the most difficult to cope with.

The loquacious or inexperienced Members ramble on, blurring question after question into a jumble of words, leaving the Prime Minister with the option to pick on just one of the points and rebut it. The Leader of the Opposition used to be allowed three interventions (it was to become six when Labour introduced one half-hour Wednesday slot for PMQs), usually in the form of soundbites artfully contrived for the evening news, at which Tony Blair in his previous incarnation proved a master.

Prime Ministers can become obsessed with this grilling, subjected to it as they are week in and week out. Mrs Thatcher in Cabinet time and again would turn on a colleague whose policies were under scrutiny with the remark: 'You don't have to answer for the government twice a week in the House of Commons.' A high proportion of the morning preceding PMQs is given over to studying the briefing, skilfully prepared by officials and party researchers expert at spotting the likely elephant-traps lurking in the latest headlines. To that extent the Prime Minister will have forewarning. A Member of Parliament, anxious to attract news coverage, will almost certainly zero in on something topical. For this reason, it is the duty of officials to be sure that the briefing packs cover every eventuality. They do the job superbly well.

On several occasions I stood in for John at Prime Minister's Questions. My opposite number across the dispatch boxes on these occasions was usually John Prescott. I understood all too well why prime ministers approach this ordeal with such anxiety. You are there in the spotlight, against all comers. The mood of the House can change in an instant from heavy drama and legitimate indignation to uproarious farce, as the well-aimed joke ricochets around the chamber. You have to spot the moment at which the combative party point has to be replaced by instant sympathy for the genuine grievance presented by a backbencher. The one protection a Prime Minister enjoys is that only the Leader of the Opposition can intervene more than once and the Prime Minister gets the last word in each exchange.

When I first entered the House of Commons in 1966, the chamber was invariably packed for opening speeches and closing speeches in any important debate. Today, the chamber is full only rarely. For PMQs, the place is still packed. You are very much on your own. I found it the most nerve-racking experience of my political life, although my apprehension began to diminish as I gained in confidence and learnt some of the tricks of the trade.

In early November 1995, John had to leave for the Commonwealth

Heads of Government meeting in Auckland, New Zealand, and thus was unable to attend the annual Remembrance Sunday service at the Cenotaph in Whitehall on the following Sunday. He asked me to take his place, although he was bitterly criticised by Mrs Thatcher for doing so. There are few more moving occasions in the British calendar than that simple ceremony when, in stillness and silence, a nation remembers the sacrifice of the dead of two world wars. No nation conducts these affairs with greater dignity or simplicity than the British. I was carefully briefed for the role I had to play: the timing, the position, the sequence of events. After the members of the royal family have laid their wreaths, there is a significant pause before the music strikes up, whereupon the Prime Minister – or in this case his deputy – moves forward to the Cenotaph itself. I have never known such a long moment as the doubts grew in me that I had misread the instructions. I was as sure as I could be that I had been told to wait for the music but there was no music. I knew that I was meant to move. I decided that something had gone wrong and began to move forward. As my foot was raised from the ground, the music began. 'Brilliant,' they said afterwards. 'We have never seen the timing more immaculately coincide.' Sometimes the luck breaks your way.

Beyond the Prime Minister himself, there was one other colleague with whom I developed a special relationship: Ken Clarke, the Chancellor of the Exchequer. Ken and I certainly did not agree about everything. He is not the sort of man with whom anyone will agree about everything – which is what makes him such fun. He enjoys the argument. I think he was an agnostic about much of my competitiveness agenda, but we were both essentially radicals at the centre of British politics. We enjoyed an easy relationship and had much in common. We laughed at the same jokes, took a relatively relaxed approach to handling the inevitable and endless crises in which we were involved, had lives outside politics and shared, I think, a broad historic perspective about the sort of party to which we belonged.

As Chancellor, Ken chaired EDX, the Cabinet committee charged with the scrutiny of public expenditure and the delivery of the targets that Cabinet had set. My task, as Deputy Prime Minister, self-evidently was to help Ken successfully conclude these very difficult negotiations with colleagues. I was dismayed at the quality of briefing available from the Treasury. There simply is not the culture of comparative statistics that would be second nature to the private sector: no columns of figures comparing what was actually spent or achieved over the previous five years on a given service. Much more likely were convoluted essays. There was very little, if any, attempt to distinguish between revenue cuts and capital cuts.

I managed towards the end of my time in government to secure briefing material from the Treasury set out in what became known as the 'Heseltine Tables', which were actually no more than what would be regarded in the private sector as basic management information. I vividly recall looking across one column of figures which showed that the gross costs of legal aid had risen from £700 million to £1.6 billion over a period of seven years. Government ministers are often lawyers. There was little sympathy for the onslaught I proposed on such a bill.

I took a particular interest in benefit fraud and NHS prescription fraud, both of which had been scrutinised by the Efficiency Unit. I proposed that Alan Kemp should review with Department of Social Security officials what more might be done to discourage benefit fraud, and within a month they had produced a sixty-recommendation report. As a result of this and similar research Alan carried out at the Inland Revenue and Customs and Excise, even the Treasury – which had always believed that claims based on potential savings from fraud tended to disappear like winter snow – accepted that savings worth several billion pounds should be assumed in the Public Expenditure Survey. Concurrently, with the help of Peter Levene's Efficiency Unit, we persuaded the Department of Health to launch an official scrutiny of the potential for fraud by doctors, pharmacists and patients in the area of medical prescriptions.

A not dissimilar debate took place on the issue of unemployment: too many people were obtaining support from the social security system while operating in the twilight world of the black economy. In the late 1980s, I had argued for what might loosely be called 'workfare' and on my return to government I pressed my case in numerous Cabinet committees. The Treasury, the Department for Education and the Department of Employment were all sceptical of my view that a more disciplined system would be not just fairer but more effective. By the time I moved to the Cabinet Office we had got as far as two experimental schemes in Maidstone and Hull. I saw for myself in Maidstone that the results could be dramatic: freeloaders could be forced off the public payroll, while the genuine long-term unemployed could be helped by training, work experience or re-education.

John Major gave me his authority to find the best way of building on this success. In Bournemouth at the beginning of October 1996, on the periphery of the Tory Party Conference, I secured agreement with Gillian Shephard (at Education) and Ken Clarke (at Employment) that we would take what we had learnt several steps further by widening the schemes and their locality. In government after 1997, Labour took our ideas from the experimental stage to a national policy. 'Hand up not hand out' they called it. I give them credit only for the slogan.

In politics crises can arise at any time. Sometimes they are predictable; more often not.

On Monday, 18 March 1996, Douglas Hogg, the Minister of Agriculture, Fisheries and Food, asked to see me on a matter of great urgency. He arrived in my office at 4.00 p.m. His message was a simple but profoundly distressing one. It was public knowledge that Bovine Spongiform Encephalopathy (BSE) was widespread in the beef and milking herds of the United Kingdom, but the scientific advice to government had always been that this posed no threat to human health. Yet Douglas now told me that Professor John Pattison, the chairman of the Spongiform Encephalopathy Advisory Committee (SEAC), had just advised him that there had been a number of cases of a new variant of Creutzfeldt Jakob Disease (CJD), a particularly nasty form of human spongiform encephalopathy, appearing in younger people. There was no known treatment or cure or indeed any firm means of diagnosis except via post-mortem. It was now the view of SEAC that exposure to BSE was the most likely explanation, though probably this had all happened before the new measures to destroy specified bone offals (SBO) at abattoirs had been introduced in 1989 (although not all that effectively as it turned out; Douglas had already had to tighten up the regime the previous summer). In other words, there would appear to be a lengthy incubation period. However, the scientific advice was inconclusive.

The implications were devastating, particularly as in answer to one of my questions Douglas told me that, while there were only ten confirmed cases of the new variant of CJD at the time, the scientists were unable to give any reassurance as to whether it was likely to be contained at this sort of level or whether it could become an epidemic. I told him that I would arrange for the Prime Minister to be informed at once and that he should prepare a paper setting out all the facts as he knew them and outlining the options that the government might have. I made it clear that this paper should cover the range of potential risks and relevant solutions. Douglas pointed out that, at the extreme, this might involve the slaughter of the whole of the national herd; I said he must hold back nothing. Within half an hour I joined the Prime Minister, who was in the middle of a meeting with Brian Mawhinney, the party Chairman, and explained briefly the seriousness of the situation. None of us had the slightest doubt of the urgency of the matter and the Prime Minister himself chaired a meeting of colleagues that evening to go over the ground. It was decided that a further meeting would be necessary the following morning, so that we could prepare an immediate statement to Parliament. We lived by then in a culture of leaks. It was vital that, when the information in our possession was made public, it should be given in an orderly way, with as many facts as we were able to establish, and to the House of Commons. The first appropriate moment for a parliamentary statement would be that Tuesday afternoon at 3.30.

On Tuesday morning the relevant colleagues were assembled together with the chairman of SEAC, the chief veterinary officer and officials from No. 10, the Cabinet Office, the Ministry of Agriculture, Fisheries and Food (MAFF), the Department of Health and the Treasury. The meeting listened to reports which had been commissioned overnight. We had to determine what action to take and agree the wording of the statement. Progress was being made towards these objectives when Professor Pattison was asked whether there was any specific risk to young children. He answered truthfully that he was unable to give a categorical assurance on the point, and on further probing agreed he might be able to be more forthcoming in twenty-four hours' time. We were faced with an appalling dilemma. Did we risk further delay in making a parliamentary statement, with all the attendant possibility of leaks, or did we authorise a parliamentary statement which under questioning would elicit answers of the sort that we had just heard? We decided that it was better to have as fully prepared a case as possible and to run the risk of another day's delay.

On Wednesday morning the full Cabinet met and a statement was approved. In view of the dual responsibilities of MAFF and the Department of Health, it was agreed that in the House of Commons that afternoon Douglas Hogg would concentrate on the agricultural and Stephen Dorrell, as Secretary of State for Health, on the medical aspects of the problem. I had telephoned Stephen the night before and alerted him that he should be prepared to make the opening statement.

The Opposition, in the shape of Harriet Harman, behaved predictably and disgracefully. Stephen was accused of reckless disregard for public health, of a dogmatic approach to deregulation and of undermining the strength and independence of his Department's chief medical officer. But disaster did not strike straight away. The headlines worked themselves slowly up to a climax. How were the British public and a wider European audience supposed to react to such treatment by the British press? Take, for example, the *Daily Mail* in its front-page headlines over four days: Thursday, 21 March: 'Beef and Children: The Awful Questions'; Friday the 22nd: 'Could It Be Worse Than Aids?'; Monday the 25th: 'Four Million Cattle to Die'. If ever there was a prediction headed for self-fulfilment, this was it. No one should have been surprised the following day when it emblazoned across its front page: 'Now the Ban Is World Wide'. Nothing that had been said in Parliament could justify such headlines. The consequence then was immediate: a collapse of public confidence and not just in the United Kingdom.

I attended all the meetings in the first days of the crisis. Indeed, John had asked me if I would take the lead in co-ordinating our response; but, after a discussion during which I pointed out that one of my companies owned a herd of some sixty cattle, we decided that the role was best entrusted to Roger Freeman. It was a Herculean assignment and one that was to get a great deal more difficult as the weeks went by. Roger and a team of officials were focused and tireless in carrying out their task.

The atmosphere of crisis at the time left the government with no realistic option but to introduce increasingly draconian slaughter policies at ever escalating cost. Mercifully, an epidemic has not materialised, although sadly the total number of definite and probable cases of new variant CJD had reached seventy-four by the summer of 2000. I also recognise that scientific advice still points to the unknown length of any incubation period. Three and a half million cows had to be slaughtered and over £4 billion of British and European taxpayers' money spent. Certainly there was much justifiable unease about factory-farming methods and inadequate regulation by MAFF which lay behind the public reaction to the crisis. But the sensational way in which the events were portrayed undoubtedly imposed unnecessary costs upon the taxpayer and dealt a devastating blow to British farmers from which many will never recover. My worst fears, as I listened to Douglas Hogg on that Monday afternoon, had proved horribly justified.

The problems over BSE inevitably became interwoven with the European tensions dividing the Conservative Party. The reaction in the British media to the domestic crisis spread immediately to the rest of the world. Sales of British beef plummeted. Public anxiety in our export markets left other governments with no realistic choice, as they saw it, but to ban imports of our beef. The Americans had already done so in 1985, along with that from any country which had native cattle cases of BSE. They were entitled to do this on health and safety grounds under the GATT rules. Their ban was extended in 1989 to include live cattle from any country with confirmed cases of BSE. So our beef wasn't selling in the United States anyway. But now it wasn't selling anywhere else either. Even Chris Patten, the Governor of Hong Kong, found himself with no option but to close the colony to British beef.

In Europe our partners wasted little time in acting. The European Union Standing Veterinary Committee banned all beef exports from the United Kingdom into the EU. Green politics has a much greater hold on the Continent – particularly in Germany – than in Britain. I have, however, always regarded the European ban as a highly protectionist and politically motivated move, although our failure to give advance warning of our announcement to Brussels did not help. They did not ban the consumption of British beef in Britain itself, which, if they believed it was unsafe, they certainly should have done.

I was not involved in any of the interminable negotiations that went on with the Europeans in a vain attempt to get them to reverse their decision. I shared my colleagues' resentment and frustration at the inconsistencies and deceptions that were apparent in the false assurances and broken promises of the next several months. I strongly supported the policy of non-co-operation which we finally, in exasperation, resorted to later that spring and which committed us to vetoing any European proposal requiring unanimity – in the way that other countries, such as France, Italy and Spain, had done on other occasions when they believed their essential national interests to be threatened. But it is a blunt weapon at the best of times, and one reason why it is so rarely used is that it rapidly affects a range of unrelated decisions. No such reservations influenced the Eurosceptics on our back benches and their allies. The turn of events was grist to their mill.

Even the Labour Party, prepared to exploit any crisis for every potential ounce of political flesh, recognised the prevailing public mood and supported our policy of non-co-operation. It did at least focus the minds of Europe's leaders. At the Florence Summit on 24 June 1996, some concessions moved the agenda a step on and lowered the temperature a degree or two, but the problems dragged on for the rest of the Parliament. Despite Labour's overblown claims, in the event, as I write four years later the French are still defying the rest of their European colleagues, who in late 1999 at last voted to lift the ban. Little consolation it undoubtedly is for many in the beef industry, but there is now every prospect that the matter will finally be resolved: France has been taken to the European Court, although no one can for certain predict the outcome nor how long deliberations will take. For those who believe Britain's best interests are served at the heart of Europe, this has been a testing experience. And, after fifteen years, the American ban still remains; very few people are even aware of it and there is no recourse to law to resolve the matter.

It is always a sad and difficult situation when a senior minister has to deal with the resignation of a valued junior colleague. This is true whatever the circumstances, but was particularly so in the case of David Willetts. Known affectionately by friend and opponent alike as 'two-brains' because of his undoubted ability, David had replaced John Horam as the junior minister in the Cabinet Office late in 1995 and was elevated to the grand-sounding post of Paymaster General in 1996. I had hardly come across him as a colleague before he joined the OPS team, although it had been to speak for him as a newly selected candidate that I had journeyed to Havant on the memorable night of Geoffrey Howe's resignation in the autumn of 1990. David was certainly a valuable addition to our forces. He worked hard to carry out effectively EDCP's remit to co-ordinate announcements and the handling of the media across Whitehall.

But he did not remain in his post right up to the election. He became embroiled in one of those transparent charades that cause such phoney shock-horror headlines over the alleged behaviour of a Member of Parliament. Before being appointed to junior ministerial rank, David had served in the government Whips' Office. Early on in that capacity, he had had a conversation with Sir Geoffrey Johnson-Smith, the chairman of the Select Committee on Members' Interests, about an inquiry the Committee was undertaking, and had written a note to the Chief Whip reporting their talk. His note concluded with the enigmatic words: 'He wants our advice.' This phrase undermined the illusion that is carefully fostered that select committees are independent of the government or party machine and that their deliberations are confidential. Here, so to speak, was a government whip caught with his hand in the till, prepared to influence the outcome of the Committee's deliberations. Or so it was alleged. Over a year later the smoke and steam of righteous indignation exploded across Westminster. The Committee of Standards and Privileges heard the evidence. The House was still smarting from the affront to its *amour propre* represented by the Nolan Inquiry into the rules governing the conduct of MPs, and the newly constituted Committee was determined to flex its muscles.

David tried, rather unsuccessfully, to explain away the words, but nobody was persuaded and he was forced to resign. I had a long conversation with him in my office the night before (thereby incurring the undying wrath of a select band of potential supporters whom I had been scheduled to meet and rally to the party's cause). I told him not to worry. It would do his career no harm whatsoever, and would soon be forgotten. Everyone knew that the whips hear precisely what is going on in the select committees and that committee members from both sides of the House act as conduits to the custodians of their party's interests. 'Next time, don't put it in writing' was my advice. David went on to play a pivotal role in the drafting of our manifesto for the forthcoming election and I was delighted after the election to see him back and well up in the pecking order of Opposition spokesmen.

Fortunately, the business of government had its happier aspects. I was sitting with John Major in the Cabinet Room one day in 1995 when he asked me whether I would be prepared to become a Millennium Commissioner and thus join one of the distribution bodies that was to be set up to dispose of the proceeds of the national lottery. John's vision for the lottery was truly magnificent. I had supported it from the beginning. Here was an opportunity to raise sums of money for what might loosely be called good causes on an unprecedented scale. John would be entitled to claim that, through the lottery, he created the greatest age of patronage in British history. The annual cash generated by the lottery was to be divided: a fifth each would go to charities, sport, arts, the heritage and, for a period up until the turn of the century, the Millennium Commission. The Commission was to be chaired by the Secretary of State for the Department of National Heritage, who to start with was Peter

Brooke, later to be succeeded by Stephen Dorrell and then Virginia Bottomley.

The Commission was established on a non-partisan basis, although Michael Montague (who sadly died in 1999) was invited to join as a representative of the Labour Party. But politics never entered into our discussions. This was a well-rounded group from varied backgrounds, charged with determining how to make available in time for the celebration of the millennium dramatically large sums on projects which could be defined only as millennial. It was up to us to decide what that actually meant.

Apart from Peter Brooke and myself from the Conservative Party and Michael Montague for Labour, the Commission consisted of Sir John Hall, the highly successful businessman who had made his reputation and fortune with the Metro Centre construction in Gateshead; Simon Jenkins, the ex-editor of *The Times* and the *Evening Standard*; Patricia Scotland, the eminent QC who had come to this country at an early age from Dominica; Lord Glentoran, an Olympic gold-medallist in 1964 and the former chairman of Redland Tile and Brick; the Earl of Dalkeith, deputy chairman of the Independent Television Commission, a member of Scottish Natural Heritage and the heir to the Duke of Buccleuch (who as Johnny Dalkeith had served with me in the House of Commons in the 1960s); and Heather Couper, broadcaster and writer on science-related subjects.

The Commission was fortunate in persuading Jennie Page to leave English Heritage to mastermind the vast challenge of establishing a cash-distributing organisation on the scale required to match the bewildering range of projects submitted for approval. Without doubt, Jennie is one of the finest public administrators of her time, as was to become spectacularly clear.

So the new Commission met to discharge its responsibilities. We were given an early indication of the scale of money that might be available to us. It seemed that over the five years we might expect to receive something in the order of £1.25 billion. In the event the success of the lottery raised that figure to a final budget of about £2 billion. Originally, we had no power under the legislation to initiate projects. We could only advertise the availability of cash and invite submissions. As we were to discover through our experience with the Dome, this was too restrictive and the 1998 National Lottery Act gave distributors the power to solicit applications.

I had two very clear aims from the outset. The first was that we should concentrate on capital investment as opposed to revenue subsidy and that we should not contribute more than 50 per cent of the cost of the capital projects to which we gave our approval. Experience had taught me the dangers of public subsidy for revenue purposes. A tail of perpetual commitments builds up. Once a particular organisation has got used to the idea that its expenditure will be met by public subvention, it rapidly assumes that what it received one year is the starting point for its bid for the next. We had an opportunity to start afresh and concentrate on new building and investment. I also believed strongly that, in order to have some confidence that the people on the ground would actually deliver the projects which they submitted to us, it was prudent that they should be expected to raise at least half the cost of the project themselves. The Commission accepted this approach. In the event we distributed grants of £1,260 million in support of projects costing £3,000 million. In addition we made payments to individuals engaged in local community work, and in such cases we paid up to 90 per cent of the total, but the level of individual grants was limited to a few thousands of pounds.

My second ambition was that we should repeat what I believed to have been massively successful national endeavours: the Great Exhibition of 1851 and the Festival of Britain of 1951. As a nation, I believed that we should stake our claim to the future with a statement of great confidence and pride in ourselves. I knew that those two earlier events had in their day been hugely controversial. The 1851 Great Exhibition had actually had its planning stage brought to a halt by restless Conservative Members of Parliament, incensed at the design. Their objections had prevailed, which had led to the commission from James Paxton of the famous glass structure that became known as the Crystal Palace. I could remember visiting the 1951 Festival of Britain. Curiously enough, it was managed by a friend of my father's, Sir Leslie Joseph, a figure well known in Swansea as the entrepreneur behind the Coney Beach amusement facility at Porthcawl on the South Wales coast. A further coincidence was to be brought home to me when, after the election of 1997, I found myself working on the Dome project with Peter Mandelson, whose grandfather Herbert Morrison had been the Labour Cabinet Minister responsible for the Festival of Britain.

I had experienced the dramas of getting the Liverpool Garden Festival up and running in the early 1980s. I knew the sort of flak that would attend not just the initial decision, but every stage of the preparations. But I equally believed that, once the event was established and successful, the doubters would be among the first to claim credit. There were others on the Commission who shared either one or both of my objectives and I was delighted that, from an early stage, they were accepted as part of our strategic overall objective.

Inevitably, all of our activities became overshadowed by the centrepiece, the Dome itself. Because we did not yet have the power to initiate a project, we had to advertise our requirements and await offers or proposals. We sought flexibility to enable us to marry the best project with the most suitable site. The sites would almost certainly be in the public sector, whereas the bids would come, we thought, from the private sector.

The site competition narrowed to a choice of four locations: the National Exhibition Centre (NEC) at Birmingham, Pride Park in Derby and two in London, Stratford and Greenwich. The choice of the site in Greenwich, owned by British Gas, attracted much political controversy. It was badly polluted and difficult to reach by car. To make the matter more complex, far and away the most imaginative presentation for the project came from Gary Withers of Imagination, a company specialising in the provision of high-quality and visually attractive events for private sector companies. But his scheme was linked to the NEC in Birmingham. In other words it was a package. Gary Withers was the clear project winner, but the NEC as the possible site had serious problems. The traffic forecasts threw significant doubts over the ability of the local infrastructure to cope with the volume of cars that would be attracted on any one day to the event. The proposal simply involved extensions to the existing exhibition centre and was, therefore, without what might be regarded as a unique physical presence of its own. Furthermore, London was the capital. We had searched London for a suitable site, exploring the areas west to Heathrow and also the possible use of Hyde Park. But, certainly in the minds of some of us, the 300 acres of dereliction on the Greenwich peninsula added an extra dimension of urban regeneration that would prove a lasting legacy.

We decided to go for Greenwich and to invite Gary Withers to mastermind the project on that site. I had great sympathy for the NEC, whose case was articulated forcibly by my friend and colleague Norman Fowler, the Member of Parliament for Sutton Coldfield. But I have never doubted that we made the right decision about the location. Experience had by this time already shown that there would be no private-sector-led venture, that the government would have to play a significant part in driving the project through and that the project, as envisaged, was quite beyond anything Gary's company had previously undertaken. I had worked with creative geniuses in the publishing world. They have great strengths and compensating weaknesses. Gary was full of ideas and was wonderful fun, but he was facing a test on a scale so outside his experience that one day his intermittent threats to depart the scene might become reality.

The Commission had initially committed £200 million to the project. The chosen vehicle for delivery was Millennium Central, a private sector company chaired by Bob Ayling, then chief executive of British Airways. In 1997 it became a government-owned company with a new name, the New Millennium Experience Company (NMEC). Jennie Page moved from the Millennium Commission to become its chief executive, in order to concentrate her formidable powers on the delivery of the largest and most controversial of the Commission's projects. In this she succeeded – in spite of the unprecedented scale and the number of hurdles that had to be jumped. That condenses into one simple sentence three and a half long, dedicated years of hard work and total commitment. The difficulties that beset us were legion: the acquisition of the site from British Gas by English Partnerships; the preparation of a detailed plan, which led in turn to significant increases in the budget; and an ever widening range of problems at the interface of local and national government. The Dome not only resembles a mushroom; the project grew like one.

We had always counted on private sector sponsorship. We now had to raise it. And we had to do so against a background of mounting criticism in the national media. The press continually demanded neat answers and precise solutions about the project when none could possibly exist at such an early stage. The moment we announced our sponsorship target of £150 million, they were after us for a list of which companies were on board. When a chief executive sounded interested, they would immediately find someone else in the company to express dismay.

As one of the principal proponents of the Dome and as a Millennium Commissioner, I knew I now had to try and persuade other people to put their money where my mouth had been. With the help of Peter Levene, I invited the captains of many of Britain's major companies to a crowded meeting in the largest conference room that 70 Whitehall could provide. We made a presentation of our plans and ambitions, outlined the scale of the cost and announced our target of £150 million. And we persuaded the Millennium Commission that the target was achievable (in the event we exceeded it).

It was, I have to admit, hard sledding, but at the time of the election in 1997 we were approaching something like the halfway mark with what promised to be relatively firm commitments. Yet almost every contract had to be fought and struggled over. The exception was a letter, claimed to be unprecedented, containing an offer of £6 million from Arnold Weinstock of GEC. Arnold has a reputation for his personal generosity to charitable causes, but he is also known as a formidable protector of his shareholders' money. It was a wonderful act of faith on his part. Usually, chairmen would give positive indications; their underlings would then seek to agree detailed arrangements that projected their most favourable corporate image. This tended to turn the project from a celebration of national endeavour into something approaching a trade fair. Initially interested chairmen, aware of media hostility, found that they were likely to run into a serious barrage of internal and shareholder criticism themselves. Persuading companies to sign up to the last detail proved a tortuous process. In practice even on the Dome's opening night some £40 million of the £150 million was still uncontracted, although firmly committed.

Several months before the election I had become persuaded that, if there were to be any prospect of moving through the growing welter of technical, legal, commercial and personal problems with which we were beset, only a senior government minister could act as trouble-shooter. I appeared to be the obvious candidate. The key players began to meet in my office for a regular weekly meeting. Then one day in January 1997 Jennie Page and Simon Jenkins came to see me. They told me the game was up. A new and apparently insurmountable problem had arisen, and there was no way through or round it. The directors of the management company, led by Bob Ayling, had taken a decision: they were not prepared to serve without a government guarantee. Any such guarantee would lead to a reclassification of the costs as public expenditure. There was no way the government would accept this.

There appeared to be no way forward. At that moment, in the context of the Dome, I was on my own. But I was determined that we would find a way through. And so, indeed, we did. I devised a proposal by which the government agreed that, if the project went belly-up, the life of the Millennium Commission would be extended so that additional lottery funds would protect the cash position of the Commission and the Dome. Realistically, at that stage no government would have taken a decision to let the project fail. Virginia Bottomley, who had been steadfast in her support for the project, announced the new arrangements on 18 January.

As the next election approached, new uncertainties thrust themselves forward. Company chairmen, anxious to escape the sales pitch, asked what would happen if there was a new government. Executives responsible for the Dome had authority to proceed to specific stages of construction but could not move on to the detailed planning of content. Up to then Michael Montague, the Labour Party's representative on the Millennium Commission, was in touch, as we understood it, with Jack Cunningham, the Shadow spokesman for National Heritage. Michael had given the Commission categorical assurances that the decisions we were taking enjoyed the support of the Opposition.

Towards the end of 1996 it became essential, however, to get a more formal undertaking from the Opposition. Despite repeated assurances that we were about to receive appropriate confirmation from Jack Cunningham (himself to be later appointed a Commissioner in July 1998), it never came. We were faced with an inescapable crisis. There were still a few months to go before the election itself and, given the stage we had reached, if those months passed with no decision, the Dome might not be ready for the opening night at the beginning of the new millennium.

There was nothing for it but to put the issue fairly and squarely to Tony Blair. There followed a quite ruthless exploitation for party political purposes of what had been up to then and was thereafter – despite an ill-judged Conservative Opposition supply day debate in February 2000 – essentially a non-partisan affair. I met Tony Blair on 16 January 1997 in his office in the House of Commons, explained the assurances that Montague had given and the need for decisions if the programme was to continue to time. I warned that the Millennium Commission would not commit any further funds if there were the slightest question that the project might be abandoned after the election. For the Dome to meet its targets we depended on our ability to raise funds in the private sector. No decision on his part meant no confidence on the part of business. No confidence meant no funds.

I was not the only person to put these arguments to Blair. Jennie

Page and Bob Ayling also met with him. But the Labour Party detected political advantage in taking a macho stand over tough expenditure criteria. They had had full knowledge of every decision and full access to all the information available to the Commission when those decisions were taken. Their representative had assured us of their support. Yet they could not resist the temptation to parade their credentials as custodians of the public purse and shamelessly pursued tactics to suit their own political agenda.

Eventually, after the most protracted and tense negotiations, a form of words was extracted from the then Labour Opposition which enabled the project to proceed, although this included a requirement for a post-election review. They duly won the election and there was such a review. But it produced nothing of consequence: no change of plan, no change of discipline, not a single thing that had not already been built into the procedures and decisions which had underlain the process from the beginning. We had, however, lost precious weeks in what was always the tightest of schedules.

The general election behind us, my membership of the Millennium Commission remained unaffected. Peter Mandelson, as the new Minister without Portfolio in the Cabinet Office, was put in charge of the Dome project and invited me to come and discuss my experiences with him. I explained how, as a minister, I had found myself drawn into a central position in the decision-making process. I advised that it was essential for a similar relationship to continue in the new government. He invited me to join a committee that would meet regularly, at 5.00 p.m. every Tuesday until the Dome opened, to provide continuity. Simon Jenkins accepted a similar invitation.

Two and a half years later the Millennium Dome opened as promised and within budget – a remarkable achievement. On the evening of 31 December 1999, my family and I had the privilege of sailing down the Thames in the company of Her Majesty the Queen and the Duke of Edinburgh to attend the spectacular opening ceremonies in Greenwich.

Fate has seldom dealt so unjust a blow as it did that evening to Jennie Page. She had achieved a near miracle in driving the Dome to completion. However, a serious last-minute breakdown in security arrangements kept thousands of visitors stranded for hours at Stratford on the opening night, among whom were a number of editors of national newspapers. They were not amused. Jennie carried the can. Low initial attendance figures and a refusal by a handful of sponsors to pay up on time led to a cash-flow crisis. Bob Ayling, chairman of NMEC, concluded with his colleagues that a new chief executive with personal experience of large-scale crowd control in visitor attractions could alone restore confidence and end the ceaseless press criticism. The best candidate available was Pierre-Yves Gerbeau, late of Disneyland Paris, who insisted on a free hand. The board chose him and Jennie went.

Those of us close to the project had no choice but to support the board once it had so voted. Jennie is a public servant of outstanding merit and all of us felt deeply saddened at the roughness of the decision. Ironically, only a few weeks later Bob Ayling was himself dismissed from the post of chief executive at British Airways in the same peremptory manner by his chairman, Lord Marshall. This was in part because of falling profits and a number of alleged failures within the company, but it was also because BA's own millennium project, the London Eye – a gigantic Ferris wheel on the banks of the Thames at Westminster Bridge – had cost three times its original budget. It has proved enormously popular, but its universal acclaim was not enough to save him.

That was not to be the end of the matter. Repeated requests for extra grant to finance a mounting deficit caused by lower than budgeted revenues and increased costs undermined the confidence of the Millennium Commissioners in the corporate governance of NMEC. In May 2000 the Commission approved, with great reluctance, further financial support – albeit less than requested – but determined that a clear signal of its dissatisfaction required a change in the company at boardroom level. Bob Ayling handed over the chairmanship to David Quarmby, previously head of the British Tourist Authority. This was a decision accepted by ministers but not led by them.

Critical to the Millennium Commissioners' decision to opt for Greenwich had been the longer-term prospects of regenerating this outstanding site. I had deeply regretted that I had left it out of the London Docklands Development Corporation designation back in 1979. That would have avoided twenty lost years. In the event the decision to go for Greenwich has been abundantly justified. The site has been cleared of its pollution and toxicity. Long-term public and private investment has poured into this historic wasteland. The most modern retailing facilities have been built by Sainsburys and Homebase. A multiplex cinema, the Express (Holiday Inn) Hotel and new school, health and community facilities are planned and will be just the prelude to the transformation which the Millennium Commission sought for this deprived community, many of whose younger generation have received training and work experience in the Dome itself, thus giving them a much enhanced employment future than would otherwise have been the case.

But the decision to build the Dome in Greenwich had one other factor in common with UDCs. In both cases we were faced with a flood of questions about what we intended to do with the land once reclaimed and then an even more vehement barrage of criticism when we admitted our inability to answer those questions except in the most general terms. I would have been laughed to scorn if, in 1979, I had predicted a development of the scale and quality of Canary Wharf on the Isle of Dogs. The Commission was convinced that, if we were the catalyst that ensured the decontamination and reclamation of the Greenwich site and a new Underground link, the market would do the rest. We were concerned to ensure, however, that the overall plan for the site should be of outstanding merit and we welcomed the involvement of Richard Rogers in its development.

As to the after-use of the Dome building itself, we believed this was best left until it had been built. It would sell itself – as indeed it has – and government and the Commission could form a judgement about real options rather than indulge in largely pointless speculation. Our faith has been vindicated. The peninsula is being restored to life, to the immense benefit of the London Borough of Greenwich, its inhabitants and a wider public.

In the summer of 1996, on 15 June, in one of its last mainland attacks, the IRA tore the heart out of Manchester with a bomb in the packed Arndale Shopping Centre. Mercifully, no one was killed. But massive damage – some £300 million worth – was done. Two days later I travelled up to meet the new Labour leader of the City Council, Richard Leese. As I have shown, I knew Manchester well, having first become involved with it over the redrawing of its city boundaries when I was a junior minister at the DOE in the early 1970s. In the early 1980s, as Secretary of State in the same Department I had (with Tom King) played a critical role in the arrangements to develop the G-MEX exhibition centre there. I had also been influential in finding a way to finance the Bridgewater Hall, the concert centre which replaced the old Free Trade Hall as the home of the Hallé Orchestra, and I had provided the funding in the early 1990s to get rid of one of western

Europe's worst slums, the Hulme Estate, through the City Challenge venture. In addition I had worked closely with the city over its abortive Olympic bid. The new sports stadium, the Velodrome, the Olympic-size swimming pool and securing the Commonwealth Games in 2002 were a significant legacy of that otherwise disappointing decision. As I remembered all this on the train journey north, I resolved that what we needed was to turn disaster into opportunity. But how? This was a Labour council and unlikely to feel particularly at ease with a Conservative minister. I decided however to have a go.

Fortunately, as soon as we got together in the City Hall, Richard Leese asked me first for my views, without offering his own. I had thought carefully about what I wanted to say to him. I told him I believed this was a remarkable opportunity for the city to create a great legacy from the outrage. Rather than simply patching things up, I suggested that they appoint – as a result of an international competition – the most imaginative urban landscape architects they could find, who should be invited to come up with ideas to rebuild not just the damaged streets but a much wider area around the heart of Manchester. To be feasible, I said, this idea would require a genuine public-private sector partnership but they had already seen how this could work through the City Challenge scheme on the Hulme Estate. I suggested they should invite Alan Cockshaw, the chairman of AMEC, who had played such a crucial part in that project, to join them as leader of the private sector team.

I waited with apprehension for the objections. They did not come. Instead Richard Leese said: 'I agree. That is what we'll do.' It was a remarkable moment. I promised to give whatever support I properly could as a minister and undertook to keep closely in touch, both of which I did. We never had a disagreement and I was able to ensure in one way or another that central government provided the financing on the scale necessary to complete the project.

If ever good can come from evil, the renaissance of Manchester is an example. The decision we took to embrace an area significantly larger than that directly affected by bomb damage had offered the winning design consultants, Edaw and Associates, the opportunity to give life to the ambitions of the City Council. The city centre was to be extended and to a standard quite beyond anything it had previously known. Four years later I walked the streets of the city with Howard Bernstein, the chief executive of the City Council. The transformation is a triumph. The lavatory-tile façade of the old

Arndale Centre has been reclad to create an acceptable contrast to the dramatically impressive new and enlarged Marks and Spencers. The Old Wellington (mid-sixteenth century) and Sinclairs (early eighteenth century) pubs were literally moved brick by brick to release space for development. As part of the Manchester millennium centre project, the cathedral square has been recaptured with extensive pedestrianisation linking the old Corn Exchange building back into a newly vibrant city centre. In all, some £63 million of public money has already levered in over ten times that sum in private investment and the process is rippling on, as higher standards and growing confidence reinforce our original concept.

But, as a politician, what really pleased me was the acknowledgement by Richard Leese that the public-private partnerships forged by the City Challenge scheme to rebuild the Hulme Estate had worked well and that this had influenced his agreement to my proposals. From the earliest days of government in 1979 it had been my primary purpose to create this fusion of local strengths to rebuild our rundown cities.

The last months of the Major government were as dominated by Europe as its earliest days. We had got the Maastricht Treaty through but the Eurosceptics felt they had the bit between their teeth and, like a runaway horse, there was no stopping them. Euroscepticism had been growing apace. The collapse of the Soviet Union had left a void in the demonology of politics. The recession of the early 1990s had coincided with a flood of directives from Brussels implementing the single market and demanding legislative time in the House of Commons. Colleagues were receiving a steady stream of correspondence from a wide variety of industries and interest groups complaining about the changes that the Single European Act had initiated half a decade before. There were plenty of claimants anxious to lead the growing army of Eurosceptics. Mrs Thatcher more than fulfilled her threat – when John Major became Prime Minister – to be a back-seat driver, with incessant leaks of her bizarre contradictions of much that she herself had done in government. A strange collection of never-promoted, never-would-be-promoted and once-promoted-but-now-demoted backbenchers spent every waking moment on College Green outside the Palace of Westminster, feeding the airwaves of the national media with their views. The Australian-North American Rupert Murdoch and the Canadian Conrad Black, owners of an assortment of British newspapers, were up in the front line and the *Daily Mail*, a Europhile newspaper under its previous editor David English, was now stridently Eurosceptic under his successor Paul Dacre. But the most intense pressure on John Major came from within his own Cabinet.

All this had the effect of bringing me into an ever closer alliance with Ken Clarke. In Cabinet committees or in Cabinet itself, whenever an issue concerning Europe arose, the line-up was predictable. Michael Howard, the Home Secretary, invariably waded in first and he would be joined by Michael Portillo, now Defence Secretary; John Redwood, Secretary of State for Wales until he resigned in June 1995 to oppose John in the leadership contest; Peter Lilley, Secretary of State for Social Security; Michael Forsyth, Secretary of State for Scotland; and William Hague, who succeeded Redwood as Secretary of State for Wales. The strain on John Major was intense. But it was not the formal discussions among colleagues that most concerned him. It was the unremitting flow of leaks to the national press which effectively brought to an end collective responsibility. The government was deeply and irreconcilably divided over Europe and the Eurosceptics didn't mind exploiting it. John's famous expletive about the 'bastards' was merely a revealing glimpse of the volcano of emotion and indignation that was a constant theme of the last years of the government. John was under remorseless pressure to move the party, one stage after another, into ever more determined Euroscepticism.

Ken and I decided that we alone – Douglas Hurd had stepped down from the Foreign Office in July 1995 – could act as an anchor to a ship that otherwise would slip fast downstream. I do not know what conversations John and Ken may have had privately on all these issues. But, for my part, I explained to John how strongly I felt. I told him that I discussed these matters continually with Ken and that the two of us would stick together to prevent the government's public position from being hijacked by the sort of pressure which we knew him to be under. Interestingly, when the dialogue became one of detail, it was frequently the case that the Cabinet was perfectly able to find a set of proposals or a form of words upon which to unite. Malcolm Rifkind, as the new Foreign Secretary, had chaired a Cabinet committee preparing for the EU's next Inter-Governmental Conference (IGC). The object was to publish a White Paper on European policy. Ken and I, all the Eurosceptics and most other senior members of the government sat on the committee. Malcolm himself traditionally belonged to the

Europhile wing of the party, although he too found the balancing act difficult and I detected a shift in his position as Euroscepticism gained in ascendancy. After lengthy discussions, however, we reached agreement across a wide spectrum. I have to admit I knew that some of the words and ideas would never survive the detailed negotiations of European summitry, but they were reasonable opening bids.

One of the few issues of real moment to come out of this saga was the question of a referendum. I am personally opposed to the use of referenda. I am not alone in this conviction. Mrs Thatcher voiced the doubts I still feel when she spoke in the House of Commons on 11 March 1975. It was her maiden speech as the leader of the Tory Party. Labour had proposed a referendum on our membership of the European Economic Community; in her response she said: 'Perhaps the late Lord Attlee was right when he said that the referendum was a device of dictators and demagogues.'

Throughout his last months in No. 10 John was looking for what he hoped – vainly as it turned out – would be a gesture that could bring the Eurosceptics back on side and thus end the divisiveness that was so damaging the reputation of the government. He must have discussed the possibility of a referendum over the single currency with Ken. Certainly he did with me. I remained, as I told him, resolutely opposed. I remembered how Harold Wilson, unable to unite the Labour Party over the issue of Europe in 1972, had escaped the political straitjacket by promising a referendum on our membership should he win the next election. It was a device to unite the Labour Party and had nothing to do with any genuine interest in consulting the British people. I had despised Wilson for it. The idea that the intricacies of a single currency were to be debated in terms that were all too predictable, given the Eurosceptic nature of the foreign-owned British press, seemed to me the worst example of the sort of thing that Mrs Thatcher had so accurately described in 1975. I was also very doubtful that such a device would reunite the party. I believed the Eurosceptics would simply regard the concession as a sign of weakness, pocket it and up the ante. That was how they always operated.

I was always conscious, however, of my commitment to John that I would do whatever I could to help him shoulder the onerous responsibilities he carried. The issue of a referendum on the single currency was raised in Cabinet in early March 1996 and John had said publicly that we were considering it. One night in the Prime

Minister's room in the House of Commons, John, Ken and I were engaged in yet another discussion about the European situation and I made a suggestion that I thought might enable John to offer a sufficient gesture to the Eurosceptics to get us through the next election with at least a semblance of unity, although I knew there remained a high risk that they would simply regard it as another victory in a ceaseless struggle. I said to Ken that perhaps it would be possible for us to agree to a referendum but only 'in the next Parliament', on the ground that there could be no commitment in the next election manifesto for accession to the single currency in view of the Maastricht opt-out. Ken, with much reluctance, agreed to this approach.

I have regretted my suggestion ever since. First, and above all, it did nothing to improve the fortunes of the government. I remember John in the middle of the election campaign itself returning from the West Country perplexed that no one there even knew that we had made such a commitment. Second, as Ken and I had both feared, it merely allowed the Eurosceptics to move on to demand the next concession, without a backward glance. Thirdly, it ensured that the Labour Party were forced to follow suit by committing themselves to a referendum as well. And, finally, the qualifying words 'in the next Parliament' rapidly fell from usage, despite my insistence that they should remain in the policy documents that were associated with the general election campaign. I remain to this day convinced that the referendum is incompatible with our constitutional traditions. That the all-important question of Britain's adoption of the single currency was to be decided by this misbegotten device was one of the many pernicious effects of the Euroscepticism that so distorted the politics of the 1990s.

Chapter 21

END OF THE ROAD

On 4 July 1995, having secured re-election as Leader of the party, John Major appointed Brian Mawhinney as party Chairman to mastermind our campaign for the next election. Although we had never worked closely before, Brian and I enjoyed a good relationship and I looked forward to its extension. I was aware of the ever present risk that Central Office would become a world apart from Downing Street, with growing suspicion poisoning the atmosphere between the two. The Chairman of the party has a difficult responsibility to fulfil. He has to give a lead but he has to do so in the knowledge that he is reflecting the views and instincts of the leader of the party, who inevitably carries the main strain of the campaign. Brian was determined from the outset that he would not get far out in front on the decisions that he needed to share with the Prime Minster, and in this I believe he was right. He had told me that he wanted me to play a full role in Central Office activities. As the election drew closer he offered me an office there and extended a general invitation to their deliberations. I was determined to afford him every support. Given that we were to suffer a humiliating defeat, one might have expected there to be bitter recriminations afterwards, but certainly among the principal players there have been none.

There were three haunting themes against which we conducted the campaign: a party divided over Europe, sleaze and insufficient public appreciation of the improving economic prospect. They were played out against a general mood which meant that, whatever we said, the public at large saw little, if any, threat in the newly packaged, freshly minted product called new Labour. If there were beds around in that campaign, they were not there for reds to hide beneath. There was also, after eighteen years, a general desire for a change.

It required no deep psephological knowledge to understand that, as we faced the end of the 1992–7 Parliament, the politics and the economics were out of kilter for us. The predictions of economic recovery were all too clear, but would they materialise quickly enough for the benefits to flow through into people's pockets? It didn't seem likely, but it focused attention on the strategic judgement: when should we have the election? My view, based on this analysis, was that we had to go on for as long as we could, accepting the dangers inherent in such a strategy.

I produced a graph going back over the previous fifty years to indicate the basis of my conviction that re-election demanded sustained economic prosperity for twelve months before an election. The rule is not absolute but it is better than any other I know. In the event, the passage of time, as we waited for economic delivery to materialise, did nothing to help. Revelation after revelation of scandal gave the Opposition easy headlines. We became a government increasingly tainted by sleaze. The Hamilton case and that of at least ten other parliamentary colleagues had been referred to Sir Gordon Downey, the new Parliamentary Ombudsman appointed in the wake of the Nolan Committee. He had reported on the majority of these cases with the inevitable publicity that followed, but he had not yet reported – and we had no knowledge of when he would do so – on Neil Hamilton and a handful of others. We were trapped. We had set up Sir Gordon as an independent authority, and, quite properly, could not anticipate his findings.

During the election campaign itself a junior colleague in the Commons, the MP for Beckenham, Piers Merchant, took time off from electioneering to do a little canoodling in a public park, and thereby attracted increasingly lurid headlines. In the face of those he still wouldn't go, firmly refusing to take the hints I publicly delivered to him on the BBC's *Today* programme. Allan Stewart was forced to stand down as our candidate for Eastwood in Scotland as rumours began to circulate about his private life. Micky Hirst had to resign as party Chairman north of the border as a result of sexual allegations. On top of that, Tim Smith was swamped by further revelations of his involvement with Mohammed al-Fayed and had to resign as candidate for Beaconsfield. We found it impossible to move the debate on from sleaze.

I did as much campaigning as most of my colleagues, travelling widely and undertaking a daily round of radio and television studios.

I have listened to replays of some of my broadcasts. I can be heard attempting to move off the subject of sleaze and on to the state of the economy and the general issues that ought to have dominated the campaign. All that comes across is a senior minister apparently wriggling to get off the hook. My colleagues fared no better. The economic statistics made no impression. The shadow of sleaze hung heavy. The people heard and had had enough. They wanted us out.

The Eurosceptics never let up. We were a deeply divided party. For good commercial reasons Central Office organises at election times a scheme whereby they will print, on favourable terms based upon the bulk of orders, colleagues' election addresses. I was dismayed to learn that well over 100 of our candidates had submitted election address texts which contained a commitment that the candidate concerned would not sign up to a single currency in the next Parliament. This was inconsistent with the policy I had driven through and made a mockery of any attempt to find a common approach. It revealed clearly how limited the concession of a referendum had proved to be and it was bound to provide an open goal for our critics. I discussed the issue with John and Brian, who were equally concerned. My first argument was that we should refuse to print any election address unless it was in accordance with official party policy, but it was felt that the inevitable row that would be precipitated by sending back large numbers of election addresses to adopted candidates would simply fuel the flames.

I persuaded John and Brian that I should appeal to the 92 Group of Tory backbenchers, to which most of the Eurosceptics belonged. I accepted that such an intervention was extremely unlikely to do any good, but I felt that every effort for unity had to be made. The meeting was packed. I explained the damage that such flagrant defiance of party policy would do. Two of the members present, Michael Brown and Winston Churchill, said they had been persuaded by my arguments, but there were no other takers. Although one member told me I was a traitor, in the main it was a reasonably good-natured meeting. I had worked with many of those present over my years in Parliament and when a minister. Some had even supported me against Mrs Thatcher. I did not detect much personal hostility. But I had to report to John that I had made virtually no impression and that we were hell-bent on a course of self-destruction. It was, of course, from within this group – after the election and after the lurch in policy towards Euroscepticism – that the most eloquent appeals for unity were to be heard.

The election campaign itself was conducted from Central Office with twice-daily meetings attended by key political colleagues and staff. We would consider the polls, including those we had commissioned. The message was unmitigated gloom, with the exception of a single rogue poll in the *Guardian* which showed a dramatic closing of Labour's lead. That lasted only until the publication of the next one. Three of the most sophisticated political consultants in the country, Maurice Saatchi, Tim Bell and Peter Gummer, masterminded the advertising and public relations strategy and were regular attenders of our meetings. Brian presided, taking what decisions he could against a background of limited funds. The atmosphere was in retrospect surprisingly buoyant. This was not a defeated army, given up and routed from the battlefield. That might have been naive of us, but there is an adrenalin in these things and just a fragment of enough truth in the fallibility of opinion polls to provide the heart and stomach for the fight.

I was constantly asked by journalists for my prediction of the outcome. For the first half of the campaign I repeated a forecast I had first made the previous October of a Conservative majority of sixty. I doubt if anybody believed me or if I was even convinced myself. But at least nobody could find in that confident claim any hint of defeatism. Indeed, halfway through the campaign in answer to John Humphrys' question 'Do you still believe in your forecast of sixty?', I expanded on my prediction with a smile. 'Nudging up,' I replied. At least it seemed to amuse the normally mournful Humphrys, though the bet I took with Bob Worcester of the MORI polling organisation was to prove rather more expensive. It cost me a £150 cedar tree, which I had to deliver to him after the election. I had forgotten the bet. He hadn't.

The divisions in the party ensured that Europe was an issue. I therefore make no apology for the one Tory newspaper advertisement of the campaign for which I was directly responsible. One afternoon in Central Office we were discussing Tony Blair's European policy, which I felt posed a serious threat to the concessions that John Major had so skilfully achieved at Maastricht. In particular Blair was committed to imposing on Britain the Social Contract, much beloved of the German government. At home I have hanging a cartoon by Vicky drawn in the early 1960s in which the diminutive figure of Harold Macmillan is seen sitting in the lap of a huge President Kennedy. The caption to the cartoon attributes to Quintin Hailsham the words, 'We have a veritable giant emerging on the world scene.' I remembered this cartoon and, as I sat next to Brian, listening to the discussion, I sketched a picture of Chancellor Kohl of Germany with the tiny figure of Tony Blair sitting on his knee. Brian was immediately amused by it and it became what I still regard as one of the most effective messages of our campaign. This was not a Eurosceptic concept – it was a Blair-sceptic concept.

But the fact is that nothing mattered. The UK Independence Party and the Goldsmith Referendum Party both fielded candidates against us and in the more marginal seats this posed a serious threat, although post-election research shows that they drew almost as many votes from our opponents as from us. I have seen no independent analysis indicating that Conservative candidates who took an overtly Eurosceptical line did better than those who stuck loyally to the official party line. I do not say it was cause and effect, but nobody who surveyed the wreckage of Michael Portillo's campaign in Southgate can argue that Euroscepticism had proved a winner. (There were local issues in Southgate which would have influenced the result, but then again his acknowledged Euroscepticism was not demonstrated to be a crowd-puller in his remarkably low-poll by-election victory in Kensington and Chelsea in November 1999.)

On 28 April, the Monday before polling day, John told me that if the results were as bad as Brian Mawhinney was predicting he would resign immediately. He wanted to give me time to prepare my response. He said he hoped I would take his place. Despite the gloomy background to what he had to say, I have ever since thought of that as a great compliment, coming as it did from a man whom I had grown not only to like and respect but to admire.

I now felt free in what little time there was to spare from the campaign itself to consider the likely turn of events. Richard Ottaway, who had returned to my team to help with electioneering, has commented that he noticed that for the first time I was prepared to speculate about the possibility of the leadership in a way I had never done before. He did not know of my conversation with John and the feeling of release that it had created. That same night over dinner with our wives at Drones restaurant I pondered who would be left on our benches when Parliament reassembled who would be of sufficient status to hold the party to its 'One Nation' stance. I believed that the task would fall to John, Ken Clarke, Malcolm Rifkind and myself. I was, however, not sure that I would stand. The party's serious Eurosceptic bias might project Michael Portillo to the top. To stand against him and lose would be a rather dreary way to end my career. I was also sixty-three and would be approaching sixty-eight at the next election. There was in addition the prospect of the continuing battle with the Eurosceptics. They had behaved disgracefully in government; freed of all restraint in opposition, there was no telling what might happen.

Over the next few days Richard reported a wave of new converts to my cause, including Jeffrey Archer, who was already canvassing for the chairmanship of the party.

I spent polling day in my Henley constituency and, as I have always done, travelled in a reverse direction from my wife Anne, visiting committee room after committee room. We met at lunchtime and in the afternoon each covered the ground that the other had covered that morning. Then we returned to London. One of my children pointed out that they had never seen my office – the one which had attracted so much publicity. So the Heseltine tribe set off for Whitehall. Could we be blamed for a certain sense that there might not be another opportunity? In my outer office there was a large white board which Mark Gibson had used for the daily diary and to keep his colleagues' minds focused on the immediate challenges as they arose. On it the office had scrawled a message: 'Hello boss. We have a long list of ideas for you to get stuck into on 2 May.' I was touched and wrote underneath my final words in public office: 'Another triumph – shame about the electorate.'

We went on to dine, together with Eileen Strathnaver, at the Royal Horseguards Hotel and then to Central Office to listen to the early results. The warning signs were already there. All through the day seasoned activists in my own constituency branches, who had been involved in many a campaign, were sending the same messages back to the constituency headquarters: 'The vote is down.' The first results were enough to indicate what was to come. Anne and I left Central Office at about midnight for my local count at the Icknield School in Watlington. It was quickly beyond any doubt that eighteen years of Conservative government were over. It was not unexpected – we had had time to get used to the idea. My result followed the national trend; the majority was well down, from the 19,000 I gained in 1992 to 11,000. I went through the form of giving short-clip interviews to the numerous television and radio programmes that had come to cover my poll and get my reaction to the national results. I did not feel well, but I assumed that this was not unexpected at the end of a gruelling campaign.

In the small hours of Friday morning Anne and I returned to Thenford. Strange to say, I have no memory of the rest of that day. But a friend remembers clearly talking to me on my car phone, as I was being driven up to London in the middle of the day, and Andy, my driver, confirms this. I went directly to Buckingham Palace, where I was received by Her Majesty the Queen, to whom I returned my seals of office. I then turned round and, no longer a minister, went straight back to Thenford. I believe I made a few telephone calls; I undoubtedly spoke to John Major, but I can no longer recall our conversation. Then Anne and I took a walk around the arboretum. There is a solace to be found among trees.

I discussed the leadership with Richard late in the afternoon and left it that we would talk again over the weekend. I told him that I intended to call one or two key figures to see if their support would be forthcoming before making up my mind. I telephoned Richard again just before going to bed and asked him to ring me at 9.30 the next morning. But that conversation never took place; by then I was in hospital.

Very early on the morning of Saturday, 3 May, I awoke in significant discomfort and asked Anne to call a doctor. Our own doctor in the country, Tim Cherry, was not available but his senior partner, Dr Stephen Large, appeared remarkably quickly and organised an ambulance to take me to the Hornton District Hospital in Banbury. It was soon diagnosed that I had suffered an attack of angina. Once again the national press arrived. Brian Mawhinney asked Anthony Gordon-Lennox from Central Office press department to help Anne cope with the pressures. Outside the hospital on that Saturday lunchtime Anne announced (and, despite some speculation by the press and various pundits, this was with my complete agreement) that I would not be a candidate in the forthcoming leadership election.

I was moved shortly afterwards to the Harley Street Clinic in London and once again Peter Mills conducted an angiogram. This time one of the inner walls of an artery had bulged inwards, narrowing the channel through which the blood could travel. Before my very eyes, a small tube was inserted into the artery, thus restoring me to normality. As I rapidly recovered, I began to have mild second thoughts about my future. John had, after all, indicated his wishes. Many Conservative MPs had suggested a similar degree of commitment and, but for the doubts that would now inevitably be raised about my health, I remained probably in as strong a position as anyone to lead the party. I did my best, though, to banish all such belated aspirations from my mind – even reminding myself that, if I went back into the game, I would find myself facing a Labour Prime Minister who was twenty years my junior.

I had no doubt that the right choice for the Conservative Party was Ken Clarke. John had been as good as his word and had announced his forthcoming departure on the Friday after polling day – without having any possible foreknowledge of the fate that would befall me. I publicly threw my weight behind Ken and was not surprised to find that the majority of Conservatives in the country, not just the activists in the party, shared this view. As Chancellor he had enhanced the economic inheritance that now passed to the new Labour government. He had wide experience of government, he was a character apart from the conventional wisdom, indifferent to the political correctness so deeply ingrained in lesser men. He is what he is. You get what you see. And people like that. But he is a Europhile. There is not the slightest shred of evidence to suggest that the Conservative Party had gained from its shift to Euroscepticism, but for many in the party Europe had become not just an issue, but *the* issue. To those still in thrall to the Thatcherite instinct he was unacceptable simply because of his pro-European views. He had been a robust, reforming minister and a tough Chancellor. But he was doomed to fall at what they believed to be the only fence on the course.

So far as I was concerned, the writing was on the wall the moment I saw the results of the election for the chairmanship of the 1922 Committee. It was basically a contest between Archie Hamilton, an amiable but limited backbencher who had briefly been PPS to Mrs Thatcher, and John MacGregor, a highly capable former holder of five different Cabinet posts but associated in his early political career with Ted Heath. Hamilton won by a sufficient margin to convince me that no centre candidate was likely to win the leadership itself. I told Ken that night that he couldn't win. The usual manoeuvring and canvassing revealed that this judgement was likely to prove correct. William Hague had become the chosen vehicle for Ken's defeat.

I had been an admirer of William's from his earliest appearance on the national stage when he made the speech at the 1977 party Conference in which he included the memorable words to the older representatives: 'It's all right for some of you; half of you may not be here in thirty or forty years' time: but I will be and I want to be free.' He had stolen the show. I know, because otherwise the show on that day would have been mine. We have often laughed about the way in which he had eclipsed my standing ovation. Time and again in government we worked together, and I found him an admirable and loyal colleague. I have disagreed with him only on one issue – and that is Europe.

Indeed, William invited me to run as the Party's official candidate for Mayor of London after Jeffrey Archer withdrew from the race in late November 1999. We met in William's office one evening and he discussed the prospect and the campaign at some length. I was flattered to be asked, and very aware that William was himself taking something of a risk in view of our very different opinions about Europe. The fact that we both felt this hurdle could be jumped I saw as a strength and not a weakness. I pondered overnight, and with some reluctance concluded that the reasons why I had not stood for the leadership itself remained overwhelming. I conveyed my decision to him the next morning.

I was not against Hague for party leader; I was for Clarke. It became evident that the choice was between the two. Ann Widdecombe had finished off Michael Howard's chances with her memorable phrase that he had 'something of the night about him'. John Redwood was a leader destined to remain yet again in waiting, and he clearly recognised his likely future when he agreed to see Ken after the second ballot. The three of us met at Tim Sainsbury's home in Vincent Square. John explained that he had been asked by his supporters, of whom there were up to three dozen – he had received twenty-seven votes in the first ballot and thirty-eight in the second – to see if a deal could be done. He had been told that they would follow his, John's, decision and that he could therefore deliver sufficient votes to ensure Ken's election. (Ken had received a slightly disappointing sixty-four votes in the second ballot, an increase of only fifteen on his showing on the first ballot, in which Peter Lilley and Michael Howard had also participated.) Redwood, clearly trying to salvage something from the wreckage of his hopes, made very few demands as a condition of his support and those he did make were perfectly consistent with Ken's declared public policy aims (though he did, slightly embarrassingly, make it clear that he was eager to be Shadow Chancellor). It was, to put it mildly, an unlikely alliance but in practice there was nothing to lose. Ken could not win on his own and, if the Redwood offer had been built on anything but sand, it could have turned the scales.

In the event, the alliance was greeted with at best disbelief and at worst distaste not just by the national press but by quite a few colleagues in the House of Commons. Anyway, Redwood could not deliver the votes and it became rapidly apparent that the alliance – likened by some unkind spirits to the Molotov-Ribbentrop Pact of 1939 – had diminished rather than increased the support for Ken; it certainly alienated more potential recruits to Ken's cause than it attracted committed followers from Redwood's camp.

Yet there was genuine dismay at the prospect of Hague's victory among a fair number of MPs. This should not be construed as a criticism of the man himself. It was felt that he was too young, too inexperienced and unproven for the task. It was at this juncture that events took, for the last time, a bizarre and unpredicted turn. Several colleagues came to me and said that there was growing apprehension and alarm. 'Ken can't do it but you could. You're the only one who can now defeat William. You have to persuade Ken to back out and let you stand in his place.' I talked to Ken about this, told him again that he couldn't win – a fact which he now readily appreciated – and added that there seemed to be a body of our colleagues who thought that I could. Ken accepted what I said without rancour and undertook to talk to his wife Gillian. He did so very speedily, came back and said that, if I would enter the lists, he would withdraw. I think Gillian was rather relieved at the prospect. I met John Major, accompanied by Gary Streeter, who had been a junior minister towards the end of our time in government, in the Leader of the Opposition's office in the Commons. John urged me to put my name forward, said he thought that I would win and – most important of all – promised me his support. Gary Streeter endorsed his judgement and said that he had discussed the matter with Patrick McLoughlin, a former colleague in the DTI and now Deputy Chief Whip, who believed that my entry into the battle would change everything. I was torn. I had made up my mind to take no part in the contest and had said so publicly. I was looking forward to an active executive role at Haymarket which I had effectively left twenty-seven years before. There was the arboretum – and the book Anne and I had long talked of writing about its creation. These were exciting things to be doing; I had a clear view of how the rest of my life would pan out. Anne had been delighted at the prospect that I would no longer carry the strain of high office. But, of course, we are all human.

Some other colleagues in the Clarke camp had been consulted and there was a welcome for the idea of my coming in on the third ballot, as the rules allowed. Nothing, however, was settled. I promised that I would think about it overnight and Michael Mates undertook to canvass opinion and let me know by eight o'clock the next morning what he had found out. I returned home to Chapel Street and told Anne what had happened. She was, of course, as I knew she would be, far from happy. She had had to carry the burden of fear not just over the 1993 Venice heart attack but also of the angina scare of only a few weeks before. She had believed that the pressure was at last off. I promised that I had made no decision and that, before I did, I would speak to Peter Mills, my consultant. I got through to him at half-past seven the next morning. We went over the territory. He said there was no medical ground upon which he could tell me that I should not do it. 'Of course there are no guarantees, but there is nothing that makes me say to you that you would be taking unwarranted risks with your health other than might be expected from someone of your age and medical history.' Then he pounced: 'But may I talk to you as a friend as opposed to your medical adviser?' He went on to say, 'Don't you think you've done enough for your party? I know people are saying to you that you're the only one that can pull the thing off. But you've given your life to this cause. Haven't you done enough?'

We discussed another aspect and one which weighed with me hugely. All political careers are tough. There is no job description. There is no time limit to the commitment. You throw yourself into it because you love it. Others do the same. Each in his or her way gives everything. People often ask how you carry the strain. They fail to understand that it isn't a strain. It isn't a strain in large measure because the prizes are there to be won – first, the ability to serve and, later, a sense of achievement at having done so. In all careers there are rewards and it is the excitement and the adrenalin that flows in their pursuit that turns what others might see as a strain into a way of life, a vision, a challenge, a sense of purpose that drives you on.

But the prospect facing me was a four-year grind towards what might well be another electoral defeat. That *would* be a strain. It would be overshadowed by references to a caretaker leader attempting to hold together a divided party when what was wanted was a new broom and a new Eurosceptic direction. I thanked Peter Mills for his advice and for his words of friendship and put the telephone down.

Michael Mates rang a few moments later to say he had good

news. The deal was on. Everybody was very pleased, even elated. 'I'm sorry, Michael,' I said. 'There's just one problem. I won't do it.'

I have never regretted that decision.

Appendix

RESIGNATION STATEMENT, 9 JANUARY 1986

I have today tendered my resignation from the government. Not because of the discussion at today's Cabinet but because of the way in which the reconstruction of Westland plc has been handled over a period of months. This has raised profound issues about defence procurement and Britain's future as a technologically advanced country, issues that however have never been properly addressed by the government. Indeed, as I shall show, a deliberate attempt has been made to avoid addressing them. This is not a proper way to carry on government and ultimately not an approach for which I can share responsibility.

The background to the government's policy on helicopter procurement is the 1978 Declaration of Principles agreed by France, Germany, Italy and the United Kingdom. This provided that each country would make every effort to meet their needs with helicopters developed jointly in Europe. That policy has thus far been followed through in our future planning. It is entirely consistent with the wider approach to defence procurement set out in the 1985 Statement on the Defence Estimates which emphasised the importance of Europe coming together in an equal partnership with the United States within the North Atlantic Alliance. My own commitment to that Alliance and to the strongest and most friendly relations with the United States on a basis of equality could not be clearer.

When Westland plc ran into financial difficulties, partially because of their failure on the civil market, this was not my immediate ministerial responsibility. I am not the sponsoring Minister for the helicopter industry. It would have been quite wrong for me to try to take the lead role in what was a DTI responsibility. It would have been wrong also for the Ministry of Defence alone to bail out the company with orders for which there was not an approved military requirement. I did, however, make clear throughout that the helicopter capability provided by Westland was essential in some form to our defence needs.

When Sir John Cuckney, who had become the chairman of Westland with my full support and encouragement, first approached the government about its attitude to potential partners for Westland, there was a close identity of view between the Ministry of Defence and the Department of Trade and Industry. In view of this identity of view, it was still unnecessary for me to take any direct initiative. It was recognised that with a Sikorsky shareholding Westland might tend to become little more than a production facility for Sikorsky and to lose its own helicopter design and development capacity, that a link with European companies would fit better into the developing pattern of European collaboration and that, in many ways, British Aerospace would be the most welcome partner. The need to explore urgently the European option was recommended by the Secretary of State for Trade and Industry on 4th October. When, on 17th October, Sir John Cuckney met the Secretary of State for Trade and Industry he said that he was well aware of the government's preference for a European minority shareholder in Westland and attached weight to that preference. The problem was how to bring this about in a timely way.

Over the following weeks there were a number of discussions involving both the European companies and Westland and contacts between European ministers. I kept in close touch with these and with the financial position of the company. At one stage I intervened to direct that the MOD's accounting officer should make a payment of £6 million to Westland that was correctly being withheld from them on grounds of prudent government accounting but that I was satisfied should be made because of the wider issues involved. As time went on I became increasingly concerned about progress in the discussions particularly at a company level. On 26th November, I met Sir John Cuckney and discussed with him where matters stood. He explained the need for urgent action and the attractions of participation by Sikorsky. However, he did not rule out other options provided that they had as much to offer as the Sikorsky alternative. His problem was that he lacked the management resources himself to explore them. I asked if I could help, having already agreed with the Secretary of State for Trade and Industry that this was acceptable. He welcomed my proposal that I should assist in this process. The lessons of the negotiations over the European Fighter Aircraft were in my view clear: without ministerial involvement, it would be very difficult to achieve timely success. I was not prepared to seek the support of my European ministerial colleagues, unless their efforts would be fairly and properly treated.

Since Sir John Cuckney had in no way ruled out the European alternative and welcomed my offer to explore it, I discussed it with Dr Woerner the following day and arranged that national armaments directors of the United Kingdom, Germany, Italy and France should meet on 29th November, and that the companies involved should also come together that day. The national armaments directors reached provisional agreement on the way forward including a recommendation that, in an extension of the 1978 agreement their needs within the main helicopter classes should be covered solely in the future by helicopters designed and built in Europe. They also agreed to complete the rationalisation of their requirement for helicopters, carrying forward the objectives set out in 1978. As soon as this agreement had been reached I personally gave a copy to Sir John Cuckney.

Sir John Cuckney's response was that the agreement that had now been reached would effectively preclude Westland from proceeding with a tie-up with Sikorsky. The subsequent ministerial discussions took place only in the context of this issue, rather than the wider dimension of the government's approach to the ownership of a major defence capability. There were three ministerial meetings chaired by the Prime Minister at the beginning of December, two of them ad-hoc groups on 4th and 5th December and finally a discussion in the ministerial Sub-Committee on Economic Strategy on 9th December. The Prime Minister attempted at all three meetings to remove the recommendation of the national armaments directors and thus leave the way clear for the Sikorsky deal.

The ad-hoc meetings were both ill-tempered attempts to overcome the refusal of some colleagues to thus close off the European option.

The Prime Minister, failing to secure that preference, called a meeting of the Sub-Committee on Economic Strategy on Monday 9th December. I proposed delay until the following Friday to give the Europeans time to come forward with a proper proposal. If they failed, I said that I would back Sikorsky.

Virtually every colleague who attended the enlarged meeting and thus came fresh to the arguments supported me, despite the fact that Sir John Cuckney had been invited to put his views to the meeting.

That meeting concluded that the Sub-Committee were not yet ready to reject the NADs' recommendation and a number of ministers would have a clear preference for the European alternative to a Sikorsky deal, if it could be developed into a form which Westland would regard as preferable to the Sikorsky arrangement. Time was limited and, as I have said, I was given to the following Friday to come up with such a proposal. The Prime Minister clearly stated on that Monday that ministers would meet again to consider the result on Friday at 3 p.m. after the Stock Exchange had closed. There would thus be a further opportunity for colleagues to consider the outcome and to inform the board of their views if they wished. I was content. There was time. There would be further collective discussions.

The Cabinet Office subsequently began arrangements for that meeting and a number of Whitehall departments were contacted about the availability of their Minister. These arrangements were, however, cancelled on the instructions of the Prime Minister. Having lost three times, there was to be no question of risking a fourth discussion. As a result the meeting on 9th December represents the only occasion on which there was a collective discussion of the issues involved, as opposed simply to the question of their public handling by the government. By 13th December I produced proposals for ministerial agreement. A complementary offer by the companies concerned to participate in the reconstruction of Westland was also made that day. They were not addressed collectively, but I circulated them to colleagues.

Following the decision not to proceed with the meeting on 13th December, I sought on a number of occasions to have the issues properly addressed. The first attempt had been at the Cabinet on Thursday 12th December. The Prime Minister refused to allow a discussion in Cabinet that day. I insisted that the Cabinet secretary should record my protest in the Cabinet minutes. When the minutes were circulated there was no reference to any discussion about Westland and consequently no record of my protest. Before the next Cabinet meeting I complained to the secretary of the Cabinet. He explained that the item had been omitted from the minutes as the result of an error and he subsequently circulated an addendum in the form of a brief note of the discussion. Such an error and correction was unprecedented in my experience. The minutes, as finally issued, still did not record my protest and I have since informed the secretary of the Cabinet that I am still not content with the way in which this discussion was recorded.

The world is aware that on 13th December the board of Westland rejected, after the briefest discussion, the proposals put forward by a consortium which now included Britain's leading aerospace company, British Aerospace plc.

On 16th December the Secretary of State for Trade and Industry made a statement to the House that, since the Westland board had rejected the British/European consortium proposals, the government was not bound by the NADs' recommendation. Effectively he thereby left the way clear for the Sikorsky/Fiat bid.

There followed increasing concern over the defence implications of this decision. The officers of the backbench Defence Committee of the Conservative Party put out a statement in support of the approach I was taking. I did not solicit that statement. Subsequently on 18th December the House of Commons Defence Committee, following a private meeting with me, also drew attention to the defence implications. At the Cabinet discussion on 19th December, there was again no attempt to address these fundamental issues. It was laid down that it was the policy of the government that it was for Westland to decide what was the best course to follow in the best interests of the company and its employees; that no minister was entitled to lobby in favour of one proposal rather than another; and that major issues of defence procurement were for collective decision. Information about the implications of defence procurement for Westland's workload should be made equally available to both groups as well as to Westland. I explicitly explained at that meeting that, as the Ministry of Defence was the major customer of Westland, I was bound to answer questions whether from UT/Fiat or from the European consortium about defence procurement aspects. I also drew attention to the fact that I believed that on the following day events would unfold that demanded collective judgement. I knew at the time, but could not prove, that the British/European proposals would appear next day. I therefore told the Cabinet that while it was acceptable that Thursday for the government to adopt an apparently neutral approach, events would shortly unfold which would demand collective judgement.

Events did so unfold. The following day 20th December the British/European consortium put forward an offer to Westland that was widely described as superior in every way to the Sikorsky/Fiat alternative. It was rejected out of hand by the Westland board.

I wrote on 23rd December to my colleagues setting out my views on the implications of both offers and their comparative merits and asking that the government should exercise its proper responsibility on so important a matter of defence industrial policy. I explicitly recognised that the holiday period was a difficult time for such a judgement. But before the directors came out with a final recommendation last Sunday, it would still have been possible for the government to meet and to restate the preferences so clearly expressed at the outset. My request for a meeting was refused by the Prime Minister.

Two further events must be recorded. Sir John Cuckney wrote on 30th December to the Prime Minister seeking assurances about the position of the company should they proceed with a Sikorsky/Fiat link. These assurances were sought directly in relation to a letter sent by the Ministry of Defence at my direction to the company. The fundamental issue raised by Sir John Cuckney related to defence procurement issues for which I was the Secretary of State with the individual ministerial responsibility. In the proper conduct of government business Sir John's letter would have been referred to my Department for advice and a draft reply. In this case the Prime Minister's private secretary sent the letter to the Department of Trade and Industry and asked for a draft reply, cleared as appropriate with other departments and the Law Officers. He asked for it to be submitted by 4 p.m. the following day. The letter from 10 Downing Street set out the line which the Prime Minister proposed to take.

When I received my copy of the letter the following morning, I pointed out that these were matters within my ministerial responsibility but the letter was not transferred to my Department for answer. I also pointed out that the line which the Prime Minister proposed to take was materially misleading. The Department of Trade and Industry prepared a draft reply which was referred to the Law Officers only at my express request. A reply with which all concerned could live was eventually hammered out at about 10 p.m. on New Year's Eve.

I subsequently amplified those parts of the reply that sought to hide the reality of Westland's position in relation to potential European partners and prospects for orders from the Ministry of Defence in the medium term, in a letter of 3rd January to Lloyds Merchant Bank, which I copied to Sir John Cuckney.

I was informed the following day by the Solicitor General that on the basis of the evidence which he had thus far seen my letter contained material inaccuracies. He wrote to me in this sense on Monday 6th January. Within two hours of my receiving his letter damaging selective passages had been leaked to the Press Association. I cannot comment on the source of these leaks on which there will no doubt be a full inquiry in the normal way. No one can doubt their purpose. I subsequently on 6th January set out to the Solicitor General some of the further evidence at my disposal about the attitude of other governments and other companies and informed Lloyds Merchant Bank by letter on that day that my answer needed no correction.

The government, in its official position, has sought to suggest that it has adopted an even-handed approach between the viable offers. In practice throughout the attempt has been made to remove any obstacles to the offer by Sikorsky/Fiat even to the extent of changing existing government policy. Although, as I explained earlier, at the outset there was a clear recognition of the attractions of involvement by British Aerospace, I understand that last night the Secretary for Trade and Industry, in the presence of another Minister in his Department and his officials, told Sir Raymond Lygo of British Aerospace that the role which British Aerospace were taking in the European consortium was against the national interest and that British Aerospace should withdraw. So much for the wish of the sponsoring Department to leave the matter to the shareholders on the basis of the most attractive choice available to them.

Finally we come to today's Cabinet. It was suggested that any questions in connection with the competing offers for Westland should be referred by all ministers to the Cabinet Office to be handled by them in the first instance. To have done so would have been to imply doubt and delay in any and every part of the assurances I had publicly given on behalf of my Ministry and of my European colleagues. Such a procedure would have allowed the advocates of the Sikorsky proposals to make mayhem over what is now the superior British/European offer. While I agreed that all new policy issues could be referred to the Cabinet Office, I refused to abandon or qualify in any way assurances I have given or my right as the responsible Minister to answer questions on defence procurement issues in line with policies my colleagues have not contradicted.

The Prime Minister properly summed up the view of Cabinet that all answers should be referred for collective clearance. I could not accept that constraint in the critical few days before the Westland shareholders decide. I had no choice but to accept or to resign. I left the Cabinet.

To be Secretary of State for Defence in a Tory government is one of the highest distinctions one can achieve.

To serve as a member of a Tory Cabinet within the constitutional understandings and practices of a system under which the Prime Minister is *primus inter pares* is a memory I will always treasure.

But if the basis of trust between the Prime Minister and her Defence Secretary no longer exists, there is no place for me with honour in such a Cabinet.

Illustration Credits

Associated Press; BIPPA; Peter Brookes/The Times; John Bull; John Cole at Studio Five; Coventry Express; Crown Copyright/MOD; Daily Telegraph; Andrew Dunsmore; Express Newspapers; GLC/Godfrey New; Hants/Times Newspapers Ltd, 30 May 1976; Jak/Evening Standard; Neville Labovitch; Mac/Daily Mail; NATO; PA Photos; Kenny Parker, Oxford; Photo Coverage Ltd; Reuters; Times Newspapers; West Midland Photo Services.

All photographs are from the author's collection, unless otherwise stated.

Every reasonable attempt has been made to identify owners of copyright. Errors or omissions will be corrected in subsequent reprints.

Index

ABM (Anti-Ballisitic Missile) Treaty 255
Abraham, Trevor 445
Abrahamson, General James 256
Accountancy Age 84, 91
Accountant 84
Ad Weekly 84
Adams, Gerry 481
Adeane, Lord 235
Advanced Passenger Train 132
Aérospatiale 297, 329
Agnelli, Gianni 298, 302
Agusta 297, 331
Air France 137, 141, 142
Aircraft and Shipbuilding Industries Bill,
   1975 164–65, 167–68, 169–75, 212
Aitken, Jonathan 462–64
Al-Fayed, Mohammed 465, 524
Al-Yamamah contract 286
Alington, C. A. 18
Allen, Peter 445
Amateur Tape Recording 77
Amery, Julian 36, 124, 243
Amess, David 410
Ancient Monuments Board 234, 235
Anderson, Eric 18
Angus, Sir Michael 468
Any Questions 24
Archer, Jeffrey (Lord) 461–62, 528,
   531
Ariane launcher 145, 146
arms procurement, cooperative 293,
   297, 324
Armstrong, Sir Robert: and MH's business
   affairs 90; and Levene 272; and
   shipbuilding 278; and Westland Affair
   301, 314, 327–28
Atkins, Sir Humphrey 172, 173, 174, 177,
   323, 326, 327
Atomic Energy Authority 470
Atwell, John 147
Audit Commission 206
Autosport 83, 93
AWACS 270, 299
Ayling, Bob 511, 512, 514, 515

Bagehot, Walter xiii
Bailey, Christopher 167, 169–70, 174
Bailey, David 65
Baker, Colin 450
Baker, Eileen 113 *see also* Strathnaver,
   Eileen

Baker, John 435, 436, 443
Baker, Kenneth 186, 347, 351, 353, 366, 473
Banham, John (Sir) 206
Banks, Major Mike 103
Barber, Tony 155
Barings 81
Barker, Lex 153
Barlas, Richard 170
Barnett, Correlli 493
Barnett, Ken 119, 187, 188
Baron, Sir Tom 199, 226, 251, 252, 268
Barratt, Lawrie 226
Barrow-in-Furness 30–31, 244, 250–51
Bartlett-Williams, Mrs 5
Bass 39
Bastion Contruction 72
Bastion Property 60
Bean, Basil 227
Beaumont, Rev. Timothy (Lord) 67, 68,
   74
Bechtel 398
beef exports 505–6
Bell, Martin 466
Bell, Tim (Lord) 526
Bellow, Irwin (Lord Bellwin) 190–91
benefit fraud 501
Benn, Tony 156, 162, 163–64
Beresford, Sir Paul 359
Berman, Ed 199
Bernstein, Howard 517
Berry, Tony 279
Bessell, Peter 97, 100
Bevan, Aneurin 29, 36, 56
Bevan, Peter 10
Bevan, Tom and Elvira 10
Bevans, Mary Marie (grandmother) 4
Bevins, Anthony 194, 360–61, 363
Biffen, John (Lord) 110
Bingham, Lord Justice 447
Birch, Margaret 96
Birmingham 215, 510
Bishop, Victor 87–88
Black, Conrad 518
Black Hawk helicopter 294–95, 296, 302,
   305, 318, 329, 330, 331, 332
'Black Wednesday' 431
Blackwell, Sir Basil 316
Blair, Tony 409, 430, 513–14, 527
Blaker, Peter (Lord) 31, 240, 249
Bloom, Margaret 491
Blue Ribbon Club 30

Blue Streak rocket 144
Blyth, James (Lord) 286
BMARC 463
Body, Richard 475
Boeing 331
Bonham Carter, Mark (Lord) 97
Bonham Carter, Lady Violet 36
Booth, Roger 34
Boston, Peter 60–61
Boswell, Jonathan 34
Bottomley, Virginia 508, 513
Boundary Commission 103–4
Bow Group 48, 95
Bowe, Colette 224, 308, 314, 327
Bowness, Alan (Sir) 225
Bowness, Peter (Lord) 202
Boxer, Mark 64
Boyd-Carpenter, John 153
Boyle, Sir Edward 115, 117
Boyson, Rhodes (Sir) 451
Brain, Ron 130, 212
Braine, Sir Bernard 243
Bramall, Field Marshal Edwin (Lord) 264, 267, 290
Brezhnev, President Leonid 253
Briggs, Asa (Lord) 33
Bright, Graham 473
Brighton: hotel bombing 279–80
Bristol Channel Shiprepairers 167
Bristow, Alan 315, 316, 317–18, 319
Bristow Helicopters 315
British Aerospace 274, 286, 298, 300, 301, 302, 305, 308, 309, 315, 326, 536, 539, 541
British Aircraft Company 135, 136, 137
British Airways 141, 142
British Coal 435, 436, 438, 439, 443
British European Airways 131, 141
British Fashion Council 422–23
British Gas 436: remuneration 467, 468; monopoly after privatisation 471–72
British Institute of Management 77, 78
British Leyland 176
British Overseas Airways Corporation 131, 137, 141, 142
British Printing Corporation 66, 82–83, 87–88
British Rate and Data 77
British Shipbuilders 277, 278
British Standards Institute 75
British Steel 416
Brittan, Leon: and Westland Affair 294, 296, 297, 302, 305, 306, 308–9, 326, 327; and GATT 426
Brixton 215
Broadbent, Sir Euan 282
Broakes, Nigel (Sir) 146–47, 214
Brockhurst school 16–17
Brodie, John 339

Bromley-Davenport, Sir Walter 114
Bromsgrove junior school 14
Bronowski, Jacob 36
Brooke, Peter 507–8
Broughton 10
Broughton Hall school 9, 14–18
Brown, Cedric 467, 472
Brown, Michael 525
Browne, Percy 97
Brunson, Michael 455
Bryan, Paul (Sir) 47, 111
BSE (Bovine Spongiform Encephalopathy) 502, 505
Buckley, Paul (Sir) 84–85
Budge, Richard 443, 444
Budgen, Nick 498
Buerk, Michael 354
Burke, Tom 345, 379, 401
Burma 290–91
Burns, Simon 450, 451
Burton, Bruce 34
bus companies 112–13, 168
Bush, President George 403
Business in the Community 210, 429
Business Link 429–30
Butler, Sir Robin: and PIIs 447; sleaze investigations 465; and MH's Deputy Prime Ministership 483, 484; and civil service reform 491–93
Butler, Adam (Sir) 240
Butt, Ronald 360

Cabinet Office: confusion of responsibilities 488–89; MINIS 489; privatisations 490–93
Caborn, Richard 442
Caines, Jean 456
Callaghan, Jim (Lord): succeeds Wilson 169, 179; and Alexandra Heseltine 179–80; character 179; calls election, 1979 180–81; and nuclear issues 250; on resignation 328
Cammell Laird Shipbuilders 277–79
Campaign 63, 93
Campbell, Alastair 154
Canary Wharf 200, 380, 397, 398, 412–13
Candole, James de 367
Caravan Life 77
Carey, Mr 13
Carlisle, Mark 229
Carman, George 449
Carr, Robert (Lord) 160, 161
Carrington, Lord 185, 235, 371
Cartiss, Michael 458, 459
Cartledge, Sir Bryan 337
Cash, Bill 364
Castle, Barbara (Baroness) 36, 112, 113–14, 119, 168

Castro, Mauricio de 325
Central Policy Review Staff 146
Chalker, Lynda (Baroness) 186
Chamber of Shipping 150
Chamberlain, Neville 6
Chancellor of the Duchy of Lancaster 489
Chandler, Colin 286
Channon, Paul (Lord Kelvedon) 124,
  163, 325
Charterhouse bank 89, 90
Chataway, Christopher 96, 102, 211
Cherry, Tim 529
Cherwell 59
Chevaline programme 244
Chevenix-Trench, Anthony 23
Chichester-Clark, Captain H. P. 100
Chief of the Defence Staff 263–64, 267
Chinook helicopter 331
Church Commissioners 62
Churchill, Winston (Sir) 37
Churchill, Winston (MP) 327, 441, 525
City Challenge 205, 395–97, 517, 518
City Grant 225
City Pride 205
Civil Aviation Authority 152
Civil Service College, Sunningdale 492–93
CJD (Creutzfeld Jakob Disease) 502, 504
Clark, Alan 448
Clarke, Kenneth: and MH 381, 500–1;
  and English development agency 400;
  PII signed by 447; and Post Office
  privatisation 450; and potential for
  leadership 472, 473; as Secretary for
  Education 494
Clinton-Davies, Stanley (Lord) 153
Clitheroe 6, 14
Clore, Charles (Sir) 64
Clough, Arthur Hugh 373
CND (Campaign for Nuclear
  Disarmament) 241, 244, 249–50
coal: market for 435, 437, 441–42, 442, 443;
  electricity still generated by 442–43 see
  also following entry
coal mines: closures 435–44; problems of
  434–35; redundancies 436, 437, 438, 442,
  443; help for mining communities 440,
  443; remains of 442–43; privatisation
  443–44
Cobley, Jim 98
Cockburn, Bill 450
Cocks, Colin 9
Cocks, Michael (Lord) 172, 173–74
Cockshaw, Sir Alan 396, 517
Coe, Sebastian (Lord) 496
Collett Dickenson Pearce 65
Collins, John 402
Commonwealth Immigrants Bill, 1968
  114–15

Companies Act, 1985 322, 323
Companies House 470
Competitiveness White Papers 421, 470,
  493, 495
Computing 92
Concorde 131, 135–43
Coningsby Club 48
Connaught Hotel restaurant 51
Convention on Climate Change 403
Cook, Robin 443, 448, 449, 451
Cooke, Robin 32
Cooper, Sir Frank 316, 317
Cooper, Peter 80, 82
Corman, Charles 61, 81, 90, 339
Cornmarket Press 59, 60, 76
Cosgrave, Liam 36
Cotton, Jack 64
council house sales 181–82, 194–97, 204,
  226, 229, 383
council tax 390–91
county council elections, 1978 180
Couper, Heather 508
Courtauld Institute 404
Cousins, Frank 131
Coventry Express 96
Cranborne, Robert (Viscount) 243, 483,
  486–87, 496
Crane, John 147
Crawte, Leslie 35
Critchley, Julian (Sir): schooldays 17; and
  Shrewsbury debate on public schools 23;
  at Oxford 28, 30; elected to Parliament
  32; exam results 35; tenant of Thurston
  Court Hotel 41; as editor 65–66
Critchley, Dr Macdonald 13–14, 17
Crosland, Tony 119, 151, 153, 201
Crossbow 95
Crossman, Dick 36, 118
Croucher, Sergeant-Major Bert 53
Crowther, Geoffrey 76, 77, 78
cruise missiles 244, 245, 247, 251, 252, 253
Cublington 151, 152
Cuckney, Sir John: and Westland 296, 297,
  299, 303, 304, 305, 315, 317, 319, 321, 323,
  325, 327, 330, 331, 536–37, 538, 540
Cuninghame, Sir Andrew 32
Cunningham, Jack 513
Curtis, Denis 76, 288
Cutler, Sir Horace 180
Cwmllynfell 56

Dacre, Paul 519
Daily Express 361
Daily Herald 24
Daily Mail 17, 139, 160, 361, 504, 519
Daily Mirror 101
Daily Telegraph 237, 311, 314–15, 351,
  361, 420

Dalkeith, Earl of 508
Dalyell, Tam 280, 281–82, 284
Dassault 274, 275
Dassault, Marcel and Serge 275
Davies, David 10
Davies, Denzell 280, 281, 283
Davies, Gwen and Betty 5
Davies, Ifor 55–56, 57
Davies, John 130–31, 141
Davies-Scourfield, D. G. 49
Dawe, Tony 237
Dawnays 10, 45
Day, Graham 278
De Ramsey, Lord (John) 403
defence industry 270–79; cooperative
  procurement 293, 297, 324
Defence Ministry: structure 240; MH takes
  over 257; organisational framework
  261–62; reform of 261–65; role of
  Secretary of State 262; unified structure
  of services 262–63; MINIS 263; culture
  266–67; costings 267–72; procurement
  268–72; and industry 269–70, 273;
  collaborative procurement 274–76
Defence Review, 1981 241–42, 243, 266
Defence White Paper, 1985 276, 293
Deloitte, Plender and Griffiths 25
Delors, Jacques 349, 354
Denholm, Ian 150–51
Denmark: referendums 457, 458
Denning, Lord 271
Denny, Major 43, 49, 58
Derelict Land Grant 214
Design Council 429
Dibden, Charles (ancestor) 3–4
Dibden, Eve Mary (great-grandmother) 3
Dibden, Thomas Colman (ancestor of
  MH) 3, 122
Dickens, John 61, 70–71
Dimbleby, David 231
Directory of Opportunities for Graduates 60
Directory of Opportunities for Qualified Men
  60, 75, 76, 81
Directory of Opportunities for Schools Leavers
  60, 75, 76, 81
Dobbie, Dr Bob 420, 421, 493
Docker, Sir Bernard and Lady 35
Docklands Light Railway (DLR) 200, 397–98
Dockyard Services Bill 271
Donovan, Terence 65
Dorrell, Stephen 503–4, 508
Douglas, Senator Paul 31
Douglas-Home, Sir Alec xiv, 80, 96, 158,
  160, 261
Downey, Sir Gordon 524
Downing Street: IRA attack on 391
Drew, Sir Arthur 235
Drogheda, Lord 78

DTI see Trade and Industry Department
du Cann, Edward (Sir) 159, 193
Dudden, Rev. Frederick Homes 26, 33
Duguid, Andrew 325
Duncan, Alan 477
Dundrum 6
Dundrum Public Elementary school 13
Durant, Tony 364
Durham 180
Dutt, R. Palme 36
Dykes, Hugh 451

Eccles, David (Viscount) 379
Economist 76, 78
EDCP (Committee on the Co-ordination
  and Presentation of Government Policy)
  496–97
Edelman, Maurice 169
Eden, Anthony 182
Edmonds, David 189, 223, 411
education 494–95
Edwards, George 150
Efficiency Unit 501
Eggar, Tim 436, 441, 443, 469, 471, 472
EH101 helicopter 329, 331
electricity: privatisation 434–35, 469–71
Emley, John 316
English, David 478, 519
English Estates 400
English Heritage 235
English Partnerships 163, 342, 511
Enterprise Zones 214, 397
Environment Act,1995 403
Environment Department: council house
  sales 181–82, 194–97, 204, 226, 229;
  MINIS 191, 192, 403; size of 192; housing
  reforms 197–99; rates, replacing 201, 207;
  and local government 202–6; revival of
  inner cities 209–29, 395–97; quangos 232,
  234; responsibilities of 232–33; regional
  offices merged into multi-disciplinary
  395; new premises needed 412–13
Environmental Impact Assessments 402
Equitas 424
Europa rocket 144
Europe: controversy over 343; split in
  Conservative party 348, 351, 354, 472,
  475–76, 505, 519 see also Eurosceptics
European Communities (Finance) Bill 475
European Community 144, 428: and
  GATT 426
European Economic Community: UK
  joins 148
European Fighter Aircraft 274–76, 294,
  296, 537
European Launcher Development
  Organisation 144, 145
European Monetary System:

Exchange Rate Mechanism 349, 417, 431–32
European Space Agency 144–46, 273, 293
European Space Research Organisation 144, 145
European Union: and GATT 426–27; expansion of 473
Eurosceptics 417, 432, 473, 475–76, 476, 498, 505, 518, 520, 525, 527
Evans, David 362, 477
Evening Standard 134, 361
Ewing, Humphry Crum 55

Fabricant, Michael 477–78
Falkland Islands: War 237, 238, 241–43, 280–84; airport 284, 285; MH visits 284–86; sinking of the *General Belgrano* 280–84
Fanshawe, Lord 318–19
Farr, John 243
fashion industry 422–23
fat cats 467–69
Fatstock Marketing Corporation 39
Faure, Hubert 317
Ferranti 269
Fiat 298, 302, 305, 321, 539, 540, 541
Fieldhouse, Admiral Sir John 267, 271, 280
Financial Institutions Group 224, 225
Financial Times 78, 257
Finsberg, Geoffrey 234
Foot, Michael 36, 170–71, 173, 244
Ford cars 75
Ford, Richard 360
Forsyth, Michael 519
Forte, Lord 318
Fortescue, Tim 97
Foster, Dr Richard 214
Fothergill, Stephen 437
Foulness 152
Fowler, Norman (Sir) 162, 457, 510
Fox, Sir Marcus 131, 441
France 254, 274, 275, 286, 287, 288, 289, 293, 428
Franks, Cecil 251
Fraser, David xiv, 85–88, 91
Fraser, Hugh 160, 161
Freeman, Roger 496, 504
Fry, Peter 171
Fuge, Charlie 22–23
Fulton Commission 491, 492

Galpin, Sydney 74
Galtieri, General 243
Gammans, David 36–37
Gardiner, George 232
Garel-Jones, Tristan 368, 371, 447
Garlick, Sir John 187, 188, 190, 212
Gas Act, 1995 472
Gatehouse, Stella 30

Gateway Supermarkets 4
GATT 425, 426–27
GE 275
GEC: electronic traffic signals 122–23; and Westland Affair 299, 300, 302, 305, 308, 315
Gee and Co 84
General Belgrano 280–84
General Electric 273
Gerbeau, Pierre-Yves 515
Gibson, Mark 488, 497, 528
Gilbert, Sir Arthur 405–6
Gilbert, Dr John 327
Gill, Christopher 476
Gilmour, Ian 105, 112, 229
GKN 331
Glaxo 471
Glentoran, Lord 508
Goodhart, Philip 226
Goodison, Nicholas 320
Goodlad, Alastair 496
Gordon-Lennox, Anthony 529
Gorman, Theresa 365, 372, 476
Government Offices for the Regions 225
Gow, Ian 96
Gower constituency 47–48
GP 77, 93
Granville, Keith 141
Gray, John 390
Grayson, David 429
Greater London Council: Conservatives in control 180; abolition 393
Green Alliance 345
Greenbury, Sir Richard 404, 468, 469
Greenham Common 245, 246, 249, 251, 253
Greenwich Dome 398, 509, 510–16
Greer, Ian 465
Gregory, Andy 335
Gregson, Sir Peter 420–21, 426
Grenada: invasion of 258–59
Grenfell, Dai 55
Gribben, Roland 420
Griffiths, Eldon 124
Griffiths, J. Gwyn 57
Grist, Ian 365
Groundwork Trust 210–11
Grugeon, Sir John 202
Guardian 29, 246, 361, 436, 464, 526
Guards Depot, Caterham 49, 50, 51
Gummer, John 394, 401, 403
Gummer, Peter 526
Guthrie, General Sir Charles 54

Hague, William 114, 162, 519, 530–31, 532
Haig, General Alexander 299
Hailsham, Quentin (Lord) 303, 380, 526–27
   see also Hogg, Quentin
Hall, Arnold 150

Hall, Sir John 508
Hall, Professor Peter 398
Hall, Ron 69
Hamilton, Archie 473, 530
Hamilton, James 131, 146
Hamilton, Neil 433, 464–66, 524
Hampson, Keith Dr xv, 240–41, 340, 351, 363, 367
Hansard 490
Hanson, James (Lord) 316–17, 321, 331
Hardwick, Nick 385
Harman, Harriet 504
Harper, Keith 437
Harris, Sir William 123
Harris, David 355
Harrison, Ernie 147
Hattersley, Roy (Lord) 197–98, 250
Haughton, Dan 148
Havers, Sir Michael 196, 203, 304, 306, 314
Haviland, Julian 342
Hawk aircraft 239–40
Hawker Harrier Jump Jet 136
Hawker Siddeley 132, 150
Hay, John 106
Hayes, Sir Brian 325
Hayes, Dr Geoffrey 7, 41, 45
Haymarket Publishing Group 64, 76, 81, 82–88, 91–92
Hazell Watson and Viney 76, 82
Healey, Denis (Lord) xiv, 160, 175
Heath, Sir Edward 47, 81; and MH's business affairs 90; at Tavistock 100; talk of replacing 103; Cabinet reshuffle 117; creates DTI and DoE 124; and third London airport 153; election 1974 155–56; and Keith Joseph 157, 159–60; character 158; leadership challenge to 159–60
Hefner, Hugh 66
Heisbourg, François 275
Heiser, Sir Terry 187, 188, 378, 379, 398, 412
helicopters 294: 329–30 see also under names of and Westland Affair
Heller, Robert 78, 86–87
Henderson, Sir Denys 468
Henderson, Paul 444
Henley-on-Thames 106
Her Majesty's Stationery Office 489, 490–91
Hernu, Charles 274, 275
Heron, Michael 450
Heseltine, Alexandra (daughter) 124, 179–80, 336: birth 101
Heseltine, Annabel (daughter) 124, 172: birth 71
Heseltine, Anne (wife): with MH to hear Heath 48; first meeting with MH 69; wedding 69, 96; background 70; first child 71; second child 101; third child

103; and mace brandishing 172–73; and MH's heart attack 453–57
Heseltine, Eileen Ray (mother) 3, 4, 9, 10–11, 71, 100
Heseltine, John William Dibden (grandfather) 3–4
Heseltine, Kearley and Tonge 4
Heseltine, Marie Berthe (grandmother) 4
Heseltine, Michael: birth 3; childhood 5–11; contracts meningitis 5–6; fascination with nature 7; fishing 7–8; angling champion 7–8; love of gardening 11, 15–16; schooling 13–24; writing problems 13, 14; childhood exhaustion 15; Victor Ludorum 15; arboretum created by 16, 179; bird-watching interests 16, 21–22, 285–86; at Shrewsbury 17, 18–22, 23; Common Entrance results 18; abandons medical ambitions 20; school certificate results 20; accepted at Pembroke College, Oxford 25–26; ambition to be accountant 25; at Pembroke 26; chooses PPE 27; and Oxford Union 27, 28, 31–38; politics a likely career 27; maps out career on back of envelope (allegedly) 29; opposes nuclear weapon tests 29; speaking tour while at Oxford 30–31; elected to Oxford committees and posts 32; finals 34–35; President of Oxford Union 34, 35–38, 40; accountancy articles 39; commercial instincts 39–40; commercial experience at Oxford 40; into partnership with Josephs 40; buys and sells Thurston Court Hotel 40–41; buys New Court Hotel 41; moves to smaller accountancy firm 43–44; accountancy losing attractions for 44; father's death 44; affection for father 45; early uncertainties about capitalism pass 46; puts name down for Conservative candidacy 47; buys first Jaguar 48; selected as Conservative candidate for Gower 48; national Service 49–55; receives commission 53; campaigning in Gower 55–57; ends partnership with Josephs 57; Gower result 57; New Court Hotel sold 57; more property developments 57–58, 60–62, 70–73; National Service ends 58; into partnership with Labovitch 59; becomes publisher 60; starts property development company, Bastion Property 60; publishing career 62–69, 75–88, 92–93; Chepstow Villas home 69; Stafford Terrace home 69; wedding and honeymoon 69, 96; first child 71; business has financial problems

72, 73–75, 85; and banks 73–74; Edgware Road premises 77; sets about acquiring businesses 77; Harrow Road premises 79–80; selected as candidate for Tavistock 80; Haymarket absorbs BPC magazines 82–83; loses control of company 83; Oxford Street premises 84–85; and unions 86–87, 181; and big-company systems 87–88; ministers' rules and commercial activities 88, 90; relationship with BPC sours 88–89; BPC bought out 89–90; shares put in blind trust 90; as consultant to company 91, 92; role in company after Conservative defeat, 1974 91; company to remain private 92; returns to Haymarket after 1997 election 92–93; becomes managing director of Bow Group Publications 95; Conservative candidate for Coventry North 95–97; and race issues 96, 114–16, 221, 230–31; selection for Tavistock 97–100; second child 101; wins Tavistock 101; fights Tavistock for second time 103; speaks in national election campaign 103; invitations to speak around country 104; Tavistock constituency disappears 104; search for new constituency 104–5; third child 104; selected candidate for Henley-on-Thames 106; new boy in Parliament 109–10; maiden speech (on incomes policy) 110–11; and Peter Walker 111–12, 187; announced as front bench spokesman on transport 113; opposes Transport Bill 113, 114, 115; first speaks at party conference 114, 175; reputation as speaker grows 114; and workings of the House 116–17; opposes Ports Bill 117–18; early relations with Thatcher 117, 161, 175, 176; becomes front bench spokesman on Transport 118; appointed parliamentary under-secretary at Ministry of Transport 121; resigns chairmanship of Haymarket 122; opens roads 124; caught speeding 124; and local government 126–28, 153, 392–94, 411; becomes Minister for Aerospace 129, 130; and London's South Bank planning 130; aerospace responsibilities 131–32, 143–50; and London's third airport 131, 151–53; government R&D 132–35, 146–48; shipping responsibilities 132, 150–51; closes down hovertrain project 133; and Concorde 135–43; in USA 148–49; 'Tarzan' and 'Hezza'

coined 153; Trade and Industry spokesman 156, 163; and Edward Heath 157–58; re-elected for Henley, 1974 159; brandishes mace 172–73; apologises to House 174; at party conference 1976 175; appointed Environment spokesman by Thatcher 175, 177; acquires Thenford House 177–79; and arboretum 179; and council house sales 181–82, 194–97, 204; at DOE 186–236; becomes Secretary of State for Environment 186; private office 188, 189; working methods as Secretary of State 188–89; agenda at DOE 189–90; management style 190–94; and MINIS 190–94, 263; reducing government expenditure 190; and Civil Service 191–92, 491–93; Thatcher approves of management style 192–93; housing reform 194–99; and rent control 197–98; home building 199, 200; special advisers 199, 200; and London Docklands Development Corporation 200, 380; cuts in local government 202–6; and rates 206–8; and revival of inner cities 209–15, 295–97; Toxteth riots 1981 Liverpool 216–29; awarded honorary degree by Liverpool University 228; 'It Took a Riot' 228; and public investment 229; and the Treasury 229, 235, 236, 416; Tory party conference, 1981 230; DOE's responsibilities 232–33; and media 233–34; and architectural competitions 234; and quangos 234–35; becomes Secretary of State for Defence 237; flies Hawk aircraft 239–40; MOD structure 240; mystery why Thatcher promoted him 241, 243; nuclear weapons issues (as Secretary of State for Defence) 243–58; refuses to debate with CND 245, 246; and NATO 247; speaking engagements, 1983/84 247–48; visits Berlin 249; and Grenada 269; and EFA 275–76; conference speeches a tradition 279; and sinking of *General Belgrano* 280–84; visits Falklands 285–86; visits troops in Lebanon 288–89; and commemoration of Normandy landings 289–90; and commemoration of VE Day 290; visits Far East 290–91; and Westland Affair 293–333, 535–42; resigns as Defence Secretary 310, 535–42, 542; and Stock Exchange enquiry 320–21; still in demand for speaking engagements 336; relationship with media changes 337–38; writes *Where There's a Will* 339, 341–42, 350; Downing Street undermining of 340, 341; on life

as a backbencher 340–41; as potential
rival to Thatcher 341, 347, 352; his
proposals adapted 342; attitude to
Europe 343, 475, 476–77, 518–21; writes
*The Challenge of Europe: Can Britain
Win?* 343; writes *Unemployment: No
Time for Ostriches* 344; 1987 election
campaign 346; and poll tax 346, 353–54,
379, 411; didn't want to challenge
Thatcher 352, 353, 361–62; open letter
to constituency chairman 355; and
reply to his letter 357–60; stands against
Thatcher 362–70; press statement on
announcement of leadership candidacy
362–63; commitment to abolish poll
tax 362; leadership contest 362–74;
prospects of becoming Prime Minister
vanish 369–70; leadership election
result 372; turns down Home Office
377–78; Secretary of State for the
Environment 378–413; on nature of
government in 1990 380–81; relationship
with Kenneth Clarke 381, 500–1, 519,
530, 531; relationship with Major 383,
485; and Portillo 387–88; and Channel
Tunnel Rail Link 399; environmental
objectives 401–2; and Manchester
406–7; Conference speech, 1991 408;
performance graded on leaving
DOE 411–12; at DTI 415–84; and
competitiveness 415, 416, 417, 419,
420, 421; privatisation 415, 416, 469–71,
490–93; and the economy 416–17;
and private and public sector cooperation
416; takes title of President of the Board
of Trade 418–19; and interventionism
419–20, 434; and sponsorship 422; as
Deputy Prime Minister 424, 434, 449,
479, 480, 483, 485–21; and arms exports
425; and exports 425–27; and support
for smaller companies 427–30; changes
DTI 430–31; party conference, 1992 431;
and deregulation 432–33, 495; and PII
certificates and Scott Enquiry 445–48;
heart attack 453–57, 533; and China 460;
and Archer 461–62; as potential rival
to Major 472–73, 476; suggestions that
he become leader 472; Major wants to
involve him closer to centre 478–79;
Major's leadership re-election 480,
481, 482, 483; relations with Cabinet
colleagues 485–86, 487–88; recruits
press officer 488; responsibilities as
Deputy Prime Minister 489; becomes
Millennium Commissioner 507–16;
and Dome project 509–14; attitude to
referendums 520; campaigning for
1997 election 524–25; general election,

1997 528–29; angina attack 529, 533;
and party leadership struggle, 1997
529–31; asked to run for Mayor of
London 531; potential to become leader
of party in 1997 532–33; resignation
statement as Defence Secretary 535–42
Heseltine, Rupert (son) xvi, 13, 23, 455
Heseltine, Rupert Dibden (father): army
career 6, 9, 54; son's birth 3; background
4; post-war career 10; works for
Conservative Party 26–27; death 44; TA
and 49
Heseltine, Yvonne ('Bubbles'; sister) 3, 8, 11,
45, 100
Higham, Charles 63
Highlight Interior Decorators 71
Hillier, Harold 179
Hirst, Michael (Sir) 524
Historic Buildings Council 234, 235
Hitchen, Brian 465
Hoban, Michael 23
Hobbs, Richard 424
Hocking, Philip 96
Hoffman, Mr 325
Hogg, Douglas 502, 503, 505
Hogg, Quentin 114, 115 *see also* Hailsham,
Quentin
Hogg, Sarah (Baroness) 390, 391
Hong Kong 418, 459–60
Horam, John 506
Horne, David 305, 306, 315, 320
Horne, Mike 488
Horrabridge 101–2
Horsfall, Sergeant Peter 50–51, 52, 53
House of Commons: research assistants
113; Select Committee on Science and
Technology 133–34, 135; Public Accounts
Committee 143; pairing system 171–74;
Select Committee on Defence 302, 308,
323–24, 326, 327, 539; Select Committee
on Trade and Industry 322, 323, 324,
441–42; Select Committee on Members'
Interests 506–7 *see also* legislation
house prices 391–92
housebuilding, private sector 195
Housego, David 139
Housing Act, 1980 194, 195, 199
Housing Action Trusts 384, 411
hovertrain 132–35
Howard, Michael 205, 401, 487, 519, 531
Howard, Sergeant Eric 53
Howard, Tony: at Oxford 32, 34, 36, 37,
38; tenant of Thurston Court Hotel 41; at
Stafford Terrace 69
Howat, Sue 359
Howe, Geoffrey (Lord) 55, 161; becomes
Shadow Chancellor 161–62; as
Chancellor 203, 212, 215; and urban

renewal 213; Enterprise Zones 214; and
USA 255, 258; and Grenada 258; and
Brighton bombing 279; resignation 348,
354–55, 360, 362; resignation speech 359,
361, 362; supports MH in leadership
challenge 371
Howell, David (Lord) 109
HS146 aircraft 132, 150
Hull 215
Hulme Estate, Manchester 396, 406,
517, 518
Humphrey, Bill 210
Hunt, David (Lord) 365, 393, 478
Hunt, Sir Rex 242, 285
Hurd, Douglas (Lord) 105: PSA and
192; becomes Foreign Secretary 351;
and Conservative leadership 367;
leadership challenge 370, 372; and China
459–60
Hussein, King 355
Hydraulics Research Station 192

Imagination 510
Independent 363
Independent European Programme
Group 276
Industrial Expansion Act, 1968 141
industrialists 168–69
INF Treaty 253
inflation 206, 208
Ingham, Bernard 307, 339, 355, 356
Inland Revenue 405, 406
Inner City Enterprises 225
Inner London Education Authority 393
Insolvency Service 470
insurance industry 423–25
Integrated Pollution Control 402, 403
International Monetary Fund 175
IRA (Irish Republican Army) 279–80, 391,
406, 423, 432, 516
Iran: arms to 463
Iran, Shah of 137–38, 139
Iraq: exports to 444, 446
Irving, Clive 69
Isaacs, Sir Jeremy 34, 37
Isis 37, 38
Italy 274, 287: and arms procurement
293
Ive, Ken 43–44
Izbicki, John 69

Jackling, Roger 266
Jackson, Michael 84
Jagan, Cheddi 37
James, Dr Elwyn 5
James, Howell 497
Jellicoe, George (Earl) 125, 137, 140
Jenkin, Patrick (Lord) 110, 208

Jenkins, Dame Jennifer 235, 384
Jenkins, Peter 409–10
Jenkins, Roy (Lord) 216
Jenkins, Simon 404, 508, 512, 514
Jiang Zemin, President 460
Johnson-Smith, Sir Geoffrey 506
Jones, Sir Trevor 214
Jones, Elwyn 44
Jones, Philip (Sir) 136, 143
Jopling, Michael (Lord) 361, 373
Joseph, Keith (Lord) 157, 159–60, 164, 212,
213
Joseph, Sir Leslie 509
Josephs, Ian 28–29, 31, 40, 41, 43, 57
Jubilee Line 200, 397–98
Jumblatt, Walid 288

Kalman, Andras 70
Kaufman, Gerald 198, 250
Keith, Kenneth 141
Keliher Hudson and Kearns 76
Kemp, Alan 488, 490, 501
Kennedy, Senator Edward 255
Kent, Nick xv, 359, 367
Kenyan Asians 114–15
Kerby, Captain Henry 26
Kerr, Sir John 427
Kershaw, Sir Anthony 282
Key, Robert 406
Key Victoria 170
King, Lord 318
King, Tom: MH asks for him as minister
186; and local government 201, 204; and
rates 207, 208; and inner city revival
210; responsibilities of 233; Gulf and
challenge to Thatcher 360, 361, 370;
supports Hurd in leadership battle 370
King-Farlow, John 32
Kinnock, Neil 354, 374, 407, 409
Kitley 116
Knight, Geoffrey 136, 139
Knight, Jill (Baroness) 109
Knowles, Richard (Sir) 396
Kohl, Chancellor Helmut 355, 527

Laboratory of the Government Chemist
470
Labour Party: anti-nuclear principles and
CND 30; and BSE 505–6
Labovitch, Clive 44, 57; publishing
career 59–61, 81–82; departure
of 80–81
Laing-Mowlem-Amey Roadstone
Construction 285
Lambert, Richard 434
Lambton, Viscount 125
Lamont, Norman (Lord): in MOD 240;
and MH's leadership challenge 370–71;

and Somerset House 405; and Black
Wednesday 431, 432; and pit closures
437, 444
Lancaster, Roy 179
Land Commission 62
Lane, Tony 131
Lang, Ian (Lord) 393, 424, 449, 483
Large, Dr Stephen 529
Large-Scale Voluntary Transfer 384
Lawson, Dominic 331
Lawson, Nigel (Lord) 151, 206, 230, 344,
348: resignation as Chancellor 349–50;
supports MH in leadership challenge 371
Layard, Professor Richard (Lord) 344
Leach, Admiral Sir Henry 243
Lean Look exercise 266
Leasehold Reform Act, 1967 198
Lebanon 287–89
Lee Hsien Loong 140
Lee Kuan Yew 140
Leese, Richard 516, 517, 518
Lefauve, Marie Berthe (grandmother) 4
legislation: categories of 165–66; progress
of 166–67; hybridity 167, 168, 169, 212
Leigh, Edward 449, 450
Lennox-Boyd, Alan (Lord) 48
Lennox-Boyd, Mark (Sir) 366
Levene, Peter (Lord): as Lord Mayor
93; and MOD 268, 269, 271, 272; and
Westland Affair 296; and DLR 398; MH's
access to 488; and Greenwich Dome 511
Lewis, Mr 21–22
Lewis-Lloyd, Miss 6
Leyland Daf 176
Li Lanqing 460
Lilley, Peter 400, 402, 445, 496, 519, 531
Lipsey, David (Lord) 369
Liverpool: urban revival 209, 210, 211,
212, 213; docks 211; UDC in 213, 214,
216, 227; and Heseltine 216–29; ethnic
population 217–18, 221, 222; Stockbridge
Village Trust 222; Anglican Cathedral
224; Tate Gallery 224; Cantril Farm
estate 226; Garden Festival 226–27;
Wavertree 226; cleaning up the Mersey
402 see also Toxteth
Llanwrtyd Wells 14
Llewellyn, Sir Godfrey 49
Lloyd, Ian 354
Lloyd, Jim 225–26
Lloyd, Peter 314
Lloyd, Selwyn (Lord) 70
Lloyds of London 423–25
Lloyds Merchant Bank 304, 305, 315, 336,
540, 541
local government: cuts 202–6;
accountability 205; central government's
control of 205; and UDCs 213

Lockheed 148
London: third airport 131, 151–53;
dereliction of East End 153, 212–13;
development in East End 398–99 see also
following entries
London Docklands Development
Corporation 200, 380, 397, 398, 515
London Eye 515
London Fashion Week 422–23
Luscombe, Harold 103
Lutyens, Edwin 242
Lyell, Nicholas (Sir) 447
Lygo, Sir Raymond 308–9, 316, 326, 541
Lynk, Roy 439

Maastricht Bill 457–59, 474, 518
Maastrict Treaty 417, 432, 521, 526
McAlpine, Alistair (Lord) 366, 454–55
McAlpine, Romilly (Lady) 454–55
McCallum, Ian 202
McCallum, R. B. 33–34
McColl, Ian (Lord) 496
McCullin, Don 65
MacDonald, David 406
MacDonald, Kenneth 270
McDonnell Douglas 309
Macfarlane, Sir Neil 365
MacGregor, John (Sir) 530
Mackay of Clashfern, Lord 405
Macleod, Iain 65, 115, 120, 131, 207, 377
McLoughlin, Patrick 53
Macmillan, Harold (Earl of Stockton) xxii
57, 65, 261, 417
Macmillan, Maurice 67
MacPherson, Angus 139
Magee, Bryan 37
Major, John: becomes Foreign Secretary
349; becomes Chancellor 351; leadership
challenge 364, 370, 371, 372; toothache
366; and poll tax 390–91; signs
Convention on Climate Change 403;
1992 election 407–9; and PIIs 447;
and Post Office privatisation 450;
murmurings against his leadership
continue 472; resignation as leader
of party 478, 480; re-election 481–83;
and changed cabinet atmosphere 488;
supporting MH for leadership 493
Mallaby, Sir Christopher 310
Man about Town 64–67, 69, 73, 77, 84
Management Today 78, 84, 93
Manager 77–78
Manchester 215, 396, 406–7, 516–18
Manchester Guardian 37
Mandelson, Peter 509, 514
Mann Island, Pilotage Building 214
Manpower Services Commission (MSC)
428

Maplin Development Bill 152
Maplin Sands 153
Marathon Shipbuilders 170
maritime communications satellite
  (MAROTS) 144
Marlow, Tony 473, 476
Marsh, Richard (Lord) 119
Marshall, Sir Douglas 100–1
Marshall, Lord 515
Marshall, Michael 327
Mascall, Norman 67–68
Massiter, Cathy 250
Masters, Lindsay: background 62–63;
  recruited by Labovitch 62; and Critchley
  66; stays with MH when Labovitch
  leaves 81; shares 82, 90–91, 92; and
  Campaign 83–84; credit card cut in
  half 85–86; takes over responsibilities
  as managing director 87; and unions
  87; becomes chairman 88; retires from
  chairmanship 93–94; becomes managing
  director 113
Mates, Michael: and Westland Affair 323;
  and Whitelaw 327; becomes friendly
  with MH 340; and poll tax 353; and
  MH's leadership challenge 363–64,
  367, 533–34; and Eurosceptics 476; and
  Major's re-election campaign 482
Matrix Churchill Affair 444–49
Maude, Francis 495, 496
Maudling, Reginald 158, 162
Mawhinney, Brian (Sir) 496, 503, 523,
  527, 529
Maxwell-Hyslop, Robin 32, 168, 170, 174
Mayhew, Patrick (Lord) 31, 304, 305–6, 308
MBB 297
Mellish, Bob 214
Mellor, David 364, 497
Melville, Herman 218
Mendoza, Maurice 234
Merchant, Piers 524
Mersey, cleaning 402
Merseyside Task Force 225
Meyer, Sir Anthony 351, 368
Meyers, David 288
Mikado, Ian 36
military industrial base 273
Millennium Central 511
Millennium Commission 507–16
Millennium Dome 509–14
Miller, Major Alastair 54
Miller, Lieutenant-Colonel Sir John 53–54,
  186, 290
Mills, Peter 455, 529, 533
Milne, Peter 278
MIMS 77, 93
MINIS (Management Information System
  for Ministers) 190–94, 263, 403, 421, 489

Mitchell, Andrew 473
Mitterand, President François 275, 289
Mobil Oil 465
MOD *see* Defence Ministry
Mogg, John 306
Molesworth 251–53, 381
Moman, Praveen 342
Monbiot, Raymond 357, 359
Moncrieff, Chris 311
Mons officer cadet school 53
Montagu, Nicholas 405
Montague of Beaulieu, Lord 235
Montague, Michael 508, 513
Moore, Charlie 7, 10
Moore, John 366
Morgan, A. E. 77
Morgan, Christopher 336, 347
Morrison, Charles (Sir) 112
Morrison, Herbert (Lord) 509
Morrison, Peter 351–52, 366, 367
Morrison, Tom 357, 359
Morton, Martin 30–31
Moser, Edward Branthwaite 18
Moses, Alan 447
Mottram, Richard (Sir) 240, 276, 280, 297, 330
Mountbatten, Lord 261, 264
Mourne Grange 13
Mozambique 389
Mulley, Fred 119, 120
Murden, Michael 278
Murdoch, Rupert 320, 321, 366, 478, 518

NADS (national armament directors) 297,
  298, 299, 537
Narberth 6
National Coal Board 435
National Engineering Laboratory 470
National Freight Corporation 194
National Gallery extension 234
national insurance 495–96
National Liberal Party 48fn.
National Lottery Act, 1998 508
National Newsagent 89
National Physics Laboratory 471
National Power 435, 436
National Research and Development
  Corporation 132
National Rivers Authority 402
National Union of Mineworkers 155,
  215, 439
NATO (North Atlantic Treaty
  Organization) 253, 254, 259
Nature Conservancy Council 233
naval dockyards 271–72
Neale, Gerry 366
Neave, Airey 133–34, 135, 159, 162
Needham, Richard (Sir) 423, 425–26
Neil, Andrew 366

Nelson, Anthony 424
Nettlebed 177
Neville-Rolfe, Lucy 495
Neville-Rolfe, Marianne 492, 495
New Millennium Experience Company (NMEC) 511, 515
Newbury 245, 246
News Chronicle 24
News of the World 366
Newton, Tony (Lord) 496
NH90 helicopter 331
Nicholls, Aubrey 96
1922 Committee 161, 351, 441, 475, 530
92 Group 232: 525
Nolan Enquiry/Report 466–67, 507, 524
Northern Ireland 481
Nott, John 109, 193, 236, 241–42, 266, 267
Notting Hill riots 220
nuclear deterrent, independent 244
Nuclear Inspectorate 469
nuclear power stations 469–70
Nyanza Terrace 6

Oakley, Robin 360
Observer 338, 365
Odermatt, Marc A. 325
Office of Public Service 489
oil prices 153, 155
O'Malley, Brian 169
Onslow, Cranley (Lord) 131, 363, 366
Opportunities for Graduates 60
Ottaway, Richard xv, 433, 472, 473–74, 482, 496, 527
Ove Arup 399
Owen, David (Lord) 216, 283
Owen, Peter 355, 357
Oxford Carlton Club 30
Oxford Conservative Association 26
Oxford, Ken 222
Oxford Union 27, 28, 31–38
Oxford University Conservative Association 30, 168
Oxford University What's What 59

Page, Graham 124, 125, 127, 130
Page, Jennie 508, 511, 512, 513–14, 515
Palace of Westminster 234
Palmar, Derek 39
Palmer, John 74
Pamflete 83, 102
Pantysifi 10
Parcelforce 450
Park, John Fergus 16, 17
Parkinson, Cecil (Lord) 131, 134, 230, 370
Parkinson, Michael 69
Parris, Matthew 360
Parsons, Sir Anthony 265
Parsons, Billy 72, 73

Patent Office 470
Paterson, Robert 76
Patten, Chris: at DOE 345, 379–80, 400, 401; 'double whammy' 409; loses seat, 1992 417–18; Governor of Hong Kong 418, 459–60
Pattie, Geoffrey (Sir) 146, 240, 309
Pattison, Professor John 502, 503
Pawsey, Jim 451
PAYE deductions 495–96
Peacock, Elizabeth 441
Pearce, Idris 55
Peat, Henry 39
Peat, Marwick, Mitchell and Co. 39, 43
Pelling, Tony 210
Pendry, Tom 171, 172, 173
People 497
Pepys, Samuel 271
Perkins, Neville Ward 27, 35
Perrick, Eve 80
Perrick, Penny 80
Pershing II missiles 244
Personal Business Advisers 429, 430
Peyton, John (Lord) 121, 124, 161
Phillips, A. H. 21
Pickard, Sir Michael 200
Pike, John 257
Pilkington, Sir Alastair 210
Pilkington Glass Company 210
pirate radio stations 111
Pirbright 53, 54–56, 186
pit closures 435–44
Playboy empire 66
Polaris system 244
political advisers 378–79
poll tax: faults of 207, 388–89; consequences 345–46, 348, 353–54, 371; MH's commitment to abolish 363
Pollock, John 83
pollution 401, 402
Pollution, Her Majesty's Inspectorate of 402–3
Ponting, Clive 281–84
Pope, Alexander 362
Portillo, Michael: and MH 387–88; and poll tax 387, 391; and Europe 388, 519; and pit closures 436, 437, 444; and Eurosceptics 527–28; Enfield Southgate campaign, 1997 527
Ports Bill, 1969 118–19, 165, 171
Portsmouth News 354
Post Office: privatisation 449–51
Powell, Charles (Lord) 279, 306
Powell, Enoch 65, 115, 116, 215, 369
Powell, William 367
PowerGen 435, 436
Practical Camper 77
Prentice, Reg 212–13

Prescott, John 499
prescription fraud 501
Preston 215
Price, Charles 328–29
Priddle, Robert 131, 139
Pridmore, James (grandfather) 4–5, 6–7
Pridmore, Mary Marie (grandmother) 4
Prime Minister's Questions 498–500
Prior, Jim (Lord) 161, 172, 230, 270
Priority Estates project 194
private secretary: role of 188–89
privatisation: sleaze and 467–68
Property Services Agency 192, 285, 411–12
psychiatric hospitals: closure of 386
Public Interest Immunity Certificates 445–48
public sector: private sector partnership 394–95
Publishing News 82
Pullen, Maggie 357–58, 410
Purnells 82
Pym, Francis (Lord) 105, 135, 185, 473

Quarmby, David 515
Queen 64
Queen Elizabeth II Conference Centre 235–36

Race Relations Bill/Act 115–16
Rachman, Peter 43
radio spectrum: selling 470
Radiocommunications Agency 470
Rafale 274
Raison, Tim 216
Raphael, Adam 338
rates: abolition 181, 201, 207; highness of 206; and taxpayers 206; property revaluation 207
Reagan, President Ronald 254, 255, 258, 289
Redcliffe-Maud, John (Lord) 126, 127
Redmayne, Martin 65
Redwood, John 340, 519; and leadership of party 476, 482, 531, 532
Rees, George 53
Rees, Hugh 55
Rees and Kirby 4
Rees-Mogg, William (Lord) 343, 448, 474
Referendum Party 527
Reichman, Paul 397–98
Reid, Jim 429
Remembrance Travel 291
Remnant, Jimmy (Lord) 81
rent control 197–98
Renton, Tim (Lord) 105, 363
research laboratories 470–71
Reynolds, Albert 481
Richardson, George 33

Ricketts, Colonel Johnny 51, 53, 54, 285
Riddick, Graham 466
Ridley, Nicholas (Lord): background 242; and Falklands 242–43; and housebuilding 344; and Europe 354
Rifkind, Malcolm 399, 447, 519–20
Right-to-Buy *see* council house sales
Rio Earth Summit 403
riots 215, 216
Rippon, Geoffrey (Lord) 152, 161
R.J.B. Mining 444
Robbins Tea 4
Robert Fleming Merchant Bank 316
Roberts, Sir Wyn 365
Rodgers, Bill (Lord) 216
Rogers, Richard (Lord) 516
Rolls-Royce 148, 273, 274, 294
Rootes cars 75
Roper, Lanning 179
Rosancik, Harry 63
Roskill Committee 151, 152
Rossdale, Richard Dr 455
Rossi, Hugh (Sir) 181
Rothschild, Jacob (Lord) 146, 405, 406
Rothschilds 89, 444
Rouane, Rusty 43
rough sleepers 384–87
Rowe & Pitman 316
Rowland, David 424
Royal British Legion 291
Royal Commission on the Historical Monuments of England 235
Royal Mail 416, 449, 450
Royal Ordnance 272
Royal Society for the Protection of Birds 233
Royle, Anthony 318
Ruddock, Joan 244–45
Rulton, Ron 106
Rumble, Gordon 72
Rumble, Ron 72
Ryder of Eaton Hastings, Lord 176, 458, 465, 475
Ryder, Richard (Lord) 368, 450

Saatchi, Maurice 85, 488, 526
Saatchi & Saatchi 85, 88
Saddam Hussein, President 361
Sainsbury, John (Lord) 433, 495
Sainsbury, Tim (Sir) 186, 216, 240, 405, 425, 427, 433, 436, 439, 457, 531
St. John-Stevas, Norman (Lord St. John) 28, 162
Salter, Molly 15
Sandys, Duncan 484
Sargeantson, Roderick 178
Sassoon, Vidal 422
Saudi Arabia 286–87

Scargill, Arthur 436
Schenk, Roland 84
Schiess, Guillermo 325
Schultz, George 259
Science Research Council 145
Scotchman, I. G. S. 18
Scotland, Patricia (Baroness) 508
Scott, Sir Richard: Inquiry 446, 447, 448–49, 462
Scott, Kellan 14
Scottish Development Agency 162, 163
SD3–30 aircraft 132, 148
SDI (Strategic Defense Initiative) 254–58
SDP 216, 247
SEAC (Spongiform Encephalopathy Advisory Committee) 502
Serco 146
Serpell, Sir David 90, 189
Shamir, Yitzak 355
share options 468
Shephard, Gillian 436, 439, 494–95, 502
Shepherd, Guy 22–23
Sheppard, Allen (Lord) 404
Sheppard, David (Lord) 217
shipbuilding industry 277–79
Shipley, Blackburn, Sutton and Co. 44
Shock, Maurice 33
Shoppers' Guide 75–76
Shore, Peter 187, 214
Short, Ted 111
Shorts 132, 148, 329
Shotover 6
Shotover House 54
Shrewsbury School 17, 18–22, 23
Shuman, Howard 31
Sieff, David 210
Sikorsky: and Westland 37, 294, 296, 297, 298, 299, 301, 302, 305, 314, 315, 318, 320, 321, 330, 331, 536, 539, 540, 541
Silver, Clinton 423
Silver, George 29
Silverhill pit 439
Simon, Sir John 48fn.
Simon, David (Lord) 468
Singapore 291
Single European Act 348, 477
Sitwell, Peter Wilmot 316
Skyvan 132, 148
Sladden, Mr 5
sleaze 460–69, 524, 525
Small Business Service 430
Smallwood, Brian 19
Smart, Jack 202
Smith, John 408, 409, 474
Smith, Peter 474
Smith, Tim 465, 524
Smythe, Wing Commander 101
SNECMA 275

Snow, Peter 410
Soames, Lord 229
Somerset House 404–6
Sorenson, Eric 225
Sortridge 101
Soundess House 134
South Wales Evening Post 56
Southall 215
Spain 274, 294
Spectator 115
Speed, Keith 262, 327
Spencer, Jonathan 424
Spiller, Roger 250
spin-doctors 497
Spottiswoode, Clare 471
SS-20 missiles 253
SSSIs (Sites of Special Scientific Interest) 233
Stanier, John 266
Stanley, John (Sir) 186, 195, 196, 212; in MOD 240, 280
Star Wars see SDI
Stevens, Jocelyn (Sir) 64, 235
Stewart, Allan 524
Stewart, John 34
stock options 468
Stoddart, David 133, 134
Stoke 227
Stokes, Lord 78
Storie-Pugh, Colonel Piers 291
Strathnaver, Eileen (Lady) xv-xvi, 336, 364, 369, 378, 488, 497, 528
Streeter, Gary 532
Stringer, Donald 357, 358
Strong, Dick 89, 90
Studholme, Sir Henry 97, 98, 99, 101, 158
Sud Aviation 137
Summers, Jean 178
Sun 361
Sunday Express 14, 366, 465
Sunday Telegraph 365, 366
Sunday Times 69, 77, 172, 179, 365, 366, 372, 467, 472
Super Puma helicopter 329
Swan Hunter 277, 278
Swansea: MH's childhood in 3–11; parks 7; bombing of 8
Swansea West Conservative Association 26

Tapsell, Peter (Sir) 32, 326, 365
Taverner, Jean 43
Tavistock 97–100, 102–3, 116
tax cuts 201, 207, 350
Taylor, Sir Godfrey 202
Taylor, Ian 463, 470
Taylor, John 97
Taylor, Simon 83
Tebbit, Norman (Lord) 173, 229, 276–77, 278, 279, 298, 366

Tenants Charter 194
Thatcher, Denis 318
Thatcher, Margaret (Baroness): never regards MH as 'one of us' 111; and Barbara Castle 113–14; Shadow Transport spokesman 117; sketch of 117; becomes Education Shadow 118; deputy Shadow Chancellor 160; wins leadership of party 160; Heseltine disagrees with 176; and Leyland 176; approves of MH's management style 192–93; hectoring style 193, 232, 488; and local government expenditure 204; and rates 208; domination of 232; and Falklands War 243, 280, 281; and President Reagan 255; and Grenada 258; MOD and 262; and centralisation 265–66; and sinking of *General Belgrano* 280–84; and Al-Yamamah arms deal 287; and Westland Affair 296, 298–300, 302, 303, 304–6, 308, 310, 312, 313, 326, 329, 338; and Europe 343, 348–49, 354, 356; and poll tax 345, 356; popularity wanes 347, 352; Bruges speech 348; leadership challenges to 351, 362–70; unease at style of government 351; losing by-elections 356; Heseltine stands against 362–70; swears cabinet not to vote for MH 365; attacks MH 366–67; withdraws from leadership contest 369; change of atmosphere after departure 371, 488; grudge against Major 382; and 1992 conference 432; as back-seat driver 518
Thenford House 177–79
This Common Inheritance White Paper 401
Thomas, George (Lord) 170
Thomas, Peter 161
Thompson, George Kenneth 14–15, 17
Thompson, Heather 15
Thompson, Sir Kenneth 213, 214
Thomson, Roy 77, 78
Thornber, Ken 357
Thorneycroft, Peter (Lord) 162
Thornton, Clive 215
Thornton, Peter 143
Thorpe, Barry 50
Thorpe, Jeremy 97, 156
three-day week 155
Tickell, Sir Crispin 402, 403
Time & Tide 68
Times, The 138, 139, 172, 173, 228, 311, 314, 331, 333, 352, 355, 356, 360, 365, 367, 373, 461, 462, 474
Tindall, Simon: as salesman 63; and *Topic* 68; and financial problems 74; and *What Hi-Fi?* 77; and unsolds 79; stays with MH when Labovitch leaves 80; shares 82, 90–91, 92; and *Autosport* 83; and consumer magazines 87

Tollemache, Hon. Tim 53
Tomalin, Nicholas 68–69
Topic 67–69, 73
Tornado aircraft 286–87
Touche, Remnant and Co 81
Tower Colliery 444
Toxteth 211, 215, 217–23, 227
Toynbee, Polly 409
Tracked Hovercraft 132
Trade and Industry Department: creation of 421; Competitiveness Division 421; MINIS 421; and Department of Energy 422; and exports 425–27; trade side split 425; Heseltine changes 430–31
Training and Enterprise Councils (TECs) 428, 429, 430
Transport Act, 1968 112, 113
Treacher, Bob 389
Tredinnick, David 466
Trethewey, Christopher 101
Trevelyan, Dennis 272
Trident system 244, 245, 247, 251
Trippier, David 365, 400–1
Tristar airliner 148–49
Trubshaw, Brian 138, 139
Trustam-Eve, Sir Malcolm 62
Turner, Lawrence 27
Turton, Peter 69

UK Independence Party 527
unemployment 210, 214, 215, 231, 344, 501–2
Union of Democratic Mineworkers 439
Union of Soviet Socialist Republics (USSR) 243, 253–54, 255
United Scientific Holdings 268, 316, 317
United States of America: SDI 254–58; UK and 254; technology and 256, 257; Grenada invasion 258–59; and Middle East 287, 288; beef ban 506
United Technologies Corporation (UTC) 296, 298, 299, 305, 320
Uplands Crescent, Swansea 4, 5, 6, 8
Urban Development Corporations 211, 212, 213, 214–15, 399–400
Urban Development Grant 225
Urban Programme 214, 394–95, 396

V2 rockets 9
Vallance, Sir Ian 468
Varley, Eric 163, 164
Vaughan, Gerry 458
Vaux, Margaret 55
Vernon Holdings and Partners 77
VJ Day 9
Volume Housebuilders 199, 200, 215

W30 404 helicopter 329

Wakeham, John (Lord) 279, 312, 313, 326, 368
Wales, Princess of 423
Walid Jumblatt 288
Walker, Sir Gervas 202
Walker, Peter (Lord) 90; tours West
  Country 111–12; campaign against
  Transport Bill 112, 113; and
  Mrs Thatcher 112, 163; Shadow
  Minister for Housing 117; Secretary
  of State for the Environment
  124–26; and local government
  reorganisation 126–28; takes charge
  of DTI 131; and council house
  sales 181
Wallington, Jeremy 69
Wallis, Ed 436, 443
Walters, Sir Alan 349
Walters, Dennis 364
Ward, John 496
Ward, Phillip 389, 390
Waring and Gillow 85
Warren, Kenneth (Sir) 324
Warren Springs Laboratory 471
water quality: responsibility for 402–3
Waterstone, Nigel 496
Weatherill, Jack (Lord) 113
Wei Ling 140
Weidenfeld, George (Lord) 343
Weinberger, Cap 254, 257, 259
Weinstock, Arnold (Lord) 122-24,
  270, 512
Weissmuller, Johnny 153
Wells, Henry 62
Welsh Development Agency 162, 163
West Germany 274, 286, 428; and arms
  procurement 293, 294
Western European Union 254
Westland Affair: policy background
  293–94, 535; company's financial
  difficulties 294, 295, 535; cooperative
  arms procurement 294; USA and
  294; board of company 301, 302, 303,
  539, 540; share dealings 319, 320–24;
  shareholders harried 319; shareholders
  meetings 319, 321; Sikorsky buys shares
  320; Stock Exchange enquiry 320–21,
  322–23, 323; DTI investigation 325;
  manufacture Black Hawk 330; company
  merged with Agusta 331; Sikorsky sells
  shares 331; MH's resignation statement
  535–42
Westminster, Palace of 234
Westminster Dredging Company 174
'wets' and 'drys' 229, 231, 232, 241
What Car? 87, 91
What Hi-Fi? 77

Wheeler, John 198
Whitbread, Judith 98
White, Sir Gordon 317
White, Richard 146
Whitelaw, William (Lord) 103, 121,
  156, 160, 161, 177; and rates 208; and
  Liverpool 216; and Westland Affair 312
Whitmore, Clive (Sir) 240, 263, 272; and MOD
  263, 272, 276, 278, 280, 300, 308, 309
Whitney, Ray 482
Widdicombe, Ann 531
Wild, Robert 22–23
Willetts, David 354, 496, 506–7
Willey, Fred 198
Williams, Anne see Heseltine, Anne
Williams, Sir Brandon Rhys 198
Williams, Shirley (Baroness) 216
Williams, William and Edna 70
Wills, Peter 320, 321, 322, 323
Wilson, Brian 463
Wilson, Harold (Lord) 36, 104, 109, 162,
  169, 162–63, 338
Wine and Spirit 89
Wingate, Orde 291
winter of discontent 181, 182
Winterton, Ann 441, 451
Winterton, Nicholas 441, 451
Withers, Gary 510
Woerner, Manfred 254, 274, 297, 537
Wolfenden, John (Lord) 21, 36
Wolff, Michael 158
Wolsey, Tom 65
Wolverhampton 215
Wood, Russell 20
Woodhead, Christopher 494
Worcester, Bob 526
workfare 501–2
World Affairs Council 149
World War Two: declaration of 6
Worlock, Derek 217
Wrottesley, Mr Justice 17
Wyatt, Woodrow 96
Wyman, Peter 496

Yates, Ivan 31
Yes, Minister 189
Young, David (Lord) 428, 478
Young, Sir George 105; at DOE 383, 384–85
Young, Leslie 214
Younger, George (Lord): and rates 207,
  208; and MOD 270, 311, 330, 331;
  Thatcher's campaign manager 351,
  366, 368
Ystradgynlais 57

Zincone, Robert 330